World Music
Traditions and Transformations

World Music
Traditions and Transformations

Michael B. Bakan
The Florida State University

Boston   Burr Ridge, IL   Dubuque, IA   Madison, WI   New York   San Francisco   St. Louis
Bangkok   Bogotá   Caracas   Kuala Lumpur   Lisbon   London   Madrid   Mexico City
Milan   Montreal   New Delhi   Santiago   Seoul   Singapore   Sydney   Taipei   Toronto

Higher Education

Published by McGraw-Hill, a business unit of The McGraw-Hill Companies, Inc., 1221 Avenue of the Americas, New York, NY, 10020. Copyright © 2007 by Michael B. Bakan. All rights reserved. No part of this publication may be reproduced or distributed in any form or by any means, or stored in a database or retrieval system, without the prior written consent of The McGraw-Hill Companies, Inc., including, but not limited to, in any network or other electronic storage or transmission, or broadcast for distance learning.
Some ancillaries, including electronic and print components, may not be available to customers outside the United States.

This book is printed on acid-free paper.

3 4 5 6 7 8 9 0 WCK/WCK 0 9 8

ISBN: 978-0-07-241566-7
MHID: 0-07-241566-5

Vice President and Editor-in-Chief: *Emily Barrosse*
Publisher: *Christopher Freitag*
Marketing Manager: *Pamela Cooper*
Developmental Editor: *Chris Narozny*
Editorial Assistant: *Marley Magaziner*
Lead Project Manager: *Susan Trentacosti*
Manuscript Editor: *Betsy Blumenthal*
Lead Designer: *Gino Cieslik*
Text Designer: *Amanda Cavanaugh*
Photo Research Coordinator: *Natalia Peschiera*
Photo Researcher: *Christine Buese/Photosearch, Inc.*
Art Editor: *Emma Ghiselli*
Production Supervisor: *Jason I. Huls*
Lead Media Project Manager: *Marc Mattson*
Lead Media Producer: *Jocelyn Spielberger*
Composition: *10/12 Fairfield Light, Thompson Type*
Printing: *45# Pub Matte Plus, Quebecor Versailles*

Cover photo: Sekehe gong (gamelan group) performing in Banjar Teges, Bali, Indonesia. Photograph by Brittany Beihl. Used by permission of Brittany Beihl.

Credits: The credits section for this book begins on page 369 and is considered an extension of the copyright page.

Library of Congress Control Number: 2006939430

The Internet addresses listed in the text were accurate at the time of publication. The inclusion of a Web site does not indicate an endorsement by the authors or McGraw-Hill, and McGraw-Hill does not guarantee the accuracy of the information presented at these sites.
www.mhhe.com

I dedicate this book with love to
Megan, Isaac, and Leah, and to the
memory of my mother, Rita Bakan.

If ever you should leave my world,
And take with you my sustenance,
I would turn into a hollow hulk,
and walk the streets alone,
And hear the people say "Was that a man?"
And then I'd answer them this way:
That was a man whose every thought was joy;
That was a man who knew all bliss;
What he had was better yet than any man
*   should have.*
And so from him they took it all,
And what remains is here before you.
What he was he is no longer.

("Do Not Leave Me," by Paul Bakan,
February 23, 1954)

Michael B. Bakan is Associate Professor of Ethnomusicology in the College of Music at Florida State University, where he also directs the university's Balinese gamelan ensemble, Sekaa Gong Hanuman Agung. He has been the recipient of numerous awards and honors, including the prestigious Florida State University Undergraduate Teaching Award. His first book, *Music of Death and New Creation: Experiences in the World of Balinese Gamelan Beleganjur* (University of Chicago Press, 1999), was selected to the *Choice* Outstanding Academic Titles list for the year 2000 and was recognized as one of the two "most significant publications on Balinese music in almost half a century" in *The Times* (London). His many other publications encompass topics ranging from Indonesian music and world percussion to electronic music technology, early jazz history, multicultural music education, and the ethnomusicology of autism. He is the Series Editor of the critically acclaimed ABC-CLIO World Music Series, published in four volumes in 2004 and 2005, and also of a new world music book series that is being published by Routledge.

As a percussionist, Bakan has performed with many renowned world music, jazz, and Western classical music artists and ensembles, including the Toronto Symphony Orchestra, the Music at Marlboro Festival Orchestra, John Cage, A. J. Racy, Phil Nimmons, I Ketut Sukarata, and the championship beleganjur groups of Batur Tengah and Tatasan Kaja in Bali, Indonesia. He is also an active composer, with traditional and experimental works for Balinese gamelan, world music/jazz fusion pieces, film scores, and modern dance compositions to his credit.

Bakan formerly taught ethnomusicology at Bowling Green State University and has been a visiting professor or invited lecturer at the University of Washington, Indiana University, the University of Chicago, the University of Illinois, and the University of Colorado. He previously served as president of the Society for Ethnomusicology's Southeast/Caribbean Chapter. He lives in Tallahassee with his wife, Megan, their two children, their dog Wallace, and multiple outdoor cats.

brief contents

contents

World Music: Traditions and Transformations is an introductory-level survey of diverse musics from around the world. It assumes no prior formal training or education in music and avoids the use of Western music notation almost entirely. It is written primarily for classes of undergraduate nonmusic majors, but is also appropriate for music majors, as well as for courses enrolling both music and nonmusic students.

In writing this book, I have tried to create an engaging, clear, and accessible text that college and university instructors from a variety of backgrounds can use to make world music a vehicle of exploration, discovery, intellectual stimulation, and fun for their students. The work is the product of some seven years of research and writing and a decade-and-a-half of teaching. Really, though, its genesis dates back much farther, in particular, to the occasion of my third birthday, when I discovered a love of music that has inspired a commitment to sharing music with others ever since.

My birthday gift from my parents on that memorable day was the album *Beatles VI*. I still recall the magical feeling that came over me the first time I heard it. It filled me with wonder, delight, curiosity, and an exhilarating sense of discovery. I have experienced similar feelings many times since then: the first time I heard John Coltrane, Stravinsky's *The Rite of Spring*, Balinese *gamelan* music. Each of these encounters compelled me to listen again and again, moving deeper and deeper inside the music and coming away every time with more appreciation, more understanding, more love of music and fascination with the people and processes behind its creation.

Today, I continue to relish such magical moments of musical discovery and exploration when they come along, and they still do. But even more satisfying is getting the chance to help other people experience them, especially my students. That is the great reward of teaching introductory courses in world music such as the ones for which this text is intended. Teaching world music offers abundant and special opportunities to enrich our students' lives on many levels. Getting inside of music and seeing how it works, how it lives, and what makes it meaningful to people across a broad range of global contexts not only has the potential to expand our students' musical horizons and appreciations, but also can lead them to deeper understandings of their world, of cultural diversity and multiculturalism, of each other, and, not least importantly, of themselves.

Organization and Approach

This book is organized in two parts. Part I, consisting of the first six chapters, provides an inviting and nonthreatening introduction to the "elements of music" that is global in its inclusivity, encompasses cultural as well as purely musical elements, and is written with the explicit goal of being readily accessible to readers with no background in music. The depth of coverage in these chapters is geared specifically to preparing students for the materials they will encounter in Part II, not more, and is accordingly limited and focused.

Chapter 1 examines the fundamental question "What, in the world, is music?" Chapter 2 looks at how music lives as a phenomenon of culture and explains the book's core concept of *musicultural tradition*. Chapters 3–6 explore how music works as a medium of organized sound, with discussions of rhythm (Chapter 3); pitch (Chapter 4); dynamics, timbre, and instruments (Chapter 5); and texture and form (Chapter 6).

The various elements introduced in these chapters, both musical and cultural, are brought to life and made accessible via a combination of musical examples and illustrations of four kinds:

- Participatory exercises based on songs that will likely be familiar to most students ("The Alphabet Song," "Mary Had a Little Lamb," "The Star-Spangled Banner").

- Recorded examples representing diverse music traditions from around the world (these are included on the text's accompanying 3-CD set—see p. xxii).

- Online Musical Illustrations featuring audio-recorded examples of specific music elements (these are located at the Online Learning Center at www.mhhe.com/bakan1—see p. xxiv).

- User-friendly visual illustrations that are closely integrated with the musical examples discussed.

With respect to the world music recordings, these serve a dual purpose in this opening set of chapters. Beyond providing illustrations of specific music elements (syncopation, melodic contour, call-and-response, etc.), they also initiate the global musical journey that then continues on a different plane in Part II. Collectively, the Part I recordings give students both a musical preview of traditions that are explored more fully in later chapters and a whirlwind tour of numerous other traditions that are not: Native American dance song; traditional Aboriginal Australian music; Greek *syrtaki*; Zimbabwean world beat; Roma (Gypsy) brass band music; Mongolian *khoomii* multiphonic singing; Fijian hymnody; American blues; Japanese *koto, shakuhachi,* and *gagaku.*

Building from the foundation established in Part I, Part II features eight chapters, each consisting of an exploration of a single musicultural tradition. These chapters all link a central topic of musical focus to a central topic of cultural focus, which in turn form the main musicultural lens through which the tradition as a whole is then examined. In the chapter on Balinese music from Indonesia, for example (Chapter 7), we learn how the procedures for creating interlocking patterns in gamelan music embody core cultural values of communal interdependence that are evident in Balinese social interaction as well.

In this and the other Part II chapters, the main musicultural thread identified at the outset is woven through a series of recorded examples representing traditional, neo-traditional, and post-traditional manifestations of the music tradition at hand. The journey of Chapter 7 takes students from a traditional Hindu-Balinese cremation procession to a hip-hop/gamelan fusion piece produced in the United States; that of Chapter 14 extends from an archaic style of mystical Jewish chanting preserved in Bukhara, Uzbekistan, to the Jewish mysticism-inspired techno-electronica music of the contemporary British band Zöhar.

This *focused, musicultural approach*—encompassing traditional, neo-traditional, and post-traditional modes of expression within a series of compelling world music case studies—is intended to facilitate both depth of understanding and breadth of perspective without becoming overwhelming. While maintaining a scope that is manageable and appropriately contained, it allows students to engage with the complex realities of how music traditions move fluidly across conventional boundaries of history, geography, and identity. And it is an approach that aligns well with the conception of tradition that guides this entire work, namely, that *tradition is a process of creative transformation whose most remarkable feature is the continuity it nurtures and sustains.*

Key Features

Beyond its unique treatment of the elements of music (Part I) and its focused, musicultural approach (Part II), this text and its accompanying media offer a number of other valuable and attractive key features. These are described below.

World Music: Traditions and Transformations 3-CD Set

The 3-CD set was produced by Sony BMG Music Entertainment and includes over 100 musical selections (a combination of excerpts and complete tracks). The majority of these are drawn from high-quality, professional recordings by the likes of **Ravi Shankar, Tito Puente, Santana, Shakti, Angélique Kidjo, Hossam Ramzy, John Coltrane, The Chieftains, Eileen Ivers,** and **Yo-Yo Ma.**

The CD tracks are closely integrated with the text through Guided Listening Experience narratives, Guided Listening Quick Summaries, Musical Guided Tours, Music Making Exercises, and visual illustrations. Importantly, *the music itself drives this text, rather than being supplemental to it.* Each chapter was conceived and built "from the music up."

Getting Inside the Music Features

In keeping with its "music first" priority, *World Music: Traditions and Transformations* offers a number of mutually reinforcing vehicles for getting students inside the music they explore to see how it works and what makes it musiculturally meaningful:

- **Guided Listening Experience** narratives linked to the main musical examples of the Part II chapters highlight key elements of music sound, musical design, and cultural meaning as they unfold. They are written to be accessible and engaging for nonmusic majors, while improving students' listening skills and taking them deeply into the music without becoming overly technical.

- Boxed **Guided Listening Quick Summaries** immediately follow each of the main Guided Listening Experience narratives. These timeline boxes concisely summarize the principal features emphasized in a format that is easy to follow during listening.

- **Musical Guided Tours** take you inside the music in a different way. These brief and straightforward audio-recorded lecture demonstrations (which also appear in transcribed form in the text) enable students to hear and understand how music works *from the inside out,* step by step and part by part. They will learn, for example, how polyrhythms are generated in West African drum ensemble music (Chapter 10); how Irish traditional dance tunes are melodically ornamented and combined to form medleys (Chapter 9); and how the multiple musical layers and interlocking patterns of Balinese gamelan music are structured and organized (Chapter 7). There are eight Musical Guided Tours, one for each of the chapters in Part II.

- The **Making Music Exercises** included in some chapters provide another avenue of access to music's inner workings. Here, students are given simple, step-by-step instructions on how to actually *perform* on some level the music they are studying, either on their own or interactively with the recordings. (These exercises also work well as in-class group activities when directed by the course instructor.) They get to keep tal with Ravi Shankar; mark out Egyptian dance rhythm patterns with Hossam Ramzy; and actually *experience,* rather than just learn in the abstract, the meanings of key musical terms like melody, rhythm, and tempo.

- Finally, there are 26 **Online Musical Illustrations** that demonstrate key musical elements and features discussed in the text, from scales and instrumental timbres; to the paired tuning of Balinese gamelan instruments; to the traditional, neo-traditional, and post-traditional treatments of a single melodic figure in three contrasting Irish music performances.

Maps and Timelines

Chapter maps and chapter timelines are located at the beginning of each chapter in Part II. These collectively outline the geographical, historical, and musical trajectories of their respective chapters. They are designed to facilitate efficient, organized reading strategies and are valuable study resources as well.

Key Terms Lists, Pronunciation Guidance, and Glossary

A concerted effort has been made to limit the amount of foreign and technical terminology in the text. Given the subject matter, however, the presence of such terminology is an inevitable reality to some degree. In the interest of helping students and instructors alike to comfortably navigate the book's terminological terrain, the following features are included:

- A list of **Key Terms** at the end of every chapter; the key terms are highlighted in boldface print in the chapter text, generally at the point of their first appearance. (Other foreign terms that are not key terms are italicized where they first appear.)
- "Commonsense"-style phonetic **pronunciation guidance** in the margins for key terms and other terms or names that may present pronunciation difficulties.
- A **Glossary** that includes both definitions and pronunciation guidance for key terms, as well as reference to the main chapter in which the term appears.

Photographs, Visual Illustrations, and "Insights and Perspectives" Boxes

This book is enriched by abundant photographs, figures, tables, and other illustrative materials that bring the music and text vividly to life and enrich the clarity and enjoyment of the reading and music-listening experience. "Insights and Perspectives" boxes, which provide additional coverage or alternate points of view on materials in the main text, are another important feature.

Study Questions, Discussion Questions, and "Applying What You Have Learned" Sections

A list of study questions is included at the end of each chapter, along with discussion questions and suggestions for student projects and assignments that build upon or extend from chapter materials ("Applying What You Have Learned"). Students are also directed to the Online Learning Center at www.mhhe.com/bakan1 for additional resources and study aids at the conclusion of each chapter.

Flexibility

The text is designed to be flexible and adaptable to varied teaching situations and instructor needs and interests. This is the case in both Part I and Part II.

Though designed as an integrated unit, the set of six preliminary chapters that constitutes Part I may be approached in a variety of ways. Different student backgrounds (e.g., nonmusic majors versus music majors), pedagogical aims (e.g., greater "music" emphasis versus greater "culture" emphasis), or course settings (size of class, semester versus quarter) may inspire instructors to approach the teaching of these chapters in different ways (a number of suggestions are included in the Online Instructor's Manual at www.mhhe.com/bakan1—see p. xxiv). Some instructors may even elect to teach the chapters in an alternate order, for example, beginning with the elements of music sound addressed in Chapters 3–6 before addressing the more conceptual and cultural issues of Chapters 1–2.

As for Part II, there is a great amount of flexibility. Any number of these chapters (or all of them) may be taught in any order the instructor prefers. Though cross-references between certain chapters do occur and there are overarching themes that can be productively developed across chapters (e.g., music and nationalism, music and identity), each Part II chapter is ultimately a stand-alone unit. Some instructors may opt to cover all eight chapters, while others may prefer to select just five or six to allow time for more in-depth study. Some may follow the book's order of chapters, whereas others may prefer to use a different organizational strategy, for example, moving from "near to far" geographically, starting, say, with the Latino/American and Irish music chapters (Chapters 11 and 9) before tackling Bali or India (Chapters 7 and 8). Again, the Online Instructor's Manual provides suggestions on some possible approaches.

Consistency of Presentation and Authority in a Single-Authored Text

In contrast to several other introductory world music texts currently available, *World Music: Traditions and Transformations* is a single-authored work rather than a product of collaboration between multiple authors contributing individual chapters in their respective areas of specialization. A veritable explosion of new and excellent publications and other media in the world music arena in the last few years has made the prospect of a single-authored text of this type feasible and viable. Single authorship allows for a level of consistency of presentation in both the conception and writing of a work of this scale that is difficult, if not impossible, to achieve in a multi-authored textbook.

As for the accuracy and authority of the text, each chapter has benefited from a rigorous process of review. Especially noteworthy in this regard was the review process for the chapters of Part II, which were all reviewed by leading ethnomusicologists with specializations in the areas covered.

Supplementary Features

World Music: Traditions and Transformations offers helpful online resources for both instructors and students. The **Online Learning Center, Student Edition,** at www.mhhe.com/bakan1, provides students with a wealth of materials for course preparation and study, including chapter overviews, sample multiple-choice quizzes, sample music-listening quizzes, exam study guides, Internet links, annotated lists of resources and references for further study and research (books, articles, recordings, videos and DVDs, Internet resources), guidance on pronunciation of foreign language terms (beyond that included in the main text), and an image bank. Downloadable MP3 files of six of the book's eight audio Musical Guided Tours are located at the Online Learning Center (the other two audio Musical Guided Tours are included on the 3-CD set). So too are the 26 audio Online Musical Illustrations, which are likewise downloadable (with the exception of one).

The **Online Learning Center, Instructor Edition,** also located at www.mhhe.com/bakan1, gives instructors access to all the materials of the Student Edition plus much more. The most notable component of the Instructor Edition is the aforementioned **Online Instructor's Manual.** This includes lesson plans, ideas for in-class participatory exercises, supplementary information on chapter topics that can be used to enliven and enrich lectures, additional lists of resources for research and class use, sample syllabi and course schedules tailored to different course contexts (e.g., single semester, quarter, nonmusic major, music major), and a test bank including hundreds of questions.

PageOut (www.pageout.net) is an online resource designed and provided by McGraw-Hill that helps instructors put their course online. Combining easy entry, design templates, and a set of course management tools, PageOut is the easiest way to create a professionally designed Web site for your course.

Acknowledgments

I am immeasurably indebted to the many reviewers, colleagues, friends, and loved ones who have contributed to this work. It is impossible for me to list all those to whom I owe a debt of gratitude, but I must at least extend my deep thanks to the scores of ethnomusicologists and world music course instructors across the United States, Canada, and the United Kingdom whose comments, corrections, criticisms, and suggestions in reviews have helped shape this book: Noel Benkman, *Chabot College*; Eric Charry, *Wesleyan University*; Judah M. Cohen, *Indiana University*; Paula Conlon, *University of Oklahoma*; Steven Cornelius, *Bowling Green State University*; Robert Danziger, *California State University–Stanislaus*; Gavin Douglas, *University of North Carolina at Greensboro*; Ralph T. Dudgeon, *State University of New York*; Jonathan Dueck, *University of Maryland College Park*; Ron Emoff, *Ohio State University at Newark*; Michael Frishkopf, *University of Alberta*; Stephen Fuller, *St. Cloud State University*; Chris Geyer, *University of Indianapolis*; Rolf Groesbeck, *University of Arkansas–Little Rock*; Patricia Ann Grutzmacher, *Kent State University*; James A. Grymes, *University of North Carolina at Charlotte*; Aurelia W. Hartenberger, *Maryville University*; Ramona Holmes, *Seattle Pacific University*; Eric Hing-Tao Hung, *University of Montana*; E. Morgan Jenkins, *Pennsylvania State University–Mont Alto*; Barbara Rose Lange, *University of Houston–Moores*; Peter Manuel, *John Jay College* and the *Graduate Center, City University of New York*; Luke Palmer, *Pennsylvania State University–Berks*; Greg Petersen, *Rogers State University*; Harold Popp, *Wichita State University*; Tomm Roland, *University of Nebraska, Omaha*; Gil Seeley, *Lewis and Clark College*; Stephen Slawek, *University of Texas at Austin*; Paul Ely Smith, *Washington State University*; Jonathan Stock, *University of Sheffield*; Sean Williams, *Evergreen State College*; and Tom Zlabinger, *York College*.

I also extend my deep appreciation to Trevor Harvey, who realized the book's figures and tables and co-produced and mastered the 3-CD set, the Online Musical Illustrations, and the six online Musical Guided Tours; Carolyn Ramzy, Plamena Kourtova, Peter Hoesing, and Sarah Arthur, for cheerfully and efficiently completing the multitude of nit-picky tasks I assigned to them as my graduate assistants; Michael Redig, for his outstanding photographic contributions; Deng Haiqiong and Lynnsey Weissenberger, for their excellent Musical Guided Tour performances and advice; and Jane Scott, Meg Jackson, Ross Brand, Jeff Jones, Brittany Beihl, Pacho Lara, Mariano Rodriguez, León Garcia, Brittany Roche, Elizabeth Timan, Bryan Burton, Melinda Cowen, Jim Cox, Richard Zarou, Damascus Kafumbe, Lisa Beckley, Rachel Harris, Roderic Knight, Roger Vetter, Margaret Puente, Tito Puente Jr., Joe Conzo, Ted Levin, A. J. and Barbara Racy, Aisha Ali, Steve Stuempfle, Allan Marett, Katherine Hagedorn, Erran Baron Cohen, Michelle Kisliuk, Li Xiuqin, Jane Sugarman, Charles Atkins, Jen Brannstrom, Alec McLane, Valerie Gillespie, Jon Waxman, Daniel Avorgbedor, Joe Williams, Steven Loza, Ruth Wieder Magan, Rabbi Schneur Oirechman, Ellen Koskoff, Michael Tenzer, I Ketut Gedé Asnawa, I Ketut Sukarata, I Ketut Suandita, Sherry Simpson, Henry Hall, Min Tian, Jill Braaten, Caren-Alexandra Entwistle and Jon Entwistle of ARC Music Productions International Ltd., and Atesh Sonneborn of Smithsonian Folkways Recordings for their assistance, contributions, and wise counsel on a variety of matters.

My colleagues in the College of Music at Florida State University (FSU) have been extraordinarily supportive, and I especially want to thank Dale Olsen, Jeffery Kite-Powell, Douglass Seaton, Frank Gunderson, Ben Koen, Denise Von Glahn, Charles Brewer, Don Gibson, Jon Piersol, Clifford Madsen, Jane Clendinning, Pam Ryan, Patrick Meighan, Jerrold Pope, Barbara Ford, Dee Beggarly, Leo Welch, Wendy Smith, Linda Ross, Sally Gross, and Brian Gaber for their help. Numerous undergraduate and graduate students at FSU beyond those already acknowledged also have played an essential part in this work. I trust that you know who you are if you are reading this. Please forgive me for not mentioning you individually.

The editorial and production team at McGraw-Hill has been consummately professional and a joy to work with. Special thanks to Cindy Sullivan for "discovering" me and getting me in the loop; the editorial team of Chris Freitag, Melody Marcus, Beth Ebenstein, and Marley Magaziner; development editors Chris Narozny and Kate Engelberg; copyeditor Betsy Blumenthal; designer Gino Cieslik; project manager Susan Trentacosti; art editor Emma Ghiselli; photo research coordinator Natalia Peschiera; media producers Jocelyn Spielberger and Marc Mattson; and production supervisor Jason Huls. Special thanks, too, to Tom Laskey of Sony BMG Music Entertainment, whose tireless patience and perseverance over a span of many years were essential to achieving the outstanding quality and content of the 3-CD set; and to lead photo researcher Christine Buese of Photosearch, Inc., for her exemplary work.

To the many musicians who are featured on the CD set—those whom I know personally and those whom I do not, those who are living and those who have passed on—this book is a tribute to all of you and to musicians everywhere who make music work and make it live.

Michael B. Bakan
The Florida State University

about this book: an introduction for students

". . . the value of a piece of music as music is inseparable from its value as an expression of human experience."

John Blacking, *Music, Culture, & Experience*

World Music: Traditions and Transformations is an introductory-level survey of diverse musics from around the world. It assumes no prior formal training or education in music of any kind. You do not have to have had music lessons or classes to understand this book; nor do you need to know how to read music or play an instrument. The only real prerequisite is your willingness to explore music as the global phenomenon of human expression and experience it truly is, and in turn to approach the diversity of music you encounter with an open mind, open ears, thoughtfulness, and active engagement.

Throughout this world music journey, you will be invited to listen deeply to music, think broadly about what it means and why it is significant in human life, and even "perform" it yourself in some instances. The purpose of this multifaceted, experiential approach is not just to increase your understanding of what music is and how it works, but also to increase your appreciation and enjoyment of music overall. Experiencing, learning about, and taking pleasure in music go hand in hand; at least they ought to. Each of these interrelated ways of engaging with music enriches the other. All of them together have the capacity to enhance our appreciations of cultural diversity, intercultural tolerance, human creativity and resourcefulness, and the common spirit of humanity that unites us all.

World Music

"World music" is a slippery term. It is broad enough to encompass any and all music that exists or has ever existed in the world, yet it lacks the precision to accurately apply to any *specific* music tradition; it is open to many interpretations. A *raga* from India is neither more nor less deserving of the designation "world music" than a Mozart piano sonata. Yet most Westerners, if asked, would classify the former as an example of world music but not the latter; and most connoisseurs of Indian music would strongly disagree with this type of a classification scheme altogether.

Here, our approach will be to conceive of the study of world music simply as an exploration of selected music traditions from *throughout* the world. Each of the traditions chosen is traced from its point (or points) of beginning to wherever its multidirectional pathways of continuity and transformation may lead. The geographical and cultural "hubs" of given musics—the places identified with their origins, the communities and societies with which they are connected, the musicians recognized as their leading exponents—are most certainly accounted for, but so too are the complex, intersecting webs of geography, culture, technology, and sound that situate these hubs in more broadly global frameworks. All manner of musical expression, from the most resolutely traditional and geographically specific to the most commercially oriented, cross-culturally diverse, and radically experimental, are included.

A Focused, Musicultural Approach

This text is organized in two main parts. Part I, comprising Chapters 1–6, offers a general introduction to music as a phenomenon of sound and a phenomenon of culture. Drawing upon a combination of simple, familiar songs (such as "The Alphabet Song") and an eclectic range of music from around the world for its examples and illustrations, the six Part I chapters collectively address three fundamental questions:

- What is music?
- How does music live in people's lives?
- How does music work?

These chapters establish the basic foundation and framework for what follows in Part II.

Each of the eight chapters of Part II (Chapters 7–14) offers an exploration of a single *musicultural tradition*. The merging of the words "music" and "cultural" into the compound term *musicultural* (a new term) is intended to emphasize the inseparability of music as sound and music as "an expression of human experience" (Blacking 1995:31). Each chapter links a central topic of musical focus to a central topic of cultural focus. Together, these provide the principal musicultural lens through which the music tradition as a whole is then viewed. For example, in Chapter 7, a standard approach to rhythmic organization used in music from the island of Bali, Indonesia, is linked to fundamental cultural values and practices relating to Balinese concepts of social interdependence. This link then becomes the basis of an exploration of Balinese music traditions and transformations covering everything from ritual music played at Hindu-Balinese cremation ceremonies to a hip-hop/Balinese fusion piece.

Traditions and Transformations

Looking at relationships between established world music traditions and the processes of transformation that challenge and redefine them is central to this work. Every chapter in Part II builds around this issue of tradition and transformation in one way or another, and in each case a conception of *tradition as a process,* specifically, *a process of creative transformation whose most remarkable feature is the continuity it nurtures and sustains,* is at the heart of the discussion.

We encounter a series of first traditional, then neo-traditional, and finally post-traditional musical examples as each chapter unfolds (these are included on the text's accompanying 3-CD set—see p. xxx). On one level, key similarities and connections between the different examples are highlighted. This is done in order to illustrate how foundational features of musical style and meaning endure even in the face of far-reaching musical and cultural change. Examining the music on this level offers insights into what defines a tradition at its core, regardless of the eclectic musical surfaces that may become attached to it along the way. It helps us to comprehend, for example, how an ancient mystical prayer chanted in a traditional, Central Asian Jewish style dating back centuries belongs to the same music tradition as a Jewish mysticism-inspired techno-funk recording by the contemporary British band Zöhar (Chapter 14).

On a second level, contrasts and departures from convention that *distinguish* the different musical examples of each chapter one from the other—in terms of both their musical content and cultural meanings—also are emphasized. These serve to demonstrate the creative range and possibilities for transformation that are inherent in the flexibility of the tradition itself. As I try to show in each chapter, it is this flexibility that enables traditions to retain their vitality and relevance as they move through time across history, are transported to diverse locations around the globe, absorb and influence elements of other traditions, and become important and meaningful to different people for different reasons in different situations.

Depth versus Breadth: A Difficult Balancing Act

Many students reading this text will likely be contending with not just one but *two* rather complex subjects for the first time: the study of music and the study of culture. The focused, musicultural approach described earlier is intended to guide you toward appreciating the richness and depth of both—and of the fascinating domains of interaction that arise between them—without overwhelming you in the process. I have learned over the years that the richest appreciations, deepest understandings, and most enjoyable experiences of world music come not from trying to "cover everything" in a single course (an impossibility in any case, as I will discuss shortly), but rather from a more narrowly defined approach that explores a relatively small number of well-chosen traditions and topics.

That said, trade-offs and compromises are inevitable. In the present work, certain traditions and topics are included at the exclusion of many others that are every bit as interesting, important, and worthy of our attention. For example, there is a chapter on Chinese music (Chapter 13), but no chapter on Japanese or Korean music. Moreover, the Chinese music chapter focuses almost exclusively on the tradition of a single music instrument (the *zheng*), with only brief accounts of a handful of the thousands of other instrumental, ensemble, vocal, and theatrical traditions encompassed under the massive umbrella of "Chinese musical culture." In the chapter on Latino/American music (Chapter 11), a particular lineage of musical tradition and transformation is traced from its West African and Spanish roots to Cuba, Puerto Rico, and the United States; but Mexico, Central America, and South America are largely absent from the discussion. The single chapter devoted to musics of Africa (Chapter 10) focuses almost entirely on traditions originating in western Africa, with little attention to the rest of this huge and musically rich and diverse continent.

In Part I, I have tried to account for at least some world music areas and traditions not covered in the main chapter case studies of Part II (albeit superficially). Recordings representing Native American, African American, Aboriginal Australian, Mexican, Brazilian, Andean South American, Japanese, Mongolian, Tuvan, Polynesian, Micronesian, Romanian, Greek, and Spanish musics, as well as music traditions from several regions of Africa (i.e., southern, central, and eastern) are to be found among the selections on the CD set linked to the Part I chapters. Yet even if I were to add an entire chapter on each of these, we would still be just scratching the surface of what the universe of world music actually contains in all its comprehensive breadth. Our planet is host to thousands—indeed hundreds of thousands—of distinct music traditions and cultures, each fascinating and important in its own right.

A variety of factors guided my choices of what topics and areas to include in the eight chapters of Part II. In opting to include chapters on music traditions originating in China and India, for example, I was definitely swayed by the fact that these two nations together account for more than one-third of the world's entire population! At least as significant, though, was my interest in two particular musicians, Deng Haiqiong from China and Ravi Shankar from India. I felt that their particular musical odysseys, both in their native lands and internationally, offered wonderful opportunities for exploring tradition and transformation in world music.

My interest in the individual musician as a focal point for exploring musical tradition and transformation also influenced my decision to build the chapter on Latino/American music (Chapter 11) around the iconic figure of Tito Puente, and, more specifically, around his most famous composition, "Oye Como Va." Many other factors entered in here, too, a major one being that I wanted at least one chapter devoted specifically to a music tradition of the Americas. As for my decisions to include a chapter on Balinese music (Chapter 7) and one on Jewish music (Chapter 14), it was significant that these were two areas in which I have conducted specialized research.

I could continue with further examples, but the ones I have provided are probably sufficient to demonstrate that there is no one ideal, or even one best, rationale for deciding what to include and what not to when approaching a topic as vast as "world music." Practical considerations (What can one reasonably expect to cover in a single course?), representational considerations (including a range of musics that are diverse, cover a wide geographical range in their totality, and represent a number of the world's major music-culture regions), thematic considerations (choosing musics and topics that lend themselves well to a tradition-and-transformation approach), and personal considerations (areas of research specialization, interest in specific musicians) all entered into my decision-making processes. Above all else, though, my priority has been to make choices that collectively yield an introduction to world music that students will find accessible, enlightening, and exciting.

Getting Inside the Music

The *World Music: Traditions and Transformations* 3-CD set is in many respects the heart of this entire work. The book is driven by the music, rather than the other way around. Each chapter has been conceived and written "from the music up." The musical examples *themselves* tell the stories of musicultural tradition and transformation illuminated by the text. The main purpose of the text, then, is to help you hear those stories better, to get you inside the music on multiple levels and to provide a contextual framework to better understand and appreciate it.

The 3-CD set, which was produced by Sony BMG Music Entertainment, includes more than a hundred musical selections (a combination of excerpts and complete tracks). Most of these are drawn from professional, commercial recordings. Among the many artists and groups represented are some of the most well-known, highly respected, and influential in the world of music, past and present: Ravi Shankar, Tito Puente, Santana, Shakti, Angélique Kidjo, Taj Mahal, Toumani Diabate, Hossam Ramzy, John Coltrane, The Chieftains, Eileen Ivers, Yo-Yo Ma.

For each of the main musical examples of Part II included on the CDs, Guided Listening Experience narratives followed by concise, bullet-style Guided Listening Quick Summaries help you to explore how the music is organized *as* music and how key musical elements reflect larger musicultural issues. To get the most out of the Guided Listening, I suggest the following general approach:

- First, just listen to the example, without reading.

- Second, read through the Guided Listening Experience narrative to learn how the music is organized and how it reflects key cultural themes of the chapter.

- Third, listen to the example *at least* one more time, following along with the Guided Listening Quick Summary timeline and attempting to identify as many of the musical features highlighted as possible.

(*Note:* I also suggest having all three disks of the CD set on hand when doing your reading and listening assignments, since you will occasionally need to move between disks to access examples referenced in the text, especially in the chapters of Part I.)

Musical Guided Tours in each of the Part II chapters provide another opportunity for getting inside the music and understanding how it works. These take the form of brief, audio-recorded lecture demonstrations (which also appear in transcribed form in the text) that break down particular styles of music explored into their constituent parts, then put them back together again. Through these tours, you will hear how the interlocking parts in Balinese music are organized, how multiple rhythmic patterns are layered in West African drumming performances, and how Irish musicians "decorate" their dance tunes with musical ornaments. The Musical Guided Tours are interesting and instructive in and of themselves, but they also are useful for developing listening skills that can be productively applied to the Guided Listening Experiences.

Six of the eight Musical Guided Tours are located at the *World Music: Traditions and Transformations* Online Learning Center, Student Edition (www.mhhe.com/bakan1), where they are available as downloadable MP3 files; the other two are included on the 3-CD set (the text directs you to the appropriate location in each chapter). Also available at the Online Learning Center are 26 Online Musical Illustrations, which provide audio-recorded examples of key musical elements and features discussed in the text. These, too, are downloadable (with the exception of one). The Online Learning Center additionally offers a wealth of other materials for enhancing your learning and study experience: chapter overviews, sample multiple-choice quizzes, sample music-listening quizzes, exam study guides, Internet links, guidance on pronunciation of foreign language terms (beyond that included in the main text), an image bank, and annotated lists of reading, listening, viewing, and Internet resources.

A final way of getting inside the music to better understand, appreciate, and enjoy it is to actually *perform* music yourself. Many chapters include simple performance exercises that allow you to experience how music works firsthand by either making it or interacting in specific ways with the recordings. These kinds of "hands-on" experiences can be tremendously helpful in increasing your understanding of how music works. They also can be a lot of fun, especially when you team up with friends or fellow students—or even your whole class—to try them out.

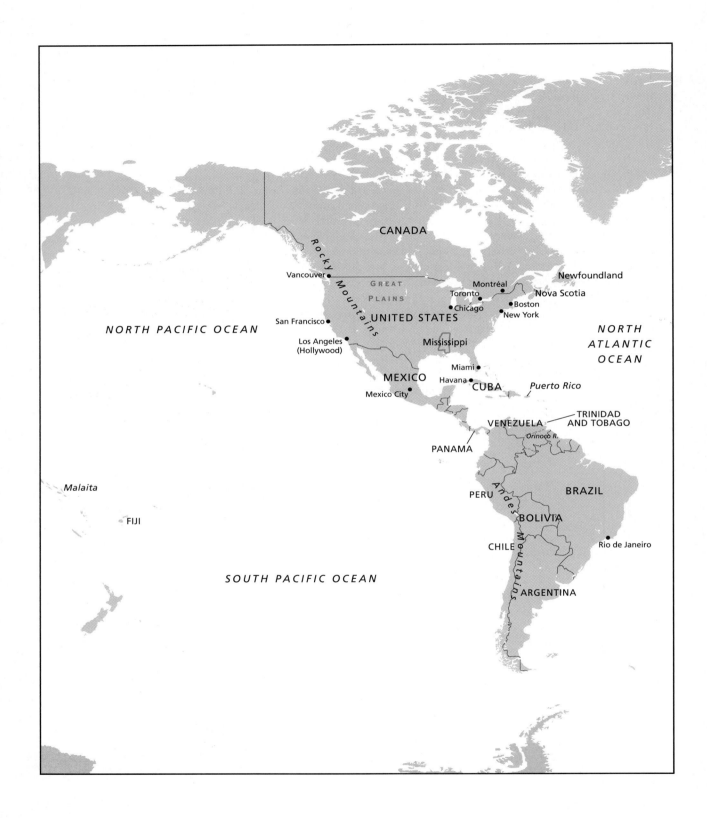

CANADA

Vancouver •

Rocky Mountains

GREAT PLAINS

Montréal
Toronto
• Chicago

Newfoundland

Nova Scotia

• Boston
New York

UNITED STATES

San Francisco •

NORTH PACIFIC OCEAN

Los Angeles
(Hollywood) •

Mississippi

*NORTH
ATLANTIC
OCEAN*

Miami •

MEXICO

Havana •

CUBA

Puerto Rico

Mexico City •

VENEZUELA

TRINIDAD
AND TOBAGO

PANAMA

Orinoco R.

Malaita

PERU

Andes Mountains

BRAZIL

FIJI

BOLIVIA

CHILE

Rio de Janeiro •

SOUTH PACIFIC OCEAN

ARGENTINA

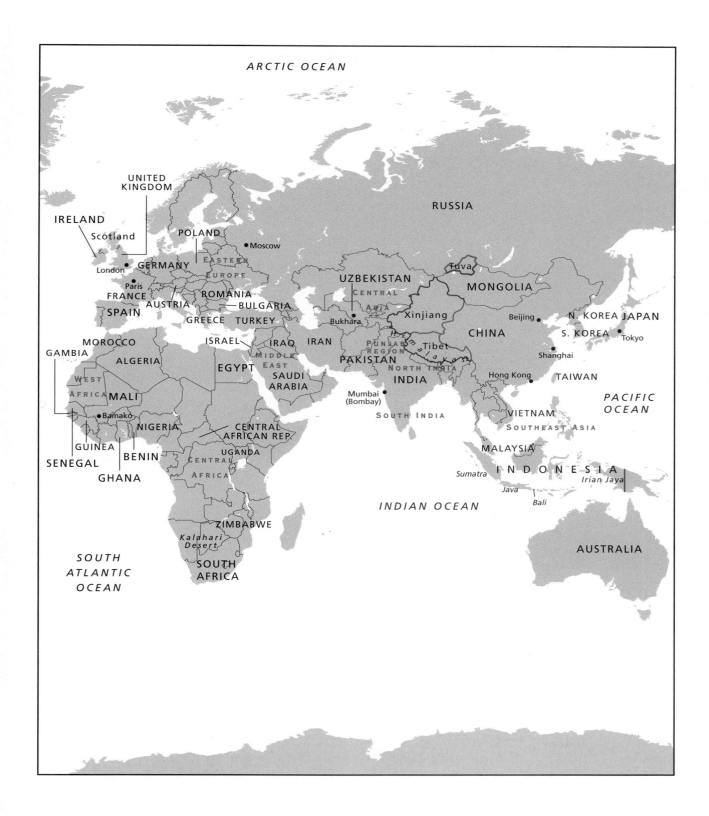

ARCTIC OCEAN

IRELAND

Scotland

UNITED KINGDOM

POLAND

• Moscow

RUSSIA

London

GERMANY

EASTERN

EUROPE

Paris

FRANCE

AUSTRIA

ROMANIA

SPAIN

BULGARIA

GREECE

TURKEY

UZBEKISTAN

Tuva

CENTRAL
ASIA

MONGOLIA

Bukhara

Xinjiang

Beijing

N. KOREA JAPAN

MOROCCO

ISRAEL

IRAQ

IRAN

CHINA

S. KOREA

Tokyo

GAMBIA

ALGERIA

MIDDLE
EAST

PUNJAB
REGION

Himalayas

Tibet

Shanghai

WEST
AFRICA

EGYPT

SAUDI
ARABIA

PAKISTAN

NORTH INDIA

Hong Kong

TAIWAN

MALI

INDIA

PACIFIC
OCEAN

Bamako

Mumbai
(Bombay)

SOUTH INDIA

NIGERIA

GUINEA

CENTRAL
AFRICAN REP.

VIETNAM

SENEGAL

BENIN

UGANDA

SOUTHEAST ASIA

GHANA

CENTRAL
AFRICA

MALAYSIA

INDONESIA

Sumatra

Irian Jaya

Java

INDIAN OCEAN

Bali

ZIMBABWE

Kalahari
Desert

AUSTRALIA

SOUTH
ATLANTIC
OCEAN

SOUTH
AFRICA

what, in the **world,** is **music?**

The piano recital is about to begin. The first piece listed on the program is *4'33"* (*four minutes, thirty-three seconds*), by a composer named John Cage.

The pianist is greeted by warm applause as she steps out onto the stage and bows to the audience. She sits down at the piano, puts a musical score up on the stand, and clicks a button on a stopwatch. Closing her eyes and gracefully placing her hands over the piano keys, she appears poised and ready to play. But then she doesn't play anything. Thirty seconds go by, then a minute. Nothing but silence. She reaches up and turns a page. Still no music. Two minutes go by. Another page turn; *still* no music. The "silence" becomes almost overwhelming. Every sound in the concert hall—the muffled coughs, the squeaking seats, the whirring of the air-conditioning system—seems as though it is coming through an amplifier.

Finally, four minutes and thirty-three seconds after sitting down at the piano, the pianist reaches over, turns off the stopwatch, stands up, and bows, never having played a note. Some members of the audience applaud enthusiastically. Others do not seem to know quite what to do.

This is music?

Qur'an, Qur'anic (koar-AHN, koar-AH-nik)

Shift the scene now to a mosque. A passage from the **Qur'an,** the holy book of Islam, is being recited. The words flow forth in melodious tones: beautiful, profound, elegantly crafted—in a word, musical. Yet this is categorically *not* music according to the Muslim people who have gathered at the mosque to pray. In fact, to refer to it as such is not just wrong from an Islamic perspective, but offensive.

Is *this* music?

A third scene now. A teenage boy sits in his room on a Saturday afternoon listening to his favorite CD, *Wrecking Everything,* by the thrash metal band Overkill. The music is turned up loud, very loud. The boy's father is downstairs working on his taxes. He is tired and has a headache. After a while, he loses his patience, charges up the stairs, and storms into his son's room. "Turn that garbage off!" he shouts. "How can you listen to this junk? It's nothing but noise. It's not even music!"

Not for him perhaps, but it certainly is for his son.

Is this music?

■ ■ ■

A Point of Departure: Five Propositions for Exploring World Music

Determining when you are experiencing "music" and when you are experiencing something else is not always a straightforward matter. One person's music may be another person's noise, prayer recitation, even silence. The question "What is music?" can yield radically different responses even within a single family or tight-knit community. Expand the scope to a global scale and the divergence of views multiplies exponentially.

All of this raises at least two interesting questions:

1. What factors account for people's many and vastly different views of what music is, and what it is not?

2. Given that there is not even general agreement about what music is in the first place, how might we establish a reasonable, common point of departure from which to begin our exploration of music—world music—as the global and extraordinarily diverse phenomenon of humankind that it is?

The **five propositions** that follow address these questions in both direct and indirect ways. In the process, they collectively provide a point of departure regarding what music is—and what it is not—that underscores the approach of this text as a whole. This approach is based on the idea that it is important to have an open-minded and inclusive perspective on what music is when exploring world music. In keeping with this idea, these five propositions represent perspectives that are widely shared among people interested in the study of music as a worldwide phenomenon. The propositions are by no means definitive or closed to debate, however. They are presented here mainly to establish a common ground for our musical journey, but also will hopefully stimulate you to think about and discuss your own, possibly different, ideas about what music is.

Proposition 1: The basic property of all music is sound

Music is made up of sounds. To distinguish music sounds from other kinds of sounds (noise sounds, speech sounds, ambient sounds, etc.), we will use the term **tone** to designate a music sound. A tone, then, is *a sound whose principal identity is a musical identity, as defined by people (though not necessarily all people) who make or experience that sound.*

Every tone possesses four basic physical properties: duration (length), frequency (pitch), amplitude (loudness), and timbre (quality of sound, tone color). We will learn more about these four properties of tones in successive chapters.

timbre (TAM-ber)

Additionally, tones are defined by the musical environments that surround them. Each tone gains musical meaning through its relationships with other tones. It is through these relationships between tones that the building blocks of music—melodies, chords, rhythms, textures, all of which also will be topics of later chapters—are formed.

Tones also acquire *cultural* meanings from the symbolic associations that people attach to them, associations that extend far beyond the domain of music sound itself. A tone with a particular set of physical properties may be used in one instance to summon deities in a religious ritual. But that exact same tone also may appear in a commercial jingle for a fast-food restaurant, where the purpose is to convince people to buy more burgers and fries. How any given tone is understood, then, has at least as much to do with what people make of it as with the physical properties of the sound itself.

Any and all sounds have the potential to be tones, that is, to be music sounds. This includes obvious candidates such as notes that are sung or played on a piano, guitar, or violin, but it also includes the sounds of slamming shutter doors, pig squeals, water rushing in a stream, or anything else. As we shall explore later in the chapter, the classification of sounds as music sounds (tones) or as nonmusic sounds is principally a product of people's intentions and perceptions regarding sounds. Theoretically, at least, there are no limits, but people do make decisions about what they will and will not accept as a music sound, just as they make decisions about what they will and will not accept in most other areas of life. That is why some people identify the sounds of Qur'anic recitation or of thrash metal as music sounds, while other people categorically do not.

But what about John Cage's *4′33″*, a work in which the most basic property of music—that is, that it be based in sound—seems conspicuously absent. Surely here, in what is often referred to as "Cage's silence piece," we have crossed the line of what any reasonable human being might justifiably classify as music. Or have we?

Perhaps not. Actually, there *are* sounds—many sounds—in every performance of *4′33″*. There are the sounds of the performers' footsteps as they walk out onto the stage, of the audience applauding, of the clicking on and off of the stopwatch, of the turning of pages at prescribed time intervals, of the random assortment of coughs, chair squeaks, heating and air-conditioning system hums, and whatever else may emerge during a given performance. It is not an absence of sounds, then, that makes *4′33″*'s status as a piece of music controversial. It is, rather, the fact that most people are not accustomed to hearing the types of sounds that occur in a performance of the piece *as* music that mainly accounts for the controversy it has generated for over a half century since its premiere performance (by the composer) in 1952. Indeed, one of the main "points" of *4′33″* is that it creates a framework for music listening that compels people to reorient their hearing, to hear "the music" inherent in a range of sounds and silences whose musical qualities are conventionally ignored or go unnoticed by music listeners.

John Cage.

Proposition 2: The sounds (and silences) that comprise a musical work are organized in some way

One marker of difference between music sounds and other types of sounds is that music sounds always emerge within some kind of organizational framework, whereas other sounds may or may not. Music, then, is a form of *organized sound*. This is plainly evident when we listen to a well-known Western classical music work such as Ludwig van Beethoven's Symphony #9 **(CD ex. #1-1),** but the organizational element is no less significant in music that seems, at least to many Western listeners, to defy recognizable principles of organization. This latter category may include music from a foreign culture that is based on unfamiliar organizational schemes, such as the Japanese *gagaku* music heard in **CD ex. #1-2.** It also may include music originating in our own culture that intentionally *subverts* the common and familiar organizational principles that make music recognizable, things like conventional types of melodies, rhythms, and instrumental sounds. Much of John Cage's music fits this description.

**gagaku
(gah-GAH-koo)**

Proposition 3: Sounds are organized into music by people; thus, music is a form of humanly organized sound

The baseline assertion that helps us begin to distinguish between music sound and a great many other types of organized sound is that *music is a human phenomenon*: it is a form of "humanly organized sound" (Blacking 1973). There is no doubt that many animals express themselves and even communicate using organized systems of sound that have musiclike qualities. It may even be true that some animals (e.g., whales, dolphins) conceptualize certain types of sounds they create in ways that are closely akin to how people conceptualize music. Research suggestive of such possibilities already exists, and it is likely that future research will be even more revealing.

For our present purposes, however, it is proposed that music, understood as such, is essentially a human invention. It is something that people either make, hear, or assign to other kinds of sounds. Birds and whales did not "sing" until human beings saw fit to label their distinctive forms of vocalization with that musical term (which, again, is not necessarily to say that they do not have a well-defined concept of what they *are* doing when *we* say they are singing—a good subject for research, speculation, and debate). Moreover, birds and whales do not necessarily "make music" any more than pigs do, but the "songs" of birds and whales seem to have been more amenable to musical interpretation *by people* than the grunts of pigs (see also Nettl 2006:23).

In short, returning to a point made earlier, any and all sounds have the *potential* to be employed and heard as musical sounds. However, only when a human being *uses* a given sound for musical purposes, or *perceives* or *describes* that sound in musical terms, does the sound actually enter into the domain of "music." Once again, it is not what a sound is *per se,* but rather what people make of it, that is the main criterion.

Japanese gagaku orchestra.

Proposition 4: Music is a product of human intention and perception

Expanding on another premise alluded to earlier in the chapter, there are two basic processes of human cognition involved in determining what is and what is not music: intention and perception. When any sound, series of sounds, or combination of sounds is organized by a person or group of people and presented as "music"—that is, with the *intention* that it be heard as music—our point of departure will be to treat it as music. Similarly, when any person or group of persons *perceives* a sound, series of sounds, or combination of sounds as "music," our point of departure will be to treat that as music too.

The value of this approach—which I refer to for convenience as the **HIP (human intention and perception) approach**—is that it (1) privileges inclusiveness over exclusiveness and (2) emphasizes the idea that music is inseparable from the people who make and experience it.

John Cage created *4'33"* with the intention of making a piece of music; musicians who perform the work approach it as a piece of music; and at least some members of the audiences who hear it performed are likely to perceive it as music. Thus, it fits the criteria of "music" in the HIP model. Granted, a performance of *4'33"* may be interpreted as many things other than a music performance—for example, as a philosophical statement *about* music, a commentary on the experience of music listening, or a challenge to conventional expectations of music listeners—but these other points of view only enrich how *4'33"* may be understood and appreciated *as* music.

Islamic Qur'anic recitation, an example of which may be heard on **CD ex. #1-3,** can be treated as music because its melodic and rhythmic organization is likely perceived by *you* (if you are not a Muslim) in musical terms. The undeniably "musical" quality that Qur'anic recitation suggests to Western listeners—and indeed the close similarity of such recitation to forms of organized sound that Muslims themselves *do* recognize as music (see Chapter 12)—makes the question of why it is not considered music by Muslims all the more interesting. The answer is that many Muslims believe music to be essentially a profane art that has no place in religious observance: if it is part of worship, it is not music, regardless of what it sounds like. In this case, religious and cultural principles take priority over ostensibly musical properties of sound. (As we will see in Chapter 12 [p. 272], attitudes in Islamic societies concerning the relationship between worship and music are considerably more varied and complex than the present discussion suggests.)

As for the example of the father dismissing his son's favorite thrash metal CD as being "not even music," the HIP approach favors the idea that this *is* indeed music. The musicians created it with the intention that it be heard as music, and the teenage boy heard it as music. It thus meets the basic criteria of music status. This does not mean that the father's opinion on the matter should not be part of the discussion, however. Examining *why* different people in the same situation accept or reject something as music is one of the best paths to understanding the roles and functions of music in human life. In this case, differences in age and generational status

Muslim men praying together inside a mosque in Alexandria, Egypt.

between the boy and his father would seem to be decisive factors in explaining their very different views on what is, and what is not, music.

Proposition 5: The term *music* is inescapably tied to Western culture and its assumptions

We can now say that music is a category of humanly organized sound that takes its core identity from the musical intentions and perceptions of its makers and listeners. That would be a solid point of departure for our journey were it not for the fact that many of the world's peoples do not even have a word equivalent to *music* in their languages. Furthermore, even in languages that do possess a term closely akin to *music,* such as Arabic, the term may not always apply where we would expect it to, as the example of Qur'anic recitation illustrates.

And so we are left with a dilemma: even though every human culture in the world has produced forms of organized sound that we in the West consider music, many of these cultures do not categorize their own "music" as music at all. It seems that our concept of music, however broad and open-minded we try to make it, cannot transcend its Western cultural moorings. We are apparently doomed to a certain measure of **ethnocentrism;** that is, we cannot help but impose our own culturally grounded perspectives, biases, and assumptions on practices and lifeways that are different from our own.

What options do we have for confronting this dilemma? We can

1. Avoid dealing with these problematic phenomena of sound in musical terms altogether.

2. Impose Western musical concepts on them, in essence "converting" them into music on our terms (for example, treating Qur'anic recitation as music regardless of the Muslim claim that it is not music).

3. Try to find some way to integrate and balance our own perceptions of what we hear as "music" with the indigenous terms and concepts used by other people when describing the same phenomena.

The third of these options is the one that for the most part guides the approach of this text, both in relation to the fundamental question of what is and is not music and in terms of two closely related issues that we address in the forthcoming chapters: how music lives and how music works.

Summary

This chapter began with the question posed by its title: *What, in the world, is music?* Following a series of three brief scenarios that challenged conventional notions of what music is, five propositions about music were offered to provide a conceptual framework for addressing this question. These propositions posited that

1. The basic property of all music is sound.

2. The sounds (and silences) that comprise a musical work are organized in some way.

3. Sounds are organized into music by people; thus, music is a form of humanly organized sound.

4. Music is a product of human intention and perception.

5. The term *music* is inescapably tied to Western culture and its assumptions.

In addition to providing a basic framework for exploring the question of what is and what is not music, these five propositions also were presented, collectively, as a general point of departure for exploring world music from open-minded and broadly inclusive perspectives.

Key Terms

Qur'an (Qur'anic recitation)
five propositions (about music)
tone

HIP (human intention and
   perception) approach
ethnocentrism

Study Questions

- What were the five propositions for exploring world music presented in this chapter?

- What is the HIP (human intention and perception) approach, and why is it important in the study of world music?

- Why do Muslims not consider Qur'anic recitation music, even though it sounds like music to other people?

- What is ethnocentrism?

- Why can John Cage's *4'33"* be categorized as a piece of music even though it does not seem to sound like one?

Discussion Questions

- Do you think John Cage's *4'33"* should be classified as music or not? On what grounds might you argue for or against its musical status?

- Do you think animals make music, or is music specifically a human phenomenon? How would you support an argument for either side of the debate?

- Do you agree with the five propositions for exploring world music presented in the chapter? Are there any you think are open to challenge? If so, why, and how? Can you think of any alternate or additional propositions that would help to clarify what is—and what is not—music?

Applying What You Have Learned

- Go to the quietest place you can find: a secluded forest, a remote mountainside, an isolated room. Sit or lie down, close your eyes, and listen to the "silence." What sounds do you hear? Is there a sense in which they take on a *musical* character after a while? Describe the experience as a *musical* experience.

- Create a list of different kinds of sounds, classifying them into "music" and "nonmusic" categories. Use your own *subjective* criteria to decide what to include on each list. Are there instances where the types of sounds that you think of as music would not qualify as music according to the criteria of this chapter (e.g., animal sounds), or where sounds that you categorize as nonmusic would be classified as music using the HIP approach? If so, what do you think accounts for these "discrepancies"?

Resources for Further Study

Visit the Online Learning Center at www.mhhe.com/bakan1 for additional learning aids, study help, and resources that supplement the content of this chapter.

chapter two

how **music lives:**
a musicultural approach

In the first chapter, we were introduced to the idea that music is defined not only by its sounds, but also by the environments in which it lives and the meanings people attach to it. This chapter explores that idea in more detail.

Music becomes significant mainly in the context of human life: in what people do, who they think they are, what they believe, what they value. When we explore what people do, think, believe, and value as members of groups and communities, we are exploring what is known in the social sciences as *culture*. Music is a phenomenon of culture, and, as such, it is best understood in relation to culture, more specifically, in relation to the *cultural context*—or contexts—in which it lives.

Understanding music as a phenomenon of culture is always important, but is perhaps especially so when dealing with music in a global perspective.

Often, it is the beliefs and practices of cultural life that are embedded in music, rather than the sounds themselves, that reveal the most profound insights into what makes music meaningful and significant in people's lives. **Ethnomusicology**—an interdisciplinary academic field that draws on musicology, anthropology, and other disciplines in order to study the world's musics—makes a first priority of engaging music in ways that reveal such insights. Ethnomusicologists are interested in understanding music as a **musicultural** phenomenon (a new term), that is, as a phenomenon where *music as sound* and *music as culture* are mutually reinforcing, and where the two are essentially inseparable from one another. Our purpose throughout this text will be to understand and appreciate the musics we encounter in this way, and this chapter, therefore, lays the groundwork for examining how music lives in human life, not just as sound, but as culture as well.

■ ■ ■

Culture in Music

In 1871, Edward Tylor, a seminal figure in the history of anthropology, defined **culture** as "that complex whole which includes knowledge, belief, art, law, morals, custom, and any other capabilities and habits acquired by man [humankind] as a member of society" (quoted in Barnard 2000:102). Scores of other definitions of the term *culture* have been proposed since, yet Tylor's classic formulation has proven extraordinarily durable. It still provides a good baseline for comprehending the concept of culture in our modern world.

As the Tylor definition implies, the study of culture encompasses most everything having to do with people's lives as members of human communities: their religions and political systems; their languages and technologies; their rituals and dances; their modes of work and play; the things that make them laugh and cry; what they wear and what they eat; and, of course, the music they make and listen to.

But what is the community, or what are the *communities,* that define a culture? Throughout human history, cultures have always been changing, merging, malleable, overlapping, in flux; and that is likely more true today than in any previous era. Globalization, mass media communications, the Internet, multinational entertainment industry corporations, easy access to international travel, and other forces of modernity often make it difficult, if not impossible, to draw a clear line in the sand distinguishing one culture from another, musically or otherwise. An example: What is "the culture" of residents of Germany who are of Turkish descent but who define and express themselves mainly through an American-derived style of hip-hop music, with lyrics that alternate between passages in Turkish and passages in German? There is no clear answer to such a question; indeed, there is no clear best point of departure from which to begin to address it.

Yet despite such complexities, cultures—and the cultural traditions through which they become manifest—are real and they do endure, even as they transform. Certain groups of people—tribes, clans, religious sects, ethnic groups, societies, nations—do indeed behave, think, and believe differently than others on the whole, and the degrees of difference and similarity between different cultural groups vary: the musical cultures of Egypt and Lebanon are in many ways distinct, yet they clearly have more in common than the musical cultures of Egypt and Finland.

Music is a mode of cultural production and representation that reveals much about the workings of culture, from the resilience of traditional ways to people's remarkable capacities for cultural adaptation, innovation, and transformation. In the collective sounds and meanings of the world's musics lies a remarkable pool of resources for comprehending what unites and separates us as individuals, as communities, as musicultural beings, and as members of the global culture of humanity to which we all belong.

Meaning in Music

Music comes into existence at the intersection of sound and culture. It is not until some kind of *meaning* is connected to sounds—sounds that might otherwise be heard as random or arbitrary—that these sounds come to be perceived as music. Meaning, then, is the essential glue that binds together sound and culture to form music.

As was mentioned briefly in Chapter 1, the tones of music are meaningful in at least two ways. First, they have meaning relative to one another. For example, the familiar children's song "Mary Had a Little Lamb" consists of a series of tones, or *notes* (a common term used to refer to the specific tones in a piece of music), that occur in a particular order. Each of these notes acquires meaning relative to the others: the note on which you sing the first syllable of the word "Mary" at the beginning (i.e., "Ma-") sounds higher than the note for the second syllable ("-ry"); and the note for the word "had," which follows "Mary," sounds lower than those used for either "Ma-" or "ry." The relative highness or lowness of each of these three notes in comparison with one another (a function of the musical element of *pitch,* which we will explore in Chapter 4) invests each with a particular meaning in the context of that song. This kind of meaning is essentially limited to the sounds themselves, in other words, to music solely as a phenomenon of sound.

At the second level of meaning, the one that concerns us here, musical sounds acquire meaning in relation to things beyond themselves. Imagine being raised in a culture where the exact same melody that we associate with "Mary Had a Little Lamb" was the basis of a funeral lament instead of a children's song. Hearing the melody would cause you to have entirely different feelings, memories, and thoughts. The song's meaning would be completely transformed.

This example illustrates what is so often true of music: that its meaning is determined as much or more by matters of context as by "the notes" themselves. This is musical meaning at the level of a phenomenon of culture, not of sound alone. Musical meaning as a phenomenon of culture accounts for why shamans (traditional healers) among the Warao, an Amerindian people of Venezuela, believe that there are certain kinds of songs that have the power to heal people and other kinds of songs that have the power to make people sick (Olsen 1996: 262–63). It also accounts for why the singing style heard in **CD ex. #1-4,** an example of a Chinese opera song (see Chapter 13, pp. 302–03), is perceived as beautiful by its Chinese admirers but may be perceived quite differently by people who do not share their culturally informed points of view regarding musical aesthetics.

Identity in Music

How people make and perceive meaning in music is inextricable from how they think about and represent themselves and one another. Conceptions of music

The late Jaime Zapata, a powerful Warao shaman.

Costumed Beijing Opera performer.

Mongolian khoomii singer Amartuwshin Baasandorj, who is featured on CD ex. #1-5.

throughout the world are closely tied to conceptions of **identity,** that is, to people's ideas about who they are and what unites them with or distinguishes them from other people and entities: individuals, families, communities, institutions, cultures, societies, nations, supernatural powers.

To a significant degree, music always provides partial answers to two fundamental questions: *Who am I?* and *Who are we?* If you are a hip-hop DJ or enthusiast, your involvement with that music will inevitably contribute to your conceptions of who you are—the "I" portion of your identity. It also will cause you to identify and socialize with certain individuals, groups, and communities more than others—the "we" portion of your identity. On the "I" level, connecting yourself to hip-hop and its musicultural world (or worlds!) may impact your self-esteem, your fashion sensibilities, your approaches to expressing yourself and communicating with others. On the "we" level, it may lead to new friendships with like-minded listeners, or to a shift away from spending time with old friends and acquaintances who do not share your passion for hip-hop.

Music also frames identity in regards to a related pair of questions: *Who is she (or he)?* and *Who are they?* When you first encounter a Mongolian singing performance like the one featured on **CD ex. #1-5,** or a performance of a Central Javanese *gamelan* orchestra from Indonesia such as that heard in **CD ex. #1-6,** you immediately begin to form ideas about what the people making the music are like and what kind of a culture they come from. If you go a step further and study the music and the culture in some depth, you may discover that some of your initial impressions were on track, but that others were misguided.

gamelan (gah-muh-lahn)

Go deeper still and you are likely to encounter a host of interesting music-culture parallels, but also an abundance of contradictions and ambiguities revolving around the interrelationships of music, culture, and identity. Disparities exist between how musicians represent themselves and their culture versus how they are represented by others. Misleading stereotypes relating to ethnicity, gender, and race abound, distorting musical and cultural meanings while shaping them at the same time. You also may find your own assumptions about the music you hear—

A Central Javanese gamelan.

your notions about whether it is traditional or modern, authentic or inauthentic—turned upside down in the face of historical and contextual realities.

Listen to **CD ex. #1-7,** which features the opening portion of a Rabbit Dance song performed in a style that is closely identified with Amerindian music cultures of the Great Plains region of North America (spanning from the Mississippi River westward to the Rocky Mountains). With its evocative title, descending vocal lines, intense singing style, and percussive accompaniment, "Rabbit Dance" sounds very traditional. But listen now to **CD ex. #1-8,** which picks up where the previous selection left off. Focus on the words. Surprised? As it turns out, this is a quite different kind of song than it first seemed to be, and this difference suggests that the identities of the people singing it—that is, who they are—may be *quite* far removed from what you had initially presumed.

This example points to the fact that identities—of people, of groups, of types of music—are very complex. They consist of many different components. Some of these components are mutually reinforcing; others seem contradictory; many of them overlap. I think of myself as a Canadian, though I reside in and have spent more than half of my life in the United States. As a musician, I conceive of myself mainly as a jazz drummer, though I am much better known in my profession as a Balinese gamelan musician (this despite the fact that I have not an ounce of Balinese blood in me). To some people, I am a teacher; to others, an ethnomusicologist and book author; to still others, a father and husband. The music I compose and perform contains elements of all these different aspects of my identity, and often reflects the complex relations that exist between them.

If you think about who you are—as an individual, as a cultural being, and in terms of your impressions of who *other* people think you are—you will quickly realize that your identity, too, is complex and multifaceted. You also may discover that it is intimately bound up with the way music functions in your life. Music symbolically reflects and embodies the social realities and ideals of the people who make and listen to it in significant ways. It can tell us much about who these people are and what matters to them, but we need to know how to listen in a culturally informed way to get the message.

Identity is located in music at many different levels. Societies, cultures, nations, transnational communities, and other large-scale social structures fundamentally define people's conceptions of who they and others are, at home and throughout the world. It is these large-scale units of social organization that provide the broad frameworks, or outlines, for the shaping of identity through music, and to which we now turn our attention.

Native American dance performance.

Societies

A **society** may be defined as *a group of persons regarded as forming a single community.* When we study the relationship of music and society, our interest is in how music functions among the members of such a group of persons to foster their sense of community, and sometimes to challenge it.

While the term *society* may be applied to communities of virtually any size, it is most often used in connection with large-scale social entities, such as nations. Because of their size, societies are usually *imagined communities* (Anderson 1991). This means that they are unified as communities not because all of their members actually know each other on a "face-to-face" basis, but rather because they share a connection to one another through certain ideas and **social institutions** that define the social order.

All societies are built around aggregates of intersecting social institutions. These may be governmental, economic, legal, religious, family-centered, activity- or interest-based, service-oriented, or purely social in nature. Sororities and fraternities, churches and synagogues, political parties and village councils, banks and corporations, hospitals and schools, marching bands and rock bands, dance clubs and sewing clubs are all examples of social institutions.

Social institutions function and take on meaning within and across a range of different family-based, administrative, and political spheres of a society: families, peer groups, tribes, clans, neighborhood organizations, villages, towns, cities, counties, states and provinces, large regional areas, nations. They also may take on significance in interactions between different societies, for example, in a cultural exchange program for high school orchestras from the United States and Taiwan. At every level of society, music may serve to mark the society's identity in significant ways, whether through the performance of a family band at a local dancehall or an international concert tour of a national music-and-dance troupe.

The study of music and society focuses on how musicians and musical institutions act and function relative to their societies. It explores how they enter into, are affected by, change and are changed by, and contribute to the interplay of, the social institutions that keep the engine of a society running, or that may in some instances cause it to stall.

Looking at the domain of gamelan music in Bali, Indonesia (which is explored again in greater detail in Chapter 7), offers key insights into the relationship of music and society. A gamelan consists of a large number of instruments—mainly percussion instruments such as gongs, drums, cymbals, and xylophone-like bronze **metallophones**—played by a large group of musicians in an intricately coordinated way. We earlier heard an example of gamelan music from the island of Java **(CD ex. #1-6).** Gamelan music from Bali, Java's neighboring island to the east, tends to have a strikingly different sound and character, as can be readily heard by comparing the Balinese gamelan selection of **CD ex. #1-9** to its Javanese counterpart. Though employing similar types of instruments and based on related histories and musical principles (see Chapter 7, pp. 92–95), they represent very different musicultural worlds.

The principal social institution linked to musical performance on Bali is the *sekehe gong,* or gamelan club. A sekehe gong is typically made up exclusively of people from a particular *banjar,* or village ward; strict rules prohibit individuals from other banjars from joining. The sekehe gong has an important function within the banjar, furnishing gamelan music for important religious ceremonies and other occasions. It also represents the banjar in music competitions against clubs from neighboring banjars.

Traditionally, all of the members of a sekehe gong were male. Western influences on Indonesian national policies in recent decades, however, have led to changing conceptions of women's roles in Indonesian society, and one outcome of this has been the advent of women's sekehe

metallophones (meh-TAL-lo-phones)

sekehe gong (SUH-kuh ["uh" like "oo" in "look"])

banjar (BAHN-jahr)

Sekehe gong performing during a religious ceremony.

gong in the banjars of Bali. The women's clubs tend to perform in a much more limited range of contexts than their male counterparts: while they may be featured at political rallies and other events of a nationalistic bent, they rarely play during traditional Balinese religious rituals. The women's groups also have generated much controversy in different sectors of Balinese society, being championed by some as icons of progressive modernity while being chastised by others as a threat to the integrity of traditional cultural values.

Through this brief portrait of the social institution of the Balinese sekehe gong as a nexus of Balinese musical life and society, we begin to see the fruitful lines of inquiry that the study of music in its relation to society can reveal, whether our interests lie in the areas of gender, nationalism, religious ritual, or social relations.

Cultures

We have already examined *culture* as an overarching concept for exploring the subject of music in context. In this section, we explore culture at a more specific level of meaning, looking at it as a particular kind of social entity that at once complements, overlaps with, and is distinctive from society. Whereas a society is defined principally in terms of its social institutions and their operations and interactions, *a culture is defined mainly by a collective worldview shared by its members.* Put another way, societies are rooted in social organization, whereas **cultures** are rooted in ideas, beliefs, and practices that underscore social organization: religions, ideologies, philosophies, sciences, moral and ethical principles, artistic creations, ritual performances. To illustrate the distinction, we will continue with our profile of the Balinese sekehe gong, now emphasizing its links to Balinese culture rather than Balinese society.

An important duty of every banjar's sekehe gong is to perform on a set of processional gamelan instruments called the *gamelan beleganjur* during cremation processions (see Chapter 7, pp. 99–103). Music played on this particular type of gamelan is believed to possess special powers that ward off evil spirits, spirits who endeavor to capture the souls of the dead and drag them to the underworld of the Balinese cosmos. Only men are thought to have the requisite strength to harness the power of the gamelan beleganjur and properly direct it musically, thus

beleganjur (buh-luh-gahn-YOOR)

Balinese women's sekehe gong.

*emansipasi
(ee-mahn-see-
PAH-see)*

berani (buh-rah-nee)

ensuring deflection of the demons and safe passage of deceased souls from the earthly world to the upper world of gods and deified ancestors. The cultural importance of the correct gender identity of belganjur performers (i.e., male) is therefore great: the very sanctity of human souls in the afterlife depends on it. For this reason, belganjur music has conventionally been performed exclusively by men, even outside of traditional ritual contexts. This practice is consistent with a Balinese cultural worldview.

In the mid-1990s, however, the Balinese arm of the Indonesian national government, responding to the call of a politically motivated *emansipasi* (women's emancipation) agenda for the nation, sponsored the formation of women's belganjur groups in several Balinese *banjars*. As a Balinese societal phenomenon, this development represented merely an extension of an existing social institution, the banjar-based *sekehe gong*. As a Balinese *cultural* phenomenon, it was considerably more radical and problematic. While some Balinese viewed it as progressive in a positive sense, others, such as the venerable musician I Wayan Beratha, found it reprehensible. "[T]he proper spirit of [belganjur] music is masculine and courageously bold (*berani*)," explains Beratha, echoing a Balinese cultural conviction that is shared widely among both men and women, "and to have girls play it both cheapens the music and puts the girls in an awkward and inappropriate situation" (quoted in Bakan 1999:248).

The case of women's belganjur groups in Bali illustrates how examining music in relation to society, on the one hand, and in relation to culture, on the other, offers different kinds of insights into how music lives in the lives of people and the communities to which they belong. It is from the blending of these different yet complementary perspectives that *sociocultural* understandings of music emerge. Cultivating such understandings is central to the approach of ethnomusicology and to the musicultural approach of this text.

Nations and nation-states

Societies and cultures are often defined in relation to nations. Moreover, the idea of nation figures prominently in how many music traditions of the world have been developed, conceptualized, and even self-consciously invented over the course of history, from ancient kingdoms and empires to modern nation-states.

It is important when dealing with the relationship of music to nationhood to recognize a distinction between two terms: **nation-state** and **nation.** The members of a nation-state share a national society and culture *and* a national homeland. Canada is a nation-state. Its people, the Canadians, are unified by a national government and a network of other social institutions (society), by shared ideas about and expressions of what constitutes Canadian identity (culture), and by the geographical landmass of Canada itself (homeland). Palestine, by contrast, is a nation but *not* a nation-state. The Palestinians share a society, a culture, and a strong sense of nationhood, but they do not (as of this writing) have political autonomy over the geographical area they claim as their homeland. Palestine is thus a nation without a state.

Nation-states and nations without states alike are catalysts for nationalist music traditions and musical nationalism. **Nationalist music** is often promoted by governments and other official institutions to symbolize an idealized "national identity." The range of raw materials from which nationalist musics are constructed is very broad—some are rooted in rural folk music forms, others in contemporary popular music styles, still others in centuries-old classical music traditions.

Some embrace Westernization and modernization as symbols of national progress, while others eschew all outside influences in their efforts to promote a "pure" notion of national ideals inscribed firmly in indigenous musical soil.

But all nationalist musics share the common feature of a nation-building or nation-consolidating agenda, and typically emerge and develop through some form of collaboration between musicians and political authorities. The Indonesian nationalist-inspired incorporation of women's beleganjur groups into the local musical culture of Bali is an example of this. In later chapters, we will witness the close interaction of music and nationalism in the musical cultures of China, Egypt, and elsewhere.

On the flipside of nationalist musics are often to be found musics of resistance, protest, and subversion. As surely as music has the power to reinforce national solidarity and ideals, it also has the power to profoundly challenge and undermine them. The Civil Rights movement in the United States and the anti-Apartheid struggle in South Africa were two instances where music played a central role in articulating and bringing to mass public attention the plights and aspirations of peoples who had long been marginalized and oppressed. Directly and indirectly, African-American and Black South African musicians such as James Brown and Miriam Makeba contributed significantly to overturning the laws, policies, social institutions, and public attitudes in which the racist infrastructures of U.S. and South African nationhood had historically been grounded. It is noteworthy, too, that these same musicians and their music have been absorbed into the mainstream of national imagery symbolism in the United States and South Africa in contemporary times. This kind of transformation of meaning, where musics of protest and resistance are essentially recast as nationalist musics in different times and circumstances, has been a common feature of the dynamic relationship between music and the construction of nationhood in many countries.

South African singer and national icon Miriam Makeba.

Diasporas and other transnational communities

The term **diaspora** refers to an international network of communities linked together by identification with a common ancestral homeland and culture. People in diaspora exist in a condition of living away from their "homeland," often with no gurarantee, or even likelihood, of return. The term dates back to the original Diaspora, in which the ancient Jews were expelled from their ancestral homeland (present-day Israel) millennia ago and began a centuries-long odyssey of dispersal (i.e., diaspora) throughout many parts of the world (see Chapter 14, p. 329).

Diasporic communities are found around the globe. The African diaspora, which was initiated by the insidious institution of the Euro-American slave trade centuries ago, ultimately led to the establishment of large diasporic communities and cultures in the Americas—in Cuba, Brazil, the United States. More recent waves of diasporic movement from the African continent have occurred in Africa's post-colonial era, especially since the end of World War II. These have led to the growth of sizable diasporic cultures in Europe, especially in major urban centers such as London and Paris. The vast geographical and cultural expanse of the African diaspora today encompasses all of these diverse communities. Their collective contributions to the global landscape of musical culture cannot be overestimated. From American jazz and hip-hop, to Brazilian samba and Cuban rumba **(CD ex. #3-2)**, to popular recordings by contemporary African emigré music stars like Angélique Kidjo that are produced in the major studios of Paris, London, and New York **(CD ex. #2-26)**, music of the African diaspora has defined and influenced global music making at just about every conceivable level for a half century and more.

emigré (e-mi-gray)

Brazilian samba group.

The Irish diaspora also has had a profound historical and modern impact on the world of music. This diaspora began with the Irish potato famine of the 19th century, when the threat of starvation led Irish people to leave their homeland by the thousands to seek refuge in foreign lands such as the United States and Canada (see Chapter 9). Since that time, a series of subsequent transnational waves of migration have continued to redefine and recast the dynamic relationship between the Irish homeland and its diasporic outreach. Musicians such as the Irish-American fiddler Eileen Ivers have crystallized the richness and multidimensionality of Irish diasporic music in highly innovative and globally influential ways. An example of Ivers' innovative, transnational musical approach is featured in **CD ex. #2-20,** which we will explore more fully in Chapter 9, pp. 179–83.

Diasporic communities also might be regarded as belonging to a larger class of *transnational communities,* overlapping with other immigrant communities, migrant worker communities, and a diverse range of social groups whose geographical diffusion around the globe defies ready categorization in terms of conventional notions of society, nation, and culture. **Virtual communities,** that is, communities forged in the electronic sphere of cyberspace rather than in more conventional ways, represent the latest chapter in the complex story of transnational identity formation. Through electronic technologies such as the Internet, established notions of what constitutes a community, a social group, a society, a culture, a nation, or a diaspora are being radically transformed. The dissemination of music via these electronic media is in many cases proving to be a major piece of the puzzle in new forms of transnational identity formation.

The Individual in Music

Cultures, societies, nations, and transnational communities provide important frameworks for understanding identity through music. They do not, however, actually do or think *anything,* let alone make music. Rather, it is individual people, flesh-and-blood human beings operating alone

Do You Belong to a Virtual Music Community?

Do you download or swap music files on the Internet, surf the Web for information about your favorite musicians, or correspond via e-mail or text message with friends about upcoming musical events? If so, you are part of the vast world of virtual music communities, whether you know it or not. The Internet has radically transformed the world of music and musical communities, making it possible to be a part of informal or formal global networks of people—communities, in essence—bound together wholly or in part by their shared musical tastes, interests, and listening experiences.

or as members of groups, who make and listen to music and who find meaning and define their identities in relation to it.

In a certain sense, all individuals may be viewed as communities unto themselves. Each of us is an ever-evolving repository of multiple identities, and we bring the full range of these varied identities to all that we experience in music and all that we express through it. This is why the music of an individual like the late salsa and Latin jazz superstar Tito Puente is best understood in relation to the multifaceted identity he brought to his musical career (see Chapter 11). Puente, whose classic original recording of his signature song, "Oye Como Va," is heard on **CD ex. #3-5,** was a native and lifetime resident of New York City. He nonetheless identified himself ethnically as a Puerto Rican, while claiming that Cuban music formed the foundation of his *musical* identity (Loza 1999). This complex of identities sheds light on the character of Puente's music, since he was a true master of **musical syncretism,** the merging of formerly distinct styles and idioms into new forms of expression. His multidimensional identity is also relevant when we consider his *family* legacy as a musical patriarch, since his

Tito Puente.

son, Tito Puente Jr., has made significant contributions to the continuing development of Latin dance music into the new millennium (see Chapter 11, pp. 230–231).

Ethnomusicologists in recent years have become increasingly interested in focusing their studies on particular musicians rather than on the cultures or societies to which they belong more broadly. Timothy Rice, in his important book *May It Fill Your Soul: Experiencing Bulgarian Music* (1994), traces the lives in music of two Bulgarian musicians, the *gaida* (Bulgarian bagpipe) player Kostadin Varimezov and his wife, the singer Todora Varimezova. He also devotes considerable attention to what he experienced personally and musically while conducting **fieldwork** in Bulgaria. Fieldwork is a hallmark of ethnomusicological research. It involves living for an extended period of time among the people whose lives and music one researches, and often learning and performing their music as well. In chronicling the stories of Kostadin, Todora, and himself, Rice offers many insights into Bulgarian culture, society, and nationhood, but he does so while maintaining a consistent focus on the individual musician as the primary location of musical identity and meaning. Many of the later chapters in this text reflect a similar philosophy in their focus on individual musicians.

gaida (GUY-dah ["gai" rhymes with "high"])

Spirituality and Transcendence in Music

In most world cultures and societies, music plays an integral role in worship, religious ritual, and the expression of faith. It may serve as a bridge between the earthly world and worlds beyond, bringing people closer to invisible realms or into communion with supernatural forces. In such instances, music facilitates *transcendence.* Examples of music-related transcendence are found in many cultures. During Balinese cremations, it is believed that the soul of the deceased ascends to the upper world of the cosmos on a "ladder" of beleganjur music (Chapter 7, p. 103). The legendary Jewish mystic known as the Baal Shem Tov is said to have risen through music to heaven and finally to have *become* music following his death (Chapter 14, p. 325). Practitioners of Afro-Cuban Santería, or Orisha, religion employ specific drum rhythms (such as those heard on **CD ex. #3-1**) as a form of invitation to deities (orishas) to temporarily descend to the earthly world and participate in sacred rituals presented in their honor. When the summoned orishas descend, they become manifest through ritual dances of spirit mediums, people who undergo *transubstantiation* (transformation into altered states of being) when "possessed" by the visiting orishas (Chapter 11, pp. 222–23).

Music's expression of spirituality also may take the form of a reflection of a divinely created cosmic order. As we will explore in more detail in later chapters (i.e., Chapters 6, 7, and 8), music in Hindu cultures such as Bali and India is often built over *musical cycles,* which are patterns that are repeated over and over during the course of a performance while other aspects of the music change and evolve. These fundamentally cyclic *musical* designs reflect core Hindu *cultural* ideas and beliefs about the balanced order of the universe. Each musical cycle symbolically encompasses a process of birth, preservation, and death leading to rebirth, from which the cycle is regenerated again and again, ad infinitum. This is a musical correlate of the Hindu belief in reincarnation, and in turn of the divine convergence of the "Three Shapes" (Trimurti) of the

**Santería
 (San-te-REE-yah)**

Orisha (o-REE-sha)

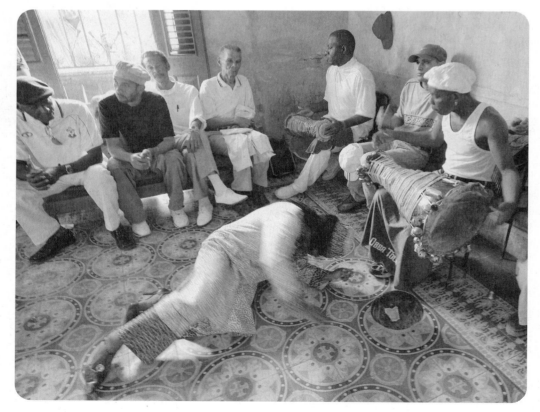

Dancing for the orishas. (*Note:* This photograph originally was published by The Associated Press. The taking of photographs at ceremonies such as this one is generally proscribed, but photojournalists sometimes negotiate terms under which it is permissible.)

Hindu godhead—Brahma, the Creator; Vishnu (Visnu), the Preserver; and Shiva (Siva, Siwa), the Destroyer—who together ensure an eternal continuity of cosmic order.

Music's spiritual importance also resides in its unique capacity to bring members of communities together in social solidarity and in a single, unified expression of their faith. When people make music together, they are often "at their best" in terms of displaying a sense of common purpose and endeavor in their worship. **CD ex. #1-10,** a performance of a Christian church hymn from the island of Fiji, captures this spirit of the communal expression of faith with poignance and power.

Church choir, Fiji.

Music and Dance

Music may move people to transcendent states, but it also has the capacity to move them in a more literal way by inspiring them to dance. The integral connection of music and dance is a feature of music cultures worldwide. In many instances, in fact, music and dance are regarded as mutual reflections of one another, the one expressing itself in organized sound, the other in organized movement. The myriad forms and contexts of dancing accompanied by music occur in just about every kind of social and cultural situation imaginable, from the most sacred of religious rites to the most secular spectacles of revelry. In the musical journey of this text, we will encounter dancing and dance music in several musicultural traditions: Irish dance tunes (Chapter 9), Latin dance music (Chapter 11), traditional women's dance in Egypt and international belly dance (Chapter 12). Each case offers a unique scenario of dance as a sociocultural phenomenon and as an activity through which people define identity and meaning in their lives.

Dance, and the music that accompanies it, may serve as a lens through which to view social celebration, community solidarity, the physical expression of culture, and the performance of identity. It also may provide revealing and sometimes troubling insights into how people treat and classify each other in terms of issues of gender, race, and ethnicity. In the Middle East, professional female dancers who dance publicly in the company of men are generally accorded low social status. Their artistry—and their art—is marginalized due to the social stigma attached to it. Indeed, the historical association of music with women's dancing in Islamic societies has been a major factor in music's reputation as a profane art that must be kept separate, physically and conceptually, from the sacred practices of Islamic worship (see Chapter 12, p. 272).

Rationalizations for racism and racist social policies levied against African peoples and people of African descent in the Americas were historically supported by theories of racial inferiority that were tied to dance and music as well. The purported "natural rhythm" of Africans and people of the African diaspora, together with their integral use of dance to express core values of cultural identity and faith, were turned against them. African rhythm and African dance were cast by Western exploiters as symbols of African "primitiveness," and in turn were used to justify the inhumanely oppressive institutions and policies of the European colonization of Africa and the Euro-American slave trade. The vestiges of such attitudes are still with us today in cultural and ethnic stereotypes relating to music and dance.

Racist stereotyping of "African" dancers.

The communal performance of music, often presented in conjunction with some form of dramatic or dance presentation, is a prominent feature of **rituals** in many world cultures. Rituals are special events during which individuals or communities enact, through performance, their core beliefs, values, and ideals. They often take the form of communal performances of myths, legends, epics, or sacred texts or stories that are foundational to a culture's identity. As a result, rituals reveal a great deal about the *worldviews* of the people who perform them, that is, about the ways in which these people conceive of their world and their place and purpose within it. Rituals have been a major focus of attention for anthropologists and others interested in the study of culture, including ethnomusicologists, who have long been fascinated by the prominent role of music in ritual performances.

Rituals may be sacred or secular. They are used to mark important life-cycle events and rites of passage in all cultures. They play a prominent role in healing practices the world over. They have long served to legitimize the authority and power of political leaders and social institutions, or alternatively to subvert and challenge them. Even when rituals are not explicitly spiritual or religious, they tend to have a transcendent quality to them, since they are, by definition, events that are set off from the regular course of everyday reality. This basic distinction from "ordinary life" is frequently symbolized by the presence of music in the ritual space, which marks that space as special.

zaar (zahr)

The Egyptian *zaar* (zar) is a healing ritual in which music functions prominently (see Chapter 12, pp. 263–267). During a zaar, specific kinds of rhythms like the ones heard in **CD ex. #1-11** are played on drums and other percussion instruments. These rhythms accompany a dance performed by a woman who is believed to have fallen ill as a result of being entered, or

asyad (ahs-sigh-yed)

"possessed," by an *asyad,* a type of supernatural being. The afflicted woman's dancing, which is

A zaar ritual.

driven by the powerful percussive rhythms of the music, is performed with the intention of convincing the intruding asyad to depart. If the woman returns to a state of health, this is taken as an indication that the ritual has succeeded, that the patient has been liberated from her affliction and the asyad has moved on. The entire event may be viewed as a performance of worldview and belief, one that, like many rituals, moves its participants from one state of being and perception to another.

Alan Maralung.

Music as Commodity and the Patronage of Music

Support and ownership of music are major factors that influence how music lives in communities, cultures, and societies. Some music is regarded as the property of a family lineage (e.g., in India) or an entire village community (e.g., in Bali). Other music is not regarded as property at all, rather being thought of as an integral facet of communal life that is absorbed into the broader fabric of culture.

Ownership of music by individuals is also common. We in the West are very familiar with the idea of a song or other musical composition being privately owned. The laws of copyright protect musical works as a form of intellectual property. A songwriter or composer who holds the copyright to a piece of music holds the exclusive legal right to sell, market, and distribute that music as he or she sees fit. In this context, the music is a commodity.

The idea of private music ownership is by no means limited to the modern West. In some Aboriginal Australian and Amerindian cultures, songs bequeathed to particular individuals in dreams or visions are regarded as their exclusive property. No one else may perform these songs, with the possible exception of people who receive them as gifts from their original owners.

Different models of ownership of music become complexly intertwined when cultural representatives of different societies join forces. **CD ex. #1-12,** "Ibis," is a case in point. This is a song owned by Alan Maralung, a revered Aboriginal Australian singer who is now deceased. It is one of a large number of songs that Maralung claimed as his own on account of reportedly having received them directly from supernatural beings.

In his singing of "Ibis," Maralung is accompanied by two instruments: a pair of wooden sticks that are struck together and a *didjeridu*. The didjeridu is a truly remarkable instrument. In its traditional form, it is constructed of a long branch of eucalyptus wood—usually 1 to 1.5 meters in length—which has been hollowed out by termites. (More modern adaptations sometimes use PVC pipe or other materials in place of eucalyptus.) By blowing into the didjeridu in a variety of ways, the player is able to produce a wide range of sounds, as can be heard in the example. (The didjeridu is discussed further in Chapter 5, pp. 60–61.)

didjeridu (DIJ-er-ee-DOO)

According to the rules of his culture, Maralung exclusively owns this song and all others that were likewise bequeathed to him during his lifetime. No one else may perform or claim these songs, at least not without having received his explicit endorsement. But how does the status of the song and its ownership change in light of the fact that it has been released commercially by an American record company (Smithsonian Folkways), and that it has in turn been presented to you—in excerpted form—on the CD set accompanying this text? As Ronald Radano and Philip Bohlman assert in the book *Music and The Racial Imagination,* "The condition of ownership has . . . been stripped from world music, for anyone able to buy CDs or turn on the radio or television can possess it" (Radano and Bohlman 2000:9). Their claim is debatable, but the issues it raises are significant.

Didjeridu being played.

Now that "Ibis" has been commodified and Maralung has passed away, does Smithsonian Folkways or McGraw-Hill (or do I) have specific *ethical* responsibilities regarding the song's use and distribution? Did Maralung himself act appropriately in allowing the song, a gift from a supernatural being, to be commodified and distributed internationally in the ways it has been? These are complicated questions, but ones worth considering.

Closely aligned with issues of music ownership and commodification is the matter of music patronage. Music patronage involves the support of musicians and musical institutions, whether that support be financial, social, institutional, educational, or of some other type. In former times (and still sometimes today), kings, queens, princes, and princesses were leading music patrons, supporting musicians and even entire musical cultures in their royal courts and music ministries (see, for example, Chapters 10 and 13). Churches and other religious institutions also have been important music patrons historically.

But the tradition of patronage of musicians by brothel owners, country dancehall proprietors, and the like probably dates back at least as far as royal patronage. Different musical traditions have always been closely linked to different social classes, and sources of musical patronage—who pays the piper, in essence—have always borne directly on connections between music, class, and social status. Sources of musical patronage also have had important implications on how different musical traditions and styles are classified relative to one another. They have as much or more to do with the use of designations like folk music, popular music, religious music, art music, court music, classical music, entertainment music, and commercial music as the musical styles linked to those terms themselves. The same style of music—even the same piece—is likely to be classified quite differently and take on different meanings and identities if it is played in a concert hall than if it is heard as part of the soundtrack for a television sitcom.

Today, government arts agencies, university music departments and conservatories, private arts funding organizations, music industry corporations, Internet music providers, radio and television advertisers, nightclub proprietors, music festival producers, book publishers, and makers of films and television shows, music videos, cell phones, and video games all have a role to play in the complex networks of local, national, and international finance that constitute the contem-

Sting performing with Algerian *rai* music star Cheb Mami.

porary universe of music patronage. So too do lawyers, rock star world music producers (Paul Simon, Peter Gabriel, Sting), journalists, music critics, and general music consumers who attend concerts, buy CDs, and download music files from the Internet. The global culture of music patronage is highly complex, and nowhere more so than in the world of "world music."

Technology itself is also a key player in the patronage of music. The technologies used to produce, record, transmit, and disseminate music largely shape and determine what kind of music gets heard and by whom, who supports that music, and indeed what music actually sounds like. Humans are ultimately the source of all musical production, even of computer-generated music; it is human intention and perception put into practice that constitutes the lowest common denominator of music, as we saw in Chapter 1. But technologies—from the didjeridu, to the multitrack recording studio, to the i-Pod—largely shape both musical sound and the cultural frameworks and attitudes that give that sound meaning and identity.

The Transmission of Music and Musical Knowledge

Music is a social fact. One way or another, it becomes meaningful by entering the realm of social life. Once there, it moves among people and communities, sometimes locally, sometimes globally. The processes by means of which music moves from one person to another, from one generation to another, from one community to another, and potentially throughout the whole world, are processes of *music transmission.*

Music may be transmitted directly from one person to another, "face-to-face" in the context of a performance or some kind of a lesson (formal or informal) where it is taught and learned. It also may be transmitted via music notation (e.g., as sheet music) or in some other graphic form. Additionally, music can move from person to person and place to place through electronic media—on CDs, DVDs, films and television shows, radio, the Internet. A combination of these different modes of transmission is often involved as well. Finally, transmission of knowledge and information *about* music—books, treatises, scholarly articles, popular magazines, Web sites, documentary films—plays an integral role in the transmission of music itself, influencing what music does and does not get heard (and by whom) and how that music is produced and received.

Production and reception

All forms of music transmission share two basic features: the production of music and the reception of music. Sometimes the roles of music maker and music receiver are clearly separated, as in a Western classical recital where a pianist (the performer) performs a piece of music written by someone other than herself (the composer) and plays it for a gathering of people who sit and listen quietly and do not participate actively in the performance other than to applaud at the end of it (the audience). The performer in this case is a *music specialist*—often a professional, a virtuoso, a "musical artist." The audience is made up of music consumers—often paying customers—who are there to be entertained, or perhaps to be enlightened, or just to be seen.

In other instances, distinctions between the processes of music making and music reception are much less clear. In many African societies, for example, recognized distinctions between "performer" and "audience" do not exist to nearly the extent that they do in the West, at least in some contexts; all members of the community are expected to participate actively (perform) *and* to encourage and appreciate the performances of their fellow community members (i.e., to be part of their "audience").

The way in which music is taught and learned constitutes one of the most important domains of music transmission. Sometimes the passing on of music and musical knowledge implicit in the teaching-learning interaction is informal and unstructured. Musical knowledge, ability, and experience are acquired in the normal course of communal life; musicality develops through a kind of osmosis, as a product of being in and being a part of musical environments as one grows up and "learns" one's culture. In other cases, music learning is highly formal and structured.

Western concert performance.

West African communal performance.

An Indian music lesson.

Students of Indian classical music (see Chapter 8) are expected to devote themselves to their *gurus* (musical mentors) with total and unwavering commitment for a period of many years as they learn the intricacies of their demanding musical art. In contrast to their counterparts in the classical music worlds of the West or Japan, whose learning methods include the use of music notation (a musical score of some kind that is "written out"), Indian musicians trained in the traditional manner usually rely exclusively on memorization and performance models provided by their gurus to cultivate the foundations of their musical artistry.

Music creation processes

The issue of transmission in music also is informed by what kind of musical material is actually transmitted. Different types of music creation processes turn musical ideas into musical works and performances in different ways. Among the most important of these processes are the following: composition, interpretation, improvisation, and arranging.

The process of **composition** involves planning out the design of a musical work prior to its performance. This may be done by an individual (the composer) or by a group of musicians working collectively. The transmission of composed music may occur via a notated score, a live performance, a recording, or a computer-generated sound file. The traditions of Balinese gamelan **(CD ex. #1-9),** the

Japanese shakuhachi flute (**CD ex. #1-13**), and Western symphonic music (**CD ex. #1-1**) all emphasize the process of composition, that is, they are traditions in which the musical content and form of works are quite exactly determined in advance of actual music performance.

shakuhachi (sha-koo-HAH-chee)

Interpretation is the process through which music performers—or music listeners—take an existing composition and in a sense make it their own through the experience of performing or listening to it. Interpretation is present to some degree in all music performances, even of works in which composers provide performers with very precise instructions on how to approach the piece. Interpretation accounts for why no two performances of Beethoven's Ninth Symphony (**CD ex. #1-1**) are exactly alike, even though all of them are generated from essentially the same original musical score.

Improvisation involves composing in the moment of performance. In certain musical idioms—jazz, Indian raga (Chapter 8; **CD ex. #2-12**), Arab taqsim (**CD ex. #1-14;** see also Chapter 12, p. 259)—improvisation, rather than composition *per se,* is the principal criterion for assessing musical artistry. While the process of improvisation is sometimes characterized as a form of spontaneous musical invention, this is for the most part misleading. The majority of improvisatory traditions are grounded in highly systematic and rigorous conventions. Though the improvised performance *is* spontaneous, it is also the product of much disciplined training and practice.

taqsim (tak-SEEM ["k" sound in back of throat])

Arranging is the craft of taking an existing musical work and transforming it into something new, while still retaining its core musical identity. The Beatles song "Yesterday" exists in thousands of arrangements, which use different instrumentation formats, formal plans, and other features. Blending of elements from diverse musical traditions can result in particularly interesting arrangements, such as the Scottish bagpipes-and-drums arrangement of the Christian hymn "Amazing Grace" of **CD ex. #1-15** and the Egyptian rhythm-anchored take on the Mexican song "La Cucaracha" of **CD ex. #1-16.**

Music in the Process of Tradition

In much the same way that music exists at the intersection of sound and culture, tradition exists at the intersection of culture and music. It is through tradition, and within the contexts of *music traditions,* that musics become culturally meaningful, socially functional, and representative of individual and communal identities at all levels.

Tradition, like culture, is a term that can mean many different things. For some, it suggests that which is old, stable, entrenched, static, of the past. That is not the sense in which the word tradition is used in this text, however, at least not the primary one. Rather, as was mentioned briefly in the Introduction to this book, **tradition** is here conceived of as a *process,* in particular *a process of creative transformation whose most remarkable feature is the continuity it nurtures and sustains.*

This concept of tradition as process is well articulated by the ethnomusicologist Henry Spiller. "To my mind," writes Spiller, "what qualifies music as traditional is not how old it is, but rather how well it teaches, reinforces, and creates the social values of its producers and consumers. Traditional music is not something that is stuck in the past; it grows and changes, just as the people who make and listen to it grow and change, just as the values they share with those close to them change (albeit a bit more slowly). Truly traditional music, then, exploits new resources, acknowledges new requirements, and responds to new situations. Traditional music provides a place for people to try out new approaches to their existing values, to experiment with new ideas, and to synthesize the new with the old" (Spiller 2004:xix).

I agree with everything Spiller states in the above passage, though I prefer to describe what he identifies as "traditional music" as *music of tradition* instead. Music of tradition can be very modern, radical, and experimental. It can draw upon a great variety of different kinds of music and the resources of many different cultures. It can embody multiple meanings and levels of meaning and may reflect, embody, and inform many different identities. It also can be ancient and archaic, very specific in its cultural meanings, or deeply conservative in the values it expresses. Or it can represent the synthesis of a host of seemingly incongruous elements, from the most resolutely traditional to the most ultramodern.

Two related examples of blues music will help to illustrate the concept of music of tradition, a concept that is integral to the development of every chapter in Part II of this text. First, listen to **CD ex. #1-17,** a classic performance of the song "High Water Everywhere" by the seminal Mississippi blues musician Charlie Patton. Patton lived from around 1891 until 1934 (some sources place his birth date as early as 1881) and is often described as the founding father of the Mississippi Delta blues tradition. This performance, then, might be characterized as an example of "traditional blues" in a quite literal sense—music that is old and "authentic," that takes us back to the roots of the blues tradition.

khoomei (khoo-may)

khoomii (khoo-mee)

Now listen to **CD ex. #1-18,** "Kargyraa Moan," by the modern blues musician Paul Pena. This piece represents a synthesis of two great music traditions. The first is American blues, which was Pena's musical home base, as it were. (Pena died in 2005.) The second is *khoomei,* which comes from the distant land of Tuva, in Central Asia. Tuvan khoomei is closely related to the Mongolian style of singing known as *khoomii* that we listened to earlier, in **CD ex. #1-5.** Like their Mongolian counterparts (see Chapter 5, p. 61), the various types and subtypes of Tuvan khoomei rely upon the ability of a singer to manipulate his or her vocal apparatus in such a way that *multiple* tones, rather than just a single tone, are produced at once.

Through an amazing musicultural odyssey (chronicled in the equally amazing, Oscar-nominated documentary film *Genghis Blues*), Paul Pena, who was both blind and plagued by numerous health challenges, discovered Tuvan khoomei, mastered one of its main substyles (called *kargyraa*), developed a unique musical synthesis of khoomei and blues, traveled to Tuva, competed in the Tuvan national khoomei competition, and emerged a winner of the contest. The version of "Kargyraa Moan" featured here was recorded live, in Tuva, during Pena's triumphant performance in that competition.

Paul Pena.

On the surface, Pena's combining of blues and khoomei elements in "Kargyraa Moan" seems quite radically innovative, and it is. Yet Pena viewed his bridging of these seemingly disparate musical worlds less as a departure from his deep blues heritage than as a tribute and a return to it. When he first encountered the multitone style of Tuvan *kargyraa*, with its distinctive, guttural, "growling" sounds, Pena was certainly drawn in by the novelty of what he heard. But his attraction to kargyraa also came from the fact that it strongly reminded him of the singing styles of Charlie Patton and other "rough-voiced" blues greats like Tommy McLennan and Howlin' Wolf who had been his original inspiration. This profound sense of connecting back to the roots of his own musical past *in* blues *through* khoomei proved key in Pena's impassioned and tenacious pursuit of a new and unique musical vision.

Whatever form or forms it takes, music of tradition always comes out of a particular musical, social, and cultural history that prefigures it and that is at some core level inscribed in the sound and meaning of the music itself. It always expresses something essential about who people are and what matters to them. Music of tradition tells us about the people responsible for the music's creation, and for its preservation and sustenance. Indeed, it has the capacity to tell us something important about the members of *all* communities for whom it comes to have meaning and significance. In an earlier publication, I defined ethnomusicology as "the study of how music lives in the lives of people who make and experience it, and of how people live in the music they make" (Bakan 1999:17–18). In essence, that is what this book is about, too, as it explores diverse traditions of world music and the process of tradition that runs through all of them in unique and compelling ways.

Summary

In exploring how music lives, this chapter focused on the intersection of music as sound and music as culture that gives rise to meaning, identity, transmission, and creation in music. It is at this intersection of sound and culture that music exists as a musicultural phenomenon.

We began by situating this chapter and this text more broadly in relation to the discipline of ethnomusicology. An anthropological (and in turn ethnomusicological) definition and concept of culture was then introduced. From there, we distinguished different types of musical meaning (sound-based versus cultural context-based) and explored how identity becomes tied to music and musical expression on many levels: society, culture, community, nation, diaspora, the individual. We then looked at how diverse musics and identities come together and create new forms of musical and musicultural expression through processes of syncretism. We also explored important connections that exist between music and spirituality, dance, ritual, commodity, and patronage; and surveyed musical transmission and processes of music creation (composition, interpretation, improvisation, and arranging).

The final section of the chapter focused on music as tradition, positing that tradition is a process of creative transformation whose most remarkable feature is the continuity it nurtures and sustains. Transformation, even radical transformation, is very much a part of musics of tradition worldwide, as later chapters of this book will explore in myriad ways.

Key Terms

ethnomusicology
musicultural
culture (Tylor definition)
identity
society
social institutions
cultures (as social entities distinct
   from societies)

nation-state
nation
nationalist music
diaspora
virtual communities
musical syncretism
fieldwork
rituals

composition
interpretation
improvisation
arranging
tradition (as a process)

Study Questions

■ What is ethnomusicology? What does it mean to study music from a musicultural perspective?

■ What is Edward Tylor's definition of *culture*? When was it first published?

■ What distinguishes societies from cultures? What different kinds of insights do societal and cultural approaches to the study of music reveal? How was the Balinese example of this chapter used as an illustration?

■ What are some of the principal types of social institutions we might look to if we wished to gain an understanding of music and society?

■ Why are some nations *not* nation-states? How do nationalist musics develop and contribute to concepts of nationhood?

■ What is a diaspora? What can we learn about diasporic processes and phenomena from studying music? Give examples.

■ What is musical syncretism?

■ What is involved in doing ethnomusicological fieldwork?

- What were the main processes of music creation and transmission discussed?
- What is music of tradition, and how was the example of Paul Pena used to illustrate this concept?

Discussion Questions

- How is music as a phenomenon of society distinct from and/or related to music as a phenomenon of culture? Draw from examples in this chapter and either real or hypothetical examples of your own to explore and discuss this question.
- How do the Internet and other mass media influence the ways in which people conceive of their identities and the identities of others relative to music? What kinds of virtual music communities do you belong to (or could you belong to), and why? Does today's high-tech world make the potential for building community through music greater or less great than it was in the past? Why, and in what ways?
- What are some of the principal social institutions that are involved in music production and reception in your world? How do these various institutions contribute to the ways in which you experience, understand, and value the musics that are a part of your life?
- This chapter introduced numerous themes and issues for exploring music as a phenomenon of culture. There are a great many more that one might consider: children's music, music and the elderly, music among people with disabilities. How might one go about examining these areas, and what others can you think of that could lead to deeper understandings of music and human experience?

Applying What You Have Learned

- Think of a song or other piece of music that has been a part of your life for a long time. Has the significance or "meaning" of that song changed over the years? If so, what has changed in your perception of the song, and what factors in your life—personal, cultural, or other—might have contributed? Write a brief account chronicling your personal history of this song, focusing specifically on what it means to you today and what it has meant to you at different points in the past.
- Draft a chart listing all of the different kinds of music you listen to, indicating when you usually listen to them and for what purposes. What do you listen to when you're trying to relax, or when you're working out, or studying? What do you like to dance to? What music makes you feel romantic, nostalgic, happy, sad, patriotic, subversive? Are there specific kinds of music that you identify with your ethnicity, or with your cultural or national identity? On the basis of this chart, create a "music identity profile" of yourself, considering how music in your life contributes to your sense of who you are on multiple levels.
- Do your own ethnomusicological fieldwork project. Get to know some musicians in your local community and spend time observing, taking part in, and documenting their musical lives. This may involve attending rehearsals and performances in which they are involved (or other musical events), spending time with them socially, conducting interviews and engaging in informal conversations, and learning about the music they play and why it is important to them. Keep a journal of your observations, impressions, and experiences over a period of several weeks, then write a brief ethnomusicological report on your findings.

Resources for Further Study

Visit the Online Learning Center at www.mhhe.com/bakan1 for additional learning aids, study help, and resources that supplement the content of this chapter.

how **music works,** part I:
rhythm

Having explored the questions of what music is and how music lives in Chapters 1 and 2, we turn our attention in this chapter, and also in Chapters 4–6, to another fundamental issue: how music works. Collectively, this set of four chapters provides a general introduction to music sounds and to the way they are organized; in other words, to the basic *elements of music*. We want to know what the building blocks of musical sound, structure, and form are; to develop a shared vocabulary for describing and comprehending them; and to be introduced to them in a way that is accessible yet prepares us well for the diverse world music journey ahead.

Moreover, we want to engage with the elements of music not as mere abstractions, but rather as identifiable components of sound that we are able to *actually hear.* In working toward this goal, we employ examples of two kinds to illustrate the main terms and concepts introduced. These are

■ Well-known songs that are likely to be familiar, such as "The Alphabet Song," "Mary Had a Little Lamb," and "The Star-Spangled Banner" (the national anthem of the United States).

■ Recordings covering a wide range of world music traditions and cultures.

With respect to the first of these two categories, some of the examples (especially the children's songs) may strike you as overly simplistic, even a bit silly, but they have the advantage of being straightforward and recognizable. With regard to the world music recordings, the main emphasis is not on learning and memorizing all of the different names of cultures, styles, and instruments that come up. Rather, it is to become acquainted with general aspects of how music works with the aid of examples that will likely *not* be familiar to you. In the process, you will have an opportunity to sample some of the world's rich musical diversity as a prelude to the more focused case studies of the chapters in Part II.

This chapter explores the element of rhythm specifically, but we begin on a more general level with a brief introduction to the four basic properties of tones that were first mentioned in Chapter 1.

■ ■ ■

The Four Basic Properties of Tones

Every sound we hear in a piece of music—and indeed every sound we hear in our world—is defined by four basic properties: duration, frequency, amplitude, and timbre. Such terms may sound technical and intimidating to the musical novice, but their essential meanings relative to music are not so complicated. **Duration** relates to *how long or short* a tone is. It is the basis of *rhythm* in music. **Frequency,** which becomes manifest in music as *pitch,* corresponds to *how high or low* a tone is. **Amplitude** relates to *how loud or soft* tones are. The relative loudness and softness of different tones (with silence at one extreme of the loudness-to-softness continuum) are what define *dynamics* in music. **Timbre** is analogous to the *actual sound quality or "tone color"* of tones, to what they "sound like": tones played on a trumpet are timbrally distinct from tones played on a saxophone, even if both instruments are heard playing the same frequency (pitch) for the same duration (rhythm) at the same amplitude (dynamic level).

Duration, frequency, amplitude, and timbre, then, are the four basic properties of tones, the building blocks of musical sound. Their respective musical correlates—rhythm, pitch, dynamics, and tone color, respectively—are the foundational elements of music. (See Table 3.1.)

Rhythm

When we speak of **rhythm,** we are dealing with *how the sounds and silences of music are organized in time.* In understanding rhythm, two terms used in Western music provide a good start-

TABLE 3.1	The four basic properties of tones and their musical correlates.	
	Property of Tone	**Musical Correlate**
	Duration	Rhythm
	Frequency	Pitch
	Amplitude	Dynamics
	Timbre	Tone color, sound quality

ing point: note and rest. An individual musical tone may be referred to as a *note*. A pause between notes is a *rest*.

Try performing "The Alphabet Song" by tapping it out on your desk, *without* actually singing "the tune." The result is a performance of *the rhythm of that song*. You will notice that some of the notes are longer than others; in other words, that the notes have different *durations*. The notes for the first few letter names—"a, b, c, d, e, f"—are shorter by half than the note on the letter "g" which follows them. A little further on, you get to "l, m, n, o," which turn out to be twice as short as "a, b, c, d, e, f" were, and four times shorter than "g" was. (See Figure 3.1.)

Thus, we find that there are three different lengths of notes in the opening section of "The Alphabet Song." In Western music terminology, the faster-moving notes are usually called **sixteenth notes,** the medium-speed ones **eighth notes,** and the slower ones **quarter notes.** Figure 3.2 shows how these different-length notes appear in Western music notation.

Many types of music in the world, including several explored in this text, use rhythms that "translate" quite well into sixteenth, eighth, and quarter notes. These terms will therefore be used in connection with the discussions of musical rhythm in various chapters, though it should be understood from the outset that they do not necessarily reflect how people in other cultures conceive of or describe their *own* rhythms.

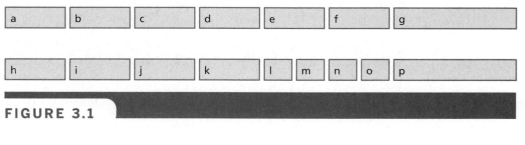

FIGURE 3.1

Notes of different duration in "The Alphabet Song."

FIGURE 3.2

"The Alphabet Song" rhythm in Western notation.

Beat

In "The Alphabet Song"—and, indeed, in much music—the lengths of the different notes are organized in relation to a steady, underlying pulse known as the **beat.** The beat is what you tap your foot to when you listen to a song, or what you move your feet to when you dance. The beat in "The Alphabet Song" is defined by a steady stream of quarter-note pulses. Each one of these pulses is called *a* beat, while the continuous stream of quarter-note pulses that underlies the entire performance is called *the* beat.

To make the relationship between a song's beat and its rhythm concrete, sing "The Alphabet Song" while clapping the beat in steady quarter notes (Figure 3.3).

The beat of a piece of music may be marked out explicitly in sound (as when you sang "The Alphabet Song" while clapping along) or it may just be implied, that is, felt but not actually heard (as when you sang the song earlier without clapping). Either way, it provides the foundation upon which all other rhythmic aspects of the music are organized.

Subdivision

When there is more than one note per beat in a piece of music, the result is what is known as rhythmic **subdivision.** A stream of eighth notes sung or played against a steady quarter-note beat (e.g., "h–i–j–k" in "The Alphabet Song") creates *duple subdivision,* that is, two evenly spaced notes for every beat. A stream of sixteenth notes against a quarter-note beat (e.g., "l-m-n-o" in "The Alphabet Song") creates *quadruple subdivision,* with a ratio of four notes to one (4:1) per beat. (See Figure 3.4.)

In many types of music, *triple subdivision* of beats, in which each individual beat is divided into three smaller, evenly spaced rhythmic units, is common. The rhythm of "Row, Row, Row Your Boat" (Figure 3.5) is based on triple subdivision. This is especially clear beginning on the ninth beat of the song, where each syllable of the text line "Mer-ri-ly, mer-ri-ly, mer-ri-ly, mer-ri-ly" accounts for precisely one-third of a beat.

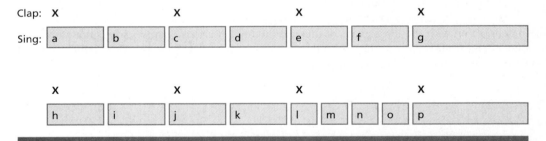

"The Alphabet Song," with beats marked out.

FIGURE 3.3

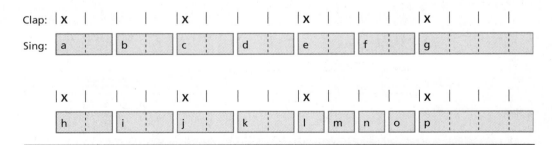

Examples of duple and quadruple subdivision, "The Alphabet Song."

FIGURE 3.4

A common type of rhythm in music with triple subdivision is the one in which *only the first and third note of each three-note grouping is actually sung or played,* with the second (middle) note being "left out." The rhythm of "**gent**–ly **down**–the **stream**" in "Row, Row, Row Your Boat" is a good example (see Figure 3.5). This **1** (2) 3 **1** (2) 3–type rhythm (Figure 3.6) is also a signature feature of popular dance rhythms in many world music traditions, such as the blues shuffle (**CD ex. #1-19**) and the Celtic hornpipe (**CD ex. #1-20**).

Many other types of rhythmic subdivision beyond the duple, triple, and quadruple forms illustrated here exist as well. In some instances, beats may be divided into 5, 7, 11, or even 13 smaller units (subdivisions); or the basic level of beat subdivision may represent some multiple of twos or threes (e.g., 6, 8, 9, 12, 16). For the most part, however, these more complex types of subdivision are beyond the scope of how we will explore the musics we encounter on our journey, so we need not examine them further here.

Meter

Moving in the opposite direction from rhythmic subdivision of beats, we discover that beats themselves are often grouped together in a systematic way. In Western music, each group of beats is called a **measure** (or bar), and the number of beats in a measure defines the music's **meter.** To clarify the difference between subdivision and meter, subdivision is what results when smaller units of rhythm are inserted between beats, whereas meter is what results when series of successive beats are grouped together in patterned ways.

Meters of two (duple meter), three (triple meter), and four (quadruple meter) are very common in the West, and indeed in many parts of the world. Meters based on other kinds of beat

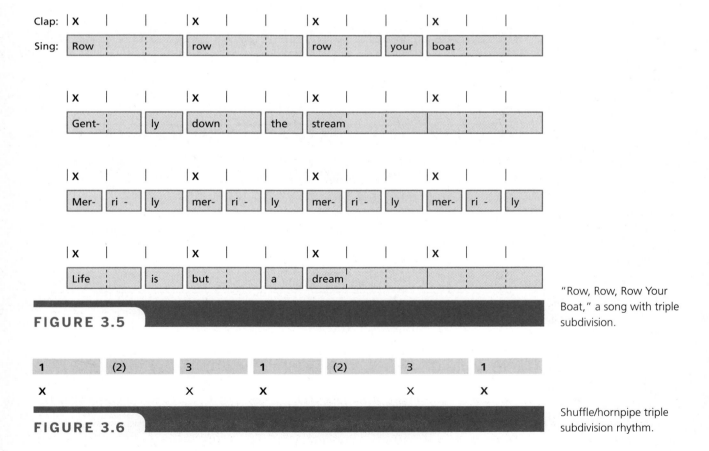

FIGURE 3.5

"Row, Row, Row Your Boat," a song with triple subdivision.

FIGURE 3.6

Shuffle/hornpipe triple subdivision rhythm.

groupings—with 5, 7, 11, 13, or even 31 beats per measure—also occur, and there are instances where the meter *changes* from one measure or section of a piece of music to the next as well. For the moment, though, we will limit our discussion mainly to relatively simple kinds of meters.

"The Alphabet Song" is an example of a piece with a meter of four. A consistent, four-beat pattern—strong beat (**S**)–weak beat (w)–medium beat (M)–weak beat (w)— is repeated over and over throughout the entire song. Using Figure 3.7 as a guide, try singing the first part of "The Alphabet Song" as you mark out the meter with handclaps and waves. Use a loud clap for the strong beats (**S**), a silent wave of the right hand for the weak beats (w), and a light clap for the medium beats (M).

"The Star-Spangled Banner" is a song in a meter of three, that is, in triple meter. With the aid of Figure 3.8, try singing the first part of this song as you mark out the beats of the standard triple-meter pattern—strong beat–weak beat–weak beat (**S** w w **S** w w, etc.)—using handclaps for the strong (**S**) beats and silent waves for the weak (w) beats.

Let us now turn our attention to a couple of recorded world music examples in which the meters are relatively straightforward and easy to identify. The Egyptian dance rhythm heard on **CD ex. #1-11** is in a duple meter; each of the low-pitched "Dum" strokes on the drums marks one beat; higher-pitched "tek" strokes fall in-between the main beats (i.e., subdividing the beats) at different points (Figure 3.9). Try marking out the main "Dum" beats with handclaps as you listen to this piece.

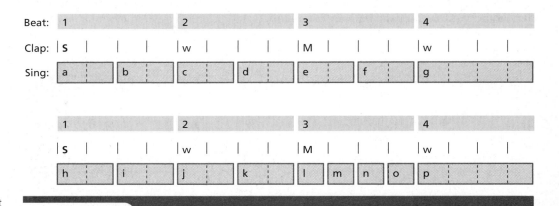

Four-beat (quadruple) meter in "The Alphabet Song."

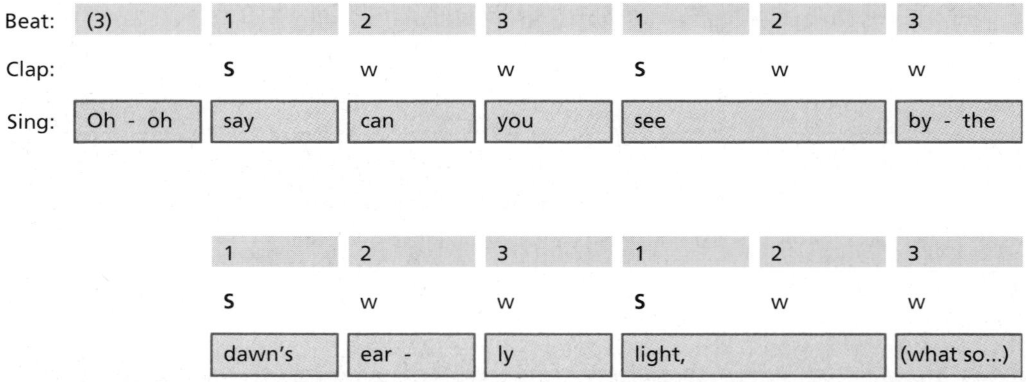

FIGURE 3.7

Triple meter in "The Star-Spangled Banner."

FIGURE 3.8

Beat:	1		2		1		2	
Strokes:	**Dum**	tek	**Dum**	tek	**Dum**	tek	**Dum**	tek

FIGURE 3.9

Egyptian dance rhythm in duple meter.

The famous Mexican *mariachi* tune "Cielito Lindo" (Pretty Cielito), featured on **CD ex. #1-21,** is a triple-meter song with the characteristic triple-meter structure (again, **S** w w **S** w w, etc.). Each strong (**S**) beat is marked by a low, bass note; each weak (w) beat by a strummed guitar chord (we will learn about chords in Chapter 4), as is charted out on page 38 in Figure 3.10. As you listen to "Cielito Lindo," try to mark out the pattern of the meter with claps on the strong (**S**) beats and silent waves on the weak (w) beats.

"Cielito Lindo" (See-el-ee-toe Lin-doe)

insights and perspectives

Four-beat meters also can employ different patterns of strong and weak beats than the standard one illustrated in Figure 3.7. In styles such as rock, blues, funk, and hip-hop, the second and fourth beats (or *backbeats,* as they are called in such contexts) typically are given *more* emphasis (strength) than the first and third beats. This entirely changes the feel of the rhythm, that is, the music's *groove.* You can get a sense of this difference by performing "The Alphabet Song" as you mark out the meter in a way that emphasizes the backbeats. Use a silent wave of the hand to mark each weak beat (w) and a loud clap to mark each strong beat (**S**).

Charles Atkins.

Beat:	1				2				3				4			
Clap:	w				s				w				s			
Sing:	a		b		c		d		e		f		g			

	1				2				3				4			
	w				s				w				s			
	h		i		j		k		l		m	n	o	p		

Just with this simple shift of emphasis on beats, the groove acquires a bit of a rock music feel.

In rock, funk, and blues (the latter exemplified by **CD ex. #1-19,** "A Funny Way of Asking," by Charles Atkins), a "thwack" on the high-pitched snare drum of the drumset is often used to emphasize the backbeats.

Beat:	1	2	3	1	2	3	1
Clap:	S	w	w	S	w	w	S
Music:	**Bass**	strum	strum	**Bass**	strum	strum	**Bass**

Triple meter in "Cielito Lindo."

FIGURE 3.10

Mariachi band.

insights and perspectives

Three Beats or Seven?

In Eastern European countries like Bulgaria and Romania, music with meters of 5, 7, 11, or 13 beats is common. **CD ex. #1-22** features a Roma brass band from Romania playing a dance tune with a meter of seven fast beats per measure (2+2+3). That is how Western music analysts describe this meter, in any case. Roma themselves would say this is essentially a *triple* meter, with two "short" beats followed by a "long" beat every measure. The "shorts" and "longs" correspond to different dance steps.

This is a good example of the difference between cultural insiders' and outsiders' perceptions of music. In this case, as in many (e.g., the music versus nonmusic status of Qur'anic recitation discussed in Chapter 1), there is validity to both perspectives. Each sheds light on the subject at hand in a different way.

In musical traditions of India, Indonesia, China, the Middle East, and other parts of the world, meters are sometimes very long and complex. Rather than consisting of two, three, or four beats, or even five or seven beats, a "measure" may consist of as many as 68, 108, or 256 beats! For these longer types of meters, we usually speak of a **metric cycle** rather than a measure or bar when describing how the beats are grouped and organized. In later chapters, we will encounter music with metric cycles of 8 beats (Bali—Chapter 7), 16 beats (India—Chapter 8), and 68 beats (China—Chapter 13), among others.

Accent and syncopation

The notes of rhythms that are given special emphasis and a little extra "oomph" during a musical performance are called **accents,** or accented notes. Usually an accent is produced by simply playing one note more loudly than the notes surrounding it.

Accents often fall directly with the main beats, but they may fall in-between the beats as well. An accented note that falls between beats is called a **syncopation.** Some music features little syncopation (the Beethoven's Ninth Symphony excerpt of **CD ex. #1-1**) or none at all (a conventional rendition of "The Alphabet Song"). Other music features an abundance of syncopation, in which case it may be described as highly syncopated music (James Brown's "I Got You [I Feel Good]"). Listen to **CD ex. #1-23,** focusing on the rhythm of the vocal shouts. This is an example of *bhangra* music from India. The rhythmic accompaniment of the drums outlines a strong, steady beat in quarter notes. Against this, the shouts of "Hoi!" create syncopated accents.

The term *syncopation,* like most Western music terminology, is culturally loaded. Much West African music is described by Western listeners as "highly syncopated" (for illustrations, listen to **CD ex. #1-41** or **CD ex. #2-22**) but the majority of West Africans do not think of it that way at all. From their perspective, the "syncopation" designation is simply not relevant because they hear and feel the music in a different way.

Tempo

The element of **tempo** is one of the easiest aspects of rhythm to comprehend. The word *tempo* (Italian for time) simply refers to *the rate at which the beats pass in music.* Tempos range from very slow, to slow, medium-slow, medium (moderate), medium-fast, fast, and very fast. Try singing "The Alphabet Song" at several different tempos (just alter the speed of the beats to change the tempo). Note how the feeling and character of the music seem to transform as the tempo changes. Tempos may be *constant* (steady, unchanging, metronomic) or they may be *variable* (speeding up and/or slowing down within the course of a performance). They may *accelerate* or *decelerate,* suddenly or gradually.

A gradual acceleration in tempo is used as a device to heighten musical excitement in many music traditions. An

West African drum ensemble.

bhangra (BHAHNG-rah)

The Athenians, a Greek syrtaki group.

A South Indian music performance, featuring vina (right) and mrdangam.

syrtaki (seer-tah-kee)

example of this effect may be heard in the excerpt of the popular Greek *syrtaki* song "Zorba the Greek" on **CD ex. #1-24.** As you listen to the selection, try clapping along with the beat and notice how dramatically the tempo increases.

Free rhythm

Thus far, our discussion of the elements of rhythm has related specifically to music in which there is a discernible beat, and, in turn, usually a discernible meter and tempo as well. Such music is called *metric music* (i.e., measured music). Not all music is metric, however. Much of it is *nonmetric*, or in **free rhythm.** Music in free rhythm does not have a discernible beat. It tends to float across time rather than march in step to it. **CD ex. #1-25** begins with music played in free rhythm on an instrument from South India called the *vina.* Then, just before the drum (called a *mrdangam*) enters, a beat is established and the drum part marks out a metric cycle (of eight beats). Note the difference between the nonmetric and metric sections, and see if you can "find the beat" once the drum part begins.

vina (VEE-nah)

mrdangam (mir-DUNG-ahm)

Summary

Rhythm was the focus of this chapter. Our examination of rhythm followed a brief overview of the four basic properties of tones—duration, frequency, amplitude, and timbre—with rhythm defined as the fundamental musical correlate of duration. We explored rhythm through both participatory exercises based on familiar songs and discussions of recorded examples representing diverse world music traditions. Elements of rhythm including beat, subdivision, meter, metric cycle, accent, syncopation, tempo, and free rhythm were introduced.

Key Terms

duration	eighth notes	metric cycle
frequency	quarter notes	accents
amplitude	beat	syncopation
timbre	subdivision	tempo
rhythm	measure	free rhythm
sixteenth notes	meter	

Study Questions

- What are the four basic properties of tones and how is each defined?
- What is rhythm?
- What is the relationship of quarter notes to eighth notes, eighth notes to sixteenth notes, quarter notes to sixteenth notes?

- How is the rhythm of a piece of music defined by its relation to elements such as beat, subdivision, meter, accents, syncopation, and tempo?

- What musical examples used in this chapter were in duple meter? Triple meter? Other meters? Which illustrated duple subdivision? Triple subdivision?

- What is a backbeat, and in what types of music are you likely to find backbeat accents?

- What is the difference between metric music and music in free rhythm?

Applying What You Have Learned

- Listen to a variety of songs and pieces from your personal music collection (focusing especially on ones with which you have the greatest familiarity) and try to identify different elements of rhythm present in them. Locate the beat of the song, then see if you can determine the level of subdivision (e.g., duple, triple, quadruple, other) and the meter (again, duple, triple, quadruple, other) by using the listening skills you have developed in this chapter.

- Listen to two or more pieces of music from your personal collection that are representative of the same musical style (e.g., two hip-hop tunes) and identify as many elements of rhythm as you can; next, listen to one or two other pieces in a contrasting musical style (e.g., country and western) and do the same. Compare your findings. What does this reveal about *general* similarities and differences in rhythmic approach between the two styles?

- Take a familiar song ("Mary Had a Little Lamb" will do) and sing it several times in a row, each time at a different tempo—slow, medium, fast, very fast, variable. How does changing the tempo change the feeling and spirit of the song overall? What does this tell you about the significance of tempo in music?

- Get together with a friend or two and play a rhythm game. Clap out the rhythm of a familiar song (e.g., "The Alphabet Song," "The Star-Spangled Banner") without actually singing the tune and see if your friend(s) can identify the tune on the basis of that rhythm performance alone. Then switch roles and have someone else clap out tunes while you try to identify them.

Resources for Further Study

Visit the Online Learning Center at www.mhhe.com/bakan1 for additional learning aids, study help, and resources that supplement the content of this chapter.

how **music works,** part II:
pitch

Pitch is the element of music that pertains to *the highness and lowness of musical tones.* In terms of the four basic properties of tones (duration, frequency, amplitude, timbre), pitch is related specifically to *frequency.*

Musical tones, and indeed all sounds, result from vibrations (usually in air) that create *soundwaves.* The rate of vibration in a soundwave varies from one tone to another. Tones with many vibrations per second have high frequencies. Those with fewer vibrations per second have lower frequencies. Correspondingly, high-frequency tones have higher pitches than low-frequency tones.

To track the pitch of a song is to track how the notes go "up" and "down" from one to the next. The particular sequence of pitches that unfolds is what we hear as the song's **melody.** Every melody has its own distinctive features:

- A *melodic range:* the distance in pitch from the lowest note to the highest note.
- *Melodic direction:* some combination of ascending and/or descending movement as the melody progresses from note to note.
- *Melodic character:* melodies in which there are numerous large "leaps" in pitch from one note to the next (disjunct melodies); versus others that move mainly in small, smooth "steps" (conjunct melodies); versus others that stay on or close to a single pitch, with little up-and-down motion (static melodies); versus still others that combine various types of movement.
- *Melodic contour:* the overall "shape" of a melody, which is a product of its range, direction, and character combined.

Pitch and melody in "Mary Had a Little Lamb" and a Native American Eagle Dance song

Hum the tune of "Mary Had a Little Lamb," leaving out the words. This is the *melody* of the song. Now go back and start again and add in the words, but sing just the first five notes. Notice how your voice—or, more specifically, the *pitch* of your voice—first moves down two steps ("Ma-ry had"), then comes back up two steps ("a lit-"[tle lamb), arriving back at the starting pitch on the fifth note (Figure 4.1). This descending-ascending arc of pitches is immediately identifiable as the beginning of the melody of "Mary Had a Little Lamb." Its *melodic direction* is a distinctive feature of the song's *melodic contour.*

If you sing through "Mary" from start to finish, you will notice that the pitches never get very much higher or lower than the pitch of the starting note. This is because it is a song with a limited, or narrow, *melodic range.* You also will notice that your voice never has to move very far from one note to the next as you sing, indicating that the *melodic character* is mainly conjunct rather than disjunct (i.e., successive notes are close together in pitch, rather than far apart).

Arapaho (Ah-RA-pa-ho)

The melodic range of the song heard in **CD ex. #1-26** is considerably larger than that of "Mary Had a Little Lamb," and other characteristics of the melody are different in distinctive ways as well. This is an Eagle Dance song of the Northern Arapaho people. Arapaho traditional songs, like those of other Native American music cultures of the Great Plains region (see also Chapter 2, pp. 12–13), have a signature pattern of melodic contour: they usually unfold as a series of *descending melodic phrases.* An approximation of the contours of the three descending phrases of the "Eagle Dance" excerpt included on the CD is charted out in graphic form in Figure 4.2.

Names of pitches in Western music

In order to distinguish between different pitches, the Western music system assigns letter names to them, from A to G: A B C D E F G. There are also some pitches that fall "in the cracks" between the ones with just plain letter names. There is, for example, a pitch that falls exactly halfway between C and D. If we identify that pitch as being a bit higher than a regular C, it is

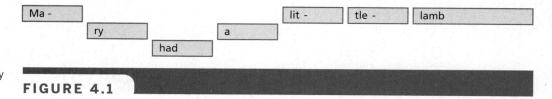

Melodic contour of the opening notes of "Mary Had a Little Lamb."

FIGURE 4.1

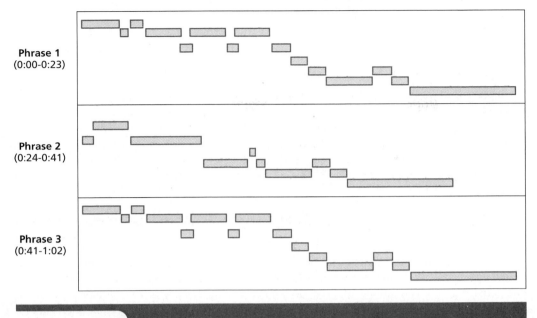

Phrase 1
(0:00-0:23)

Phrase 2
(0:24-0:41)

Phrase 3
(0:41-1:02)

Melodic contour
of "Eagle Dance"
(CD ex. #1-26).

referred to as C-sharp (C♯). If, alternatively, we identify it as being a bit lower than D, it is called D-flat (D♭). In the always metaphorical language of music terminology, "sharpening" a note means making it a bit higher, while "flattening" it means making it a bit lower. Notes that are neither sharpened nor flattened are called "naturals" (e.g., C-natural, D-natural).

Labeling the pitches of tones with letter names as described above only works in some cases. Tones that are sung or played on instruments like the piano, guitar, violin, flute, or trumpet can usually be identified in this way. This is because these tones have what is known as *determinate pitch*. But tones produced on other types of instruments—shakers, cymbals, triangles,

Native American
singing/drumming
group.

The melodic direction of a song may have important *cultural* ramifications. Earlier (Chapter 2, p. 11), we learned that Warao shamans in Venezuela use certain types of songs to cure illnesses and other kinds of songs to *cause* illnesses. Research on the music of the Warao by the ethnomusicologist Dale Olsen convincingly demonstrates that the shamanistic curing songs consistently have ascending melodies, while the shamanistic "inflicting songs" (the ones performed with the intent of causing illness) consistently have descending melodies (Olsen 1996: 262–63). This is a clear instance of music as sound and music as culture integrally informing one another.

many kinds of drums—cannot be identified by a single pitch designation. Rather than being dominated by just one pitch, these tones of *indeterminate pitch* generate many different pitches that compete for the ear's attention with no clear "winner" among them. The basic difference between tones of indeterminate and determinate pitch is reflected in the shapes of their soundwaves, which can be captured visually in computer graphics such as those reproduced in Figure 4.3.

The Western pitch system and the octave

octave (OCK-tiv)

Our concern here is with tones of determinate pitch. The pitch-related aspects of most Western music are based on a system of 12 such distinct pitches. These are laid out as white keys and black keys on a piano keyboard (Figure 4.4).

Playing all 12 notes in sequence from low to high or from high to low yields what is known as the *chromatic scale*. A **scale** is *an ascending and/or descending series of notes of different pitch*. Songs and other pieces of music are typically "built" from the notes of particular scales, much as words, sentences, and stories are built from the letters of the alphabet.

Listen to the ascending chromatic scale illustration of **Online Musical Illustration #1** (located at the Online Learning Center at www.mhhe.com/bakan1). You may observe that it ends rather oddly, almost as though it is unfinished. It seems to need one more note to provide closure. Now listen to **Online Musical Illustration #2.** This one ends in a more satisfying

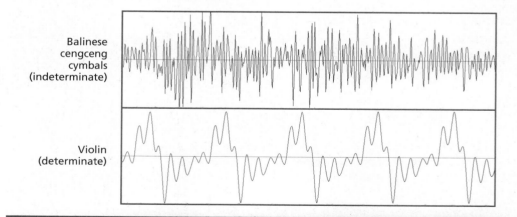

Balinese
cengceng
cymbals
(indeterminate)

Violin
(determinate)

Computer-generated images of indeterminate and determinate pitch soundwaves.

FIGURE 4.3

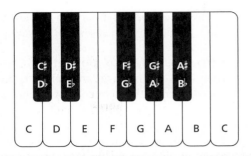

FIGURE 4.4

Labeled pitches on the piano keyboard.

way. That is because the note added, the 13th and final one in the sequence, is of the same pitch as the *first* note of the scale: both the first and last note have a pitch of C.

This may be a bit confusing, since the last note is clearly higher in pitch than the first one. How can they be "the same"? The answer: they are the same pitch an **octave** apart. The octave is a musical phenomenon that is nearly universally recognized in the world's music traditions (though it is known by many different names in different cultures and languages). Its existence explains why a man and a woman can sing the exact same melody together even though the woman's voice produces much higher pitches than the man's. Men and women sing in different octave **ranges,** otherwise known as *pitch ranges* or *registers*. The phenomenon of the octave also explains why a version of a tune played on a tuba (an instrument with a very low pitch range) is

insights and perspectives

When High Is Low and Low Is High

In our discussion of aspects of pitch like the octave, pitch ranges, and melodic direction in this chapter, there has been an implicit assumption that we all know what the difference is between "high" and "low" where pitch is concerned. It is part of our "commonsense" knowledge in this culture that the voice ranges of women are generally *higher* than the voice ranges of men, or that a relatively small instrument like a flute plays higher pitches than a very large instrument like a tuba.

Yet ethnomusicological research reveals that such seemingly basic, common-knowledge "facts" about musical sound—known to nonmusicians and musicians alike—may be more culture-specific, indeed more arbitrary, than they first appear to be. The Are'are (Ah-ray Ah-ray) people of Malaita (Solomon Islands, Micronesia) recognize that there are different pitches in their music, and that the musical tones range in pitch from low to high. However, their cultural conception of pitch is completely the reverse of ours. What they refer to as low pitches are what we in the West think of as high pitches; what they identify as high pitches are what we call low pitches (Zemp 1979). Therefore, from an Are'are perspective, the most "commonsense" assumptions that Westerners have about pitch are turned, quite literally, upside down.

recognizable as having the same melody as a version played on a flute (an instrument with a much higher pitch range). It is the same melody in both cases, but played in different octave ranges.

Common scales in Western music: Major, pentatonic, minor, and blues

In the conventional pitch system of Western music, the octave is divided into the 12 evenly spaced pitches of the chromatic scale, and this sequence of pitches climbs higher and higher (or descends lower and lower) as it spans across different octave ranges. In some styles of music, all 12 pitches of the chromatic scale are employed and have more or less equal "status." More often, however, songs and other pieces are constructed from the notes of musical scales that use only certain, select pitches out of the 12 available ones. These include the major scale, the pentatonic scale, minor scales, and the blues scale. Though these scales are specifically linked to the Western music tradition and its particular system of pitch organization, there are at least two reasons why they nonetheless provide a viable point of departure for understanding what musical scales are and how they work in the world's musics more generally. The first reason is that Western scales (and pitch-related aspects of Western music overall) have either influenced or been fully adopted into many music traditions worldwide during the modern era. The second reason is that by examining how some common Western scales work, we can develop a set of basic terms, concepts, and listening skills that will serve us well in exploring the scales and pitch systems of other world music traditions we encounter, even ones that have no direct relationship to Western music.

MAJOR SCALE While the chromatic scale incorporates all of the white and black keys of the piano keyboard within an octave range, the **major scale** can be produced with the white keys only, starting on the pitch C (Figure 4.5). There are seven pitches per octave in the major scale. Each represents one *scale degree,* or "step." For example, in the C-major scale shown in Figure 4.5, the pitch C is the first scale degree, or **tonic;** D is the second scale degree; E, the third scale degree; and so on. **Online Musical Illustration #3** provides an illustration of a C-major scale, moving through all seven scale degrees and ending with the pitch C an octave above the starting note. Major scales can be created with any of the 12 chromatic pitches as the tonic, but only the C-major scale can be produced using the white keys only.

Many songs in the Western music tradition are built predominantly or even exclusively from the notes of major scales (e.g., "The Alphabet Song," "Mary Had a Little Lamb"). Such songs are described as being in a major **key.** Music in major keys tends to have "happy" connotations for Western listeners, mainly because people in the West have been *culturally conditioned* to perceive major-key music in this way.

PENTATONIC SCALE Closely related to the major scale is the **pentatonic scale.** As its name implies, the pentatonic scale includes just five pitches per octave, rather than seven. Actually, *any* scale with five pitches per octave can be classified as a pentatonic scale. A great variety of such five-tone scales are used in different world music traditions, in Indonesia, China, Japan,

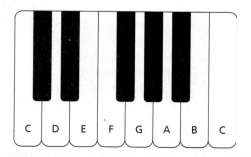

C-major scale pitches on the piano keyboard.

FIGURE 4.5

Uganda, and elsewhere. When we refer to *the* pentatonic scale in connection with Western music, however, the reference is usually specific. This is essentially a major scale with the fourth and seventh scale degrees omitted. Thus, a pentatonic scale with a tonic of C includes the notes C D E G A, leaving out F (the fourth scale degree) and B (the seventh scale degree) of the "equivalent" C-major scale (Figure 4.6). You can hear what this scale sounds like by listening to **Online Musical Illustration #4.**

Like major scales, pentatonic scales can be created with any one of the 12 chromatic pitches as their tonic. Starting from a tonic pitch of F#, for example, you can produce a pentatonic scale by playing just the black keys on a piano keyboard (Figure 4.7).

The melody of the Native American Rabbit Dance song we listened to in Chapter 2 **(CD exs. #1-7 and 1-8)** employs a pentatonic scale. The tonic pitch here is D and the scale consists of the notes D E F# A B **(Online Musical Illustration #5).** There is more to the issue from a musicultural perspective, however. Whether the use of this scale in the song was a product of Western influence on traditional Great Plains–style Native American music, a coincidence of "spontaneous invention" (nearly identical types of scales developing *independently* in two musicultural traditions), or a combination of the two is hard to know. This creates an interesting "ethnomusicological paradox." On the one hand, "Rabbit Dance" seems like an excellent example to use to illustrate what music based on the pentatonic scale sounds like. On the other hand, "Rabbit Dance" does *not* belong to the Western music tradition. Describing this music in terms of pentatonic scales and pitches identified by letter names likely has little or nothing to do with how the musicians heard on the recording think about the song.

MINOR SCALES **Minor scales,** like major scales, employ seven pitches per octave, but the sequences of pitches are somewhat different. Additionally, minor scales come in a couple of varieties, whereas there is only one basic type of major scale. Finally, minor scales may use a different sequence of pitches going up (ascending) than they use coming down (descending), as opposed to major scales, which use the same set of pitches regardless of melodic direction. **Online**

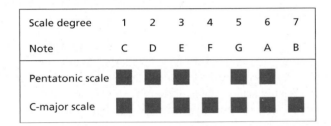

Scale degree	1	2	3	4	5	6	7
Note	C	D	E	F	G	A	B
Pentatonic scale	■	■	■		■	■	
C-major scale	■	■	■	■	■	■	■

FIGURE 4.6

Comparison of pitches of the C-major scale and the C-pentatonic scale.

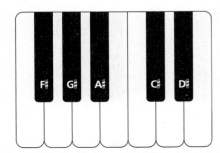

FIGURE 4.7

"Black key" pentatonic scale starting on F#.

Musical Illustration #6 provides an illustration of, first, a major scale; second, a type of minor scale called the *harmonic minor scale;* and third, a type of minor scale called the *melodic minor scale,* the only type that uses a different set of pitches when it ascends than when it descends.

The most important distinction between major and minor scales has to do with the distance in pitch between the second and third scale degrees of each. The distance between any two notes, whether in a scale or a melody, is called an **interval.** The interval between the second and third degrees in a major scale is always a bit larger than that between the second and third degrees of a minor scale. This small difference has a big effect on how we perceive music in major and minor keys. It alone can account for conventional Western distinctions between a melody that sounds "happy" (major key) and one that sounds "sad" (minor key). You can hear this in the comparison of two different versions of "Mary Had a Little Lamb" performed by the saxophonist Patrick Meighan in **Online Musical Illustration #7.** The first version is in a major key; the second, in a minor key. Notice how much "sadder" this normally "happy" song becomes merely on account of the lowering of a single pitch (i.e., the third scale degree) in the version based on the minor scale.

BLUES SCALE Beyond generating the major, pentatonic, and minor scales, the 12 pitches of the Western chromatic scale have been drawn upon historically to yield various other types of scales as well. The **blues scale,** in essence an amalgamation of features of major, minor, pentatonic, and traditional African scales, is among the best known of these. A blues scale starting on the pitch C includes six pitches: C E♭ F F♯ G B♭ (**Online Musical Illustration #8).** Three of these—E♭, F♯, and B♭—are described as the "blue notes" (Figure 4.8). These largely account for the "bluesy" sound of music based on this scale.

The blues scale is used not just in blues music *per se.* It is also present in many other styles of music around the world that have been influenced by blues and other African-American music traditions. Wherever it is used, the blues scale gives music a distinctive and readily recognizable sound and character. You can get a good sense of this by listening to bluesman Charles Atkins' "A Funny Way of Asking." The melody, sung by Atkins (**CD ex. #1-19,** starting at 0:21), is fully rooted in the blues scale.

Modulation: Moving from one scale and key to another

In the musical illustrations and examples we have listened to and discussed so far, a single tonic pitch, or "home note," has been identified for each scale and piece. As was alluded to earlier, this tonic pitch and its related scale usually determine the *key* of a piece of music in the Western tradition. For example, if you were to perform "Mary Had a Little Lamb" with a tonic pitch of C and using the C-major scale, the performance would be in the *key of C major.*

In some music, different sections of a piece will be in different keys; that is, they will draw their pitches from different scales and/or have a different "home note." Moving from one key to

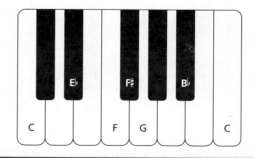

Blues scale, starting on the pitch C.

FIGURE 4.8

another during the course of a musical work is called **modulation. Online Musical Illustration #9** offers an example of a modulation. First you hear the tune of "Mary Had a Little Lamb" played in the key of C major. Then there is a modulation (i.e., the key changes) and "Mary" is played again in a different key (specifically, F major).

Pitch and scales in non-Western musical systems

The Western pitch system, with its 12 equally spaced pitches per octave, characteristic scales, and rules for moving within and between different keys, is but one of a great many pitch systems found in the world of music.

In traditional Indonesian *gamelan* music (see Chapter 7), there are two major pitch systems, one called *slendro* and another called *pelog.* Neither of these systems has anything to do with the 12-part division of the octave used in Western music, nor with major, minor, pentatonic, blues, or other Western scales. Rather, they are unique unto themselves. An example of a slendro-based scale and a pelog-based scale, respectively, may be heard in **Online Musical Illustration #10.** Both of these scales use five notes per octave—that is, they are pentatonic—but neither is the same as the Western pentatonic scale discussed earlier (though the slendro scale does sound something like it!). The notes of these scales may sound "out of tune" to your ears, but this is only because you are unaccustomed to these pitch systems. Western scales would likely sound equally "out of tune" to you if you had been raised listening only to gamelan music.

slendro (slen-djroh)

pelog (PAY-lawg)

Indian classical musicians recognize at least 22 distinct pitches per octave. Again, these do not derive from the Western pitch system. Like their Western counterparts, Indian musicians often build pieces and musical performances from "scales" comprised of seven ascending and seven descending pitches, but they have many more pitches upon which to draw in generating these "scales," which form the basis of the complex *ragas* discussed in Chapter 8.

raga(s) (RAH-gah)

Middle Eastern music in the Arab tradition (see Chapter 12) is also built from systems of tiny intervals, or **microtones.** Instead of 22 pitches per octave, though, the Arab music system has 24. An illustration of a scale in which the octave is divided into 24 microtonal intervals may

Slendro gamelan instrument (left), pelog gamelan instrument (right).

be heard in **Online Musical Illustration #11.** Additionally, in Arab music, as also in Indian, highly sophisticated systems of melodic **ornamentation,** that is, systems for "decorating" the main pitches, are integral to the pitch system overall. **CD ex. #1-27** offers an example of music in which the melody is highly ornamented. The featured instrument is a specially constructed Egyptian accordion capable of producing 24 pitches per octave rather than the customary 12, that is, equipped to produce the microtonal intervals of Arab music of this type. As you listen, see if you can distinguish the "main" melody notes from the ornamental notes.

insights and perspectives

Articulation

Another important element of music that is well illustrated by **CD ex. #1-27** is **articulation.** Listen again to the accordion solo of that example, noting how some of the notes are held long, being sustained all the way to the notes that follow them, while others are clipped off and played with a sharp attack, creating a bit of space before the next note arrives. There are two Italian terms that Western musicians commonly use to describe these different articulations: the longer, sustained treatment of a note is called **legato** (le-GAH-toe), while the shorter, clipped treatment results in notes that are **staccato** (stah-KAH-toe). An analogy from spoken language may be helpful. The vowel sounds—ahh, eeehh, ohh, oohh—are usually spoken with "legato" articulations; in contrast, most consonant sounds—the sounds made by the letters p, t, k, d—are uttered in a "staccato" manner.

insights and perspectives

Scale Versus Mode

As we have seen, the term *scale* refers exclusively to an ascending/descending sequence of pitches that provides the fundamental pitch "building blocks" for generating pieces of music in a given musical system. Related to but broader than the idea of a scale is that of a **mode.** Whereas a scale essentially comprises a "raw" sequence of pitches, a mode is something more comprehensive and multidimensional. The rules of the mode tell the musician not only *what* pitches can be used in a given piece or performance, but also offer instructions on *how* to use each of those pitches. Rules pertaining to how certain notes of the mode's scale are to be ornamented, how to move from one pitch to another in an appropriate manner, and which notes should receive relatively more or less emphasis are built into the melodic system of a mode.

So too are a variety of features that might be classified as *extramusical.* Particular modes may be identified with certain emotions, times of the day, seasons of the year, or episodes of dramatic performances or rituals. In short, a mode is like a musical road map that provides musicians and listeners with detailed instructions on how to progress through the terrain of a composition or performance with maximum efficiency and effectiveness, and without getting lost. Several of the music traditions explored in later chapters, including the Hindustani (Hin-dus-TAH-nee) raga tradition of northern India examined in Chapter 8, are essentially mode-based. Rather than try to generalize about how modes work here, we will explore the particulars of individual modal systems as they arise in the later chapters.

Pitch, Chords, and Harmony

Notes of different pitch may occur either one after the other (sequentially) or simultaneously. Generally speaking, a series of notes presented one after the other yields a melody, whereas a group of two or more notes of different pitch sounded simultaneously yields a **chord.** A chord that "makes sense" within the context of its musical style is called a **harmony.** Western music has its own rules and aesthetics of harmony. Other musical traditions have theirs too, and these often have nothing whatsoever to do with what we in the West perceive as sounding "right" or sounding "wrong."

This final section of the chapter provides an introduction to the topics of chords and harmony. It should be noted, however, that the approach to exploring how music works used in this text does not require nearly as detailed an understanding of these complex topics as it does of other pitch-related aspects of music we have addressed, such as melody, pitch systems, scales, and the octave. The following discussion is therefore rather brief and cursory, providing only as much information as is specifically needed to prepare us for the musical journey that lies ahead.

Single chord–based music and music with chord progressions

In some traditions and styles of music, an entire composition or performance may be built from the foundation of a single chord. This is the case in much hip-hop, techno, and funk, styles that often rely on musical devices other than changing chords to generate musical interest. (Listen, for example, to the passage from 3:45–4:15 of **CD ex. #3-33** [Zöhar's "Ehad"].)

In other kinds of music, it is common to have movement from one chord to another, producing what is known as a **chord progression.** Usually, the chord progression is designed specifically to support a melody to which it is linked. This produces a *chordal accompaniment* to the melody.

CD ex. #1-28, a performance of the classic *bossa nova* song "Wave" (written by the great Brazilian composer Antonio Carlos Jobim) offers a good example of melody with chordal accompaniment. The melody is heard in the saxophone part (played by the famous saxophonist Paul Desmond). The chord progression is outlined in the electric guitar part and is anchored by the string bass. Beginning at 0:13 of the example, notice how every time the bass (the lowest-pitched instrument) moves from one pitch to another the guitar mirrors this motion by moving from one *chord* to another. Sometimes one of the instruments anticipates or follows the other as they move from note to note, chord to chord, but they remain in close coordination, and the chord progression they collectively create always fits together well with the saxophone melody.

*bossa nova
(bah-sah NO-vah)*

Jobim (Joe-BEEM)

Harmonization of melodies

In "Wave," the melody and the chords were performed by separate instruments playing different parts. But it is also possible (and common) to have music in which *chords are actually built from the notes of the **melody** itself.* When this occurs—that is, when each melody note is reinforced by an additional note or notes of different pitch to create a chord—the result is what will be referred to in this text as **harmonization.** The voice parts of the chorus (choir) in the famous "Ode to Joy" section of Beethoven's Symphony No. 9 **(CD ex. #1-1)** provide an excellent illustration of such harmonization. Each note of the melody is expanded into a chord of three or more pitches in the parts sung by the different sections of the choir. The rich harmonization helps to transform a rather simple melody into a powerful and grandiose musical statement at the climactic point of this very famous musical work.

Arpeggios (broken chords)

In some cases, the different notes of a chord are played *in sequence*—"melody style," so to speak—rather than all together at once. This quasi-melodic presentation of a chord is called an **arpeggio** (arpeggiated chord). Arpeggios also may be called *broken chords* (since the notes of the chord are "broken up"). With arpeggios, the line between what is a melody and what is a

*arpeggio(s)
(ahr-PEH-jee-oh)*

chord may get blurry. Listen to the Spanish *flamenco* guitar solo excerpt of **CD ex. #1-29.** It features many arpeggios, the presence of which contributes greatly to the passionate quality of this beautiful music.

Other chords, other harmonies

As was alluded to earlier, the rules and aesthetics of chords and harmony need not have anything to do with Western music standards or conventions. Listen again to **CD ex. #1-2,** the Japanese gagaku selection from Chapter 1. This, too, might be described as a type of harmonized music with chords—there are even some arpeggios—but the chords and harmonies depend on the logic of a system of pitch organization that is radically different (and much older!) than the one to which we in the West are accustomed. To Western listeners, gagaku harmonies tend to sound "strange," but again, Western harmonies would likely sound just as strange, just as *dissonant,* to someone who had been raised listening only to gagaku music.

zheng (jung [rhymes with "lung"])

    CD ex. #1-30 presents another musical scenario that defies our usual expectations of chords and harmony. This is a piece by a Taiwanese composer featuring a Chinese instrument called the *zheng* (the focus of Chapter 13), but the organization of the music's pitch elements—melody, chords, harmony—is based neither in Taiwanese nor Chinese music traditions. Rather, it is derived exclusively from a *Western* musical system. The composer studied music composition at the University of Michigan, and the ways in which the pitches take shape in the form of melodies, chords, and harmonies are largely a product of her training there. Why, then, does this music, too, sound "strange" by conventional Western standards? Clearly, the Western musical foundations used to create works like Beethoven's Ninth Symphony are not in operation here, at least not in the same way. Indeed, this music appears to venture considerably further from such foundations than the bossa nova, flamenco, blues, or even Egyptian music examples heard earlier. The reason for this is that this piece was created using principles of pitch organization that *intentionally defy* the norms and rules of more conventional approaches to harmonic and melodic organization in Western music. Composers who create such music may be anchored in the Western music tradition by virtue of their training and experience, but they relate to that tradition with the intention of transforming and extending it, seeking sometimes radically new modes of musical expression because they have a different kind of musical statement to make.

Summary

The musical element of pitch was the topic of this chapter. We learned that the pitch of any given tone is determined by its frequency, or rate of vibration. We also learned that some tones have a determinate pitch whereas others are of indeterminate pitch.

    Melody was our point of departure for looking at and listening to how pitch works in actual musical contexts. Melodic range, direction, character, and contour were shown to be basic features distinguishing one melody from another. From there, we moved on to the pitch system of Western music, common Western scales (major, minor, pentatonic, blues), and pitch systems in other world music traditions that are essentially unrelated to the Western system and build from different principles of organization. Pitch-related elements such as modulation, microtones, and melodic ornamentation also were introduced.

    The final part of the chapter was devoted to how pitch relates to chords and harmony. Again, both Western and non-Western systems were examined.

Key Terms

melody	minor scales	ornamentation
scale	interval	mode
octave	blues scale	chord
ranges	modulation	harmony
major scale	microtones	chord progression
tonic	articulation	harmonization
key	legato	arpeggio
pentatonic scale	staccato	

Study Questions

- As rhythm is to duration, pitch is to _____?

- What is a melody? What were the four principal features of a melody identified?

- What was distinctive about the melodic direction in "Eagle Dance" (CD ex. #1-26), and how is this musiculturally significant? How is the specific cultural function of a Warao shaman's song revealed by *its* melodic direction?

- What are pitch ranges, and how do they relate to the phenomenon of the octave?

- What does it mean to say that a particular song is "in the key of C major" or "in the key of D minor"?

- What are distinguishing features of the major scale, pentatonic scale, minor scales, and blues scale?

- What does it mean when we say that there is a modulation in a piece of music?

- What, in general, distinguishes a scale from a mode?

- What is the difference in sound between a chord that is harmonized (as defined in this chapter) and one that is arpeggiated? What is a chord progression?

Applying What You Have Learned

- Listen to several pieces from your personal music collection and try to identify instances where the music is built from major, pentatonic, minor, or blues scale-based melodies and chords. Use the listening skills you have developed in this chapter—as well as your subjective impressions of the music (does it sound "happy," "sad," "bluesy," etc.)—to make your determinations.

Resources for Further Study

Visit the Online Learning Center at www.mhhe.com/bakan1 for additional learning aids, study help, and resources that supplement the content of this chapter.

how **music works,** part III:
dynamics, timbre, and instruments

Dynamics, timbre, and music instruments account for what the different tones of music *sound like*. This, then, is a chapter that explores the characteristics and qualities of music sounds themselves and that also examines the material resources involved in their making.

Dynamics

When we speak of *dynamics,* we are simply referring to how loud or how soft the different tones in music are; in other words, to their *amplitude.* Music is filled with "small" and "big" sounds covering a continuum from silence at one extreme to potentially deafening loudness at the other. The various designated gradations along this continuum of loudness that are recognized by music makers and music listeners (e.g., very soft, soft, medium, loud, very loud) account for dynamics.

The computer-generated image reproduced in Figure 5.1 is a graphic representation of the dynamics of the tone heard in **Online Musical Illustration #12.** This tone starts soft, then has a **crescendo** (it gets gradually louder), and then a **decrescendo** (it gets gradually softer). Notice how the vertical thickness of the image increases as the amplitude (dynamic level, volume) of the represented tone grows, then decreases as the tone becomes softer again. Compare this image to that of Figure 5.2, which represents a tone with *terraced dynamics,* as heard in **Online Musical Illustration #13.** In terraced dynamics, the amplitude level changes quite suddenly—from soft to loud, or from loud to soft—rather than gradually.

In scientific terms, the amplitude of a tone is measured in *decibels.* The higher the decibel count, the louder the sound. But this kind of "absolute" measurement is less significant for our purposes than thinking of how loud or soft the different notes in a piece of music are *relative to each other.* This is mainly what accounts for what we perceive as dynamics. A given performance of music may change from one dynamic level to another as it progresses, or it may remain constant throughout. Where changes in dynamics do occur, they may be gradual (crescendo, decrescendo) or sudden (terraced dynamics). Where multiple tones are heard simultaneously, their respective dynamic levels may be the same or different; for example, in a piece for flute and piano, the two instruments may play a note at the same dynamic level or at different dynamic levels at any given point, depending on the desired musical effect.

Our perceptions of dynamics are often context-dependent. A "loud" dynamic level in a heavy metal rock band's performance is going to be much louder, in *absolute* terms (i.e., in decibels), than a "loud" dynamic level in a solo flute recital. On the other hand, the **dynamic range**—

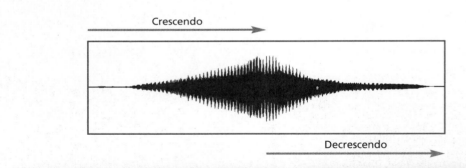

Computer-generated image of a tone with crescendo and decrescendo.

FIGURE 5.1

Computer-generated image of a tone with terraced dynamics.

FIGURE 5.2

Hearing and Charting Dynamics: A Listening Exercise

Effective use of dynamics can contribute much to the power and beauty of a musical performance. Listen to **CD ex. #1-31,** an excerpt from a performance by vocalist Ruth Wieder Magan of a composition for solo voice based on the text of an ancient mystical Jewish prayer (this recording is explored in detail in Chapter 14, pp. 342–347). How do dynamics (and dynamic contrast especially) contribute to the musical effect of the performance? How do the changing dynamic levels correspond to other musical elements we have discussed, such as melodic direction and ornamentation? Additionally, how would you describe the rhythm here: is it metric or "free rhythm"? You may wish to create a graphic image of the dynamic "landscape" of what you hear (either freehand or using a computer). Draw a line across the page from left to right, leaving spaces where there are silent pauses and using a *time scale* of one inch for every five seconds of music. Make the line thin where the notes are soft, thicker where the notes are louder. How does your chart of the dynamics in this performance compare to those of your classmates? How might you explain any differences you observe?

that is, the range between the softest and loudest notes—in the flute performance will likely be greater than that of the rock band, since Western classical music usually relies more on *dynamic contrast* to achieve its aesthetic goals than does heavy metal music.

Timbre

To describe timbre is to attempt to account for the *character or quality of a musical tone or tones.* Differences in timbre are primarily what enable us to distinguish between the sounds of a trumpet and a flute, or between those of an **acoustic** (unamplified) guitar and an electric (amplified) guitar. Tones of the exact same pitch, register, duration, and amplitude played on these

A steel drum (pan) band, which features a set of instruments with a highly distinctive timbre.

different instruments sound different. It is their distinct timbres that distinguish them from one another. Different types of **ensembles** (music groups, whether vocal, instrumental, or a combination) also have characteristic timbres. A choir (ensemble of singers) sounds categorically different than a symphony orchestra, which, in turn, has a completely different timbre than a heavy metal rock band. The *genuinely* "heavy metal" sound of a Caribbean-style steel drum (pan) band like the one heard on **CD ex. #1-32** takes us into yet another timbral universe.

In **Online Musical Illustration #14,** the first sound you hear is a tone played on a saxophone. The second is a tone of essentially the same pitch, register, duration, and amplitude played on a flute. What differentiates these two tones is their distinct timbres, which can be represented visually using computer-generated images called *spectrograms* (Figure 5.3).

The different shapes of these spectrograms, and in turn the different timbres of the tones they produce, can be explained by the fact that every tone is actually comprised of multiple pitches, not just the single pitch that you generally perceive when a note is played on an instrument such as a saxophone or a flute (e.g., the pitch C, or A, or F#). Each one of these many pitch components of a tone is called a *partial.* A spectrogram is essentially a snapshot of all of the partials contained in a tone, as well as of the loudness (amplitude) of each of the partials relative to all the others. The actual timbre you hear when a tone is played on a saxophone or flute is the audible equivalent of that snapshot. Just as the flute and saxophone tones look different in computer images, they sound different in terms of their respective timbres.

A tone consists of two types of partials: the fundamental pitch (represented as the darkest part of a spectrogram) and a series of *overtones,* or **harmonics.** In conventional saxophone or flute tones such as those heard earlier in Online Musical Illustration #14, the fundamental pitch is so much louder than the harmonics that it essentially absorbs them. We hear the note as having a pitch of F, or of B♭, or whatever the fundamental pitch is. We *do* hear the overtones, too, but not as distinct pitches; rather, they merge together with each other and with the fundamental pitch to generate the tone's distinctive timbre.

In some music traditions, the ability of performers to manipulate the relationship between the fundamental pitch of a tone and its harmonics through techniques that generate a great variety of timbres has been developed to a very high art. This is certainly the case with the Aboriginal Australian **didjeridu,** which we heard earlier on **CD ex. #1-12** ("Ibis," by Alan Maralung).

As we learned in Chapter 2, a traditional didjeridu is constructed from a long wooden branch (usually eucalyptus) that has been hollowed out by termites. A ring of beeswax or eucalyptus gum may be affixed to the narrower end of the instrument into which the player blows, serving as a kind of "mouthpiece" (see Figure 5.4; see also the photo on p. 23). Using a difficult technique called *circular breathing,* which involves breathing in through the nose and out through the

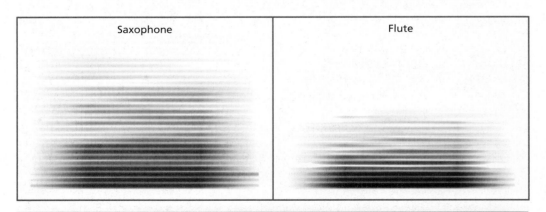

| Saxophone | Flute |

Spectrograms of saxophone and flute tones.

FIGURE 5.3

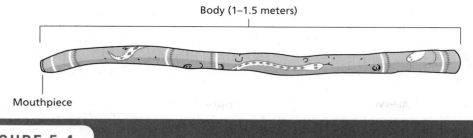

Body (1–1.5 meters)

Mouthpiece

FIGURE 5.4

Didjeridu.

mouth at the same time, the skilled didjeridu player is able to produce a continuous tone uninterrupted by breath pauses. But while the tone goes on continuously, its timbre is constantly being transformed. Changing the shape and positioning of his or her mouth relative to the instrument and employing a variety of different blowing techniques, the player manipulates the relationship between the fundamental pitch and its harmonics in myriad ways, thereby creating a veritable world of timbral diversity from a single tone.

The marvelous sound and wide timbral scope of the didjeridu is illustrated in a traditional context in "Ibis" **(CD ex. #1-12). CD ex. #1-33** features the instrument in a more contemporary musical setting: a funk-inspired didjeridu duet called "Axis."

Like the didjeridu, the human voice is capable of some rather remarkable feats of timbral manipulation through the use of harmonics. Vocal traditions of Central Asian cultures in Mongolia and Tuva display the potential of the voice in this regard to a degree that is almost unfathomable. The Mongolian *khoomii* ("overtone singing") song of **CD ex. #1-5,** to which we were introduced in Chapter 2, is an excellent example. Other than the accompanying instrumental part (played on an instrument called a *tobshuur*), all of the different layers of sound—including the high-pitched "whistling" lines (which are not *really* whistling at all) and the ultra-low-pitched guttural tones—are produced by the voice of a single vocalist, Amartuwshin Baasandorj (he can be seen on p. 12). He manipulates the relationships between the fundamental pitches and harmonics of the tones he sings to yield a dazzling array of timbres. By shaping and positioning his mouth and altering his vocal apparatus in many ways, Baasandorj changes the balance of fundamental pitches and harmonics so dramatically that he is not only able to produce a broad palette of timbres, but is actually able to create the effect that he is singing not just one, but multiple tones *at the same time*. Thus, singing of this type is sometimes described as *multiphonic* singing (i.e., "multiple sound" or "multiple tone" singing).

Differences in timbre enable us to distinguish not only between different types of tones—vocal tones, trumpet tones, flute tones, didjeridu tones—but also between similar types of tones performed by different musicians. An experienced jazz listener will be able to tell you whether the tenor saxophonist on a particular recording is John Coltrane or Lester Young from hearing just a single note; and even a casual listener will likely be able to pick out the voice of Dave Matthews, Bob Dylan, or Louis Armstrong from a recording with just a few notes to go on. **Online Musical Illustration #15** includes a series of individual instrumental and vocal tones, each performed by a different musician. All five of these tones are essentially identical in pitch, register, and duration, but their timbres differ from one another to varying degrees. The first two tones you hear are played, consecutively, on the alto saxophone by two saxophonists with distinctive "sounds." These are followed by three tones sung one after the other by three vocalists (male, male, and female, respectively). What words might you use to describe and compare the distinct timbres of the two saxophone tones? Or to compare and contrast the different timbral qualities of the three vocal tones?

Trying to come up with just the right words to describe and compare different timbres is challenging. This is because the descriptive language associated with timbre in English and other

Western languages tends to be rather impressionistic, consisting of a veritable grab-bag of different types of metaphors. The timbres of music are described variously in terms of textures (gravelly, velvety, airy—not to be confused with *musical* textures, to which subject we will return in Chapter 6), human anatomy (nasal, guttural, throaty), metaphysics (ethereal, heavenly, otherwordly), emotions (cheery, somber, melancholy), technological "spheres" (industrial, techno, space-age), socioeconomic classes (rich, majestic), and food (creamy, sweet).

The "master metaphor" for timbre is color, by virtue of the fact that timbre is very often *defined* as "tone color." Yet paradoxically, color designations are rarely used in connection with actual timbres: the "blue notes" in blues music and related styles (see page 50) get their name from their pitches, not their timbres; "red hot" music is usually described as such due to its fast tempos and loud dynamics rather than anything to do with its palette of tone colors.

Altogether, the timbral lexicon available to us, in English at least, is anything but precise or objective. (Terms used to describe timbres in some other languages, such as Japanese, are in many respects richer and more exact.) Often, the most distinctive verbal "description" we can provide of a tone's timbre is to identify the name of the *instrument* that produces it. **Online Musical Illustration #16** illustrates this point. In it, you will hear a series of tones played on various world music instruments. No matter how the tones are produced on any one of these, it would be difficult to mistake one instrument for another, since the basic timbre of each is so distinct. A list of the instruments featured in the example is provided in Table 5.1.

Music Instruments

Music comes into being through the medium of music instruments. A **music instrument** is here defined as *any sound-generating medium used to produce tones in the making of music.* This includes the human voice; all manner of traditional instruments associated with the world's music traditions (guitar, violin, trumpet, flute, didjeridu, steel drums, cymbals, maracas); and the entire spectrum of instruments and devices used in computer-generated and electronic music (synthesizers, digital samplers, sound modifiers—these will be discussed later in the chapter). It also may include the sources of any other natural, "found," or newly invented sounds that music makers use with the *intention* that they be heard as musical tones, or that music listen-

TABLE 5.1	World music instruments featured in Online Musical Illustration #16.	
	Time	**Description**
	0:00–0:06	Indonesian angklung
	0:07–0:18	Mexican guitarrón
	0:19–0:26	Ugandan madinda (amadinda "xylophone")
	0:27–0:37	Native American powwow drum
	0:38–0:48	Javanese gong
	0:49–0:53	Japanese sho (mouth organ)
	0:54–0:59	West African axatse (rattle)
	1:00–1:07	Appalachian dulcimer
	1:08–1:19	Balinese suling (bamboo flute)
	1:20–1:24	Andean sikuri (panpipes)

ers *perceive* as music when they hear them: gumballs rattling in a machine, a jackhammer hammering, a bird "singing."

Every music instrument has its own unique timbre and range of timbral possibilities. This is likewise true for every different combination of instruments used in an ensemble. The **instrumentation** employed in any musical work or performance—that is, the types of instruments (potentially including voices) and the number of each—largely dictates the timbral landscape of the music.

Music instrument classification

The world of music instruments is vast and diverse. Thousands upon thousands of instruments are used to make music, and individual instruments may even be used to produce tones in several different ways (plucked violin versus bowed violin, struck tambourine versus shaken tambourine). Instrument classification systems have developed over the course of the millennia and in many parts of the world. These systems have been used to account for both the shared features and unique qualities of particular instruments and types of instruments. In many instances, they also have been employed to link specific instruments to certain rituals, classes of people, or supernatural powers. The oldest documented instrument classification systems come from countries such as India and China and have histories dating back more than 3,000 years.

Elaborate instrument classification systems also have been preserved in oral/aural tradition–based societies (societies that until modern times did not have traditions of writing or literacy). The Are'are people of Malaita—whose "inverse" conceptions of pitch we encountered earlier (see p. 47)—have a fascinating system for classifying music instruments. Their principal category of instruments is called *'au*. *'Au* means bamboo. Since the primary melodic instruments among the Are'are are bamboo panpipes of a type similar to those heard in **CD ex. #1-34** (which actually features Kwara'ae-style *'au* music, also from Malaita), the Are'are classify *all* instruments capable of producing melodies (other than the voice) as "bamboo instruments" (*'au*). Modernization has brought an interesting twist. Since electronic devices such as tape recorders and radios are capable of "producing" melodies, the Are'are classify them as *'au*, that is, as bamboo instruments (Zemp 1978)!

The best-known *Western* instrument classification system employs three main categories: strings, winds, and percussion. The string category includes violin, viola, cello, string bass, guitar, mandolin, and harp. Wind instruments include trumpet, French horn, trombone, tuba, flute, clarinet, bassoon, and oboe. Percussion encompasses all drums, shakers, cymbals, triangle, and xylophone. This system works quite well for most standard Western orchestral and band instruments but has limitations in its ability to logically account for the complexity of music instrument diversity on a global scale.

More flexible and globally inclusive is the **Hornbostel-Sachs classification system,** which was published in 1914 by two eminent German musicologists. This system identifies four principal instrument categories, with numerous subdivisions for each: **chordophones, aerophones, membranophones,** and **idiophones** (Hornbostel and Sachs 1992 [1914]). A fifth category, **electronophones** (or electrophones), was added later.

CHORDOPHONES Chordophones are *instruments in which the sound is activated by the vibration of a string or strings (chords) over a resonating chamber.* The guitar, harp, violin, banjo, mandolin, hammered dulcimer, Middle Eastern *'ud* **(CD ex. #1-14),** South Indian vina **(CD ex. #1-25),** and Indonesian rebab (the two-string fiddle heard at the beginning of **CD ex. #1-6**) are all chordophones. East Asian *board zither chordophones* such as the Japanese *koto* **(CD ex. #1-35)** and the Chinese *zheng* **(CD ex. #1-30)** represent an important chordophone subcategory that has been in existence for many, many centuries.

Although all chordophones depend on the activation of some kind of "string" (or "strings") to produce sound, the methods of *sound activation* vary. Plucking, bowing, rubbing, or even

dulcimer
(DULL-si-mer)

'ud (ood)

rebab (ruh-BAHB)

zither (ZI-ther
[rhymes with
"hither"])

koto (KOE-toe)

zheng (jung [rhymes
with "lung"])

Chordophone
instruments.

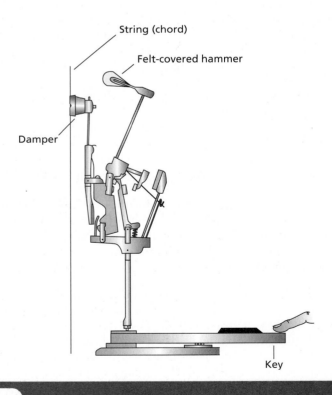

String (chord)

Felt-covered hammer

Damper

Key

Internal mechanism
of a piano.

FIGURE 5.5

striking the strings are all possibilities, and various implements—fingertips, plectra (e.g., a guitar pick), bows, or mallets—may be involved. The piano is a chordophone of a rather unique type. When you press down on the piano keys, sound is generated by the setting in motion of small, felt-tipped hammers that strike the strings hidden inside the body (resonator) of the instrument (Figure 5.5).

The guitar is a plucked chordophone, meaning that the strings are plucked to activate the sound. Its basic construction is similar to that of many chordophones. It includes a body, or *resonator*, with a soundhole in the middle of it; a number of strings that are affixed to a *bridge* near one end of the instrument; and a *neck* over which the strings (usually six) pass, attaching to *tuning pegs* on the *head* at the other end. *Frets* placed along the length of the neck of the guitar divide the instrument's multi-octave pitch range into chromatic intervals (all 12 pitches of the chromatic scale) from top to bottom (Figure 5.6).

With the possible exception of the guitar, the violin (Figure 5.7, p. 66) is probably the most widely used of all chordophones on a global scale. Like the guitar, it has a resonator (body), a bridge, strings (four), and a head with tuning pegs. The head is usually called a *scroll* on account of its distinctive shape. Instead of a round soundhole in the center of the body, the violin (like its relatives, the cello, viola, and string bass) has two S-shaped soundholes on either side of the strings. (The soundholes may alternately be described as f-shaped.) Additionally, it differs from the guitar in having no frets. As we encounter chordophones other than the violin and guitar in later chapters, we will frequently come across the same kinds of terms relating to features of their design and construction.

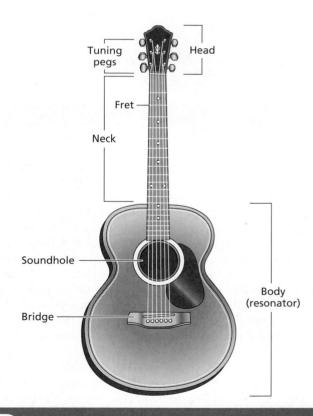

Tuning pegs

Head

Fret

Neck

Soundhole

Body (resonator)

Bridge

FIGURE 5.6

Guitar.

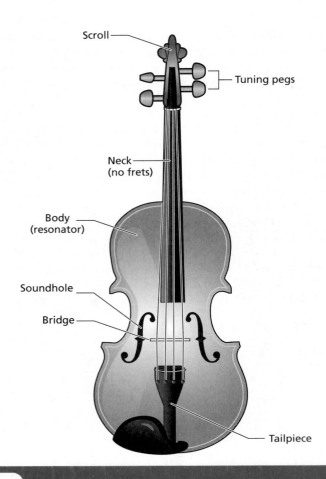

Scroll

Tuning pegs

Neck
(no frets)

Body
(resonator)

Soundhole

Bridge

Tailpiece

FIGURE 5.7

Violin.

AEROPHONES The sounds of aerophones emerge from vibrations created by *the action of air passing through a tube or some other kind of resonator.* The Western flute, clarinet, bassoon, and oboe are aerophones, as well as Western "brass" instruments such as the trumpet, trombone, French horn, and tuba. The pipe organ (the traditional church organ, that is, not the electronic organ) is also an aerophone, since its sound, too, is activated by the passage of air through tubes. Other aerophones include the bamboo panpipes heard earlier on **CD ex. #1-34,** the Japanese *shakuhachi* flute **(CD ex. #1-13),** the Irish tinwhistle **(CD ex. #1-20),** and the didjeridu **(CD exs. #1-12 and 1-33).** Some aerophones, like the Western flute, are side-blown instruments; others, like the shakuhachi, are end-blown instruments (see the photo on p. 67).

shakuhachi (sha-koo-HAH-chee)

The Aboriginal Australian bullroarer is an aerophone of a completely different type. It is usually made of a thin, flat piece of wood that is attached to a string and swung rapidly above the head in circles to produce a "whirring" sound whose pitch rises and falls depending on how fast the object is swung. There is no tube through which vibrating air passes, no resonator; just a slab of wood that "cuts" the air to produce sound-producing vibrations.

There is one final, very important subcategory of aerophones that warrants discussion: the human voice. Technically, the voice differs from other instruments in the aerophone category only because the "tube" and "resonator" of the instrument are within the human body rather than external to it. On cultural levels, however, the difference between the voice and other aerophones—and between the voice and other music instruments generally—is usually perceived as being much greater than this purely technical explanation would suggest. Because our voices are inseparable from who we are—as individuals, social beings, repositories of culture—it is counterintuitive for us to classify the voice as just another variation on the aerophone theme. Whether singing opera, blues, or Mongolian khoomii; rapping or reciting poetry over musical accompaniment; or reciting the Qur'an in "melodious" tones, people tend to think about their voices as either representing a separate category of music instrument or as not belonging within the category of music instruments at all.

MEMBRANOPHONES The third class of instruments in the Hornbostel-Sachs system, the membranophones, includes *instruments in which the vibration of a membrane (natural or synthetic) stretched tightly across a frame resonator produces the sound.* Drums are the predominant type of instrument in this category, though there are others, like the kazoo, which are perhaps less obvious inclusions. The snare drum, bass drum, and tom-toms of the Western drumset are all membranophones, as are the timpani (kettledrums) of symphonic orchestras and bands, shallow-shelled *frame drums* such as tambourines, and the Indian mrdangam drum we listened to earlier in **CD ex. #1-25.** So too are countless thousands of other types of drums originating from all around the globe.

Membranophones are played in many ways: with sticks, fingers, the palms of the hands, foot pedals, and even mouths (kazoo). Membranophones also may take on a variety of musical

Taylor & Boody's "Opus 20," the organ of First Presbyterian Church, Tallahassee, Florida.

Western flute (side-blown) and Japanese shakuhachi (end-blown).

Aerophone instruments.

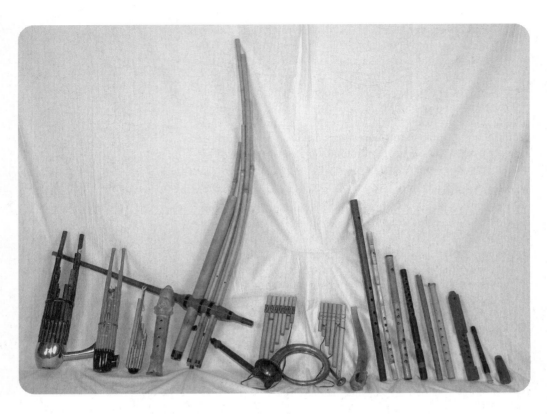

functions. We usually think of drums principally as rhythmic instruments, but in some musics they operate in a decidedly *melodic* way. **CD ex. #1-36** (from the Indonesian island of Sumatra) exemplifies this. In the example, a set of melodically tuned drums (the *taganing*) is heard "doubling" the melody of a wailing aerophone (the *sarune*). Sometimes it is clear that both instruments are playing the same melody; at other times, they seem to be playing variant versions of it.

Besides "pure" membranophones such as those already mentioned, there is a large class of "hybrid" membranophones as well. Tambourines and other drums with jingles, cymbals, shells, or other rattling devices attached to them or built into their frames do belong to the membranophone class, but they combine membranophone features with features of the fourth class of instruments in the Hornbostel-Sachs system, the idiophones.

sarune (sah-roo-nay)

Taganing drum-chime
(Sumatra, Indonesia).

IDIOPHONES Idiophones are *instruments in which the vibration of the body of the instrument itself (rather than a string, air tube, or membrane) produces the sound.* "Idiophone" literally means "self-sounder." The vibrating material and the resonating chamber are one and the same (though an external resonator may be added to increase the instrument's volume). The idiophone class includes *just about all percussion instruments other than drums*: gongs, triangles, shakers, cymbals, spoons, castanets, handclaps. Xylophone-type instruments also belong to the idiophone class, including the beautiful *metallophone* instruments featured in Indonesian gamelan orchestras **(CD ex. #1-9).** Other melodic instruments, like steel drums (pans) **(CD ex. #1-32)**

Membranophone instruments.

and the extraordinary *mbira dzavadzimu* of the Shona people of Zimbabwe heard in **CD ex. #1-37,** are idiophones as well. The mbira is made of rows of tuned metal "tongues" (lamellae) that are attached to a wooden board frame. A calabash gourd resonator is held under the instrument to amplify its sound. The player plucks the "tongues" with the thumbs of both hands. Buzzing devices (sea shells, bottle caps) are attached to the instrument to enhance its timbre. The gourd resonator and the buzzing devices have a profound effect on the overall timbre of the mbira. This can be heard in **Online Musical Illustration #17,** which demonstrates, first, the sound of an mbira without a resonator or buzzers; second, the same sound enhanced by a resonator; and third, the "complete" mbira timbre, with resonator and buzzers.

mbira dzavadzimu (em-BEE-rah dzah-vah-DZEE-moo)

Shona (SHO-nah)

lamellae (lah-mel-lay)

There is a great range of performance techniques for idiophones, including striking, rubbing, shaking, plucking (mbira), stamping, and clapping. A tambourine functions as a membranophone *and* an idiophone when the membrane (head) is struck, causing the membrane itself to sound as well as the jingles. If a tambourine is shaken, however, it is heard as a pure idiophone, since the shaking action does not activate the membrane sufficiently to make it audible. This difference is illustrated in **Online Musical Illustration #18,** where you first hear a tambourine as a combined idiophone/membranophone when it is struck, and then as a pure idiophone when it is shaken.

"Compound" instruments that consist of a number of *separate* instruments conceived of as a *single* instrument may combine a variety of idiophones and membranophones. The most familiar instrument of this kind is the **drumset,** which is

Mbira dzavadzimu.

Idiophone instruments.

common in rock, jazz, and many types of world music. In its most standard, conventional format, the drumset includes a booming, deep-pitched, foot-pedal operated *bass drum*; a "thwacking," bright-sounding snare drum; several cymbals, including a pair of cymbals, the *hi-hats*, that are mounted on a stand attached to a foot pedal and can produce both long and short (staccato) notes; and two or more *tom-toms*, resonant drums of different sizes and pitches that are not as deeply pitched as the bass drum (Figure 5.8). Many of the musical examples discussed in this

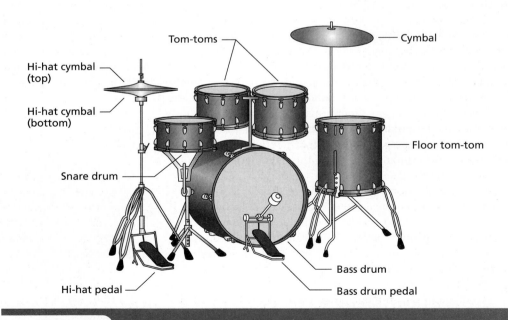

Drumset.

FIGURE 5.8

text (e.g., **CD exs. #1-47, 2-13, 2-15, 2-20,** and **3-33**) include performances on drumsets played in a variety of musical styles.

ELECTRONOPHONES Finally, we come to the electronophones, the newest and by far the fastest-growing category of instruments. There are two main categories: the *"pure" electronophones,* such as synthesizers and digital samplers, in which electronics are used to generate the sound *and* to amplify and enhance it; and the *"hybrid" electronophones,* such as the electric guitar, which are basically modified versions of conventional acoustic instruments (i.e., chordophones, aerophones, membranophones, and idiophones) that make use of electronic methods of sound amplification and processing. If you have to plug in an electronophone to make it function as the instrument it was designed to be, it is a pure electronophone; if it can function, at least marginally, without electric power, it is a hybrid electronophone. For example, if you tried to play a song on a keyboard synthesizer (a pure electronophone) without plugging it in, you would hear nothing except the little clicking sounds of the keys being pressed down. But if you tried to play the same song on a solid-body electric guitar (a hybrid electronophone) without plugging it in, you *would* be able to hear the melody, albeit very softly.

Electronically generated music usually emerges not from a single, self-contained instrument, but rather from systems or networks of interconnected instruments and devices. For all their complexity and variety, the various electronic music instruments included in such systems can be broken down into two main, interrelated categories: *sound generators* and *sound modifiers.* Sound generators are used to produce sounds; sound modifiers are used to alter and enhance them.

The sound generators category of electronophones includes instruments such as computers, synthesizers, and digital samplers. Several different technologies of *sound synthesis* are used to generate tones on these instruments. The technology of **digital sampling** allows for any existing sound to be recorded, stored as digital data, and then reproduced either "verbatim" or in electronically manipulated form (often via a piano-type synthesizer keyboard). The fluid merging of acoustic and electronically generated sound made possible by digital sampling and other advanced technologies has been an important factor in the efflorescence in recent decades of *electro-acoustic music,* which combines sonorities of purely acoustic and purely electronic origin in innovative ways.

While the digital sampling process originates with a sound (or sounds) recorded from an external source, a second technology, *digital synthesis,* creates electronic sounds from scratch, as it were. Computers or other devices (e.g., synthesizers) are used first to *create* an electronic soundwave and then to *process* that soundwave until the desired timbre is achieved. Like digital sampling, digital synthesis has reached a level of extraordinary sophistication. A skilled sound synthesist can generate tones that sound almost exactly like conventional music instruments, or that are so fantastic and otherworldly that you can hardly believe what you are hearing.

Online Musical Illustration #19 features several electronically generated tones and tone sequences, some created through digital sampling, others through digital synthesis. Table 5.2 on page 72 identifies which technology was used to generate these sounds.

The sound modifiers, including amplifiers (devices that add volume to the sound of the instrument) as well as a vast array of what are known as *effects devices,* are used to transform tones through the addition of features such as reverberation (reverb), echo, vibrato (tremolo), and distortion. The amplifier is to an electronic music instrument what the resonator is to an acoustic one; similarly, different "effects" are often to music electronics what different *acoustical spaces* (the physical environments in which music performances are heard) are to music that is not electronically processed. Musicians have long recognized the transformative potential of different acoustical spaces, like the echo of a canyon or the hollow reverberation of a large cathedral. The science of musical effects devices aims to simulate such spaces electronically, and, in the spirit of electronic music generally, to do things to and with sound that musicians of the pre-electronic age likely never even imagined.

TABLE 5.2	Digitally sampled and synthesized tones heard in Online Musical Illustration #19.

Time	Description
0:00–0:10	Digital sampling (source: Middle Eastern 'ud)
0:11–0:19	Digital synthesis
0:20–0:31	Digital sampling (source: viola)
0:32–0:39	Digital synthesis
0:41–0:54	Digital sampling (source: brass aerophones [horns])
0:55–1:03	Digital synthesis

TABLE 5.3	Examples of electronic sound modification illustrated in Online Musical Illustration #20.

Time	Description
0:00–0:03	Basic tone
0:04–0:08	Basic tone plus reverberation (reverb)
0:09–0:13	Basic tone plus vibrato (tremolo)
0:14–0:18	Basic tone plus echo
0:19–0:22	Basic tone plus reverb, vibrato (tremolo), and echo
0:23–0:29	Basic tone plus reverb, vibrato (tremolo), echo, and distortion

In **Online Musical Illustration #20,** a "basic" tone with a flute-like timbre is presented and then processed and altered in a variety of ways using electronic sound modifiers. The different types of sound modification employed are outlined in Table 5.3.

Electro-acoustic music production and recording studio.

Perhaps the most important electronophone subcategory of all is that which encompasses the full range of *music recording technologies,* past and present. The production of recordings, and the very capacity to create them, has revolutionized the making, reception, perception, and meaning of music on a global scale since the invention of the phonograph (the original music recording machine) by Thomas Edison in 1877. One of the many recording technologies that has had a huge impact on how music is made since at least the mid-1960s is **multitrack recording.** Through the use of multitrack recording machines and computer-based multitrack *sequencers,* it is possible to layer dozens upon dozens of separate musical *tracks* one atop the other in a recording studio. This is called **overdubbing.** Overdubbing technology, combined with an endless variety of electronic and computer technologies that allow for the creation of new sounds and the processing and transformation of existing ones, has changed

TABLE 5.4	Common music instruments, classified in Hornbostel-Sachs system categories.			
Chordophones	**Aerophones**	**Membranophones**	**Idiophones**	**Electronophones**
Guitar	Flute	Snare drum	Gong	Computer
Harp	Trumpet	Timpani (kettledrums)	Shaker	Synthesizer
Violin	Pipe organ	Kazoo	Hand clap	Digital sampler
Zheng	Didjeridu	Mrdangam	Mbira	Electric guitar

the very conception of what it means to "make music" in cultures worldwide. So too have a plethora of computer aids that allow an individual to "perform" music without having to actually play it in "real time." (Instead, you can insert notes one by one, like typing letters on a computer keyboard rather than speaking the words those letters spell.) A number of the musical selections we will explore during the course of our journey, even ones that sound "traditional," make extensive use of these advanced music production and recording technologies.

Summary

This chapter introduced three important elements of music that collectively make manifest the characteristic sounds and sound qualities of musical tones. These three elements are dynamics, having to do with the relative loudness and softness of tones; timbre, which relates to sound quality or "tone color"; and music instruments, the actual material objects (including the human body) responsible for generating the tones we hear in music.

With respect to dynamics, we learned that dynamic ranges in music may cover a spectrum from silence to deafening loudness, that dynamic contrast is an important aspect of much music, and that the dynamic ranges found in different types and styles of music vary.

Timbre was shown to be an element of music for which the available terminology in the English language is highly subjective: in the absence of precise terms to describe the different qualities of sound in music, we tend to borrow words from other domains—like "gravelly" or "majestic"—to describe musical sounds. Nonetheless, describing timbre is decisively important in terms of distinguishing between different music traditions, styles, instruments, and even performers on the same instrument (including singers). Furthermore, the timbral quality of any given musical work or performance is crucial to its identity and affect. On a technical level, timbre was shown to be a product of relationships between the *partials* that constitute musical tones, that is, between the fundamental pitch and harmonics (overtones).

As the actual physical objects that in a sense give birth to music in performance, music instruments—including the most ubiquitous of all, the human voice—play a crucial role in all music traditions. Our exploration of music instruments was mainly linked to the Hornbostel-Sachs classification system, with its four-part division of chordophones, aerophones, membranophones, and idiophones, and a fifth division, electronophones, that was added after the original Hornbostel-Sachs publication.

Key Terms

crescendo
decrescendo
dynamic range
acoustic (as in acoustic
 instrument)
ensembles
harmonics

didjeridu
music instrument
instrumentation
Hornbostel-Sachs classification
 system
chordophones
aerophones

membranophones
idiophones
electronophones
drumset
digital sampling
multitrack recording
overdubbing

Study Questions

- As rhythm is to duration and pitch is to frequency, dynamics are to _____.

- What happens to a tone that crescendos? To one that decrescendos?

- How do didjeridu players and khoomii singers bring out multiple pitches from a single, fundamental tone?

- What are the four principal categories of the Hornbostel-Sachs classification system? What is the important fifth category that was added later?

- What specific features of a tone are revealed by a spectrogram? What do spectrograms tell us, in technical terms, about why different instruments and voices have different timbres?

- In discussing electronophones, what is the basic distinction between a sound generator and a sound modifier? Between a "pure" electronophone and a "hybrid" electronophone? Between sounds generated by digital sampling and sounds generated by digital synthesis?

Applying What You Have Learned

- Select recordings by three of your favorite singers and listen to them, focusing specifically on the timbre of the singer's voice. Write out a detailed description of what each singer's voice sounds like (i.e., its timbre), then compare the three voice timbres and draw distinctions between them. What is it about the timbre of each voice that stands out to you and is appealing? Does this comparison of timbre reveal anything about why you like these particular artists, each for different reasons in different situations?

- Randomly scan through the various selections on the CD set accompanying this text, listening to a variety of examples. For each example you select, try to isolate and describe at least one instrument you hear (sometimes there will be only one). Indicate whether you think the instrument is a chordophone, aerophone, idiophone, membranophone, or electronophone. Describe its timbre to the best of your ability. Also describe the dynamic range and any other features of dynamics you hear in the music. If possible, create a graphic portrait of the "dynamics landscape" of the piece (as you did in the Hearing and Charting Dynamics exercise in the chapter).

Resources for Further Study

Visit the Online Learning Center at www.mhhe.com/bakan1 for additional learning aids, study help, and resources that supplement the content of this chapter.

how **music works,** part IV:
texture and form

Much as the characters in a novel relate to and interact with one another in certain ways, the "characters" in a musical work—the notes, rhythms, melodies, patterns, and vocal and instrumental parts—relate to and interact with one another in certain ways as well. The kinds of relationships that emerge and evolve between them define the element of music called **texture. Form** is the element of music that pertains to the large-scale dimensions of musical organization. When we study form, we are interested in how musical works and performances achieve their coherence and stylistic identity through the patterns, cycles, and processes of development, repetition, variation, and sectional organization that shape them. This concluding chapter of our general survey of *how music works* provides a brief and accessible introduction to the textural and formal aspects of musical design.

Single-Line Textures

"Roza DeShabbos"
(RAW-za
d'SHAH-bus)

Many kinds of relationships exist in life, and many types of textures occur in music. **Single-line textures** are the simplest type. They are otherwise known as *monophonic* textures. "Roza DeShabbos," the sung Jewish mystical prayer of **CD ex. #1-31,** is monophonic. Though the performance is complex and varied in its musical symbolism, melodic ornamentation, and dynamics (see Chapter 14, pp. 342–47), it never extends beyond the texture of a single melodic line sung by a solo vocalist.

Single-line textures are not limited to solo performances. If everyone in your class were to sing "The Alphabet Song" together, with all of you singing the same sequence of pitches in the same rhythm, this too would generate a monophonic texture (even if we allow for the different octave ranges of the men and women in the class). Likewise, if you all tapped out the rhythm of "The Alphabet Song" together on your desks *without* singing the melody, you would be creating monophony, but in this case the monophonic texture would be purely rhythmic, with no melodic component. To account for the fact that multiple performers, rather than just one, were involved in these performances, we would attach the term **unison** to our texture description (i.e., *unison monophony*).

Sufi (SOO-fee)

In music that features just a single melodic (or rhythmic) line, but where that line is performed in varied versions at the same time (usually by two or more performers), the texture is described as **heterophony.** This is the type of texture created between the singers and the flute (called a *nay*) in **CD ex. #1-38** (a Sufi chant from Egypt; see Chapter 12, pp. 271–72). Notice how the singers and the flute player are performing the same melody, but the flute's version has more ornamental decorations, and the flute player sometimes starts his notes a fraction of a beat after the singers (Figure 6.1). This variance is what makes the texture heterophonic.

Multiple-Part Textures

Textures in which there are two or more distinct parts are called **polyphonic.** Though the *melodic* texture of the Sufi chant of **CD ex. #1-38** is heterophonic, the texture of the music *overall* is polyphonic, since the drumming part adds a distinct textural layer. Polyphony may result from the playing (or singing) of different parts on different instru-

Sufi music ensemble, with nay player in the center.

Visual illustration of heterophony between nay (flute) and voices in CD ex. #1-38.

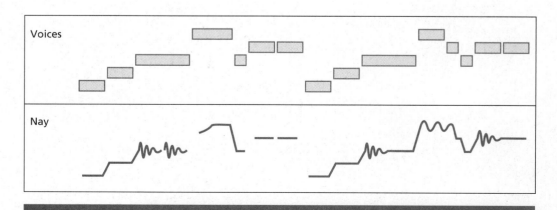

FIGURE 6.1

ments, or it may occur in the part of a single instrument that can play more than one note at the same time, such as a piano or guitar. Even a single human voice can create polyphony, as we heard in the Mongolian khoomii selection of **CD ex. #1-5.**

A melody accompanied by a **drone** is one of the simplest types of polyphonic textures. In a melody-plus-drone texture, the melody unfolds over a sustained, continuous tone, as in the Scottish bagpipe performance of "Amazing Grace" on **CD ex. #1-15.**

Harmonized textures emerge when notes of different pitch occur together to form chords, or "harmonies." In many world music traditions, each note of a melody may become the basis of its own chord. The Fijian hymn singing of **CD ex. #1-10** provides one particularly beautiful illustration of what this type of harmonized texture can sound like. A different kind of harmonized texture occurs when a single line of melody is supported by *chordal accompaniment* in a separate part performed on a designated *chording instrument*. The relationship between the saxophone's melody and the guitar's chordal accompaniment in the bossa nova "Wave" (**CD ex. #1-28**), which we listened to earlier in connection with Chapter 4, offers a good example.

Multiple-melody texture occurs in polyphonic music where two or more essentially separate melodic lines are performed simultaneously. The Zimbabwean popular music excerpt of **CD ex. #1-39** features a multiple-melody texture, with one group of male vocalists singing a unison melody in a low register and a second group singing a harmonized melody in a higher register. These two layers of vocal melody interweave over an accompaniment of chordal and rhythmic instruments.

Javanese gamelan music of Indonesia, such as that heard in **CD ex. #1-6,** provides profusely rich and varied multiple-melody textures. It typically features many different layers of melody all being sung and played at once. In the example, both male and female vocalists and musicians performing on a diverse array of instruments spin out melodic layer upon melodic layer. Each of these layers is unique, yet all of them are interrelated.

A very different, yet equally stunning and complex, type of multiple-melody texture is illustrated in **CD ex. #1-40.** This is a traditional elephant hunting song of the BaMbuti people of Central Africa. Here, the different strands of vocal melody seem to flow over each other like a waterfall.

Multiple-part textures need not be built from or even include melodies; two or more distinct *rhythmic* lines performed at the same time can also create polyphony. **Polyrhythm** is the term used to describe music in which there are several different parts or layers, with each defined mainly by its distinctive rhythmic character rather than by melodies or chords. **CD ex. #1-41** is a West African, drumming-based selection with a richly polyrhythmic texture (at least that is one way of describing it—see "Insights and Perspectives" box).

insights and perspectives

The Debate over Polyrhythms in West African Music

Some scholars of West African music claim that the use of the term *polyrhythmic* in connection with music of the kind heard in **CD ex. #1-41** is misleading, arguing that it is a designation that does not accurately reflect how the West African musicians who actually play such music conceptualize it. Rather than perceiving this as music of "many rhythms" (i.e., polyrhythms), it is possible instead to perceive it as music defined by a single, unified rhythmic expression with multiple manifestations.

The technicalities supporting either side of this interesting debate are well beyond our scope here (though the exploration of West African musicultural traditions in Chapter 10 sheds some light on the issue). The controversy is still worth noting, however. It provides yet another good example of how the study of music as sound can rarely, if ever, be appropriately separated from the study of music as culture.

BaMbuti ritual performance, Central Africa.

Multiple melodies and multiple rhythmic lines can be stacked one atop the other to create polyphonic textures of many different kinds, as we have seen. Moving in the opposite direction, a *single* melodic or rhythmic line may be *divided* among two or more instruments or voices. When this occurs, the result is textures based on **interlocking. CD ex. #1-42** features music from the Andes mountains of Bolivia, South America. The melody is divided between two Andean panpipes (*zampoña,* or *sikuri*), whose parts on the recording are clearly split between the left and right speakers. (This can be best heard through headphones.) Each panpipe has only *half* of the pitches of the complete scale needed for the melody, and each provides about half of the total number of melody notes in the interlocking texture. (This kind of texture, where two or more instruments "split" a single melody between them, is sometimes called *hocket*.) Figure 6.2 provides a graphic representation of the interlocking panpipe parts heard from 0:03–0:10 of the CD example. Interlocking textures also figure prominently in the music of Bali, Indonesia, which is explored in Chapter 7.

hocket (HAH-ket)

Call-and-response is another very important musical process linked integrally to the subject of musical texture. As its name implies, call-and-response involves back-and-forth alternation between different instrument or voice parts. The conversational element of music present in so many traditions is nowhere more apparent than in call-and-response dialogue. This dia-

Left:	███ ██ █ ███████ ███ ██ ██ █ ██ ███ ████ █████
Right:	██ ██ ███ ███████ ████ █ ██████ █████ ████

Graphic representation of interlocking panpipe parts in CD ex. #1-42.

FIGURE 6.2

logue may take any of a variety of forms. It can occur between a lead singer and a group of background singers, a singer and an instrumentalist, two groups of instrumentalists, two groups of singers, or any other such combination. **CD ex. #1-43** (another portion of the West African piece we listened to in **CD ex. #1-41**) features call-and-response between a lead vocalist and a group of vocalists. The call-and-response vocal parts are presented over an accompaniment of polyrhythmic percussion.

Form: The Designs of Musical Works

Understanding how the *form* of a piece of music works has mainly to do with comprehending how the piece is laid out from beginning to end, with how it unfolds as it progresses. In some musical styles, works unfold in one continuous motion, so to speak. Repetition, patterning, and sectional organization are essentially absent. In such music, the form is described as *through-composed*. More often, however, repetition, patterning, and sectional organization largely *define* the designs of musical forms. It is these types of forms that will be our focus here.

Repetition and patterning

Repetition and *patterning* are key features of most music. Certain elements—melodies, rhythms, chord progressions, metric cycles, even entire large sections of complex musical material—are presented and then recur in the course of a piece or performance, perhaps just once, perhaps many times. The repetition of these materials may be exact or it may be varied from one occurrence to the next. *Varied repetition* is common in many music traditions.

The presence of repetition and patterning in musical forms largely accounts for why when you listen to music, at least in familiar styles, you often have an intuitive sense of what is coming next. Even if you have not been formally trained to do so, you perceive a sense of order, of sequence, in the music's design: you feel when something you heard before is about to come back, or when the catchy "hook" of the song is about to arrive. Of course, this does not always happen. There may be surprises as well, unexpected twists and turns that take the music—and thus you, the listener—in directions unanticipated. Indeed, the effectiveness of a musical work or performance on its audience generally has much to do with how well it achieves a balance between predictability and unpredictability in its formal design, both in and of itself and relative to the stylistic conventions of the musical tradition to which it belongs.

ostinato
(ah-sti-NAH-toe)

"Xai" (like English
"shy")

nkokwane
(en-koh-kwah-nay)

OSTINATO-BASED FORMS Some musical works and performances are built entirely from the repetition or varied repetition of a single musical pattern or phrase. A short figure that is repeated over and over again is called an **ostinato.** The ostinato is typically the smallest unit of musical organization upon which forms are built. An example of an ostinato-based musical form is found in **CD ex. #1-44.** This is a piece entitled "Xai" ("Elephants"). It comes from the Qwii people (a.k.a. Bushmen, San) of the Kalahari Desert of southern Africa. The instrument is an *nkokwane,* a Qwii hunting bow that doubles as a struck chordophone instrument. The "string" of the bow is struck with either an arrow or a stick. Two different tones (with different pitches) are produced, as well as a wide range of timbres.

The basic ostinato pattern of "Xai" repeats roughly every two seconds (or every six "beats"). As you listen, notice how the ostinato is subtly varied from statement to statement, rarely being repeated exactly the same way twice. The continual presence of the ostinato and its perpetually varied repetition offer both continuity and variety, sameness and contrast.

Ostinato-based forms may gain richness and complexity through a texture of **layered ostinatos.** In this type of texture, two or more ostinatos are "stacked" one on top of the other. An example of a layered ostinato texture may be heard in **CD ex. #1-45** (from "Oye Como Va," by Tito Puente, to which we will return in Chapter 11). First you hear the ostinato melody (or *riff*) of the saxophones being played and then repeated. Next, at 0:15 of the excerpt, a layer of trombone ostinato is laid overtop the saxophones. Finally, a third ostinato layer, featuring trumpet, comes in over the saxophones and trombones at 0:31 (Figure 6.3).

CYCLIC FORMS Cyclic forms are similar to ostinato-based forms, but the repeated unit of the **cycle** is typically longer than that of an ostinato. The majority of blues songs are in a cyclic form called the **12-bar blues.** Each cycle is 12 measures (i.e., 12 bars) long and has the same basic chord progression as the others. Charles Atkins' "A Funny Way of Asking" (**CD ex. #1-19**) is a

Nkokwane ("musical bow") played by Qwii musician. In this instance, one end of the bow is inserted into the performer's mouth, which serves as a resonator. In other cases, a calabash gourd is used as the resonator.

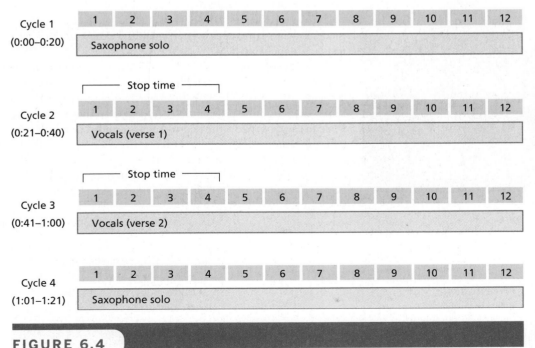

0:00	0:15	0:31	0:46
Ostinato 1	Saxophone ostinato		
Ostinato 2		Trombone ostinato	
Ostinato 3			Trumpet ostinato

FIGURE 6.3

Layered ostinatos in Tito Puente's "Oye Como Va" (CD ex. #1-45).

12-bar blues form song. All of the 12-measure cycles are the same length and have the same chords, but they differ in their instrumentation and textures. As you listen, mark the beginning of each of the first four 12-bar blues cycles with a clap and note the contrasting musical features that distinguish one cycle from the next, as outlined in Figure 6.4.

Another tradition in which cyclic forms predominate is Indonesian gamelan music. The Balinese gamelan selection of **CD ex. #1-9** has a cyclic form defined by its *gong cycle,* a recurring sequence of strokes played on gongs of different size and pitch. Balinese gong cycles range from two beats to 256 beats in length. The one heard here is 32 beats long. The main strokes are played on three large, low-pitched gongs. In the diagram in Figure 6.5 (see p. 82), the lowest-pitched gong is designated as "G," the next higher-pitched one as "L," and the highest one as "P." The dots represent beats in the cycle that are not punctuated by a large gong, but are rather marked by the steady pulse of a muted, small gong-type instrument called a *kempli.* Six gong cycles are included in the excerpt, and each cycle is about 12 seconds long. Figure 6.5 provides a timeline chart of the gong cycle form. As you listen to the example, try to keep track of the gong cycles by following the chart. Listening with headphones will enable you to hear the gong strokes with optimal clarity.

Cycle 1
(0:00–0:20)

1	2	3	4	5	6	7	8	9	10	11	12

Saxophone solo

Cycle 2
(0:21–0:40)

Stop time

1	2	3	4	5	6	7	8	9	10	11	12

Vocals (verse 1)

Cycle 3
(0:41–1:00)

Stop time

1	2	3	4	5	6	7	8	9	10	11	12

Vocals (verse 2)

Cycle 4
(1:01–1:21)

1	2	3	4	5	6	7	8	9	10	11	12

Saxophone solo

FIGURE 6.4

Charles Atkins' "A Funny Way of Asking": 12-bar blues form timeline chart (CD ex. #1-19).

Cycle 1	(0:00–0:11)	G ● ● ● P ● ● ● ● ● ● ● P ● ● L ● ● ● P ● ● ● ● ● ● ● ● P ● ● ●
Cycle 2	(0:12–0:22)	G ● ● ● P ● ● ● ● ● ● ● P ● ● L ● ● ● P ● ● ● ● ● ● ● ● P ● ● ●
Cycle 3	(0:23–0:34)	G ● ● ● P ● ● ● ● ● ● ● P ● ● L ● ● ● P ● ● ● ● ● ● ● ● P ● ● ●
Cycle 4	(0:35–0:45)	G ● ● ● P ● ● ● ● ● ● ● P ● ● L ● ● ● P ● ● ● ● ● ● ● ● P ● ● ●
Cycle 5	(0:46–0:57)	G ● ● ● P ● ● ● ● ● ● ● P ● ● L ● ● ● P ● ● ● ● ● ● ● ● P ● ● ●
Cycle 6	(0:58–end)	Same pattern, fading out…

Gong cycle form in a Balinese gamelan piece (CD ex. #1-9).

FIGURE 6.5

Forms with contrasting sections

We now shift our attention to forms with multiple, identifiably distinct sections (called *formal sections*). The different sections in such forms often contrast with one another musically. For example, a section of a piece in a minor key is followed by a contrasting section in a major key, or the instrumentation changes from one section to the next, or a section in free rhythm is followed by one with a steady tempo and a clearly marked meter. **CD ex. #1-46,** which is representative of a now-international Jewish style of dance music called *klezmer* that originated in Eastern Europe and was traditionally played at Jewish weddings and other celebrations (and often still

klezmer (KLEZ-mer)

is), features contrasting formal sections in free rhythm and metered rhythm (Figure 6.6). The piece opens with a melody played in free rhythm—and with abundant heterophony—on several instruments (clarinet, violin, hammered dulcimer). We will call this the "A" section. Then, starting at 0:51, a string bass establishes a lively, duple-meter dance rhythm. This marks the beginning of the contrasting second, or "B," section of the piece, in which the melody (starting at 0:55) now unfolds over a steady, danceable beat.

Klezmer band The Burning Bush.

One of the most popular formal designs for songs in many cultures is the **verse-chorus form.** Here, there are two basic sections, the verse (the A section) and the chorus (the B section). If there are words, the text typically changes from one verse to the next, while the chorus keeps coming back each time with the same text. Musically speaking, the chorus is usually the section of the form that contains the "hook" of the song, the catchy part that listeners are most likely to remember. In addition to the main verse and chorus sections, verse-chorus forms

0:00		0:51	
"A" Section		**"B" Section**	
• Free rhythm		• Duple meter, danceable beat	
• Heterophony		• Melody (0:55)	

Klezmer example timeline form chart (CD ex. #1-46).

FIGURE 6.6

may include additional formal sections as well: an introduction, interludes, transitions (sometimes called *bridges*), a special ending section (sometimes called a *coda,* literally "tail"). These added sections enhance the music with the variety and contrast they bring to it and often provide opportunities for instrumental solos. The way in which the various sections are ordered in sequence defines the *arrangement* of the piece (see also Chapter 2, p. 27).

"Ingculaza (AIDS)" **(CD ex. #1-47)** is a song with a verse-chorus form by the Zimbabwean *world beat* musician Dumisani "Ramadu" Moyo. (*World beat* is a term used to identify commercial music styles that blend elements of diverse world music traditions and Western popular music.) This is a social commentary song about the AIDS pandemic in Africa. More specifically, it is about the devastation the disease has wrought in Ramadu's home village. The song is sung in Ramadu's native language, Ndebele. The distinctive "click" sounds that are integral to Ndebele (and to other southern African languages) are heard at several points. The song text, a portion of which appears in translation below, metaphorically personifies the disease and grapples with the problem of how the tragedy of AIDS might be abated:

"Ingculaza" (In-cool-ah-zah)

Dumisani "Ramadu" Moyo (Doo-mee-sah-nee Rah-mah-doo Moy-yo)

Ndebele (IN-duh-bel-ee)

> *Everybody in my village is crying about you*
>
> *You have taken away my sisters, brothers and innocent souls including*
>
> > *children*
>
> *What shall we do?*
>
> *How should we behave?*
>
> *The answer is simply to "prevent rather than cure"*
>
> *in order to have a healthy community with a good life and a happy future.*
>
> (Moyo and Heller 2002)

Dumisani "Ramadu" Moyo.

The form of "Ingculaza," which is charted out in the box below, includes two sung verses (the A sections of the chart) and three sung choruses (the B sections). The last chorus is *looped* (repeated over and over without pause) as it grows progressively more expansive and texturally dense before fading away to silence. The performance commences with an instrumental introduction before the opening verse. There is also an improvised electric guitar solo. Listen to this beautiful song now, following along with the timeline chart and tracking the formal sections and musical features it outlines.

Form Chart: "Ingculaza (AIDS)," by Dumisani "Ramadu" Moyo (CD ex. #1-47)

I (INTRODUCTION)

0:00–0:28

- Single harmonized vocal phrase near beginning.
- Gradual crescendo.
- Layered ostinatos (guitar, percussion).

A (VERSE 1)

0:29–1:00

- Unison male group singing over drone-based harmony.
- Syncopated guitar ostinato.
- Percussion.

B (CHORUS 1)

1:01–1:22

- Chord progression replaces drone-based harmony.
- Vocal parts harmonized.
- Rhythmic accompaniment changes.

A (VERSE 2)

1:23–1:54

- Harmonized vocals contrast with the unison vocal texture of Verse 1.
- Thicker texture than in Verse 1.

B (CHORUS 2)

1:55–2:15

- Essentially the same as Chorus 1.

S (SOLO)

2:16–2:59

- Improvised electric guitar solo.
- This solo section takes the place of a potential third verse in the formal design of the arrangement.
- Electric guitar features a "fuzzy" timbre, created by electronic distortion effects devices.
- Lead vocalist (Ramadu) talks over the electric guitar solo; does not sing.
- Final, transitional passage of solo (beginning at 2:49) builds toward climactic arrival of the final chorus (Chorus 3) at 3:00.

B (CHORUS 3)

3:00–end

- Chorus is looped (repeated) several times to reinforce the "hook" of the song.
- Texture becomes increasingly dense as music builds.
- Multiple melodic lines: lead vocalist, background vocalists (harmonizing), solo electric guitar.
- Selection ends with music fading away to silence .

Summary

In this chapter, we learned that texture is the element of music that accounts for relationships between the different parts (instrumental and/or vocal) in a musical work, while form is the element that accounts for how musical works on the whole are organized.

A basic distinction between single-line (monophonic, heterophonic) and multiple-part (polyphonic) textures was made, and a variety of different types of multipart textures were defined and illustrated through recorded examples and visual illustrations. Musical processes that generate distinctive textures, such as interlocking and call-and-response, also were introduced.

Several types of musical forms were examined, and a distinction between forms that are through-composed and those that feature repetition, patterning, and sectional organization was set forth. The focus of our discussion then turned to a variety of specific types of forms. Ostinato-based forms, cyclic forms, and forms with contrasting formal sections such as the verse-chorus song form were highlighted.

Key Terms

texture	drone	ostinato
form	harmonized texture	layered ostinatos
single-line texture	multiple-melody texture	cycle (in a cyclic musical form)
unison	polyrhythm	12-bar blues (form)
heterophony	interlocking	verse-chorus form
polyphonic	call-and-response	

Study Questions

- How are the terms *texture* and *form* defined in relation to music?

- What distinguishes between monophonic, heterophonic, and polyphonic textures?

- What is a drone? What musical example was used to illustrate melody-plus-drone texture?

- What is the difference between a harmonized texture and a multiple-melody texture?

- On the basis of the musical examples in this chapter, what musicultural traditions might you look to for abundant examples of polyrhythmic textures? Of interlocking textures?

- What is an ostinato-based form? In the piece "Xai," was the ostinato figure repeated literally each time, or with variation from one statement to the next?

- What types of instruments underpin the cyclic design of the music in a Balinese gamelan piece such as the one you listened to in this chapter?

- What is the standard cyclic form of much blues music?

- In a verse-chorus form song with words, are the words usually the same from one chorus section to the next or different? What about in the successive verses of the song?

Applying What You Have Learned

- Take a familiar piece of music from your personal collection and write a description of its texture and form. In terms of texture, what kinds of relationships do you hear between the different voices/instruments? Is there unison singing or playing? Heterophony? Harmonization? Call-and-response? Interlocking? Does the form of the piece appear to be ostinato-based? Or does it seem to conform to the model of a 12-bar blues tune, or a verse-chorus tune, or some combination of different types of formal designs? Use your listening skills from this chapter to take you as far as you can go with this exercise, but don't get frustrated if you find that you cannot account for all that you hear. There is much in actual music making in terms of texture and form that goes well beyond what we have been able to accommodate here in this brief introductory chapter. Just have fun with this, and try to hear as much as you can.

Resources for Further Study

Visit the Online Learning Center at www.mhhe.com/bakan1 for additional learning aids, study help, and resources that supplement the content of this chapter.

interlocking rhythms and interlocking worlds in **Balinese gamelan** music

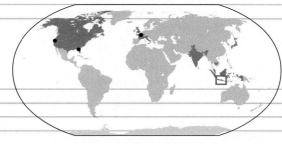

Related locations:

Cambodia	Irian Jaya
Canada	Sumatra
France	
India	Berkeley, California
Indonesia	Paris, France
Italy	Tallahassee, Florida
Japan	
Malaysia	
United Kingdom	
United States	

gamelan
   (gah-muh-lahn)

beleganjur (buh-luh-
   gahn-YOOR)

Of all the chapters in this book, this one is for me the most personal. It concerns a place and a musical culture that have been central to my life and identity for many years. We therefore begin with an account of my first visit to this special place, Bali, and of my discovery there of a musical tradition that has had a profound impact on me ever since, **gamelan beleganjur.**

Bali is a small island located in the Southeast Asian nation of Indonesia. I first ventured there in 1989 while an ethnomusicology graduate student. I have since traveled to Bali many times, and my professional life has come to revolve largely around studying, performing, and teaching Balinese music. Many of my most cherished life lessons—about trust, compassion, and the

World events		Music events
Hinduism and Buddhism brought to Bali ● from Java, blending together with one another and with earlier Balinese belief systems to form the base of the Hindu-Balinese Agama Tirta religion	**13th century–1906 Pre-colonial era**	● Advanced culture and arts with *gamelan* music as central component of ritual, social, and political life
Frequent warring between rival Balinese ● kingdoms		
	1889	● French composer Claude Debussy hears gamelan at the world's fair in Paris; influences his compositional approach
Bali colonized by Dutch ●	**1906–1908**	● *Gamelan gong kebyar* and kebyar musical style emerge in the wake of Dutch colonization, sociopolitical transformation
	1932	● German film *Die Isle der Damonen* (The Isle of Demons), featuring *Kecak* performance
Republic of Indonesia declared (though ● full national independence not achieved until 1949)	**1945**	
	1950s–present	● Extensive experimentation on the part of both Indonesian and Western musicians with the blending of gamelan and Western music elements
	1986	● First *gamelan beleganjur* contest, Denpasar
		● New contest musical style, *kreasi beleganjur,* emerges
	1990–1992	● Beleganjur groups directed by composer I Ketut Suandita win three consecutive annual championships in the major Denpasar beleganjur contest
	1997	● Premiere performance of "B.A.Ph.PET," a post-traditional work for gamelan and scratch turntable soloist by Michael Bakan

joys and challenges of experiencing music in a distant land with people whose musical and cultural backgrounds are very far removed from my own—I learned in Bali.

Soon after arriving in Bali in 1989, I headed into town one day to do some shopping. On my way back, I stumbled upon a brick-paved temple courtyard where four teenage boys were sitting around relaxing and chatting. Resting in a haphazard arrangement near the boys were four small knobbed gongs and a bundle of mallets. Apparently some kind of a gamelan rehearsal was about to begin. This excited me, for I had heard little gamelan music of any kind since my arrival.

It took a long time—perhaps half an hour—for all the musicians to arrive and for the rehearsal proper to begin, but it was well worth the wait. I counted 21 musicians in all. The music they played was powerful: loud, brash, and forcefully energetic. It sounded nothing like any of the gamelan music I had heard before coming to Bali, and nothing like the rather uninspiring "tourist performances" I'd attended since arriving either. It pumped along with a contagious groove and mesmerizing rhythmic drive. The two drummers and eight cymbal players propelled the music forward with dazzling unison figures and continuous streams of interlocking rhythm that unfolded over the anchor of a steady, recurring cycle played on large gongs suspended from ornately decorated stands. Meanwhile, rapid-fire melodies played in interlocking patterns by four musicians on a set of four small hand-held gongs elaborated a two-tone ostinato melody played on a pair of somewhat larger instruments of the same type an octave below.

The rhythmic complexity, the precise execution, the inventiveness of the musical arrangement with its endless variations and contrasting sections—all of these were breathtaking. I was transfixed, and I listened carefully, transcribing the rhythms in my head as best I could. After a while, the playing stopped. There was some talking among the musicians and the next thing I knew, one of the cymbal players was looking at me, smiling, beckoning me to come over. As I walked toward him, he held out his cymbals.

I take the cymbals and sit down next to a slim, mop-topped member of the group. He appears to be the leader of the cymbal section. He smiles and introduces himself as Madé. As the drumming introduction starts up, I glue my eyes on Madé's hands. He springs into action and I follow. (At this point, listen to **CD ex. #2-1** as you continue to read.)

CENG - - - CENG - CENG - - - CENG CENG, go the cymbals; then again,

CENG - - - CENG - CENG - - - CENG CENG. Then softer,

ceng - - ceng - - ceng - - ceng - ceng - CENG CENG CENG, leading directly into an

intense passage of interlocking cymbal rhythm,

CENG-ceCENG-ceCENG-CENG-ceCENG-ceCENG-

CENG-ceCENG-ceCENG-CENG-ceCENG-ceCENG-, then, back to unison:

CENG-CENG-CENG-CENG-CENG-CENG-CENG-CENG CENG

Then a repetition of the whole last chunk:

CENG-ceCENG-ceCENG-CENG-ceCENG-ceCENG-

CENG-ceCENG-ceCENG-CENG-ceCENG-ceCENG-

CENG-CENG-CENG-CENG-CENG-CENG-CENG-CENG CENG, and on we go.

**CENG ce-CENG
(CHAYNG
chuh-CHAYNG)**

The author performing in a contest with a gamelan beleganjur group in Bali, Indonesia, 1990.

What joy! Here I am, halfway around the world, playing a kind of music I've only just discovered with a group of musicians I've never met before and with whom I don't even yet share a common language. But we are playing together, the music sounds good, and we're having a great time.

When our session ends, I ask the cymbal player, who speaks some English, what kind of music we've been playing.

"Gamelan music," he says.

"Gamelan what?" I ask. "What kind of gamelan music?"

"Gamelan beleganjur," he replies.

I jot the unfamiliar name down on a notepad. A new chapter of my life begins.

▪ ▪ ▪

Introduction

This chapter explores musical traditions of Balinese gamelan, with a particular focus on the *gamelan beleganjur,* the Balinese "gamelan of walking warriors." The term **gamelan** essentially means "ensemble" or "orchestra" (though the word literally means "to handle"). It is used in reference to a diverse class of mainly percussion-dominated music ensembles found on Bali, Java, and several other Indonesian islands. Related types of ensembles also are found elsewhere in Southeast Asia, for example, in Malaysia and Cambodia. Though they usually consist of a large number of individual instruments played by multiple performers, each gamelan is conceived of in its entirety as a *single* music instrument. Each is regarded as being unique and distinct from all other gamelans, even from other gamelans of the exact same type. Individual gamelans even have their own proper names, like Gamelan of the Venerable Dark Cloud.

The gamelan beleganjur is a *processional ensemble* (i.e., the musicians walk or march as they perform, as in a Western marching band) consisting of multiple gongs, drums, and cymbals (see the photos on pp. 96, 100, and 105). It has played an integral role in Balinese ritual and ceremonial life for many centuries. Traditionally associated with warfare, battles with evil spirit forces, and rituals for the dead, this ensemble has more recently become the basis of an exciting type of modern Balinese music contest as well. From the interlocking rhythms of its music to the interlocking of worlds it animates—human and spirit, traditional and modern, Balinese and Western—the gamelan beleganjur is an ideal lens through which to view vital processes of tradition and transformation in Balinese music.

Balinese Gamelan Music in Context

Like all music traditions, Balinese gamelan traditions are framed by broader musical, historical, cultural, and societal contexts. In this section, we briefly overview some of these in preparation for the more focused exploration of beleganjur and related gamelan musics that follows in the later portions of the chapter.

Bali and the Republic of Indonesia

Bali is one of more than 13,000 islands in the Southeast Asian nation of Indonesia (Republic of Indonesia), which spans from Sumatra in the west to Irian Jaya in the east. Close to 6,000 of Indonesia's islands are inhabited. Bali is very small—you can easily drive around its perimeter in a day—but it is densely populated. Three million people live there, the majority in the fertile rice-growing lands of the southern and southeastern portions of the island. Bali is home to a very large tourist industry, annually hosting hundreds of thousands of visitors from other parts of Indonesia and throughout the world.

The capital of Indonesia is Jakarta, the country's largest city with a population of more than 11 million. Jakarta is also one of the world's most densely populated metropolises. It is located in the northwestern portion of Java, Bali's neighboring island to the west. More than 100 million people, about half of Indonesia's entire population, live in Java. Surakarta and Yogyakarta are other major Javanese cities. Both are located in the province of Central Java. They are home to the great musical traditions of **Central Javanese court gamelan** (*gamelan kraton*), an example of which we heard earlier on **CD ex. #1-6** (to which we will return). Another major historical and contemporary center of gamelan activity is the city of Bandung, where the distinctive language, culture, and music of the Sundanese people of West Java predominate.

Indonesia became an independent nation in 1945, though full national sovereignty was not achieved until 1949. Most of its lands, including Bali, were formerly Dutch colonies or Dutch-occupied territories within the sprawling Dutch East Indies Company (Bali did not come under Dutch colonial rule until 1906–1908, much later than Java and many other Indonesian islands). The national language is **Bahasa Indonesia** (Indonesian), a derivative of Malay, though more than 300 other languages are spoken by members of the country's 300-plus ethnic groups, each of which has its own distinctive culture. The Balinese are one of these many ethnic groups, accounting for less than 2 percent of the Indonesian population. Almost 40 percent of Indonesians are of Javanese ethnicity, and another 16 percent are ethnically Sundanese.

Indonesia's national slogan, **Unity in Diversity** (Bhinnéka Tunggal Ika), was instituted to provide a framework for the preservation, development, and nationalization of the country's diverse cultures and cultural traditions. Certain traditions, including various forms of Central Javanese gamelan and Balinese gamelan, have figured especially prominently in the national image of Indonesia promoted under the cultural nationalism agenda of Unity in Diversity, both within Indonesia and internationally. The modern, contest style of beleganjur music, which originated in Bali's capital city, Denpasar, in 1986, has received abundant government support as a musical emblem of Balinese-Indonesian cultural nationalism.

Bandung
(Bahn-doong)

Bahasa Indonesia
(Bah-HAH-suh In-doh-NEE-see-uh)

Bhinnéka Tunggal
Ika (Bee-nay-kah
Toon-gahl EE-kah)

Denpasar
(Duhn-PAH-SAHR)

Religion in Bali and Indonesia

Indonesia is the world's largest Islamic nation, both geographically and in population. Almost 90 percent of Indonesians are Muslims, though the religion is practiced in many varied forms that represent syncretisms with earlier layers of Hindu, Buddhist, and indigenous belief systems. Bali is the only province of Indonesia where Hinduism is the majority religion. Indeed, Bali is the only world society outside of the Indian subcontinent where the majority of the population is Hindu.

Though historically derived from Hinduism in India and sharing many key features with it—cremation of the dead, belief in reincarnation, cyclic concepts of time, entrenchment in great mythic Hindu epics such as the Ramayana and the Mahab-

Agama Tirta
(Ah-gah-muh
TEER-tuh)

wayang kulit (wah-yahng KOO-leet)

harata, a prominent place for music and related arts in religious life—Balinese Hinduism is a unique religion. It is known either as Agama Hindu (Hindu Religion) or **Agama Tirta** (Religion of Holy Water) and is in fact a syncretic faith blending elements of Hinduism and Buddhism (both originally brought to Bali from Java beginning in the 13th century) with earlier layers of indigenous Balinese spiritual belief and practice. Gamelan music has always been central to the practices of Balinese Hinduism and is performed at virtually all religious ceremonies. Most of the major forms of Balinese gamelan and related arts—dances, dance-dramas, shadow puppetry (*wayang kulit*)—trace back historically to the same Hindu-Javanese culture (the Majapahit) that brought Hinduism to Bali many centuries ago.

Gambuh, an ancient Balinese dance-drama.

Not all Balinese are Hindus. In certain Balinese villages such as Tenganan and Trunyan, people follow indige-nous religious faiths that have not absorbed the Hindu or Buddhist layers of influence that largely define Agama Tirta. These are the villages of peoples known as the **Bali Aga,** or "Original Balinese." Though there are similarities between the Bali Aga and Hindu-Balinese cultures, there are also profound differences. Cer-tain sacred Balinese gamelans believed to predate the arrival of Hindu-Javanese culture centuries ago, such as the iron-keyed *gamelan selonding* of Tenganan and certain other Bali Aga villages, are regarded with rev-erence not only among the Bali Aga themselves but among the Balinese population at large.

It is also important to note that though Islam is not nearly as prevalent in Bali as it is elsewhere in Indonesia, there is a sizable Muslim population on the island. A number of villages and towns in northern Bali are predominantly Muslim.

Balinese shadow puppet performance (wayang kulit).

Triloka
(Tree-LOH-kah)

Trimurti
(Tree-MOOR-tee)

In the Hindu-Balinese conception of the universe (i.e., Hindu-Balinese *cosmology*), there are three worlds (*Triloka*). The Upper World is the domain of the gods and venerated ancestors, who reside in the heavens above Mount Agung, the volcano that gave birth to Bali with its own emergence. It is here that the Trimurti, the "Three Shapes" of the su-preme Hindu deity—Brahma, the Creator; Wisnu (Visnu, Vishnu), the Preserver; and Siwa (Siva, Shiva), the De-stroyer—are believed to dwell. The Middle World of Bali-nese cosmology is Bali itself, the earthly realm of the Bali-nese people. The Lower World, beginning where land meets sea and descending from there, is the realm of evil spirits and malevolent creatures, such as *bhutas* and *leyaks,* who pose a constant threat to humankind. As we will explore, gamelan beleganjur music performed during Hindu-Balinese cremation processions functions in important ways in the battles between the human and evil spirit forces that animate these events.

Gamelan in Bali and beyond

Few world cultures have held so tenaciously to the cultivation of their indigenous musical tra-ditions as have the Balinese, and few musical traditions have inspired such awe among world music connoisseurs as has Balinese gamelan.

Indonesia is a nation of extraordinary musical diversity that goes far beyond gamelan music. Non-gamelan-based religious, folk, and popular traditions of many kinds; regional and national musical styles; and contemporary, experimental music genres blending traditional Indonesian and international elements abound. Resources for exploring some of the fascinating non-gamelan music traditions of Indonesia are included at the Online Learning Center (www.mhhe.com/bakan1). Here, though, we limit our focus exclusively to gamelan.

kebyar (kuh-BYAHR)
The best-known Indonesian gamelan traditions are Central Javanese court gamelan and Balinese **gamelan gong kebyar,** examples of both of which we have already heard in connec-tion with earlier chapters (**CD ex. #1-6** and **CD ex. #1-9,** respectively). These two traditions share a common line of historical descent originating with Javanese gamelan traditions of several

centuries ago. The following general musicultural features are characteristic of both, and of gamelan musics generally:

- Related types of instruments (bronze gongs, bronze metallophones, drums, end-blown bamboo flutes).
- A basis in cyclic musical forms.
- Related tuning systems, scales, and modes.
- Multipart textures in which the higher-pitched instruments play at faster rhythmic rates than the lower-pitched instruments.
- Melodic organization in which a slow-moving core melody is embellished by faster-moving melodies played on other instruments.
- Close associations with various forms of dance, dance-drama, and other arts (e.g., shadow puppetry).
- A common historical foundation in Hindu religious cultures, which is reflected symbolically in the music.

Yet while Central Javanese court gamelan music and Balinese gamelan gong kebyar music exhibit key similarities, they sound very different from one another. This can be heard by listening to the Javanese selection of **CD ex. #1-6** and the Balinese selection of **CD ex. #2-2** one after the other. Make a subjective comparison, noticing how distinct they are in their styles and in the musical impressions and moods they create. Each of these pieces might be considered emblematic of its own tradition. The Javanese piece (entitled "Ketawang: Puspawarna") captures the majestic, expansive, almost ethereal quality of Central Javanese court gamelan. In contrast, the Balinese piece ("Jaya Semara," composed by I Wayan Beratha) captures Bali's signature gamelan sound: resonant bronze gongs, shimmering bronze-keyed metallophones, rapid-fire melodies played on metallophone instruments and sets of small tuned gongs, intricate drumming, and a frenetic pace and energy. This is the sound of *kebyar,* a Balinese term that literally means "to flare up like a match," though it is sometimes also translated as "lightning." It is fiery,

"Ketawang: Puspawarna" ("Kuh-tah-wahng Poos-pah-WOR-nuh")

"Jaya Semara" ("Jah-yuh Suh-MAH-ruh")

Balinese gamelan gong kebyar.

The Paired Tuning of Female and Male Instruments

One of the most striking features of the sound of a gamelan gong kebyar is its shimmering quality. This owes much to the unique **paired tuning** of sets of Balinese gamelan instruments. The gamelan gong keb-yar features a number of melodic metallophone instruments called **gangsa** (GAHNG-suh), which come in different sizes and octave ranges. There is either one pair or two pairs of gangsas in each octave range. One instrument of each pair is identified as the "female," the other as the "male." The bronze keys of each male-female instrument pair are tuned to produce the exact same sequence of pitches. However, each female note is tuned slightly *lower* than its male counterpart. **Online Musical Illustration #21** illustrates this. First you hear a five-note ascending scale played on a female metallophone; then you hear the same scale played on that metallophone's male counterpart instrument. Notice how all five notes in the "male" scale are slightly higher in pitch.

Listening to these two different versions of the same scale, you might think that the two instruments are simply out of tune relative to each other. This apparent "out-of-tuneness" is intentional, however, for when the male and female notes are played together, the blending of their different pitches creates an acoustical beating effect called **ombak** (OAM-bahk), or "wave," that is the essence of the gamelan's brilliant, shim-mering sound. Ombak is illustrated in **Online Musical Illustration #22.** In the example, you first hear a single tone played on the female instrument, then the "same" (slightly higher) tone played on the male in-strument, and finally both female and male struck simultaneously to produce the ombak wave effect. After this, you hear the full scale of five notes illustrated earlier, but this time with *all* five notes played together on both the male and female metallophones, producing a series of ombak tones from bottom to top.

Balinese say that it is the ombak effect that breathes life into the sound of a gamelan. Without it, a gamelan is *mati*, literally, dead. Symbolically, then, it is the union of female and male elements that creates life in the gamelan, just as it is through the union of female and male in human life that new life is created. On another symbolic level, the lower-pitched tuning of the female instruments may be interpreted generally as a manifestation of Hindu-Balinese notions about gender, where femaleness is associated with the earth and maleness with the sky. (This is similar to the concept of Mother Earth and Father Sky in certain Native American cultures.)

explosive music, born of a time in the early 20th century when Balinese society was in the midst of tremendous social upheaval, moving toward modernity under Dutch colonial rule after some five centuries of Hindu-Balinese monarchies (see Tenzer 1998 [1991], 2000 on kebyar).

Focusing in now specifically on gamelan music in Bali, we discover that the gamelan gong kebyar, though it is the best-known form of Balinese gamelan on an international scale by far, is, like its musical relative the gamelan beleganjur, but one of more than two dozen distinct types of gamelan found on the tiny, hyper-artistic speck of the earth that is Bali. Each type has its own sound and characteristic style. Some feature bronze gongs and metallophones like those heard in the gamelan gong kebyar. Others do not, relying instead on instruments made with sounding materials of iron, hardwood, bamboo, and other substances. There is even one kind of gamelan, to which we will be introduced later, that uses no instruments *per se* at all, only voices. The music of some gamelans, like that of the grand and ancient *gamelan gong gedé* ("gamelan of the great gongs"), is in many ways closer in character to the regal Central Javanese gamelan tradi-tion than to the fiery style of kebyar. And other gamelan musics bear little apparent resem-blance to either of these. Different types of Balinese gamelan also are distinguished by cultural rather than specifically musical criteria. Each one has a unique, designated role within Balinese culture, being associated with particular rituals, ceremonies, dances, dance-dramas, shadow puppet plays, competitive events, and regional styles.

The culture of gamelan in Bali is not only rich and diverse, but also extraordinarily active. There are literally thousands of functioning gamelan clubs (*sekehe gong*) on the island dedicated to the preservation and cultivation of its myriad gamelan traditions. In the most densely populated areas, such as the capital city region of Denpasar and Ubud to its north, one can hear a different gamelan rehearsing on the corner of virtually every square block in the weeks leading up to a major gamelan competition.

Of all the many different traditions that are carried on by Bali's scores of gamelan clubs, none is more ubiquitous or fundamental to the meeting of ritual and social requirements of Balinese life than the gamelan beleganjur.

sekehe (SUH-kuh)

The Gamelan Beleganjur: An Introduction

We begin our journey through the world of gamelan beleganjur with our first Musical Guided Tour, in which the following elements are introduced and explained:

- The instruments of the ensemble.

- The basic **gong cycle** (i.e., the recurring sequence of strokes on different gongs that serves as the music's foundation).

- The relationship between the music's core melody and the elaboration of that melody in other instrumental parts.

- The standard rhythms and interlocking rhythmic and melodic patterns employed.

- The stratified structure of the music, in which higher-pitched instruments play at faster rates than lower-pitched ones.

Gangsa-type metallo-phones of a gamelan gong kebyar.

Though specifically intended as an introduction to the gamelan beleganjur and its music, this tour also focuses on musical elements and types of instruments that are characteristic of many other types of Balinese gamelan, including the gamelan gong kebyar. Many of these characteristics are even found in Central Javanese gamelan and gamelan traditions of other islands and cultures.

The text in the box found on pages 96–97 is a transcript of the audio Musical Guided Tour. As you listen to this tour at the Online Learning Center (www.mhhe.com/bakan1), follow along with this transcript.

Kilitan Telu Interlocking Rhythms: A Musical Symbol of Communal Interdependence

The integrated, interlocking texture of the kilitan telu rhythmic patterns, as described and illustrated in the preceding Musical Guided Tour, is interesting not only on a purely musical level, but as a symbol of broader Balinese cultural values as well. Specifically, the kilitan telu and other, related forms of interlocking patterns used in Balinese music are poignant musical symbols of *communal interdependence* in Balinese society. In most every realm of life, from rice cultivation to the meeting of civic duties and religious practice, Balinese people give high priority to working

The basic tempo-keeping instrument of the gamelan beleganjur is a medium-small gong called either *kempli* (kuhm-PLEE) (meaning "the instrument that makes the sound *pli* [plee]") or *kajar* (from the root *ajar,* meaning "to line things up"). It keeps a steady beat, like this [♪].

The root foundation of beleganjur music is a *gong cycle* of eight beats called **gilak** (GEE-lahk). It employs two very large gongs called the **gong ageng** (gohng ah-GUHNG), or "great gongs"; plus a medium-sized gong, the *kempur.* Here is the lowest gong ageng, which is identified as the female gong [♪]; now the slightly higher-pitched male gong [♪]. Finally, here is the kempur [♪]. Combined together with the time-keeping kempli in the context of the eight-beat gilak gong cycle, these instruments sound like this [♪]. An additional, clangy-sounding gong called the *bendé* [♪] is usually added to the gilak gong cycle in beleganjur as well. Here is its contribution [♪]. The order of the gong strokes also may be reversed in gilak, which gives the gong cycle a rather different character, like this [♪].

The next musical layer above the gong cycle is the melodic layer. This has two components:

- A core melody played on a pair of tuned, hand-held gongs (the *ponggang*), which sounds like this [♪]; and

- Rapid-paced elaborations of the core melody played on a set of four smaller, higher-pitched, hand-held gongs called **reyong.** Each reyong "pot" is played by a different player. Player 1 performs this pattern

The instruments of the gamelan beleganjur: bendé, gong ageng (female, male), and kempur in back row, left to right; kendang (drums); reyong (4), kempli, kempluk (optional instrument, not discussed), and ponggang (2) in second row, left to right; ceng-ceng (8 pairs) in front row.

on the highest pot [♪]. That pattern is then doubled on the lowest pot, like this [♪]. The second-highest pot fills in some of the rhythmic spaces, like this [♪]. Then the third-highest pot fills in the rest [♪]. Here now is the complete reyong part together with the core melody and the gongs [♪].

The third and final layer of the beleganjur musical texture is provided by drums and cymbals. There are two drums, which are called *kendang* (kuhn-DAHNG). One is the female drum [♪]; the other, slightly higher in pitch, is the male drum [♪]. They are played in complex interlocking patterns, like this [♪]. The two drummers are the leaders of the beleganjur ensemble.

The rhythms of the crash cymbal parts are closely aligned with the drumming. There are eight pairs of cymbals, called *cengceng* (chayng-chayng), and eight cymbal players. The cymbal section alternates between performing unison rhythmic figures like this [♪] and interlocking patterns like this [♪]. The most common rhythm for cymbal interlocking is a simple pattern that sounds like this [♪]. By having some of the cymbal players play that pattern on the beat [♪], others play it starting just after the beat [♪], and the rest play it starting just ahead of the beat [♪], but all at the same time, a continuous stream of interlocking rhythmic sound is generated [♪]. This pattern of rhythmic interlocking is called **kilitan telu** (kee-lee-TAHN tuh-LOO). It is the basis of a great variety of different interlocking textures in Balinese music, some melodic, others purely rhythmic.

By way of conclusion, here is the complete gamelan beleganjur, played in a traditional style that incorporates all of the elements outlined above [♪].

together collectively in pursuit of community-directed goals and values. Individuality and individual expression, so highly prized in Western cultures, tend to be less emphasized as important priorities among Balinese people (though this is not universally the case, especially nowadays). The kilitan telu elegantly symbolize a Balinese cultural vision of an integrated, interdependent community. Each of the three rhythms is essentially identical to the other two except for where it starts relative to the kempli's beat, yet no one of the three rhythms is considered complete by itself; it *needs* the other two. The kilitan telu whole, as represented by the continuous stream of interlocked rhythm created when all three of the rhythms are played together, is greater than the sum of its individual parts.

Balinese Kecak and the kilitan telu

The rhythmic patterns and interlocking principle of the kilitan telu span out in myriad forms across the full spectrum of Balinese gamelan music, from beleganjur cymbal patterns to the intricate melodic elaborations of kebyar-style gangsa metallophone parts in pieces like "Jaya Semara" (**CD ex. #1-9 or 2-2**). Another context in which these same rhythms figure prominently is **Kecak,** a Balinese dance-drama with music provided by a gamelan comprised not of instruments *per se,* but exclusively of voices, sometimes upwards of 200 of them! Appropriately, this massive vocal ensemble is called a *gamelan suara,* meaning "voice gamelan."

Kecak (Ke-CHAHK)

The musical roots of Kecak are found in an ancient trance ritual called Sanghyang Dedari, in which mesmerizing, rhythmic vocal chanting of the kilitan telu patterns performed by a small group of men surrounding an oil lamp is used to induce trance in female spirit mediums. During the ritual, these spirit mediums are enlisted to summon ancestral spirits to aid the village community in times of crisis, especially in situations where the villagers fear that they are under siege by malevolent spirit beings.

In Kecak, the small vocal group of Sanghyang Dedari is expanded to a huge vocal ensemble, and gamelan-like gong cycles, melodies, and complex textures are recreated in vocalized form using onomatopoeic syllables for the different gamelan instruments (for example, "sirrr" for the large gong and "pur" for the kempur). The interlocking rhythmic patterns of the kilitan telu—performed with the vocal syllable *cak* (chak)—remain central to the music. **CD ex. #2-3** is an excerpt from a Kecak performance that illustrates this spectacular and unique sound.

A Balinese performance of Kecak.

The Kecak dance-drama itself involves the enactment of an episode from the Ramayana, the great Hindu epic. The most popular plot is the Abduction of Sita, about the kidnapping of a beautiful princess (Sita) by an evil king (Rawana) and her eventual rescue by her beloved Prince Rama and an army of monkeys. The musicians of the vocal gamelan double as actors, playing the roles of the monkeys in Rama's army.

In Bali, Kecak is promoted as an authentic, traditional Balinese dance-drama. In fact, it was a genre invented through a collaboration between Balinese musicians and dancers and an expatriate German painter named Walter Spies in connection with a 1932 German film entitled *Die Isle der Damonen* (The Isle of Demons) (see Dibia 1996:6–9). Henceforth, Kecak was developed into a Ramayana dance-drama for tourist performances, and that is its primary cultural niche to the present day.

Experiencing Balinese interlocking, Kecak-style

To get a sense of how it feels to perform interlocking Balinese rhythms like those heard in Kecak, try performing the interlocking kilitan telu rhythms charted out in Figure 7.1 with some of your friends. Use the sound "chak" to articulate the notes with your voice, and if there are at

	1	2	3	4	5	6	7	8	(1)
Pung	X	●	●	●	X	●	●	●	(X)
Chak 1	X	●	X	X	●	X	X	●	(X)
Chak 2	●	X	●	X	X	●	X	X	(●)
Chak 3	●	X	X	●	X	X	●	X	(●)

Kecak performance exercise: Interlocking kilitan telu rhythms.

FIGURE 7.1

least three of you participating, have one person mark out a steady pulse on the syllable "pung" while the others do interlocking "chak" patterns. Repeat the eight-beat cycle of Figure 7.1 multiple times without pause if you can.

The Gamelan Beleganjur in Battles of Good versus Evil

Sanghyang Dedari is not the only ritual context in which Balinese people react as communities to perceived threats from malevolent spirit forces. In other such rituals, beleganjur music often plays a key role. According to Balinese lore, the gamelan beleganjur was originally created by evil spirit beings of the Lower World. Later, it is said that it was transformed into a powerful force for good after coming into the possession of Balinese people of the Middle World. The role of beleganjur music as an important source of mediation between the different worlds of the Balinese cosmos—Lower, Middle, and Upper—has continued ever since.

In ritual contexts such as cremation processions, beleganjur music is performed for the purpose of intimidating and driving away malevolent spirit beings who are said to travel to the earthly Middle World in order to cause harm to people and departing souls of the dead and to disrupt the delicate balance of the cosmos. Despite its underworld origin, the imposing sound of beleganjur music is believed to have the power to frighten evil spirits, who it is hoped will be inclined to scatter in fear rather than face human adversaries equipped with the potent weapon of a gamelan beleganjur.

Beleganjur music in Hindu-Balinese cremation processions

Beleganjur music is played in all kinds of processions, but its performance is nowhere more crucial than in the context of the Hindu-Balinese ritual processions that occur in connection with cremation rituals (*ngaben*). The act of cremation is regarded as the first essential step that frees the soul, or **atma,** of the deceased from its ties to the earthly world so that it can commence its afterlife journey to worlds beyond. Ideally, this journey leads to the paradise-like Upper World of the gods and ancestors, where the atma goes to await reincarnation and a return to the Middle World in some form, or, in the most sublime of outcomes, to experience liberation from the cycle of reincarnation altogether and gain a permanent home in the Upper World.

First, though, the body or exhumed remains (bodies of the dead are sometimes buried for a lengthy period of time prior to being cremated) must be ritually prepared and taken in a large cremation tower (*wadah*) from the family home compound of the deceased to the Temple of the Dead (dedicated to Siwa) at the far end of the village. This journey takes the form of a communal procession. The procession ideally involves the participation of all members of the deceased's **banjar.** The term *banjar* is usually translated as "village ward" or "hamlet," though "neighborhood organization" may be more apt. A banjar typically consists of between 50 and 500 families and is responsible for planning and producing most of the core communal, religious, and social activities of its membership (Eiseman 1990:72–73). The planning and production of cremations and other mortuary rituals represent the highest calling of the banjar community.

The procession to the cremation grounds is thought to be fraught with peril. Deceased souls who have yet to be cremated are considered to be dangerously vulnerable to the meddlesome practices of bhutas, leyaks, and other evil spirits. It is feared that

ngaben (nya-buhn)

banjar (BAHN-jahr)

Cremation tower being carried in procession.

As in other Hindu societies such as India, social organization among the Balinese has traditionally relied upon a *caste system*. A caste is a hereditary social class. In caste societies, every individual is born into a specific caste. One's caste may determine anything from educational and professional opportunities in this life to one's spiritual destiny in lives beyond.

The Balinese caste system is different from the caste system of India (where the whole concept of a social system organized around caste is now officially banned by law, though the vestiges of a caste-based social order are by no means entirely gone—see also Chapter 8, p. 126). In the Balinese system, there are four castes: the priestly caste, the warrior caste, the merchant caste, and the commoner caste (*sudra*—literally "outsider"). About 90 percent of Balinese Hindus belong to the commoner caste. There is no "Untouchables" (Dalit) caste in Bali, in contrast to the traditional Indian caste system.

Functionally, caste affiliation in Bali has mainly to do with one's religious life and obligations: temple affiliations, cremation rites, in some cases priestly duties. Beyond the religious sphere, in social and professional life, caste is much less operative, though not necessarily irrelevant. With the exception of certain sectors of the priesthood, Balinese from all castes associate freely with one another in daily life and business and are generally free to pursue the educational and professional paths of their choice and to take part equally in civil affairs.

kidung (kee-DOONG)

Beleganjur ensemble, positioned immediately behind tower, performs in a cremation procession.

these malevolent spirits will abduct the uncremated, unliberated atma and drag it down to the underworld. The banjar community uses all resources at its disposal to ensure that this does not happen. The performance of beleganjur music is among the most important of these. The music is believed to help both the atma of the deceased and the banjar community in several different ways, both during the course of the procession and during the act of cremation itself.

At the start of the procession, the beleganjur group assembles and lines up immediately behind the cremation tower. It maintains this position throughout the procession. Men and women singing sacred verses (*kidung*) also gather in close proximity to the tower. Although the singing is entirely unrelated to the beleganjur music, the two together contribute to a rich musical cacophony that helps to generate the desired state of *ramé*, or "crowdedness," that is a hallmark of virtually every Balinese ritual or social occasion. Other types of processional gamelan may contribute to this ramé soundscape as well, and the general rule is that the more kinds of music there are—the more "crowded" and multifarious the soundscape is, in other words—the better.

The tower consists of multiple tiers that represent the three worlds of the Balinese cosmos. The body of the deceased is placed near the top of the tower, symbolizing the hope of its ascent to the Upper World. It is wrapped in a long white cloth, symbolizing purity. The number of tower carriers depends on the size of the tower. It may range from a half dozen men for a small tower to upwards of 20—and in some cases many more than that—for a large one. The largest towers are reserved for wealthy and high-caste individuals (see "Insights and Perspectives" box above).

Beleganjur Music Performed during a Balinese Cremation Procession

- CD Track #**2-4**
- Featured performer(s)/group: Beleganjur group of Banjar Belaluan Sadmerta, Denpasar, Bali, Indonesia
- Format: Excerpt
- Source recording: Field recording by the author

This selection is an excerpt from a field recording of an actual cremation procession that I made in Bali in 1995. The recording was made on a portable Digital Audio Tape (DAT) recorder using a binaural stereo microphone. The right and left channels of the microphone were separated into tiny units that attached to the right and left arms of my eyeglasses. Thus, as I move from one position to another while following along with the procession (or even just turn my head in one direction or another), the "aural picture" changes accordingly: sometimes the gongs are more in the foreground, other times the cymbals or drums. This moving soundscape effect is most pronounced if you listen with headphones.

What is heard in the recording is the opening minutes of a rather small cremation procession. As the selection begins, we find ourselves on the street outside the home of the deceased. The members of the banjar have been summoned to congregate and prepare to begin the procession to the cremation grounds. A group of women and men sing sacred verses (kidung) as poetic offerings to the gods and ancestors, imploring their benevolence to ensure a good cremation and safe passage of the departed soul to a good afterlife. The body of the deceased, adorned in a long white cloth, is being placed in the upper tiers of the cremation tower. We hear clicks and taps as final adjustments are made to the tower and the body is eased into its proper place. The tower bearers stand ready to lift the heavy tower onto their shoulders and prepare themselves for the long march ahead. Procession organizers move about the area, telling people to step backward or forward into proper formation and closing off the street to traffic. The beleganjur group takes its place immediately behind the tower. (*Note:* There is no reyong section in the ensemble in this example, as is sometimes the case in ritual beleganjur performances.)

At 0:36, the lead drummer (performing on the "male" drum) starts to play, cueing the rest of the musicians to raise up their instruments and "announcing" to the entire congregation that the procession is about to begin. He is joined in a brief interlocking flourish by the second drummer (playing the "female" drum) at 0:40, and this cues the entry of the full ensemble at 0:41. Just as the first gong stroke and cymbal crash are sounded, the tower carriers hoist the cremation tower up on their shoulders and the procession begins, with everyone moving at a quick and energetic pace. Unison cymbal rhythms, reinforced by the drumming, are pounded out over the propulsive gong tones of the gilak gong cycle. The unison rhythms give way to a brief passage of interlocking rhythm at 0:53.

Next, at 0:56, the drums and cymbals lay out momentarily while the gong cycle continues. Then there is some interlocking drumming that leads into a long passage featuring interlocking patterns in both the drum and cymbal parts. The cymbal section is heard playing the kilitan telu rhythmic patterns discussed earlier (1:06–1:38). The dynamic level of the cymbal section and the drums rises and falls at different points, reflecting and influencing the pace and energy of the procession. The lead drummer keeps a careful eye and ear on the proceedings, calibrating and adjusting the musical intensity in accordance with functional needs. At 1:39, the cymbals drop out and the two drummers come to the fore. They play an intricate drum duet called *Jagul*, which is a common feature in beleganjur performances of all types, traditional and modern. The cymbals sneak back in at 1:50, then launch into kilitan telu interlocking at 1:54, again rising and falling

Jagul (Jah-GOOL)

in dynamics, then ending with an emphatic CENG! CENG! at 2:05. The drummers and cymbal players rest as the gong cycle continues and the music fades out to end the excerpt.

guided listening quick summary

Beleganjur Music Performed during a Balinese Cremation Procession (CD ex. #2-4)

0:00–0:35

- Sound of crowd assembling, singing of sacred verses (kidung).

0:36–0:55

- Entry of lead drummer (0:36), cueing beleganjur ensemble and signaling beginning of procession.
- Full ensemble enters over gilak gong cycle at 0:41 (as tower carriers hoist tower onto their shoulders and the procession begins); unison rhythms in cymbals.
- Brief passage of kilitan telu cymbal interlocking cymbal at end of section (0:53–0:55).

0:56–1:05

- Gong cycle only (no drums or cymbals), followed by interlocking drumming and return of cymbals.

1:06–1:38

- Long passage featuring kilitan telu cymbal interlocking.

1:39–1:49

- Jagul drum duet section.

1:50–end

- Cymbals reenter, more kilitan telu interlocking; excerpt fades out after 2:05 as gong cycle continues.

Crossroads battles and a musical ladder to the Upper World

The beleganjur ensemble's assigned task in the cremation procession is far from over at the point where the music fades out at the end of the preceding musical selection (**CD ex. #2-4**). The gamelan beleganjur plays continuously from the start to the finish of the procession, providing a steady yet dynamic sonic backdrop to the ritual proceedings. Ideally, the procession should move along at a quite rapid rate, and the presence of energetic beleganjur music serves to ensure that a good pace and high level of energy are maintained. Like a conductor directing the entire procession, the lead drummer pays close attention to what is going on around him. If he perceives a lag in the procession's energy or speed, he provides a cue to kick the musical intensity and tempo up a notch. If, on the other hand, he detects an *excess* of energy or undue haste among procession participants, he may slow down the tempo of the music or have the drums and cymbals lay out for a while to settle things down.

On a purely human, Middle World level, the performance of beleganjur music serves important functions in the procession. On other levels, the music is played with the intention of opening channels of communication and productive interaction between the earthly, human world and denizens of the worlds beyond it, be those deities and ancestors of the Upper World or demonic forces of the Lower World. Regarding relations with the former, beleganjur music, with its powerful sound and presence, heralds the impending departure of the soon-to-be-cremated atma from this world and its readiness to venture onward. It is used to send an optimistic musical announcement to the gods and ancestors, alerting them to the hoped-for and anticipated arrival in the Upper World of a soul that has completed its worldly duties and is ready to move on to the next stage in the long cycle of births, deaths, and rebirths.

Regarding relations with the evil bhutas and leyaks, the assigned task of the beleganjur group is most crucial of all, especially at crossroads along the procession route. Balinese believe that crossroads are the locations where bhutas and leyaks congregate in greatest abundance. They are very dangerous places, especially for vulnerable, uncremated souls of the dead, upon whom the evil spirits are most likely to prey. Special ritual actions are performed, therefore, at all crossroads during the procession to protect the atma from potential harm. Most importantly, the cremation tower is spun around in a circle at least three times, as quickly as possible (see the photo on p. 99). This is done because it is believed that the bhutas and leyaks can only travel in straight lines. Thus, the spinning of the tower is thought to confuse them and prevent them from invading the tower to capture the atma.

The spinning of the tower at crossroads is accompanied by beleganjur music of especially great volume and energy. This intense music serves several purposes. First, it is believed that it has power, in and of itself, to frighten and deflect potentially meddlesome bhutas and leyaks. Second, it is used to inspire physical strength and courage among the carriers of the heavy tower, who face a formidable challenge in their efforts to spin the tower with sufficient speed and energy. Third, it is hoped that it will embolden the atma of the deceased itself, who it is believed otherwise may be tempted to flee the tower in fear of the advancing evil spirits, destroying its prospects for a good cremation and a successful afterlife.

The crossroads style of beleganjur music is usually marked by a change in the rhythmic patterns of the drums and cymbals. In particular, driving interlocking rhythms of straight "eighth notes" in the cymbal part, with strong accents on every main beat, replace the more intricate "sixteenth-note" interlocking patterns of kilitan telu performed during most other parts of the procession. These more driving rhythms belong to a style of playing in beleganjur called **malpal.** An example of malpal played at a crossroads during a cremation procession may be heard on **CD ex. #2-5.**

Finally, the procession reaches the cremation grounds. The beleganjur group concludes its performance with a climactic passage played just after the tower is lowered to the ground. The body (or its remains) is then removed from the tower, ritually prepared for cremation, and encased in an animal-shaped sarcophagus while the beleganjur musicians briefly rest. Then, as soon as the burning of the sarcophagus begins, they start playing again, performing music of a quieter and more meditative character in a song of farewell that is said to accompany the departing soul on its journey. This music may be described metaphorically as a ladder upon which the atma, having achieved the first stage of its liberation from the bonds of earthly life and the precarious state of death before cremation, may finally begin its ascent to the Upper World. The full liberation of the atma will not occur until weeks, possibly even years, after the actual cremation. That requires the performance of a post-cremation purification ritual called *memukur.* Still, there is much joy for the banjar community in the completion of a successful cremation, which represents the crucial first step of a good afterlife for one of its own.

memukur
(muh-moo-KOOR)

Walking Warriors:
Worldly Battlegrounds of Beleganjur Music

In exploring the performance and functions of beleganjur music in Hindu-Balinese cremation rituals, we have learned of the music's importance as a music of battle, in particular, as a music of battles fought between human communities and their evil spirit adversaries over control of the fates of deceased souls.

In former times, beleganjur music also was performed for battles of a different kind: battles of war fought by the armies of rival Balinese kingdoms. Bali was ravaged by frequent and brutal wars throughout much of its precolonial history. The current map of Bali shows the island divided into eight principal regencies (*kabupaten*). Each regency bears the name of a former Balinese kingdom. Over the course of centuries, these eight kingdoms (and several lesser ones) engaged in many wars against one another. Warfare itself was glorified. Balinese kings (*rajas*) were regarded by their subjects as semidivine beings. To fight for one's king and his kingdom was thus to fight on behalf of the deities. The great Balinese warrior was a heroic figure.

Warfare itself was accompanied by grand pageantry and ritual, and music played on the gamelan beleganjur, the "gamelan of walking warriors," was key. Balinese armies marched into battle to the accompaniment of beleganjur. The music served to inspire the warriors to bravery and to strike terror in the hearts of their enemies. With a faint hum of gongs advancing like a distant storm before an explosion of lightning cymbals and thunderous drums, beleganjur music heralded the impending doom of battle with foreboding power and force. Human rather than spirit adversaries represented the principal targets of beleganjur's threatening tones in this context, but the basic theme of a music used for battle connects the worlds of beleganjur as a music of cremation rituals and as a historical music of actual warfare.

Lomba beleganjur: The modern beleganjur contest

Though beleganjur's traditional role as a music of warfare has been rendered obsolete in modern times, the revered image of the heroic Balinese warrior of old has by no means disappeared. It is kept alive in many different contexts, from the famous Baris "warrior's dance" to countless dance-dramas and shadow puppet plays (*wayang kulit*) that chronicle the martial exploits of both the historical and mythical Balinese past.

This heroic warrior's image resurfaced anew in the mid-1980s with the invention of the modern beleganjur contest, or *lomba beleganjur.* In a lomba beleganjur, numerous beleganjur groups representing different banjars, districts, or regions of Bali compete against each other in a formal competitive environment. The first lomba beleganjur was held in Denpasar in 1986. More than two dozen groups from the city and its surrounding region (Badung) competed. The performers were all male, predominantly teenagers and young men in their early 20s.

The contest was a great success and within short order had become the model for scores of similar events held all over the island. These contests range from small regional competitions featuring just a handful of groups to islandwide championships played out before audiences of thousands in high-profile, politically charged events. The larger contests are frequently held in conjunction with election campaigns and political rallies. Many are sponsored by Balinese cultural agencies of the Indonesian government. The synthesis of Balinese cultural pride and mod-

Badung
(Bah-DOONG)

Baris dancer in warrior costume.

ern Indonesian nationalist values that these contests are said to invoke fits well with an idealized, Unity in Diversity—based image of Indonesian cultural nationalism.

Women's and children's beleganjur groups have emerged since the 1990s, though the contest style of beleganjur, in common with beleganjur played in traditional ritual contexts such as cremations, is still mainly identified with men, and indeed with core Balinese conceptions of manhood and masculinity (see also Chapter 2, pp. 14–16).

Kreasi beleganjur: The contest musical style

The lomba beleganjur contest event has given rise to a dramatic, neo-traditional beleganjur musical style with its own, unique performance aesthetic. This is known as **kreasi beleganjur,** or "new creation beleganjur" music.

Traditional beleganjur music such as that performed in cremation processions is quintessentially *functional*. Its sole purpose is to support the ritual it accompanies. Displays of compositional innovation and virtuosic display are neither of interest nor of relevance. What counts is simply that the music do its job, as it were, be that to ward off evil spirits or inspire physical strength in the cremation tower carriers.

Group performing in a beleganjur contest.

kreasi (kray-YAH-see)

Kreasi beleganjur is something else altogether. It is flashy, fast, complex, inventive, full of musical contrasts and surprises, and enhanced by elaborate pageantry, colorful costumes, and impressive choreographed movement sequences (see the photo on p. 107). Yet for all of that, it remains strongly rooted in the musical soil of traditional beleganjur. The standard gilak gong cycle and cyclic core melody of traditional styles continue to be foundational in kreasi beleganjur. The conventional kilitan telu cymbal patterns, interlocking drum rhythms, and melodic elaboration patterns of the reyong are largely carried over as well.

Even the basic processional performance medium of traditional beleganjur is retained. Several judging stations (*pos juri*) are set up along closed-off streets on the contest procession route, one at the beginning, one at the end, and two or three at designated points in between. The competing groups follow along this route at intervals, playing in a more-or-less traditional beleganjur style during the processional portions of their performance (see the photo above) and transitioning to a more virtuosic, choreographed, and musically varied demonstration style (*demonstrasi*) at each judging station, where adjudicators evaluate the performances. Contest audiences may be very large; thousands of spectators come to the biggest events. They also can be quite raucous and unruly, pressing forward and encircling the musicians with almost suffocating closeness as the contest officials attempt to push them back out of the performance area. At a good contest, the energy is electrifying as the musicians and the crowd feed off of each other's excitement and intensity.

The exciting, virtuosic style of a beleganjur contest demonstration performance is well illustrated by **CD ex. #2-6.** This is an excerpt from a field recording I made in Bali in 1995 that features a composition by the great beleganjur composer and drummer I Ketut Sukarata, who was one of my two principal Balinese music teachers (the other was I Ketut Gedé Asnawa, who is credited for having essentially "invented" the kreasi beleganjur genre). The group featured is from the Sanur Beach region of southeastern Bali, where the contest was held. We first

I Ketut Sukarata
(Ee Kuh-TOOT
Soo-kah-rah-tuh)

Asnawa
(Ah-snah-wuh)

Sanur (Sah-NOOR)

I Ketut Sukarata.

hear them approaching from the distance, playing in a traditional, processional style. The master of ceremonies builds up anticipation as they approach the judging station. Applause from the crowd marks their arrival there. All of the instruments except the gongs drop out for a while. Then the full group reenters overtop the continuing gilak gong cycle—first drums and reyongs, then cymbals—and the music becomes highly energetic. It is also much flashier and more precise in the execution of unison and interlocking parts than anything we heard in the earlier cremation procession recordings. And the musical arrangement is more varied and complex.

This is music where precision, virtuosity, and originality, not just functionality, are both valued and formally graded. Its "job" is to impress and entertain the adjudicators and audience rather than to serve functional ritual requirements. The goal of the performers is to win the contest rather than battles against malevolent spirit adversaries.

Tradition and innovation in kreasi beleganjur: An elusive balance

Kreasi beleganjur differs from traditional beleganjur in the high value it places on the following:

- Compositional originality.
- Ensemble virtuosity (*note:* not *individual* virtuosity—the group, rather than the musician, is always the "star").

- Emphasis on showmanship, both in the playing of the music itself and in **gerak** (literally "movement"), which are choreographed sequences performed by the musicians (see "Insights and Perspectives" box on the next page).
- Varied textures, in which different sections of the ensemble (drums, cymbals, reyong) are featured in turn.

In all of these priorities, kreasi beleganjur exhibits strong influences drawn from the style of kebyar music, such as that heard and discussed earlier in **CD ex. #2-2** ("Jaya Semara"). Kreasi beleganjur therefore may be said to represent a "kebyarized" form of traditional beleganjur music.

Kreasi beleganjur also differs from its traditional counterpart in its employment of musical designs with *contrasting formal sections*. The demonstration portions of a kreasi beleganjur contest piece usually have three distinct parts:

- An opening section played at a fast tempo, with lots of rhythmic variations featuring different instruments.
- A middle section played at a slower tempo, in which the style of the reyong playing is more lyrical and melodic.
- A third section in which there is a return to the fast tempo and energetic rhythmic character of the opening section, but with different variations.

There is no correlate of this three-part, fast-slow-fast formal plan in conventional, traditional beleganjur music. The borrowing here comes from the musical forms of older, classical styles associated with other types of Balinese gamelan (e.g., gamelan gong gedé, *gamelan gambuh*). In addition to **kebyarization,** then, it can be said that kreasi beleganjur is also influenced by musical processes of **classicization.** One additional influence in the works of at least some leading beleganjur composers is foreign musics. I Ketut Sukarata, for example, has gained notoriety for his incorporation into beleganjur of rhythms adapted from hip-hop, funk, and disco musics.

The key to creating a successful, prize-winning kreasi beleganjur contest piece is to be found in achieving a balance between beleganjur traditionalism and modernity. On the one hand, a high priority is placed on adhering to key elements of musical form and style that define traditional beleganjur music:

- Only the traditional beleganjur ensemble instrumentation may be used, and the basic musical roles and playing styles of the various instruments, for the most part, should be maintained (e.g., gongs should play the gong cycle, reyong should elaborate the core melody).

Gerak: The Choreographic Element in Kreasi Beleganjur

Gerak are the choreographed movement sequences in kreasi beleganjur performances. They are executed by the musicians themselves as they play. This is one of the highlight features of the beleganjur contest style. The root of gerak is to be found in choreographic sequences that alternately invoke and "comment upon" the central figure of the archetypal traditional Balinese warrior and his *kepahlawanan,* or "heroic," character. Classic poses of battle and martial arts maneuvers are precisely executed by the musicians in their mutually reflective duet of sound and movement. These choreographic images are juxtaposed to others that draw from various beleganjur-related domains, such as the spinning of the cremation tower at a crossroads during a cremation procession. Gerak also may be used to humorous effect. The gerak sequences for Sukarata's "Brek Dan" ("Break Dance"), for example, caricatured the sometimes comical moves and grooves of nightclub dancers in Bali.

All told, kreasi beleganjur gerak represents a melange of diverse choreographic and symbolic expression. Lighthearted, satirical moments ebb and flow against the current of more solemn and reverential kepahlawanan characterizations. Gerak offers a poignant reflection of the complex and multidimensional nature of contemporary Balinese-Indonesian identities and values, one that is completely consistent with the character of kreasi beleganjur music itself.

Gerak maneuver in a beleganjur contest.

- Signature musical elements of traditional beleganjur, such as the gilak gong cycle, standard core melody, and conventional interlocking patterns, should be retained.

- A dignified and "heroic" (*kepahlawanan*) musical character befitting the dignity of traditional beleganjur music in Balinese culture should be present in the performance.

Sometimes, no amount of skill, creativity, or propriety is enough to ensure competitive success in a lomba beleganjur. In a 1992 islandwide contest that was sponsored by the then-ruling GOLKAR political party in conjunction with its national election campaign, GOLKAR officials sat on the contest results until after the election results were in. They then discovered that the beleganjur group selected as champions by the adjudicating committee—a truly outstanding ensemble by the measures of all contest criteria—came from a banjar that had only given moderate support to GOLKAR in the election. The banjar of the second-place finishers, however, had supported GOLKAR almost unanimously. Lo and behold, when the results of the contest were announced, the second-place finishers, rather than the rightful winners of the contest, were awarded the championship.

On the other hand, this traditional base should be embellished by elements of novelty, innovation, variety, virtuosity, showmanship, kebyarization, classicization, and sophistication of formal design, as outlined above.

It is a difficult balance to achieve. Groups that fail to bring enough creativity and novelty to their performances are met with indifference by audiences and adjudicators alike. They even may generate audience hostility. I once witnessed a group that was literally booed off the "stage" during a beleganjur contest on account of their unoriginal, mediocre musical presentation.

Too much innovation and novelty can be even more problematic. Groups whose performances are judged to be at odds with the integrity of traditional beleganjur musical character or lacking in the proper kepahlawanan "heroic" spirit may be disqualified from a contest on these grounds alone.

Achieving the elusive balance:
The kreasi beleganjur music of I Ketut Suandita

**Suandita
(Swahn-DEE-tuh)**

If there is any figure in the kreasi beleganjur world whose music epitomizes the achievement of an ideal balance of traditionalism and creative innovation, it is I Ketut Suandita. Suandita grew up playing beleganjur, kebyar, and other styles of gamelan and studied composition with I Ketut Gedé Asnawa and other master teachers. By the age of 23, he had achieved the unprecedented distinction of being the composer of the winning composition in Bali's most prestigious beleganjur contest three years straight (1990, 1991, and 1992). Not only that, but he directed three

I Ketut Suandita (right).

different groups from three different villages to those championships, and performed as the lead drummer for two of them. This would be roughly comparable to coaching three different teams to the National Basketball Association (NBA) title in three consecutive years, while being the star player on two of those teams. Leading Balinese authorities such as Asnawa describe the early 1990s as a "golden age" of kreasi beleganjur, pointing to Suandita as the exemplary beleganjur composer of that period.

The secret to Suandita's success derived from his singular ability to adhere closely to the foundational style and character of beleganjur musical tradition while at the same time extending that tradition into uncharted, innovative, and musically compelling territory.

guided listening experience

"Wira Ghorava Cakti '95" (Kreasi Beleganjur), by I Ketut Suandita

- CD Track #: **2-7**
- Featured performer(s)/group: Beleganjur group of Banjar Meranggi, Denpasar, Bali, Indonesia
- Format: Excerpt
- Source recording: Field recording by the author

Suandita's distinctive kreasi beleganjur style is well exemplified in the work "Wira Ghorava Cakti," a prize-winning piece performed here (in an excerpt from a 1995 performance) by the group from the banjar of Meranggi that Suandita directed to the 1992 beleganjur championship. This ensemble is considered to have been one of the best contest beleganjur groups ever.

"Wira Ghorava Cakti" never loses sight of its traditional beleganjur roots and stays firmly within the neo-traditional sphere of the kreasi beleganjur medium. Elements such as the gilak gong cycle, ostinato core melody, and kilitan telu cymbal patterns are still present, though they may drop in and out of the texture at different points or be presented in varied or manipulated forms (see below). Overall, however, this is a piece that moves much farther from conventional beleganjur style than works like the Sukarata kreasi beleganjur composition of **CD ex. #2-6.**

Among the innovative musical elements of this piece are the following:

- At certain points, the gong cycle and time-keeping kempli drop out completely (reflecting kebyar influence), leaving the drums, the cymbals, or the reyong to play unaccompanied in passages featuring complex interlocking textures. The solo reyong passage at 0:19 is an example.

- Instead of having just three interlocking rhythms divided among the eight cymbal players (i.e., the standard kilitan telu patterns), Suandita assigns a separate rhythmic pattern to *each* cymbal player. Most of the added patterns actually derive from the fundamental kilitan telu rhythm (x-xx-xx-), but the more varied rhythmic texture generated by eight cymbal parts creates a distinctive musical effect. This can be heard in the section at 0:07, and again in the more extended passage beginning at 0:38.

- There is much more variety of rhythms and textures in this piece than there is in more conventional kreasi beleganjur pieces such as **CD ex. #2-6,** let alone in traditional ritual beleganjur performance styles.

- Though the standard kreasi beleganjur distinction between fast and slow sections is present, Suandita blurs the distinction between the two through frequent shifts in tempo, texture, and rhythm. This is most clear in the "slow" section beginning at 1:29, which sometimes almost creates the impression of being played at a slow tempo *and* a fast tempo at the same time. This effect is especially pronounced at 2:12.

"Wira Ghorava Cakti" ("Wee-rah Go-rah-vah CHAK-tee")

---

guided listening quick summary

"Wira Ghorava Cakti '95," by I Ketut Suandita (CD ex. #2-7)

0:00–0:06
- Excerpt begins with impressive interlocking drumming, syncopated cymbal rhythms; gilak gong cycle provides foundation.

0:07–0:18

- Brief passage featuring distinctive Suandita-style cymbal interlocking, with different rhythmic patterns performed by each of the eight cymbal players (0:07–0:09).

- Reyong, drums, and other instruments come in from 0:10 on.

0:19–0:27

- Unaccompanied reyong feature (gong cycle absent); superb example of fast, intricate reyong interlocking.

0:28–1:14

- Gong cycle returns; talents of full ensemble on display; good examples of eight–part cymbal interlocking from 0:38.

1:15–1:28

- Transition to slow-tempoed section of the piece; contrasting musical character.

1:29–2:11

- Slow section proper begins (over a dramatically slower gilak gong cycle).

- Unpredictable changes in tempo, texture, and rhythm intentionally used to blur distinction between "slow" and "fast" parts of piece as music progresses.

2:12–end

- Drums and cymbals play at double the tempo of the other instruments, creating an effect of two levels of tempo (slow and fast) occurring at once.

- Excerpt fades out as performance continues (3:00).

Crossing International Borders

Composers from outside of Indonesia have long held a fascination for gamelan music. Ever since the famous French composer Claude Debussy heard a Javanese gamelan at the 1889 world's fair in Paris, many non-Indonesian composers have been influenced by, and in some cases written works for, Javanese and Balinese gamelan: John Cage, Lou Harrison, Colin McPhee, Benjamin Britten, Philip Glass, Steve Reich, Michael Tenzer, Wayne Vitale, Evan Ziporyn, Barbara Benary. Even pop stars like Janet Jackson (on "China Love") and Beck (on "Loser") have used digital samples of gamelan on some of their recordings.

musik kontemporer (moo-SEEK koan-tuhm-poh-RAYR)

Astita (Ah-stee-tuh)

Indonesian composers have likewise been influenced by Western and other international musics, both in the popular music arena and in the experimental, avant-garde genre of Indonesian *musik kontemporer* ("contemporary music"), which combines Indonesian and non-Indonesian musical elements in novel ways. A number of prominent Balinese composers, including Asnawa and his brother I Komang Astita, have composed internationally acclaimed musik kontemporer works.

Gamelan performance groups are active today in many countries, from the United States and Canada, to the United Kingdom, Italy, and Japan. The majority of these groups specialize in Javanese gamelan traditions, but there are a number of Balinese gamelan ensembles as well. The best-known of the latter is Gamelan Sekar Jaya, based in Berkeley, California. Additionally, there are Balinese gamelan programs at a number of universities, including UCLA, the University of British Columbia, Bowling Green State University, and Florida State University (FSU).

The final piece of music we will explore in this chapter is one that I composed in 1997 for the student Balinese gamelan group I direct at Florida State University. It is entitled "B.A.Ph.PET."

"B.A.Ph.PET," by Michael Bakan

- CD Track #: **2-8**
- Featured performer(s)/group: Charles Tremblay (scratch turntable soloist) with the Florida State University Balinese Gamelan
- Format: Excerpt
- Source recording: From the personal archive of the author (all rights reserved)

"B.A.Ph.PET" is a post-traditional Balinese gamelan piece scored for gamelan gong kebyar instruments, the four reyong "pots" of a gamelan beleganjur, keyboard synthesizer, synthesized drums and percussion, electric bass, and scratch turntable soloist. The scratch turntable part is improvised; all of the other parts are composed. The turntable soloist is Charles Tremblay, who was an FSU student, gamelan member, and dance club DJ working in the Tallahassee area when this recording was made. Charles, a percussionist by training, performed with the FSU gamelan for several years. He was a standout member of the group, excelling especially in the difficult art of Balinese kendang drumming. For his final concert with the ensemble, I decided to create a work that would highlight his talents as a turntablist while at the same time expanding my own horizons as a composer of intercultural gamelan music. "B.A.Ph.PET," short for "Big Attitude Phat Pet" (in reference to a dog belonging to a friend of mine who possessed rather extraordinary singing abilities), was the result.

The gamelan aspect of "B.A.Ph.PET" incorporates many conventional Balinese elements: a gong cycle foundation, a steady-paced core melody, melodic elaborations featuring interlocking parts, a stratified structure of faster-moving parts in the higher-pitched instruments and

Florida State University Balinese gamelan, with Charles Tremblay playing kendang (drum).

Two scratch turntablists. Afrika Bambaataa, the "Godfather of Hip-Hop," is seen in the left-side photo.

slower-moving parts in the lower-pitched ones. All of these elements, however, are tied to Western-style chord progressions and synthesizer melodies in some portions of the piece. And they are progressively encompassed by hip-hop/funk drum rhythms, bass lines, and improvised turn-tabling during the second part of the work, which commences at 1:26.

The reyong and upper-range gangsa metallophone parts of "B.A.Ph.PET" all derive from a shortened variant of the basic kilitan telu rhythm. Rather than the full pattern of [x-xx-xx-], a truncated pattern of [x-xx--] is used instead (see Figure 7.2). This pattern, played on a single, muffled reyong "pot" and repeated over and over as an ostinato, is the first thing you hear. Gradually, the other three reyong pots join the first, one by one, to create a unison rhythmic pattern on a dissonant, four-note chord that one would not expect to hear in traditional or neo-traditional Balinese music.

The other gamelan instruments enter one after another, section by section. When the gangsa metallophones come in, their parts build from the same truncated kilitan telu rhythm that was introduced earlier by the reyong. Rather than playing in unison, however, all of the gangsa players perform variant versions of this basic pattern on notes of different pitch, and all of the patterns start at different points relative to the main beat. The final result, once all of the gangsas have entered (0:35), is a six-note, ascending-and-descending melodic ostinato resulting from all

Basic kilitan telu rhythmic pattern compared to truncated "B.A.Ph.PET" rhythmic pattern.

	1	2	3	4	5	6	7	8	1	2	3	4	5	6	7	8	(1)
Kilitan telu	X	•	X	X	•	X	X	•	X	•	X	X	•	X	X	•	(X)
B.A.Ph.PET	X	•	X	X	•	•	X	•	X	X	•	•	X	•	X	X	(•)

FIGURE 7.2

of the interlocking patterns being played together. This ostinato continues in tandem with the synthesizer melody introduced at 0:54. The musical particulars are different, but the basic principles and procedures of generating interlocking parts that we explored earlier in connection with beleganjur and Kecak music are also present here.

The second part of the piece commences with a return to the single reyong pot texture of the opening at 1:26, followed by the entrances of synthesized drums (1:30), electric bass (1:33), and scratch turntable soloist (1:39) in quick succession. Beginning at 2:29, the gamelan instruments gradually reenter amidst this radically transformed musical enviroment in the same order as before, and playing essentially the same parts. The music builds progressively, both in instrumental layers and in intensity, through to the full ensemble climax near the end (3:55).

guided listening quick summary

"B.A.Ph.PET," by Michael Bakan (CD ex. #2-8)

PART I

0:00–0:13

- Begins with single reyong pot playing truncated, kilitan telu–derived rhythmic pattern.
- The other three reyong pots enter successively playing the same rhythm, together building a dissonant cluster of notes (chord).

0:14–0:53

- Gong ageng enters, followed by gangsa metallophones.
- Gangsas enter one by one and eventually generate an ascending-descending, six-note ostinato melody (0:35) based on the truncated kilitan telu rhythmic figure and interlocking parts.

0:54–1:25

- Synthesizer melody unfolds over steady, slow-moving core melody in lower-register metallophone gamelan instruments.
- Sequence of low gong strokes (supplemented by electric bass tones) combines elements of a Balinese-style gong cycle and the bass line of a Western-style chord progression.

PART II

1:26–1:41

- All instruments drop out except for single reyong pot (like at the beginning).
- Synthesized drums enter (1:30).
- Electric bass enters, establishing funk groove (1:33).
- Scratch turntable sneaks in and builds with a crescendo (1:39–1:41).

1:42–3:37

- Improvised scratch turntable solo—soloist: Charles Tremblay (*note:* new bass line begins at 2:16).
- Second, third, and fourth reyong pots reenter, one after another, beginning at 2:29.
- Gangsas also come back in sequentially (from 2:41), gradually splitting apart (after all starting their patterns on the *same* pitch this time around) to create the same six-note melodic ostinato as before beginning at 3:24.

3:38–end

- Return of synthesizer tune over gamelan core melody, low gongs, and bass, plus all other instruments; dense, multiple-layer texture.
- Climax of piece arrives at 3:55, followed by fade-out ending.

Summary

Though it covered a broad range of gamelan and gamelan-based music traditions—Central Javanese court gamelan, Balinese gamelan gong kebyar, Balinese Kecak, and intercultural fusion music—the principal focus of this chapter was the gamelan beleganjur. We began with a narrative about my own discovery of beleganjur music during my first trip to Bali in 1989. We then situated the gamelan beleganjur in its broader musical, social, and cultural contexts before focusing in on it more specifically. Following an introduction to the beleganjur instruments and their music via a Musical Guided Tour, we explored the ensemble's multiple roles and functions in traditional Hindu-Balinese cremation rituals (ngaben). From there, we moved on to the modern, contest style of kreasi beleganjur. We concluded with an experimental, cross-cultural piece combining elements of gamelan beleganjur, gamelan gong kebyar, and American hip-hop and funk musics.

A unifying theme of this entire journey was the principle of interlocking. A specific, ubiquitous set of interlocking rhythms, the kilitan telu, was tracked through virtually all of the music introduced. Sometimes left intact in its conventional form and at other times transformed through various types of manipulations, this enduring component of Balinese musical identity took on many different forms but was always found to be present in one guise or another. Moreover, the interlocking principle underlying the kilitan telu was shown to inform larger cultural practices and values that are central to Balinese life, such as the high priority placed on communal interdependence.

Whether across oceans, between cosmic realms, or between music instruments, the concept of interlocking permeates gamelan music and its culture on many levels. It is a key to understanding both the resilience and vitality of the Balinese musicultural tradition.

Key Terms

gamelan beleganjur
gamelan
Central Javanese court gamelan
Bahasa Indonesia
Unity in Diversity
Agama Tirta
Bali Aga
gamelan gong kebyar
paired tuning

gangsa
ombak
gong cycle
gilak
gong ageng
reyong
kilitan telu
Kecak
atma

banjar
malpal
kreasi beleganjur
gerak
kebyarization (in kreasi beleganjur)
classicization (in kreasi beleganjur)

Study Questions

- What is a gamelan?

- The best-known gamelan traditions of Indonesia are from what two islands?

- What kinds of instruments are used in the gamelan beleganjur? Is it usually played from a seated position or in processional style?

- What is the capital city of the Republic of Indonesia? What is the capital city of Bali?

- What are the best-known gamelan traditions of Java and Bali, respectively? (*Hint:* gamelan beleganjur is *not* a correct answer.)

- What were the *general* musicultural features of gamelan music outlined in the chapter?

- What is ombak? Paired tuning?

- How does the kilitan telu set of rhythmic patterns, as well as other sets of interlocking patterns that are pervasive in Balinese music, represent a musical manifestation of important *cultural* values in Balinese society? What other kinds of cultural (including religious) symbolism are present in gamelan music?

- In what ways does beleganjur music function as a "weapon" in the battles against evil spirits that occur during Hindu-Balinese cremation processions?

- In what year was the first beleganjur contest held? Where did it take place?

- What features of musical form and style distinguish kreasi beleganjur from traditional beleganjur (and what common features link the two)?

- What is gerak, and what is its importance in kreasi beleganjur performance?

- Who are three important kreasi beleganjur composers?

- What innovations did the composer Suandita introduce into kreasi beleganjur music?

- What famous 19th-century French composer first heard gamelan at the world's fair in Paris in 1889 and subsequently was influenced by the experience?

- How does the piece "B.A.Ph.PET" build upon standard musical conventions and instrumentation of Balinese gamelan music? In what ways does it depart from gamelan tradition?

Discussion Questions

- The history of the Balinese dance-drama Kecak provides an interesting example of the kind of complex relationships between tradition and modernity that define many world music traditions. Though it is promoted as "traditional Balinese," it is in fact a product of 20th-century intercultural innovation. Try to think of types of music with which you are familiar that are marketed as "traditional" and "authentic" despite being modern and contemporary in many if not most respects. Discuss these in class.

- In this chapter, "B.A.Ph.PET" is presented as a piece belonging to the tradition of Balinese gamelan. What do you think of this? Should music of this kind be played using gamelan instruments, or is that inappropriate? Is there any point at which musicians should be expected to draw the line in terms of how far they go in their efforts to fuse very different music traditions?

Applying What You Have Learned

- Listen once again to the Balinese gamelan gong kebyar piece "Jaya Semara" (**CD ex. #2-2**) and the Central Javanese court gamelan piece "Ketawang: Puspawarna" (**CD ex. #1-6**) and compare the two in a brief written report. Using the information and listening skills you have developed in connection with the chapter, try to connect your initial, subjective impressions of the similarities and differences between these pieces with a more technical, objective assessment. What are similar and different about the instrumentation? About the role and style of the drumming? The relationship between core melody and melodic elaboration? The gong cycles? On the basis of what you come up with, what can you say about what links and distinguishes these two related yet very different musical traditions on purely music sound–based levels?

- Look closely at the kilitan telu rhythmic patterns charted in Figure 7.1 (p. 98). Try to figure out how all three patterns are in fact the "same" rhythm placed at different points relative to the main beat. One of these rhythms is known as the "follower," another as the "anticipator." Can you tell which is which and explain why?

- A metaphor of battle is central to the cultural functions of beleganjur music on many levels. Thinking about what you have learned about the beleganjur tradition in this chapter, create a list of different ways in which this battle metaphor plays out in actual Balinese cultural practice, both in traditional ritual contexts and in modern beleganjur contests.

Resources for Further Study

Visit the Online Learning Center at **www.mhhe.com/bakan1** for learning aids, study help, and additional resources that supplement the content of this chapter.

raga, Ravi Shankar, and **intercultural** crossings in **Indian music**

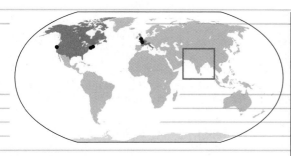

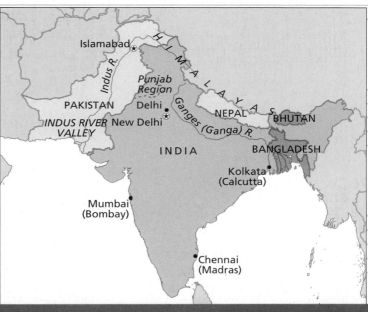

Related locations:

Canada	Boston
France	London
Italy	New York
United Kingdom	Paris
United States	San Rafael, California

Music, for the Indian, is the food of his soul. . . . Music, being the finest of arts, helps the soul to rise above differences. It unites souls, because even words are not necessary. Music stands beyond words.

Hafez Inayat Khan, *The Mysticism of Sound and Music*

India. For many, the very name conjures up images of the exotic, the spiritual, the mystical. Historically, much has been made of India's supposed difference from the West. Indeed, India often has been typecast as the star player of "the mysterious East" in the Western popular imagination, as the quintessential "exotic Other." This tendency to exoticize India, its people, and its culture has had consequences. Rather than try to truly understand and appreciate Indian cultural systems and practices on their own terms, Westerners have too often been content to simply cast them as "fascinating," "amazing," "deeply spiritual," "extraordinarily complex." There has been a tendency to leave the matter at that and go no further, or perhaps to spend a few minutes or hours learning about complex disciplines such as yoga or meditation

World events		Music events
Advanced urban civilization, Indus River Valley (now part of Pakistan)	**c. 3000 BCE**	
Possible time of emergence of distinct northern and southern Indian cultures; key elements of Hinduism (worship of many deities, caste system, Vedas) date from this period as well	**c. 1500 BCE**	
Buddhism and Jainism originate in India	**5th century BCE**	
Islam first introduced to India	**8th century CE**	
Southern expansion of Central Asian Islamic kingdoms into India	**c. 1000 CE**	
Islamic influence begins to exert a strong influence on Hindustani culture in north of India	**13th century**	Beginning of divergence of Hindustani and Karnatak musics into distinct traditions
Spice trade brings significant European presence and influence to India (including introduction of Christianity)	**15th–16th centuries**	
Sikh religion, combining elements of Hinduism and Islam, is founded	**16th century**	Karnatak and Hindustani music recognized as fully distinct (but historically related) traditions
Turko-Persian Mughals rule much of northern India	**1526–1857**	Mughal influence on Hindustani music is profound
		Sufism important factor in cross-pollination of Hindustani and Turko-Persian music under the Mughals
	1562–1607	Life of Tansen, legendary musician revered as the wellspring of Hindustani musical culture
Britain becomes the predominant colonial power in India	**19th century**	
India officially becomes a part of the British empire	**1858**	
	1920	Ravi Shankar born
	1930s	Ravi Shankar lives abroad and tours internationally with brother Uday Shankar's troupe; meets both future *guru* Allaudin Khan (Baba) and the violinist Yehudi Menuhin during his time in Paris
	1942	John McLaughlin born

and think that this is enough to get the gist of what Indian culture is all about. Such tendencies have resulted in the creation of many stereotypes concerning Indian culture and values, stereotypes that Indian people themselves, both in India and in the West, have tenaciously challenged over the course of a long and often troubled history of relations with Western powers.

The great classical music traditions of India have played a key role both in promoting these facile stereotypes of "Indian exoticism" and in challenging them. No single musician has been of more central

World events		Music events
Led by Mahatma Gandhi, India achieves national independence from Britain	1947	
	1950s	Establishment of important musical partnership between Ravi Shankar and Yehudi Menuhin
	1951	Trilok Gurtu born
	1952	Vishwa Mohan Bhatt born
	1961	Ravi Shankar collaborates with Bud Shank and other jazz musicians on *Improvisations*
		John Coltrane records "India"; acknowledges his admiration for Ravi Shankar in a published interview that same year
	1964–1965	Coltrane studies briefly with Shankar (dies in 1967 before having the opportunity to undertake more extensive studies with Shankar)
	1965	George Harrison of the Beatles plays a sitar solo on "Norwegian Wood"
	1966	Harrison studies sitar with Ravi Shankar; subsequent deepening of Indian influence on Beatles
	1967	Harrison's "Within You, Without You" released on Beatles' album *Sergeant Pepper's Lonely Hearts Club Band*
	1960s	Shankar becomes an unwitting international pop culture icon: enmeshed in "great sitar explosion," hippie counterculture
	1975	Pioneering Indian-jazz fusion group Shakti formed by John McLaughlin
	1976	Release of album *Shakti, with John McLaughlin,* featuring "Joy"
	1987–1992	Trilok Gurtu performs and records with Oregon, John McLaughlin Trio
	1988	Gurtu releases first album under his own name, *Usfret*
	1991	Gurtu releases *Living Magic*

importance, on both sides of the issue, than Ravi Shankar, the great sitarist and exemplar of the **Hindustani raga** tradition of northern India. Throughout his multidimensional career, as performer, composer, and teacher, Shankar has had a consistent mission: to demystify Indian music for an international public. He has aimed to help people all over the world to see, hear, and appreciate Indian classical music on its own terms, as a deeply tradition-bound yet inexhaustibly creative medium of expression, rather than as something merely exotic or mysterious.

Ravi Shankar (RUH-vee SHUN-kuhr)

Hindustani raga (Hin-dus-TAH-nee RAH-gah [or RAHG])

Ravi Shankar playing the sitar (center), accompanied by Alla Rakha on tabla (left) and a tambura player (right).

barhat (bar-hut)

gharana (gha-RAH-nah)

Vishwa Mohan Bhatt (VISH-wah MO-hahn Bhatt [like "but"])

Shakti (SHAK-tee)

Trilok Gurtu (TREE-lok GUR-too)

Yet ironically, through these very efforts, Shankar himself frequently has ended up being cast as the symbol *par excellence* of the kind of Indian exoticism he so abhors. Even more problematically, his international promotion of Indian music in some instances has inadvertently led to the music's misappropriation, especially during the 1960s, when the sounds of Indian raga came to be associated with hallucinogenic drug use in the American youth counterculture movement. Because of these kinds of paradoxes, which have characterized his career at least since the beginning of his famed association with the Beatles in the 1960s, Ravi Shankar might be viewed as a microcosm of the complexly paradoxical world of "world music" at large.

Ravi Shankar—his music, his life, his career, his range of influence—is the centerpoint around which this chapter revolves. The principal musical element explored is the venerable musical tradition with which Shankar has been mainly identified throughout his life, Hindustani raga. In particular, we will look at (and listen to) the way in which a raga unfolds in performance as a process of growth—musical, personal, social, and spiritual.

We will expand on this concept of growth to explore domains beyond the purely musical. In the terminology of Hindustani music, the Hindi word **barhat** refers to the note-by-note expansion of the melodic range of a raga during performance. This term derives from a verb meaning to increase, multiply, extend, advance, push ahead, progress, grow. Though barhat is a term that is specific to a particular dimension of melody in Indian music, this notion of growth, expansion, or progression is relevant to other matters we will explore as well. Beyond their note-by-note expansion, ragas grow during the course of performance in other ways, through changes in rhythm, tempo, dynamics, and instrumentation. Within the process of raga performance, too, musical forms emerge, and social relationships between musicians, and between musicians and listeners, deepen and take on new meaning. On a social structure level, the **gharana,** the "musical families" that have preserved, cultivated, and developed the different "schools" of traditional raga performance in India and beyond, often over the course of many generations, also are defined in large measure by the ways in which *they* grow, multiply, and advance the raga tradition. Finally, there is the growth, extension, and pushing ahead of Indian classical music that has occurred in connection with the fascinating intercultural history of musical encounter between India and the West for more than half a century. This history provides a revealing window through which to view key issues explored in this text: tradition, transformation, and intercultural processes in music.

From the vantage point of Ravi Shankar's musical and professional life and the wide web of influence he has spun (see Figure 8.1), this chapter explores concepts of growth on all of these interrelated levels. It does so most specifically through a survey of, first, the actual Hindustani raga tradition, represented here in recordings by Ravi Shankar and one of his protégés, Vishwa Mohan Bhatt; and, second, intercultural music-making grounded in the syncretism of Indian classical music and jazz, here represented by the musics of John Coltrane, John McLaughlin and Shakti, and Trilok Gurtu specifically.

■ ■ ■

Indian Music in Context

The vast Indian subcontinent is both geographically and ecologically diverse, with terrain and ecosystems ranging from tropical jungle to mountain forests. It is bounded by oceans to the east, south, and west, and by the Himalayas to the north. Mountain passes in the northwest served as

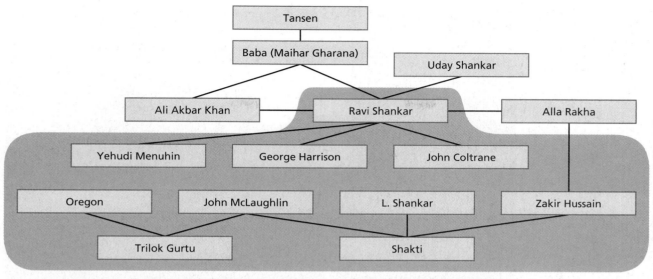

FIGURE 8.1

Ravi Shankar: Lineage and influences.

the main entryway to India for nearly all migrating groups and invaders prior to the first arrival of Europeans in the 15th century. Over millennia, innumerable groups moved into the subcontinent, resulting in a great deal of intermingling among cultures but also much retention of regional distinctiveness.

The Indian population is one of the most diverse in the world—physically, ethnically, linguistically, and culturally. More than 200 languages and 1,600 different dialects are spoken; Hindi and English are recognized as national languages. Although there is great diversity throughout the subcontinent, broad ethnic, linguistic, and cultural distinctions exist between northern and southern India; for example, the languages of northern India belong to a different linguistic group than the languages of southern India.

The origin of this distinction may have been a historical event that occurred about 1500 BCE. Prior to this time, as far back as 3000 BCE, an ancient urban civilization existed in northwestern India, in the Indus River Valley (now part of Pakistan). The high level of development of this civilization was similar to that of ancient Mesopotamia (present-day Iraq). About 1500 BCE, a wave of invaders pushed the indigenous inhabitants south; some experts believe this movement may be the original source of the distinction between northern and southern Indian cultures, though not everyone agrees. Some elements of the **Hindu religion,** the majority faith in India, date to this time. These include the worship of many deities and the caste system of rigid hierarchical levels in society.

Fundamental to the origin of Hinduism were the four **Vedas** (Rig Veda, Sama Veda, Yajur Veda, and Atharva Veda). These ancient, seminal Hindu scriptures in the Sanskrit language (in which the word for musician, *baqawathar,* also means "he who sings the praises of God" [Metting 2001:252]) are believed by Hindus to be of divine rather than human origin. Their texts have been carried through the ages to the present in the form of Vedic chants, which feature melodic recitation of the Veda texts. According to Ravi Shankar, Indian classical music evolved from Vedic chant through a centuries-long process of musical transformation (Metting 2001:252). There is no musicological evidence to support the claim of any direct connection between the two, however. The existence of direct historical links between Indian classical music and a body of Hindu devotional songs and hymns known as **bhajan** is more clear. **CD ex. #2-9** is an excerpt of a bhajan devoted to the Hindu deity Krishna sung with instrumental accompaniment (we will discuss Indian instruments later).

Veda(s) (VAY-dah)

bhajan (BUH-jin [rhymes with "bludgeon"])

Performance of a bhajan.

Sufi vocalist Shafqat Ali Khan.

In the 5th century BCE, two other religions, Buddhism and Jainism, originated in India. Islam was first introduced in the 8th century CE, and Islamic kingdoms extending into northern India were established by Turks, Persians, Mongols, and other peoples from Central Asia beginning in about 1000. The differences between Hinduism and Islam are profound: "Hinduism recognizes many gods, whereas Islam recognizes only one; Hinduism cherishes religious images, whereas Islam prohibits them; and Hinduism promotes vegetarianism [and venerates cows], but Islam, although it has dietary restrictions, allows the killing and eating of many animals, including cows" (Molloy 2002:180). Much of the political unrest within India in modern times—and between India and some of its neighbors—stems from centuries-old tensions among different religious groups, especially Hindus, Muslims, and Sikhs. (Sikhism is a religion founded in the 16th century that combines elements of Hinduism and Islam).

Nonetheless, Hindus and Muslims in India have in many instances forged synergistic bonds through culture, and music is an area where this has certainly occurred. Such synergy owes much to Sufism, a mystical form of Islam (see Chapter 12, pp. 271–72) that has exerted an especially strong influence on Indian culture, including music. Sufism, in contrast to other forms of Islam, shares with Hinduism the belief that music may serve as a pathway to communion with the divine. This has facilitated musical, religious, and cultural syncretism historically. Sufi musicians and musical traditions have had, and continue to have, a great impact on the broader musical culture of the Indian subcontinent. **CD ex. #2-10** offers an example of Sufi song originating from the Punjab region (which is divided between Pakistan and India). The vocalist is Shafqat Ali Khan.

The musical style heard in CD ex. #2-10, including the singing and the driving rhythms of the drumming, is related to that of a type of music called *qawwali*. Qawwali, also from Punjab, became a major world music phenomenon through the international popularity of the late singer Nusrat Fateh Ali Khan. In qawwali, the lead singer is joined by an accompanying ensemble of vocalists and instrumentalists. The powerful and emotional singing style of qawwali, combined with the compelling rhythms of the drumming and unison handclapping by members of the group, account for much of the genre's broad appeal internationally.

European influence on India began in the 15th and 16th centuries when the Portuguese, French, Dutch, and English, arriving by sea in pursuit of the spice trade, set up fortified posts and attempted to establish exclusive commercial agreements for their trading companies and countries. Some Europeans tried to import Christianity but met with limited success. In the 19th century, Britain became the predominant colonial power, officially adding India to its empire in 1858. Led by Mahatma Gandhi, India achieved national independence in 1947. With much violence and bloodshed, two primarily Muslim areas in the northwest and northeast became Pakistan and East Pakistan (now Bangladesh). Today, India is officially a secular state, but more than 80 percent of the population is Hindu.

The late qawwali superstar Nusrat Fateh Ali Khan.

Musical Diversity and Two Great Traditions

Just as there is great cultural, ethnic, and linguistic diversity in India, there is also great diversity in Indian music. Literally thousands of genres, subgenres, and styles of folk, religious, devotional, popular, and film music are found in India and throughout the subcontinent.

Filmi git, Indian film songs, are the dominant popular music of modern India. The Indian film industry, centered in Mumbai and known as "Bollywood," is the largest in the world (the "Bo" portion of "Bollywood" is derived from Mumbai's old name, Bombay). Filmi git's audience extends from hundreds of millions of people in India to millions more living in South Asian diasporic communities around the world.

A major component of contemporary music heard in Bollywood productions is **bhangra,** which originated in Punjab. Traditional bhangra features lively Punjabi folk songs and dances accompanied by powerful rhythms played on a large, barrel-shaped drum called a *dhol.* Rhythmic shouts ("hoi!") from the dancers add extra rhythmic punch. Since the 1980s, the folk base of bhangra has been merged with other Indian popular music styles and with everything from hip-hop to reggae. This modern bhangra style has become very popular among South Asian diasporic communities in North America, the United Kingdom, and elsewhere and has achieved a considerable following among non-Indian world music audiences. It is heard on many Indian film soundtracks and on commercial recordings by Indian, Pakistani, and South Asian diasporic musicians. Jasbir Jassi is a leading star of modern bhangra. **CD ex. #1-23** (discussed earlier, in Chapter 3, p. 39) is an excerpt from his catchy hit tune "Kudi Kudi" ("Girl, Girl"), replete with dhol drumming and electronic drum grooves, abundant use of synthesizers, and energetic, syncopated "hoi!" shouts.

In the domain of Indian classical music, there are two great traditions: the **Karnatak** (Carnatic) tradition of southern India and the Hindustani tradition of northern India.

filmi git
(FIL-mee GEET)

bhangra
(BHAHNG-rah)

Jasbir Jassi (Jahs-BEER JUH-see)

"Kudi Kudi" (like "curry curry," with "r" touching roof of mouth)

Karnatak
(Kar-NAH-tuck)

Scene from a Bollywood film.

A bhangra street performance. The musician on the right is playing a dhol drum.

The Hindustani tradition is the better known of the two outside of the Indian subcontinent, partly because of the global stature of Ravi Shankar and partly because of immigration patterns: historically, most Indian immigrants have come from northern India and have brought this music with them to countries such as the United Kingdom, the United States, and Canada.

The Karnatak and Hindustani traditions have been recognized since the 16th century as distinct music cultures with related but separate histories. Though they share many features, they also exhibit significant differences (Table 8.1). These may be attributed to a variety of factors, including the different political histories, languages, and local cultures of southern and northern India. One important factor of difference was the greater impact of Islamic cultures on the Hindustani north beginning in the 13th century. Especially influential on Hindustani music and culture were the Muslim, Turko-Persian Mughals, who ruled over much of northern India from 1526 to 1857. Much cross-pollination between the existing Hindustani music culture and the Turko-Persian music culture brought by the Mughals occurred during this period. (Sufi influence was pervasive under Mughal rule.) Though Islamic invasions did eventually reach and affect southern India, the impact was not nearly as great as in the north, and this is reflected musically.

As for similarities, both Hindustani and Karnatak music build from highly complex and elaborate melodic systems called **raga,** employ systems of rhythm and meter known as **tala** (literally, "time"), and are deeply steeped in the spiritual and cultural traditions of Hinduism. They both belong within larger frameworks of what is known as *sangita* in their respective cultures. Sangita is a term that is often translated as "music," but that also encompasses the music-related arts of dance and drama.

In both Karnatak and Hindustani cultures, singing is regarded as the highest form of musical expression. The sound of the human voice is believed to be the closest possible approximation of **Nada Brahma,** the "Sound of God," the divine source of all sound and music. Instrumental traditions in Hindustani and Karnatak music alike are closely connected to parallel vocal traditions. This is especially the case in Karnatak music, but in Hindustani music, too, the merit of instrumental performances is determined largely by how well they accord with an ideal of singing-based models. It is therefore somewhat paradoxical that instrumental music, rather than vocal music, has become iconic of Indian classical music outside of India. This, like so much else pertaining to the international image of Indian music, is largely attributable to the dominant international impact of Ravi Shankar. Whereas instrumentalists such as Shankar have long been the leading international celebrities and cultural ambassadors of Indian classical music (and the principal subjects of introductions to Indian music like this one, which tend to deal almost exclusively with instrumental music), in India itself it is vocalists who reign supreme; instrumentalists occupy considerably lower rungs on the ladder of musical status.

Standard in both Karnatak and Hindustani instrumental music are ensembles consisting of three instruments (trios). Each of the three instruments has a primary responsiblity of contributing one layer to the music's overall texture, which comprises *a single-line melody, a drone, and rhythmic accompaniment.* (Chords and harmony, as such, are not part of traditional Indian classical music textures.) One of the most common trio configurations in Karnatak music features the **vina,** a plucked chordophone, as the solo melodic instrument; the **tambura,** another plucked chordophone, as the principal drone-providing instrument; and the **mrdangam,** a double-headed drum, as the rhythmic accompaniment instrument. This trio of instruments is featured in **CD ex. #1-25,** which we listened to earlier in connection with Chapter 3 (see p. 40).

tala (TAH-lah [or TAHL])

vina (VEE-nah)

tambura (tum-BOO-rah)

mrdangam (mir-DUNG-ahm)

TABLE 8.1   Comparison of Karnatak and Hindustani music traditions.

Similarities

- Raga as basis of melody
- Tala as basis of rhythm/meter
- Part of larger sangita traditions (encompassing music, dance, drama)
- Singing highest form of musical expression
- Instrumental traditions closely connected to parallel vocal traditions
- Related histories (especially pre-16th century)
- Related types of instruments

Differences

- Recognized as distinct traditions since 16th century
- Hindustani: Greater influence from Islamic cultures (especially Mughal)
- Karnatak: Less influence from Islamic cultures
- Hindustani: More international exposure and recognition outside of India
- Karnatak: Status of singing more elevated relative to instrumental music
- Hindustani: Sitar, tambura (Hindustani), tabla instrumental trio common
- Karnatak: Vina, tambura (Karnatak), mrdangam instrumental trio common
- The specific ragas, talas, and music terminologies are different in the two traditions

Among the most common instrumental trio configurations in Hindustani music is that which includes the **sitar,** a plucked chordophone, as the lead melodic instrument; the Hindustani version of the tambura as the drone instrument; and the pair of drums known as **tabla** as the rhythmic accompaniment instrument (see the photo on p. 120). We will learn more about this ensemble shortly.

sitar (si-TAHR [rhymes with "guitar"])

tabla (TUB-lah [like "tub" in English])

Because this chapter focuses on the Hindustani tradition of Ravi Shankar, we can offer here only these few observations on the Karnatak tradition. For students who wish to learn more about this other vast and rich classical tradition of India, as well as about the myriad other musical genres of India and the subcontinent, further resources are listed at the Online Learning Center (www.mhhe.com/bakan1). For a comparison between the Karnatak and Hindustani music traditions, see Table 8.1.

Karnatak instrumental trio: mrdangam, vina, and tambura.

The Hindustani Raga of Northern India

We turn now to a journey through the world of North Indian music from a vantage point specifically linked to the life, career, and influence of Ravi Shankar. In this section, we explore the unique sounds, rhythms, and instruments of North Indian classical music. In the next section, we touch on Shankar's encounters and associations with Western musicians, including the Beatles, and we explore the music resulting from the integration of raga and jazz in the works of such artists as John Coltrane, John McLaughlin and the group Shakti, and Trilok Gurtu.

Ravi Shankar and the Maihar Gharana

As Indian music scholar Gerry Farrell has written, Ravi Shankar is the only Indian musician "to have become a household name in the West" (Farrell 2000:564). He was born Ravindra Shankar Chaudhuri into an upper-class, Hindu family of the priestly Brahmin caste in 1920 (see "Insights and Perspectives" box on the caste system). His father was a prominent educator, politician, and activist for Indian national independence.

Early on, young Ravi showed prodigious talent as both a dancer and musician. In the 1930s, while still in his teens, he joined an Indian music-and-dance troupe formed by his older brother, Uday, and with that group toured the great capitals of Europe as a sitar player and dancer. He spent extended periods of time in both London and Paris during this early part of his career. While in Paris, he befriended the famous, young English classical violinist Yehudi Menuhin. Years later (in the 1950s), Shankar and Menuhin would form an important intercultural musical partnership that helped bring Indian classical music to widespread international attention, a subject to which we will return.

It was also during his early years in Paris in the 1930s that Shankar met the great raga master Allaudin Khan, otherwise known as Baba (literally, "Father"). A few years later, Shankar would return to India to be initiated as a musical disciple (*sisya*) of Baba. Living with Baba for some eight years and forsaking virtually all in life except musical study under the strict watch of his extraordinarily demanding **guru** (mentor), Shankar was transformed from a precocious musical talent into an inspired and disciplined young master of the art of raga. In becoming a disciple of Baba, Shankar also became a member of the highly famed and influential "family" or "school" of raga study and performance known as the Maihar Gharana, of which Baba himself was the founder.

With the aid of Baba, Ravi Shankar came to be revered as one of the master sitar players, raga performers, and Indian music gurus of his generation. Through his collaborations with Yehudi Menuhin and other Western musical luminaries from the worlds of classical and jazz music, he also became a pathbreaking innovator of intercultural musical experimentation and India's princi-

Maihar (MA'EE-har [as in first syllable of "mighty"])

insights and perspectives

The Caste System in India

Like Hindus in Bali (Chapter 7, p. 100), Hindus in India have traditionally recognized a caste system. Caste divides society into social classes based on family birthright or occupational specialization. The Indian caste system is more highly structured than its Balinese counterpart, though practices and policies based on caste division are officially illegal in modern India. Efforts to eradicate the caste system in India have been largely inspired by concerns about the plight of members of the lowest caste, the Dalit, or "Untouchables," who have been subject to many abuses and severely limited opportunities historically. But while the caste system is legally banned, its vestiges survive in many areas of Indian social and cultural life.

The caste system is supported by ancient Hindu scriptures, which posited that there are different types of people who should perform different roles in society, and that stratification of this order is essential to the maintenance of a balanced social and spiritual order. There are five principal castes: Brahmin (priest), Kshatriya (warrior), Vaishya (merchant), Shudra (peasant), and Dalit (untouchable). The Brahmin caste, to which Ravi Shankar and his family belong, is the highest of the five. Members of this caste have traditionally been assigned responsibilities and afforded opportunities not available to members of the other castes.

The Gharana

The gharana is the principal social institution through which knowledge of raga is disseminated and legacies of raga performance are transmitted from musician to musician and generation to generation. Although the term *gharana* is sometimes translated as "musical family," the basic criterion of membership in a gharana is not typically blood or marital relations between its members (though such relations often do exist), but rather indoctrination into a particular lineage, or "school," of raga performance. According to raga scholar Stephen Slawek, what unifies the members of a gharana first and foremost is a shared "style or approach to performance practice that sets them apart from other ghārānas" (Slawek 1991:170).

Members of the gharana trace their heritage through their own guru back through the guru's guru and so on through the generations to the founder of the gharana. The gharana's founder, in turn, typically traces his lineage to the legendary 16th-century musician Tansen (1562–1607), who is revered as the wellspring of Hindustani musical culture. Tansen himself is believed to have received his extraordinary musical and spiritual gifts from divine powers.

Like the ragas they preserve and cultivate, gharanas develop through a process of growth. The founder is the seed from which the gharana as a whole blossoms and comes to fruition. Through the collective efforts and devotion of his sucessors, the gharana "musical organism" grows. Each line of succession across the generations, each individual member, becomes a branch or leaf on the gharana "tree"—all grounded in the same trunk and nourished by the same root.

pal musical ambassador to the world. But it was as a result of his relationship with a quiet English rock guitarist, George Harrison of the Beatles, that Shankar was catapulted rather tumultuously and incongruously into the role of global superstar celebrity. As such, he inspired revolutionary changes in rock and world musics, becoming an unwitting pop culture icon of 1960s "hippie" counterculture and ultimately emerging, in Harrison's words, as the "Godfather of World Music."

Beyond all this, Ravi Shankar is famous as a father in the more literal sense. He is perhaps best known among younger music enthusiasts today not for any of his own professional achievements, but as the father of two musician daughters: Anoushka Shankar, who is continuing his Maihar legacy as a sitarist; and singer-songwriter Norah Jones, who might be seen as extending her father's "other" legacy as a force of influence in the worlds of Western popular music and jazz.

Anoushka Shankar playing the sitar.

"An Introduction to Indian Music," by Ravi Shankar

For an introduction to the sound of the Hindustani raga and a primer on core features, terms, and concepts relating to Hindustani raga music, we now turn to a brief recorded lecture demonstration that Ravi Shankar created for the purpose of introducing the art of Hindustani raga to new listeners. We will treat this as the chapter's Musical Guided Tour. Shankar uses some terms that we have not yet discussed in detail, including raga, tala, **alap, tintal, theka,** and **sam,** but we will explain these terms shortly. For now, just listen to Shankar's explanations and experience the sound of Indian music. Try to hear the various features and characteristics of raga identified: the melodic forms of the raga "scale," the melodic ornaments and microtones,

alap (ah-LAHP)

tintal (TEEN-tahl)

theka (TAY-kah)

sam (like English "some")

Anoushka Shankar: Carrying on the Legacy

Anoushka Shankar is a highly accomplished professional musician and has been touted as the only classical sitarist in the world trained exclusively by Ravi Shankar. Her first solo CD, *Anoushka,* was a chart-topper in the world music area. Additional albums have followed (including the acclaimed *Rise,* released in 2005) and she has frequently appeared both live and on recordings performing together with her father (for example, on the album *Full Circle*). Like Ravi Shankar, Anoushka has charisma, talent, and eclectic musical tastes and interests. She has risen to prominence among the ranks of international Indian classical music artists.

the distinctive sound of the drone, the beat-counts of the talas. A transcript of Shankar's lecture demonstration is included in the Musical Guided Tour box at the bottom of this page.

The sitar-tambura-tabla trio: Instruments and texture

Now that we have had an opportunity to hear what the sitar, tambura, and tabla sound like and how they function together within an ensemble setting, we are ready to take a more detailed look at these fascinating instruments. Though the sitar-tambura-tabla combination is but one of many ensembles employed in Hindustani music, it has in a sense become emblematic of Indian music on an international scale. This has much to do with the influence of Ravi Shankar, whose introduction of Indian music to the West was largely achieved through his international performances and recordings within this ensemble context.

"An Introduction to Indian Music" (CD ex. # 2-11)

Ragas are precise melody forms. A raga is not a mere scale [♪]. Nor is it a mode [♪]. Each raga has its own ascending and descending movement [♪] and those subtle touches and usage of microtones, and stresses on particular notes, like this [♪]. With the tambura, the drone instrument, in the background [♪], the soloist does a free improvisation known as *alap,* after which he starts the theme based on a rhythmic framework known as *tala.* He can choose from many talas, such as *tintal,* a rhythmic cycle of sixteen beats [♪], or *jhaptal,* having ten beats [♪]. The tabla are the drums, which keeps [sic] this framework, just plays the *thekas,* or beats, in the beginning, as you heard just now. Then starts the gradual progression of playing first smaller patterns, then longer ones. In the beginning, the accompanying tabla gives, if I may say so, a reply to the lead instrument, such as the sitar. At times they may play together a long rhythmic pattern, and return with a climax to *sam,* or the "one" [i.e., beat one of the tala's metric cycle], which is the most important thing, like this [♪]. Although the role of the tabla is relatively free, it is the lead instrument which directs the whole progress of the improvisation.

The Western listener will appreciate and enjoy our music more if he listens with an open and relaxed mind, without expecting to hear harmony, counterpoint, or other elements prominent in Western music. Neither should our music be thought of as akin to jazz, despite the improvisation and exciting rhythms present in both kinds of music.

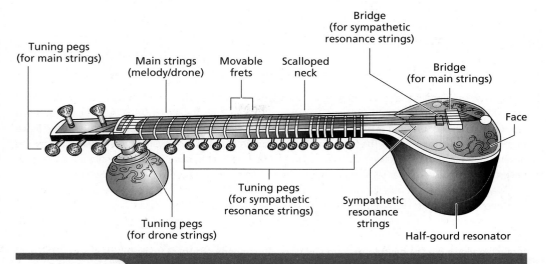

Tuning pegs
(for main strings)

Main strings
(melody/drone)

Movable
frets

Scalloped
neck

Bridge
(for sympathetic
resonance strings)

Bridge
(for main strings)

Face

Tuning pegs
(for sympathetic
resonance strings)

Sympathetic
resonance
strings

Tuning pegs
(for drone strings)

Half-gourd resonator

FIGURE 8.2

Sitar.

SITAR The sitar, the instrument Ravi Shankar plays, is a long-necked, plucked chordophone (Figure 8.2). Its resonating body (resonator) consists of a half gourd covered over by an artistically decorated wooden "face." The long wooden neck is hollowed out, or *scalloped,* in a way that allows the strings running across it to be pressed in and out with the fingers of the left hand. This "bending" of the strings facilitates the production of many different kinds of melodic ornamentation. Twenty arched metal frets are attached to the instrument's neck. Rather than being fixed in place as on a guitar, they are attached with nylon threads, making it possible to move them to different positions to achieve different pitches. This is an important feature, since Indian music involves a system of tuning that incorporates microtones, requiring very precise pitch intervals that could not be achieved with any single setup of frets as one finds on a guitar.

There are six or seven strings running across the main platform of the sitar's neck. Some of these are designated for melody while others supply drone tones. Additionally, there are 13 thinner strings called *sympathetic resonance strings* running underneath the frets. These special strings magnify certain high overtones emerging from the melody and drone strings. The combination of all three different kinds of strings—melody, drone, and sympathetic—combined with certain other unique design features, accounts for the unique timbre of the sitar. The instrument is held diagonally across the lap by a player seated cross-legged on the floor. As on a guitar, the right hand is used to pluck the strings and the left to finger the neck (see the photos on pp. 120 and 127).

TAMBURA Although the sitar is capable of supplying its own drone tones, another instrument, the tambura, is dedicated specifically to droning and serves no other function. The construction and shape of the tambura's body and neck are similar to those of the sitar. It has four or five strings, which are tuned to the most fundamental pitches from which the sitar melody builds during a performance (including the tonic, known as **vadi**). Thin threads underneath the strings pick up high overtones and

Hindustani tambura.

vadi (VAH-dee)

Though it is better known in the West than its counterparts, the sitar is just one of a large variety of melodic instruments used in Hindustani raga performance. These include the *sarod* (sa-ROAD), which is also a plucked chordophone. It has a shorter neck than the sitar, no frets, and a fingerboard on the neck made from metal rather than wood. The lower part of the instrument's body is covered with animal hide instead of wood. The most famous player of the sarod in the modern era has been Ali Akbar Khan, another principal proponent of the Maihar style. He is the son of Ravi Shankar's guru, Allaudin Khan (Baba).

Baba himself was a specialist on the sarod and also the violin, which was adopted as an Indian concert instrument long ago and is prized for the voice-like quality of its tone. Some Indian violinists hold the instrument in the conventional Western playing position, but most sit cross-legged and hold it in a downward-pointing position so that the scroll (the "head" where the tuning pegs are located) rests on the player's foot. This allows the left hand to slide up and down the fingerboard more freely, which makes it easier to produce the proper melodic ornaments. Other Hindustani melodic instruments include the bamboo flute *bansuri* (BAHN-sree) (also prized for its voice-like timbre), the oboe-like *shahnai,* and the bowed chordophone *sarangi* (SAH-rahng-ee).

Sarod, played by Ali Akbar Khan.

Violin, played by N. Rajam.

Bansuri, played by Benjamin Koen.

Shahnai, played by Bismillah Khan.

Sarangi, played by Ram Narayan.

Muslim Musicians in Hindustani Musical Society

Ravi Shankar has performed with many illustrious tabla players, but none greater than Alla Rakha (AL-lah RUH-khah). Their decades-long association represented one of the most significant musical partnerships of the 20th century. Rakha's legacy continues through his son, Zakir Hussain, possibly the greatest tabla master of his generation and a maverick intercultural music pioneer in his own right.

Ravi Shankar is a Hindu, whereas Alla Rakha was a Muslim. "Interfaith" musical partnerships such as this are, and long have been, common in the Hindustani musicultural world. Additionally, it is noteworthy that the percentage of Hindustani musicians who are Muslims is disproportionately large relative to the general population of northern India.

It may seem peculiar that the realm of Hindustani instrumental music, in which music is treated explicitly as a path toward spiritual enlightenment, is so heavily populated by followers of Islam, a religion that, in its familiar orthodox manifestations at least, views music as suspect where religious worship is concerned. As with other religions, though, Islam is highly diverse and takes many forms. The kind of Islam that developed in northern India (at least among denizens of the Hindustani music culture) shared with Hinduism a concept of music as a sacred, devotional art. Historically, this was partly the result of its absorption of Hindu influences, and, as was alluded to earlier, partly a product of the fact that Sufism was a major force in the spread of Islam to India.

contribute to the tambura's distinctive, multidimensional timbre. The tambura is held vertically in the player's lap and plucked continuously to produce a constant, underlying drone.

When one thinks of the word *drone,* a single, monotonous tone being sounded incessantly comes to mind. The drone of the tambura, however, is something else altogether. It swirls and whirls around the fundamental pitch, bringing out different tones and overtones to create a wavelike timbral effect.

TABLA Unlike its southern, Karnatak relative, the mrdangam, the tabla is not a single double-headed drum, but rather a pair of single-headed drums played by one player (Figure 8.3). The higher-pitched, right-hand drum, called the *dahina* (or *tabla*) has a tapering cylindrical shape and is made of thick wood. The lower-pitched, left-hand drum, the *bayan,* has a kettle-like shape and is usually made of metal. Both drums have goatskin heads. To each is affixed a thick

**dahina
(DAH-hee-nah)**

**bayan (BAH-yin
[rhymes with
"Ryan"])**

Black weight spots

Tuning
straps

Metal
body

Wood
body

Bayan   **Dahina**

FiGURE 8.3

Tabla drums.

and prominent black "weight spot" that largely accounts for the distinctive sound and large range of timbres produced. The heads are attached to the bodies of the two drums by laced leather straps. The intricate tabla tuning method involves adjusting the tension on the straps (and thus on the heads) to change the pitch. The dahina is tuned to produce a clear, ringing tone. The bayan, in contrast, has a deep, resonant tone. Its pitch can be bent up and down by pressing the heel of the hand into the drum head while playing with the fingers. The drums are played with the bare hands from a cross-legged, seated position (see the photos on pp. 120 and 145). The range of hand and finger strokes employed is nothing short of dazzling.

Raga defined

In "An Introduction to Indian Music" that we listened to earlier, Ravi Shankar explained that ragas were "precise melody forms." More specifically, each raga is *a complete and self-contained melodic system* that serves as the basis for all the melodic materials in any composition or performance created *in* that raga. There are many different Hindustani ragas (the index of the *Garland Encyclopedia of World Music* India volume lists 58 of them [Arnold 2000:1066]). Each has a distinctive set of features that includes the following five:

- *An identifying set of pitches,* more or less a "scale" (based on a sequence of tones known in Indian music as a *that* [pronounced like "tot"]), usually consisting of seven ascending pitches and seven descending pitches per octave. As was illustrated in the Shankar example, the ascending and descending versions of this "scale" may employ different sets of pitches and different twists and turns of the basic melodic contour. The pitches of a given raga "scale" are drawn from a tonal system consisting of at least 22 distinct pitches (microtones) per octave (see also Chapter 4, pp. 51–52).

- *A unique repertoire of melodic ornaments and melodic motives,* many of which incorporate microtonal inflections, that is, subtle melodic figures that employ "the notes between the notes" (pitches located *between* the raga's main pitches) in some systematic fashion.

- *A system of rules and procedures* for dealing with the various pitches, ornaments, and melodic motives of the raga in relation to one another; this system of rules functions like a musical road map that is internalized in the musician's mind after years of study and practice, and that guides the course of improvisation during a raga performance.

- *A repertoire of set (precomposed) compositions* that is unique to that particular raga. The same system of rules and procedures that guides improvisation in the raga is embedded within each of these set compositions as well. Set compositions may have been passed down in oral/aural tradition through many generations or may be of more recent vintage. They may be very short or very long. In the course of a performance, the musicians draw upon their knowledge of the raga's repertoire of set compositions, selecting specific ones to incorporate into the broader framework of their overall improvised performance.

- *A host of extramusical associations,* which may link a given raga to a particular time of day (e.g., a "morning raga," an "evening raga"); season of the year (e.g., a "summer raga," a "winter raga"); ceremonial event; or designated emotional state of mind, or *rasa* (e.g., joy, sadness, peacefulness).

Performing a raga demands strict adherence to the rules and procedures of that raga; you cannot switch between one raga and another in midstream. If Ravi Shankar chooses to play a particular raga in performance, every note, ornament, and set composition he plays must fit within the parameters of that raga. He cannot borrow and incorporate elements or set pieces from a different raga, and were he to do so, this would be a rather serious offense.

Tala: Meter and rhythm in raga performance

The rhythmic framework of a raga performance, and especially the metric cycle in which the music is grounded, is called the *tala.* Just as there are many different ragas, there are also many

Standard Features of a Tala Summarized

- Each tala has a specific number of beats (e.g., 16 beats for tintal, 10 beats for jhaptal); the number ranges from as few as 3 beats per cycle to more than 100 beats per cycle.
- The metric cycle of the tala has a specific pattern of relatively stronger and weaker beats.
- The basic, "skeletal" drumming pattern that defines the tala is called the *theka*.
- The first beat of each tala cycle—which simultaneously functions as the last beat of the preceding cycle—is called *sam*.

different talas. Like meters in Western music, each tala has a specific number of beats. Talas range in length from simple cycles of three or four beats to exceptionally complex ones of over a hundred beats. In his "Introduction to Indian Music," Shankar mentioned two popular talas, the 16-beat tala called *tintal* and the 10-beat tala called *jhaptal*. We will learn to mark out and "perform" the 16-beat tintal pattern later in the chapter.

As with Western meters, the various beats in a tala receive different degrees of emphasis relative to one another; that is, there are strong, medium, and weak beats (and often finer gradations, in addition). As we learned in Shankar's "An Introduction to Indian Music," the first beat of each cycle of a tala (which generally doubles as the *last* beat of the preceding cycle) is called *sam*.

The skeletal drum pattern that outlines the basic structure of the tala cycle is called the *theka*. This pattern is rarely heard unembellished in actual performance, except when the tabla first enters. After this, the drumming tends to become highly elaborate in its varied rhythmic exploits and improvisations, to the point that the skeletal theka is largely obscured (though it still continues to *function* implicitly as the rhythmic foundation for the piece). Raga is an art of adornment, elaboration, virtuosity, and improvisation, and this applies as much to the tabla player in the treatment of the tala as it does to the sitar player in the treatment of raga melody.

How a raga "grows"

The way a raga is developed in performance, explains Indian music scholar George Ruckert, is described in terms of its *barhat,* or growth. Various metaphors are used, from the growing of a seed to the act of making love (Ruckert and Widdess 2000:84). From the "seed" of the raga itself, a seed containing all of the directions, resources, and methods necessary to bring to fruition a rich and self-contained musical world, the musician grows his unique yet deeply tradition-bound rendering of "the raga," essentially creating it in the very moment of performance. The raga is internalized not as some tangible music entity like a "piece of music" in the Western sense, but as a *template for musical action in the musician's mind* that has been developed through many years of devoted study and practice. It is a generating source from which musical ideas and inspirations grow and flow, or, in Ruckert's words, "a map a musician follows in his or her creation of a musical performance: a catalog of melodic movements that the artist unfolds, details, and expands while following a traditional performance format that has been passed down orally from teacher to student," generation after generation (Ruckert and Widdess 2000:66). With a deep awareness of the unique features, rules, procedures, and philosophical and spiritual underpinnings that define the particular raga he is playing—for example, Raga Nat Bhairav—a master musician such as Ravi Shankar explores the musical, symbolic, and spiritual potential inherent in that raga. He adheres strictly to the raga's dictates while simultaneously pushing it to the limits of its potential, cultivating the achievement of a state of musical and spiritual transcendence for himself and his listeners.

jhaptal (JUP-tahl ["jhap" rhymes with "cup"])

Raga Nat Bhairav (RAH-gah nut BHAY-ruv)

The number of paths on which to travel in journeying through a raga's realm of possibilities is essentially limitless. No two performances of a given raga are ever identical, not even two different performances by the same musicians. On the other hand, every path the raga may lead to is carefully marked by the signposts of a standard formal plan that nurtures the growth process inherent in every raga performance. We turn to a discussion of this formal plan next, and after that to a participatory musical activity and a raga Guided Listening Experience.

Form in raga performance

According to Ruckert, the overall pattern in the various forms and styles of raga starts with slow and abstract movement and proceeds through a section of slow rhythm that grows more metrical as it accelerates to a presto [very fast-tempoed] conclusion (Ruckert and Widdess 2000:84). This process of gradually progressing from slow melodic motion in a free and unmetered rhythm at the beginning, to very fast melodic motion that is highly structured rhythmically and metrically by the end, is symbolic of the growth process that is a general characteristic of raga performance.

ALAP The "slow and abstract movement" portion of an instrumental raga performance is contained in its opening section, the alap. As we heard in Shankar's "Introduction to Indian Music," the alap is improvised by the melodic soloist (e.g., the sitar player) with only a drone accompaniment. It is an exploratory journey through the raga's melodic essence and range of possibility. There is no drumming, no meter, no set compositions. Woven into the alap are successive passages in which each of the principal tones of the raga is introduced and deeply explored. Each one is presented alone, "dressed up" in characteristic ornaments and microtonal nuances, and contributing to distinctive melodic figures and motives that may be developed more extensively later on in the performance. As the various individual pitches are introduced, the broader dimensions of the raga's overall musical organization begin to blossom. At the same time, the raga's designated mood-state, its rasa, starts to emerge and grows increasingly clear. Hearing an alap is like going to see a play and being introduced to all of the characters before the play proper begins, in a way that gives a deep sense of who these characters are and how they will operate and interact as the play unfolds.

Finally, the alap serves as an introduction not just to the raga but to the soloist playing it as well. Improvisational ability constitutes the true measure of a raga performer, and the alap is regarded as the quintessential test of improvisatory skill in a raga performance. It is in this improvised opening that the true mettle and skill of the soloist are assessed by the audience.

As the alap unfolds, the rhythm becomes more and more animated and the melodic range expands and grows as the soloist explores the raga in various octave registers. Then, at some point, a more-or-less regular rhythmic pulse is usually established, though still without a set meter or any drumming accompaniment. (This section of the alap may be referred to as the *jor.*) The arrival of this rhythmic pulse might be likened metaphorically to the first detectable heartbeat of a developing fetus. Following the establishment of the rhythmic pulse, the performance may end, or it may continue forward into a second main section, the **gat.**

gat (like English "gut")

GAT The arrival of a gat in an instrumental Hindustani raga performance is announced by the entry of the tabla drums. A regular pulse is firmly and unambiguously established at this point. After an introductory rhythmic flourish, the tabla immediately begins marking out in drum strokes the tala metric cycle that will serve as the rhythmic foundation throughout the rest of the performance.

With the commencement of the gat, a raga performance becomes a brilliant display of musical/social interaction. The sitar player may be the "soloist" and the tabla player the "accompanist," but these labels are frequently eclipsed by the sense of equal partnership that is achieved in their musical dialogue. As the gat unfolds, the tabla part moves fluidly between accompanying the solo instrument in some parts, engaging in dialogue with it in others, and playing complex rhythmic unison passages together with it in still others. The intensity and depth of interplay increase as the performance progresses and grows. As was mentioned earlier, the gat combines passages of improvisation with strategically placed set compositions, with all of this material emerging from

Two Kinds of Time

So far, our exploration of raga has focused specifically on how a raga "grows" during the course of a performance. This growth has been depicted as gradual and continuous, a progressive process of development across time. In addition to this kind of time, another kind of time—represented by the tala—is running concurrently. As the raga grows and progresses throughout the gat, it does so framed against the cyclic regularity of the tala. Thus, the progress of raga growth is "measured" against the constancy of tala time. Just as the growth of a tree is both measured and profoundly affected by the cyclic passage of time from day to day, season to season, year to year, so too is the melodic growth of the raga marked and in large measure determined in reference to the constant, cyclic time of tala.

the raga itself and presented in the established tala (the same raga may be combined with different talas in different performances). As the music moves forward through these various kinds of passages, two general patterns emerge: first, there is a gradual, progressive increase in tempo, which by the end of the performance may be extremely fast; second, the successive patterns, phrases, and set compositions become longer and more complex, with a single segment sometimes encompassing several tala cycles. Again, parallels to processes of growth are obvious. All of the different formal sections, intricate melodies, and complex rhythms combine to create a musical whole that is greater than the sum of its parts and that builds progressively to a climactic finish (see Figure 8.4). The ultimate goal is to take the raga to such heights through this process of growth that the music approaches the ideal of Nada Brahma, "the Sound of God," the divine source of all sound and all ragas. Thus, playing a raga is more than mere music making; it is a spiritual practice.

Keeping tal with Ravi Shankar

Were you to attend a live raga performance in India (or even outside of India), you might be surprised to see members of the audience quietly clapping, touching their fingers together, and moving their hands in the air in time to the music as the musicians play. This patterned method of marking musical time is called **keeping tal** (short for "keeping tala"). In this section, we will learn how to keep tal with selected passages of "An Introduction to Indian Music."

Slow, abstract → Fast, metered

Alap	Gat
• Progressive introduction of raga's tones, stylistic elements • Gradual expansion of melodic range; suggestion of rhythmic pulse toward end • Improvised	• Arrival of drumming and establishment of the tala announces gat • Progressive intensification through overall increase in tempo, complexity of cycles • Growth of musical interaction between performers • Alternation of composed and improvised sections • Performance builds to climactic finish

FIGURE 8.4

Form in raga performance.

CLAPS, WAVES, AND FINGER COUNTS Keeping tal is essentially just a more sophisticated version of what we in the West do when we tap our feet to the beat while listening to music. What makes keeping tal a bit more complex than your standard foot tap is that it not only marks the beats, but also provides *a visual system for differentiating their relative strengths and functions within the tala's metric cycle.* For example, in the 16-beat metric cycle called tintal (Figure 8.7), three different kinds of hand gestures are incorporated into the keeping tal pattern: claps, waves, and finger touches. Beats 1, 5, and 13 are each marked by a handclap. These are the *tali,* or "full," beats of the metric cycle of tintal. Beat one receives a bit of extra emphasis since it marks the all-important principal beat, sam. Beat nine, conversely, is marked by a silent wave (Figure 8.5), which is executed by turning your right hand over from back to front, so that you end up with the palm facing upward. This wave gesture signifies the *khali,* or "empty," beat of the tintal cycle. It arrives exactly halfway through the cycle and essentially represents the *opposite* of the very "full" sam beat, where all the different elements of the music come together (*sam* literally translates as "together"). As we saw in Chapter 2 (pp. 20–21), Hindu cosmology defines the universe largely in terms of balanced opposites, or binary oppositions (light-dark, sacred-profane, male-female, etc.), and this full/empty, clap/wave opposition symbolizes this concept in musical terms.

khali (KAH-lee)

All of the other beats in tintal are marked by finger touches (Figure 8.6), in which you touch your right thumb with the tips of your right ring, middle, and index fingers one after the other on successive beats (i.e., ring finger on beat 2, middle finger on beat 3, index finger on beat 4; likewise for beats 6, 7, and 8; 10, 11, and 12; and 14, 15, and 16, respectively). These are the subordinate beats of the cycle.

In Figure 8.7, the basic hand gesture pattern for keeping tal with tintal is marked out. The claps are marked by an "x," the wave by an "O," and the finger touches by dots. Uppercase "X" is used for beat one, or sam, as a reminder to give that beat extra emphasis.

LEARNING TO KEEP TAL As the first step of learning to keep tal, try to mark out the entire tintal pattern using the appropriate hand and finger gestures while keeping a steady tempo. Repeat the cycle two or three times directly, without pausing between cycles. Practice by "singing along" with the model of **Online Musical Illustration #23.**

Once you are able to mark out the cycle on your own, cue up "An Introduction to Indian Music" (**CD ex. #2-11**) to the tintal musical illustration located at 1:45–2:00. Keep tal along with Shankar's counting of the beats, making sure that your various claps, waves, and touches line up with the correct beats. You will notice that Shankar adds an accent to his verbal counts on each of the main clap and wave beats (1, 5, 9, and 13).

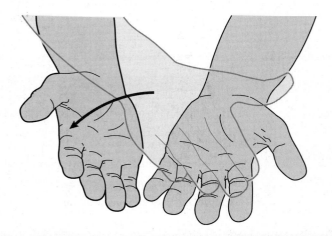

Khali (silent wave) hand gesture.

FIGURE 8.5

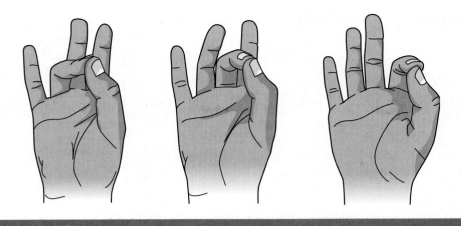

FIGURE 8.6

Finger touches.

1	2	3	4	5	6	7	8	9	10	11	12	13	14	15	16
X	•	•	•	x	•	•	•	O	•	•	•	x	•	•	•

FIGURE 8.7

Keeping tal pattern for tintal.

Finally, try to keep tal with the mini-performance located at 2:58–3:30. Here the tempo is extremely fast, to the point where you probably will not be able to mark all of the subordinate beats with finger counts. Therefore, just focus on executing the claps and waves of the main beats: 1, 5, 9, and 13. See if you can count the number of tala cycles in the performance overall.

In doing this final exercise, be prepared for the possibility that keeping track of the tala may get especially difficult toward the end, where the rhythm loops around and cuts across the main beats in mind-bending ways. The reason for this is that the musicians are finishing their performance with something called a **tihai,** in which the same rhythmic pattern is played three times in succession, with the final statement of the pattern landing precisely on sam to end the piece. The tihai functions as a rhythmic *cadence,* an ending pattern that provides a satisfying sense of closure at the end of a musical performance or section of a musical performance.

tihai (ti-HA-EE ["ti" as in "tiff," not "tea"])

insights and perspectives

The Rhythm of Tihai

Because the basic rhythmic pattern of the tihai is of an irregular length, it creates a highly syncopated effect and the sense of rhythmic "dislocation" seems to intensify with each repetition (sometimes varied repetition) of the pattern. This creates an exciting rhythmic tension that is satisfyingly resolved when everything comes back together emphatically on the performance's final, climactic note. The musicians must carefully calibrate the length of the tihai to ensure that it does indeed land back on sam as it is supposed to. Most raga performances end with a tihai, and many of the internal sections within a raga performance do as well. Listen once more to the final section of the **CD ex. #2-11** performance, from 3:23–3:30. Try to identify the tihai pattern as it recurs three times.

"Raga Nat Bhairav" (Hindustani Raga), Vishwa Mohan Bhatt

- ■ CD Track # **2-12**

- ■ Featured performer(s)/group: Vishwa Mohan Bhatt (modified guitar [a.k.a. Mohan vina]), Kumar Bose (tabla), Shefali Nag (tambura)

- ■ Format: Complete track

- ■ Source recording: *Raga-Ragini: Indian Quintet* (Chhanda Dhara SNCD 74188)

To hear how a raga comes to life in actual performance, we will listen to a recording of Raga Nat Bhairav. This is one of several ragas belonging to the family of Raga Bhairav (like the individual members of gharanas, individual ragas are grouped together as members of musical families). It is named for Bhairav, one of the many names used for Shiva, the Hindu deity of destruction. In particular, according to sarod master Ali Akbar Khan and his protégé George Ruckert, the raga relates to Shiva "in his powerful form as a naked ascetic with matted locks and body smeared with ashes." Raga Bhairav is a morning raga. It is to be played in a mood of devotion in the early morning hours. The "vibrations of the notes in Bhairav clear your whole mind—like taking a shower in the morning," and the rasa, or emotional state of mind, evoked in Bhairav is a complex one, covering "a great range of emotional qualities, from sadness to valor, peace to agitation" (Khan and Ruckert 1998:31).

Raga Nat Bhairav represents a relatively recent addition to the Raga Bhairav family. It was popularized by Ravi Shankar beginning in the mid-1940s, and he is known to have described it as one of his favorite ragas to perform. Though classified as a Bhairav raga, it is actually a composite of two different raga forms: Raga Bhairav and Raga Nat.

The performance of Raga Nat Bhairav included on **CD ex. #2-12** features not Ravi Shankar, but rather one of his best-known disciples, Vishwa Mohan Bhatt (b. 1952). Through his ties to Shankar, Bhatt's musical lineage also encompasses Shankar's guru, Allaudin Khan (Baba); the Maihar Gharana founded by Baba; and the 16th-century musician Tansen to whom Baba traced his own musical heritage.

Bhatt has achieved renown both as a consummate performer of traditional Hindustani raga and as a cross-cultural music innovator. A 1993 album he made with the American guitarist Ry Cooder, *A Meeting by the River,* received a Grammy Award as best world music album for that year.

Vishwa Mohan Bhatt began his musical studies on sitar and violin at a young age, but switched to the guitar when he was about 15. By inventively reworking and reconfiguring the Western guitar to make it more sitar-like, he transformed it into an instrument capable of achieving all of the microtonal nuances and inflections needed for raga performance. The modified, "Indianized" guitar Bhatt fashioned (which he himself dubbed the Mohan vina) featured 19 strings rather than the customary 6: 3 melody strings, 4 drone strings, and 12 sympathetic resonance strings (which bring out certain overtones of the melody and drone strings, as on a sitar).

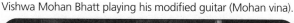

Vishwa Mohan Bhatt playing his modified guitar (Mohan vina).

Rather than using the fingers of his left hand to depress the strings as is done in normal guitar technique, Bhatt adapted a *slide guitar* technique, holding a special bar in his left palm and running it along the strings to change pitches. This slide technique is the key to his ability to produce the microtones and complex melodic ornaments of raga. It also accounts for his playing position. Bhatt sits cross-legged on the floor with his instru-

Slide guitar

Slide guitar techniques are used in many musical traditions around the world. Use of the slide guitar has been prominent in blues since the earliest days. The Hawaiian slide steel guitar tradition is another important example. During the 20th century, a great many musical styles, from American country-and-western to a variety of African popular genres, adopted (and adapted) the Hawaiian version of the slide steel guitar.

ment laid across his lap—strings facing the ceiling—rather than playing his guitar in the standard, Western manner. This position allows him maximum dexterity in using the slide technique. Largely by virtue of Bhatt's pioneering efforts, the guitar is now recognized in Hindustani musical culture as an appropriate instrument for raga performance.

Vishwa Mohan Bhatt's performance of Raga Nat Bhairav includes all the basic features of a full-scale raga performance, but they are condensed into a highly compressed form. Whereas most raga recordings run to at least 15 minutes in length—and live performances of ragas to an hour or more—this recording achieves its process of growth and development in just over seven minutes.

ALAP The opening three minutes of "Raga Nat Bhairav" are taken up by the improvised, nonmetric alap. The first sounds heard are the drone and a sequence of four guitar notes—in Western terms, D (high), D (low), A, and D (high, again)—which establish the basic tonality (the "key") and context for the performance overall. At 0:06, the melodic exploration of the raga proper commences. Beginning on the tonic pitch (D), or *vadi,* Bhatt winds his way downward through one complete octave, introducing all of the principal pitches of the raga as he goes. At 0:48, he switches direction and progresses back *up* the octave to the starting vadi pitch, arriving there at 1:06 (then lingering until 1:14) while introducing his listeners to the ascending form of the raga along the way.

Like most ragas, Raga Nat Bhairav has distinct descending and ascending melodic characteristics. However, unlike some other ragas, the fundamental sets of pitches in both the descending and ascending versions of the basic "scale" prove to be the same: in Western translation, D E F♯ G A B♭ C♯ (D). During Bhatt's brief introductory exposition of Raga Nat Bhairav's principal tones and related features (beginning–1:14), each of these pitches becomes the subject of a miniature musical portrait, replete with characteristic ornamentation, special melodic motives, and particular ways of moving to, from, and around the main tones. Each portrait tells a story, and, collectively, they tell the tale of this raga in slow, abstract, melodic motion: its identification with morning, its membership in the Raga Bhairav family, its distinctive rasa.

Bhatt's tale of Raga Nat Bhairav continues to develop in more elevated octave territory during the latter part of the alap, from 1:15–2:58. Moving higher and higher, pitch by pitch, he goes progressively deeper in his explorations of the distinctive characteristics of the different tones and of the raga as a whole. The energy gradually grows and the rhythm becomes more active. A dramatic run up and down the full raga scale from 2:46–2:58 brings with it a feeling of completion and finality.

Then, at 2:59, a sense of a steady rhythmic pulse emerges, carrying the alap through to its conclusion and into the gat 10 seconds later. From start to finish, the overall effect of this alap is one of building, of intensification, of a blossoming forth of the raga's latent potential.

GAT At 3:09, the entrance of the tabla announces the official commencement of the gat, which occupies the remainder of the performance. Tintal is established as the tala here. As the gat continues, the music grows through an integrated sequence of set compositions and improvisatory passages. Certain (though not necessarily all) of the set compositions are recognizable as such since they feature passages where the guitar and tabla play together in rhythmic unison. As you listen, try to locate these passages.

Picking up where the alap left off, there is a progressive sense of forward motion and building intensity in the gat. A gradual acceleration in the music's tempo is one key indicator of this, and at some points, especially near the end, the tempo gets ratcheted up quite suddenly and dramatically. By the final minute of the performance, the music is racing along at a formidable clip, providing a marked contrast to the relaxed tempos of earlier sections.

Musical growth in the gat is also evident on a more subtle level. As the music moves from one section of the gat to the next, there is a general tendency toward introducing musical patterns and segments of greater and greater length, of what you will recall Ravi Shankar referring to in "An Introduction to Indian Music" as "the gradual progression of playing first smaller patterns, then longer ones." The complexity of raga musical form and structure makes it difficult for the novice listener to actually identify the different levels of this progression, but even just listening with an awareness that this process *is happening* may enable you to begin hearing musical expansion of this order after a few careful listenings.

Finally, there is a sense of growth in the social relationship of Bhatt and the tabla player, Kumar Bose, which becomes manifest in the musical dialogue between the guitar and the drums over the course of the performance. As the piece develops, the dynamics of social/musical interaction shift several times. Sometimes, the guitar is clearly the solo voice, with the tabla acting very much in a supportive, accompanying role (e.g., 3:49–4:05). At other times, however, the tabla emerges from the background as more of an equal partner to the guitar. This relative equality may take the form of tight, unison passages where the guitar and tabla execute the same complex rhythms together, as though they were two manifestations of a single voice (6:50–7:10, the last 10 seconds of which comprise an exciting, concluding tihai). Alternatively, it may be expressed by the two instruments playing *different* lines simultaneously, like two people saying very different—yet related and complementary—things at the same time (3:19–3:29, 5:11–5:36). Finally, the usual soloist-accompanist relationship is occasionally reversed, with the tabla player becoming the "soloist" and the guitarist the accompanist. An example of this can be heard at 5:36–5:43. As the musical dialogue goes through these various twists and turns, the relationship between guitar and tabla becomes increasingly rich and multidimensional; in other words, it grows. Through their mutual exploration of Raga Nat Bhairav, Bhatt and Bose grow together, and in the process they nurture the growth of the raga itself.

guided listening quick summary

"Raga Nat Bhairav," Vishwa Mohan Bhatt (CD ex. #2-12)

ALAP

0:00–0:47

- Introduction of drone and fundamental tones D (vadi) and A at beginning.
- Opening section of alap melodic development from 0:06; descent through one octave of the raga "scale" starting on vadi (D), with exploration of each main pitch of the raga.

0:48–1:14

- Ascent back up through the octave to the starting vadi pitch, with exploration of the ascending form of the raga.

1:15–2:58

■ Further development of the alap improvisation with progression into higher octave registers. Telling of the raga's "story" continues as energy intensifies and rhythmic activity increases gradually. Dramatic run up and down the full raga scale (2:46–2:58) brings a feeling of completion, finality.

2:59–3:08

■ A sense of steady rhythmic pulse emerges, carrying alap to its conclusion and toward the gat.

GAT

3:09–end

■ Gat commences with the entrance of the tabla at 3:09.

■ Tabla outlines the metric cycle of tintal, which serves as the rhythmic foundation for the remainder of the performance.

■ Raga continues to grow throughout the gat as the music moves through a series of set compositions and improvisatory passages.

■ General progression from shorter to longer patterns and segments.

■ Various modes of guitar-tabla interaction and dialogue: guitar leads (e.g., 3:49–4:05), tight unison (e.g., 6:50–7:10), equal yet complementary interaction (e.g., 3:19–3:29, 5:11–5:36), tabla in foreground (e.g., 5:36–5:43).

■ Performance concludes with a climactic tihai (7:00–end).

Intercultural Crossings

During the mid- to late 1960s, when Vishwa Mohan Bhatt was cultivating his distinctive brand of guitar raga, two other highly influential guitarists, George Harrison and John McLaughlin, were making their own unique contributions to the establishment of an important East-West/sitar-guitar nexus that would have a profound impact on the future course of world music history. Not surprisingly, the journeys of both Harrison and McLaughlin were well marked by the teachings and influences of Ravi Shankar, and this was likewise the case for a host of other important pioneers of Indian-Western musical fusion who preceded and followed them, including Yehudi Menuhin, John Coltrane, and Trilok Gurtu.

This part of the chapter surveys dimensions of the intercultural musical landscape that has emerged out of interactions of Indian, Western, and other musicultural traditions since the 1950s. The primary emphasis is on relationships that formed between Indian musicians and jazz musicians during this period and the music and innovations that resulted from their collaborations. As we will see, Ravi Shankar is the common thread that binds together the vastly diverse musical artists and styles covered.

It should be be noted that the discussion here represents a very narrow view of the globalization of Indian music in the modern era, and even of Ravi Shankar's own contributions to that phenomenon. A more comprehensive treatment would cover non-Indian music conservatories devoted exclusively to the teaching of Indian classical music (e.g., the Ali Akbar College of Music in San Rafael, California), Indian music performance courses taught at North American and European universities, the stories of scores of non-Indian musicians who have traveled to India to study and become highly accomplished performers of Indian music, and international cultural organizations that sponsor Indian classical music performances. It would also cover the vibrant and vital Indian music scenes that have come into being in large, urban communities of the South Asian diaspora in North America, the United Kingdom, and other places in recent decades. In short, what is presented here represents a small but significant thread in a much larger fabric of Indian music's global outreach.

Early inroads: *West Meets East, Improvisations,* and the music of John Coltrane

By the mid-1960s, Ravi Shankar was a well-known figure in Western classical music circles. The fact that the violin virtuoso Yehudi Menuhin had undertaken serious studies of Indian classical music performance with him beginning in the 1950s had garnered much public attention. And when Menuhin began to concertize and record with Shankar, the art of Hindustani raga, the fruitful potential of cross-cultural musical collaboration, and indeed the singular artistry of Ravi Shankar himself, all came to the prominent attention of Western classical music audiences in one fell swoop. Especially influential was the seminal Shankar-Menuhin recording *West Meets East* (1967), the first of a series of popular recordings featuring the two master musicians performing Indian music together.

Several years before the release of *West Meets East,* Shankar had already extended his musical range into cross-cultural, experimental musical projects with prominent American jazz musicians. Though Shankar resisted facile comparisons between raga and jazz, rightly insisting that they were entirely distinct and historically unrelated musical traditions, he did acknowledge that certain similarities between the two—especially their shared emphases on virtuosity and improvised solos—furnished a fertile meeting ground for musical cross-pollination. In addition, as Gerry Farrell has noted in his book *Indian Music and the West,* Shankar found that jazz musicians "were quick to grasp the rhythmic subtleties of Indian music, in ways that [Western] pop and classical musicians were not" (Farrell 1997:189). A pioneering Indian-jazz fusion album entitled *Improvisations,* featuring Shankar with flutist Bud Shank and several other well-known jazz musicians, was released in 1961 to critical acclaim.

It was also in the year 1961 that a quintet led by the late, great jazz saxophonist John Coltrane recorded a Coltrane composition entitled "India" (**CD ex. #2-13**). This piece featured an Indian-inspired style of jazz music with extended passages of improvisation over drone-based harmonies (chords played overtop an underlying, tonic drone). Over the next few years, this style became the foundation of Coltrane's highly innovative approach to jazz, an approach in which Indian music became, according to Farrell, "a musical reference point in artistic consciousness that also worked freely with influences from Africa and the Middle East, as well as blues, folk, and Western classical music" (Farrell 1997:191).

Prior to recording "India" in 1961, John Coltrane had been devoting much of his time and energy to listening to and closely studying Indian music recordings, especially recordings by Ravi

John Coltrane playing the soprano saxophone.

Shankar. Referring to Shankar in a 1961 interview, he commented that "I collect the records he's made, and his music moves me. I'm certain that if I recorded with him I'd increase my possibilities tenfold . . ." (Porter 1998:209).

Alas, Coltrane never did record with Shankar, though he did study with him briefly in the winter of 1964–1965. Recalling their lessons together many years later, Shankar said of Coltrane that he was "amazed by our different system of improvisation, . . . by the complexity of our talas, and more than anything by how we can create such peace, tranquillity and spirituality in our music" (Shankar 1999:178).

When Coltrane and his wife Alice gave birth to a son in 1965, they named him Ravi. Coltrane had planned to undertake more serious studies with Shankar, but the plans never materialized due to his failing health. He succumbed to cancer in 1967 while still a young man.

Ravi Shankar, the Beatles, and the "great sitar explosion"

At about the same time that John Coltrane was engaged in his brief course of study with Ravi Shankar, George Harrison, a musician from a very different world, was embarking upon his own Indian music odyssey. Legend has it that Harrison first happened upon a sitar during filming of the Beatles movie *Help!* The instrument was being used as a prop on one of the stage sets. Harrison picked it up, plucked a few notes, and, liking the sound, began teaching himself to play it.

In 1965, a sitar solo played by Harrison was included in "Norwegian Wood," one of the songs on the Beatles album *Rubber Soul*. In that context, the instrument was merely a novel timbre, adding "exotic color" to the song's acoustic, otherwise folk-rock texture. The cultural impact was significant, however. Suddenly, the sound of the sitar was being heard by Beatles fans the world over, reaching and intriguing millions of listeners with no prior exposure to it.

The following year, 1966, Harrison began his formal sitar studies with Ravi Shankar. At first, Shankar was not quite sure what to make of this quiet, humble, English rock guitarist. It was one thing for Shankar to work with a musician like Yehudi Menuhin, who, like himself, was a leading proponent of a long-established classical music tradition. Working with jazz musicians also had proved a reasonably comfortable stretch, due to the fact that jazz shared with raga certain key musical features and priorities. Rock music, however, was completely alien territory for Shankar. Coming from a culture where the worlds of classical and popular music existed in quite strictly separated realms, he was surprised to encounter a pop musician with aspirations of learning a classical music tradition, and a tradition of a foreign music culture at that. But Harrison seemed serious and motivated, so Shankar agreed to teach him. At the time, he had no idea that this simple decision to take on a new student would contribute to a musical and cultural revolution and to a radical transformation of his own life and career.

By the time the Beatles album *Revolver* came out in 1966, the Indian musical imprint was quite pronounced on certain tracks. And by the time Harrison's own song, "Within You, Without You," was released on *Sergeant Pepper's Lonely Hearts Club Band* in 1967, this imprint was firmly embedded in the music's sound, instrumentation, structure, and lyrics. In addition to employing sitar, tabla, and several other traditional Indian instruments, "Within You, Without You" incorporated raga-like features in its melodies and forms and tala-inspired meters and rhythms. Moreover, Harrison's introspective lyrics reflected his growing interest in Hindu philosophy and spiritual practices.

Once the sitar had made its debut on a Beatles record, it was not long before it became a favored "exotic" sound in the live and recorded performances of other leading rock, pop, and folk bands, the Byrds, the Yardbirds, and the Rolling Stones among them. Soon, other signature elements of Indian music—drones, "Indian" vocal effects (slides, slurs, etc.), raga-like scales, mystical or quasi-religious lyrics—also were finding their way into many rock and pop tunes.

"Sitar rock" had become part and parcel of the rock and pop music landscape, but core principles of Hindustani raga were not exactly being adopted into rock contexts as part of this trend. As Farrell explains, pop musicians of this period had neither the technical ability nor the aesthetic perspectives to work within, say, a genuine raga framework, with the result that "the elements of Indian music that appeared in pop were fragmented, their musical meaning changed through being out of context" (Farrell 1997:182). In the case of the post-1966 Beatles, the appropriation of Indian musical elements was generally approached with seriousness of purpose and a sense of adventurous creativity. In most other instances, however, rock sitar solos and other Indian music markers served as little more than trendy tokens of exoticism (which is not to say that they necessarily lacked effectiveness *within* their own new musical contexts).

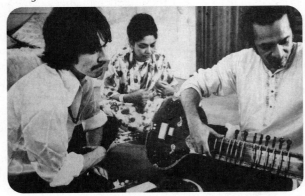

George Harrison with Ravi Shankar.

Ravi Shankar found the often trite and gratuitous uses to which the sitar and other Indian instruments and musical devices were put by these rock and pop bands of the "great sitar explosion" of the 1960s and 1970s disturbing, though he tried to keep an open mind and maintain an attitude of acceptance. As he wrote in his 1968 autobiography:

> Though the sitar is being exploited now by pop groups on both sides of the Atlantic and will no doubt continue to be used this way for some time, those who sincerely love Indian music as *classical* music should not be upset by this. One instrument can serve many styles of music. (Shankar 1968:93)

Even more troubling for him than the musical effects of the great sitar explosion, though, were its cultural side effects. The sitar and all things Indian came to be equated with drug-induced, altered states of consciousness. Indian music became the vehicle of choice for "tripping out" and "getting high" on LSD and other drugs. For Shankar, this was abhorrent, though once again he ultimately found cause for optimism in the growth and progress of more enlightened attitudes and behaviors:

> I have been facing a surprising problem with some of my concert audiences since about 1965, especially in England. I found many young people who were "high"; sitting in the front rows of the hall, they were altogether in another world. Often, too, they sat there in front of me carrying on indecently with their girl friends or boy friends [sic], and many of them even lit cigarettes (if that, in fact, was what they were) whenever they pleased. Their conduct disgusted me, for too many people in this dazed stupor send out bad vibrations that are extremely upsetting.
> . . . but I am now happy to note that things have changed to such an extent that this problem has practically disappeared. My audiences everywhere are so much more clean and respectful, serious and receptive—especially in the United States. (Shankar 1968:96)

A new level: John McLaughlin and Shakti

In the late 1960s, a period that witnessed the untimely death of John Coltrane, the great sitar explosion, and the gradual disintegration of the Beatles, the career of a brilliant young British jazz guitarist, John McLaughlin (b. 1942), was just beginning to take off. Moving to New York in 1969, McLaughlin was hired by jazz trumpet great Miles Davis, who had already helped to launch the careers of many other top jazz musicians, including Coltrane.

McLaughlin brought to his work with Davis an extremely eclectic musical background. As a child, his first love was Western classical music—Beethoven, Schubert, Brahms. But before he had reached his teens, he had come to love many other kinds of music as well: Mississippi Delta blues, Spanish flamenco, jazz, rock. As he developed into a gifted guitarist and composer, all of these early influences came to shape his unique, hybrid style. So too did his early passion for Indian classical music, though the full impact of that particular tradition would not come to the fore until after his tenure with Davis.

By the early 1970s, McLaughlin had left Davis to pursue other projects. In 1971, he formed **Mahavishnu (MAH-hah-VISH-noo)** an influential jazz-rock fusion band called the Mahavishnu Orchestra. ("Mahavishnu" means "divine compassion, power, and justice" in Sanskrit.) In addition to its jazz and rock elements, the Mahavishnu Orchestra's music showed strong Indian music influences, such as complex, tala-like metric cycles and raga-inspired scales, melodies, and musical forms. During his Mahavishnu period, McLaughlin took music lessons with Ravi Shankar, studied yoga, and became a disciple of the Hindu spiritual teacher Sri Chimnoy, ultimately converting to Hinduism himself. With single-minded devotion, he penetrated deeply into the ways of Indian culture both musically and spiritually. Jazz writer John Ephland has characterized the course of McLaughlin's experiences as "the eventual immersion of one person into another culture, allowing himself to be transformed in the process" (Ephland 1991[1976]:4).

Shakti.

In 1975, McLaughlin's ever-deepening Indian immersion process led him to form a new group called Shakti (meaning "creative intelligence, beauty, and power" in Sanskrit). Indian instrumental sounds and musical features had become quite common in jazz, rock, jazz-rock fusion, and other Western music genres by this time, but Shakti took the idea of Indian-jazz fusion to a new level. Other than McLaughlin himself, all of the players were Indian classical musicians by training. Though Ravi Shankar was not actually a member of Shakti, his presence was strongly felt. The group's violinist, L. Shankar, was his nephew, and the young tabla player, the aforementioned Zakir Hussain, was the son of Shankar's own long-time musical partner, the tabla player Alla Rakha.

The other two members, R. Raghavan and T.H. Vinayakaram, were master percussionists of the southern, Karnatak tradition. Thus, from an Indian perspective, Shakti was actually a fusion group *within* a fusion group, fusing Indian and Western forms to be sure, but also Hindustani and Karnatak traditions.

For his work with Shakti, John McLaughlin developed a special kind of acoustic guitar modified with sitar-like features (scalloped fingerboard, extra strings) that made it possible for him to closely approximate the kinds of microtonal inflections and timbral nuances required of the group's heavily Indian-rooted fusion style. This unique instrument, similar in purpose to Vishwa Mohan Bhatt's modified guitar (Mohan vina) but quite different in design, provided McLaughlin with a distinctive sound that was ideally suited to Shakti's musical style.

guided listening experience

"Joy," Shakti

- CD Track # **2-14**
- Featured performer(s)/group: Shakti, with John McLaughlin (guitar), L. Shankar (violin), Zakir Hussain (tabla), R. Raghavan and T.H. Vinayakaram (mrdangam/South Indian percussion)
- Format: Excerpt
- Source recording: *Shakti, with John McLaughlin* (Columbia/Legacy CD 46868)

The trademark virtuosity of Shakti is well displayed in a piece entitled "Joy," which was included on the band's debut 1976 recording, *Shakti, with John McLaughlin*. "Joy" is not a raga, but it draws upon raga elements, combining them with jazz-derived forms and structures to create an exciting synthesis.

The opening melody of the piece, played mainly in rapid unison rhythms by McLaughlin (guitar) and L. Shankar (violin) to fiery drumming and drone accompaniment, builds from a raga-type scale that closely resembles those used in the Bhairav family of ragas. The melody consists of a series of contrasting melodic sections, most of which are played once and then repeated (sometimes more than once, and sometimes with variations). In its entirety, this melody is almost a full two minutes long (0:00–1:53). It ends with a return to the first melodic section of the piece, which we will call the A section, at 1:39–1:53.

The tala-like metric cycle of the first two melodic sections of "Joy" (i.e., A and B) is very interesting. Each of these sections has a total length of 16 beats, as in tintal. However, some of the individual melodic phrases within each cycle are lengthened or shortened by a *fraction* of a beat, creating a rhythm that feels highly assymetrical, despite the fact that the metric cycle overall is a symmetrical 16 beats. (This *fractional tala* type of metric structure is common in some neo-traditional schools of raga performance as well.) The metric structure of the opening may be charted out as follows:

I. **A** section—cycle length 16 beats (0:00–0:06):

- 1st phrase: 4½ beats
- 2nd phrase: 3½ beats
- Repeat of 1st phrase: 4½ beats
- Repeat of 2nd phrase: 3½ beats

II. **A** section repeated—cycle length 16 beats (0:06–0:12)

III. **B** section—cycle length 16 beats (0:13–0:19):

- 1st phrase: 3½ beats
- 2nd phrase: 4 beats
- 3rd phrase: 4 beats
- 4th phrase: 4½ beats

IV. **B** section repeated—cycle length 16 beats (0:20–0:26)

Following this opening part, the piece moves on to several other episodes of compelling melodic development. At 0:40, the violin takes over as the main melodic instrument, breaking away from the unison texture of violin and guitar that predominates elsewhere. Excellent examples of characteristic, raga-like melodic ornamentation are featured in this passage. A long section of growing intensity and excitement marked by almost perpetual rhythmic motion in the unison violin/guitar parts begins at 1:03. The music progressively builds up tension that is finally resolved with the earlier mentioned partial return of the opening melody at 1:39.

Next comes a tabla solo by Zakir Hussain (1:54–2:05), which in turn leads into an improvised guitar solo by McLaughlin that continues as the excerpt fades out (2:06–end).

guided listening quick summary

"Joy," Shakti (CD ex. #2-14)

0:00–1:53

- **A** section of melody, played twice, 0:00–0:12: "assymetrical" rhythm of melody juxtaposed to symmetrical, 16-beat metric cycle underpinning.

- **B** section of melody, played twice, 0:13–0:26: similar to **A,** but with different rhythmic manipulations of melodic phrases.

Trilok Gurtu: Global fusion artist extraordinaire

The innovative spirits of Ravi Shankar, John Coltrane, *and* John McLaughlin and Shakti all live on in the music of an artist who today stands at the vanguard of Indian music-jazz fusion, Trilok Gurtu. Gurtu was born into a musical family in Bombay (now Mumbai) in 1951. His mother, Shobha Gurtu, was a famous classical Indian vocalist; his grandfather was a concert sitarist and musicologist; and his brothers Narendra and Ravi were, like himself, percussionists. He played tabla from age five, studying with some of India's finest tabla masters.

With his talent and pedigree, Gurtu could have successfully pursued a career as a classical tabla player in India, but his diverse musical interests compelled him to seek a less conventional path. Growing up in cosmopolitan Bombay, the young Trilok was exposed to music of all kinds: jazz, soul, rock and roll. He was as taken with the musical creations of John Coltrane, James Brown, Jimi Hendrix, and The Supremes as he was with Ravi Shankar and Ali Akbar Khan. He also got involved with the world of Indian film music as a studio musician and toured and recorded with bhangra bands.

In 1976, following several years of touring with Indian pop bands and some time living in Italy, Gurtu moved to New York. There he played drumset and percussion with well-known jazz artists like Charlie Mariano and Don Cherry, as well as the Brazilian percussionist Nana Vasconcelos. He applied for admission to the prestigious Berklee College of Music in Boston, a premiere training ground for jazz musicians, but was turned down.

Trilok Gurtu.

While the rejection was a bitter pill to swallow, it turned out to be a blessing in disguise. Following the Berklee snub—and likely inspired by it—Gurtu dedicated himself to developing his own, unique sound. Rather than play tabla *or* drumset, he invented a whole new kind of intercultural percussion "floor kit." To play, he would kneel on the floor, a pair of tabla directly in front of him, surrounded by a massive array of drums, cymbals, gongs, cowbells, woodblocks, metal chains, and automobile brake drums, as well as his signature bucket of water, in which he would immerse various sound-producing objects to change their pitches and timbres. From this strange playing position, engulfed by this even stranger mishmash of a setup, Gurtu would produce tapestries of sound blending rhythms from jazz, rock, North Indian, South Indian, African, Brazilian, Indonesian, Chinese, and Japanese musics, the likes of which had never been conceived of—let alone heard—before.

Gurtu's unique approach soon began to attract attention in many different musical quarters. He performed with fellow Indian percussionist Zakir Hussain and with the Norwegian jazz saxophonist Jan Garbarek. In 1987, he joined the innovative jazz-world music fusion group Oregon. Two of Oregon's founding members, guitarist Ralph Towner and percussionist Collin Walcott, had been students of Ravi Shankar before forming the group. When Walcott died tragically in an automobile accident in 1984, the three other members of Oregon determined that he was irreplaceable and that if the group were to continue, they would do so without a percussionist. But when they discovered Gurtu, they changed their minds. Gurtu toured and recorded with Oregon between 1987 and 1991.

For roughly the same period, Gurtu also enjoyed a productive musical association with John McLaughlin. Following Shakti's groundbreaking work of the 1970s and 1980s, the group disbanded for a number of years. (A new incarnation, Remember Shakti, was formed in 1997.) During the Shakti hiatus, John McLaughlin remained very much in the forefront of cutting-edge music, producing one excellent project after another. One of these was the John McLaughlin Trio, in which Trilok Gurtu was the percussionist. The trio toured internationally and produced two albums (*Live at the Royal Festival Hall* [1990] and *Que Alegria* [1992]) between 1988 and 1992.

While jumping between tours and sessions with Oregon and the John McLaughlin Trio, Gurtu also found time to form his own world fusion bands and to produce excellent albums under his own name, such as *Usfret* (1988) and *Living Magic* (1991). These albums, plus a series of subsequent ones taking us up to the present, highlighted his talents not only as a percussionist but as a composer and bandleader as well.

guided listening experience

"Living Magic," Trilok Gurtu

- CD Track # **2-15**
- Featured performer(s)/group: Trilok Gurtu group, wth Trilok Gurtu (percussion "floor kit"), Daniel Goyone (piano/synthesizer), Shanthi Rao (vina), Nicolas Fiszman (electric bass)
- Format: Excerpt
- Source recording: *Living Magic,* by Trilok Gurtu (CMP CD 50)

For his 1991 album *Living Magic,* Trilok Gurtu assembled an all-star international cast of musicians hailing from Asia, Africa, South America, Europe, and North America to help bring his creative vision to life. Merging Indian musical elements with jazz and enhancing this core foundation with instruments, rhythms, and performance styles derived from many other musicultural traditions—as well as with high-tech musical electronics and sophisticated compositional techniques drawn from contemporary Western art music—Gurtu and his collaborators created a masterpiece of syncretic, global music fusion.

The title track, "Living Magic," was co-composed by Gurtu and the band's keyboardist, Daniel Goyone. It can be listened to on many levels. Rhythmically, its complexity is formidable. Mutations of different conventional tala cycles and Western meters yield unusual metric cycles of 7 beats, 10½ beats, and even 13¾ beats. Melodically, too, the music is very complicated. It combines Western tonal features and raga-like Indian melodic formations with atonal melodies, the latter generated by a sophisticated compositional procedure called *dodecaphony,* or 12-tone serialism, which was first developed in the early 20th century by the Viennese-born composer Arnold Schoenberg.

Analysis of such rhythmic, metric, and melodic complexities is well beyond our scope here, but one feature of "Living Magic" that is quite easy to hear is the raga-like process of growth that unfolds as the piece progresses. In what follows, that growth process is tracked through the first three-plus minutes of the piece. Note the use of quotation marks around the "Alap" and "Gat" section headings. These are used since there are sections of "Living Magic" that are alap-*like* and gat-*like,* but there is neither an alap nor a gat proper in the piece.

"ALAP" In essence, "Living Magic" develops and grows much like a standard raga performance does. It begins with an improvisatory, alap-like introduction of slow and abstract movement in free, unmetered rhythm. The melodic instrument heard is the South Indian vina, played here by Shanthi Rao. Rao begins the performance much as Bhatt did his in "Raga Nat Bhairav," outlining the fundamental pitches—in this case F (the vadi) and C—before proceeding with the improvised, free rhythm melodic development.

What is strikingly different here are the treatment and timbres of the melodic instrument and the underlying drone. Rather than emanating from specific drone strings on the vina or a dedicated drone instrument such as a tambura, this drone is produced and progressively thickened and transformed with the aid of electronic sound-processing devices. Reverberation, echo, and other electronic effects are used to pick up, extend, and timbrally reconfigure certain key vina notes played by Rao, converting them into a stack of densely layered, electro-acoustic drone tones while the vina melody evolves and grows in volume and timbral complexity. This drone-growing and timbral manipulation process begins at about 0:13, and, for the next minute or so, more and more tones are layered one on top of the other as the music crescendos. By 1:09, the electronic drone texture has become so dense and timbrally unique that it barely even sounds like a drone in the conventional Indian music sense anymore. Through its growth and transformation, it has morphed into a nebulous wash of ambient, electro-acoustic sound. Meanwhile, the vina has become a very different-sounding instrument overall.

At this same point in the piece (1:09), a faint, low-pitched rumble sneaks into the thick timbral stew as if from out of nowhere. Within about three or four seconds, the rumble has increased in volume and rhythmic focus, revealing its source to be an electric bass played at a steady tempo. By about 1:31, the bass line is revealed as an ascending and descending ostinato pattern that outlines a complex metric cycle. Increasingly animated drumming and brief flourishes of piano improvisation embellish the texture.

"GAT" Although a clear sense of meter has been set by 1:31, it is not until 2:11 that a decidedly gat-like formal section begins. At this point, the lead melodic part is taken up by a synthesizer (played by Daniel Goyone). The melody develops over the firm anchor of Gurtu's precisely metric (sometimes polymetric) drumming, and over a new bass line ostinato that outlines another complex, tala-like metric cycle.

The excerpt on your CD fades out beginning about one-and-a-half minutes into the "gat" section of "Living Magic." On the complete, original recording, the piece continues for an additional three minutes. Over this span, it progresses through a series of precomposed and improvisational passages, growing in overall intensity through to the end. Though the musical style is deeply indebted to jazz, this does not negate the fact that the formal design and progression of the piece *overall* are highly consistent with the standard alap-gat model of growth in raga performance, a principal focus of this chapter.

We can conclude, then, that while "Living Magic" is clearly not an example of raga performance, it offers a creative, intercultural manifestation of the same basic process of musical growth. With works such as this one, artists like Trilok Gurtu are extending and expanding the creative range of the art of raga, putting their own unique stamp on the identity of the "global gharana" that has emerged in the wake of Ravi Shankar's profound influences on the development of modern world music culture.

guided listening quick summary

"Living Magic," Trilok Gurtu (CD ex. # 2-15)

"ALAP" SECTION

0:00–1:08

- Introduction of fundamental pitches on the vina (F [vadi] and C) commences the performance; alap-like development follows.

- Electro-acoustic, multitone drone derived from electronically processed vina tones begins to emerge and grow (0:13).

- Progressive growth occurs as "alap" develops, underscored by thickening, intensification, and timbral transformation of the drone and the sound of the vina overall.

TRANSITIONAL SECTION (BRIDGING "ALAP" AND "GAT" SECTIONS)

1:09–2:10

- Bass line in a highly complex, tala-like metric cycle gradually emerges and takes on a distinct shape (1:09–1:30).

- Continued growth in dynamics and intensity as tala-like metric cycle becomes firmly established in the bass part (by 1:31); piano flourishes and drumming fill out the texture.

"GAT" SECTION

2:11–end

- Arrival of synthesizer melody, more clearly metric bass and drum accompaniment, and a new tala-like metric cycle mark the commencement of the gat-like section of the piece. Excerpt fades out as performance continues.

Summary

This chapter explored the global musical legacy of Ravi Shankar, tracing that legacy from its Maihar Gharana roots, through Shankar's own work and that of his disciples such as Vishwa Mohan Bhatt, and finally to the West, where the impact has been great in many musical domains, from classical to rock. Of the many possible roads that could have been traced relative to a subject as complex as "Indian music" and a career as multifaceted as Shankar's, the ones emphasized here were those leading to (and from) the Hindustani raga tradition itself and to what might be termed raga-jazz fusion.

Processes of growth, musical and otherwise, were the chapter's major musicultural theme. We explored how raga performances themselves and other musical performances informed by raga tradition exhibit processes of musical growth in related ways. We also saw how social institutions such as gharanas, the "families" or networks of musicians that cultivate raga performance traditions, grow and evolve. The idea of gharana—of an expansive and ever-evolving network of musicians emerging from a central, pioneering figure—was applied to the global web of musical influences and phenomena spun by Ravi Shankar. In this regard, special attention was devoted to a number of musicians—John Coltrane, John McLaughlin and his Shakti collaborators, Trilok Gurtu—who have syncretized elements of Indian music and jazz to create innovative and unique forms of musical expression.

The great classical tradition of Hindustani raga is very much alive today, in India and around the world, in the carrying on of the tradition itself and in its myriad transformations. Ravi Shankar has been a central figure in the tradition and transformation of raga, and in the process he has contributed as much as any individual to the shaping of world music on a global scale.

Key Terms

Hindustani raga	tala	tintal
barhat	Nada Brahma	theka
gharana	vina	sam
Hindu religion	tambura	vadi
Vedas	mrdangam	gat
bhajan	sitar	keeping tal
bhangra	tabla	tihai
Karnatak	guru	
raga	alap	

Study Questions

- What are some of the basic features of Hinduism?

- What are the two great classical traditions of Indian music? How are they related, and how are they different?

- Which tradition do the sitar and tabla belong to? The vina and mrdangam?

- Identify three melodic instruments of Hindustani music other than the sitar.

- What is a gharana? What gharana was Ravi Shankar raised in and who was his guru?

- Who were the important exponents of Hindustani raga tradition discussed in this chapter? Who were the important exponents of Indian-Western music fusion?

- What kind of instrument does Vishwa Mohan Bhatt play?

- What are some of the defining features of Raga Nat Bhairav? Who first popularized this raga? Who performed it on the recording we explored in this chapter?

- Beyond their specific musical outcomes, why were Ravi Shankar's relationships with Yehudi Menuhin and George Harrison so significant historically?

- What are the names of Ravi Shankar's two famous musician daughters? Which one plays the sitar?

- What kinds of Indian (and Pakistani) traditional musics other than the Hindustani and Karnatak classical traditions were discussed in this chapter? Describe each.

- What were the five principal features of a raga outlined in the chapter?

- What kinds of metaphors are used to describe the barhat, or growth, of a raga?

- What are the main formal sections of a Hindustani raga (i.e., when it is performed)?

- What are the different hand gestures used in keeping tal, and which appears where in the 16-beat metric cycle of tintal?

- What were some of the landmark collaborations and recordings in the history of Indian music-jazz fusion?

Discussion Questions

- Do you think it is more appropriate to classify Vishwa Mohan Bhatt's "Indianized" guitar (Mohan vina) as principally a Western instrument or an Indian instrument? What kinds of criteria might you use to decide?

- What *general* principles relating to processes of musical tradition and transformation are exemplified by the discussion and musical examples of this chapter? Do all of the musical examples explored seem appropriate choices for exploring "the Indian music tradition"? Do any of the examples fall outside of the boundaries of that tradition, in your opinion?

Applying What You Have Learned

- Since the time of the Beatles, the sounds of sitars and other traditional Indian instruments (either the actual instruments or digitally sampled versions) have become commonplace in much Western popular music. Recordings of groups and artists ranging from the Rolling Stones to Ricky Martin feature an "Indian" element. Beginning with keyword searches on the Internet (e.g., search "Rolling Stones AND sitar" or "Ricky Martin AND sitar"), try to locate several examples of such music and create a list. If possible, listen to the examples you find and describe what Indian music elements you hear and how they function in the music.

- As a paragon of Indian classical music and the "Godfather of World Music," Ravi Shankar has influenced countless musicians around the world on many levels. The artists discussed in this chapter represent just a small (but important) sampling of what might be described as Shankar's "global gharana." Do an Internet search of "Ravi Shankar" and use this search to locate musicians who have collaborated with him, who acknowledge his influence, or who otherwise are identified in connection with him. Create an annotated list summarizing your findings.

Resources for Further Study

Visit the Online Learning Center at **www.mhhe.com/bakan1** for learning aids, study help, and additional resources that supplement the content of this chapter.

chapter nine

tradition and transformation in **Irish** traditional **music**

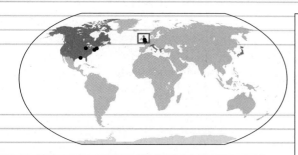

Related locations:

Canada	Appalachian Mountains,
Greece	United States
Italy	Brittany, western France
Japan	Newfoundland, Canada
United Kingdom	Nova Scotia, Canada
United States	Southwest Louisiana
	(Cajun region)

Boston
Chicago
Liverpool, England
London
New York

Think of Ireland and any of a host of thoughts and media images may come to mind. Rolling green pastures stretching to the sea, a lone shepherd off in the distance herding his sheep, the roar of the surf crashing on a secluded rocky shore. The poetry of William Butler Yeats, the novels of James Joyce, the urban squalor of a gritty industrial town on a gray and rainy day. Four-leaf clovers and leprechauns. Newsreel chronicles of the carnage and suffering of a bitter civil war fueled by religious divisions. Old friends gathering over a pint of stout at the neighborhood pub to tell stories to one another and laugh together.

And music, always music. Music in the home, at the pub, on the street corner, in the concert hall. Music in the Irish homeland and across the seas to

World events		Music events
Beginnings of Celtic culture in Ireland ●	**4th century** BCE	
Beginning of Irish potato famine ●	**1840s**	
Mass starvation and emigrations (to U.S., ● Canada, elsewhere), initiating Irish diaspora		
	1919	● Seamus Ennis born
Political division of Ireland (Republic of ● Ireland, Northern Ireland)	**1920**	
Irish Free State ●	**1921–1949**	● Decline in Irish traditional music (especially after 1930) despite efforts to preserve, promote, and nationalize it
First president, Eamon DeValera ●		
Economic devastation of Irish inner cities ●		● Seamus Ennis emerges as a central figure in preservation, performance, and dissemination of Irish music
	1926	● Radio Éireann established
	1931	● Sean Ó'Riada born
	1930s–1940s	● Irish traditional music thrives and develops in Irish diaspora communities (U.S. and elsewhere)
Republic of Ireland becomes fully ● independent nation	**1949**	
Massive urbanization, shift from ● agricultural to manufacturing-based economy (and industrialization of agriculture)	**1950s**	
Economic upturn for Ireland ●	**1960s**	● First decade of Irish music revival
		● Shift toward neo-traditional musical styles, ensemble rather than solo performance
		● Growing cross-pollination between Irish and Irish diaspora musicians on both sides of the Atlantic

wherever Irish people and people of Irish descent live or have left their mark: in Boston and New York, Liverpool and London, Nova Scotia and Newfoundland, the Cajun belt of Louisiana, the Appalachian mountains of the eastern United States. Irish music is a core emblem of Irish identity in Ireland and beyond, and its influence permeates musical traditions and transformations around the globe. It is there in everything from American country music, to the rock styles of U2 and The Pogues , to the adventurously international Irish-world music fusion approaches of contemporary groups like the Afro Celts and Eileen Ivers and Immigrant Soul.

The core of Irish music itself, and of myriad musical styles that claim Irish music as their root, is what is known as **Irish traditional music.** Common to all of the diverse types and styles of music that fall within the Irish traditional rubric—traditional, neo-traditional, and post-traditional—is a basis in rural, Irish folk music tradition. This tradition can only be traced back a couple of centuries with any authority, though its roots are widely presumed to date back much farther.

World events		Music events
	1960	● Sean Ó'Riada forms the group Ceoltóirí Cualann, ushering in a transformation of Irish traditional music
	1963	● Founding of the iconic Irish music group The Chieftains
	1965	● Irish-American fiddler Eileen Ivers born (Bronx, New York)
	1970s	● Second generation of Irish music revival
		● Planxty, Clannad, the Bothy Band, and De Danaan fuse Irish music with rock, jazz, other styles
	1971	● Sean Ó'Riada dies
	1980s	● Altan and other new groups established, preserving traditional styles while continuing to push Irish traditional music in new directions as well
	1982	● Seamus Ennis dies
	1990s–present	● *Riverdance* becomes an international sensation (fiddler Eileen Ivers featured)
		● Eileen Ivers, Afro Celts, and other contemporary musicians and groups create highly innovative styles rooted in Irish traditional music
		● Emergence of a truly international pan-Irish musical culture
	1990	● Altan releases *The Red Crow*
	1999	● Ivers releases *Crossing the Bridge*, featuring "Gravelwalk"

In this chapter, we trace a path through Irish traditional music covering traditional, neo-traditional, and post-traditional musical styles. We will explore this progression through the medium of Irish dance tunes. The resilience of the Irish dance tune tradition and the malleability of dance tunes themselves make this an ideal topic for exploring tradition and transformation in Irish music, and also for exploring issues of tradition-alism and modernity in Irish culture and society more broadly. Additionally, the Irish dance tune medium offers a revealing vantage point from which to view Irish music as a **pan-Irish** cultural phenomenon. Today, notions of what constitutes Irish identity and Irishness are perhaps defined as much by developments occur-ring outside of Ireland as by developments occurring within Ireland itself: Irish culture has become transna-tional in the form of pan-Irish culture. Music, and dance music especially, is a prominent part of pan-Irish culture, and this is another topic we will explore.

▪ ▪ ▪

A Preliminary Listening Experience

A good place to start our Irish music journey is with a listening-based comparison of three different performances of a characteristic melodic figure that occurs in many Irish traditional dance tunes. These performances may be heard back-to-back in **Online Musical Illustration #24** at the Online Learning Center (www.mhhe.com/bakan1); each is about 15-20 seconds long. The first one is a solo Irish fiddle version with no accompanying instruments. The second is in a different style and features an ensemble of acoustic instruments. The third is a heavily rock-influenced rendition. In the terms of this chapter, these three very different performances may be said to represent, in order, a traditional, a neo-traditional, and a post-traditional approach to the same type of melodic material.

Listen to all three of the performances now, one after the other. Make note of any similarities or differences you hear. On the basis of this exercise alone, what can you now say about style and identity in "Irish traditional music"?

Irish Music in Context

The story of Irish music told in this chapter unfolds against a backdrop of Irish national history and the modern history of the Irish people, both in Ireland and internationally. We therefore begin with the following overview, which provides a general background for understanding the different styles and examples of music addressed later in the chapter in cultural context.

Since 1920, the island of Ireland has been divided politically between the Republic of Ireland (Ireland) and Northern Ireland. The Republic of Ireland is an independent nation with its capital in Dublin. Northern Ireland, with its capital in Belfast, is a province of the United Kingdom (U.K.), which also includes England, Scotland, Wales, Cornwall, and the Isle of Man.

A group of Irish musicians performing in County Donegal, Ireland.

Northern Ireland covers Ireland's northeastern portion, accounting for about 15 percent of the island's landmass. It is an area whose people have suffered through a long history of often-violent struggle between the Irish Protestant majority of the province (accounting for about two-thirds of the population) and its Irish Catholic minority (about one-third of the population). Persecution of Catholics, terrorism, conflicts between the Republic of Ireland and Britain (U.K.) over political control of the region, and failed British attempts to subdue the province through the imposition of martial law and other hard-nosed policies have been major factors accounting for Northern Ireland's troubled history. The 1970s and 1980s brought especially hard times, and though the situation is now improved (as of this writing), the provisional state of relative peace is tenuous and there remains much volatility.

In contrast to Northern Ireland, the Republic of Ireland, whose musical traditions are the main focus of this chapter, is host to a predominantly Catholic population. Approximately 93 percent of the nation's 3.6 million people identify themselves as Catholics. English and Irish (i.e., **Irish Gaelic**) are the two official languages, though English is dominant in 95 percent of the country, with Irish Gaelic mainly spoken in concentrated areas known as the Gaeltacht (see map on p. 153). The Republic of Ireland covers approximately 85 percent of the total landmass of Ireland, including the entire southern and central regions of the island as well as the northwestern-most area, County Donegal, one of the Republic's 26 counties. Each county is known for its distinctive cultural traditions and character. Regional musical styles are key to the cultural identities of the different counties, much as the distinctive sound of Irish traditional music is a signature of Irish culture generally. The names of counties such as Donegal, Galway, Sligo, Limerick, Kerry, and Clare are well known to lovers of Irish traditional music through the musical styles and great musicians associated with them, both in Ireland itself and around the world.

Donegal (Dun-ee-GAHL)

The Republic of Ireland achieved full independence in 1949. Prior to that, from 1921–1949, it was known as the Irish Free State and was a quasi-autonomous, self-governing dominion within the British Commonwealth. The founding of the Irish Free State came in the wake of many hundreds of years of struggle by Irish Catholics against British (Protestant) rule, domination, and repression. Pivotal to this history was the infamous **Irish potato famine,** which began in the 1840s. The famine and subsequent evictions led to the deaths of 1.5 million Irish people and massive (often fatal) attempts at emigration, resulting in the rapid reduction of the population from 8 million to 3.5 million. The Irish blamed the British for not doing enough to assist them during the famine, and this galvanized an Irish nationalist movement marked by violent resistance to British control of Ireland and calls for Irish self-rule. This movement would ultimately lead to the founding of the Irish Free State (later the Republic of Ireland) and the partition of Ireland into the Republic and the province of Northern Ireland.

Irish-American women and men all dressed up for an evening of social dancing, New York City, 1905.

It was the famine, too, that provided the main impetus for what would come to be known as the **Irish diaspora.** Millions of Irish people left Ireland for other lands during this and subsequent periods. A great many settled in major American cities such as Boston and New York, establishing large Irish immigrant communities and making major contributions to the sustenance and transformation of Irish cultural traditions, including music.

The founding of the Irish Free State in 1921 marked a new chapter in the development of Irish nationalism. Eamon DeValera, the American-born first president of the country, envisioned an Ireland based almost entirely on a village economy. His well-intentioned policies led to the economic devastation of Ireland's inner cities, as described in books like Frank McCourt's *Angela's Ashes.* Under the Irish

Free State, government-sponsored initiatives were established to preserve Irish traditional culture, including rural oral/aural traditions of poetry, song, and instrumental music. The forces of modernization and urbanization were seen as major threats to the survival of these traditions. A national radio station, **Radio Éireann,** was established in 1926. Irish traditional music became a powerful symbol of Irish national identity and a tool of Irish nationalism, and nationwide radio broadcasts of performances featuring musicians from different counties all over the island played a very important role. The preservation, collection, and dissemination of Irish traditional music became priorities of Irish cultural nationalism. Yet despite such efforts and initiatives, Irish traditional music held a relatively marginal status in Ireland during this period. It was seen as important, but was not widely popular among the general public.

The post-1949 era ushered in a period of massive urbanization, reliance on manufacturing rather than agriculture as the main basis of the economy, and large-scale industrialization of agriculture itself in the newly independent Republic of Ireland. These changes led to both increased prosperity and fears of culture loss. Both factors contributed to the **Irish music revival** of the 1960s, a phenomenon that would have profound implications on the future course of Irish music, both in Ireland and abroad. Growing interaction and cross-pollination between performers of Irish music in Ireland and in the United States, Canada, England, and other lands, from Italy to Japan, yielded many new musical innovations and musicultural developments, some of which had a major impact on music "back home" in Ireland. The internationalization of the phenomenon of the Irish music **session** (*seisiún*), an informal gathering where musicians join together to play Irish tunes amidst socializing, was perhaps the most significant of these. This, together with developments such as innovative fusions of Irish traditional music with rock, jazz, and other international musical styles, led to the consolidation of a transnational musical culture rooted in Irish traditional music by the end of the 20th century, that is, to a pan-Irish musical culture.

The Irish harp, national symbol of Ireland.

An Introduction to Irish Traditional Music

In terms of international popularity, Irish traditional music has the distinction of being "Europe's most commercially successful traditional music" (O'Connor 1999:170). The designation "Irish traditional music" is applied very broadly to an array of different types of music, from centuries-old folk tunes of rural Irish counties to more contemporary styles that may build from Irish musical stock while incorporating influences from outside the tradition. Historical documentation of Irish traditional music accounts for just the last two to three centuries of its development, but historians and Irish musicians alike believe that its roots are in antiquity.

The core identity of Irish traditional music, today as in the past, is to be found in a musical repertoire that was already well established prior to the 20th century. This repertoire consists of five main categories of music:

■ The revered **sean nós,** or "old way," songs, which are sung in Irish Gaelic.

■ Slow instrumental melodies called *airs,* which are often performed in free rhythm.

- Songs sung in English.
- The musical tradition of the Irish harp (the harp is the national symbol of Ireland).
- Instrumental dance tunes and medleys

Sean nós singing is regarded by Irish music connoiseurs as representing the heart of Irish traditional music. It involves a style of singing that features elaborate and subtle forms of melodic ornamentation, distinctive rhythmic phrasing, and deeply felt emotional expression. On all of these levels, the influence of sean nós is directly or indirectly apparent in most other types of Irish music, whether vocal or instrumental, traditional or modern. The texts of sean nós songs include nature poetry, love songs, and religious songs that express "a somewhat mystical brand of Irish Catholic belief" (Hast, Cowdery, and Scott 1999:60–61).

If sean nós is indeed the heart of Irish music, then instrumental dance music is its public and highly visible face. Music designed to accompany dancing has long been the most popular type in Ireland and throughout the Irish diaspora. Even as actual dancing has become increasingly divorced from dance music over the years, the dominant popularity of Irish dance tunes has endured.

The Musical Guided Tour for this chapter offers an introduction to foundational elements of Irish dance music style, focusing on basic dance rhythms, dance tune forms, and characteristics of melody and ornamentation. The fiddler is Lynnsey Weissenberger, an active performer of the music who lives in Florida. Lynnsey has studied and apprenticed with the renowned Irish fiddler James Kelly, won several fiddling competitions including the official State of Florida Fiddle Contest in 2005, and performed on one occasion with the leading Irish music group The Chieftains. Her mentor, James Kelly, who now also lives in Florida, is a major international figure in Irish traditional music. A former member of Planxty (an important Irish band discussed later in the chapter) who has performed with The Chieftains and other Irish music luminaries, he grew up in Dublin and is the son of fiddler John Kelly. John Kelly was a member of the highly influential Irish group Ceoltóirí Cualann (also discussed later in the chapter). From the age of three, James learned to play the fiddle from John. His informal course of musical training also involved learning from the legions of renowned musicians from counties all over Ireland who would come to the Dublin home of the Kellys to visit, play music, and share tunes with his father.

Ceoltóirí Cualann
(Kyol-TOR-ee
KOO-lin)

The transcript in the box on page 160 corresponds to the audio Musical Guided Tour. As you listen to this tour at the Online Learning Center (www.mhhe.com/bakan1), follow along with this transcript.

Traditional Irish Dance Tunes and Medleys: Two Examples

Since at least the mid-20th century, Irish traditional dance tunes and medleys have usually been performed ensemble-style by groups of instrumentalists playing a variety of instruments. There are two main contexts for such performances. One is the **ceílí,** an informal social gathering that is normally held at a neighborhood pub or dance hall and involves dancing. The other is the aforementioned Irish music *session,* in which musicians playing different instruments come together to perform the older traditional tunes and newer ones modeled after them, but not to accompany dancing (at least not typically). Sessions are much more common than ceílís today, since fewer people actually dance to Irish dance tunes than in the past. Beyond their status as communal music-making events, sessions provide "a time for friendships to be validated, for chat and fun . . ." (Moloney 1992:184). They occur in a wide range of social settings and contexts, as can be seen from the following reminiscences of Michael Moloney, a leading Irish session musician and scholar of Irish music:

ceílí (KAY-lee)

As a musician myself I have participated in more sessions than I can count or remember over the past twenty-five years in Ireland, England, and America. As I write, images come

Irish dance tune melodies are set to common dance rhythms such as the **jig** [♪], the **hornpipe** [♪], and, most popular of all, the **reel** [♪].

All of the tunes are based on three different types of scales. One of these, the Dorian scale, sounds like this [♪]. It is closely related to certain forms of the minor scale discussed in Chapter 4. Here is part of a reel based on the Dorian scale. In other words, it is a reel in a Dorian *key*. The title of the tune is "The Morning Dew" [♪].

Second, we come to the Mixolydian scale. It is essentially a major scale with a lowered seventh scale degree. It sounds like this [♪]. Lynnsey will now play part of a jig using the Mixolydian scale. The tune is called "Fraher's Jig" [♪].

Third, and finally, many Irish tunes use the familiar major scale. Here is a passage from a hornpipe in a major key called "Cronin's Hornpipe" [♪].

Ornamentation of melodies is an essential feature of Irish music performance. Indeed, Irish tunes are rarely performed without ornamentation. Listen to "Fraher's Jig" in a version with no ornamentation [♪]. Now here is "Fraher's Jig" again, the proper way, with ornamentation [♪].

Many different types of **ornaments** are used. Some embellish the basic melody; others add rhythmic interest to it. Five of the most common ornaments are the *roll*, the *cran*, the *treble*, the *cut*, and the *triplet*. Let's hear what these sound like.

First, here is an illustration of a roll, followed by a short section of a reel including several rolls [♪].

Next, we hear a cran, followed by a portion of a jig that has crans in it [♪].

Our third type of ornament is the treble, heard first in isolation and then in a musical context [♪].

Now, ornament number four, the cut, heard by itself and in the context of a tune [♪].

Fifth and finally, an illustration of the triplet: ornament first, followed by a musical example featuring triplets [♪].

Now that we have been introduced to some common dance rhythms, scales, and ornaments, we move on to a brief introduction to musical form. The form of an Irish dance tune usually consists of several sections, or *parts,* as they are known. When the tune is performed, it is common for each of these parts to be played twice in succession, the second time usually with variations. Lynnsey will now play a jig called "Paddy Clancy's." The form is AABB, probably the most common of all Irish dance tune forms. I will count the measures as Lynnsey plays and clap and call out the appropriate letter name (A or B) at the arrival of each part. Listen carefully, and you will notice how Lynnsey varies the melody and the ornaments each time she repeats a part. Notice also how the melodies of the A and B parts are different from one another; in other words, how they *contrast* [♪].

In performance, two or more tunes (typically three) are often strung together to form a set of tunes called a **medley.** All of the tunes in the medley are of the same tune type, for example, all reels, or all jigs. Now, as a musical conclusion, Lynnsey will play a medley consisting of two reels ("The Scholar" and "Sligo Maid"). This medley incorporates virtually all of the elements of Irish dance tune style we have discussed in this tour [♪].

to mind of sessions in small pubs in Ireland with musicians pressed tightly together in a corner in the familiar semicircle that Irish traditional musicians always form wherever they gather; with the sounds of the instruments struggling to break through a wall of sound created by a babel of voices raised in consort around the bar. I remember similar sessions in little villages in County Clare where people "have great respect for the music[,]" when

An old-time Irish country dance.

the pub patrons stopped their conversation and listened almost reverentially to the music for hours on end.

I remember sessions in villages on the coastline of west Clare or in little towns in County Kerry . . . where my mother's people came from, . . . in noisy pubs so densely crowded that it seemed almost impossible to push through to the bar to get a drink. It is a long way from the wild yells and whoops of such sessions to the quiet humid stillness of the campground area in White Springs, Florida, . . . where I have sat in the late night darkness with fiddler James Kelly from Dublin [and several other musicians] . . . playing reels . . . while shadowy figures listened silently in the eerie gloom. (Moloney 1992:187–88)

Tinwhistle player Jim Cox and fiddler Lynnsey Weissenberger.

The playing of Irish dance tunes occupied a rather different social milieu in earlier times, especially before urbanization and modernization began to transform the social life of Irish dance music around 1920. During this earlier period, social dancing to music at rural domestic gatherings (the forerunners of the modern ceílí) was the main order of the day. At such events, a solo player or an *ad hoc* group of instrumentalists would typically provide music for the dancers. There was no real separation between the dance tune performance and the dancing itself, which were viewed as integral to one another, unlike today.

The musicians played on instruments such as the fiddle, the **tinwhistle** (a small, end-blown flute with six fingerholes), and the **uilleann pipes** (a form of Irish bagpipe to which we will

**uilleann
(YOO-lee-yin)**

Seamus Ennis playing the uilleann pipes.

soon return). Stringing together two or more tunes in a single dance rhythm—a series of reels, or of jigs or hornpipes—musicians would generate impromptu dance tune medleys. A medley might continue for as long as the dancers wished to keep dancing, or for as long as the musician or musicians could think of more tunes to add, whichever came first. The music and the dancing, along with good and abundant food and drink, were key to fostering a spirit of camaraderie, solidifying communal bonds, and creating a joyful social environment. In good times and bad, through moments of celebration and hardship, music and dancing were fundamental to Irish social life.

In the face of modernity and massive urbanization, the old instrumental dance music styles fell into decline, but government-sponsored initiatives led to efforts to preserve and revitalize them in some instances. Key to these efforts was the important Irish musician and folklorist Seamus Ennis, the featured performer in the two very traditional-style solo Irish dance music selections of **CD ex. #2-16** and **CD ex. #2-17.**

guided listening experience

"The Cuckoo's Hornpipe," Seamus Ennis

■ CD Track # **2-16**

■ Featured performer(s)/group: Seamus Ennis (tinwhistle)

■ Format: Complete track

■ Source recording: *Two Centuries of Celtic Music,* by Seamus Ennis (Legacy CD 499)

Seamus Ennis
(SHAY-muhs EN-nis)

Celtic (KEL-tick)

"The Cuckoo's Hornpipe," as its title indicates, is a tune in the dance rhythm of the hornpipe. The hornpipe is a dance most closely identified with English traditional music, but it is also very popular in Irish and other **Celtic** traditions (see "Insights and Perspectives" box on Irish and Celtic music on p. 164). The standard hornpipe rhythm is in a two-beat meter and is performed at a medium to medium-fast tempo. It has a "lilting" rhythmic quality, which results from a steady alternation of notes of uneven length (with underlying triple subdivision of the beat) (Figure 9.1).

In the example, Seamus Ennis is heard in a solo tinwhistle performance. This simple aerophone is usually made of metal (tin or other), though it also can be made of wood or plastic. Another common name for the instrument is *pennywhistle*. The tinwhistle is one of three popular flute-type aerophones used in Irish music, the other two being the larger, lower-pitched, and darker-toned **Irish wooden flute** and the more recently invented (in the 1970s) *low whistle,* a larger version of the tinwhistle with a lower range.

1	2	1	2
DAH da	DAH da	DAH da	DAH da

Hornpipe rhythm. **FIGURE 9.1**

Virtually anyone can get a decent sound out of a tinwhistle, and its small size makes it a manageable instrument in tiny hands. It has therefore long been a favorite music learning instrument for Irish children. In the hands of master players like Seamus Ennis, however, it is transformed into a musical vehicle of surprising expressive range and subtlety.

The form of "The Cuckoo's Hornpipe" is the most standard one in Irish traditional dance music: AABB, with eight two-beat measures per part (i.e., per lettered section). Since varied repetition occurs throughout the performance, however, a representation of the form as AA'BB' is most accurate. The AA'BB' form is repeated once in its entirety, with an extra A section added on at the end to round things out. Thus, the complete form is: AA'BB' AA'BB' A.

Ennis performs "The Cuckoo's Hornpipe" with a high degree of ornamentation of the basic melody. The same types of ornaments demonstrated earlier on the fiddle in the Musical Guided Tour, such as rolls and triplets, are here transferred to the tinwhistle. The locations of some spots where these types of ornaments occur are highlighted in the Guided Listening Quick Summary below.

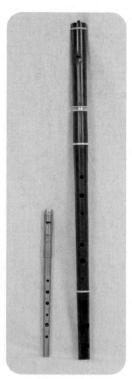

Tinwhistle and Irish wooden flute.

guided listening quick summary

"The Cuckoo's Hornpipe," Seamus Ennis (CD ex. #2-16)

FIRST STATEMENT OF MELODY (AA'BB'):

0:00–0:11—A (First part: eight measures)

- Melody mainly in lower register of tinwhistle's range.
- Tempo accelerates through first few seconds; note "lilting," duple meter hornpipe rhythm (**DAH** - da DAH - da **DAH** - da DAH - da).
- Second half basically a repetition of the first, with a different ending.

0:11–0:21—A' (Second part: eight measures)

- Variations from first **A** part: different opening melodic figure, use of different melodic ornaments (e.g., more triplets, such as at 0:13 and 0:19).

0:21–0:31—B (Third part: eight measures)

- New, contrasting melodic material, mainly in higher register of the instrument.
- More profuse melodic ornamentation than in the **A** parts.
- Louder dynamic level and more boisterous character.
- More notes with short articulations (fewer of the notes are sustained).

0:31–0:40—B' (Fourth part: eight measures)

- Similar to preceding part, but some notes are left out here and the timbral quality is a bit "rougher" than before.

SECOND STATEMENT OF MELODY (AA'BB'):

0:40–0:49—A (First part: eight measures)

- More breaths between notes than in earlier **A** parts. (Possibly Ennis is getting tired, running out of breath.)
- Alteration of some of the main melody notes compared to earlier **A** parts (e.g., at 0:45–0:47).

0:50–0:59—A' (Second part: eight measures)

- More notes with short articulations.
- Melody jumps up to the higher octave range on the final note, adding excitement leading into the **B** section.

insights and perspectives

Irish Music and Celtic Music and Cultures

The identities of Irish music and culture, historical and contemporary, have always been importantly defined by their foundation in a *Celtic* cultural lineage. During ancient times and up through the early era of Christianity, so-called Celtic peoples ranged across much of Europe, from Britain to France and Spain and as far east as present-day Ukraine and Turkey. Today, the cultural legacy of these peoples survives mainly in Ireland, Scotland, Wales, and Brittany (westernmost France), as well as in certain regions of eastern Canada (especially in the provinces of Newfoundland and Nova Scotia) and other areas. The history of Celtic culture in Ireland, in particular, extends back to the 4th century BCE.

Celtic cultural survivals are most clearly evident in a family of related Indo-European languages known as the *Celtic languages.* There are two groups of languages within the Celtic languages family. The first is made up of Irish Gaelic, Scottish Gaelic, and Manx Gaelic. The second includes Welsh, Breton, and Cornish. These are minority languages wherever they are spoken and historically have been "victims of suppression by English and French authorities" (Kuter 2000:319). Since the 1920s in Ireland and the 1980s in Scotland and Wales, however, they have gained increased prominence and use as they have become associated in important ways with cultural revival initiatives belonging to larger nationalist movements in these countries. The growing stature and popularity of "Celtic music," both in specific association with these cultural revival movements and as a category of world music on an international scale (albeit a difficult if not impossible one to precisely define) has followed suit. Though there is no identifiable "set of sonic traits that can qualify or disqualify music as Celtic" (Kuter 2000:320), there are certain key unifying characteristics of musical style that are shared widely among the traditional musics of Celtic regions. These characteristics, all of which are displayed prominently in Irish traditional music, include

■ Prevalence of melodies based on specific types of scales and modes (e.g., the major, Dorian, and Mixolydian types illustrated earlier).

■ Identifiable styles of melodic ornamentation (though there is much variation in types of ornamentation from one "Celtic" country to another).

■ Use of certain types of instruments (e.g., fiddles, bagpipes, flutes).

■ Dance tunes based on common dance rhythms (usually in duple or four-beat meters).

■ Standard forms for songs and dance tunes (e.g., AABB forms for dance tunes).

■ A close integration of music making with dancing, especially in connection with social gatherings that also feature uninhibited feasting and drinking (see Kuter 2000:320–22).

guided listening experience

"The First House in Connaught/The Copper Plate Reel" (Medley), Seamus Ennis

- CD Track #**2-17**
- Featured performer(s)/group: Seamus Ennis (uilleann pipes)
- Format: Complete track
- Source recording: *Two Centuries of Celtic Music,* by Seamus Ennis (Legacy CD 499)

This second traditional-style dance music performance by Seamus Ennis consists of a medley of two tunes rather than a single tune, and is played on the uilleann pipes rather than the tinwhistle. It also features a multipart texture rather than a single-line texture, since the uilleann pipes are capable of producing polyphonic textures.

The uilleann pipes are regarded as the most distinctively Irish of all Irish traditional music instruments. While the fiddle and the tinwhistle were originally brought to Ireland from other lands, the uilleann pipes—pipes, for short—were developed from imported continental European prototypes into a uniquely Irish instrument (Shields and Gershen 2000:384). This Irish variant of the bagpipe, which had evolved into its current form by about 1800, differs greatly from the familiar Great Highland bagpipe of Scotland that most of us think of when the word *bagpipe* is used (**CD ex. #1-15**). It is distinct from the Bulgarian, Italian, Latvian, Indian, and other international variants of the bagpipe as well.

Compared to the Scottish bagpipes, the uilleann pipes are an instrument with a rather soft dynamic range and a more delicate, refined timbre. Additionally, they are designed to be played from a seated position rather than standing up. Though the person playing the uilleann pipes may

Uilleann pipes of Ireland (left), Great Highland bagpipe of Scotland (right).

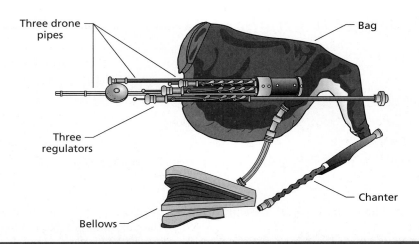

Three drone pipes

Bag

Three regulators

Chanter

Bellows

Uilleann pipes.

FIGURE 9.2

look as if he is holding an octopus in his lap, all those pipes can be reduced to three functions, providing drones, melody, and chords (Figure 9.2).

In common with its Scottish cousin, the uilleann pipes include three *drone pipes,* each of which plays the same tonic pitch in a different octave range (though the tonic pitch of the uilleann pipes is D, whereas that of the Scottish pipes is B♭). Sound is produced when air is forced through the pipes by a *bellows,* which is essentially a bag with collapsible sides. The bellows is inflated to capacity *before* the instrument is played. It is then held in the crook of the player's left arm and squeezed by the left elbow ("uilleann" means elbow in Irish Gaelic). This squeezing action forces sound-producing air through the three drone pipes attached to the instrument, as well as through a fourth pipe, the *chanter,* or melody pipe, and three additional ones, the *regulators,* which are used to generate chords.

The chanter is the only pipe on the uilleann pipes used for melodies. It is also the only one with *fingerholes,* which are pressed down in different combinations to produce the main melody pitches and a variety of melodic ornaments. By covering or leaving open certain holes in certain combinations, the performer effectively changes the length of the pipe, and thus the pitch: the "longer" the pipe becomes, the lower the pitch produced. This same principle applies to the use of fingerholes on the tinwhistle, and on aerophones generally.

The three regulator pipes (regulators) are the only pipes on the instrument capable of producing chords. On each regulator are located four or five keys. Each produces a different pitch when it is pressed down. By pressing down different combinations of keys on the different regulator pipes, the player generates groups of notes. These may function as chords that underscore the melody (though typically only to a relatively limited degree) or they may provide rhythmic effects and punctuate the ends of melodic phrases. Both the drone and regulator pipes may be switched on or off by the player during the course of performance.

As can be imagined from the foregoing description, uilleann pipes players quite literally have their hands full just dealing with the instrument's practical logistics. Between moving one's fingers over the chanter, pumping the bellows, switching the regulators on and off and pressing their keys, and keeping all seven pipes going at once, there is much to keep track of. And those are just the rudiments. The real art of playing the uilleann pipes *musically* is another matter altogether, and Seamus Ennis stands as one of the great masters of all time in this regard.

The medley of two reels included on **CD ex. #2-17** provides a wonderful example of solo uilleann pipes music in the traditional dance tune style, as well as a fine display of Seamus Ennis's unique artistry on the instrument.

	1				2				1				2			
Reel	**Dah**	da	da	da	**Dah**	da	da	da	**Dah**	da	da	da	**Dah**	da	da	da

	1		2		1		2	
Hornpipe	**Dah**	da	**Dah**	da	**Dah**	da	**Dah**	da

FIGURE 9.3

Comparison of reel and hornpipe rhythms.

The dance rhythm featured throughout is that of the reel. Compared to the hornpipe, the reel rhythm is more "even" sounding (**DAH** da da da **DAH** da da da) than lilting (**DAH** - da **DAH** - da **DAH** - da **DAH** - da) (Figure 9.3). (Technically, this can be explained by the underlying quadruple subdivision of beats in the reel, as opposed to the triple subdivision of beats in the hornpipe.) The tempo is relatively fast, making the music quite energetic in character.

The tune form is again AA'BB'. Both tunes of the medley adhere to this format, and both are played twice in their entirety.

The texture is melody-plus-drone throughout. The addition of regulator chords at certain points enhances the basic melody-plus-drone texture. The regulator chords are mainly used for rhythmic effect and punctuating the ends of phrases (cadences). Their use is sometimes surprising; for example, at 1:20–1:22, if you were not aware that what you were hearing was indeed a regulator chord, you might mistake it for an Irish taxicab blasting its horn outside the recording studio! Melodic ornamentation is again used profusely.

A final interesting feature of this performance is what might be described as its irregularities. There are a couple of points where Ennis drops a beat from the regular two-beat meter pattern, and there is even a moment where a full measure seems to disappear. The rhythm sounds a bit "shaky" here and there as well. Far from being detrimental to the effect of the performance, these irregularities give it an attractive feeling of raw spontaneity that is a marked contrast to the more slick and polished musical productions we will encounter later on our journey. They are at the core of a traditional-style musical art that emphasizes creating music in the moment of performance and never playing a tune or part of a tune exactly the same way twice. This is an art of which Ennis (as well as some of the musicians mentioned earlier, such as John Kelly and James Kelly) was a true master.

guided listening quick summary

"The First House in Connaught/The Copper Plate Reel" (Medley), Seamus Ennis (CD ex. #2-17)

"THE FIRST HOUSE IN CONNAUGHT" (MEDLEY TUNE #1)

FIRST STATEMENT OF MELODY (AA'BB'):

0:00–0:10—A

- First drone, then chanter melody, then a regulator chord at the end (at 0:09) are heard.
- Note rhythmic character of the reel (**DAH** da da da **DAH** da da da).
- Note melodic ornaments and different articulations (including many staccato [short] notes, which are characteristic of this older style but less so of more modern uilleann piping styles).

0:10–0:18—A'

- Regulator chords (0:14–0:15).
- Dropped beats near beginning and end of this part (e.g., at 0:16–0:18).

0:18–0:26—B

- "Shaky" rhythm in some passages.
- Melodic range higher than in the preceding **A** parts (as in **B** parts of "Cuckoo's Hornpipe" and tunes of this type generally).

0:27–0:34—B'

- One full measure (two beats) is dropped at the end of this part.

SECOND STATEMENT OF MELODY (AA'BB'):

0:34–0:42—A
0:43–0:51—A'

- Note prominent use of regulator pipes.

0:51–0:59—B
0:59–1:07—B'

- The first couple of melody notes are played an octave *lower* than in earlier **B** parts (varied repetition).

"THE COPPER PLATE REEL" (MEDLEY TUNE #2)

FIRST STATEMENT OF MELODY (AA'BB'):

1:08–1:15—A

- New tune begins (though this is not necessarily obvious for listeners new to the style!).

1:16–1:24—A'

- Listen for "car horn" regulator chord (1:20–1:22).

1:24–1:32—B
1:32–1:40—B'

SECOND STATEMENT OF MELODY (AA'BB'):

1:40–1:48—A
1:49–1:56—A'
1:57–2:05—B
2:05–end—B'

- The most elaborate ornamentation of the entire performance occurs in this final part (as was also the case in "Cuckoo's Hornpipe" and is common in Irish traditional music performances generally).

The life and legacy of Seamus Ennis

Beyond his stature as one of the great uilleann pipers of the 20th century, Seamus Ennis (1919–1982) was one of the most important figures in the preservation, cultivation, and dissemination of Irish traditional music (see the photo of a young Seamus Ennis on p. 162). He was born into a musical family in Jamestown, Ireland, near Dublin. His father, James Ennis, was a master uilleann pipes player, champion Irish dancer, and member of the famous Fingal Trio. This was one of the first Irish music groups to be featured on national radio broadcasts (on radio station 2RN, the forerunner of Radio Éireann). They had a major influence on later generations of Irish musicians. Falling asleep to the sounds of his father's piping was one of Seamus's earliest childhood memories, and the household in which he grew up was one of abundant musical riches. Local and visiting musicians would regularly come by to socialize and play music with his father, the music often accompanying dancing in the home.

Seamus began playing the uilleann pipes as a child and was a recognized master of the instrument by age 21, when he was featured on an outstanding series of Radio Éireann broadcasts in 1940. He never took formal lessons on the instrument, neither from his father nor anyone else, learning to play in the traditional oral/aural tradition way. His father was the only piper he ever credited as a major influence on his playing, especially for explaining how to deal with some of the "difficult bits" of piping technique and ornamentation. James also taught Seamus to read and write down music, skills that most other Irish traditional musicians of their time did not possess.

Seamus's music literacy aided him significantly in his professional career. It was an important qualification in his job as a folk music collector for the government's Irish Folklore Commission. This position gave him the opportunity to travel throughout Ireland, locating the best local musicians and singers and transcribing their songs, airs, and dance tunes. He spoke excellent Irish Gaelic, and this, combined with the fact that he himself was an outstanding musician, made for easy rapport with the musicians he met wherever he went. "He was clearly accepted and well-liked by those from whom he sought music," writes Irish music specialist Ronan Nolan, "and was able to instantly spot the genuinely good players and singers. Being a musician himself meant that he was in turn fully accepted by them—a case of like recognising like" (Nolan 2003).

Moving on from the Irish Folklore Commission, Seamus was appointed an Outside Broadcast Officer for Radio Éireann in 1947. The radio station had an already-established practice of bringing traditional singers and musicians from counties all over Ireland to perform for national broadcasts. The next venture was to devise a way that these musicians could be recorded in their home environments, in the villages and towns where they lived. For this, a special mobile recording unit was created. Seamus traveled the countryside with this unit, locating top local musicians and recording them for national radio broadcasts. These programs "increased public awareness of the richness of Irish traditional music, and a generation of older rural singers and musicians became known to, and admired by, the Irish public," both in rural and urban areas (Shields and Gershen 2000:391). They also made musicians from different Irish counties and regions familiar with the styles of one another. Now a musician from County Kerry in the south could listen to dance tunes and airs played by musicians of County Donegal in the north. As musicians in rural areas came to know and be influenced by each other's styles via radio, and as urbanization brought musicians from different places together in major cities like Dublin, a more pan-Irish approach to Irish traditional music began to emerge. Ennis was a key figure in this development, as in many others.

In 1951, Ennis moved to London to work for the British Broadcasting Corporation (BBC). He became part of a major BBC project devoted to the preservation on recordings of surviving folk culture traditions of Ireland, England, Scotland, and Wales (song, instrumental music, oral poetry, myths and legends, storytelling). Between 1951 and 1958, he made recordings and broadcasts throughout the United Kingdom and Ireland and also hosted a pioneering BBC folk music radio program (*As I Roved Out*).

Ennis returned to Ireland to live in 1958, doing freelance work for Radio Éireann as well as some shows in the new medium of television. He traveled the country playing music during the 1960s and became an important icon of the Irish music revival during that period. In 1964, he went to the United States to perform at the Newport Folk Festival, introducing traditional Irish music to a new, mass international audience. He died in 1982 at the age of 63. He continued to play right up to the end, and spent his final years living in a mobile home in the county where he was born. Today, his stature as a piper is almost legendary: "Seamus' playing of the uilleann pipes," writes Ronan Nolan, "was always instantly recognisable for his tone, technique and particular versions of tunes and the variations which he employed while playing them. Any tune, no matter how commonly played by musicians at sessions or elsewhere, became different when he played it and despite the amount of skill and technique which he used, the tune was never stifled or

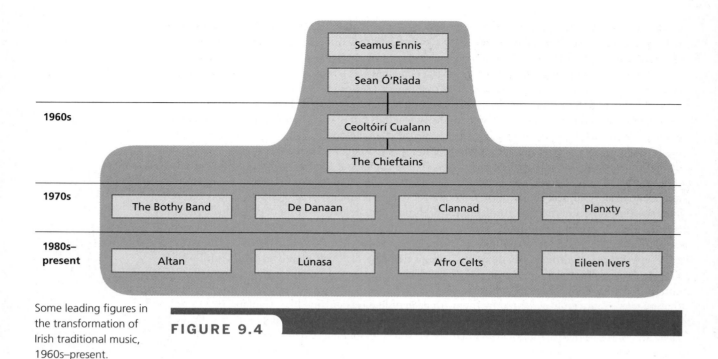

1960s		Seamus Ennis	
		Sean Ó'Riada	
		Ceoltóirí Cualann	
		The Chieftains	
1970s	The Bothy Band	De Danaan	Clannad	Planxty
1980s–present	Altan	Lúnasa	Afro Celts	Eileen Ivers

Some leading figures in the transformation of Irish traditional music, 1960s–present.

FIGURE 9.4

bent out of shape in any way and this was because Seamus had a great respect for the music and its idiomatic integrity" (Nolan 2003).

Neo-Tradtitional Irish Music and the Irish Music Revival

Through the 1950s, Irish society experienced profound socioeconomic changes. Large-scale industrialization in commercial areas such as food processing and beverage making (beer, ale) led to massive urbanization and ultimately to an economy based principally on manufacturing rather than agriculture. Agriculture itself also became heavily industrialized, yielding major economic gains. Ireland prospered during the 1960s as an outcome of these changes. This prosperity, together with renewed fears of culture loss and a growing interest on the part of many younger Irish people in traditional Irish culture, sparked a major cultural revival movement.

The Irish music revival, which began in the 1960s, was a key component of this movement. Recordings of traditional musicians from counties all over Ireland were produced in record numbers and were broadcast and distributed nationwide. Many local, regional, and national traditional music competitions, such as the prestigious All-Ireland music competitions (called *fleadhs*) were established or revived, spurring great public interest in the music and inspiring many Irish youth to return to their "roots" by taking up traditional Irish instruments and learning the old music styles.

fleadhs (flahs)

As the music was revived and revitalized, it also was transformed. It moved from the countryside and the home to the pub, the dance hall, and the concert hall. Approaches to the playing of dance tunes and medleys became more formal and structured, with well-planned musical arrangements often taking the place of the older, more spontaneous performance styles. In addition to traditional melodic instruments, chordal and rhythmic accompaniment instruments now became standard as well, and in many cases these newly added instruments even became the principal focal points of the new-style arrangements. Casual groups of musicians who had formerly gathered to play for dancing turned into established bands that performed, recorded, and toured professionally (Figure 9.4). With this move toward professionalism, the status of the old tunes themselves often was changed too. Traditional dance tunes that in the past had been regarded as common property now came to be increasingly identified with specific arrangements and recordings by specific performers and bands. This initiated a general trend toward the commodification of Irish traditional music, a trend that has only grown and intensified over the years. Finally, the performance of dance tunes and medleys became largely unhinged from dancing itself, as music's social function in Irish society came to reflect new social values and environments.

Sean Ó'Riada and the transformation of Irish traditional music

Key to the transformation of Irish music leading up to and during the Irish music revival was Sean Ó'Riada (1931–1971). Seamus Ennis's status as an icon of Irish traditional music in the 20th century is matched, if not exceeded, by that of Sean Ó'Riada. As important as Ennis was to the preservation and cultivation of older styles of Irish folk music, Ó'Riada was to their transformation and modernization. Both men were seminal figures during and leading up to the Irish music revival that crystallized around 1960, gained new momentum in the 1970s with the emergence of a new generation of outstanding musicians and bands, and continued henceforth into the 1980s and beyond (Figure 9.4).

Sean Ó'Riada (SHAWN oh REEyah-dah)

Sean Ó'Riada (left) and Ceoltóirí Cualann.

In 1960, Sean Ó'Riada organized a group of leading Irish traditional musicians into the ensemble Ceoltóirí Cualann, or Musicians of Cualann (a region of Dublin). Together with these musicians, among them John Kelly, he essentially invented a fresh, neo-traditional Irish musical idiom that was soon absorbed into the Irish traditional music mainstream itself. Ó'Riada combined old-fashioned solo instrumental traditions and playing styles with sophisticated arranging techniques and an ensemble-based sound. Innovative use of chords, multiple-melody textures, changing combinations of instruments, and alternating solos on different instruments were among the features that defined his distinctive approach.

Ceoltóirí Cualann employed a core instrumental lineup of uilleann pipes, two fiddles, tinwhistle, button box accordion, and **bodhrán** (a handheld frame drum with a goat skin head). The uilleann pipes, which, despite the valiant efforts of advocates like Seamus Ennis, had declined greatly in popularity during the preceding decades, were featured prominently in Ó'Riada's arrangements for Ceoltóirí Cualann. This restored a largely lost status to the instrument that endures to the present in Irish music. The group's contribution to the legacy of the bodhrán was perhaps even more impressive. Formerly a domestic utensil used by Irish homemakers, the bodhrán had traditionally led a double life as an occasional rhythmic accompaniment instrument used during rural ceremonial gatherings. With the promotion of the instrument by Ceoltóirí Cualann, however, it came to enjoy a new status as the main rhythmic accompaniment instrument of the new Irish traditional music ensemble style, a status it still retains today.

bodhrán (BOH-rawn)

Bodhrán and button box accordion.

The Chieftains

Beyond its own historical importance, Ceoltóirí Cualann is also significant for a new group that emerged out of it, The Chieftains. Led by uilleann pipes master Paddy Moloney, The Chieftains are arguably the most widely influential and internationally renowned Irish traditional music group ever.

The Chieftains, with Paddy Moloney playing the uilleann pipes (front center) and guest fiddler Eileen Ivers (rear right). This photo is from a 1999 television broadcast.

Clannad (CLAHN-ad)

De Danaan (Day DAN-an)

Lúnasa (LOO-nuh-sah)

Since the release of their first record album in 1963, they have become the premier international ambassadors of Irish traditional music. Their influence may be heard in the music of virtually all subsequent leading Irish groups—Clannad, Planxty, The Bothy Band, De Danaan, Altan, Lúnasa—and they have collaborated with members of all these groups on a variety of projects. They also have been inveterate boundary-blurring musical adventurers, undertaking collaborative projects with everyone from the Rolling Stones' Mick Jagger to reggae star Ziggy Marley.

guided listening experience

"The Dingle Set" (Medley), The Chieftains

- CD Track #**2-18**
- Featured performer(s)/group: The Chieftains, with Paddy Moloney (tinwhistle, uilleann pipes)
- Format: Excerpt
- Source recording: "An Poc Ar Buile/The Dingle Set," from *The Essential Chieftains* (RCA Victor/Legacy 82876 75398 2).

This selection features a medley consisting of three reels: "Far From Home," "Gladstone," and "The Scartaglen." It was recorded live in County Kerry, Ireland, in 2000. Paddy Moloney, who is credited as the arranger, plays tinwhistle on the first tune ("Far From Home") and uilleann pipes on the last one ("The Scartaglen"). The other instruments in the ensemble are fiddles, Irish wooden flute, Irish harp, accordion, concertina (a smaller, accordion-like instrument), banjo, and bodhrán. From 1:51 to the end you will also hear the rhythmic footwork of guest artist and well-known fiddler Ashley MacIsaac (from Cape Breton Island, Nova Scotia, Canada), as he spontaneously breaks into dancing a reel.

Sean Ó'Riada's lasting influence on subsequent Irish music arrangers is evident here in Moloney's use of *changing textures* from one tune of the medley to the next. While the first and third tunes are played by the full ensemble, the middle tune ("Gladstone") is performed by the fiddlers alone. Altering the instrumentation in this way generates considerable musical variety and contrast in Moloney's arrangement.

In terms of form, "Far From Home" is in the standard AABB format already familiar to us. The tune is repeated once in its entirety (AABB AABB). "Gladstone" and "The Scartaglen" both have a formal design of AB, rather than AABB. (Reels with an AB form are called *single reels,* whereas those with an AABB form are called *double reels.*) "Gladstone" is played through twice (AB AB), while "The Scartaglen" is played through four times (AB AB AB AB).

In addition to offering an example of the consummate musicianship of an iconic Irish ensemble, this live recording also captures a special quality of exuberance in social celebration that is central to the Irish dance tune tradition overall.

---

guided listening quick summary

"The Dingle Set" (Medley), The Chieftains (CD ex. #2-18)

"FAR FROM HOME" (MEDLEY TUNE #1): AABB AABB

0:00–0:07—A
0:08–0:15—A
0:16–0:23—B
0:24–0:31—B
0:32–0:39—A
0:40–0:46—A
0:47–0:55—B
0:55–1:02—B

- Performed by full ensemble, including tinwhistle (Moloney), fiddles, Irish wooden flute, Irish harp, accordion, concertina, banjo, and bodhrán.
- Lively, up-tempo reel, with the bodhrán laying down a strong rhythmic foundation.

"GLADSTONE" (MEDLEY TUNE #2): AB AB

1:03–1:10—A
1:11–1:18—B
1:19–1:26—A
1:27–1:34—B

- Fiddles only throughout, with the rest of the ensemble laying out; instrumentation change creates interesting contrast in texture.

"THE SCARTAGLEN" (MEDLEY TUNE #3): AB AB AB AB

1:35–1:42—A
1:43–1:50—B
1:51–1:58—A (Ashley MacIsaac begins dancing here.)
1:59–2:06—B
2:07–2:14—A
2:15–2:22—B
2:23–2:30—A
2:31–end—B

- With the arrival of this final tune at 1:35, there is a return to a full ensemble texture (but with Paddy Moloney now playing uilleann pipes).
- The rhythms of the bodhrán and the rhythmic footwork of the dancer add energy and excitement as the performance drives to its conclusion.

The 1970s: Second generation of the Irish music revival

Though an ardent traditionalist throughout his life, Seamus Ennis was also an admirer of some of the newer sounds of Irish music that came out of the post-Ó'Riada era of the Irish music revival during the 1970s. During that decade, Ennis developed a close friendship with Liam O'Flynn, a younger uilleann pipes virtuoso and member of one of the leading Irish bands of the time, Planxty. "When we travelled together," recalled O'Flynn many years later, "he always drove and that could be a fairly 'hairy' experience. The conversation always turned to music[,] with fascinating stories about places, tunes, songs, players and singers. I absorbed a great deal from him in this way. Planxty was in full flight at this time and he took a terrific interest in the group. He gave us songs and tunes in abundance" (O'Flynn, quoted in Nolan 2003).

Donal Lunny of Planxty, 1970s.

Planxty was indeed in full flight. O'Flynn and his Planxty bandmates, including Andy Irvine, Christy Moore, Donal Lunny, and James Kelly, came together as products of the Irish music revival generation. Many Irish musicians who emerged during this period had grown up with other kinds of music: rock, jazz, classical. Their re-embracing of cultural roots via Irish music in many cases came later. Moreover, their ideas about what Irish traditional music was becoming were as much informed by the already-modernized styles of Ceoltóirí Cualann and The Chieftains as by the older breed of traditional Irish musicians championed—and to some extent represented—by Seamus Ennis.

This second wave of the Irish music revival, then, featured a new generation of musicians who approached the Irish music tradition from a different, more cosmopolitan and commercial vantage point. Planxty, Clannad, the Bothy Band, and De Danaan were among its most important representative groups. On one level, these bands were significant for creating a new fusion of Irish traditional music, rock, jazz, and other international popular music styles. On another level, they were important for carrying on certain elements of the repertoire of standard, old Irish dance tunes of their forebears, but for doing so with an innovative approach.

The modern ensemble sound of Irish traditional dance music

The innovative, cosmopolitan approach to playing standard Irish traditional dance tunes and medleys identified with bands like Planxty built on and extended the earlier innovations of Ceoltóirí Cualann and The Chieftains, while also adding novel elements. Planxty in particular has been credited for having ". . . really changed the way young Irish people looked on the old folk repertoire. Their arrangements of old airs and tunes, and Liam O'Flynn's wonderful uilleann piping, opened a lot of ears and inspired a lot of the new Celtic groups of the last two decades" (O'Connor 1999:179). The Irish group Altan and bands led by the Irish-American fiddler Eileen Ivers, musical examples by both of whom we will explore shortly, are among the most important of these later groups.

The list that follows this paragraph summarizes some of the main features of the modern ensemble style of Irish dance music, which will be our focus throughout the remainder of this chapter. These features are characteristic of neo-traditional dance music styles, and also prefigure post-traditional styles. They essentially distinguish these modern approaches from traditional, instrumental dance music such as that heard in the Seamus Ennis recordings we listened to earlier. The modern ensemble sound here described crystallized in some of the music of Ceoltóirí Cualann and the early Chieftains during the 1960s. It developed in new ways with Planxty and other second wave Irish music revival groups of the 1970s. It has since been extended even further in the hands of more recent groups like Altan and Eileen Ivers' bands. Today, it is ubiquitous across many realms of Irish music performance, from concerts and recordings by professional groups to informal Irish music sessions held in pubs and other venues throughout Ireland, the Irish diaspora, and the world. All of the features included on this list have become standard in contemporary Irish dance music performance (especially as performed by professional groups), though it is important to note that not every *one* of them is necessarily present in any given performance. With all of this in mind, it may be stated that in the modern ensemble style

- *Performances are by groups* and usually feature a combination of melodic and chordal/rhythmic accompaniment instruments, rather than just melodic instruments.
- *Variation in performance styles and textures in the playing of dance tune melodies is common.* Some combination of traditional Irish melodic instruments including tinwhistle, low whistle, wooden flute, uilleann pipes, accordion, concertina, and/or fiddle is usually employed. Two or more different melodic textures often occur within the same performance. These may include
  - *Unison ornamented melody.* All of the melodic instruments play the melody together, with even the ornaments being executed in precise unison by the various instrumentalists.
  - *Varied versions of a single melody (heterophony).* The same tune is played together on all of the melodic instruments, but each instrumentalist ornaments and articulates the melody somewhat differently.
  - *Divided-up melody.* The different instrumentalists divide the playing of the melody between them, so all are not playing together all the time. For example, the uilleann pipes player may play the first phrase of a tune alone, then drop out while the fiddler and tinwhistle player take up the next phrase.
  - *Jazz- or rock-influenced textures featuring solo improvsation.* In some more modern approaches, one or more instrumentalists may depart from the main melody (and from the standard, traditional melodic variation techniques of Irish music generally) to perform improvised solos indebted to jazz or rock styles.
- In addition to the melodic instruments, *chording instruments are very prominent in the musical texture.* These include strummed chordophones such as the guitar and the Irish bouzouki (see the "Insights and Perspectives" box on p. 176), instruments that were not formerly associated with Irish dance music or, at least in the case of the bouzouki, with Irish music at all. The use of a bass chordophone (e.g., string bass or electric bass guitar) also may occur.
- *Chordal accompaniment of dance tune melodies is highly developed.* In addition to the drones and drone-based harmonies of old-style Irish dance music, complex chord progressions showing influences of jazz, rock, and even Spanish flamenco music are employed. Modulations, which shift the music from one key to another at different points (e.g., from C major to D Dorian), may also figure prominently.
- *The rhythmic accompaniment patterns of the chording instruments often exhibit outside influences.* Standard Irish dance tune rhythms like the reel are enhanced by rhythmic elements adapted from jazz, rock, and sometimes African, Latin, and Balkan musics as well (see the "Insights and Perspectives" box on p. 176 regarding Balkan influences).
- *Percussion instruments are sometimes used to reinforce the dance rhythms.* These include the bodhrán, but drumset and Latin percussion instruments such as conga drums (see Chapter 11, p. 223) may be used as well.
- The former function of Irish dance music as music to be danced to is largely eclipsed by its new function as *music to be listened to but not danced to,* whether in the pub or the concert hall (though a modern revival of Irish dancing has been spurred by international theatrical productions such as *Riverdance;* for more information on that phenomenon, visit the Online Learning Center at http://www.mhhe.com/bakan1).

The Irish bouzouki is a flat-backed hybrid of the original Greek bouzouki (which is featured in **CD ex. #1-24**) and the mandolin. The bouzouki first came into Irish music through Johnny Moynihan in the late 1960s and became a signature element of groups like Planxty and the Bothy Band through the outstanding playing of Donal Lunny. It is now one of the standard chording instruments used in Irish music, along with the mandolin and the guitar. With the introduction of the bouzouki into Irish music came other changes as well. Greek and other Balkan rhythms were incorporated into Irish dance music styles, and these, together with additional borrowed rhythms from rock, jazz, and other musicultural traditions, had a major impact on Irish music.

The Irish bouzouki.

guided listening experience

"The Emyvale/Ríl Gan Ainm/The Three Merry Sisters of Fate" (Medley), Altan

- CD Track #**2-19**
- Featured performer(s)/group: Altan, with Mairéad Ní Mhaonaigh and Paul O'Shaughnessy (fiddles), Frankie Kennedy (flutes), Ciarán Curran (Irish bouzouki), and Mark Kelly (guitar)
- Format: Complete track
- Source recording: *The Best of Altan* (Green Linnet Records GLCD 1177)

Altan is one of the most popular, widely respected, and influential Irish groups of the post-1970s era. The group formed in the mid-1980s and throughout the 1990s was recognized, along with other top bands like the Bothy Band and De Danaan, as the "flagbearers for the Irish traditional band scene" (O'Connor 1999:180). At once deeply rooted in Irish musical tradition and adventurously creative, Altan is a group that has garnered acclaim from traditionalists and modernists alike.

Mairéad Ní Mhaonaigh (Mah–RAID Nah–WEE–nee)

Ciarán (KyEE-rawn)

Altan was founded by Mairéad Ní Mhaonaigh of County Donegal, a fiddler and vocalist (and the daughter of a famous Irish fiddler), and her husband, the late Belfast-born Irish wooden flute and tinwhistle player Frankie Kennedy. Together with a second fiddler, Paul O'Shaughnessy; guitarist Mark Kelly; and Irish bouzouki player Ciarán Curran, Ní Mhaonaigh and Kennedy fronted an outstanding quintet that produced several memorable albums, including 1990's *The Red Crow*, on which the dance tune medley of **CD ex. #2-19** first appeared. Subsequent years and albums witnessed a series of personnel changes (most notably following the tragic early death of Frankie Kennedy from cancer in 1994) and collaborations with a variety of guest artists. Altan's music has covered everything from Irish traditional dance medleys to Irish-rock fusion productions that combine diverse musical elements in unconventional ways.

The medley of **CD ex. #2-19** falls squarely in the former category and provides excellent examples of many features of the neo-traditional, modern Irish ensemble sound outlined in the preceding section. It is comprised of three dance tunes, all reels. The first and third tunes are single reels, with alternating A and B parts (AB AB AB and AB AB AB A, respectively). The middle tune, "Ríl Gan Ainm," which literally means "Reel Without Name," is a double reel (AABB form) and is played through twice (AABB AABB). The two fiddles and Frankie Kennedy's Irish wooden flute provide the melodic layer of the music's texture. They play mostly in tight unison, right down to the melodic ornaments.

Much of the interest of the arrangement lies in its chordal accompaniment, which is provided by the guitar and Irish bouzouki. As the music moves between several different keys over the course of the arrangement, these instruments outline the harmonic progression. Sometimes they accompany the melody with straight drone-based chords or simple chord progressions, but there are also passages where more intricate, jazz-influenced chord progressions are heard underscoring the tune.

Altan.

The guitar and Irish bouzouki also provide the music's rhythmic accompaniment layer (no percussion instruments are used in this arrangement). In some passages, the rhythmic treatment is quite straightforward; in others, influences of rock, jazz, and funk are evident in the syncopations of the guitar and bouzouki parts.

Overall, the playing of the ensemble is very tight and clean. Rhythmic execution is strict and precise, meter and tempo constant and unwavering, phrases consistent in length. Clearly, Altan is operating from a rather different musical aesthetic than was Seamus Ennis in the uilleann pipes medley explored earlier in the chapter. This is because Altan has seemingly planned out virtually every move they make, whereas Ennis was more creating in the moment. Both selections (not to mention The Chieftains example we listened to) are excellent representatives of "Irish traditional music," but they represent different dimensions of that tradition, one neither better nor worse than the other. There is an old Irish Gaelic saying that translates as "It's not the same, but it's just as nice." That saying applies well here.

guided listening quick summary

"The Emyvale/Ríl Gan Ainm/The Three Merry Sisters of Fate" (Medley), Altan (CD ex. #2-19)

"THE EMYVALE" (MEDLEY TUNE #1—FORM: AB AB AB)

0:00–0:08—A

- Key: A Dorian.
- Texture: unison melody (two fiddles, Irish wooden flute), chordal accompaniment (guitar, Irish bouzouki).

Ríl Gan Ainm
(Reel Gahn Ahm)

- Chord progression moves over an implied drone.
- Chordal accompaniment rhythmically sparse, especially at the beginning; no syncopation.

0:08–0:16—B

- Jazz-like ascending chord progression (over a continuing implied drone).

0:16–0:24—A

- Similar to opening **A** section, but with more rhythmically active chordal accompaniment.

0:24–0:32—B

- Chordal accompaniment more prominent than in the first **B** section.
- Extra emphasis on low-range notes of the guitar part.

0:32–0:40—A

- Music becomes louder and the rhythm is more active and syncopated than before.
- Flute more prominent now.

0:40–0:48—B

- Rhythmic activity and dynamic level continue to grow as the music builds in intensity.

"RÍL GAN AINM" ["REEL WITHOUT NAME"] (MEDLEY TUNE #2—FORM: AABB AABB)

0:48–1:04—AA

- Modulation to key of D Dorian signals change of tune.
- Funk-inspired, syncopated rhythmic pattern introduced in the chordal accompaniment.

1:05–1:19—BB

- Temporary modulation to key of C major.
- Chordal accompaniment less syncopated (as compared to preceding "funky" style).

1:20–1:35—AA

- Modulation back to D Dorian.
- Syncopated rhythmic accompaniment returns.
- Use of more strummed chords thickens the overall texture.

1:36–1:43—B

- Modulation to C major again, with return of straightforward, less-syncopated rhythmic accompaniment.

1:43–1:51—B

- Intensity builds; the Irish bouzouki takes a more prominent role in the texture.

"THE THREE MERRY SISTERS OF FATE" (MEDLEY TUNE #3—FORM: AB AB AB A)

1:51–2:00—A

- Modulation: key alternates between D major and B Dorian.
- Chord progression quite complex.
- Irish bouzouki plays in a style suggesting American bluegrass music influence (i.e., finger-picking style).

2:00–2:07—B

- Bouzouki part more prominent.
- Rhythmic accompaniment more rhythmically active in general.

2:08–2:31—ABA

■ Progressive building up of musical intensity.

2:31–2:38—B

■ Intensity builds to a climax.

2:39–end—A

■ Triumphant conclusion of the medley; ends satisfyingly on a big D-major chord.

The Post–Traditional World of Irish Music: Crossing Bridges with Eileen Ivers

The story of Irish music is only partially told through an exploration of music in Ireland itself. Equally significant is the history of Irish traditional music in the Irish diaspora. From the 1930s through the 1950s, there was a major decline in the support of Irish traditional music in Ireland. Political turbulence, a major economic downturn in the 1930s, and rapid modernization and urbanization all contributed to this decline. For many modern-minded Irish, the traditional music came to be associated with an antiquated and outmoded way of life that was out of step with the goals and aspirations of a modernizing Ireland.

Meanwhile, in Irish diasporic communities of the United States, Canada, England, and elsewhere, Irish traditional music was being tenaciously preserved and creatively developed as a touchstone of Irish ethnic identification with the homeland. Growing prosperity, ready access to international travel, tourism, mass media, and improved communication technologies on both sides of the Atlantic during the post–World War II era connected Irish music culture itself to the vibrant musical worlds of the Irish diaspora to an unprecedented degree. In particular, a number of early American recordings of the fiddlers Michael Coleman and James Morrison, both originally from County Sligo in Ireland, were highly influential in music circles "back home." Instruments, performance styles, and repertoires that had been kept alive in the diaspora while all but disappearing in Ireland were reintroduced to the homeland and revitalized. New musical styles and playing techniques cultivated by Irish diaspora musicians began to influence musicians in Ireland as well. Altogether, the vibrant new life of Irish music abroad galvanized musicultural life in Ireland itself, providing an important impetus for the Irish music revival of the 1960s. Since that time, the rich cross-pollination that has occurred between Irish music in the Irish diaspora and in Ireland has given rise to a truly transnational pan-Irish musical culture. If any one contemporary musician might be said to be representative of that transnational culture, it is the Irish-American fiddler Eileen Ivers.

The music and life of Eileen Ivers

Eileen Ivers has carved out a unique and important niche in contemporary, pan-Irish music. Her work spans a broad and eclectic range of musical styles, from neo-traditional Irish; to Irish-rock, Irish-Latin, and Irish-African fusion; to combinations of all of these and more. For Ivers, musical borders and boundaries are there to be broken. Yet the Irish traditional core that defines her extraordinarily diverse musical approach is always present. Irish traditional music is Eileen Ivers' homebase; she is just a frequent flyer.

Ivers was born to Irish immigrant parents in 1965 in the Bronx borough of New York City. She grew up in a large and vibrant Irish-American immigrant community where Irish music,

Eileen Ivers.

dancing, and social and cultural values were a basic part of life. But the environment in which she was raised was also a diversely multicultural one, and this affected the formation of her musical and cultural identity as much as her Irish heritage. She grew up listening to salsa, rock, jazz, Broadway show tunes, and classical music. All of these influenced her emergent and unique musical persona. As the Eileen Ivers admirer and Pulitzer Prize–winning author of *Angela's Ashes* Frank McCourt has written,

> She grew up in a boom box Bronx and she carries sounds from childhood that are surely embedded in her musical soul: the chirp and clank of an October radiator heating up; the rhythms of girls hopscotching on a nearby sidewalk; the sway and strut of a bodega beat; the roar of a baseball crowd at Yankee Stadium; mothers calling for their kids to come home; the rattle of a taxi; and, yeah, that lullaby of Broadway.
>
> She's Irish, she's American, she's international. She's the Bronx, Botswana, Balldehob [*sic*]. She's played solo and with groups in the noisiest of pubs and clubs, on cruise ships, in arenas and stadiums and Radio City Music Hall. I've seen her, heard her in all these venues and wondered, after you've been there and done that, Eileen, how are they going to keep you down on the farm? (McCourt 1999)

Ivers began playing Irish fiddle at the age of eight. Her principal mentor was the renowned fiddler Martin Mulvhill from County Limerick in western Ireland. Her talents were prodigious. She traveled to Ireland to compete in the All-Ireland Fiddle Championships and won—nine times! From there, she went from one success to another, performing with everyone from The Chieftains to the London Symphony Orchestra. She even found time to graduate *magna cum laude* in mathematics from Iona College.

In the late 1980s, Ivers began touring and recording as a solo fiddler and bandleader under her own name, crafting the unique and eclectic Irish-world music fusion sound with which she is now largely identified. Along the way came her starring musical role as featured fiddler in the Broadway production of *Riverdance* in the 1990s (for more information, visit the Online Learning Center at www.mhhe.com/bakan1), and after that co-founding membership in the groundbreaking all-women's group Cherish the Ladies.

guided listening experience

"Gravelwalk" (Medley), Eileen Ivers

- CD Track #2-20
- Featured performer(s)/group: Eileen Ivers group, with Eileen Ivers (acoustic fiddle and electric violin), Jerry O'Sullivan (uilleann pipes), Seamus Egan (Irish wooden flute), Bakithi Kumalo (electric bass), and Steve Gadd (drumset)
- Format: Complete track
- Source recording: *Crossing the Bridge,* by Eileen Ivers (Sony Classical SK 60746)

Crossing the Bridge is an album that fully demonstrates Eileen Ivers' eclectic, music-without-borders approach. In the CD's accompanying booklet, Frank McCourt describes the music of *Crossing the Bridge* as ". . . startling in its geographic variety: Spain, Africa, West Indies, Cuba, Ireland, always Ireland. And here you are digging jazz, jigs, hip hop, strains of reggae, flamenco, bluegrass. The Irish never stray far from country music. Who, after all, brought it to America?" (McCourt 1999).

The opening track of *Crossing the Bridge,* "Gravelwalk," is an innovative arrangement of a medley of three old-style Irish reels served up with hard-driving rock-Irish rhythmic grooves. Ivers' scorching electric violin solos on "Gravelwalk" belie their instrumental source. They sound like they are being played on an electric guitar rather than a violin, and the influence of guitar greats like Jim Hendrix and Carlos Santana is apparent (see Chapter 11 for more on Santana).

Ivers is joined on "Gravelwalk" by an all-star international cast of musicians, including the uilleann piper Jerry O'Sullivan, Irish wooden flute player Seamus Egan, American drummer Steve Gadd, and South African electric bassist Bakithi Kumalo. The collaboration results in an interesting and highly effective blend of diverse musical traditions and approaches that strays from, yet never loses touch with, the work's Irish musical foundation.

The track begins with ambient electro-acoustic sounds, which build and lead into the opening tune of the medley, "Fermoy Lasses." This is a standard, AABB-form Irish double reel, though Ivers twists around the conventional form a little bit in the arrangement. The presentation of the tune starts out in a fairly traditional style, with Ivers playing the melody on acoustic violin, accompanied by a drone-like bass line and straightforward rhythms in the drumset part. The uilleann pipes soon join the fiddle in playing the melody as the bass playing gets more active and syncopated.

The mainly traditional sound of the opening of "Fermoy Lasses" gets a facelift at 0:32 when Ivers switches to electric violin and manipulates the timbre of the instrument further through use of a "wah-wah" electronic effects device. This change is matched in the drumming part, as Gadd moves to a more rock-like groove with backbeat accents. As the arrangement continues, there are many modulations, as well as changes in instrumentation, musical texture, rhythmic accompaniment patterns, and overall style. Some portions of the medley sound resolutely Irish traditional, others like contemporary jazz, still others like hard rock, and quite a few like a seamless blend of all of the above. A wonderful improvised duet by Ivers (acoustic fiddle) and Seamus Egan (Irish wooden flute) that arrives in the middle of the second tune of the medley ("The Noisy Curlew") is a highlight of the performance. So too is Ivers' final electric violin solo in the last tune, "Gravelwalks to Granie," which builds and builds to an exciting climax.

"Gravelwalks to Granie" also takes us back full circle to the beginning of our journey. Listen carefully to the passage at 3:47 and you will recognize what you hear as the last of the three renditions of the characteristic Irish melodic figure featured in **Online Musical Illustration (OMI) #24** (the second of these renditions, which immediately precedes the Ivers clip in OMI #24, is by Altan and can be located in *its* original musical context at 1:05 of **CD ex. #2-19).** Comparing Eileen Ivers' "Gravelwalk" to all of the music that came before it during the course of our journey, we are once again reminded of the old Irish saying, "It's not the same, but it's just as nice."

guided listening quick summary

"Gravelwalk" (Medley), Eileen Ivers (CD ex. #2-20)

INTRODUCTION

0:00–0:20

- Ambient opening: electronic timbres, cymbal roll with crescendo (0:15), Irish wooden flute (0:18).

"FERMOY LASSES" (MEDLEY TUNE #1)

0:21–0:28—A

- Key: E Dorian; melody played on acoustic fiddle (Ivers).
- Fairly traditional accompaniment, with drone-based harmony and straightforward drum rhythms.

0:28–0:35—A′

- Uilleann pipes prominent; bass/drum accompaniment more syncopated.
- Ivers switches to electric violin with "wah-wah" effect at 0:32.

0:36–0:50—AA′

■ Melody now played on electric violin (with "wah-wah" effects).

■ Rock-style drumming with backbeats.

0:50–1:04—BB′

■ Modulation from E Dorian to G major.

■ Ivers switches back to acoustic fiddle as drumming intensifies and bass outlines chord progression (rather than drone-based harmonies).

1:05–1:19—A′A′

■ Similar to before, with Irish wooden flute prominent in melodic texture.

1:19–1:33—BB

■ Celebratory return of the **B** part material.

■ Fiddle, flute, uilleann pipes play melody; big, "orchestral" synthesizer chords add dramatic effect.

1:33–1:47—A′A′

■ As before, but with more electronic timbres.

"THE NOISY CURLEW" [A.K.A. "JACK MCGUIRE'S"] (MEDLEY TUNE #2)

1:48–2:01—AA′

■ Fiddle (Ivers) and Irish wooden flute (Egan) introduce melody without accompanying instruments; Ivers weaves chords and rhythmic patterns in as she plays the melody.

2:02–2:15—BB′

■ Similar texture, except at 2:09–2:12, where Ivers breaks away from the melody momentarily to provide a rhythmic, drone accompaniment to the flute.

2:15–2:29—A′A′

■ Improvised fiddle-flute duet with multiple-melody texture and clever interplay between Ivers and Egan.

2:29–2:43—B′B′

■ Call-and-response dialogue between the fiddle-flute duo and the full band, who trade four-measure phrases (i.e., "trading fours," a borrowing from jazz).

INTERLUDE (JAZZ-ROCK STYLE; NOT BASED ON ANY IRISH TUNE)

2:43–2:57

■ Electric bass solo (Kumalo) over driving, rock-like drum groove.

2:58–3:22

■ Electric violin solo (Ivers); rhythmic groove intensifies.

3:23–3:26

■ Transitional material (based on a "Fermoy Lasses" melodic fragment).

"GRAVELWALKS TO GRANIE" (MEDLEY TUNE #3)

3:26–3:40—AB

■ Modulation to A Dorian; relatively traditional sound and texture (acoustic instruments, straightforward rhythmic accompaniment).

3:40–3:47—C

■ Modulation to D major; prominent uilleann pipes; building intensity.

3:47–4:01—DD′

- **D** melody arrives triumphantly, along with a modulation to C major; melody instruments (fiddle, flute, pipes) continue as before; syncopated "shots" in bass and drums outline chord progression.
- Same music heard in final (third) segment of Online Musical Illustration #24.

4:01–end—ABCDD′, then D′D′D′D′ vamp to end

- Varied reprise of the whole "Gravelwalks to Granie" tune, with more electric violin soloing.
- Ivers "takes over" through the vamp at the end, driving the performance to its climactic unison finish.

Summary

In this chapter, we journeyed a long distance, from the traditional dance tune performances of Seamus Ennis to the Irish-rock-world music fusion of Eileen Ivers. Along the way, we witnessed profound musicultural transformations of Irish traditional music on multiple levels. Despite their many differences, however, the various types of music we listened to were all the same at a core level. The same kinds of tunes, instruments, dance tune forms, medley-based musical designs, and basic approaches to melodic ornamentation and variation were present in each. But the styles of performing the old dance tune melodies that were at the heart of all the music varied considerably from era to era and example to example. And the presence or absence of imported, nontraditionally Irish musical elements—as well as their degree of influence and musical use—were also important factors of difference.

Irish traditional music, like most traditional musics of the world, has endured and been transformed in response to the changing social, political, and cultural conditions that surround it. This chapter examined how Irish nationalism and transnationalism, modernization and urbanization, and musical and cultural revival have become inscribed on one particular domain of Irish traditional music: Irish dance tunes. As both a specifically Irish and an internationally pan-Irish phenomenon, the Irish dance tune symbolizes and serves as a medium for the performance of Irish identity and social life. It takes on different meanings in the home, the dance hall, the concert hall, and the recording studio. It says different things about its performers and audiences depending on who plays it, the instrument or instruments on which it is played, and the style and context in which it is performed. It also reflects very different social values and historical conditions by virtue of whether or not it is used to accompany dancing at all, and if so, what kind. Yet regardless of the musical surfaces to which they become attached or the historical or cultural realities they reflect, embody, and inform, Irish dance tunes always speak and respond to a core sense of what it is to be Irish, be that in Ireland, North America, or anywhere in the world.

Key Terms

Irish traditional music	sean nós	medley
pan-Irish	ceílí	tinwhistle
Irish Gaelic (language)	jig	uilleann pipes
Irish potato famine	hornpipe	Celtic
Irish diaspora	reel	Irish wooden flute
Radio Éireann	ornaments (roll, cran, treble,	bodhrán
Irish music revival	cut, triplet)	
session		

Study Questions

- Besides dance tunes, what are the other four main categories of Irish traditional music?
- What is sean nós, and why is it an important component of Irish traditional music?

- What were some of the major developments of (and issues in) Irish traditional music during the Irish Free State period? What impact did the urbanization and modernization of Ireland during this and subsequent periods have on music?
- What instruments are conventionally used in Irish traditional music?
- How are the uilleann pipes constructed and played? What important uilleann pipers were discussed in this chapter?
- What is the difference between a ceílí and an Irish music session?
- What were the distinctive contributions of Seamus Ennis and Sean Ó'Riada to the preservation and development of Irish traditional music?
- How did The Chieftains first form and what is their historical (and contemporary) significance?
- What features have defined the modern, ensemble style of Irish music since the Irish music revival that began in the 1960s? (Summarize list from chapter.)
- Who were some of the leading proponents of Irish traditional music of the 1970s? The 1980s and 1990s?
- How have processes of diaspora and transnationalism impacted Irish traditional music? What are examples from the chapter that illustrate this impact?

Discussion Questions

- How might the historical development of Irish music traced in this chapter be shown to directly reflect the histories of Irish nationhood, urbanization, modernization, and transnational pan-Irish identity?
- While she is widely respected and admired for her artistry, Eileen Ivers also is regarded as a controversial representative of the Irish music tradition in certain circles. What case could be made in support of her inclusion as a representative of Irish traditional music? What case could be made against that status?

Applying What You Have Learned

- The Irish music session has become a common social institution in many parts of the world today. If you live in a city or college town, there is a good chance that you can find a session or other Irish music performance to attend in your local area. Try to locate a nearby session and go to it. Bring a notepad and jot down your observations: At what kind of a venue is the session held (pub, restaurant, nightclub)? What instruments do the musicians play? What can you say about the tunes played and the styles of performance on the basis of what you learned in this chapter? What kinds of social interactions go on between the participating musicians, and between the musicians and the audience? Is there any dancing? What does it feel like for you to be a part of this environment? Use your notes as the basis of a brief ethnomusicological report on the session and your experience of it.

- Locate several recordings of Irish or Irish-influenced music. Listen to each, applying your listening skills and what you have learned in this chapter to a compare-and-contrast exploration of the music. Identify any Irish instruments you hear. Note what other kinds of instruments they are combined with. Try to determine whether any of the music uses the standard tune forms (e.g., AABB) or medley forms of traditional Irish music, and whether these appear "as is" or mixed up with other kinds of forms (e.g., verse-chorus, 12-bar blues, ostinato-based). Listen to how the melodies are played or sung, noting whether the conventional types of melodic ornaments used in Irish music are employed.

Resources for Further Study

Visit the Online Learning Center at **www.mhhe.com/bakan1** for learning aids, study help, and additional resources that supplement the content of this chapter.

chapter ten

musical **conversations:**
communication and collective expression
in West African musics

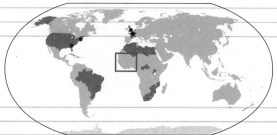

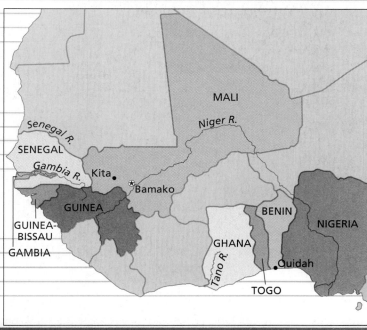

Related locations:

Algeria	Mozambique
Brazil	Puerto Rico
Central African Republic	South Africa
Cuba	Trinidad and Tobago
Egypt	Uganda
England	Zimbabwe
France	Bahia, Brazil
Haiti	Mediterranean Sea
Holland	Sahara Desert
Jamaica	
Libya	Athens, Georgia
Morocco	London
	New York
	Paris

The river crosses the path,
the path crosses the river,
who is elder?

The path was cut to meet the river,
the river is of old,
the river comes from
   "Odomankoma" the Creator

Akan (AH-kahn)

This translated passage from an ancient proverb of the **Akan** people of Ghana, West Africa, sets the tone for our exploration of West African music. Its text speaks metaphorically to the key issues that underlie the musicultural journey of this chapter: intersections, pathways, relationships, interdependence, homage.

The proverb begins in the form of a riddle: Which is older, the river or the path? Then we learn the answer. It is the river that is older. The river comes from the divine source of creation. It provides the water that is the source of life and human sustenance, and it connects Akan people who find meaning in this proverb to Odomankoma, the Creator.

Yet it is the path, cut to meet the great Tano River by Akan ancestors of long ago, that connects the Akan to the Tano, marking the routes and

World events		Music events
Advanced civilizations and powerful empires across sub-Saharan Africa: Mande, Ghana, Songhay, Dahomey, Baganda ●	**Pre-15th century**	
Sunjata Keita unifies Mande (Mali) empire, centered in Bamako, Mali ●	**13th century CE (c. 1225–1252)**	● Jeliya tradition dates from Sunjata period
Progressive colonization and foreign domination of sub-Saharan Africa ●	**15th–20th centuries**	
Decline and collapse of traditional African nations, empires ●		
Transformation of African political and cultural map ●		
Slave trade, African diaspora ●	**17th–19th centuries**	
Independent African nations established across continent in post-colonial era ●	**Post-1945**	● Sidiki Diabate and song "Kaira" closely identified with struggle for Malian independence beginning in 1940s
Ghana becomes independent nation (formerly a British colony) ●	**1957**	
Mali becomes independent nation (formerly a French colony) ●	**1960**	
Dahomey (renamed Benin in 1975) becomes independent nation (formerly a French colony) ●		
	1970s	● American blues guitarist and world music pioneer Taj Mahal first encounters the kora, ultimately leading to travels in Mali and collaborations with Malian musicians (Toumani Diabate, Ali Farka Toure)
	1971	● Release of *Ancient Strings* (Sidiki Diabate and Djelimadi Sissoko), first internationally distributed recording featuring the kora
	1994–1996	● Angélique Kidjo rises to world music stardom with dance single "Ayé" (1994), album *Fifa* (1996)
	1999	● Release of *Kulanjan,* by Taj Mahal and Toumani Diabate, featuring "Atlanta Kaira"
	2001	● Seckou Keita releases *Baiyo:* re-released by ARC Music Productions International Ltd. under the title *Mali* in 2002 (features "Dounuya")
	2002	● Angélique Kidjo releases *Black Ivory Soul,* featuring "Iwoya" (with Dave Matthews) and "Okan Bale"

roots of human existence along the way. The path must meet the river to find its earthly purpose, yet the river must be met *by* the path to fulfill its own *divine* purpose, which is of utmost importance to the Akan. Both the river and the path are essential, indivisible. Human life relies upon their union and reciprocity.

The telling of this Akan proverb can be performed in different ways. It may be recited in spoken words or it may be recited in **drum speech.** This is because the language in which it is composed, Twi, is a **tonal language.** The meaning of a word in a tonal language like Twi is determined not just by the actual sounds of its syllables, but also by the specific patterns of pitch, rhythm, and timbral inflection with which it is articulated. The exact "same" word can thus mean completely different things if the pitch, rhythm, and timbre with which it is uttered are altered. For example, *akonta,* if pronounced "a-kon-TA" (with the accent on the last syllable) is understood to mean brother-in-law, while "a-KON-ta" (accenting the middle syllable) translates as mathematics. By replicating the pitch, rhythm, and timbre patterns of verbal speech, certain Akan drums such as the **atumpan** are literally capable of speaking themselves.

An example of drum speech on the atumpan is featured in **CD ex. #2-21.** This is an excerpt from a recording of the Akan proverb of the river and the path. Each text phrase is recited verbally and then reiterated in drum language. Listen to the example now, noting how the flow of pitches, rhythms, and timbres of each spoken part (the call) is replicated in the drum-speech part on the atumpan that follows it (the response). The portion of the proverb heard in the first 25 seconds of the example is included below in Twi and also in an English translation. Additional, shorter passages of call-and-response interaction between the voice and atumpan are heard in the final 30 seconds of the excerpt, where it is actually somewhat easier to hear that the voice and drum are "saying" the same words.

Atumpan drums (right) accompanying a dance performance by an Akan woman.

Twi (Chwee)

atumpan (AH-toom-pahn)

Twi text:	English translation
Asuo twa okwan,	The river crosses the path,
okwan twa asuo,	the path crosses the river,
opani ne hwan?	who is elder?
Asuo twa okwan,	The river crosses the path,
okwan twa asuo,	the path crosses the river,
opani ne hwan?	who is elder?
Yeboo kwan no katoo asuo no,	The path was cut to meet the river,
Asuo no firi tete,	the river is of old,
Asuo no firi Odomankoma a oboo adee	the river comes from "Odomankoma" the Creator

Transcription and translation: Daniel Agyei Dwarko (in Vetter 1996: 18–19).

The river and the path are literal parts of the Akan world. They are also metaphors with multiple levels of meaning. Just as the path must meet the river, the Akan must cut their own paths toward communion with the sources of their creation: divine, ancestral, familial, natural. They also must aim to follow their individual pathways toward intersection with one another and mutual support. The ideal of mutual interdependence is of key importance for Akan people, as for people everywhere. We all have our individual paths and there is often the temptation to go it alone. Yet it is together, collectively, as members of communities

The kora, played by the late kora master Jali Mori Suso.

human and beyond, that we usually find ourselves best equipped to meet our needs, solve our problems, and pay homage to those to whom it is due. This Akan proverb encodes such messages and ideals in its literal and metaphorical depiction of the path and the river.

Much music in West Africa encodes similar ideals. Metaphorically, the artistry of West African music explored in this chapter *is* the meeting of the path and the river. Like the river, it flows to the pulse of many different rhythms, timbres, and layers that, on first impression, may suggest little sense of integrated coherence (that is, to the non-African listener). But, ultimately, the multidimensional musical flow reveals itself as an integrated collective of individual "voices" that are unified by shared values and a communal sense of purpose.

This chapter explores the musical element of polyphony, music of "many sounds," of "many parts." It might be more accurate, however, to describe this as a chapter about **polyvocality,** many *voices.* The music we will explore is not generally conceived of by its makers as music that exists solely for its own sake. Rather, it is a form of *conversation,* in which people alternately speak in turn and all at once. The ability of many voices to speak and be heard simultaneously, and in the process to express a unified diversity of views and perspectives, is valued in many modes of social and conversational interaction in West Africa. It resonates strongly in the social interaction of music making. Exploring how this works is our main musicultural focus.

The chapter begins by briefly situating West African musics within broader musical, cultural, and geographical contexts of the continent of Africa and beyond. We then explore polyvocality in a second Akan drumming-based piece. After that, the focus turns to three different pieces of music that all feature a particular instrument, the **kora.** This is a remarkable harp-like chordophone of the **Mande** peoples of western Africa with a history dating back centuries. Today, the ancient legacy of the kora is preserved in the art of **jeliya,** the musical repertoire of the hereditary "praise singer," or **griot,** families among the Mande. The kora also has taken on a new life as a prominent musical instrument in a wide range of both African and international popular, intercultural jazz, and world beat music circles.

Mande (MAHN-day)

jeliya (jay-lee-uh)

griot (GREE-oh)

African Musics in Context

"Africa," writes Peter Fletcher, "gave birth to the first human beings and—we may assume—to the first human song" (Fletcher 2001:145). Indeed, Africa retains some of the world's oldest extant musical traditions. The origins of some of these may date back to tens of thousands of years ago.

But music in Africa, in many respects, is the heartbeat of modern, global musical expression as well. The rhythms and textures of just about every major international popular music phenomenon of the past century—from mambo to hip-hop and rock to reggae—have their roots in African soil, and African musicians continue to reshape and redefine contemporary world music expression right up to the present day. These include Angélique Kidjo and Toumani Diabate, whose music we will explore, as well as Youssou N'Dour (who was featured on Peter Gabriel's hit recording of "In Your Eyes"), Manu Dibango (featured on Michael Jackson's "Wanna Be Startin' Something"), N'Faly Kouyate (kora player with the Afro Celts), and the South African vocal group Ladysmith Black Mambazo (featured on Paul Simon's *Graceland* and also on the soundtrack of *The Lion King*).

Toumani Diabate
(Too-MAH-nee
Jah-BAH-tay)

Youssou N'Dour
(Yoo-soo En-DOOR)

N'Faly Kouyate
(En-FAH-lee
Koo-YAH-tay)

The African continent, sub-Saharan Africa, and the African diaspora

Africa is a huge continent. Its landmass is second in size only to that of Asia, covering more than 11 million square miles and accounting for more than 20 percent of the earth's land surface. About

one-quarter of the world's population resides in Africa itself, and millions of people of African descent reside throughout the world in the **African diaspora,** with especially large population concentrations in the United States, Brazil, the Caribbean (Cuba, Haiti, Jamaica, Trinidad and Tobago), and major European metropolises such as London and Paris.

The northern portion of the continent of Africa covers the vast Sahara Desert and is bordered along its northern coast by the Mediterranean Sea. This region includes Egypt and the North African nations of the Maghrib, which spans from Libya in the east to Morocco in the West. Islam is the dominant religion of North Africa and Arab culture is pervasive throughout this region (see Chapter 12).

Africa south of the Sahara, or sub-Saharan Africa, is the subject of this chapter. More specifically, our focus is on selected musicultural traditions originating from western Africa south of the Sahara. West African musical traditions are rich and varied in and of themselves and have had a profound impact on the course of musical developments worldwide over the past several centuries. This was the region of the continent from which most African slaves were brought to the Americas. In the Americas, African- and European-derived musics blended to form the foundations of many new types and styles of music. It is to this development that we trace the origins of ragtime, blues, jazz, rhythm-and-blues, soul, rock-and-roll, rap, hip-hop, salsa, Cuban *son,* Puerto Rican bomba, Trinidadian steel band, Jamaican reggae, Brazilian samba, and scores of other musical genres and subgenres too numerous to mention. In turn, elements of these and many other musics of the African diaspora have been reabsorbed back into newer styles of music in Africa, and from there have gone on to influence other international styles. In short, there is a continuous feedback loop between Mother Africa, the African diaspora, and global music making on a worldwide scale.

Music, culture, and history in sub-Saharan Africa

Sub-Saharan Africa comprises a huge geographical region of extraordinary ethnic, cultural, and musical diversity. For much of its history, large portions of the region were ruled by powerful kingdoms. The empires of Mande, Ghana, Songhay, Dahomey, and Baganda that thrived centuries ago were among the world's most powerful during their respective eras. From the 15th century

Songhay (Song-HIGH)

Dahomey (Duh-HO-mee [or Dah-oh-MAY])

onward, however, European (and, later, U.S.) intervention and domination led to the dismantling of reigning African imperial powers and a transformation of the African political and cultural map. The most visible manifestations of this foreign encroachment were the slave trade of the 17th–19th centuries and the colonization of the majority of sub-Saharan Africa that occurred between the 19th century and well into the middle decades of the 20th century (and in South Africa and certain other nations, long after that as well). Beyond transforming Africa itself, colonization and the slave trade combined with other sociopolitical forces to initiate the African diaspora, which witnessed the forced or voluntary migration of millions of people from the African continent to other parts of the world, especially the Americas and certain parts of western Europe.

Since the end of World War II, the African continent has come to encompass many postcolonial, independent African nations. While great triumphs have been achieved in terms of sovereignty and civil rights in many modern African societies, struggles for freedom from colonial rule and for national independence were long, fierce, and costly on many levels. Political stability and economic prosperity have remained elusive for many African nations and peoples. Warfare, continued foreign exploitation of African lands and resources, and public health crises of catastrophic proportions such as the African AIDS pandemic have brought major challenges.

In African nationalist movements and African responses to modern sociopolitical challenges and opportunities alike, the revival, revitalization, and modernization of traditional forms of African music, dance, and ceremonial practice have figured prominently. So too has the development of new forms and styles of music aimed at responding to, reflecting, and affecting contemporary situations and circumstances. These new musical forms and styles frequently build from a combination of indigenous African and international elements, the latter most prominently influenced by U.S., Caribbean, and South American musics that evolved within the African diaspora (e.g., American popular musics and jazz, Cuban rumba [see Chapter 11, pp. 223–24], Brazilian samba). "Ingculaza (AIDS)" (**CD ex. #1-47**), a song by the Zimbabwean musician Dumisani "Ramadu" Moyo that was discussed in Chapter 6 (pp. 83–84), is a good example. It incorporates traditional African instruments (e.g., hand drums) and musical elements (e.g., singing style) into a setting that otherwise relies heavily on the instrumental and stylistic resources of African-American popular music idioms such as soul and rhythm-and-blues. This syncretic mixture of elements serves as the musical backdrop for Ramadu to address, in his native southern African language, Ndebele, the AIDS crisis in Africa.

Religion is a pervasive force in life throughout sub-Saharan Africa. Islam and Christianity are widespread, though their practice often represents a syncretism with indigenous forms of African religion that predated their arrival. There are hundreds, if not thousands, of religions practiced in sub-Saharan Africa. The diversity of religious belief and practice is immense. Paying homage and due respect—to deities, venerated ancestors, community leaders and elders, and the creative and sustaining forces of nature—is a major priority of religious practice and social life generally. Often this takes the form of communal rituals involving music and the active participation of all in attendance (whether through singing, playing music instruments, dancing, clapping, or some other mode of participation). The collective expression of the community as a whole, diverse in its individual components, polyvocal in its articulation, unified in its totality, is highly valued in the act of paying homage. The spiritual/social values of paying homage and collective expression are strongly reflected in all of the music we will examine.

Ndebele
(IN-duh-bel-ee)

Drumming

The first thing that comes to mind for many people when they think about music in Africa is drumming. Indeed, drums and drumming are prominent in the musical traditions of many African cultures. This is certainly the case in West African countries like Ghana, where the Akan drum proverb of **CD ex. #2-21** heard earlier is from. **CD ex. #2-22** features another drumming-based example of Akan music. This time, however, rather than just one drummer, there is an ensemble of percussionists. All perform on drums with the exception of one, who plays a steady, repeating rhythmic pattern (ostinato) on an iron bell called a *dawuro*. This is music of the royal Akan drum ensemble known as **Fontomfrom.** It provides an excellent introduction to the concept of a conversation played out in musical tones between multiple participants "speaking" all together at once and in turn. Listen to it now as a prelude to the discussion that follows.

Fontomfrom: An Akan royal drum ensemble

The Akan are one of several West African ethnic groups who reside principally in the nation of Ghana, a former British colony that achieved national independence in 1957. English is the official language of Ghana, but about half of Ghanaians speak some version of the Akan language as well. Twi, the language of the river-and-path drum proverb, is the most widely spoken of these.

The Akan are principally a matrilineal people, which means that they trace their descent lines through the side of the mother. All Akan who can trace their ancestry back through their mother, maternal grandmother, and earlier generations of matriarchs to a common ancestress are considered blood relatives belonging to the same clan. All members of a clan are obligated to participate in rituals devoted to honoring their family ancestors, "a practice that is still central to Akan identity even among those who have converted to Christianity" (Vetter 1996:3).

In former times, Akan chiefs ruled over Akan societies. Today, their leadership role has been overtaken to a significant degree by the Ghanaian government. Nonetheless, most small-scale claims involving land issues or domestic disputes are still mediated by village, district, or regional chiefs (Vetter 1996:12).

Akan chiefs, today as in the past, use certain types of traditional music and music instruments to symbolize their power and stature. Purchasing a royal set of drums such as a Fontomfrom and sponsoring Fontomfrom performances is a long-established tradition among Akan chiefs. These drums are played at events where the chief makes a public appearance: processions, village ceremonies, funerals. The chief may dance at such occasions to the accompaniment of Fontomfrom music, often while brandishing a royal sword. An assistant stands close by throughout the dance, ready to catch the chief should he accidentally stumble and begin to fall. It is

Fontomfrom drums being carried in an Akan royal procession. The chief is also held aloft during the procession.

imperative that he not fall, since if he does, this is taken by the Akan as a sign that he is weak or vulnerable. In some instances, the drums of the Fontomfrom ensemble may be used to make specific utterances in the "speech mode" of drum language, such as *"Nana, bre bre"* ("Chief, walk majestically"). Additionally, call-and-response dialogue, with drummed linguistic content, may occur between the different drums of the ensemble.

The Musical Guided Tour and related Guided Listening Experience which follow collectively provide a musical introduction to the Fontomfrom tradition. Fontomfrom is used here to illustrate the principle of *musical conversation* as a fundamental element of West African music. The transcript below corresponds to the audio Musical Guided Tour. As you listen to this tour at the Online Learning Center (www.mhhe.com/bakan1), follow along with this transcript.

musical guided tour

Instruments and Basic Rhythmic Patterns in Fontomfrom Music

The instrumentation of the Fontomfrom ensemble we heard in **CD ex. #2-22** consists of the *gongon* bell plus three pairs of drums. The first pair of drums is the *from* (frahm), the second is the atumpan, and the third is the *eguankoba* (ay-gwan-koh-bah) (see the photo below). All of the drums are barrel-like in shape and have a single drum head that is attached to the instrument with pegs. They are all played with wooden sticks.

The *from* is a very tall, heavy type of drum with a low pitch [♪]. The lead drummer of the Fontomfrom ensemble plays on the *from*. The atumpan are also large and heavy, though they are not nearly as tall as the *from* and are higher in pitch [♪]. The eguankoba are thin, relatively tall drums (taller than the atum-

Fontomfrom ensemble, left to right: eguankoba, atumpan, dawuro (difficult to see), and *from.*

pan, but significantly shorter than the *from*). Their pitch is higher than that of the other drums in the ensemble [♪].

Throughout the Fontomfrom piece we listened to earlier, a continually recurring rhythmic pattern was played on the gongon bell. We will call this rhythm the *time-line*. It sounds like this [♪]. Now, try to clap out the time-line rhythm together with me as I play it on the dawuro. (Use the notation below as a guide.)

1	2	3	4	5	6	7	8	9	10	11	12	(1)
X	•	X	•	X	•	X	X	•	X	•	X	(X)

The time-line rhythm of the dawuro can be felt in several different ways. One way to feel it is as a four-beat pattern with three subdivisions per beat, like this [♪]. When this music accompanies dancing, the steps of the dancers often correspond to this way of feeling the rhythm.

The different drum parts line up with, and "cut across," the time-line rhythm of the gongon in various ways. This creates a texture of *polyrhythms:* multiple layers of rhythm (in the different drum parts) that imply different beats and meters occurring all at the same time. A great range of different rhythmic variations—some set, some improvised—occur in each of the drum parts. The *from* and the atumpan parts tend to be especially varied in their rhythms. There are, however, certain standard, recurring Fontomfrom rhythmic patterns for each drum part that interlock with one another and with the gongon time-line. Here, we focus specifically on one such set of rhythmic patterns.

To begin, here is a standard pattern played on the *from* [♪]. Against the gongon time-line, it sounds like this [♪].

Next, a standard atumpan pattern [♪], which against the bell sounds like this [♪].

Finally, here is one standard eguankoba pattern [♪]. And now here it is again with the dawuro [♪]. Now the second eguankoba drum pattern [♪], and that pattern together with the gongon.

Now let's build up the full polyrhythmic texture one instrument at a time. Try to clap out the dawuro pattern continuously as the different drumming layers are gradually added in.

Here is the dawuro alone [♪]. Now we add the *from* [♪] and the atumpan [♪], the first eguankoba [♪], and the second eguankoba [♪]. A visual illustration of all the rhythms together is provided in Figure 10.1.

In this tour, we have only scratched the surface of the complexity of an actual Fontomfrom performance such as that heard in **CD ex. #2-22.** Nonetheless, the tour provides a foundation for understanding and appreciating that complexity, and at least a rudimentary sense of how the principle of multipart musical conversation in West African music works.

	1	2	3	4	5	6	7	8	9	10	11	12	(1)
Dawuro	X	•	X	•	X	•	X	X	•	X	•	X	(X)
Eguankoba 1	X	•	X	•	X	•	X	X	•	X	X	X	(X)
Eguankoba 2	•	•	X	•	X	•	•	X	•	•	X	•	(•)
Atumpan	X	X	X	X	X	•	X	X	X	X	X	•	(X)
From	•	X	•	X	X	•	•	X	•	X	X	•	( )

FIGURE 10.1

Multiple layers of rhythm in Fontomfrom (Musical Guided Tour).

guided listening experience

Fontomfrom (Akan Royal Drum Ensemble Music)

- CD Track #**2-22**
- Featured performer(s)/group: Eyisam Mbensuon (group), led by Opanyin Yaw Amoah
- Format: Excerpt
- Source recording: "Fontomfrom," from *Rhythms of Life, Songs of Wisdom: Akan Music from Ghana, West Africa* (Smithsonian Folkways SF CD 40463)

We return now to the Akan performance of Fontomfrom music featured on the CD set. This is an excerpt from a recording made in Ghana by the ethnomusicologist Roger Vetter. The first sounds you hear are rhythms played by the lead drummer on the *from* drums, which serve to announce the start of the performance. In his authority and leadership, the *from* drummer may be likened symbolically to the chief in whose honor the music is played.

The gongon bell joins the *from* almost immediately (at 0:02), playing the same time-line rhythmic pattern illustrated earlier in our Musical Guided Tour. Note that the gongon player "misses" the first note of that pattern the very first time he plays it (Figure 10.2).

The atumpan and eguankoba drums enter at about 0:08–0:09 as the dawuro continues and the *from* plays one intricate rhythmic variation after another. The other drums introduce rhythmic variations as well here, and the overall effect is dizzying in its polyrhythmic complexity. For the next 11 dawuro time-line cycles (0:10–0:26), it sounds to the untrained ear almost as though the ensemble is not even playing together at many points. In fact, the ensemble *is* playing together, very much so, but their togetherness is not of a rigid lock-step order. Rather, it has freedom, elasticity. The various drum parts flow into, around, and over each other like the rushing waters of a swift river, each changing course as needs be to accommodate the curves in the river's path.

At 0:27, there is a breath-length pause in the drumming, after which the drums re-enter over the continuing pattern of the dawuro. Now the rhythms become more steady and pattern-based. Specific, recurring patterns (similar to the ones illustrated in the preceding Musical Guided Tour) come to be associated with each of the different drum parts and are layered atop one another and varied in different ways (i.e., layered ostinato texture with variations). These patterns are not mere musical utterances, but linguistic ones as well, "spoken" in the tonal language of the drums in this conversation between members of what is essentially a drum family.

The lead drummer directs the ensemble from the *from* with rhythmic cues and commands that mark transitions and different sections of the performance. The conversational element of the music becomes most clear in those sections where the *from* and the atumpan engage in a back-and-forth series of drummed statements and replies. These call-and-response musical dialogues occur at 0:33–0:47 and 1:03–1:32.

In its totality, this music is far more than a mere drumming piece. It is also a multipart conversation and a musical model of idealized Akan social interaction.

1	2	3	4	5	6	7	8	9	10	11	12	(1)
(X)*	●	X	●	X	●	X	X	●	X	●	X	(X)

*Note: First note of pattern is *not played* first time through cycle.

Gongon time-line, "Fontomfrom."

FIGURE 10.2

Unifying Features of Music in West Africa: Musical Africanisms

Despite popular misconceptions to the contrary, there is really no such thing as "African music" *per se*. Rather, as has already been alluded to, there are many different *African musics*. These musics collectively encompass a great range of musicultural diversity and are all unique and distinct in their own right. They span the gamut from traditional ritual and ceremonial musics of rural, village societies; to national musical forms associated with modern African nations; to regional genres that transcend ethnic or national affiliation; to transnational popular and experimental musics that creatively combine African traditional and myriad non-African musical elements.

Nonetheless, despite all of this diversity, many musics of sub-Saharan Africa, and of West Africa in particular, do exhibit certain key, readily identifiable features and musicultural characteristics that are widely shared (and that are prominent in many African diasporic musics as well). Ethnomusicologists identify these as musical **Africanisms.** We have encountered some of these already; others will come up in connection with musical selections still to be explored. The following list introduces and defines six of the most salient ones:

- **Complex polyphonic textures.** Textures featuring multiple layers of instruments/voices are common in sub-Saharan Africa. The Fontomfrom music of **CD ex. #2-22** and all of the other music we will explore later in the chapter exemplify this feature.

- **Layered ostinatos with varied repetition.** A standard device for creating polyphony in sub-Saharan African music is the layering of multiple, recurring patterns (ostinatos) one on top of another. This was well illustrated in **CD ex. #2-22,** in which, as is common, the ostinato patterns tend to recur in varied forms rather than in the same form each time (varied repetition). (Listen, for example, to the passage of **CD ex. #2-22** from 1:18–1:24.)

- **Conversational element.** Sub-Saharan African musics are frequently conversational in character, whether literally, figuratively, or metaphorically. The musical conversations come in many forms. They may have a call-and-response format, as in the river-and-path drum proverb and certain sections of the Fontomfrom piece; or they may be more in the mode of having many voices all speaking at once—complementing and commenting upon one another's utterances—again, as in some passages of the Fontomfrom piece (e.g., **CD ex. #2-22,** 0:10–0:26, 0:48–1:02). The relationship between music and dance that is so central to much sub-Saharan African performance also is frequently defined by a conversational character, a dialogue of sound and movement. (*Note:* Though music is closely linked to dance in a great many African traditions, African dance and the relationship of music and dance in Africa are beyond the scope of this chapter. Lists of resources for exploring the close relationship of music and dance in African societies, and for exploring a diverse range of African musical-cultural traditions, are included at the Online Learning Center at www.mhhe.com/bakan1.)

- **Improvisation.** Improvisation is a hallmark of sub-Saharan African musical expression. Even in relatively "set" compositions that have been passed down through the generations or that are now transmitted via music notation, the incorporation of improvisation—sometimes subtle, sometimes pronounced—is usually expected. The lead drumming part of the *from* in **CD ex. #2-22** features much improvisation. The prominent place of improvisation in sub-Saharan African musics is likewise characteristic of African-American musical traditions such as blues, jazz, and rap.

- **Timbral variety.** Musicians in sub-Saharan Africa often exhibit a fascination with exploring a wide range of timbral possibilities. Rather than aiming for a "pure" tone, African singers and instrumentalists may manipulate their voices and instruments to produce "buzzing" timbres and other timbral effects. The buzzing sound of the *mbira dzavadzimu* on **CD ex. #1-37** (produced by the rattling of bottle caps that are attached loosely to the instrument's frame—see photo, p. 69) is a good example of this.

- **Distinctive pitch systems and scales.** Certain types of scales, modes, and tuning systems predominate in sub-Saharan Africa. We will encounter some of these in later musical examples.

mbira dzavadzimu (em-BEE-rah dzah-vah-DZEE-moo)

Timbila ("xylophone") orchestra of the Chopi people, Mozambique.

BaMbuti (BEH-em-boo-tee)

More than Drumming: African Musical Diversity and the Kora

Thus far, the music we have examined in this chapter has been almost exclusively drumming-based. Drums and drumming have undeniable importance in many African traditions, but it is important to realize that *drumming is **not** the basis of most music in Africa,* much of which does not include any drumming at all.

Highly developed forms of polyphonic music that are purely vocal, such as the traditional elephant hunting song of the Central African BaMbuti people heard on **CD ex. #1-40** (see pp. 77–78), are found throughout sub-Saharan Africa. The melodic complexity and sublime beauty of music played on the mbira dzavadzimu (**CD ex. #1-37,** p. 69), an instrument of the Shona people of Zimbabwe that is one of many types of *plucked idiophones* in Africa, is another highlight of non-drumming-based African musical artistry. There are also large orchestras of xylophone-type instruments

Mmen animal horn aerophones (right), Ghana.

Damascus Kafumbe playing endongo, a Ugandan chordophone.

and a great range of different kinds of aerophones, from animal horn trumpets and flutes to conch shells. Many imported instruments also have become part and parcel of the sound of much music in Africa. The acoustic guitar and the electric guitar are primary among these.

Chordophone-based traditions of many different types abound, from music of the one-stringed *nkokwane* "musical bow" of the Qwii people (Bushmen, San) of southern Africa (**CD ex. #1-44,** p. 80) to *endongo* music of Uganda. Endongo, played by one of the instrument's leading exponents, Damascus Kafumbe, is featured on **CD ex. #2-23** (note the interesting "buzzing" timbre of this instrument).

The kora, a chordophone of the Mande peoples of West Africa that combines guitar- and harp-like features, is probably the most widely known and appreciated nonpercussion instrument of sub-Saharan Africa on an international scale. It has become an international symbol of "African music" in much the way that the sitar has become an international symbol of "Indian music" (see Chapter 8). Also like the sitar, it is an instrument whose sound has come to international attention both through the global exposure of its traditional musical repertoire and through its prominent use in intercultural popular, experimental, and jazz-based music styles.

nkokwane
(en-koh-kwah-nay)

endongo
(ayn-doan-goh)

The Kora and Its Musicultural World

The kora is a 21-string *spike harp chordophone* (see the labeled diagram of Figure 10.3 on p. 198). All spike harps have a neck (curved or straight) that pierces the resonator (body) of the instrument to form a post or tailpiece at the lower end. Spike harp chordophones are unique to West Africa.

The kora has a straight neck and a resonator made from a large calabash, or half gourd. A cow-hide face stretches over the opening of the calabash and is attached to it with decorative tacks. A soundhole—circular, square, or triangular in shape—is cut into the right side of the resonator and a high *bridge* is mounted onto the face. Two parallel rows of strings pass through notches that are carved into the bridge. The strings are made of nylon fishing line; prior to the introduction of nylon, they were made from thin strips of twisted antelope hide (King 1972:121). Each string is attached to its own rawhide tuning collar on the neck and passes to one side or the other of the bridge. All 21 strings meet at the bottom of the instrument, where they are attached to an iron ring in the tailpiece (Figure 10.3).

When playing the kora, the performer holds the instrument by two handgrips mounted on either side of the neck and plucks the strings with only the thumbs and forefingers (see the photo on p. 198). The traditional method of playing is from a seated position on the floor, with the tail-piece also in contact with the floor to add resonance to the sound. Playing while sitting in a chair or while standing or moving about are also possible (see photo, p. 205). Today, the use of amplification

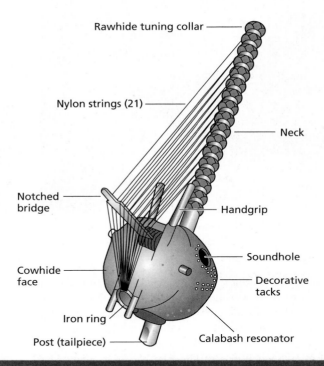

Rawhide tuning collar

Nylon strings (21)

Neck

Notched bridge

Handgrip

Soundhole

Cowhide face

Decorative tacks

Iron ring

Post (tailpiece)

Calabash resonator

FIGURE 10.3

Kora.

Right- and left-hand positioning on the kora.

Bamako (BAH-mah-koh)

compensates for the loss of resonance that normally occurs when these nontraditional methods of playing are employed.

Because it has a bridge, the kora is classified not only as a spike harp, but also as a *bridge harp* (see Knight 2001). Bridges are standard features on many types of chordophones (e.g., guitar, violin), but they are rarely found on harps. The kora's classification as a bridge harp is therefore important and distinctive.

Mande history and culture

The traditional homelands of the Mande span across the modern nations of Mali, Guinea, Guinea-Bissau, Senegal, and Gambia in western Africa. The great, ancient Mande civilization developed and spread along the three great waterways of this region: the western Niger River, the Senegal River, and the Gambia River.

In former times, the present homelands of the Mande were the domain of the powerful Mande empire, otherwise known as the Mali empire. This empire was unified by the legendary warrior and hero Sunjata Keita in the 13th century (sometime between 1225 and 1252). It was centered south of present-day Bamako, a city located on the banks of the Niger River in western Mali. Today, Bamako is the capital of the modern nation of Mali and remains the heartland of Mande culture.

Tales of the rise of the Mande empire from a small chiefdom ruled by great hunters to an expansive and powerful West African empire under Sunjata form a large body of oral and written Mande literature. Epic accounts of the founding of the empire constitute the texts of much of the traditional repertoire of Mande music. Pieces dedicated to Sunjata and chronicling his legendary achievements—from a child unable to walk, to a warrior in exile, to a great king—are numerous (see Charry 2000:40–43).

Traditional Mande culture and music, including the art of the kora, are preserved and continue to develop both within Mali itself and throughout the former realm of the Mande empire. The Mande ethnic group consists of two large, geographically defined subgroups: the Maninka of Mali and Guinea and the Mandinka of Senegal and Gambia (Senegambia). Collectively, both groups are referred to as the Mandenka, and their myriad of related languages and dialects fall within the Mande language group (i.e., Mande languages).

Colonial history also has left its strong mark on Mande culture, both linguistically and in terms of the modern map of Africa. Senegal, Mali, and Guinea are former French colonies where the official language is French. The tiny nation of Gambia, a former British colony, has English as its official language, while Guinea-Bissau was formerly colonized by Portugal and retains Portuguese as its official language.

The jeli and the art of jeliya

The principal exponents of the kora and its art have always belonged to a hereditary class of professional Mande musicians known as **jeli** (pl. *jelilu*). The jelilu are the griots (praise singers, praise musicians) of Mande culture. Living members of the principal **hereditary jeli families**—Kouyate, Diabate, Sissoko (also spelled Cissokho)—can trace their lineage back across many generations, in some cases all the way to the original Mande court musicians patronized by King Sunjata himself.

jeli (JAY-lee)

A female jeli may be referred to as a *jelimuso* (pl. *jelimusolu*). While the men both sing and play instruments, the women normally specialize in singing exclusively. In modern times, several jelimusolu have emerged as major stars of both contemporary Mande and African pan-cultural music. The most revered and famous of these is Kandia Kouyate.

Kandia Kouyate (Kahn-jah Koo-YAH-tay)

The jelilu are the purveyors of the hallowed Mande musical art of jeliya. People born into jeli families have the exclusive right—and are even bound by duty in many cases—to devote their lives to preserving and cultivating jeliya's classic repertoire. This repertoire centers on **praise songs,** which were formerly sung to honor royalty exclusively, but are now often performed in honor of modern politicians or other patrons wealthy enough to retain a jeli's services. An important new network of jeli patronage is the international world music industry. Today, it is international music promoters and record producers, rather than Mande kings and princes, who often account for the livelihoods and prestige of the top exponents of jeliya musical artistry. Not surprisingly, many leading Mande kora players of the modern era have taken up residence—full or part time—in Paris, London, and New York, availing themselves of professional opportunities in these major commercial centers of the world music industry that they would not have in the West African lands of their birth.

Kandia Kouyate.

Throughout the centuries, jelilu have served important roles not just as musicians, but also as historians, genealogists, and social and political commentators. Traditionally, they alone had the right to sing about certain sensitive issues of Mande social and political life. Moreover, only they have traditionally been permitted to perform on *designated jeli instruments,* including the kora and others. Even today, there is a stigma attached to musicians from non-jeli families who play such instruments.

Besides the kora, the **bala** (see the photo on p. 200) is one of the principal designated jeli instruments. It is a xylophone-type idiophone that is constructed of between 17 and 21 hard wooden slats (keys) of different lengths that are suspended over a wooden frame in ascending

bala (BAH-lah)

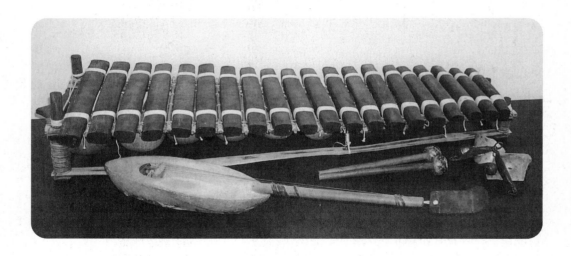

pitch order. The range of the instrument spans up to three octaves, typically with seven notes per octave. Each slat is laid over its own calabash resonator. The larger (and thus lower-pitched) the slat, the larger the resonator. The player traditionally sits on the ground behind the instrument and strikes the keys with a pair of rubber-ended mallets. Alternatively, he may mount the instrument on a stand and play from a standing position, or even sling the bala around his neck with a long strap and play "marching band" style in processions.

koni (koh-nee)

Another important instrument of the jeli is the **koni** (*ngoni*). This is a banjo-like plucked chordophone. Some sources suggest, in fact, that the koni is the modern banjo's direct African ancestor. The body, or resonator, of the koni is made from a hollowed-out, canoe-shaped piece of wood covered by a tightly stretched animal hide (see the photo above). The strings run along the neck, which consists of a round, fretless stick that is inserted directly into the instrument's body. The koni is held horizontally across the player's lap and played more or less like a guitar (or banjo). The size, pitch range, and number of strings vary. Some konis have four strings, others have five or even seven; some are quite small and have a high pitch range, others are rather large and function as "bass" instruments. In the modern era, the guitar has been adopted as a jeli instrument as well. Similarities between the koni and guitar in terms of construction and basic playing techniques likely account for the guitar's ready adaptation into the jeliya context.

You will soon be introduced to a musical example featuring kora, bala, koni, and guitar played together in an ensemble (along with traditional jeliya singing). First, however, we explore the solo kora and vocal artistry of the jeli Seckou Keita.

Seckou Keita (Say-koo KAY-tah)

Seckou Keita: Kora Master, Jeli, and Radical Royal

While it is generally frowned upon in Mande society for people of non-jeli families to play jeli instruments or otherwise practice the art of jeliya (e.g., as singers), disapproval is especially severe for persons of Mande royal lineage. According to Mande custom, anyone bearing the royal name Keita is forbidden from being a jeli, indeed from performing music professionally in any context. This custom endures to the present, but there have been individuals who have broken rank and defied it.

The best known of these radical royals is the Malian-born singer and world beat superstar Salif Keita. His music blends traditional jeliya stylistic features, a cutting-edge contemporary popular sound, and strong doses of social and political commentary. Salif Keita has done much to bring international attention to Malian traditional music and to major social, cultural, and political issues affecting Mali in particular and Africa more broadly. He is arguably the best-known and most influential living "statesman" of this impoverished and troubled nation. In his home-

Salif Keita.

Seckou Keita.

land, however, Salif Keita is a figure surrounded by controversy, not so much for the boldness of his music, but rather on account of his decision to be a professional musician despite his noble lineage.

"I am not shy to sing and play the kora"

Another Keita of royal lineage who broke rank for the sake of pursuing a musical career is jeli and kora virtuoso Seckou Keita. Keita was born into a "mixed heritage" family in southern Senegal in 1977. His father was a blue-blood Keita, his mother a descendant of the vaunted Sissoko family of jelilu. Seckou's mixed Keita-Sissoko lineage created ambiguity regarding his musical prospects. Properly, he should have eschewed any serious musical aspirations to follow the more regal path of his father's Keita lineage. But this was not to be his fate. He was raised principally by his mother's family rather than his father's, and this ultimately opened the door for him to pursue his musical passions toward the career path of a jeli while bringing relatively little disgrace to the Keita side of his distinguished pedigree.

Seckou's gratitude for being able to follow his musical destiny—his gratitude to his parents, to his grandfather, and to God—is eloquently expressed in "Sabu Nginma" ("Good Help"), a praise song featured on his international debut album *Baiyo* (2001), which was reissued under the title *Mali* by ARC Music Productions International Ltd. in 2002. In a summary English translation of the song's text included in the ARC CD booklet, Seckou recounts the fortuitous twists of fate that allowed him to practice the art of jeliya:

"Sabu Nginma" ("Sah-boo Nee-mah")

> It is not today that I have decided to be a musician and to sing. It is the luck of being born into the Griot [jeli] tradition through my mum's family, the Cissokho [Sissoko]. Oh mum! Oh dad! I am not shy to sing and play the *kora*.
>
> My mum and my dad like it. They agree that I am lucky to have this gift from God. Love has united my mum and dad despite the traditions [of social class exclusivity in

marriage]. These traditions also do not allow a king such as somebody from the Keitas to become a musician, a griot. My grandfather always said to me, "If you leave well, you will arrive well." Everyone has luck from somewhere. (Keita 2002:4)

guided listening experience

"Dounuya," Seckou Keita

- CD Track **#2-24**
- Featured performer(s)/group: Seckou Keita (kora and voice)
- Format: Complete track
- Source recording: *Mali,* by Seckou Keita (ARC Music Productions International Ltd. EUCD 1779)

"Dounuya"
(Doo-noo-yah)

A second track from the same Seckou Keita CD will serve as our musical introduction to the kora and to traditional jeliya musical style. The song is "Dounuya," meaning "The World." It was composed by Keita in an essentially traditional style and features him singing and accompanying himself on the kora.

In genuine jeliya tradition, "Dounuya" features a text that operates at several levels simultaneously. It is at once a praise song honoring the Creator (God), a critique of the shortcomings of people in their social lives, and a call for elevated virtue and integrity. In the true spirit of jeliya, too, it is a song deeply rooted in the Mande musical and cultural legacy, yet attuned to the contemporary milieu of the jeliya artist's situation. In the text, Seckou does not speak only to the Mande commuity, but to the global human community as a whole:

> I have seen something that scares me. There should not be any problems between ourselves and God. The problems come from the relationships we have with each other. All religions are the same. Anyone can pray, anyone can worship God. But we need to be circumspect in our own relationships with each other. God created the world with perfections and imperfections and gave us the choice between good and bad. Why should we choose the bad? (Keita 2002:5)

Or in other terms, as an Akan traditionalist might say, why should we follow the path that does *not* lead to the river, that takes us anywhere but to the eternal wisdom of the Creator?

In "Dounuya," Seckou's kora playing is the proverbial river that flows across and through the path of the message of his words. Following a brief introductory passage of solo kora playing delivered mainly in short (staccato), syncopated notes, the sound of the kora truly starts to flow like a river beginning at 0:10, where Keita begins playing in a style called **kumbengo.** This is the layered ostinato-based style on the kora that is normally used to accompany singing. Three kumbengo layers—one in the low-pitch register outlining a "bass line," the second occupying the instrument's middle range, and the third in the higher range—emerge and merge within seconds. They become a choir of three kora "voices" weaving in and out of one another.

kumbengo
(koom-BAYN-go)

Each layer of the kumbengo texture is at once fully itself yet completely dependent on the others for its identity and sustenance, like the interwoven drum parts in the Fontomfrom music of **CD ex. #2-22.** Here, though, a single musician is weaving together all the different layers on a single instrument and within a musical context largely defined by melodies and chords.

Though the overall kumbengo pattern recurs cyclically about every two to three seconds (0:10–0:13, 0:14–0:16, 0:17–0:19, 0:20–0:23), each recurrence is a variation on the others. No two statements of the pattern are precisely the same. They all differ in subtle nuances of rhythm, melody, ornamentation, and timbre.

Following the fourth statement of the pattern, Keita partially breaks from the kumbengo style momentarily to present a virtuosic melodic flourish called a **birimintingo** at 0:24. This antici-pates the introduction of Keita's singing voice into the multipart musical conversation at 0:30. The continuing flow of the kumbengo part, now in an accompanying role, fills in the spaces be-tween sung phrases. A return of the earlier birimintingo flourish occurs at 1:03, setting up the second sung verse of the song at 1:09. Then, a series of hammerlike, high-register kora chords (1:28–1:37) adds yet another musical layer as the singing and the kumbengo accompaniment continue. These chords have an almost disruptive effect on the smooth flow of the performance established up to that point. They also heighten its sense of musical drama, highlighting the key line of text meaning, "Why should we choose the bad [when the good is there for us to choose]?" When this rhetorical question comes back as a refrain near the end of the performance (begin-ning at 2:57), the "percussive" chords return as well.

birimintingo (beer-uh-men-TEEN-go)

From 1:41–2:14, following the completion of the second verse, the singing drops out to make way for a solo kora feature section in which the kumbengo pattern continues but is enhanced by birimintingo passages and some clever call-and-response dialogue between the middle- and upper-range voices of the kora (starting at 2:02). This solo kora texture gives way at 2:15 to the return of Keita's singing voice, but the singing is now more improvisatory, extemporaneous, gen-erally higher in pitch range, and sometimes even speechlike in character (e.g., at 2:47). This different style of vocalization is called **sataro.** The sataro section segues to the aforementioned refrain ("Why should we choose the bad?") at 2:57, replete with the hammerlike chords. The performance is rounded out by a return to the introductory solo kora material of the opening.

"Dounuya" is a song with a message. It tells us that we must improve our relationships with one another if we are to follow the path toward the good rather than the bad, the path toward rather than away from the divine source of creation. This message is stated explicitly in the text, but it is no less apparent on a symbolic, musical level in the integrated polyvocality of interaction between the voice of Seckou Keita and the multiple "voices" of his kora.

guided listening quick summary

"Dounuya," by Seckou Keita (CD ex. #2-24)

0:00–0:09

- Solo kora introduction featuring short (staccato) notes and syncopated rhythms.

0:10–0:24

- Solo kora continues, but now the playing style is kumbengo.
- Flowing, layered ostinato texture and interwoven kora lines in the low, middle, and high registers of the instrument.
- Ostinato patterns are varied each time they recur.

0:24–0:29

- Keita partially breaks from the kumbengo style momentarily at 0:24 to play a virtuosic, birimintingo flourish; this anticipates the arrival of the sung verse to follow.

0:30–1:08

- First verse of "Dounuya" song, sung by Keita as his kora playing now becomes the accompaniment; section concludes with a second birimintingo passage at 1:03.

1:09–1:40

- Second sung verse of "Dounuya" song (new text, varied melody).
- At 1:28, hammerlike chords in the kora's high register heighten the musical drama when the impor-tant line "Why should we choose the bad [when the good is there for us to choose]?" is sung.

1:41–2:14

■ This section once again features the kora alone (solo); no singing.

■ Texture highlights occasional birimintingo passages over continuing kumbengo accompaniment.

■ Interesting call-and-response dialogue between middle- and upper-range kora "voices" beginning at 2:02.

2:15–2:56

■ Keita now returns as vocalist, but performing in sataro style rather than singing as he did before.

2:57–end

■ Final vocal refrain on the line "Why should we choose the bad?" once again enhanced by hammer-like chords in the upper register of the kora.

"Kaira" ("Kai" rhymes with "pie")

A Meeting of Musical Worlds: "Atlanta Kaira"

From the traditional-style, solo jeliya performance of "Dounuya," we now move to a more neo-traditional, ensemble jeliya performance entitled "Atlanta Kaira" (**CD ex. #2-25**). "Atlanta Kaira" features an ensemble of two singers (one male, one female), two koras, a bala, a koni, and an acoustic guitar. All but the guitarist are esteemed Mande musicians in the jeli tradition. Three of the most revered jeli families—Sissoko, Diabate, and Kouyate—are represented in the all-star lineup. The Kouyate clan is represented by koni maestro Bassekou Kouyate (playing a large, low-pitched version of the instrument), the Sissokos by the young kora star Ballake Sissoko, and the Diabates by both the male vocalist Kassemady Diabate and the kora virtuoso Toumani Diabate. The female singer is Ramatou Diakite, who comes from another important Mande musical family.

Bassekou Kouyate (Bah-say-koo Koo-YAH-tay)

Ballake Sissoko (Bah-lah-kay See-soh-koh)

Kassemady Diabate (Kah-say-mah-dee Jah-BAH-tay)

Ramatou Diakite (Rah-mah-too Jah-KEE-tay)

Alhaji Bai Konte (Ahl-hah-jee Bie Kohn-tay ["Bai" rhymes with "pie"])

Ali Farka Toure (Ah-lee Fahr-kah TOO-ray)

Kulanjan **(Koo-lahn-JAHN)**

The guitarist is the maverick American blues musician and intercultural music pioneer Taj Mahal. Mahal first discovered the kora in the 1970s and became immediately enamored of the instrument. He was initially struck by parallels he observed between kora playing techniques introduced to him by the Gambian jeli Alhaji Bai Konte (one of the first kora players to tour North America) and the down-home finger-picking guitar styles he had learned from Blind Jesse Fuller and other of his old-style blues mentors. At a deeper level, what Mahal heard in the kora artistry of Konte was something truly profound and personal, something that "was at the heart of his own music—perhaps even his own identity—the African roots of the blues" (Mahal 2004).

Mahal's kora epiphany and search for his musical roots eventually led him to Mali and a host of Malian music masters including guitarist Ali Farka Toure and kora master Toumani Diabate. In 1999, more than two decades after his initial encounter with the kora, he teamed up with Toumani to produce the album *Kulanjan*. The album included "Atlanta Kaira" and a number of other selections that paired Mahal with Toumani's all-star band of Mande jeli masters. For Mahal, *Kulanjan* represented the culmination of a long and fascinating musical roots odyssey, "bringing the blues and Malian music back together again, in one huge circle of 500 years" (Mahal, quoted in Duran 2000:5). For Toumani, it was perhaps less a search for roots than a logical extension of an ever-expanding and ever more complex web of Mande traditionalism and global modernity. The following passage from Eric Charry's excellent book *Mande Music* offers a revealing glimpse into Toumani's complex musicultural world:

> In the home given to his father by the first president of Mali, Toumani Diabate lives in a world of fax machines, cell phones, recording sessions, local nightclubs, international tours, electrified jelimuso-led ensembles performing at traditional celebrations, extended family and the extended obligations therein, high infant mortality, young kora apprentices, respect for the jelis of his father's generation, and the proud legacy of the Diabate lineage

of jelis. Like many of his contemporaries, he uses modern technological tools to honor traditional commitments. Traditional musics are likewise put in modern contexts in his ensembles, mixing diverse instruments with new arrangements. Traditional and modern worldviews complement each other, meld together, and also remain distinct. . . . (Charry 2000:27)

Kulanjan manifests this complementary traditional/modern musical identity. The album was recorded not in Mali, but rather in Athens, Georgia (in the same studio where the rock band REM made many of their important albums). Some of the pieces are heavily oriented toward the blues or toward a relatively equal-parts syncretism of blues and jeliya elements. Others, most notably "Atlanta Kaira," are decisively slanted toward the pure jeliya side of the syncretic equation. "Atlanta Kaira" is less an example of cross-cultural fusion than it is a contemporary reinterpretation of the piece "Kaira" (Arabic for "peace"), a now-classic composition of the jeliya repertoire that is usually attributed to Toumani's late father, Sidiki Diabate, and is said to date from the 1940s, possibly earlier. Sidiki was known during his lifetime as the King of the Kora. He was, according to Charry, ". . . one of the greatest musical artists of his generation, whose death was cause for national mourning" in his adopted homeland of Mali (Charry 2000:27). (Sidiki was born in Gambia but moved to and settled in Mali early in life.) Beyond his renown in West Africa, Sidiki also played a seminal role in bringing the kora to broad international attention. His classic 1971 duet album with fellow kora master Djelimadi Sissoko, *Ancient Strings,* was the first internationally distributed recording to feature the instrument; the album achieved considerable commercial success.

Toumani Diabate.

Although Sidiki is often credited as the composer of "Kaira," he himself claimed merely to have "developed" it (Charry 2000:156). In any case, it is with him that the piece is mainly identified historically. Beginning in the 1940s, "Kaira" came to be closely associated with the Malian struggle for independence from French colonial rule. Its melody became well known and popular among the Malian people, inspiring many different texts reflective of different aspects of the nationalist struggle (Charry 2000:156). During this period, Sidiki traveled widely throughout Mali, performing "Kaira" and other jeliya pieces to galvanize the Malian nationalism movement. In true jeli fashion, he attuned the ancient jeliya repertoire to the needs, demands, and issues of his own time. In this way, he formed a link between the grandeur of the Mande's proud historical legacy and a vision of Mali's future as a modern Mande nation.

Sidiki's charisma and activism endeared him to the Malian people, but not to the French colonial authorities. For his efforts, he was eventually arrested by the French and imprisoned. But all this did was energize the independence movement, which then came to be known as the "Kaira Movement." When Mali achieved its independence in 1960, Sidiki was honored as a national hero. He counted among his close friends the nation's first president and became a cultural ambassador for the Malian nation and its great musical heritage within Mali, more broadly in Africa, and eventually throughout the world. "Kaira" became an emblem of himself, his musical legacy, and the country of Mali.

In the hands of his son Toumani Diabate, one of the greatest kora artists of his own generation, the development and cultivation of "Kaira" has continued. Toumani has recorded various versions of the piece, including one that served as the title track of his debut international album

(*Kaira*). "Atlanta Kaira" adds to Toumani's recorded "Kaira" legacy, paying tribute to his father not just in music but also in words. The sataro portions of the piece, sung by Kassemady Diabate, pay homage to Sidiki: his signature song has been turned into a praise song in *his* honor.

In the many polyphonic layers that emerge in the performance—the singing, the kora playing, the parts of the bala and koni, Taj Mahal's guitar—the power of collective expression so characteristic of West African music becomes poignantly manifest. In its unified collage of sound, "Atlanta Kaira" is able to tell its many stories all at once. It is a tribute to Sidiki Diabate, an exemplar of traditional jeliya ensemble art, a chapter in Taj Mahal's roots musical odyssey, a reflection of the contemporary "international jeli" culture to which Toumani Diabate belongs. All of these "voices" are allowed to speak, all at once, and none gets in the way of the expression of the other. It is the great power of music such as this to allow for such multiplicity and simultaneity of expression.

guided listening experience

"Atlanta Kaira," Toumani Diabate, Taj Mahal, and Ensemble

- CD Track #**2-25**
- Featured performer(s)/group: Toumani Diabate and Ballake Sissoko (kora), Taj Mahal (guitar), Kassemady Diabate and Ramatou Diakite (vocals), Bassekou Kouyate (koni)
- Format: Complete track
- Source recording: *Kulanjan,* by Taj Mahal and Toumani Diabate (Hannibal Records/Rykodisc HNCD 1444)

sauta (sow-tah)

"Atlanta Kaira" is played in a mode called **sauta,** which is one of the four principal modes in Mande music. Its scale sounds much like a major scale with a raised fourth degree starting on the pitch F, that is, F G A B C D E (F). This is only a rough approximation, however, since there are microtonal subtleties in sauta tuning that do not correspond to standard Western pitch intervals.

Following a solo kora introduction in free rhythm, a steady four-beat meter (with triple subdivisions of beats) is established and continues through the rest of the performance (starting at 0:42). A two-measure (eight-beat) kumbengo pattern also recurs cyclically throughout the piece from this point onward. Each two-measure cycle is about three seconds long (0:42–0:45, 0:45–0:48, etc.)

The piece shares many common features with Seckou Keita's "Dounuya" and illustrates many of the same musical Africanisms:

- Both pieces have complex polyphonic textures (solo voice plus solo kora providing the multiple parts in "Dounuya," two voices and the instrumental ensemble generating the polyphony in "Atlanta Kaira"); in both cases, layered ostinatos, varied repetition, and improvisation are pervasive.
- Both include performance in the kumbengo, birimintingo, and sataro styles that are characteristic of jeliya music.
- Both are intensely "conversational" on multiple levels, with the various "voices" sometimes speaking all together at once and other times engaging in call-and-response dialogue.
- Both provide rich examples of timbral variety, especially through manipulation of the large range of timbres available on the kora.

The overall formal design of "Atlanta Kaira" consits of six main parts:

- Solo kora introduction by Toumani Diabate (0:00–0:42).

- "Kaira" song, sung by Kassemady Diabate and Ramatou Diakite with ensemble accompaniment (0:42–1:28; note that the first 10 seconds of this part are taken up by an instrumental ensemble introduction preceding the entrance of the singers).
- Sataro #1, featuring Kassemady Diabate (1:29–2:50).
- Koni solo, featuring Bassekou Kouyate (2:51–3:32)
- Sataro #2, again featuring Kassemady Diabate (3:33–4:21).
- Second singing of "Kaira" song with ensemble accompaniment (4:22–end).

The following discussion describes each of these six sections in order. Before reading it, listen to the whole piece one time through to become familiar with it. Then read the discussion, and after that listen to the recording one more time while following along with the Guided Listening Quick Summary on pages 208–09. This is a rather involved piece. Your understanding and enjoyment of it will likely increase with every listening, so give it some extra time.

Here, now, is a section-by-section breakdown.

1. *Solo kora introduction.* This free-rhythm introduction offers a brilliant display of kora virtuosity. The cascading melodic runs up and down the sauta scale; dramatic use of contrasts in dynamics; varied articulations, ornaments, and timbres; and sudden jumps from one octave range to another highlight the characteristic flair of birimintingo style on the kora.

2. *Ensemble introduction and "Kaira" song.* The full instrumental ensemble—two koras, bala, koni, and guitar—establishes a kumbengo texture with layered ostinatos at 0:42, setting up the subsequent entry of the singers at 0:53. Each instrument has its own repeating pattern, and these recur in varied form with each repetition of the two-measure kumbengo cycle (0:42–0:45, 0:45–0:48, and so on). Additionally, different instruments break away from their basic patterns at various points to improvise in a birimintingo style. (The bala actually plays birimintingo throughout the whole ensemble introduction, not settling into its regular kumbengo pattern until after the singers enter.) The timbre of the kora should be familiar enough by now that you can identify it within the ensemble. Listen for the percussive, woody, xylophone-like timbre of the bala to locate that instrument. Listen for the "bass line," the lowest-pitched layer of melody, to identify the koni.

   Each instrument contributes its own layer to the polyphonic texture. The koni is the bass instrument, the bala moves along steadily in the middle register, and the lead kora part emphasizes the high range. The second kora and Taj Mahal's guitar, meanwhile, operate essentially as "free agents" within the overall texture. They enhance and reinforce the parts played on the other instruments, adding their own touches of improvisation where appropriate. Mahal's guitar playing is admirably unobtrusive, though the steel-string twang of his sporadic, syncopated chord work does make a distinctive contribution at some points (for example, in the passage from 0:46–0:52).

   The two vocalists enter at 0:53 and sing the main "Kaira" song over the continuing kumbengo instrumental texture, which now becomes an accompaniment to the singing. At first they sing an octave apart, then move into unison, with Kassemady singing at the higher end of his range and Ramatou at the lower end of hers. The sung melody is highly ornamented, with many twists and turns. Notice how precisely together the two singers are in articulating the intricate ornaments, both the first time the melody is sung and during its repetition (following an instrumental interlude) at 1:11.

3. *Sataro #1.* Beginning at 1:29, Kassemady Diabate performs the first of two sataros. The text pays homage to the grand legacy of Sidiki Diabate. The vocal delivery is distinctly different than in the preceding section. It is more speechlike and dramatic, almost oratorical, and the speechlike rhythms move quite freely overtop the measured instrumental accompaniment. This sataro also becomes a dialogue between Kassemady's voice and Toumani's kora. The kora eloquently fills in the spaces between vocal phrases with birimintingo passages. Occasionally,

these even dovetail and overlap with the vocal part, as though the kora is commenting on and embellishing the singer's utterances at the moment he presents them. This interaction has a very conversational character to it.

4. *Koni solo.* The section from 2:51–3:32 is purely instrumental, with no singing. The principal featured instrument here is the koni, which breaks from its bass line kumbengo part to perform an improvised solo. At some points (e.g., at 3:15), the koni player, Bassekou Kouyate, sounds almost like a blues musician. It is moments such as these that make Taj Mahal's comments about the full circle from Malian music to blues and back again seem especially poignant. Technically, the koni remains the lead instrument throughout this passage, but at various points the kora and bala players break from their kumbengo patterns to improvise and engage with the koni in a texture of conversational, collective improvisation. This too brings to mind other styles of music, especially that of early jazz groups like those led by Louis Armstrong in which collective improvisation between the trumpet, clarinet, and trombone players sometimes achieved rather similar musical effects.

5. *Sataro #2.* Kassemady reenters with a second sataro beginning at 3:33. This is similar to the earlier sataro section.

6. *Return of "Kaira" song.* The performance concludes with the singing of "Kaira" two more times, from 4:22 to the end.

---

guided listening quick summary

"Atlanta Kaira," Toumani Diabate, Taj Mahal, and Ensemble (CD ex. #2-25)

SOLO KORA INTRODUCTION (TOUMANI DIABATE)

0:00–0:42

- Played in the sauta mode.
- Good illustration of the musical range of the instrument when played in a virtuosic, birimintingo style.

ENSEMBLE INTRODUCTION TO "KAIRA" SONG

0:42–0:52

- Instrumentation: two koras, bala, koni, and guitar.
- Kumbengo texture with occasional birmintingo passages played on different instruments (bala plays birimintingo throughout this introduction).

"KAIRA" SONG

0:53–1:28

- Two singers, Kassemady Diabate (man) and Ramatou Diakite (woman) enter texture; they begin by singing in octaves, then move into unison in the same octave register.
- Melody highly ornamented and ornaments sung precisely together.
- Kumbengo accompaniment provided by instrumental ensemble.

FIRST SATARO SECTION

1:29–2:50

- Text pays homage to Sidiki Diabate.
- Dramatic, almost speechlike vocal delivery by Kassemady Diabate.
- Musical dialogue between vocal part (Kassemady) and birimintingo passages on kora (Toumani).

Angélique Kidjo: West African Collective Expression in a Global Musical World

Viewed in its entirety, "Atlanta Kaira" represents another manifestation of the multivoice conversation approach that is so pervasive in West African music. For all the musical complexity of the piece, it is readily apparent that the many "voices" it presents are all speaking at once, all with their own distinctive things to say, all interacting with one another and supporting each other in turn, all ultimately unified within the larger expression of the greater collective whole. And what is being "said," whether in words or in musical sounds, brings us back to the other central theme of this chapter: the importance of paying one's respects to the sources of creation and wisdom—whether human or divine; parents, community elders, or master musicians; chiefs, kings, or sacred rivers.

The final musical work we explore in this chapter, Angélique Kidjo's "Okan Bale," meets these same basic criteria. It moves us into a very different musical realm than we have visited so far, however, a realm of mainstream international popular music (world beat) that retains strong ties to West African music and culture. In "Atlanta Kaira," Taj Mahal and his guitar essentially met the art of jeliya on its own musical home turf and found a place of belonging there. In "Okan Bale," it is the kora and one of the instrument's leading young jeli masters, Mamadou Diabate, that venture out from *their* musical roots and homeland in search of new vistas of musical expression.

"Okan Bale" ("Oh-kahn BAH-lay")

The diva from Benin

This final portion of our musical journey through West Africa takes us first to the nation of Benin, where the sublime singer and international world beat superstar Angélique Kidjo was born and raised. Benin is a tiny country with a population of about six million people. It is sandwiched between Ghana and Togo to the west and Nigeria to the east. Centuries ago, the Beninese city of Abomey was the capital of the great West African kingdom of Dahomey. The Dahomey empire achieved tremendous power during its precolonial era reign, rivaling the Mande empire in this regard. The 17th-century Dahomey rulers became heavily involved in supplying slaves to European slave traders. Many Dahomeans were shipped to the Americas as slaves, the majority to Brazil. The musical legacy of the Dahomey, whether directly or indirectly manifested, lives on in Brazil and throughout many other areas of the African diaspora.

With the end of the slave trade and the waning of the Dahomey empire in the 19th century, present-day Benin came under French colonial rule. An independent nation, Dahomey, was formed in 1960 following the ousting of the French. Dahomey was renamed Benin in 1975.

During the 1970s and 1980s, it was governed as a socialist state. The early 1990s saw a shift to a multiparty democracractic system of governance.

The official language of Benin is French, but the traditional languages of the country's major ethnic groups, such as the Yoruba and the **Fon,** are widely spoken as well. Angélique Kidjo, a Fon, sings the majority of her songs in the Fon language. Despite the cosmopolitan internationalism of her music, this linguistic preference ties her and her musical artistry closely to her Fon heritage.

According to *The Rough Guide* to world music, Angélique Kidjo, the "diva from Benin," has "done more to popularise African music than any other woman" (Bensignor and Audra 1999:434). This claim is open to debate (a case could certainly be made for the great South African singer Miriam Makeba; see also Chapter 2, p. 17), but there can be little doubt that Kidjo stands among the most talented and influential of all contemporary African musicians, male or female.

Kidjo was born in 1960 in the coastal Benin city of Ouidah. She was raised in an artistic household by parents who belonged to an elite cultural community that helped establish Benin

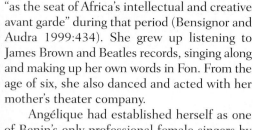

"as the seat of Africa's intellectual and creative avant garde" during that period (Bensignor and Audra 1999:434). She grew up listening to James Brown and Beatles records, singing along and making up her own words in Fon. From the age of six, she also danced and acted with her mother's theater company.

Angélique had established herself as one of Benin's only professional female singers by the time she was 20. She faced limited professional prospects in Benin, however, and moved first to Holland and then to Paris while in her 20s. In contrast to other expatriate African musicians she encountered on the Paris world music scene, she did not make a point of staying close to her homeland musical roots. Rather, she pursued a "crossover" approach right from the start, becoming part of a diverse community of French, Caribbean, African, and American musicians with broadly international musical tastes, sensibilities, and aspirations.

Her husband and producer, the French musician and record producer Jean Hébrail, was a key member of that community. The uniquely eclectic musical approach she and Hébrail developed drew on Angélique's Fon cultural roots, in both the language of her songs and her use of the vocal stylings of *zilin* and other Fon music traditions, but it was equally informed by a diversity of musical styles including American soul, rhythm-and-blues, funk, and jazz. "Throughout her career," it is written on Kidjo's Web site, "Angélique Kidjo has attempted to prove that the world is much smaller and far more culturally connected than it may appear. Her music glorifies individual cultures while also underlining their universal similarities" (Kidjo 2004).

Kidjo first hit the big time with her 1994 international dance hit "Ayé." It was her 1996 album *Fifa,* however, that truly launched her to stardom. Incorporating everything from authentic Beninese field recordings to hard-driving dance numbers and luscious ballads, *Fifa* was an instant world beat classic. Among other guest artists, it featured Latin rock guitar great Carlos Santana (see Chapter 11), one of Angélique's main musical inspirations during her formative years in Benin.

Following the success of *Fifa,* Kidjo embarked upon an ambitious undertaking: a trilogy of albums devoted to exploring the African roots of African-derived musics of the Americas. The first volume of this triology, *Oremi* (1998), drew mainly upon links between musics of Africa and the American rhythm-and-blues tradition. Part two, *Black Ivory Soul* (2002), explored the musical and cultural kinship of Africa and Brazil (especially between Benin and Bahia, the most Afro-

Yoruba (YOR-oo-buh)

Makeba (Mah-KAY-bah)

Ouidah (WEE-duh)

Angélique Kidjo.

zilin (zee-leen)

Brazilian of Brazil's provinces). Part three, *Oyaya!* (2004), delved into the nexus of African and Afro-Caribbean musics (salsa, merengue, calypso, ska).

Today, Kidjo resides principally in New York, dividing her time between there, Paris, and London, and a busy schedule of international touring and recording. As the back-cover write-up of *Black Ivory Soul* rightly proclaims, she "is more than just one of the world's best-loved African singers—she is a musical ambassador for her country, Benin, and indeed, for the entire African continent."

guided listening experience

"Okan Bale," Angélique Kidjo

- CD Track #**2-26**
- Featured performer(s)/group: Angélique Kidjo group, with Angélique Kidjo (vocals), Mamadou Diabate (kora)
- Format: Complete track
- Source recording: *Black Ivory Soul,* by Angélique Kidjo (Columbia CD 85799)

Though many of the selections on Kidjo's *Black Ivory Soul*—and the album itself—highlight musical links between West Africa and Brazil, some do not, at least not in any explicitly obvious way. These include the catchy, upbeat "Iwoya," featuring a duet between Kidjo and Dave Matthews, and the stunningly beautiful "Okan Bale," a loving tribute to Kidjo's own family. (The title may be translated as "[A] Piece of [My] Heart.")

"Okan Bale" is a lush pop ballad in a quite conventional sense. Its formal design is that of the standard verse-chorus song (see Chapter 6, pp. 82–84), with an introduction, two verses, two choruses, and bridge sections linking the first verse to the first chorus and the second verse to the second chorus.

But this is a pop ballad stamped with a decidely pan-African musicultural flavor on account of its Fon lyrics, occasional Beninese zilin-inspired vocal stylings, and, most important of all, the featured role of Mamadou Diabate's kora as a solo instrument. Mamadou is a younger cousin of Toumani Diabate. As a leading kora virtuoso in his own right, he is one of several prominent musicians carrying forth the proud, centuries-old legacy of the Diabate jeli clan.

Mamadou was born in Kita, Mali, in 1975. His father, N'fa Diabate, was a well-known kora player and Mamadou's first teacher. Mamadou left school early to pursue a career as a kora player. After winning a regional kora competition at age 15, he moved to Bamako, where cousin Toumani took him under his wing. Within short order, he was performing regularly on the Bamako jeliya circuit, backing singers at weddings and baptisms and playing for tourists at posh hotels.

Mamadou first traveled to the United States in 1996 as a member of a Malian touring troupe. He decided to stay, settling in New York. Since moving to the United States he has performed traditional Mande jeliya music at such prestigious

Mamadou Diabate.

venues as the Kennedy Center, the United Nations, and the Smithsonian Institution. He also has been featured on numerous jazz, pop, and cross-cultural fusion albums and projects. Besides Angélique Kidjo, he has worked with jazz trumpet great Donald Byrd, Zimbabwean pop legend Thomas Mapfumo, and many other luminaries.

Mamadou's playing on "Okan Bale" is florid and flowing. His cascading runs up and down the instrument and the free-floating rhythmic character of his style beg comparison with Toumani Diabate's performance in "Atlanta Kaira." The beauty of the kora is highlighted especially well in two birimintingo sections of "Okan Bale," the first beginning at 0:24, immediately before the opening (sung) verse, and the second beginning at 1:52, leading up to the second verse.

Also interesting is the way that the kora's role grows progressively throughout the performance within the verses and choruses themselves. During the first verse (0:36–0:57), the kora is virtually absent, whereas it figures prominently in the second verse (2:14–2:35), weaving in and out of Kidjo's vocal phrases. Similarly, there is no kora soloing in the first chorus (1:19–1:51), while the kora is quite active in the second chorus (2:58–end) with its waterfall-like birimintingo runs interspersed between lines of Kidjo's singing. It is almost as though the kora, growing in "stature" through the course of the performance, is taking the listener on a journey back to Mother Africa, back to the homeland, family roots, the creative source.

The intimate musical dialogue that emerges between Kidjo's singing and Mamadou's kora playing on "Okan Bale" strongly evokes the jeliya musical art. Though Kidjo is neither a jeli nor any other kind of griot, and though the musical style of "Okan Bale" is oceans apart from jeliya proper, a jeliya essence pervades the performance throughout. The theme of the song's text—praising and expressing gratitude to one's family—also may be said to link "Okan Bale," at least in spirit, to core values of jeliya:

> *I know where I come from*
>
> *From you, my family*
>
> *Let me take a moment to thank you*
>
> *Because you bring me joy and strength*
>
> *If my moves are full of blessings*
>
> *It comes from you, my family.*

Kidjo's singing and Mamadou's kora may be the featured voices of "Okan Bale," but there are other notable contributions to the multipart musical conversation: synthesizer, guitar, electric bass, background vocals rendering ethereal harmonies in breathy tones (actually overdubbed by Kidjo herself), shifting musical textures, and changing timbral landscapes. They "speak" sometimes all at once and sometimes in turn, in monologues and in dialogues. And in the end, they contribute to a poignant realization of Angélique Kidjo's grand vision: to prove that the world is indeed smaller and more culturally connected than it seems; to glorify individual cultures while at the same time revealing the universality of human experience.

---

guided listening quick summary

"Okan Bale," Angélique Kidjo (CD ex. #2-26)

INTRODUCTION

0:00–0:35

- Ethereal synthesizer tones, acoustic guitar, electric bass (playing harmonics), harmonized voices (all Kidjo's, overdubbed)
- From 0:24–0:35, Mamadou Diabate plays kora solo in birimintingo style.

FIRST VERSE (VERSE I)

0:36–0:57

- Sung by Kidjo.
- Acoustic guitar main accompanying instrument; kora essentially absent.

FIRST BRIDGE SECTION (BRIDGE I)

0:58–1:18

- Different chord progression; guitar shifts to mainly staccato articulations.
- Brief kora birimintingo at 1:07–1:09 between vocal phrases.

FIRST CHORUS (CHORUS I)

1:19–1:51

- Dialogue between lead voice (Kidjo) and harmonized background vocals (also Kidjo; overdubbed).
- Beautiful, lush chord progression (outlined largely by the background vocals).
- Role of kora limited (no solo parts).

INTERLUDE ("REPRISE" OF INTRODUCTION)

1:52–2:13

- Solo kora (birimintingo) featured again.
- Kora solo more extended and florid in style than in introduction.

SECOND VERSE (VERSE II)

2:14–2:35

- Similar to first verse, but kora takes a more active role, weaving in and out of the lead vocal line with birimintingo flourishes.

SECOND BRIDGE SECTION (BRIDGE II)

2:36–2:57

- Similar to first bridge section, but this time it is a kora birimintingo, rather than a guitar lead-in, that provides the transitional material leading into the chorus.

SECOND CHORUS (CHORUS II)

2:58–end

- Similar to first chorus, except that the kora is now much more active than before, inserting several birimintingo flourishes.

Summary

In this chapter, we explored a range of different African musics as varied expressions of a common theme: musical conversation. Musical traditions of West Africa south of the Sahara (sub-Saharan Africa), especially drumming-based traditions of the Akan people and the kora tradition of the Mande people, were the principal foci. Certain key musical Africanisms that link these particular traditions to each other and to musics of the African continent and the African diaspora more broadly were introduced. Beginning with the Akan drum proverb of the river and the path, we moved on to a discussion of Akan Fontomfrom royal drum ensemble music. From there, we shifted to the Mande world of the kora and the art of jeliya. A traditional-style solo piece for voice and kora by Seckou Keita, a neo-traditional ensemble piece featuring kora master Toumani Diabate with other Mande musicians and the American guitarist Taj Mahal, and a "world pop" ballad of Angélique Kidjo that placed the kora artistry of Mamadou Diabate in a resolutely post-traditional musical context were explored.

Throughout this journey, we encountered African musics as conversation and as polyvocal forms of collective expression. Whether speaking through their voices, through the voices of their instruments, all together at once, in call-and-response dialogues, or in some combination of different conversational modes, we discovered that certain unifying themes bridged the creators of the different types and styles of music encountered. Principal among these was a theme of communal expression of gratitude. In one way or another, all of the music in this chapter was music of homage, music performed by people out of respect for the human, natural, or divine sources of creation and support that sustain and inspire them: deities, rivers, chiefs, parents, musical elders, and mentors.

Through the musical conversations of African musics, rivers cross paths and paths cross rivers in the metaphorical expressions of musical sounds, and in the relationships these sounds embody. In the polyvocal expressions of the music are contained profound models of interaction and collective expression that manifest ideals of how people can live well together and within their world.

Key Terms

Akan	jeliya	praise songs (in jeliya)
drum speech	griot	bala
tonal language (e.g., Twi)	African diaspora	koni
atumpan	Fontomfrom	kumbengo
polyvocality (in West African music)	Africanisms (musical)	birimintingo
	jeli	sataro
kora	hereditary jeli families (Kouyate, Diabate, Sissoko)	sauta
Mande		Fon

Study Questions

■ What is the Akan drum proverb of the river and the path about, literally and metaphorically?

■ Why are certain West African drums, like the atumpan, able to literally speak?

■ How is the term *polyvocality* applied in this chapter?

■ What is the history of Mande society and culture? How has the jeliya tradition been significant to that history?

■ What cultures and music traditions of the African diaspora were mentioned in this chapter?

■ Traditionally, what was the function of the Fontomfrom ensemble and its music in Akan societies? Has modernization changed this? How?

■ What were the six musical Africanisms listed in the chapter? How do they apply to the various musical examples explored?

■ Besides the kora, what other African chordophones were discussed in this chapter, and what countries/regions do these instruments come from?

■ Besides the kora, what other Mande instruments identified with jeliya were discussed?

■ Who is/was Seckou Keita? Salif Keita? Sunjata Keita? What does the last name "Keita" imply about a Mande person's family lineage? (Likewise, what do last names like Kouyate, Diabate, and Sissoko imply re: family lineage?)

■ Who is/was Sidiki Diabate? Toumani Diabate? Mamadou Diabate? How are they related and what instrument do/did all of them play?

- What do the words *kumbengo, birimintingo,* and *sataro* mean relative to Mande musical practice? Where did you hear examples of these in the chapter's musical selections?

- What is the ethnicity of Angélique Kidjo, and how is this specifically reflected in her otherwise globally cosmopolitan music? What examples would you use to support the claim that her music *is* globally cosmopolitan?

Discussion Questions

- An integral relationship between language and music is a feature of many world music cultures and traditions. How do language and music combine and reinforce one another in the kinds of music you listen to? Can you think of instances where the line between what constitutes speech and what constitutes music blurs?

- The so-called musical Africanisms discussed in this chapter are pervasive features of many music traditions outside of Africa as well, especially traditions that belong to or have been influenced by African diasporic culture. Listen to and discuss a range of music that is familiar to you. What Africanisms do you hear in the music, and what effect do they have on how the music sounds and makes you feel?

Applying What You Have Learned

- The American musician Taj Mahal has made a career of breaking down conventional musical boundaries and redefining world music as *worldly* music. Do some research on Mahal and locate recordings of his that represent the range and diversity of his music. Write a report describing how Mahal has combined his musical foundation in blues music, his broad conception of "African" music as encompassing all forms of African and African diasporic musical expression, and his global cosmopolitanism as a world music adventurer and pioneer. (You also could choose to focus on other musicians discussed in this chapter in a report like this, such as Toumani Diabate or Angélique Kidjo.)

- Locate and listen to recordings representing several different African and African diasporic music traditions beyond those focused on in this chapter. Some possibilities: Brazilian samba, Trinidadian calypso, American funk and hip-hop, Ghanaian highlife, South African mbaqanga and isicathamiya. What distinctive features do you hear in each? Are there any unifying features that cut across some or all of the different traditions you explore?

Resources for Further Study

Visit the Online Learning Center at **www.mhhe.com/bakan1** for learning aids, study help, and additional resources that supplement the content of this chapter.

"Oye Como Va":
three generations in the life of a classic
Latino/American dance tune

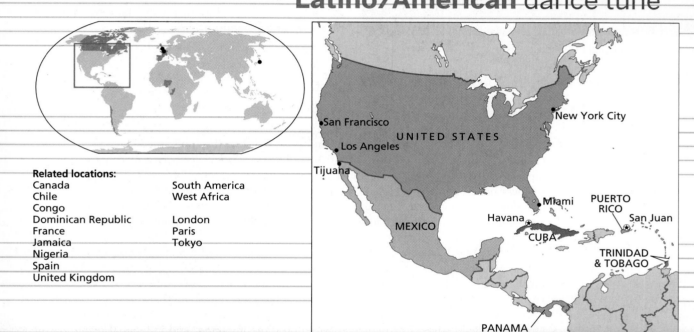

Related locations:

Canada
Chile
Congo
Dominican Republic
France
Jamaica
Nigeria
Spain
United Kingdom

South America
West Africa

London
Paris
Tokyo

timbales
(teem-BAH-lays)

Tito Puente (TEE-toh
PWEN-tay)

Los Angeles. 1988. The lights dim. The curtain rises. A crowd of a thousand-plus Latin music fans cheers wildly, for there, standing center stage behind a battery of drums and other percussion instruments called the **timbales** is The King—*El Rey*—of Latin music: Tito Puente.

This is a king who wears many crowns: king of the timbales, king of **salsa** music, king of Latin jazz. Like Elvis Presley in rock-and-roll, Louis Armstrong in jazz, and Ludwig van Beethoven in Western classical music, Puente is an icon. He is a musician whose artistry and persona essentially define the musical tradition with which he is identified.

Tito immediately takes command of the band, locking in tightly with the other members of the **rhythm section** (pianist, bassist, percussionists)

Tito Puente playing the timbales.

and "kicking" the rhythms and **riffs** of the **horn section** (trumpets, trombones, saxophones) with a barrage of drum fills and accented "shots." The energy his playing and presence generate is extraordinary, and the rest of the band rises to meet it.

Over the course of this magical night of music making, Tito Puente wows the audience with his dazzling timbales solos, his lyrical playing on the vibraphone (an instrument whose use he pioneered in Latin music), his bandleading skills, showmanship, charm, and humor. They take it all in, loving every minute, crying out "Tito, we love you!" at various points. There are many great moments, but there is one that unquestionably tops the rest as far as the response of the audience is concerned. When Tito and the band launch into an arrangement of "Oye Como Va," the most famous piece he ever wrote, the entire crowd rises from their seats as one, swaying and dancing to the **cha cha chá** beat of this classic **Latino/American** tune.

◼ ◼ ◼

Introduction

This chapter presents a story of **Latin dance music** viewed through the lens of the musicultural history of the song "Oye Como Va." According to ethnomusicologist and Tito Puente biographer Steven Loza, "Oye Como Va" is "an international anthem," "the most played Latin tune in the world," and a song which, in 1970, turned the worlds of rock and pop music "upside down" when it was recorded by the **Latin rock** band Santana and became a commercial mega-hit the likes of which had never been seen before in the domain of Latin music (Loza 1999:45, 73, 44).

The chapter begins by placing "Oye Como Va" in the contexts of Latin dance music and Latino/American culture. We then move through a survey of the key developments in Latin dance music history—especially those rooted in traditional Cuban dance music styles such as the **rumba,** the **danzón,** the **danzón-mambo,** the cha cha chá, and the **mambo**—that prefigured the musical style and social significance of "Oye Como Va." The second half of the chapter builds around Guided Listening Experiences based on three important and influential recordings of "Oye Como Va":

rumba (ROOM-bah)

danzón (dan-SOHN [last syllable in-between English "sun" and "sewn"])

◼ The original Tito Puente recording from his 1963 album *El Rey Bravo*.

◼ Santana's enormously popular, rock-infused version from the hit 1970 record *Abraxas*.

◼ A hip-hop and techno-inspired dance mix version from a 2004 Tito Puente Jr. CD entitled *Tito Puente, Jr.: Greatest Club Remixes*.

Each of these recordings tells its own tale of the form and substance of *pan-Latino cultural identity* at a particular historical juncture. Each also reflects on a broader musicultural history of interrelationships between the United States, Puerto Rico, and Cuba. It is the musical products of this history that account for most of the major styles of popular Latin dance music: mambo, cha cha chá, salsa, Latin jazz, Latin rock, and a plethora of newer styles identified by umbrella labels like Latin pop and Latin rap.

This chapter, then, takes a specific piece of music, "Oye Como Va," as its focus musical element, and looks at that composition in terms of the musicultural history of pan-Latino culture and society. A variety of topics and subjects emerge along the way. Five are of central importance:

- The Cuban cha cha chá: its musical and cultural roots and its historical transformation.
- Puerto Rican and **Newyorican** (New York/Puerto Rican) society and musicultural life.
- The life and career of Tito Puente (1923–2000).
- The musical tradition of Latin dance music (defined below).
- The integral connection between Latin dance music and the commercial music industry.

"Oye Como Va" and Latin Dance Music in Context

We begin with a deceptively simple question: Where does the song "Oye Como Va" (which basically translates as "See how she moves") come from? A simple answer: the United States, New York City specifically. New York is where Tito Puente was born and raised and where he based himself throughout his professional life. It is where the song was first performed and recorded. And it is almost surely where Puente wrote the tune in the first place.

So then, strictly speaking, "Oye Como Va" is an American song from New York (i.e., with "American" meaning "United States-ian" to be precise). That is not all there is to the matter, however. Though Puente was a lifelong New Yorker and a patriotic American citizen who served in the U.S. military during World War II, he identified himself, ethnically and culturally, as a Puerto Rican first and foremost. "Oye Como Va," and Puente's body of work overall, belongs to a grand legacy of Latino musical culture that developed principally among Puerto Ricans and Americans of Puerto Rican descent in both the United States (especially New York) and Puerto Rico. Perhaps, then, "Oye Como Va" is best described as an example of Puerto Rican music.

Alas, there is a catch to this theory, too. In terms of its fundamental *musical* identity—its core style, form, and structure—"Oye Como Va" is neither principally American nor Puerto Rican, but rather Cuban. It belongs irrefutably to the musical legacy of the cha cha chá, a Cuban dance-music genre that emerged around 1950 in the Cuban capital of Havana before being developed and gaining wide popularity in North America, Europe, and elsewhere. Furthermore, Tito Puente himself, throughout his life, insisted that his own musical identity was principally Cuban rather than Puerto Rican or American. By these measures, "Oye Como Va" would seem to be a Cuban song, or at least a song of Cuban musical extraction.

There is at least one more possibility to throw into the mix as well. "Oye Como Va" may have its musical basis in Cuba, its cultural essence in Puerto Rico, and its geographical point of origin in New York, but for millions upon millions of people around the world, it is, pure and simple, an American "classic rock" tune by Santana. Relatively few people who know and love "Oye Como Va" have any idea who Tito Puente was, let alone that he wrote and was the first to record this famous song. Nor do they know that Santana closely modeled his recorded version after the Puente original (though Santana never made any secret of that fact). Even among his legions of fans, Puente was not necessarily known as the composer of "Oye Como Va." Wherever in the world he would play, he used to report, people would come up to him and say, "Tito, could you please play Santana's tune, you know 'Oye como va'?" (Puente, quoted in Loza 1999:44). This brings us back full circle. Maybe "Oye Como Va" *is* an American song after all, but for different reasons than those outlined earlier.

The fact of the matter is that there is no single right answer to the question, Where does "Oye Como Va" come from? It comes from many different places, and in its eclectic musicultural admixture brings to bear an even more complex question: Where does "Latin dance music" come from? And by extension, who, and what, does it represent?

Latin dance music defined

"Oye Como Va," in its many incarnations (at least the ones we deal with in this chapter), belongs to the realm of Latin dance music. This is one of those terms that can mean any or all of a number of different things, so let us establish from the outset what it is assumed to mean here.

World events		Music events
European discovery of Cuba (Christopher ●········· Columbus)	**1492**	
First Spanish settlers to Cuba ●·········	**1511**	
Taino and other indigenous peoples all ●········· but wiped out in wake of Spanish conquest		
Height of slave trade in Cuba ●·········	**1790–1860**	
	Late 19th century	········● Creolized dance-music forms: *contradanza, danzón*
	1920s	········● Danzón essentially becomes national dance of Cuba
		········● Afro-Cuban *son* emerges and challenges danzón in both popularity and nationalistic significance
	1923	········● Tito Puente born to Puerto Rican immigrant parents in Spanish Harlem, New York City
	1930s	········● Xavier Cugat dominant figure in so-called Latin dance music in U.S.
	1940	········● Formation of Machito and the Afro-Cubans
	1947	········● Carlos Santana born in Mexico
	1949	········● Pérez Prado's "Mambo #5" achieves major commercial success
	1950	········● Cha cha chá originates in Cuba (Enrique Jorrin)

The "Latin" in Latin dance music refers to Latin America. Geographically, Latin America is a large and culturally diverse region of the world encompassing all of South America and the various nations and territories of Central America, Mexico, and the Caribbean. In its broadest sense, Latin American music—or Latin music, for short—is any music originating from anywhere in this vast region; and in this broad sense, too, musics of diasporic Latino communities in the United States, Canada, Europe, and elsewhere also may be included (e.g., salsa music, a genre of Latin music that was "invented" in New York City). (Visit the Online Learning Center at www.mhhe.com/bakan1 for information and resources on diverse traditions of Latin American music.) The "dance" in Latin dance music, of course, refers to music intended to accompany dancing. Thus, Latin dance music, in the broadest and most literal sense, is any and all music identified with Latin America that is intended for dancing.

This, however, is *not* the sense in which the term "Latin dance music" is used in this chapter. Instead, our scope will be far more narrow and specific. As used here, the term refers specifically to *a host of popular dance-music genres that originated in or derived from the island of Cuba; that have experienced significant histories of development in the United States and/or Puerto Rico; and that have histories of transmission closely tied to the U.S./international commercial music industry and mass media distribution.* New York City has been the main U.S. hub of Latin dance music's

World events		Music events
	1950s	● Big band mambo and "mambo craze" in U.S. (Puente, Tito Rodríguez, Machito)
		● Latin dance music scene dominated by a combination of Cuban, Puerto Rican, and Newyorican bandleaders and musicians
Fidel Castro comes to power in Cuba, ● which becomes a socialist state	**1959**	
Pan-Latino movement emerges and ● develops in U.S., and eventually internationally	**1960s–1970s**	
	1963	● Original Tito Puente recording of "Oye Como Va" released on *El Rey Bravo*
	1970s	● Birth and rise to popularity of salsa music ("salsa explosion")
	1970	● Santana's Latin rock version of "Oye Como Va" released on *Abraxas*
	1971	● Tito Puente Jr. born in New York City
	1996	● "Oye Como Va" released on *Guarachando*, by Tito Puente Jr. & the Latin Rhythm Crew
	1999	● Carlos Santana releases Grammy award-winning album *Supernatural*
	2000	● Death of Tito Puente
	2004	● Tito Puente Jr. releases *Tito Puente, Jr.: Greatest Club Remixes* (including remix version of "Oye Como Va") and *En Los Pasos De Mi Padre* (In My Father's Shoes)

development and popularization, though other cities—Miami, San Francisco, Los Angeles, and to some extent Paris, London, and even Tokyo—have played key roles as well.

A Latino/American phenomenon

The musicians responsible for shaping the history of Latin dance music (i.e., as defined immediately above) encompass a diverse and confluent range of ethnic, national, and musical backgrounds. There are the Cuban and Cuban-American pioneers: Israel "Cachao" López and Orestes López (the López brothers), Enrique Jorrin, Mario Bauzá, Machito (Frank Grillo), Pérez Prado, Arsenio Rodríguez, Mongo Santamaría, Celia Cruz. There are also the Puerto Rican and Puerto Rican–American bandleaders like Tito Rodríguez and Tito Puente, whose impact, as we shall see, has been particularly decisive. African-American jazz musicians including trumpet great Dizzy Gillespie have made seminal contributions too, as have a Panamanian salsa superstar, Rubén Blades, and a Mexican-American (Chicano) rock guitarist, Carlos Santana.

Altogether, the history of Latin dance music has been, and remains, categorically multicultural and multidimensional. More specifically, Latin dance music has been fueled by an ongoing mutual feedback loop between Latin American nations and the United States. Thus, it is appropriate to categorize this diverse matrix of Cuban-derived Latin dance music as a Latino/

Enrique Jorrin
(En-ree-kay
Horr-EEN)

Mario Bauzá
(MAH-ree-o
Bow-SAH)

Machito
(Ma-CHEE-toe)

Creolization is defined as "the development of a distinctive new culture out of the prolonged encounter of two or more other cultures" (Manuel 1995:14). It is a term that is essentially synonomous with syncretization but is more widely used in discussions of Caribbean cultures. This is why it is used in this chapter.

American phenomenon, the slash between "Latino" and "American" implying "and/or" in the widest sense. We now explore one slice of the large pie of this musical phenomenon via a journey through, first, the historical roots and, second, the actual history of "Oye Como Va."

Cuba, Creolization, and the Roots of Latin Dance Music

The roots of the Cuban dance-music styles that gave rise to the cha cha chá and, in turn, to the song "Oye Como Va," take us back to Spain and West Africa. Centuries ago, Spain colonized Cuba (as well as Puerto Rico) and instituted slavery there, bringing millions of African slaves to the island. It was through the blending of musical elements of Spanish and West African derivation—their syncretization or *creolization,* in the hands of first African slaves and then their African-derived and *mulatto* ("mixed race") descendants especially—that the distinctive forms of Afro-Cuban (African-Cuban) music that form the basis of all of the popular Latin dance music genres we will discuss were born.

An understanding of Cuban dance music and the popular Latin dance music styles that grew from it begins with an understanding of the creolization of African-derived (principally West African) and European-derived (principally Spanish) musical culture in Cuba.

Afro-Cuban roots of Latin dance music

Taino (TAH-EE-no)

The European discovery of Cuba occurred in 1492, when Christopher Columbus and his Spanish fleet arrived on the island. The indigenous population of Cuba was comprised of Amerindian peoples such as the Taino, who, tragically, were all but wiped out in the wake of the Spanish conquest. Spanish settlers began arriving in Cuba in 1511. They established large sugar cane plantations. African slaves were brought to the island in huge numbers—an estimated five million in all—to work the plantations. They came from many different African nations and ethnic heritages, but most were of either Yoruba (the largest ethnic group in western Africa; the majority of modern-day Yoruba live in Nigeria) or Congolese descent.

A very large majority of the slaves arrived between 1790 and 1860, much later than their counterparts in British colonies of the Caribbean and in the United States. (Importation of slaves to the British Caribbean colonies ceased in 1804, and the U.S. slave trade also greatly declined around that time.) This relatively late arrival of slaves in Cuba helps to explain why, even today, much Cuban music sounds distinctly more "African" (and, more specifically, Yoruba- or Congolese-derived) than other African-derived musics of the Americas (e.g., American blues, Jamaican reggae).

Other factors account for this difference as well. Due to differing approaches and attitudes toward the institution of slavery on the part of slave owners, traditional African-rooted forms of worship, music, and dance were retained in Spanish colonies such as Cuba to a much greater extent than they were in British colonies (e.g., Jamaica, Trinidad) or in the United States. Additionally, it was easier for Cuban slaves to buy their freedom than it was for their counterparts in Jamaica, Trinidad, or the United States. Thus, large communities of free blacks were established

Batá drums being played during a Santería ritual. This photograph was originally published by the Associated Press. Although photography is generally not permitted during Santería (Orisha) rituals, terms are sometimes negotiated by photojournalists that render the taking and publishing of photos such as this one permissible.

in Cuban towns and cities by the early 18th century, and they, together with slaves in these same areas, celebrated religious and social occasions in ways that were largely consistent with the practices of their African forebears. These conditions fostered an environment that "favored the dynamic flourishing of neo-African music in Cuba" (Manuel 1995:20).

Two types of traditional, neo-African music in Cuba would prove especially influential to the later development of Latin dance music: ritual drumming associated with the Afro-Cuban religion of **Santería** (a.k.a. Orisha religion) and the secular, social dance music of traditional Cuban rumba.

Santería ritual drumming is traditionally performed on a set of three drums called **batá.** Each drum is of a different size and pitch (low, medium, high). Stringed bells attached to the lowest-pitched, lead drum enhance its timbre, providing an idiophonic element to the sound. The drums are played in an intricate, interlocking style of complex polyrhythms (see Amira and Cornelius 1992). The lead drummer's part involves much improvisation, whereas the two other drummers' parts are mainly based on recurring rhythmic patterns (ostinatos). In ritual contexts, the batá drums often accompany sacred songs, such as the one heard on **CD ex. #3-1.**

The music of rumba also features a set of three drums—low-, medium-, and high-pitched—played in a complex, polyrhythmic style. The modern, barrel-shaped **conga drums (congas)** used by many contemporary Latin and popular music groups are descendants of the original rumba drums (called *ngoma*). Rumba drummers today usually play the music on congas.

All of the rhythms in rumba music in a sense derive from a single rhythm called **clave,** which is played on an instrument,

Santería
  (San-te-REE-yah)
batá (bah-TAH)
conga (KOAN-gah)
clave (KLAH-vay)

Conga drums and claves.

Son 3-2	X • • X • • X • • • X • X • • •

Son 2-3	• • X • X • • • X • • X • • X •

Rumba 3-2	X • • X • • • X • • X • X • • •

Rumba 2-3	• • X • X • • • X • • X • • • X

The four versions of the clave rhythm.

FIGURE 11.1

the **claves,** that consists of a pair of thick, round sticks that are struck together. Indeed, the clave rhythm, of which there are actually four variants (see Figure 11.1, corresponding to **Online Musical Illustration #25**), is the rhythmic basis of virtually all forms of Latin dance music, including cha cha chá tunes like "Oye Como Va." Clave is so fundamental to Latin dance music that it is often not even actually played; rather, its presence is simply *felt,* by the musicians, dancers, and listeners alike.

In traditional rumba performances, the percussion instruments (the three conga drums, the claves, and an additional wooden idiophone called *palitos* that usually plays an embellished version of the clave rhythm) accompany songs sung by a lead singer and a group of background singers (the *coro,* or chorus). The singers interact with each other in call-and-response style. The music accompanies dancing. The dance associated with the style of rumba music heard in **CD ex. #3-2,** called *rumba guaguancó,* is performed by a man and a woman who engage in what ethnomusicologist Peter Manuel has characterized as "a pantomime game of coy evasion on the woman's part and playful conquest on the man's" (Manuel 1995:25).

guaguancó (wah-wahn-KOH)

Man and woman dancing to the accompaniment of the Cuban group Rumba Morena.

Spanish-Cuban roots of Latin dance music

The other half of the story of traditional, creolized forms of Cuban dance music that preceded modern Latin dance music styles as represented in songs like "Oye Como Va" has to do with European, especially Spanish, musical influences.

Creolized dance-music styles blending African (especially Yoruba and Congolese) and European (especially Spanish) elements became highly prominent beginning in the latter part of the 18th century. Prior to that, white urban Cuban society had relied mainly on European genres such as the waltz, the minuet, and the mazurka for their dance entertainment. Increasing disenchantment on the part of the white Cuban establishment with economic restrictions and governmental corruption and inefficiency issuing from Spain led to a rejection of these cultural symbols of the European past. New, distinctly Cuban hybrid dance-music forms emerged as Cuban musicians—primarily of Afro-Cuban or mulatto descent—grafted rhythmic and other elements of African-derived traditions onto adapted European dance-music forms. These new, creolized styles, such as the *contradanza* and the danzón, became important symbols of an emergent Cuban national identity that arose in the late 1800s in connection with a strong, anti-Spanish rule nationalist movement. They reflected a shift toward a more inclusive notion of what constituted Cuban identity, one in which whites, blacks, and mulattos all had a place (though full racial equality was by no means achieved). Some of the creolized dance music styles also achieved international popularity, setting the stage for the dominance of Cuban-derived musics in the international Latin dance music culture of later periods.

By the 1920s, the danzón had essentially become the national dance of Cuba. Danzón music was mainly performed on a type of "sweet-sounding" ensemble called a **charanga.** Charanga instrumentation usually featured a wooden flute and two or more violins backed by a piano, a string bass, a *güiro* (wooden scraper idiophone), and a pair of drums that were the forerunners of the modern timbales. Maracas (shakers) were often used as well.

Around this same time, however, in the 1920s, the danzón's status as the reigning form of Cuban national dance music was challenged by the emergence of a new, more heavily African-influenced style called ***son.*** Yet despite the dramatic ascent of *son,* both in popularity and as a symbol of Cuban national consciousness (see Moore 1997; Manuel 1995, for more on this subject), the danzón and the charanga did not fade away. Rather, they rallied to meet the challenge. The charanga danzón groups, "with their quaint yet soulful flute-and-violin sound, were surviving by changing with the times and making their music hotter and more Afro-Cuban" (Manuel 1995:41). This led to the emergence of a new dance-music style, the danzón-mambo (Gerard 2001:68), and in turn to the Cuban cha cha chá style in which the direct musical ancestry of "Oye Como Va" is rooted.

Güiro and maracas.

charanga
(cha-RAHN-gah)

güiro (WEE-ro)

son (sohn
[in-between
English "sun"
and "sewn"])

Arcaño y sus
Maravillas (Ar-
CAH-nyo ee soos
Mah-rah-VEE-yas)

timbalero
(teem-ba-LAY-ro)

The Danzón-Mambo

The danzón-mambo was a highly Afro-Cubanized version of the earlier danzón. The principal charanga group responsible for its development was Arcaño y sus Maravillas (or Maravillos). This group was led by the flutist Antonio Arcaño, but two other members of the band, the brothers Orestes López and Israel "Cachao" López, were the principal innovators of the danzón-mambo style.

Elements of Afro-Cubanization were present at multiple levels in the danzón-mambo. Conga drums were added to the standard charanga percussion section of timbales, güiro, and maracas. The complex and syncopated rhythms played on the congas added a strong imprint of Afro-Cuban rhythmic character to the music. (This imprint reflected influences from *son* especially.) Additionally, a cowbell was added to the percussive arsenal of the timbales player (*timbalero*), paving the way for the development of the standard "drum kit" setup of modern timbaleros like Tito Puente (consisting of two or more metal-sided timbale drums, cowbells, woodblock, one or more cymbals, and sometimes additional instruments—see the photo on p. 218).

These various elements of Afro-Cuban musical influence were most prominent in the so-called *mambo sections* of danzón-mambo arrangements. These mambo sections highlighted rhythmically exciting music with lots of repetition and textures featuring layered ostinatos. Even the violins, whose function in earlier danzón styles had been almost entirely melodic, took on a largely rhythmic function in the danzón-mambo, playing syncopated ostinato figures that complemented the Afro-Cuban character of the percussion parts. Soaring, improvised flute solos were another signature element of style.

The historical importance of the danzón-mambo is twofold, since its influence fed directly into the two most successful and influential Latin dance-music phenomena of the early 1950s, **big band mambo** and cha cha chá. These two genres, in turn, would coalesce in the original Tito Puente version of "Oye Como Va."

Enrique Jorrin and the Cuban Cha Cha Chá

While the López brothers moved the danzón in an increasingly Afro-Cuban, *son*-influenced direction through the late 1940s, another alumnus of Arcaño y sus Maravillas, the violinist and bandleader Enrique Jorrin, took the music in another direction altogether beginning in 1950. It was in that year that Jorrin recorded a composition entitled "La Engañadora" (The Beguiler) with his own charanga group, Orquesta América. This was the first cha cha chá ever recorded. It represented a fusion of older danzón sensibilities with the retention of certain elements that had come into the music via the danzón-mambo, such as the use of conga drums.

As interesting as the musical synthesis itself in cha cha chá was its underlying motivation. More than anything, Jorrin wanted to devise a Cuban dance-music style that would appeal to non-Cuban dancers, especially Americans. He was reportedly first inspired to compose "La Engañadora" after watching a group of American dancers struggle to keep up with complex Cuban rhythms on the dance floor (Fairley 2000:389).

The key to creating accessible Cuban dance music, Jorrin reasoned, was rhythmic simplification. Thus, he dispensed with the syncopated rhythm of the timbales part heard in danzón and danzón-mambo arrangements and replaced it with a "four-square rhythm" in which the steady beat was crystal clear (at least by Latin dance music standards). Tempos were kept in a comfortable, medium range, so as not to tax the dancers' feet or aerobic conditioning too much. Even inexperienced, non-Cuban dancers were able to keep pace with the relatively simple "one - two - cha-cha-chá" footwork required. The rhythmic foundations of cha cha chá music are illustrated and explained in the Musical Guided Tour for this chapter. The transcript on page 227 corresponds to the audio Musical Guided Tour. As you listen to this tour at the Online Learning Center (www.mhhe.com/bakan1), follow along with this transcript.

Another distinctive feature of the Jorrin-style Cuban cha cha chá was the role of the singers. Singing, which had either been entirely absent or used sparingly in the danzón-mambo style, became an identifying feature of the cha cha chá. However, the harmonized vocal textures and involved patterns of vocal call-and-response found in earlier Cuban musics such as rumba and *son* were here substituted for by simpler, mainly unison singing textures.

"El Bodeguero"
(El Bo-day-GAY-ro)

Following the success of "El Engañadora," Jorrin released other popular cha cha chá recordings. One of these was "El Bodeguero" (The Grocer). **CD ex. #3-3** is an excerpt from a recording of "El Bodeguero" performed in a modern charanga arrangement that for the most part remains true to the original Jorrin style (though electronic keyboard instruments are used and there are no violins). A contemporary Cuban group, Grupo Cimarrón de Cuba, is featured. As you listen, take note of the accessible dance rhythm (which is anchored by the same types of percussion instruments and rhythmic patterns demonstrated in the Musical Guided Tour), the unison group singing texture (up until 1:20, after which the vocal parts are harmonized), and the prominent role played by the flute.

Couple dancing the cha cha chá in the 1950s.

The "Cuban light" appeal of the cha cha chá, as represented by the music of Enrique Jorrin and a host of other musicians influenced by him, proved highly marketable internationally. The dance swept across North America and Europe in the 1950s, aided greatly by the advent of two new technologies, television and the LP (long-playing) record. By mid-decade, it "had become the vogue among aficionados of Latin music in the United States and abroad" (Loza 1999:142).

Cha cha chá fizzled out after a few years, however, at least as an international mass culture phenomenon. Its decline was most certainly hastened by the rock-and-roll explosion of the mid- to late 1950s (e.g., Elvis Presley, Chuck Berry, Jerry Lee Lewis, Little Richard), but cha cha chá was also a victim of its own unabashedly populist, commercial appeal; its "commercial-

Latin Percussion Rhythms of the Cha Cha Chá

In a standard cha cha chá, the timbalero (timbales player) marks out a basic beat of steady quarter notes in a four-beat meter on a small cowbell, like this [♪]. Sometimes extra notes are added between the main cowbell beats to embellish the rhythm. Here is an example of what that sounds like [♪]. This embellished version of the cowbell rhythm is reinforced by the wooden scraper-type idiophone called the güiro, whose part sounds like this [♪]. Another timbral layer is often provided by the maracas (shakers), which play a rhythm of steady eighth notes, like this [♪]. The cowbell, güiro, and maracas together, then, create this rhythmic texture [♪].

Another percussive layer of cha cha chá rhythm is furnished by the conga drums, with their signature, syncopated rhythmic pattern called *tumbao* (toom-BAH-oh). Tumbao is a rhythm that can be traced back to traditional rumba styles (and that also finds parallels in ritual batá drumming). It came into the cha cha chá via the influences of *son* and the danzón-mambo. Alone, tumbao on the conga drums sounds like this [♪]. Together with the cowbell, güiro, and maracas, it sounds like this [♪]. An additional layer of rhythm furnished by a small pair of drums called the **bongó** (bon-GO [as opposed to the English pronunciation BAHN-go]) may be incorporated as well [♪], resulting in this overall sound and rhythmic texture [♪].

Though the clave rhythm is often not actually played in a cha cha chá performance, its presence is clearly implied by the tumbao rhythm of the conga drums. We will now play tumbao on the congas together with clave rhythm played on a pair of claves; notice how the conga part seems to trace the shape of the clave rhythm while at the same time filling in the rhythmic spaces between clave strikes [♪].

Finally, here is the full percussion section—including the claves—playing as they would in a standard cha cha chá arrangement [♪].

Bongó drums being played.

ization and Arthur Murray-style dilution . . . guaranteed its decline" (Manuel 1995:41). "A few years of lumpy rhythm sections, mooing sax section [*sic*], and musicians raggedly chanting CHAH! CHAH! CHAH! were enough" (Roberts 1979:133; c.f. Manuel 1995:41).

Yet the cha cha chá did not die. In fact, it took on new life and a new sound in the hands of the same great New York–based Latin bandleaders who had blazed the trails of the other major Latin dance craze of the early 1950s, big band mambo. For these bandleaders and their audiences, cha cha chás provided a nice contrast to the hot rhythms, fast tempos, heavy syncopations, and trenchant Afro-Cubanisms of the mambos that otherwise dominated their set lists. The four-square rhythm of the cha cha chá possessed an elegantly funky quality all its own and gave the denizens of the Latin dance ballrooms of New York and other places a chance to slow down and get acquainted between tear-it-up mambo numbers. Yet while it represented a contrast to the big band mambo style, the new style of the cha cha chá that yielded tunes like "Oye Como Va" was musically influenced in important ways by big band mambo, to which we now turn our attention.

Mambo (Big Band Mambo)

The musician commonly credited with the "invention" of the mambo (from a Congolese word meaning "chant") was the Cuban bandleader Pérez Prado, who spent the majority of his career touring and recording in Mexico and elsewhere outside of Cuba. It was Prado who had the first international mambo hit, "Mambo #5," in 1949.

Yet while Prado may have crystallized the mambo into a distinctive genre, it was the bands of a group of bandleaders in New York City known as the **mambo kings**—Machito and the Afro-Cubans and groups led by Tito Puente and Tito Rodríguez—who took mambo to its most sublime heights. Fusing the Prado-style mambo with other popular Cuban dance music elements, a deeper entrenchment in Afro-Cuban percussion and rhythm, and abundant use of borrowed elements from American jazz and mainstream American popular music of the day, they created something profoundly new and different. "For the first time," writes Cuban music scholar Charley Gerard, "a new Cuban style originated outside of the island" (Gerard 2001:2).

Mambo, as developed by the big New York Latin dance bands of Tito Puente and his contemporaries beginning in the early 1950s, was a musical genre defined by the following features:

- **Big band instrumentation.** This was adopted and adapted from the model of American big band swing and jazz of the era. The typical lineup included sections of anywhere from two to five players each on trumpet, trombone, and saxophone; plus piano, bass, and three or more percussionists (with singers possibly in addition, depending on the arrangement). The percussion section featured the three types of drums also used in Cuban *son* bands: the timbales, the conga drums, and the bongó drums, plus the additional, idiophone-type Latin percussion instruments (cowbells, claves, güiro, maracas, etc.).

- **Musical textures featuring layered ostinatos throughout the band.** All of the instrumentalists—the percussionists, pianist, bassist, saxophonists, trombonists, and trumpet players—were assigned short, recurring patterns (ostinatos, or *riffs*) that were repeated over and over, often with variations, and layered one atop the other during the course of a mambo arrangement. These layered ostinato textures, which were reflective of influences from the earlier Cuban *son* and danzón-mambo styles, created "a tight, composite rhythm that had a unique drive and an electrifying appeal to dancers" (Manuel 1995:37).

- **Driving, Afro-Cuban percussion rhythms.** The syncopated, interlocking rhythms of the percussion section in mambo, all growing from the root rhythm of clave and reflecting the characteristic Cuban rhythmic styles of rumba and *son,* served as the engine that drove the music.

- **Jazz influences.** Beyond the big band instrumentation, influences from American jazz were reflected in the harmonies (chords and chord progressions), rhythms, and arrangements of mambos, and also in the highlighting of extended, improvised instrumental solos.

- **Fast tempos and highly energetic playing.** The tempos of the mambos were upbeat and the music exciting, energetic, and eminently danceable (though not *easy* to dance to, unlike the cha cha chá).

- **Absence, or at least limited use, of singing.** Compared to related Cuban forms like *son,* there was relatively little emphasis on singing—and in turn on song texts—in mambo. "With its emphasis on short, often meaningless vocal interjections, it was the perfect style for an audience who didn't speak Spanish" (Gerard 2001:2–3). This was important, since mambo was designed to appeal to Latino and non-Latino audiences alike (and succeeded in doing so).

The big band mambo sound outlined above is well illustrated by a short excerpt from the mambo "Sambia" (**CD ex. #3-4**), a classic recording by Machito and the Afro-Cubans. Listen especially to the section of the excerpt beginning at 0:19, which follows the heavily jazz-inspired introductory section of the opening. First the saxophones present a riff (0:19–0:26), then they repeat it with the trumpets and trombones "answering" between phrases in call-and-response fashion (0:27–0:35), and finally an intricate texture of layered riffs is created by saxo-

Machito and the Afro-Cubans.

phones, trumpets, and trombones together (0:36–0:52). All the while, the driving Afro-Cuban rhythmic base of the rhythm section pushes the music along with propulsive force and energy.

Tito Puente, the Newyorican Connection, and Latino/American Music Culture in New York City

Despite its principally Cuban musical lineage, the culture of Latin dance music in New York in the 1950s and beyond represented a complex mixture of ethnicities and cultures. Of the leading mambo bandleaders, Machito and Mario Bauzá were from Cuba, but Tito Rodríguez was from Puerto Rico, and Tito Puente, as was mentioned earlier, was a Newyorican, born and raised in New York of Puerto Rican descent. The personnel of the bands were likewise ethnically diverse. The percussion section of Machito and the Afro-Cubans, for example, featured drummers from Cuba as well as Newyorican percussionists who were intensely devoted to mastering the Afro-Cuban styles (these included a young Tito Puente at one point—see p. 231). All of this re-flected larger demographics of Latino/American society during this period. As Gerard explains, "Afro-Cuban music developed its stateside [U.S.] home not in Cuban neighborhoods, which . . . were primarily white, but in Puerto Rican neighborhoods, where Afro-Cubans mixed with dark-skinned Puerto Ricans" (Gerard 2001:13). Primary among these Puerto Rican neighborhoods in both size and cultural influence was Spanish Harlem in New York City, otherwise known simply as the *barrio* (the neighborhood).

Tito Puente was born in the barrio of Spanish Harlem in 1923 to Puerto Rican immigrant parents. He grew up there, absorbing the myriad influences of traditional Puerto Rican music, Afro-Cuban music, American popular song, African-American jazz, big band swing, even Western art music. All of these were integral parts of the rich, living soundtrack that surrounded him in his native musical environment and formed the fabric of his eclectic and syncretic musical range.

"The background of the perennial bandleader," Gerard says of Puente, "is a perfect meta-phor for what made him a central figure in stateside Cuban music. He grew up speaking English on the street and Spanish at home. As a young man, he learned big band [jazz] drumming. As a

Machito and the Afro-Cubans in the History of Latin Dance Music

Machito and the Afro-Cubans, the band featured in "Sambia" (**CD ex. #3-4**), was one of the most important and influential of all Latin dance bands. It was this group, more than any other, that formed the seminal link between Cuban dance music in Cuba and Cuban-derived dance music in New York, ultimately leading to the profusion of modern, international styles of Latin dance music that would emerge.

Machito and the Afro-Cubans was formed in 1940, two years after Machito moved to New York from his native Cuba at the invitation of his longtime musical collaborator (and brother-in-law) Mario Bauzá. Bauzá had settled in New York several years earlier. In the late 1930s, so-called Latin dance music in the United States was dominated by the syrupy, sanitized Latin sound of the Spanish-born, Cuban-raised popular musician Xavier Cugat. Like Enrique Jorrin with the cha cha chá, Cugat opportunistically set out to create a style of Latin music that would have broad popular appeal beyond the Latino market, but he went considerably farther in this direction than did Jorrin with the original cha cha chá. "To succeed in America," Cugat once said, "I gave the Americans a Latin music that had nothing authentic about it" (Roberts 1979:87; c.f. Manuel 1995:69).

Publicity shot of Desi Arnaz.

Cugat's formula proved immensely successful. He became a perennial New York high-society favorite, playing "for Anglos in swanky lower Manhattan ballrooms" (Manuel 1995:69). He and his orchestra also appeared in numerous Hollywood films, introducing mainstream America to the ostensibly "Latin" dance-music sound. Cugat's popularity paved the way for later popular Latin bandleaders who worked in an essentially similar idiom, such as Desi Arnaz of television's *I Love Lucy* fame.

Bauzá and Machito, "disgruntled with the watered-down rhythms of Latin society bands" like Cugat's, launched Machito and the Afro-Cubans in response. They forged an innovative musical approach that was rooted in the classic *son* style of Cuban masters like Arsenio Rodríguez, but that also incorporated the sonic force of the jazz big band and the influences of jazz improvisers like Dizzy Gillespie and Charlie Parker, the future founders of bebop jazz. "With powerful horns and a hell-fired rhythm section, the band immediately captured the attention of the Latino community in New York" (Leymarie 2002:4).

teenager, he joined Machito's orchestra and learned how to play Cuban popular rhythms. Later, he made it his business to acquaint himself with Afro-Cuban culture. A trained musician [in Western art music] who read music fluently, he took the study of the oral tradition of Afro-Cuban folkloric music seriously at a time when many musicians thought that if you weren't from an Afro-Cuban *barrio* you could never master the idiom" (Gerard 2001:2).

This multicultural upbringing and eclectic musical background would profoundly shape Tito Puente's multifaceted conceptions of his own identity throughout his life. As we learned earlier in the chapter, he identified himself principally as a Puerto Rican even though he was born and raised in New York:

> Wherever I go . . . they ask me, "What are you?" I say "I'm Puerto Rican" . . . But I am international, too. I play for all kinds of people, and they dance to my music and I have all kinds of a following; so I don't want to tag myself . . . but when they ask me who I am, I represent Puerto Rico. (Puente, quoted in Loza 1999:224–25)

Yet when asked about his *musical* identity, his standard response, despite his greatly varied musical experience, was simply, "I play Cuban music" (Puente, cited in Manuel 1995:74).

These different types of self-identification may seem paradoxical, but they are completely consistent with the larger history of Latin dance music culture in New York City. According to Manuel, Newyorican and Puerto Rican immigrant musicians who had mastered and in a sense re-invented traditional Cuban music styles were dominating the city's Latin music scene by the 1940s (Manuel 1995:67).

Tito Puente joined Machito and the Afro-Cubans in 1942 but was drafted into the U.S. Navy shortly therearter. (He played drums and saxophone with the Navy band.) Returning to New York in 1945, he re-established his career as a dance band musician and also enrolled at the prestigious Juilliard School. He studied conducting, orchestration, music theory, and percussion at Juilliard, and became especially interested in playing the vibraphone during this period.

The vibraphone.

The post–World War II era brought massive migration of Puerto Ricans to the U.S. mainland, the majority coming to New York. This created a growing market for dance bands that played Cuban-derived Latin music, which had long been popular in Puerto Rico. An influx of important new arrivals from Cuba, including the great percussionists Chano Pozo (who developed an important association with Dizzy Gillespie) and Mongo Santamaría, altered the musical landscape as well. They brought with them the authentic rhythms of Cuban batá drumming and rumba, and these were absorbed into the musical fabric of bands like Machito's. Puente became an avid protégé of Mongo Santamaría, in particular, soaking up all he could about Afro-Cuban drum styles, music, and culture.

The year 1949 proved to be a pivotal one for Puente and Latin music. It was in this year that Pérez Prado's first big hit, "Mambo #5," launched what would soon come to be known as the *mambo craze* of the 1950s. It was also in 1949 that Max Hyman purchased New York's Palladium Ballroom and quickly transformed it into the epicenter of the burgeoning mambo world. Riding the wave of mambomania, Tito Puente formed his first Latin dance band that same year, and within short order was playing the Palladium and other top venues and rivaling the likes of Machito and Tito Rodríguez for top billing as the reigning king of mambo. His band was as hot and as innovative as any, and included conga player Mongo Santamaría and bongó player Willie Bobo alongside Puente on the timbales in what today is remembered as perhaps the greatest Latin dance band percussion section of all time.

Buoyed by his star status at the Palladium, Tito Puente went from success to success, touring widely with his band and making many records. By the time he released his most popular song, "Oye Como Va," on the 1963 album *El Rey Bravo,* he had almost 40 albums as a bandleader to his credit, including big sellers like *Dance Mania* (1958). By this time also, "mamboized" cha cha chás like "Oye Como Va" were a staple of his repertoire. We now turn our attention to this classic recording.

guided listening experience

"Oye Como Va," Tito Puente (1963)

- CD Track #**3-5**
- Featured performer(s)/group: Tito Puente band, with Tito Puente (timbales)
- Format: Excerpt
- Source recording: *El Rey Bravo,* by Tito Puente (Tico/Sonido TRSLP-1086)

Tito Puente and his band performing at the Palladium.

The Palladium must have been an amazing place to be during the heyday of the mambo. Battles of the bands between top groups like Puente's and Machito's were a highlight of the entertainment format, and audiences delighted in the sizzling results of these informal contests as each band tried to outdo the other. The Palladium was also interesting as a hotbed of multicultural interaction, its audiences often casting off the shackles of racial and ethnic division to meet out on the dance floor. "The audiences that began to form in the Palladium and other dance halls," explains Steven Loza, "were, like those of jazz, highly integrated, notwithstanding the elements of discrimination and segregation that still existed in a large part of the society" (Loza 1999:222). For noted Latin music historian Max Salazar, the mambo and the Palladium scene were nothing less than agents of profound social change in American society: "The Palladium was the laboratory. The catalyst that brought Afro-Americans, Irish, Italians, Jews. God, they danced the mambo. And because of the mambo, race relations started to improve in that era. What social scientists couldn't do on purpose, the mambo was able to accomplish by error" (Salazar, quoted in Loza 1999:68). The Palladium was also a great venue for celebrity watching. Entertainer Sammy Davis Jr., painter Jackson Pollock, beat poet Allen Ginsberg, and movie stars Marlene Dietrich and Marlon Brando were all patrons. Brando was even known to sit in on the bongó drums with the Machito Orchestra on occasion!

The original Tito Puente recording of "Oye Como Va" is essentially a cha cha chá with big band mambo instrumentation, textures, and stylistic elements. Comparing it to the more traditionally Cuban cha cha chá style of "El Bodeguero" (**CD ex. #3-3**), one discovers both similarities and differences. While the basic groove and feel of the conventional cha cha chá dance rhythm are present in both, the tempo of "Oye Como Va" is slightly faster, giving it an edge and intensity that contrasts with the more relaxed feel of "El Bodeguero." Additionally, and more importantly, the organ and bass riffs of "Oye Como Va" that swirl around the foundational cha cha chá percussion groove (which is first introduced just by clicked sticks and handclaps and is then reinforced by the full complement of timbales, congas, and güiro from 0:15 on) offer the Puente performance a deliciously funky and syncopated rhythmic flair, generating a kind of swagger that finds no parallel in "El Bodeguero." (The use of the organ itself was a novel feature introduced into Latin dance music with this recording.)

The minor key of "Oye Como Va" (A minor) also creates a contrast with "El Bodeguero," which, in common with the majority of traditional Cuban cha cha chás, is a tune in a major key. Compared to the cheerful, lighthearted quality of brightness created by "El Bodeguero," "Oye Como Va" comes off as a bit more hard-nosed and gritty, an effect at least partially attributable to its minor key.

At 0:15, the entrance of a big band–style horn section (saxophones, trumpets, and trombones) along with the full Latin percussion section puts the instrumentation squarely in the camp of big band mambo. The improvised, solo playing of the flute, however, forms a clear link to the charanga instrumentation of Cuban-style cha cha chá. Reminiscent of traditional cha cha chá,

Measure	**1**				**2**			
Beat	1	2	3	4	1	2	3	4
Rhythm	X •	X X	• X	X X	• X	X X	X X	X •

	3				**4**			
	1	2	3	4	1	2	3	4
	X •	X •	X X	• X	• X	X •	• •	X •

FIGURE 11.2

Signature unison figure, "Oye Como Va."

too, is the singing in "Oye Como Va" (0:46 –1:04, 1:56-2:18), which features a group of male vocalists who are also the instrumentalists in the band (as opposed to designated singers) singing a short and simple tune with a single-line Spanish text in which a *macho* protagonist boasts about the potency of his "groove" to a *mulatta* dancer. It should be noted, however, that the vocal texture is more harmonized here than in more conventional cha cha chá fare (compare to the first 1:20 of "El Bodeguero"), suggesting other musical influences.

At 0:38, just before the singing begins, the entire band joins together in the playing of a syncopated, unison figure that is highly compelling. Its rhythm is sketched out in Figure 11.2. This unison figure, which returns intermittently at different points in the arrangement, has over time become a recognizable musical signature of this famous song.

Following a partial return of the signature unison figure at 1:01, the band launches into the first of two instrumental mambo sections—that is, mambo sections set to a cha cha chá rhythmic groove—beginning at 1:05. The texture builds in progressively layered riffs (ostinatos) in the horn section that grow overtop a continuing cha cha chá groove in the rhythm section. As in Machito's "Sambia" (**CD ex. #3-4**), the saxophones start things off, repeating their riff over and over from 1:05 forward. Next come the trombones at 1:20, whose riff plays off of and complements the saxophone part. Then comes the trumpet riff at 1:36, providing a third musical layer that enhances the polyphonic richness and density all the more. Occasional interjections of "uh-huh" from one of the musicians, along with a whistle or two and sporadic moments of flute improvisation, are thrown into the mix as well.

Following a partial return of the signature unison figure, a second singing of the "Oye Como Va" tune, and an exciting crescendo that builds through the whole band, the second mambo section arrives at 2:19. In this mambo, the saxophone, trombone, and trumpet riffs are more syncopated and complexly related than in the first mambo. The flute soloing is more animated here, too, and sporadic singing, vocal shouts, and whistling create a partylike atmosphere. Then, like a precision knife cutting through thick brush, the signature unison figure returns one final time at 3:06 to close out the excerpt.

guided listening quick summary

"Oye Como Va," by Tito Puente (CD ex. #3-5)

INTRODUCTION (INSTRUMENTAL)

0:00–0:45

■ Piece begins with syncopated organ riff over straight cha cha chá rhythm (the latter initially marked out just by clicked wooden sticks and handclaps).

- Full percussion section and horn section enter at 0:15 (following a lead-in played on the timbales): timbales, congas, and güiro play standard cha cha chá rhythmic patterns; horns (saxophones, trombones, trumpets) double organ riff rhythm.
- Flute takes main melody beginning at 0:23 (charanga-esque).
- Signature unison figure played at 0:38.

SINGING OF MAIN TUNE, FIRST TIME

0:46–1:04

- "Oye Como Va" tune sung by group of male singers (unison/harmonized vocal texture; cha cha chá groove).
- Partial return of signature unison figure at 1:01.

FIRST MAMBO SECTION (MAMBO I)

1:05–1:55

- Saxophone riff (1:05), trombone riff (1:20), trumpet riff (1:36).
- Another partial return of signature unison figure (1:51).

SINGING OF MAIN TUNE, SECOND TIME

1:56–2:18

- As before, but ends with big instrumental crescendo (2:11) leading up to second mambo section.

SECOND MAMBO SECTION (MAMBO II)

2:19–end

- More syncopated and complexly related horn riffs than in first mambo section; building intensity.
- Flute, vocal shouts, and whistling create partylike atmosphere.
- Excerpt concludes with full statement of the signature unison figure at 3:06.

New Sounds, New Times: "Oye Como Va," the Santana Version

When "Oye Como Va" was released in 1963, Tito Puente was already well established as the king of Latin music. He was as famous and as respected as any Latin dance bandleader and was credited with numerous important innovations and achievements, musical and otherwise. "Oye Como Va" helped make *El Rey Bravo* Puente's second best-selling album up to that point (after *Dance Mania*) and became an audience favorite everywhere he played. But no one, least of all Puente himself, could have predicted the impact that "Oye Como Va" would ultimately have on the future of Latin dance music and Puente's own career.

In 1970, Santana, a San Francisco–based rock band with a Latin dance band twist, recorded a rock-infused cover version of "Oye Como Va" and included it on their second album, *Abraxas.* The album became a mega-hit, selling millions of copies. "Oye Como Va" was one of two hit singles to come out of *Abraxas* (the other was "Black Magic Woman"). It rose to #13 on the *Billboard* rock charts, an unprecedented achievement for a recording of a tune that had been taken "right out of the Latin catalog" of standard dance band numbers (Loza 1999:65). With "Oye Como Va" and *Abraxas,* Latin rock, a genre invented almost single-handedly by Santana and one that remains even today principally identified with that band and its leader, guitarist Carlos Santana, was cemented into the lexicon of Latin dance music. Beyond its own success, Santana's

"Oye Como Va" also would have far-reaching effects on the career of Tito Puente, the "salsa explosion" of the 1970s, and the consolidation of a new and cosmopolitan pan-Latino identity that was closely tied to Latin dance music.

The rise of Santana and Latin rock

Carlos Santana was born in Mexico in 1947. He grew up listening to various kinds of music, especially American rock-and-roll and the recordings of Chicano (Mexican-American) musicians such as Ritchie Valens, who had the first major Latino rock crossover hit with "La Bamba."

Santana took up the guitar as a child and by his early teenage years was gigging regularly in Tijuana area nightclubs. When he was 15, he moved to San Francisco. There he encountered and became enamored of an array of musics that were new to him. This was the early 1960s, and San Francisco was host to a booming, multicultural music scene. The closest thing to a West Coast New York (albeit with a very different cultural mix and urban flavor), San Francisco teemed with concert venues, nightclubs, and record stores. The city also was taking shape as ground zero for the youth counterculture movement that would revolutionize the American cultural, societal, and political landscape in the late 1960s (see also Chapter 8, pp. 120, 141–44).

Cover of Santana's *Abraxas*.

In this urban cauldron of cultural richness, Santana discovered the new jazz sounds of Miles Davis and John Coltrane (**CD ex. #2-13**). He got deeply into the blues of Muddy Waters and B.B. King, and indeed had already established himself as "an avid exponent of the blues before his Latin-rock innovations" (Loza 1993:282). As the decade progressed, he witnessed and became an integral part of San Francisco's own thriving rock music scene, where he shared the spotlight with the likes of Janis Joplin, Jimi Hendrix, and Sly and the Family Stone.

All of these experiences shaped Santana's musical vision and his unique and ultimately influential approach to the electric guitar. But the two elements that largely set him and his music apart were his Latino identity and the pervasive influence of Latin music on his musical style. This Latino musical imprint was present in the influences he had absorbed from his childhood in Mexico. Even more important, however, were the influences of leading New York–based Latin dance bands that he became familiar with through recordings by Tito Puente, Machito, Willie Bobo, and others.

insights and perspectives

Carlos Santana and Prince

As an innovator on the electric guitar, Carlos Santana has been a major influence on legions of younger guitarists, including Prince. Rock critics have often noted a close similarity between Prince's guitar style and that of Jimi Hendrix, inferring that Hendrix was Prince's main influence on the guitar. Prince himself denies this, however.

"It's only because he's black," Prince has said regarding such comparisons with Hendrix. "That's really the only thing we have in common. He plays different guitar than I do. If they really listened to my stuff, they'd hear more of a Santana influence than Jimi Hendrix" (c.f. Starr and Waterman 2003:400).

Santana, featuring guitarist Carlos Santana (right), performing at Woodstock, 1969. The band's bassist, Dave Brown, is on the left.

SANTANA, THE BAND In 1968, Carlos Santana joined forces with several other up-and-coming young San Francisco–area musicians to form the band Santana. They came from working- and middle-class backgrounds and collectively represented something of a microcosm of American cultural diversity at the time: Latino, African-American, Euro-American. Their musical range was at least equally diverse. The group's unique sound coalesced as a synthesis of rock, blues, jazz, rhythm-and-blues, soul, Mexican, Chicano, Afro-Cuban, and contemporary Latin dance musics.

Santana's big break came when they were invited to perform at Woodstock, the historic 1969 rock music festival that would come to define an era and a generation. Santana was a little-known, upstart band at the time, but their Woodstock performance created a sensation. It launched their ascent to rock superstardom and also established their compelling Latin rock sound as a staple of American youth counterculture identity at a decisive historical moment. Tens of thousands of people moved to the groove of Santana at Woodstock, and millions more soon came to know the band through the film version of the festival, *Woodstock,* which was released not long after the actual event. As Ben Fong-Torres explains,

> [Santana] turned an also-on-the-bill stint at the Woodstock festival into a mesmerizing mini-set, and when they appeared in the Woodstock film, they galvanized audiences the way Janis Joplin had at Monterey Pop [another major rock festival of the late 1960s]. On tour, town by town, they exposed fans to their revolutionary fusion of Afro-Latin rhythms and rock and roll and got them dancing—and running off to the record store. And it got fellow musicians and producers listening—and taking notes. (Fong-Torres 1998:2)

Santana played Woodstock in August 1969. The band's debut album, *Santana,* was released on Columbia Records in the fall of that same year. It was a major commercial hit, thanks largely to Santana's Woodstock triumph. *Santana* sold more than two million copies and produced a major hit single, "Evil Ways." "Evil Ways" was, in essence, a rocked-up version of a standard Latin dance band–style cha cha chá that had been composed and first recorded by the New York Latin bandleader, and former Tito Puente band percussionist, Willie Bobo. Santana mixed the traditional Latin percussion instruments (timbales, congas, güiro) and conventional cha cha chá groove of Bobo's original with elements of rock-style drumming (played on a drumset) to create the song's distinctive Latin rock rhythmic foundation. Above this rhythmic base, the tune was delivered in a highly electrified style, with the signature solo voice of Carlos Santana's electric guitar soaring atop the texture. The rock-ified cha cha chá sound of "Evil Ways," with its prominent electric guitar part and fused Latin and rock rhythms, introduced to the world the sound of Latin rock. It also set the stage for "Oye Como Va," in which Santana applied a similar musical formula in its treatment of the Tito Puente original.

***ABRAXAS* AND "OYE COMO VA"** *Abraxas,* Santana's second album, was released a year after their debut album, *Santana*. It produced the two hit singles mentioned earlier, "Oye Como Va" and "Black Magic Woman," and became the band's best-selling album ever. It is often described as the finest album Santana ever made and regularly appears on "greatest rock records of all time" lists.

Abraxas was created "under the stress of success" (Fong-Torres 1998:1). In the wake of Woodstock and *Santana,* Carlos Santana would recall many years later, "you had a bunch of kids who, next thing you know, were going to New York and hanging out with Miles Davis and all these incredible musicians, coexisting with Jim Hendrix, Janis Joplin, and The Who" (quoted in Fong-Torres 1998:2).

Such notoriety certainly had its upside, but it came with the price of pressure to follow up with an album that was not just as good as *Santana,* but even better. *Abraxas* met the challenge. It sold millions of copies and spent 88 weeks on the *Billboard* charts, holding down the #1 spot for six weeks. The singles it yielded, "Oye Como Va" and "Black Magic Woman," have both become enduring classics of the American popular music repertoire.

guided listening experience

"Oye Como Va," Santana (1970)

- CD Track **#3-6**
- Featured performer(s)/group: Santana, with Carlos Santana (electric guitar), Gregg Rolie (Hammond B-3 electronic organ)
- Format: Complete track
- Source recording: *Abraxas,* by Santana (Columbia/Legacy CK 65490)

In most respects, Santana's "Oye Como Va" is a straight-up cha cha chá modeled after the Tito Puente original version of 1963. In comparing the two, Steven Loza states: "Santana replaced the flute and horn riffs with his guitar to great effect. Otherwise, however, Santana's arrangement is basically a duplicate (minus some extra *coro* [chorus] and horn sections in Puente's arrangement) with a different instrumental texture and a fused rhythmic base of rock-R&B and cha-cha" (Loza 1999:196). Loza is correct, at least technically. Here is a list of basic musical features that remained intact from Puente's version to Santana's:

- The "Oye Como Va" tune itself.
- The key (A minor).
- The tempo.
- The simple, one-line, Spanish-language song text.
- The singing style (unison/harmonized vocal texture; group of male singers).
- The underlying cha cha chá groove.
- The basic sequence of the arrangement.

The main areas where Santana departs from Puente are in

- The absence of the solo flute part and the horn section, both of which are essentially replaced by, and in some cases absorbed into, Carlos Santana's rock- and blues-inspired electric guitar playing.

- The embellishment of the traditional cha cha chá rhythmic groove with rock-style drumming (played on a drumset).

- The highly prominent role of the Hammond B-3 electronic organ (played by Santana keyboardist Gregg Rolie) as a solo instrument, and the heavily blues- and rock-influenced style of the improvised organ solo.

- The substitution of the horn riff–dominated mambo sections of the Puente original by improvised electric guitar and Hammond B-3 organ solos in the Santana arrangement.

Listed dryly on the printed page, the above list of differences between Puente's and Santana's versions of "Oye Como Va" may not seem like they would add up to much, but the whole is greater than the sum of its parts in terms of distinctive musical effect. These differences largely explain the rock anthem–like character of Santana's version, which is quite a dramatic departure from the mamboized cha cha chá character of Puente's rendition.

Listen now to Santana's "Oye Como Va" and make your own subjective comparison to the Tito Puente original explored earlier. How would you describe the similarities and differences, not just in terms of instrumentation and such, but also in terms of how they make you *feel*, what thoughts and images they bring to mind, perhaps even the different ways they make your body want to move? This is an excellent exercise for exploring how seemingly "technical" musical elements—changes in instrumentation, use of different technologies, subtle modifications in rhythm, different approaches to solo improvisation—can combine to transform a largely "set" musical composition and arrangement into something very different than it once was.

On your second listening, follow along with the time-line of the Guided Listening Quick Summary in the box below and listen for the elements and features identified.

---

guided listening quick summary

"Oye Como Va," Santana version (CD ex. #3-6)

INTRODUCTION

0:00–0:37

- Opens with the standard "Oye" organ riff (as in Puente original), but the Hammond B-3 organ's timbre is very different from that of the organ in Puente's version; also, no clicked sticks/clapping groove here, and the bass part is more prominent in the mix.

- Standard cha cha chá groove established with entry of percussion section at 0:08; no horns; opening flute melody of Puente version is played here on electric guitar (by Carlos Santana) and some bluesy melodic embellishments in the guitar part give the music a different character.

- Signature unison figure arrives at 0:30.

SINGING OF MAIN TUNE, FIRST TIME

0:38–0:56

- Singing is similar to that heard in the Puente version, though the vocal timbre is different.

- Partial return of signature unison figure at 0:53.

FIRST IMPROVISED SOLO (ELECTRIC GUITAR)

0:57–1:44

- Played by Carlos Santana; *electronic distortion* enhances the basic timbre of the instrument.

- Replaces the first mambo section (Mambo I) of the Puente arrangement in terms of formal design.

- Though horn section is absent, Carlos Santana's guitar solo actually builds mainly from lines adapted *from* the original Puente horn riffs (enhanced by occasional bluesy riffs at the ends of phrases).

The Hammond B-3 Organ and "Oye Como Va"

The Hammond B-3 organ, as heard in Santana's "Oye Como Va," represents one of the emblematic sounds of rock music of the 1960s and 1970s. (Another band of the period that featured the instrument prominently was The Doors.) The B-3 was invented in 1935 by Laurens Hammond and became a popular instrument in the hands of jazz organ masters like Jimmy Smith before being adopted into rock.

As was noted earlier, an organ also was used in Tito Puente's original version of "Oye Como Va," but that organ's tone and timbre lacked the punch and fullness of Gregg Rolie's B-3. It is interesting that in later recordings of "Oye Como Va" made by Tito Puente after the Santana version was released, the organ is dispensed with altogether and a piano is used in its place. It is possible that in making this substitution, Puente was trying to extricate the musical identity of *his* composition from the widespread public perception of "Oye Como Va" as a Santana tune.

■ Percussion instruments played more freely here than in Puente (e.g., improvised drum fills in conga and timbales parts) and more of a rock feel is evident in the rhythmic groove, though a cha cha chá foundation still predominates.

INTERLUDE/TRANSITION #1

1:45–2:07

■ First, return to opening organ riff (over cha cha chá rhythmic groove).

■ Second, contrasting section (1:53) with very different mood and style.

■ Third, dramatic crescendo at 2:04 (essentially an abridged, altered version of the big crescendo at the comparable point in the Puente arrangement).

SECOND IMPROVISED SOLO (HAMMOND B-3 ELECTRONIC ORGAN)

2:07–2:47

■ Played by Gregg Rolie; note distinctive timbre of the Hammond B-3.

■ Replaces second mambo section (Mambo II) of Puente arrangement in the form.

■ Rolie immediately rips into a heavy, rock- and blues-style solo that takes the piece far from its Latin roots and into new musical territory.

INTERLUDE/TRANSITION #2

2:48–2:58

■ Shorter than first Interlude/Transition section.

■ Partial return of signature unison figure at 2:56.

SINGING OF MAIN TUNE, SECOND TIME

2:59–3:21

■ Sung as before.

■ Singing followed by an extended crescendo build-up at 3:14 (again reminiscent of the Puente recording).

Beyond the Music:
Santana, "Oye Como Va," and Pan-Latino Identity

For Carlos Santana, the decision to include "Oye Como Va" on *Abraxas* was "a natural." In his own words, "I thought, this is a song . . . that when you play it, people are going to get up and dance, and that's it" (quoted in Fong-Torres 1998:6).

That *was* it, and perhaps it still *is* it, but there is more to consider as well. Santana's "Oye Como Va" did not only turn the rock world upside down. It also helped to galvanize Latin dance music and its culture; became a symbol of an emergent pan-Latino identity; and brought newfound renown, wealth, and professional opportunities to Tito Puente himself.

Santana's "Oye Como Va" and Tito Puente

Tito Puente, as the composer of "Oye Como Va," made more money from Santana's recording of the tune than he did from any of his own recordings, much more in fact. "That was the one recording that Puente could have retired on," Latin music producer and radio personality Lionel "Chico" Sesma told Steven Loza in an interview. "He probably made more money off the royalties of that Santana recorded success than he had made in his entire life before that. That must have galled him to no end" (Sesma, quoted in Loza 1999:98).

Galled him perhaps, but it also revitalized Puente's career and the Latin dance music scene more broadly. Prior to Santana's "Oye Como Va," Latin dance music had been in a state of progressive decline in terms of "mainstream" commercial popularity. The rock-and-roll explosion of the mid-1950s had squashed the mambo and cha cha chá crazes in the United States and internationally. Beatlemania and the flourishing of a plethora of new rock and pop styles in the 1960s pushed Latin dance music even further out of the spotlight. The Latin dance bands of Tito Puente and others managed to stay in business and even to thrive, but their market narrowed, being confined mainly to sectors of Puerto Rican–dominated Latino communities and some other areas. Even within U.S. Latino communities, members of the younger generations gravitated away from the Latin bands and toward rock. Exacerbating the situation was the United States' tense relationship with Cuba, which had become a socialist state under Fidel Castro in 1959 and had been largely shut off from the U.S. since the early 1960s. Though Latin dance music was rarely being marketed as Cuban music by this time, the fact of its core Cuban root identity remained. The dint of Latin music's historical association with Cuba did little to advance the music's cause in the United States in a tense political climate.

The success of Santana's "Oye Como Va" helped swing the pendulum of commercial viability back in the direction of Latin music. It brought youth culture and Latin dance music back together in a unique transformation and opened the door to a new age of Latin music culture beyond Santana's distinctive brand of Latin rock music itself. In a review of *Abraxas* in *Rolling Stone* magazine, reviewer Jim Nash wrote, prophetically, "The major Latin bands in this country gig for $100 a night, and when you see them, you can't sit still. If Santana can reach the pop audience with *Abraxas,* then perhaps there will be room for the old masters like . . . Puente to work it out at the ballrooms" (Nash, quoted in Fong-Torres 1998:6).

In the wake of Santana's hit, Puente did indeed get to "work it out" as never before, not only at the ballrooms, but eventually at major music festivals and on concert stages worldwide as well. Nevertheless, the scope of his fame never approached Santana's own. As Puente told Steven Loza in a 1994 interview, Santana's "Oye Como Va" recording "really helped me a lot to get that recognition with the people, because when he does his interviews, you know he mentions it, and his interviews are twenty times bigger than mine. All over the world, and the people that he caters to, they're twenty, thirty, forty thousand people in a stadium. I cater to a few hundred people in a ballroom. It's quite different than the music that I play" (Puente, quoted in Loza 1999:45).

The king of salsa

In another of the seemingly endless paradoxes that define the modern history of Latin dance music, Tito Puente's revitalized image as a Latin music icon occurred in connection with neither the mambo, the cha cha chá, nor any other style key to his initial rise to fame. Rather, he was reconfigured as the king of a "new" kind of Latin dance music that took shape in the 1970s, *salsa,* itself a New York (largely Newyorican) musical "invention" with decidely strong musical roots in the Afro-Cuban *son.*

Salsa, Loza explains, "basically adheres to the traditional structure and instrumentation of Afro-Cuban dance forms, but with significant embellishments, adaptations, and new formats and influences. Among the various artists spearheading this movement were Eddie Palmieri, Johnny Pacheco, Ray Barretto, and Willie Colón. Artists such as Tito Puente and Mongo Santamaría, who had been performing the same basic musical forms for the previous thirty years, adapted well and opportunistically to the new popular format . . ." (Loza 1999:16).

The timing of the "salsa explosion" of the 1970s was no coincidence. Though it was by no means the whole story or even necessarily the main part of it, the success of Santana's "Oye Como Va" in 1970 had a signficant impact. The huge spotlight of international attention that burned down on Santana was large enough to cast its light on the emerging stars of salsa as well, and the catchy marketing term *salsa* itself made for a more commercially viable product than, say, "Latin dance music."

Tito Puente had little use for the name salsa *per se,* but he recognized its promotional value and pragmatically accepted his title as the music's *de facto* king. "Salsa," he once told an interviewer, "means sauce, literally; it's just a commercial term for Afro-Cuban dance music which was used to promote the music. My problem is that we don't play sauce, we play music, and Latin music has different styles; cha-cha, mambo, guaguancó, and son. Salsa doesn't address the complexities and the rich history of the music that we play. But it's accepted now and it helped get the music promoted" (in Loza 1999:16; c.f. Sanabria and Socolov 1990:23).

"Oye Como Va" and the emergence of pan-Latino identity

Santana's "Oye Como Va" not only launched the band to new heights of fame and popularity, revived and redirected the career of Tito Puente, and helped ignite the salsa explosion of the 1970s, but also played an important role in the forging of a new Latino social consciousness rooted in the concept of pan-Latino identity. Santana's symbolic eradication of the boundaries between Latin music and rock music served as a powerful symbol of a conception of Latino/ American-ness that insisted on inclusion while demanding distinctiveness of identity, and that recognized the uniqueness of different "Latin" (Latino) nationalities and cultures while building bridges between them.

And Tito Puente, both as the composer of "Oye Como Va" and as an iconic figure of Latin dance music generally—of a music that was now being held up as a unifying symbol of pan-Latino culture—also found himself at the center of the pan-Latino social movement. His fame and notoriety, combined with his multiplex identity, musical and otherwise—Puerto Rican,

The modern realm of "Latin music" of the type dealt with in this chapter (i.e., Cuban-derived and developed largely in the United States) is today divided between two principal genres with much overlap between them. These are salsa, which emphasizes singing, is geared toward providing music for dancing, and is most popular among Latino audiences; and Latin jazz, which emphasizes fully (or almost fully) instrumental textures, extended solo improvisations, and jazz-inspired musical forms and textures, and caters largely to non-Latino audiences.

Tito Puente was and remains, even after his death, the leading figure in both areas, certainly in terms of popularity. "An inspection of any contemporary major record store," writes Loza, will reveal that ". . . the bins of Puente's recordings will predominate the various Latin jazz artists included in the collection; additionally, Puente will predominate the collection of the salsa artists. Two worlds and two markets have thus largely become associated with Tito Puente's music: the English-speaking and Spanish-speaking Americas. Added to this cultural matrix are the extended geographies of Puente's popularity, including Africa, Asia, and Europe" (Loza 1999:xvi).

Newyorican, master of Cuban music, innovator of Latin music, fervent musical traditionalist and tireless musical experimenter, savvy and industrious entrepreneur, World War II veteran—made him an obvious choice as a symbol of pan-Latino pride. At a time when there was little Latino representation in U.S. political institutions, star musicians like Puente, not to mention Carlos Santana, became flashpoints around which to galvanize political mobilization and ethnic pride movements. As Loza explains,

> Throughout the midseventies, another factor that profoundly affected Puente's role as a master musician was that of a growing and expanding pan-Latino identity in the United States. Young Puerto Ricans, Chicanos, Cubans, Dominicans, Central Americans, and other Latin Americans who were living in the country began to unite in a political, social, and cultural momentum that constantly sought symbols, leaders, and common expression in the arts. The salsa movement was in full drive, and younger musicians and artists, as had Carlos Santana, looked to Puente for inspiration and leadership. (Loza 1999:175–76)

The roots of this pan-Latino movement that crystallized in the 1970s had already begun to take shape in the 1960s, and Puente was an important figure then, too. While many Latino youth were moving away from Latin dance music in favor of the Beatles and other popular non-Latin bands, some, like Carlos Santana himself, were "discovering" the likes of Puente and Machito at the *same* time that they were discovering the Beatles and the blues, and seeing no need for selecting one over the other. For progressive-minded young Latinos like Santana, it was hip, not backward, to be into the "old" music of an artist like Tito Puente. This was the logical entry point for the formation of a new, pan-Latino musical—and in turn social, cultural, and political—identity.

In the post-1970s era, Puente and Santana have remained enduring emblems of pan-Latino identity on many levels, their distinct identities and personae bound together by the single song with which *both* of them are most closely identified, "Oye Como Va" (though, for younger generations of listeners, Carlos Santana is perhaps more closely identified with his later work, such as the Grammy Award–winning 1999 album *Supernatural*). Santana, in keeping with the tenor of his times, has been more overt in his political activism as a musical statesman of pan-Latino causes than Puente was. But Puente's role was no less important, and the longevity of his significance as both a musical and social figure has been quite remarkable.

"Perhaps one of the most significant aspects of Puente," Steven Loza wrote shortly before Puente's death, "is that he became enmeshed with various generations—the adults, the children, and the babies of the forties through the nineties. Race and intercultural relations have taken different courses during these years, but Puente has attempted to adapt to each era. It can be said that he has taken more of the multicultural versus nationalistic course, consistently emphasizing the international popularity and charisma of his music and himself. At the same time, however, he has often been active in the artistic and political solidarity of the Latino community in the United States" (Loza 1999:224).

Rubén Blades in performance.

The pan-Latino movement that arose in the United States in the 1960s and 1970s now encompasses not just diverse Latino communities in the U.S., but nations throughout Latin America, from northern Mexico to southern Chile and throughout the Caribbean. Salsa, a Cuban-derived music developed in New York, has become an international Latino music and identity emblem. The Latin rock phenomenon intitiated by Santana has inspired or given rise to myriad commercially oriented popular Latin dance music styles. Perhaps no artist has so fluidly bridged the gap between musical artistry and activism on behalf of pan-Latino causes than the Panamanian salsa star Rubén Blades. Beyond being an exceptional musician with a rare gift for infusing his songs with poignant social commentary, Blades is also a lawyer, a politician, and an actor who has appeared in several Hollywood films (*The Milagro Beanfield War, The Super*).

Directly or indirectly, the legacies of Tito Puente, Santana, and "Oye Como Va" are carried on in a great many spheres of the Latino/American musicultural world. Their convergence, however, is nowhere more clear than in the music of our final Guided Listening Experience, Tito Puente Jr.'s version of "Oye Como Va."

"Oye Como Va": The Next Generation

Since 1970, "Oye Como Va" has been recorded in myriad versions by everyone from muzak maestro Percy Faith to rapper Mr. Capone-E (Table 11.1). Of all these many renditions, the one that has arguably generated the most public attention is that of Tito Puente's own son, Tito Puente Jr., the self-anointed Prince of Latin Dance music.

TABLE 11.1	A sampling of other recordings of "Oye Como Va."	
Artist	**Year**	**Description**
Percy Faith	1971	Easy listening, orchestral ("muzak")
The Ventures	1971	Straight cover of Santana version
Fattburger	1996	Smooth jazz, melody played by flute
Michel Camillo	1997	Progressive jazz
Kinky	2004	Electronic/Latin Dance
Groove Society	2005	A cappella (unaccompanied vocal group)
Mr. Capone-E	2005	Rap/hip-hop

Tito Puente Jr. in performance.

Tito Puente Jr. was born in New York City in 1971, just as Santana's "Oye Como Va" was climbing the charts. He is 24 years younger than Carlos Santana, 48 years the junior of his late father. He grew up "feeling the rhythms of [Latin] music before he could walk or talk" (Puente Jr. 2004). His first instrument was percussion. As he writes on his Web site, "I had no choice; there were 50 sets of timbales in the garage" (Puente Jr. 2004). He would later study piano, song-writing, and record producing as well—mostly under the tutelage of his famous father—and performed from an early age with his dad and with other Latin music legends, including the late, great Cuban-American singer Celia Cruz.

As a young adult, Puente Jr. moved from New York to Miami. This move took him closer, culturally and geographically, to the source of the Latin dance music traditions that made his father famous, Cuba. It also placed him in the milieu of a city that today rivals New York as the Latin music capital of the United States, if not the world. With the possible exception of New York, Miami is the most ethnically and culturally diverse "Latin American city" anywhere. The Cuban presence—culturally, politically, and musically as well—is especially pervasive, but it is just one large piece of the city's very large pan-Latino cultural pie. "I'm thrilled with the many faces and sounds of Miami," says Tito Puente Jr. "The opportunity to listen to music from Mexico, South America, the Caribbean and other parts of the world has allowed me to expand my own musical horizons, so my music can reach more people" (Puente Jr. 2004). The pan-Latino musical mosaic of Miami is embedded in his music, much as the rich multicultural musical mosaic of New York City was embedded in his father's.

Guarachando (wa-ra-CHAN-doh)

Puente Jr. acknowledges his father as his single greatest musical influence. The year 1996 saw the release (on EMI Latin) of *Guarachando,* the debut album of Tito Puente Jr. and the Latin Rhythm Crew. The album featured an innovative arrangement of "Oye Como Va" by Puente Jr. The sound of this "Oye Como Va," and of *Guarachando* generally, was at once eclectically (and electrically) contemporary and solidly grounded in the Latin dance music tradition of the elder Puente. Puente Jr. identified the style of this music as **Latin Dance** (not to be confused with the generic label "Latin dance music" used throughout this chapter). Latin Dance is essentially a hybrid of diverse contemporary music styles—pop, rock, hip-hop, techno, Latino pop—"laced with influences of Mambo, Cha Cha and [Dominican] Merengue" (Puente Jr. 2004). This is a music that is pan-Latino—Latino/American—in a very broad sense. Puente Jr. describes Latin Dance as "a new explosion of authentic music created from the streets," but it is just as surely a novel synthesis of modern dance club music and earlier styles of Latin dance music. Echoes of his father's musical legacy resonate powerfully in Tito Puente Jr.'s work, as do the influences of later Latin music icons such as Carlos Santana.

guided listening experience

"Oye Como Va," Tito Puente Jr. (2004)

- CD Track #**3-7**
- Featured performer(s)/group: Tito Puente Jr. group, with Tito Puente Jr. (timbales, percussion, vocals), Tito Puente (Sr.) (timbales), La India and Cali Aleman (vocals)
- Format: Complete track
- Source recording: *Tito Puente, Jr.: Greatest Club Remixes* (TPJR Productions)

Tito Puente Jr.'s *Guarachando* performed well on the *Billboard* dance music charts, largely on account of the popularity of "Oye Como Va." The album also was honored with a prestigious Latin Music Award. The version of "Oye Como Va" included on your CD set is not the original 1996 recording from *Guarachando,* but is, rather, a remix version of that recording that was released on *Tito Puente, Jr.: Greatest Club Remixes* (2004). This later version is the one preferred by Tito Puente Jr. himself (personal correspondence with the author, 2006). Among other differences, it puts the virtuosic timbales artistry of his famous father on more prominent display. Also featured here are the singers Cali Aleman and La India. La India is regarded as one of the great Latin music female vocalists of the post–Celia Cruz era.

In Tito Puente Jr.'s "Oye Como Va," the traditional cha cha chá rhythmic groove and many other features of both the original Tito Puente and Santana recordings are present. They undergo various types of transformations in this novel, Latin Dance musical context, however. For example, there are instances where synthesized or digitally sampled reconfigurations of the sounds of traditional Latin percussion instruments, a mambo horn section, and even a Hammond B-3 organ (sampled directly from Santana's "Oye Como Va" recording of 1970) replace the original instruments. On the rhythmic level, a relatively conventional cha cha chá groove established at the beginning (0:07) is first embellished by the simple addition of an off-beat, eighth-note rhythm "played" on electronic hi-hat cymbals beginning at 0:15. But from 1:06 on, the basic cha cha chá feel, while never disappearing entirely, is subjected to a variety of rhythmic and timbral manipulations that move the music in a progressively more funky and technoesque direction.

A new melody that provides an interesting counterpoint to the main "Oye Como Va" tune is introduced by La India at 1:19 and becomes a central feature of the arrangement henceforth. Many of the horn riffs from the original Tito Puente version are interpolated into the arrangement as well, but now they are rendered mainly in digitally synthesized tones that give this music a very different character. And topping everything off is the brilliant timbales soloing of Tito Puente (Sr.), which increasingly becomes the driving force of the music from 2:44 to the end.

Altogether, Tito Puente Jr.'s "Oye Como Va" is a fun and creative take on this classic Latin dance tune. It succeeds in balancing tradition, transformation, and innovation, at once remaining grounded in the historical legacy from which it springs and pushing that legacy forward toward new musical vistas reflective of the time of its making (see Table 11.2 on p. 247). Listen to it now, while following along with the Guided Listening Quick Summary in the box below.

guided listening quick summary

"Oye Como Va," Tito Puente Jr. version (CD ex. #3-7)

INTRODUCTION

0:00–0:06

■ Begins with the standard "Oye" organ riff, this time in the form of a heavily processed digital sample of the Hammond B-3 organ from the Santana recording (*note:* the key is A♭ minor, in contrast to the Puente [Sr.] and Santana versions, which were both in A minor).

■ Electronically processed güiro timbre, along with other digitally sampled and synthesized Latin percussion sounds.

SINGING OF MAIN TUNE, FIRST TIME

0:07–0:24

■ Standard singing style (unison/harmonized texture; male singers); electronically enhanced cha cha chá groove (especially from 0:15).

■ Partial statement of signature unison figure at 0:22.

Tito Puente Jr.: Into the future, back to the past

Since the death of Tito Puente in 2000, Tito Puente Jr. has dedicated his career to honoring his late father by carrying on his musical legacy. A second album of his from 2004, *En Los Pasos De Mi Padre* (In My Father's Shoes), is the most explicit tribute to his father's memory to date. It is a retrospective production, including classic Puente tunes from the mambo kings days of the 1950s and the salsa explosion years of the 1970s.

"I am now performing the music of Tito Puente," explains Puente Jr. "I think it's very important that the youth of today understand the music of my father, la música de ayer [the music of yesterday], la música del Palladium. It's timeless music—music that makes you dance . . . Carrying the torch and the tradition of my father's music to a whole new generation of fans has been a lifelong dream of mine" (Puente Jr. 2004).

This carrying of the torch took an interesting twist in the early 2000s when Tito Puente Jr. became co-director of a band called The Big 3 Palladium Orchestra. His collaborators in this ven-

TABLE 11.2

TABLE 11.2 Summary comparison of Tito Puente, Santana, and Tito Puente Jr. arrangements of "Oye Como Va."

	Tito Puente	Santana	Tito Puente Jr.
Year	1963	1970	2004
Album	*El Rey Bravo*	*Abraxas*	*Tito Puente, Jr.: Greatest Club Remixes*
Instrumentation	Big band horn section (saxophones, trumpets, trombones); layered ostinato horn riffs	No horn section, though horn riff figures are worked into electric guitar solo	Simplified horn riffs played on synthesizers
	Male voices	Male voices	Male voices plus female solo vocalist (singing contrasting melody)
	Main solo instrument: flute	Main solo instruments: electric guitar, Hammond B-3 organ	Main solo instrument: timbales (no melodic instrument solos)
	Organ	Different type of organ (Hammond B-3)	Digitally sampled B-3 with heavy electronic processing
	Bass	Bass	Bass
	Latin percussion; cha cha chá groove	Drumset plus Latin percussion; cha cha chá groove reinforced by rock-style drumming	Timbales, etc., plus digitally sampled/synthesized percussion; funk/electronic grooves mixed with cha cha chá
Style	Mamboized cha cha chá	Latin rock/cha cha chá	Latin Dance/cha cha chá

ture were none other than "Machito" Grillo and Tito Rodríguez. No, not the famed mambo kings of the 1950s, but their musician sons who bear their names. Puente Jr., Grillo, and Rodríguez, all fine musicians in their own right, joined forces to initiate "a lush and fiery rebirth of the music made famous by their fathers" via this most interesting project (Puente Jr. 2004). More recently, Puente Jr. has been heading up his own large Latin dance band, The Tito Puente Jr. Orchestra, a group he formed for the explicit purpose of introducing the great music of his father to new generations of listeners and reintroducing it to earlier generations of Tito Puente admirers.

Summary

Like the great gharanas of India (see Chapter 8), the great lineages in the history of Latin dance music have produced their own formidable legacies. In this chapter, we traced one such legacy, as defined by the modern history and musicultural roots of a particular song, "Oye Como Va." We chronicled its path from Afro-Cuban ritual music, to Afro-Cuban rumba, to creolized Cuban dance-music styles such as the danzón and the danzón-mambo, to the cha cha chá and big band mambo styles of the 1950s, to the original 1963 Tito Puente recording of "Oye Como Va," to "Oye Como Va" as re-created by Santana (1970) and Tito Puente Jr. (1996/2004).

Comparing and contrasting the three versions of "Oye Como Va" explored in the second half of the chapter offered a revealing view of processes of musical tradition and transformation. Musically, commercially, socially, and even politically, each of these distinct yet related interpretations of the same song speaks both to the times and conditions of its own emergence and the historical and cultural legacy to which it belongs. "Oye Como Va" *is* an article of tradition, and like all articles of tradition, it is at once both perpetually ripe for creative transformation and possessed of the inherent capacity to remain resolutely itself regardless of the types of change to which it is subjected. Like the legacy of Afro-Cuban music, or the legacy of Tito Puente, "Oye Como Va" endures at the core of its many surfaces and interpretations.

As for Tito Puente himself, his spirit and musical legacy are being carried forward today by many great musicians, including his own talented son. Though promotional in nature, the following passage from Tito Puente Jr.'s Web site captures an essence that is real and true, and that offers a fitting point of closure for this musicultural journey through Latin dance music:

> Natural heir to the throne of El Rey, he is unmistakably the son, physically, spiritually and musically of Tito Puente, seminal bandleader, percussionist and legendary good will ambassador of Latin music.
>
> Young Tito's heart is rooted deep in the musical soul of his father. But he is staking out a future in the affectionate response of those who want a modern edge added to the sensuous music that runs through all Latin lives. Puente Jr. is taking his own eclectic sound and like his father before him—is making history and moving generations.
>
> Certainly his father is there in the wide grin, the wild timbales and the charisma that rushes past the footlights and tells the world that this is the music that moves your feet, your soul and your spirit. (Puente Jr. 2004)

Key Terms

riffs
timbales
salsa
rhythm section (piano, bass, percussion)
horn section (saxophones, trombones, trumpets)
cha cha chá
Latino/American
Latin dance music (1. generic; 2. as Cuban-derived tradition)

Latin rock
rumba
danzón
danzón-mambo
mambo
Newyorican
Santería
batá
conga drums (congas)
clave (rhythm)

claves (instrument)
charanga
son
big band mambo
bongó (bongo drums)
mambo kings (Machito, Tito Puente, Tito Rodríguez)
Latin Dance (as contemporary dance-music genre)

Study Questions

■ What three recordings of "Oye Como Va" were explored in this chapter? Who was the featured artist/band on each? What years were they recorded and on what albums did they originally appear? What similarities and differences were there between them? How was each a reflection of Latino/American music and identity at the time it was recorded?

■ How was the term *Latin dance music* applied in a relatively specific and delimited way in this chapter? What does that same term mean when used in more broad and generic terms?

■ In what senses might Tito Puente be described as an individual of complex, multiple ethnic/musical identities?

■ What are batá drums? In what type of religious ritual context are these drums used?

■ What is involved in the performance of rumba and what kinds of instruments are used?

■ Describe the following instruments: timbales, congas, bongó, claves, güiro, maracas.

■ What is the clave rhythm and why is it important?

■ Define and discuss the following dance-music genres: danzón, danzón-mambo, *son,* cha cha chá, salsa. Note musical features and important historical points.

- Who were the mambo kings?

- What were the six defining features of big band mambo listed in the chapter?

- What were defining features of Santana's novel Latin rock style? How were these manifest in the Santana version of "Oye Como Va"?

- In what ways has Tito Puente Jr. carried on his father's musical legacy? In what ways has he introduced innovations that extend the range of Latin dance music? How is his recording of "Oye Como Va" representative of this merging of tradition and transformation?

Discussion Question

- Latino/American dance music is integral to the basic fabric of musicultural life throughout the Americas. Outside of what you have studied in this chapter, what kinds of Latino/American music have you encountered in your daily life? How is this music used to reflect and express ethnic and cultural identity, and how has it shaped your own impressions or experiences of Latino culture?

Applying What You Have Learned

- Visit a local record store and browse through the "Latin music" section. Take note of what items are in the CD bins and document a representative sample of the different musical styles, artists, countries, and cultures represented. If there are listening stations in the store, take some time to listen to some of the recordings. Write a brief report chronicling your experiences. What did you learn about the diversity of Latino/American music? About musical tradition and transformation? What kinds of images and impressions does viewing Latino/American culture through the lens of this experience generate for you?

- Numerous theatrical movies and documentary films featuring Latin dance musics of the kinds discussed in this chapter are readily available for library borrowing, rental, or purchase on video and DVD. Access a copy of *The Mambo Kings, Buena Vista Social Club,* or *Calle 54* and watch it. Write a film review, integrating your observations of the film with what you have learned from this chapter and the listening skills you have developed.

- Beyond the recordings of "Oye Como Va" included in this chapter, there are dozens of other ones available. Do an Internet search to find different recorded versions. Listen to as many as you can. Create an annotated list describing the styles and other notable features of the different versions you hear. What does this exercise teach you about tradition and transformation in Latino/American music? In music generally?

Resources for Further Study

Visit the Online Learning Center at **www.mhhe.com/bakan1** for learning aids, study help, and additional resources that supplement the content of this chapter.

chapter twelve

from **baladi** to **belly dance:**
women's dance and dance rhythms in Egypt and beyond

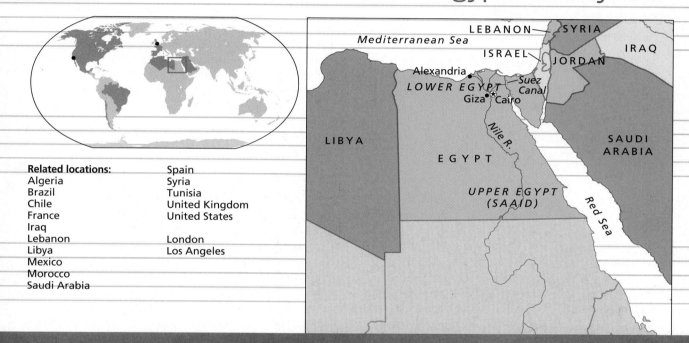

Related locations:

Algeria	Spain
Brazil	Syria
Chile	Tunisia
France	United Kingdom
Iraq	United States
Lebanon	
Libya	London
Mexico	Los Angeles
Morocco	
Saudi Arabia	

Racy (Rah-see)

riqq (ri[k]—"k" not actually sounded: glottal stop)

In 1987, during my graduate school years at UCLA, I was fortunate to have as one of my professors Dr. A. J. Racy, an eminent ethnomusicologist and one of the world's foremost Middle Eastern (alternatively, Near Eastern) music performers. I had been playing the **riqq** (Arab tambourine) in Dr. Racy's ensemble at the university for only about three weeks when I got an unexpected phone call from him one afternoon. He asked me if I was available to play riqq with him and his group that weekend.

The job, it turned out, was a lavish, $1,000-a-head black-tie affair at one of Los Angeles's finest hotels. The Lebanese ambassador to the United States was there, as well as celebrity radio and TV personality Casey Kasem (who is of Middle Eastern heritage) and other luminaries of the Arab-American world. Upwards of a thousand people filled the hotel's huge ballroom.

Dancer Aisha Ali performing.

raqs sharqi (ra[k]s shar[k]ee)

I joined Dr. Racy, the drummer Souhail Kaspar, and the rest of the musicians onstage. Dr. Racy instructed me to keep my eyes on Souhail. Souhail's lead was firm and clear, enabling me to chart my course through the labyrinth of intricate rhythms and frequent starts and stops with no major mishaps. Initially, the mood was quite relaxed. Then there was a sudden burst of energy as an elegant female dancer, Aisha Ali, flowed past us to the front of the stage. (At this point, turn on **CD ex. #3-8** and continue reading.) Souhail's playing became more animated from the moment of her entrance. The other musicians and I followed suit. Ms. Ali's dancing was truly enchanting: fluid and strong yet sublimely graceful. Every part of her body seemed to follow its own rhythm, and also to correspond to different dimensions of Souhail's drumming. Her hips swayed to the pulse of his low drum strokes. Her shoulders shimmied at the call of piercing, high-pitched rolls and accents. Her arms flowed fluidly around the beat. And for all of its many layers, this entire symphony of bodily movement was a model of perfect balance and unity. Dance and music became mutual manifestations of a single expressive gesture while dancer, musicians, and audience merged as one within the collective pulse of movement, melody, and rhythm. It was beautiful, profound, deeply moving. It was the art of Middle Eastern **raqs sharqi,** or, as it is known in the English-speaking Western world, the art of **belly dance.**

■ ■ ■

Introduction

Hossam Ramzy (Hoes-SAM RUM-zee)

tabla (TUB-lah)

dumbek/doumbec (DOOM-bek)

This chapter is about women's solo dance traditions of the Middle East and their music. More specifically, it is about certain women's dance traditions of, or associated with, the country of Egypt. The principal musical focus is on Egyptian dance rhythms. We explore such rhythms mainly through the music of Hossam Ramzy, a leading international proponent of Egyptian dance music and a master of Arab percussion.

Ramzy, who was born and raised in Egypt and now lives in London, England, plays many different Middle Eastern percussion instruments, including the riqq and the Egyptian **tabla** (not to be confused with the Indian instrument of the same name—see Chapter 8, pp. 131–32). The Egyptian tabla is a goblet-shaped, single-headed drum also known by several other names (e.g., *darabukkah, dumbek, doumbec*). It is held under one arm, usually the left, and played with both hands (see the photo on p. 253). The tabla is the lead drum in Egyptian dance music.

Hossam Ramzy has produced a large catalog of recordings of Egyptian dance music and related musical styles for ARC Music Productions International Ltd. These are used by "belly dancers" worldwide as accompanying soundtracks for their dance routines. Some are educationally oriented and used by student dancers and musicians as learning resources. Beyond his own productions, Ramzy has performed and recorded with Robert Plant and Jimmy Page (of Led Zeppelin fame), on Peter Gabriel's soundtrack for the film *The Last Temptation of Christ,* and with everyone from the Rolling Stones to Luciano Pavarotti.

Selected Hossam Ramzy recordings provide the examples through which we explore the music of Egyptian women's dance in this chapter. We will travel via these musical works from the heartland of the rural Egyptian countryside to the nation's cosmopolitan capital city, Cairo, and outward from there to the world of international belly dance. Three distinct yet closely interrelated domains of Egyptian and Egyptian-derived dance are examined. It is important from the outset to learn their names and familiarize yourself with them (see also the photos on p. 256). The three domains are

- **Raqs baladi.** "Folk dance," implying associations with rural culture or origins. This encompasses the traditional dance styles associated with women's social gatherings and rituals, as well as with certain types of folk rituals and ceremonial performances not restricted to women. While not exclusive to Egypt, **raqs baladi,** like its more modern countepart raqs sharqi (see below), is "regarded as preeminently Egyptian" (Saleh 2002:624–25).

- **Raqs sharqi.** "Oriental dance." This is the professional entertainment medium of women's dance, associated with Egyptian weddings, nightclub and cabaret performances (usually for predominantly male audiences), and Egyptian films and other mass media (e.g., music videos that are broadcast on Egyptian television stations). It combines a root identity of raqs baladi with various imported elements, most notably adopted or adapted features of European ballet and Hollywood movie musical dance numbers. The music of raqs sharqi tends to be more cosmopolitan and modern in orientation than that associated with raqs baladi. In general, raqs sharqi dancing privileges showmanship and entertainment over communal ritual and celebration. It is mainly an urban phenomenon, identified especially with the city of Cairo.

Hossam Ramzy playing the Egyptian tabla.

- **Belly dance.** This is actually the generic, all-encompassing, English-language term used in the West to refer to *all* Middle Eastern and Middle Eastern–derived forms of women's dance. Here, however, it is used specifically in reference to Western/international derivatives and offshoots of Egyptian and other Middle Eastern raqs baladi and raqs sharqi forms. Belly dancers tend to draw upon many different traditional styles—Egyptian, Turkish, Moroccan, Lebanese—to create their own forms of dance expression, though some specialize exclusively in one traditional style or another. The belly dance phenomenon also has given rise to new dance idioms, such as *American Tribal* (which emphasizes improvised group dancing and the women's community) and *Cabaret* (which, as its name implies, tends toward the seductive and exhibitionistic side of the continuum). In keeping with their internationalist character, belly dancing and belly dance music (as well as the dancers' costumes) may draw upon just about anything: ballet, modern dance, hip-hop, MTV. At some level, however, a traditional raqs baladi/raqs sharqi core identity is always present in the dance movement vocabulary. This is characterized by *an emphasis on circular and undulating movement generated from the hips and pelvic region and by maintenance of a low center of gravity in the body.*

raqs baladi (ra[k]s bah-lah-dee)

In exploring these three domains, we will track several popular, traditional Egyptian dance rhythms through a series of diverse dance-music contexts. These contexts include an ancient form of ritual called **zaar** (*zar*), the professional dance routines of raqs sharqi and belly dance performers, musical compositions originating in Egyptian commercial film, and the global sphere of contemporary, international belly dance. The structures of the individual rhythms; the instruments on which they are played; and the traditional, neo-traditional, and post-traditional musicultural contexts and meanings with which they are associated are all discussed.

zaar (zahr)

Egyptian and Egyptian-derived forms of women's dancing represent a significant yet controversial marker of Egyptian identity. Public women's dancing is a social practice that often has been criticized, both in Egypt and throughout the rest of the Arab world, as excessively sensual and at odds with Arab-Islamic mores. Though many figures of modern Arab literature and cinema have been dancers, and though characterizations of dance and dancers appear in traditional Middle Eastern poetry as well (usually as metaphors of beauty and allure), female dancers and

World events		Music events
Ancient Egyptian civilization ●	**3rd millennium BCE**	● Depictions of female dancers and dance performances in ancient Egyptian tombs suggest ancient lineage of Egyptian dance tradition
One of the most advanced cultures of ● antiquity, with major advances in sciences, arts, technology, religion, architecture, politics		
Decline of Ancient Egypt begins, following ● some 2,000 years as dominant power of region	**1070 BCE**	
Egypt becomes part of Arab-Islamic empire ●	**7th century CE**	● Islamic mores concerning public female dancing and dancers have major cultural impact; status of music relative to Islam also complex
Profound cultural transformations with ● adoption of Islam, Arabic language		
Ottoman conquest of Egypt ●	**1517**	● Ghawazi female dance tradition in Egypt may date from this time
Egypt ruled by Ottoman Turks for ● centuries (officially until 1914)		
French occupation of Egypt (Napoleon ● Bonaparte)	**1798–1801**	● Egyptian-Western encounter had important implications for developments in Egyptian dance, music
Though occupation short-lived, major ● implications for Westernization of Egypt (especially Cairo)		
French encounter with Egypt inspired ● Orientalism, exoticization in 19th century West		
French driven out of Egypt by British ●	**1801**	
Britain becomes the major power in the ● region through mid-20th century (until 1952)		
Muhammad Ali appointed governor of ● Egypt by Ottomans (with strong British support)	**1805**	● Ali institutes sweeping social reforms, including expelling all ghawazi from Cairo
Egyptian nationalism emerges under Ali ● (though he himself was not an Egyptian)		
	Late 19th/ early 20th century	● Egyptian *musical* nationalism emerges ('Abduh al-Hamuli, Sayyid Darwish)
	1910	● Birth of Muhammad 'Abd al-Wahhab, Egyptian modernist composer

their art have very often been marginalized, or omitted altogether, in the official annals of Egyptian/Middle Eastern heritage and culture history.

Adding to the complexity is the history of Western portrayals. The figure of the alluring, mysterious, Middle Eastern woman dancer has been a predominant feature of an invented, **Orientalist** image of the Middle East since the 19th century. The Orientalist fantasy has figured prominently in everything from 19th-century European paintings (see p. 257) to Hollywood movies and so-called exotic dance (striptease). It also underlies a confounding cultural paradox, which is articulated in the following comments of Wendy Buonaventura in the book *Serpent of the Nile: Women and Dance in the Arab World*:

World events		Music events
	1920s	● Emergence of Cairo commercial film industry, flourishing of casino/dance-theaters (Badiaa Masabni, central figure)
Provisional Egyptian independence under constitutional monarchy of King Faruq ●	**1922**	
	1930–1960	● Golden age of Egyptian media stars (Muhammad 'Abd al-Wahhab, Farid al-Atrash, Umm Kulthum, Samia Gamal, Tahia Carioca)
Declaration of the Jewish state of Israel ●	**1948**	
Defeat of Egypt in war with Israel ●		
	1950	● Egyptian film *Zannouba,* starring Samia Gamal with music by Muhammad 'Abd al-Wahhab ("Zeina")
Egypt gains full national independence as Arab Republic of Egypt following "bloodless revolution" ●	**1952**	
Presidency of Gamal 'Abd al-Nasser ●	**1954–1970**	
	1954	● Dancer Samia Gamal featured in international films *Ali Baba and the Forty Thieves* and *Valley of the Kings*
	1959	● Formation of Reda Troupe (Farida Fahmy)
	1964	● Legendary concert of Muhammad 'Abd al-Wahhab and Umm Kulthum
Presidency of Anwar Sadat ●	**1970–1981**	
	1970s	● Dancer Nagwa Fu'ad and drummer Ahmed Hammouda create *Tabla Solo* dance form
Hosni Mubarak becomes president of Egypt ●	**1981**	
	1990s–present	● Hossam Ramzy releases numerous recordings on the ARC label, including *Zeina: Best of Mohammed Abdul Wahab, Sabla Tolo,* and *Latin American Hits for Bellydance.*

Scantily clad entertainers who, in the commercial world, are compelled to highlight the more provocative elements of their dance are not a good advertisement for Arab womanhood. Yet their high public profile, in contrast to that of the majority of women in Muslim society, makes them the best known of Arab women outside their own country [and has rendered the art with which they are associated] the best-known manifestation of Arabic dance in the West. (Buonaventura 1989:154, 21)

Given the controversial status of women's dance in Egypt and elsewhere in the Arab world, the decision to focus this chapter on musical traditions associated with such dance at the

A group of raqs baladi performers in Egypt.

American belly dancer.

Raqs sharqi dancer performing at an Egyptian nightclub.

tarab (tah-rahb)

expense of devoting attention to more highly regarded musical traditions, such as *tarab* (see Racy 2003), may likewise be seen as controversial. (Visit the Online Learning Center at www.mhhe.com/bakan1 for information and resources on tarab and other Middle Eastern music traditions.) The reliance on recordings by Hossam Ramzy may be questioned by some too. Though Ramzy is highly respected by musicians in Egypt and throughout the Arab music world, he is reportedly less well known in Egypt itself than one might assume (that is, outside of musicians' circles). There are those who would cast him more as an international world music figure than as a representative of Egyptian music *per se,* despite his moniker as "Egypt's Ambassador of Rhythm" and his resolute self-identification as an Egyptian musician.

Whatever potential liabilities they may present, it is these very types of problems and controversies that in some sense make the point of this text's perspective on tradition and transformation in music. Whatever might be said about it, positive or negative, the art of Egyptian women's dance and the music with which it is associated are integral to both Egyptian musi-cultural heritage and the impact of that heritage on the broader world.

Egypt: An Overview

Our exploration of Egyptian and Egyptian-derived dance and dance music is framed in impor-tant ways by key developments in Egyptian political, social, and cultural history. We therefore begin with a brief overview of this history in order to establish a context for the main discussion that follows it.

The Arab Republic of Egypt (Egypt) is located in northeastern Africa. With more than 70 million people, it has the second-largest population of any African nation (after Nigeria). The vast majority of the Egyptian landmass is dominated by desert, and almost the entire pop-ulation lives either in the Nile River Valley and its fertile delta or along the Suez Canal, which was built in the late 1800s to create a connecting waterway between the Mediterranean and Red Seas. The highest population concentration is in the region of Cairo, a metropolis of some 15 million people.

Geographically, culturally, economically, and politically, Egypt—and its capital city, Cairo, in particular—has long stood as a major center of the world region known as the Middle East (or Near East), and in turn of the Arab-Islamic world. The Arab world extends from the Arabian peninsula (including Saudi Arabia) and Iraq in the east through the Levant nations of Syria, Lebanon, and Jordan; to Egypt; and across northern Africa west of Egypt from Libya to Morocco (the Maghrib). Sandwiched between the Levant nations and Egypt is the principally Jewish state of Israel (see Chapter 14), which is identified throughout much of the Arab world as Palestine.

The religion of Islam (based on the worship of Allah as the single supreme deity, recognition of the Prophet Muhammad as Allah's messenger, and the holy book the Qur'an) and the Arabic language are unifying features of this vast region. Broad similarities in cultural practices, values, beliefs, political convictions, and traditions (including music and dance traditions) across the diverse societies of the Arab world also are significant, though they are counterbalanced by pro-found cultural differences. Religious divisions within Islam, political and social injustices, and

The Sphinx, framed by one of the great pyramids of Egypt.

long histories of tension and conflict between different nations and ethnic groups within the Arab Middle East have been sources of divisiveness. Large diasporic Arab communities in North America, Europe, and elsewhere connect Middle Eastern nations culturally—and often politically—to other world regions. Moreover, the vast spread of Islam beyond the Arab world links the Arab Middle East to Turkey, Iran, Central Asia (Kazakhstan, Uzbekistan, Turkmenistan, Kyrgyzstan, Tajikistan), South Asia (India, Pakistan, Bangladesh), Southeast Asia (Malaysia, Indonesia), and even northwestern China (see Chapter 13, p. 319).

Egyptian history

Egypt's Nile Valley gave rise to one of the world's first great civilizations, Ancient Egypt, which was founded some 5,000 years ago and flourished for more than 2,000 years at the center of a succession of powerful empires. Many of the foundations of modern societies—agricultural cultivation, city-states, writing, arithmetic, geometry, astronomy, architecture—have roots in Ancient Egypt. Additionally, the archaeological record chronicles a rich culture of music making and ritual dancing. Thanks to Egypt's dry climate, many of the great temples, sculptures, and pyramids of ancient times have survived to the present day, constituting some of the priceless treasures of human history.

The decline of Ancient Egypt commenced around 1070 BCE. The empire eventually succumbed to a series of foreign invaders: first the Nubians, Assyrians, and Persians; later the Greeks under Alexander the Great (after whom the Egyptian city Alexandria is named); and then the Romans/Byzantines. Beginning in the 7th century CE, Egypt became part of a large Arab-Islamic empire that flourished for many centuries through the succession of many different dynasties (caliphates). At its height, this empire stretched from the westernmost reaches of the Indian subcontinent in the east to Spain and Morocco in the west. Egypt became an important and powerful part of the imperial Islamic world, and, during certain eras, Cairo was the capital of major Islamic empires. Islam was gradually adopted as Egypt's majority religion through the centuries, and Arabic as the country's principal language.

maqam (mah-KAHM)

Qur'anic (Koar-AH-nik)

Islam and the Arabic language served as the catalysts for new cultural formations and developments, in Egyptian religion, sciences, politics, and literature, as well as in music. The great modal musical system of *maqamat* (singular, **maqam**—see "Insights and Perspectives" box on p. 259) was introduced to and developed in Cairo and other centers, as were the revered traditions of **Qur'anic recitation** (**CD ex. #1-3**) and different forms of Islamic religious chant. According to Islamic custom, Qur'anic recitation and Islamic chant were regarded as entirely separate from music itself, despite having maqam-like "musical" characteristics (discussed further later in the chapter). Negative attitudes toward female dancers who danced in public also emerged in connection with the rise of Islam, and such attitudes were to have profound implications on future cultural developments, as we shall see.

In 1517, Egypt was conquered by the Turkish Ottoman Empire. The Ottomans were Muslims, but they were not Arabs, and they spoke Turkish rather than Arabic. Officially, Ottoman rule continued in Egypt until 1914, though the country was invaded and briefly controlled by the French (under Napoleon Bonaparte) from 1798–1801. Then, after defeating the French in alliance with the Ottomans, the British established themselves as the dominant power in the region from the early 19th century through to the establishment of Egypt as a fully independent nation in 1952. Resentment toward the Ottomans and foreign rule generally was strong in many sectors of Egyptian society throughout the Ottoman period. Opposition toward foreign domination inspired the rise of **Egyptian nationalism** beginning in the 19th century. The nationalist movement was characterized by three major currents:

Maqam: The Modal Foundation of Arab Music

The maqam system is roughly to Arab music what the raga system is to Indian music (see Chapter 8 regarding the latter). It is the foundation of one of the world's great *modal* traditions and the basis of an extraordinary range of musical idioms, improvised and composed, vocal and instrumental, solo and ensemble.

Like a raga, a maqam is built from a specific sequence of ascending and descending pitches (i.e., a scale), but it encompasses much more than that. Specific rules of melodic ornamentation, procedures for moving between different pitches, emphasis on certain notes, microtonal nuances, and characteristic melodic motives are defining features of different maqamat. A maqam also may be associated with particular emotions, healing properties, geographical locations, bodily organs, or psychological states. *Maqam Saba,* for example, is linked to the emotion of sadness.

One of the most fascinating features of the maqamat (at least as practiced since the 20th century) is their basis in a *microtonal* pitch system that divides the octave into 24 pitches separated by intervals of a **quarter tone** (see also Chapter 4, pp. 51–52). This means that there are twice as many pitches per octave than the standard 12 recognized in the Western pitch system (and in actual Arab music performance practice, many beyond that in additon [see Racy 2003:106]). The Arab music performer must have a very highly developed sense of pitch discrimination in order to capture the subtle, microtonal nuances of maqam performance.

Unlike Indian raga performances, which conventionally stay within the constraints of a specific raga throughout (Chapter 8), maqam performances often feature *elaborate schemes of modulation* that move the music from one maqam to another, ultimately arriving back at the original one. In improvised musical forms such as the instrumental *taqsim* (tak-SEEM; pl. *taqasim*), the performer's aptitude for navigating his way through a labyrinth of complex modulations is appreciated as a measure of his skill, though his ability to express and evoke appropriate moods and sentiments through his performance is perhaps even more highly prized (see Racy 2003). **CD ex. #1-14,** heard earlier in connection with Chapter 2, is an excerpt of a taqsim played on the *'ud,* a fretless, short-necked, lute-type chordophone. The performer is Mamdouh El Gebaly, who provides an excellent illustration of maqam-based improvisation. *Maqam Nahawand,* built from a scale of notes roughly equivalent to the Western pitches C D E♭ F G A♭ B (C), serves as the musical "home base" for this performance.

The 'ud, played here by the Iraqi 'ud master Munir Bashir.

- Localism (pride in Egyptianness as the antithesis of "foreignness").

- Pan-Arabism (identification with other Arabic-speaking peoples and with Arab-Islamic history and culture).

- Islamism (principal identification with the Muslim religion, and more specifically that of the Arab world).

From the 19th century onward, Egyptian music and various forms of musical folklore and theater (and later film) involving diverse styles of music and dance would play key roles in the forging of Egyptian nationalism and new conceptions of Egyptian identity.

Also integral to Egyptian nationalism from the 19th century forward was a fervent current of *modernism.* Paradoxically, this modernist current led to the large-scale appropriation of Western cultural influences and resources in many areas, including music and dance. Thus, "foreignness" was simultaneously embraced and frowned upon in the modern construction of Egyptian national identity. Though French rule of Egypt in the late 19th century had been short-lived, it was this French-Egyptian encounter that first fueled Western fascinations with Egyptian "exoticism" and antiquity, on the one hand, and Egyptian interests in Western-style modernity, on the other. This cross-cultural exchange would have ramifications in later periods on everything from Egyptian cinema and folk culture to exotica in Hollywood films and the international belly dance craze, all of which we will explore.

It is paradoxical, too, that a foreigner, Muhammad Ali, the Ottoman-appointed governor of Egypt who came to power (with strong support from the British) in 1805, is the individual often credited as the father of modern Egyptian nationalism. Ali instituted ambitious reforms aimed at modernizing and Westernizing Egypt, and in the process fostered the emergence of what El-Hamamsy has characterized as a class of Egyptians "imbued with a new national consciousness which expressed itself in a desire to improve society and to secure for themselves a greater share in its control and development" (c.f. Danielson 1997:39). This new national consciousness would ultimately permeate cultural developments in Egyptian music and related arts (including dance, theater, and film).

Faruq (Fah-roo[k])

Following a revolutionary struggle, Egypt achieved provisional independence as a constitutional monarchy under the British Crown in 1922. The country officially came under the leadership of King Faruq, though in reality the British retained a high measure of control. The Faruq era also saw the rise of the Egyptian film industry, which became a major engine of new developments in Egyptian music and dance, as well as a repository of images of Egyptianness that influenced both Egyptian nationalism and *inter*nationalism.

Gamal 'Abd al-Nasser (Gah-mal Ahb-del-NAH-sir)

Full Egyptian independence was achieved in 1952 following the "bloodless revolution" of that year (discussed later in the chapter). Since that time, Egypt's modern era of political history has been defined by the regimes of three important leaders: Gamal 'Abd al-Nasser, who ruled from 1954 until his death in 1970; Anwar Sadat, the Egyptian president from 1970 until his 1981 assassination; and Hosni Mubarak, who became president in 1981. Changing attitudes and policies toward dance and dance music have reflected larger-scale changes in Egyptian society and conceptions of identity throughout Egypt's modern, post-independence era.

Against the preceding backdrop of Egyptian history, we now turn our attention to the world of Egyptian women's dance and dance music.

The Foundations of Egyptian Women's Dance

In the West, what people know about Middle Eastern women's dance is defined mainly by the performances of professional or semiprofessional dancers in nightclubs, films, videos, public shows, concerts, and demonstrations. The principal domain of women's dancing in the Arab world, however, is neither the nightclub, the concert stage, nor the silver screen. It is, rather, the domestic women's gathering. From time immemorial, family-based communities of Arab women have gathered, out of the sight of men and in the privacy of their own homes, to socialize, eat together, share stories, sing songs, provide mutual support to one another, and teach their daughters and granddaughters important lessons about life and womanhood. Dancing has always been central to such occasions, and the forms of dance still performed at Arab women's gatherings today may derive from dances that originated in antiquity. The dances performed at women's gatherings also share much in terms of style and substance with their more professionalized counterparts, raqs sharqi and belly dance, despite their very different context and social function.

Rosina-Fawzia Al-Rawi (Roe-zeena Fow-ya Ahr-RAH-wee)

Often it is through a display of dancing at a women's gathering that a girl marks her "initiation" into the women's community. Dancer and writer Rosina-Fawzia Al-Rawi, author of the engaging book *Grandmother's Secrets: The Ancient Rituals and Healing Power of Belly Dancing* (1999), offers the following autobiographical account of her own initiation through dance as a child in Iraq:

My aunt gave me a scarf, which I tied around my hips. I listened to the music for an instant, and in I walked. All the guests turned to me and smiled encouragingly. I started moving slowly, getting in harmony with the rhythm. I felt stiff and clumsy. I suffered from all the concentrated attention.

Then my eyes fell upon my grandmother. She was sitting quietly among the guests and her eyes stroked me briefly. Her calm gave me confidence and I glided deeper into the circling movements. Slowly, the audience disappeared and soon I didn't even notice my grandmother any longer. I heard my heartbeat give me the rhythm and I felt my body dissolve in movements much older than me. Happiness and pride overwhelmed me and a deep inner knowledge curled my lips into a smile. I don't know how long I danced, because my sense of time had melted into the heat of my dancing. The inner and the outer worlds were touching. At that moment, I was neither young nor old. Eternity beckoned inside me and I gave in to the call of Life and danced with the intensity and fervor of Life itself. When I stopped and ran out of the room, I heard the guests clap and I knew that I had completed my initiation successfully. I was nine years old: a woman and a child at the same time. (Al-Rawi 1999:24)

Speculations on ancient roots

Exactly where, when, and how the ancient forms of Middle Eastern women's dance originated and evolved is largely a matter of speculation. Al-Rawi suggests that these root forms may have emerged several thousand years ago during an age that predated the great civilizations of Ancient Egypt. She portrays the cultures in which such dances first developed as ones in which matriarchal goddess cults and societies worshipped a Great Mother goddess as the source of all creation. Women belonging to such societies, she writes, would gather together during the nighttime to honor the earth, the moon, the goddesses of fertility and maternity, and the benign and malevolent spirits of nature and the netherworld through dance. Al-Rawi goes on to propose that since these ancient dances revolved around fertility, the belly and the hips—moving in circular motions that symbolized the process of giving birth and the cycle of life—played a major part in the dance movement vocabulary, as they continue to do in present-day Middle Eastern women's dance styles (thus the moniker "belly dance," at least according to some theories). In her evocative (albeit highly speculative) rendering, these ancient dances "were used to strengthen sexual energy, to awaken joy, and to praise the mysteries of life. The women danced their dance, a dance that corresponded to their body and expressed all the moods and feelings, all the longings, sufferings, and joys of being a woman. Through their dance, they came into harmony with the universe, abandoning themselves to life and to the divine. . . ." (Al-Rawi 1999:33).

The Ghawazi tradition

The tradition of professional, public women's dancing in Egypt that formed the foundation for modern women's Egyptian dance and its international derivatives is associated with hereditary families of dancers called **ghawazi** (*ghawazee*). Ghawazi dance lineages trace back many generations. There are various theories concerning the origins of the ghawazi and their art in Egypt. Edward Lane, in his classic 19th-century book *An Account of the Manners and Customs of the Modern Egyptians,* claims that "In many of the tombs of the ancient Egyptians we find representations of females dancing at private entertainments, to the sounds of various instruments, in a manner similar to the modern Ghawázee [ghawazi]. . . . It is probable, therefore, that [this tradition] has continued without interruption; and perhaps the modern Ghawázee are descended from the class of female dancers who amused the Egyptians in the times of the early Pharaohs" (Lane 1978[1895]:374–75).

Other theories place the beginning of ghawazi dance culture in Egypt in more recent historical times, suggesting that the original ghawazi may actually have belonged to families of Roma ("Gypsy") descent who came to Egypt beginning in the 16th century in the wake of the

ghawazi
(gha-WAH-zee)

Ancient Egyptian tomb painting of female dancers and musicians performing at a banquet (circa 1400 BCE).

Ottoman invasion (Saleh 2002:625). According to such theories, Roma immigrants to Egypt brought with them their distinctive traditions of dance and music, which in turn came both to influence and to be influenced by local Egyptian music and dance styles. The Roma also filled a commercial niche. In Muslim Egypt, dancing by women was something to be done in the company of women only. Dancing in public in front of men was considered shameful, and dancing for money reprehensible. Nevertheless, a large market for female dancers existed, and the ghawazi met the market demand, becoming the principal class of professional dancers, and in turn the direct progenitors of modern raqs sharqi and belly dance.

The designation "ghawazi" originally referred to the specific hereditary class of professional dancers described above, but it is now applied to virtually *all* professional female dancers in Egypt and throughout the Middle East, regardless of their family lineage or ethnic derivation. Translation of the term *ghawazi* itself sheds light on the low social status of the professional female dancer. The word means "outsider" or "invader," implying that in the Arab-Egyptian worldview, the female dancer who dances in the company of men for profit is a figure tied fundamentally to foreignness, to marginality, to aggressive intrusion.

In the early 19th century, Muhammad Ali, the Ottoman-appointed, British-supported governor of Egypt, officially expelled all ghawazi from the city of Cairo and exiled them to provincial towns in Upper Egypt (though a good many of them managed to stay in Cairo and profitably carry on their business in secrecy). This was done in the midst of Ali's sweeping reform efforts. Cairo by this time had become the cultural, political, and economic hub of the Arab world and the main nexus between the Arabic "East" and the European "West." The conspicuous presence of ghawazi culture did not conform well with Ali's aspirations for Cairo as the stellar symbol of modern Egypt. But while the expulsion of the dancers may have advanced Ali's public relations campaign on behalf of Egypt, it hurt Cairo's economy considerably, since the ghawazi, according to Lane, had accounted for more than 10 percent of city tax revenues (c.f. Buonaventura 1989:68).

Witness to a ghawazi performance

To be sure, the ghawazi were a major Cairo attraction for foreign visitors, many of whom, "if given the choice, would rather have seen the dancing than the pyramids," according to at least

insights and perspectives

The Street

Many years after Muhammad Ali's death, the ghawazi would be granted legal permission to return to Cairo (in 1866). Ironically, the center of the Egyptian dance entertainment industry today is located on the very street that bears his name, Muhammad Ali Street.

one report from that period (see Buonaventura 1989:61). The following account by the English painter and Egyptophile James Augustus St. John of a dance performance he witnessed near Cairo in 1840 provides a sense of the Orientalist fascination that the ghawazi inspired:

> Suddenly the musicians, who had hitherto gratified us only with fantasias of various kinds, and Arab melodies, struck up a dancing measure: the door was opened, and two Arab dancers entered. They were girls between the ages of 16 and 30, tall and admirably proportioned. . . .
>
> Their eyes shot fire . . . and their bodies assumed the most varied attitudes and inflexions. They twined round each other snake-like, with a suppleness and grace such as I had never seen before. Now, they let their arms drop, and their whole frames seemed to collapse in utter exhaustion. . . . All this while the music continued to play, and in its very simplicity was like a pale background to the picture, from which the glowing figures of the girls stood out in so much the stronger relief. (c.f. Buonaventura 1989: 64–65)

Zaar: Egyptian Women's Dance in a Healing Ritual

Another type of cultural performance that inspired fascination among foreign visitors to Egypt was the *zaar* (see photos on pp. 264, 22). Zaar is an ancient healing ritual rooted in ages-old shamanistic practices and involving spirit possession and trance. It is mainly a domain of women (though men may participate, especially as musicians). The practice of zaar is officially prohibited among Egyptian Muslims, but it continues to be practiced nonetheless, usually in secretive ceremonies.

Despite its officially "banned" status, zaar is paradoxically *embraced* as an integral element of Egyptian **baladi,** or folk culture heritage. Folklorized dramatizations of zaar rituals are produced in Egypt, and elements of the zaar ceremony, including its ecstatic dances and music, appear frequently in raqs baladi, raqs sharqi, and belly dance performances. In these appropriations, zaar serves as a powerful symbol of Egyptian folk roots and cultural authenticity.

baladi (bah-lah-dee)

The zaar ritual

Zaar centers on the power of the *jinn,* a form of magically empowered spirit being. Jinn (from which the English word "genie" is said to derive) have the capacity to cause evil among humans by entering their souls. Women are viewed as especially susceptible to their malevolent powers (Saleh 2002:632). If a woman is possessed by a jinn, she will be afflicted by illness. She may suffer from any of a variety of physical ailments, as well as from neurotic conditions, psychotic episodes, or psychosomatic symptoms. If possession by a jinn is suspected as the cause of the illness, a zaar may be performed in order to neutralize the jinn's power and convince it to depart the woman's soul. The afflicted woman is cured if this goal is achieved.

Dealing with jinn is a delicate matter and requires the utmost care, deference, and diplomacy. The afflicting jinn is referred to during the ceremony as *asyad,* or "master," rather than by Arabic equivalents of terms such as "spirit" or "devil," which are considered derogatory and suggest irreverence (Saleh 2002:632). Negotiation with the asyad is mainly the job of the woman who leads the ceremony. She is often elderly and is believed to have powers of clairvoyance. She is known by names such as "the old mistress" and "the one who knows." During the ritual, she strikes her spiritually empowered *duff* (a large frame drum—see photos on pp. 264, 266) and beats it against her body to put herself into a state of trance. In that state, she is addressed by the afflicting asyad, who reveals to her "the wishes and conditions under which it will leave the patient and restore peace" (Al-Rawi 1999:147).

asyad (ahs-sigh-yed)

duff (dahf)

Music is absolutely crucial to the efficacy of a zaar. Each asyad is associated with specific ritual songs. The correct songs must be selected and performed in the afflicting asyad's honor in order to placate it and convince it to depart. The songs are sung and accompanied by rhythms

A zaar ritual in Cairo, 2001.

sagat (sah-gaht)

A dancer executing a "writhing bow" back bend.

played on an ensemble of drums and other percussion instruments such as finger cymbals (**sagat**—see photo on p. 266) and a rattle made of goats' hooves.

Customizing the musical presentation to the ritual needs of the afflicted person is also critical. As the ritual progresses, the musicians experiment with different rhythms, searching for the one that best suits the needs of the affected individual. The link between healing and rhythm is profound and decisive. It is the correct rhythm of the drums, once identified, that directs and inspires the afflicted and her cohort of ritual supporters to dance their way to ecstasy and ultimately a cure. The zaar is usually a multiday affair. On the climactic, final Great Night, the afflicted woman, dressed as a bride on her wedding day, is paraded around an altar erected in honor of the asyad. Blessings are intoned and passages of the Qur'an are recited. A variety of rites, from animal sacrifices to the ritual burning of incense, are performed.

Then the ritual dancing begins. It is "violent and unrestrained, peaking in crises and subsiding when the dancers become exhausted. The convulsive movements include tripping in a tight circle, running in place, stamping, bending and plunging forward and backward, and jerking and twisting the torso and head from side to side with arms held close to the body or swinging back and forth. Emotion reaches a height as constraints are removed and repressed impulses are released" (Saleh 2002:633). Impressive feats of dexterity may be involved. An eyewitness account of a zaar ceremony in Cairo written by the British expatriate James McPherson in 1920 describes how the participants would bend their bodies "till they formed a vibrating and writhing bow, resting on the ground by the heels and back of the head, whilst the muscles of their bodies carried on the dance with unbelievable contortions" (c.f. Buonaventura 1989:162). Finally, breathing deeply to the mesmerizing beat of the rhythm, the dancers enter a state of trance and collapse to the floor, unconscious. In this moment of cathartic release, the asyad finally liberates the afflicted individual from the clutches of spirit possession so that she may return to a state of health and wholeness.

If you have ever been to a belly dance performance yourself, some of the movements described above may seem familiar. This is because much of the movement vocabulary of zaar ritual dancing has been integrally absorbed into the movement vocabularies of belly dance and raqs sharqi. Similarly, the percussive rhythms of zaar music have become a common feature of belly dance and raqs sharqi performances in which the spirit and character of the traditional zaar ritual are evoked. We will encounter such rhythms in three very different dance-music contexts in the course of this chapter (**CD exs. #3-9, 3-13, and 3-17**). We begin with a Guided Listening Experience of **CD ex. #3-9**, an excerpt from a Hossam Ramzy recording that features a composition based entirely on traditional zaar rhythms.

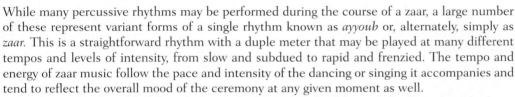

Beat:	1		2		1		2	
Strokes:	**Dum**	tek	**Dum**	tek	**Dum**	tek	**Dum**	tek

FIGURE 12.1

Basic pattern of the zaar rhythm.

guided listening experience

Traditional Zaar Rhythms, Hossam Ramzy

- CD Track **#3-9**
- Featured performer(s)/group: Hossam Ramzy (Ramzy plays all of the instruments; the different percussion parts were overdubbed in a multitrack recording studio.)
- Format: Excerpt
- Source recording: "Alla Hai," from *Baladi Plus,* by Hossam Ramzy (ARC Music Productions International Ltd. EUCD 1083)

While many percussive rhythms may be performed during the course of a zaar, a large number of these represent variant forms of a single rhythm known as *ayyoub* or, alternately, simply as *zaar.* This is a straightforward rhythm with a duple meter that may be played at many different tempos and levels of intensity, from slow and subdued to rapid and frenzied. The tempo and energy of zaar music follow the pace and intensity of the dancing or singing it accompanies and tend to reflect the overall mood of the ceremony at any given moment as well.

The zaar rhythm, like all Arab dance rhythms, is defined by a skeletal ostinato rhythmic pattern built upon two fundamental kinds of drum strokes: the low-pitched **Dum** and the high-pitched **tek.** Dum strokes mark the two main beats of the pattern, while tek strokes fill in with syncopations. Listen to the portion of **CD ex. #3-9** beginning at 0:18 and try to clap out the basic *zaar* rhythmic pattern (as outlined in Figure 12.1 above) with the drummers. Use a deep, full-handed clap for the Dum strokes and a sharp, fingertips-on-the-palm clap for the tek strokes. (You are encouraged to clap out the basic rhythmic patterns along with the recordings in this manner throughout the rest of the chapter as well.)

CD ex. #3-10 consists of a brief Musical Guided Tour in which Hossam Ramzy demonstrates the basic drum strokes and explains how they are produced. A transcript of Ramzy's presentation is included in the Musical Guided Tour box on page 266. Follow along with this transcript as you listen to the recording.

Continuing now with our discussion of **CD ex. #3-9,** we turn to instrumentation. The zaar rhythms in the example are performed and embellished by an ensemble featuring the following percussion instruments (membranophones/idiophones—see the photos on p. 266):

- The *mazhar,* a large, deep-toned tambourine with large jingles (cymbals).
- The duff, a mazhar without jingles.
- The riqq, a medium-sized, higher-pitched tambourine with jingles (the head of which is traditonally made from a fish skin).
- The tabla (darabukkah, dumbek), which functions as the lead drum of the ensemble.
- The doholla, a larger, "bass" version of the tabla.
- The sagat, or finger cymbals.

Demonstration of Dum and Tek Drum Strokes
(CD ex. #3-10)

Now I will introduce you to the [drum] sounds. Basically there are two, the Dum and the tek. The Dum is the bass beat in any Egyptian drum; the tek is the treble. On the tabla and the *doholla* [an oversized version of the tabla], the Dum is produced by striking the middle of the skin with the hand's four fingers close together, and moving the hand away as if one has touched a hot iron by accident. Here is an example of some tabla Dums [♪]. The tek on the tabla and the doholla is produced by striking the rim of the drum with one or more fingers from the right hand. In using the left hand, the tek is produced from striking the rim with the hand's third finger alone. Here is an example of some tabla teks [♪].

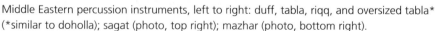

Middle Eastern percussion instruments, left to right: duff, tabla, riqq, and oversized tabla* (*similar to doholla); sagat (photo, top right); mazhar (photo, bottom right).

doholla (doe-hole-lah)

These are the standard percussion instruments used in Egyptian dance music, whether for raqs baladi, raqs sharqi, or belly dance. Some or all of them are featured in all of the pieces explored in this chapter. (*Note:* In traditional ritualistic contexts such as zaar, other "folk" percussion instruments may be used in place of the standard ones listed.)

Hossam Ramzy introduces and illustrates the sounds of several of these instruments—in order, the mazhar (0:14), duff (0:31), doholla (0:43), and tabla (1:03)—on **CD ex. #3-11.** Listen to that example now and familiarize yourself with the different instrument names and timbres. The two other percussion instruments on the above list are demonstrated by Ramzy on **CD ex. #3-12,** first the riqq (0:00–0:15), then the sagat (0:16-0:29).

Now that you have some points of orientation, listen again to **CD ex. #3-9.** It begins with an introductory series of Dum strokes. Then, at 0:18, following a lead-in by the tabla, the full "group" begins to play the standard zaar rhythm at a slow tempo. Notice how the basic rhythm is maintained by the doholla and the duff, while the tabla moves between outlining this basic rhythm and playing in a characteristic Arab style that involves "filling out the beat" with "a rich filigree of timbral and accentual nuances" (Racy 2003:116). Meanwhile, the jingles of the tambourines (riqq/mazhar) flesh out the texture with faster, ornamental rhythms. The more ornate passages of tabla playing (heard mainly from about the 1:00 point on) nicely exemplify the improvisatory art of Arab percussion performance, which is especially identified with the tabla and the riqq.

At 1:49, the tabla plays a syncopated rhythm that serves to cue the transition to the second part of the piece. This second part begins at 1:53, where the tempo is doubled and the energy increases accordingly. This faster-tempoed rhythm is the type one would expect to hear in the later portion of a zaar ritual, when the dancers begin to move toward ecstasy.

---

guided listening quick summary

Traditional Zaar Rhythms, Hossam Ramzy (CD ex. #3-9)

INTRODUCTION

0:00–0:17

- Series of unison Dum strokes in slow, sparse rhythm; same rhythmic pattern is repeated four times.

SLOW ZAAR SECTION (PART I)

0:18–1:52

- Doholla and duff lay down the basic zaar rhythm, while tabla embellishes this rhythm with improvisational elaborations (especially from the 1:00 point on) and tambourines (riqq/mazhar) add an ornamental rhythmic layer.
- Tabla cue at 1:49 signals transition to second, faster part of piece that follows.

FAST ZAAR SECTION (PART II)

1:53–end

- Tempo is doubled and energy of music intensifies; faster tempo and more energetic character reflective of what one would expect to hear during the later portions of a zaar ritual.

Music, Dance, Nationalism, and Mass Media Entertainment in 20th-Century Egypt

In 1920, the year of James McPherson's earlier-cited eyewitness account of a zaar ritual in Cairo, the Egyptian people were engaged in the first major phase of their ultimately successful revolutionary struggle for independence from British rule. Egyptian music and musical theater played an important role in this struggle, and the music and theatrical productions of one composer, Sayyid Darwish, were especially significant.

Grafting Egyptian nationalistic themes onto a base of Western-influenced Arab music that drew upon the symbolic images and musical and choreographic resources of Egyptian folk music

Sayyid Darwish (Sai-yid Der-WEE-sh)

and devotional song, Sayyid Darwish pioneered a new Egyptian music that became closely identified with Egyptian nationalism. He essentially established a new aesthetic ideal for Egyptian music and other arts. This ideal hinged on achieving an elusive balance between

- That which was *asil*, that is, authentically Arab-Egyptian in a manner that reasserted Egyptian cultural traditions and values.

- That which was *hadith*, that is, "new, useful, and, if necessary, imported," typically from the West (Danielson 1997:40).

- That which succeeded, through its synthesis of asil and hadith elements, in living up to the political and cultural challenges of its time (Racy 1981:11).

During his short life, Darwish achieved the status of a musical legend and hero of the Egyptian nation, and this status has endured. He also became a mentor and inspiration for the musical leaders that followed him, most notably the composer and singer Muhammad 'Abd al-Wahhab (see the photo on p. 270), who rose to prominence as a member of Darwish's theatrical troupe in the late 1910s. In carrying Darwish's musical legacy forward (especially in the 1950s and later), 'Abd al-Wahhab and his contemporaries formed the vanguard of the so-called new heritage (*turath jadid*) of Egyptian music.

For many Egyptians, Egyptian music proper, *purely* Egyptian music, did not even emerge until the era of Darwish and his immediate predecessors, such as the famous late-19th-century Egyptian singer 'Abduh al-Hamuli. Its purported nonexistence prior to that was attributed to the insidiousness of foreign influences. One prominent Egyptian intellectual, for example, professed in 1972 that "The Arab listener did not rid himself from Ottoman, Persian and gypsy musical gibberish . . . until less than a hundred years ago [when the singer 'Abduh al-Hamuli] began to Egyptianize and Arabize the singing of Egypt, and to depart from the lingering remnants of Ottoman singing and gypsy screaming which our country was subject to during the epochs of national and social decadence" (Kamāl al-Najmī, c.f. Racy 1981:9). It remained for Darwish to perfect the Egyptian national music idiom and tailor it to the nationalist climate of a new era, and for his protégé Muhammad 'Abd al-Wahhab, the great singer Umm Kulthum, and others to extend its range into the evolving nationalist climate of subsequent decades.

The contributions of Badiaa Masabni

Equal in significance to Sayyid Darwish's contributions to the art of Egyptian music were the contributions of Badiaa Masabni to the art of Egyptian women's dance. During the constitutional monarchy era under King Faruq that began in 1922, lavish casino-theaters, or *salas,* brought in huge profits and fostered creative developments that gave rise to a burgeoning popular entertainment industry with Egyptian dance and music at its center. Preeminent among these salas was Badiaa Masabni's Casino Badiaa. Masabni, like her musical counterparts Darwish and 'Abd al-Wahhab, was a great syncretizer and modernizer. Her innovations were put on prominent display in Casino Badiaa productions. "Her choreographers," explains Barbara Lüscher (a.k.a. Aischa), "came from abroad and her stage shows and dance theater had heavy foreign, and especially western influence" (Lüscher 2000:18). In the new style that coalesced under Masabni's watch, the arms and torso of the dancers were used much more prominently than before, with the arms often swaying in "flowing, serpentine patterns of movement" (Buonaventura 1989:149). Dances came to cover large territories of floor space, rather than being rooted to a single spot on the floor.

The look of the dancers also was transformed in a manner reflective of the influence of Hollywood glamour. "Hollywood," writes Buonaventura (1989:148–49), "exerted the greatest influence . . . and its fantasy of Oriental dance filtered through and was taken up and unconsciously parodied by Arab dancers in their desire to emulate Western behaviour and modes of fashion." Hollywood's version of the "Oriental" dance costume—sequined bra, bare midriff, and a low-slung gauzy skirt—itself a fantasy elaboration on the traditional ghawazi regalia theme, became the new dance attire of choice in Casino Badiaa. A general air of Hollywood-esque glitz and glamor pervaded the new medium as well and was appropriated as definitively "Egyptian." Music followed suit, incorporating larger ensembles combining Western and Arab instruments with song styles, rhythms, and arrangements of an increasingly Western-influenced, cosmopolitan hue. "It was in this cultural melting pot," writes Lüscher (2000:18), "that today's *Raks Sharki* [raqs sharqi] style of oriental dance, with glittering costumes and glamorous stage-show, began," moving on from there to the world of Egyptian film and eventually out into the global phenomenon of belly dance.

In the 1930s and 1940s, Badiaa's sala was *the* place to be and be seen in Cairo, and it was on her stage "that stars were born" (Lüscher 2000:18). For Egyptian dancers such as Samia Gamal (see the photo on p. 270), to whose life and career we will soon return, membership in the Casino Badiaa dance-theater troupe was a virtual prerequisite to stardom in Cairo's booming film industry.

Dance, music, and the Egyptian film industry

The Egyptian film industry emerged in Cairo in the late 1920s and quickly became the lynchpin of the city's huge and vibrant mass media entertainment industry (which, by that time, also hosted large radio and music recording industries). Egyptian film was heavily influenced by Hollywood cinema. The films built from romantic plot lines and featured "glamorous characters, exotic settings from Arab history, clearly drawn lines of good and evil, and resolutions in favor of goodness and justice" reflective of Arab-Egyptian social values of the time (Danielson 1997:88). Grand and dramatic dance spectacles featuring glamorous dancers accompanied by lively, thickly orchestrated music were a highlight of many Egyptian films.

Hollywood-esque "Oriental" dance costume modeled by the American dancer Gitana.

Farid al-Atrash (Fah-reed ahl- At-rush)

Samia Gamal (Sa-mee-ya Gah-MAHL)

From the 1930s onward, virtually all highly prolific and highly respected performing artists in Egypt—the musicians Muhammad 'Abd al-Wahhab, Farid al-Atrash, and Umm Kulthum; the dancers Samia Gamal and Tahia Carioca—were stars of both the stage and the silver screen. Conventional distinctions between "high art" and "popular entertainment" cultures, distinctions that carried considerable weight in many other societies (India, the West), had relatively less overall significance in Egypt (see Racy 1981). The modern film star, the nationalist symbol, and the icon of Egyptian cultural heritage were rolled together into one in the figure of the Egyptian media star. In an emerging nation heir to a great ancient civilization but subject for many centuries to foreign subjugation, the "new" traditions that emerged with Egyptian mass media entertainment effectively moved to the core of what Egyptian people conceived of as their own cultural heritage.

Muhammad 'Abd al-Wahhab and Samia Gamal

The golden age of the Egyptian media stars spanned from the 1930s to the 1960s. The stars of this era endure strongly in the collective consciousness of Egyptians even today, and their legacy continues to inform prevalent notions of modern Egyptianness.

In the worlds of music and dance, two media stars, the composer Muhammad 'Abd al-Wahhab and the dancer Samia Gamal, occupied somewhat parallel positions as great modernists of their era. 'Abd al-Wahhab continued the line of Sayyid Darwish, the main pioneering figure of modern Egyptian music; Gamal was a protégé of Badiaa Masabni, the main pioneering figure of modern Egyptian women's dance (raqs sharqi). Each extended the progressive vision of his/her mentor, and each, thanks to the power of mass media, achieved a level of fame and notoriety

The composer Muhammad 'Abd al-Wahhab.

in Egypt and beyond that was unparalleled by the luminaries of prior generations. They were the quintessential progressive modernists of Egyptian arts and entertainment, each in their own way representing a particular vision of what constituted Egyptianness in the minds and hearts of the Egyptian people. Collectively, their diverse personalities, public personae, and modes of artistic expression came to encompass the aspirations and ideals, as well as the contradictions and ambiguities, of Egyptian society during a defining period in its modern history.

Samia Gamal was a true innovator. She was reportedly the first Egyptian dancer to dance with a veil (though it should be noted that veil dancing is not nearly as prominent in Egyptian raqs sharqi as in international belly dance), the first to dance in high heels rather than barefoot, and one of the most influential figures involved in the syncretization of Middle Eastern and Western dance elements in raqs sharqi. As Lüscher comments, Gamal's dance style "has influenced generations of students, and continues to do so today. Her vivid and fluent veil work, her gracious arm movements and her elegant attitude combined with a real Hollywood smile made her one of the most glamorous dancers of the so-called Golden Age of Egyptian dance history" (Lüscher 2000:22).

Beyond her starring roles in many Egyptian films and stage appearances all over the Middle East, Gamal was additionally featured in European and American films of the 1950s, in-

The dancer Samia Gamal in the film *Valley of the Kings* (1954).

Accidental Innovations

It is humorous to note that many of Samia Gamal's dance innovations came less from the realization of an artistic vision than from happenstance. She reportedly first danced with a veil at the suggestion of a Russian ballet teacher, who felt that practicing her stage entrance while holding a veil in both hands behind her might improve her arm carriage. Gamal tried this out in a stage performance, the audience loved it, and soon everyone was emulating her. As for wearing high heels on stage, Gamal, who was raised in poverty, claimed that she started doing that by virtue of the simple fact she could afford the shoes and wanted people to know it.

cluding *Ali Baba and the Forty Thieves* and *Valley of the Kings* (see the photo on p. 270), both of which were released in 1954. She was also famous throughout the Arab world for her professional and romantic partnership with composer, musician, and singer Farid al-Atrash, who produced and co-starred in some of her films and was inspired in the writing of some of his most beautiful songs by his love for her.

Muhammad 'Abd al-Wahhab was born into a religious family in a working-class area of Cairo in 1910. His father was the religious leader (*imam*) of the neighborhood mosque. As a child, 'Abd al-Wahhab was educated at a religious school, where he studied the complex art of Qur'anic recitation (see "Insights and Perspectives" box on p. 272). He also attended and participated in Sufi religious rituals, where he was lauded for having the voice of an angel. This early training and experience would influence his music throughout his career; many of his songs and pieces reflect influences of Qur'anic recitation style and Sufi music (see box, p. 272).

imam (ee-MAHM)

While still a child, 'Abd al-Wahhab disgraced his family by running away from home to join a traveling circus. He soon moved on to a theater troupe, dressing up in drag and impersonating a girl singer between the main acts of the show. He eventually landed a position in the theater troupe of Sayyid Darwish, and this turn of events proved decisive in setting his future course. Though 'Abd al-Wahhab was not with Darwish for long (Darwish died of a cocaine overdose at age 32), Darwish's influence on the impressionable younger musician was an enduring one. Throughout his life, 'Abd al-Wahhab credited Darwish as a mentor.

'Abd al-Wahhab rose to fame first as a singer and later as a film actor, composer, and producer. Some of his most famous and revered songs were composed for Umm Kulthum, though the two great stars and rivals avoided collaboration for decades until finally joining forces for a legendary concert in 1964. 'Abd al-Wahhab is widely regarded today, as he was in his own time, as "the greatest Arab modernist of the twentieth century" in the area of music (Danielson 2002:600). His compositions form the backbone of the modern Egyptian musical repertoire (turath jadid). The following comments from Umm Kulthum biographer and ethnomusicologist Virginia Danielson attest to his greatness, musical range, and influence:

> An accomplished musical classicist, 'Abd al-Wahhāb was at the same time an inveterate innovator. He probed the possibilities of all musics that came his way, borrowing from the nineteenth-century European symphonic literature; Spanish, Latin American, North American, and local Middle Eastern dance rhythms; and instruments from everywhere, including the Hawaiian guitar. . . . From the perspective of the twenty-first century, 'Abd al-Wahhāb's legacy is inestimable. His grasp of international musical styles is unparalleled. His songs are a cherished part of people's memories of home and childhood [for Arabs everywhere]. (Danielson 2002:600)

Qur'anic Recitation versus Musical "Enchantment" in Islamic Society

The Arabic word for "singer" (*mutrib* [moet-rib]) translates as "one who enchants" (i.e., creates *tarab*), whereas the Arabic word for one who chants the Qur'an (*qari'*) means "one who recites." While the musical art of "enchantment" and the sacred vocal art of recitation may *sound* remarkably similar due to their common "musical" features (modes and scales, pitch contours, ornamentation, articulations), conservative Muslims reject the very idea of a *musical* identity for Qur'anic recitation or other forms of sacred Islamic vocalization. To identify an individual who recites the Qur'an as a singer (mutrib) would be offensive. The words of the Qur'an are sacrosanct for Muslims. Qur'anic recitation (**CD ex. #1-3** is an example) represents the highest expression of religious devotion to Allah (God), while "singing" and "music" *per se* are seen contrastingly as potential *threats* to Islamic piety. They have the capacity to "enchant," and thus to tempt people away from their principal sacred duties of devotion to Allah.

The clear theoretical distinction between music and nonmusic implied above is not always so clear in actual practice and individual attitudes. The mystical Sufi sects of Islam and certain other Muslim groups offer a contrasting view, sometimes claiming that music—and even dance—are important paths to spiritual transcendence, ecstasy, and communion with the divine. Additionally, there are forms of "popular Islam" in which certain types of devotional song and other kinds of music are considered to be religious or semireligious.

All of these paradoxes are underscored by, on the one hand, a "suspicion toward music because of its secular and even profane associations" that dates back many centuries (Nelson Davies 2002:158) and, on the other, a recognition (by many, at least) that sacred forms of vocal Islamic art do indeed possess musical qualities. "The prevailing impression among scholars and laypeople alike," writes ethnomusicologist Michael Frishkopf, "is that Islam forbids music in religious ritual and frowns on music in any context; the use of singing in Sufi (mystic) orders is often cited as a rare exception. But in fact melodious use of the voice is seldom absent, even in mainstream Islam" (Frishkopf 2002:165).

guided listening experience

"Zeina" (Ze-hee-NAH), by Muhammad 'Abd al-Wahhab (arrangement by Hossam Ramzy)

- CD Track **#3-13**
- Featured performer(s)/group: Hossam Ramzy group, with Hossam Ramzy (Egyptian percussion instruments), Magid Serour (qanun), Mahmoud Effat (nay), Farouq Mohammed Hassan (quarter-tone accordion)
- Format: Excerpt
- Source recording: *Zeina: Best of Mohammed Abdul Wahhab,* by Hossam Ramzy (ARC Music Productions International Ltd. EUCD 1231)

Zannouba
(Zahn-NOO-bah)

firqa musiqyya
(fir-[k]AH
moo-si-ki-YAH)

Composing dance music for films was one of the many musical areas in which Muhammad 'Abd al-Wahhab not only thrived but essentially defined the idiom. An example of his work in this area is "Zeina," which was originally composed for a dance number featuring Samia Gamal in the 1950 Egyptian film *Zannouba.* Like much of 'Abd al-Wahhab's music, "Zeina" employed the resources of a relatively large ensemble called a **firqa (firqa musiqyya).** The firqas featured

Traditional Arab Instruments of the Takht

The takht is the archetypal "classical" instrumental ensemble of Arab-Egyptian music. It is closely associated with a revered complex of musical traditions known as *tarab* (see Racy 2003). Its five instruments are the 'ud (**CD ex. #1-14**), the *qanun* (kah-NOON), the *nay* (nah-EE), the violin, and the riqq.

The 'ud is the most popular traditional music instrument in the Middle East and the lead instrument of the takht. It has a large body in the shape of a half pear and a short neck with no frets, along which run five double courses (pairs) of strings made from gut or nylon. An additional "bass" string may be included as well. It is played with a quill *plectrum* (a plucking or strumming implement; an eagle feather is the most traditional type). This instrument was the progenitor of the European lute.

The qanun is a plucked zither with a trapezoidal shape. The number of strings may vary, but the most common form of the instrument has 24 courses of three strings (for a total of 72 strings), with the three strings of each course tuned to the same pitch. Special metal bridges may be inserted under the strings to alter their tunings and allow for playing in different maqamat. The instrument is held across the lap of the player (or placed on a wooden stand) during performance and plucked with tortoise shell (traditionally) or plastic plectra that are attached to rings on the player's index fingers.

The Western violin (sometimes referred to as the *kamanjah,* after a related Arabian instrument) is the other chordophone of the takht ensemble. It is usually held under the chin and played in the conventional Western manner by Arab musicians, though there is a tradition in Morocco of balancing it vertically on the left knee and bowing it like a cello (see Touma 1996:116).

The nay is a type of end-blown flute. It is usually made of a bamboo or cane tube and has seven fingerholes, six on the front and one on the underside. The player produces sound by blowing against the edge of the open end at the top of the tube. Using a technique of overblowing, a nay player can cover a melodic range of three octaves or more. The nay comes in a number of sizes, with different ranges and capabilities for the playing of different maqamat.

The rhythmic accompaniment instrument in takht music is the riqq, or Arab tambourine, to which we have already been introduced. When employed to accompany dance or other lively music, the tabla is often added to the takht as well to provide extra rhythmic punch.

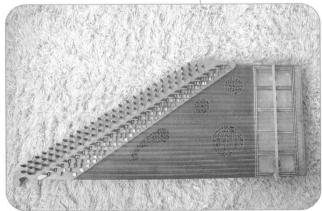

Instruments of the takht ensemble, clockwise on left: 'ud, nay, violin, and riqq. Above: qanun.

Beat:	1		2		1		2	
Strokes:	**Dum** Dum	tek	**Dum**	tek	**Dum** Dum	tek	**Dum**	tek

Masmoudi rhythmic pattern

FIGURE 12.2

takht (tah-kht [press tongue back and up to roof of mouth for "kh" sound])

on Egyptian film soundtracks of the era typically combined instruments of the traditional Arab **takht** ensemble (see "Insights and Perspectives" box on p. 273) with Western orchestral stringed instruments (a section of violins, cellos), a full complement of Arab percussion instruments, and sometimes additional Western instruments as well.

In dance pieces especially, 'Abd al-Wahhab was inclined to much experimentation with novel instruments and exciting rhythms, some drawn from the stock of traditional Egyptian folk music (baladi), others from American popular music of the day or Latin American popular dance-music genres like the rumba and the bolero. He made frequent use of the following elements: accordions, electric guitars, bass clarinets, exotic percussion instruments of various kinds; Western-style harmonizations of Arab maqam-based melodies; novel musical textures and composition and arrangement techniques. The late 1940s and early 1950s, however, saw a stylistic shift in his music, with greater emphasis placed on distinctly Arab-Egyptian–derived musical elements.

"Zeina," represented here in an arrangement by Hossam Ramzy from his tribute album to 'Abd al-Wahhab (**CD ex. #3-13**), is a good example of this. It has a maqam-based melody (in *Maqam Hijaz,* roughly D E♭ F♯ G A B♭ C [D] in Western pitch terms) featuring standard Arab-Egyptian forms of melodic ornamentation. The firqa instrumentation includes Western instruments but gives most prominent voice to traditional Arab instruments like the qanun, the nay, and Arab percussion. Most importantly for our purposes, Egyptian dance rhythms played on the standard Arab percussion instruments provide the rhythmic foundation throughout.

The arrangement begins with an introduction featuring a syncopated melody played on the qanun (zither). Each qanun phrase is "answered" by the string section (violins, cellos); during the second statement of the melody (0:11–0:20), the riqq (Arab tambourine) doubles the qanun's rhythm. At 0:21, the main melody arrives in the form of a sultry, heavily ornamented performance on the nay (flute), with swooping melodic answers provided by the string section (four violins and two cellos, plus qanun) in a call-and-response musical dialogue. The strings take the lead melody at some points (0:42–0:46, 0:56–1:06).

The percussion section comes in at 0:21 too, led by the tabla. The first rhythm heard is one of the most popular and important in raqs baladi, raqs sharqi, and belly dance. It is called **masmoudi** (or *masmudi*) and features the ostinato pattern of dum and tek strokes illustrated above in Figure 12.2.

masmoudi (mas-MOO-dee)

The masmoudi rhythm and the medium-slow tempo at which it is played provide a perfect match for the sensuous melody of the nay. Indeed, masmoudi (a.k.a. "slow maqsoum"—see "Insights and Perspectives" box on p. 275) is very appropriate for dances requiring an especially intimate character. For example, when a woman marries, she may perform a special dance for her new husband that reveals, to quote Al-Rawi (1999:141), "the full bloom of her femininity." Masmoudi is often the accompanying rhythm for such dancing, and likewise for segments of raqs sharqi and belly dance routines and cinematic dance numbers that invoke a similarly sensuous mood and character.

At 1:07 of "Zeina," the nay flute melody is repeated (i.e., *varied* repetition) over the continuing masmoudi groove. This time, however, the rhythmic accompaniment is enhanced by the rhythms played on a *quarter-tone accordion,* which is basically a standard accordion modified to accomodate the microtonal intervals of Arab music.

Then, at 1:52, there is a dramatic transformation. A sudden upward jump in tempo occurs, the rhythm changes, sagat (finger cymbals) enter the texture prominently, and (beginning at

A Rhythm by Any Other Name

The names assigned to the various Egyptian dance rhythms can vary. For example, masmoudi comes in several forms other than the one charted out in Figure 12.2, including this one:

Beat:	1				2				1				2			
Strokes:	**Dum**	Dum		tek	**Dum**		tek	tek	**Dum**	Dum		tek	**Dum**		tek	tek

and this longer one:

Beat:	1				2				3				4			
Strokes:	**Dum**		Dum		**Dum**		tek	tek	**Dum**		tek	tek			tek	tek

Moreover, the rhythm identified in the Guided Listening Experience for "Zeina" as masmoudi, that is:

Beat:	1				2				1				2			
Strokes:	**Dum**	Dum		tek	**Dum**		tek		**Dum**	Dum		tek	**Dum**		tek	

is sometimes identified by a different name, **maqsoum** (or *maqsum*) [mak-SOOM], though this is a rhythm that more usually takes the following form:

Beat:	1				2				1				2			
Strokes:	**Dum**	tek		tek	**Dum**		tek		**Dum**	tek		tek	**Dum**		tek	

Accounting for variance and ambiguity in the terminologies surrounding music is a common challenge faced by ethnomusicologists. This is but one of many possible examples.

1:55) the quarter-tone accordion, playing a new melody, replaces the nay as the lead melodic voice. The new rhythm for this contrasting section of the piece may sound familiar to you, since it is the same rhythm, zaar (ayyoub), that was featured in **CD ex. #3-9** earlier. Here, the zaar rhythm is played at an upbeat tempo, with the percussion instruments reinforced by an electric bass part. Compare this to the fast-tempoed zaar rhythm heard at 1:53 of **CD ex. #3-9.** Aside from the presence of the electric bass and the accordion, the two are virtually identical: in rhythm, tempo, and instrumenation.

Notably, this "zaar" section of "Zeina" was not part of the 'Abd al-Wahhab original version that Samia Gamal danced to in *Zannouba*. (Moreover, the original film version featured a vocalist, which this one does not.) Rather, it is a creative addition to the piece contributed by Hossam Ramzy. Its purpose in the arrangement, according to Ramzy, is to reinforce, even deepen, "Zeina's" baladi essence, in other words, its Egyptian folk root. Describing "Zeina" in the CD booklet, Ramzy states that "It sounds like a classical [Arab] song to the uneducated ear but it is a 100% Baladi and traditional piece, hence the ZAAR part (the Ayyoub rhythm) in the middle . . ." (Ramzy 1995:2).

As the zaar portion of the arrangement unfolds, it does so in an AA'BB' AA'BB' form (eight measures per lettered section), with the A sections dominated by accordion melody and the

B sections led by the nay flute and the string section together (see the Guided Listening Quick Summary). Then, at 3:00, there is a sudden break, followed by a flourish on the qanun and a return to the original "Zeina" melody and the slow, masmoudi rhythm. The melody this time is played by the accordion and the other melodic instruments of the ensemble (nay, qanun, violins, and cellos) in heterophony (i.e., variant versions of the same melody) as the excerpt fades out.

---

guided listening quick summary

"Zeina," by Muhammad 'Abd al-Wahhab* [*arrangement/performance: Hossam Ramzy and group] (CD ex. #3-13)

INTRODUCTION

0:00–0:20

- Syncopated melody, qanun; strings (violins, cellos) "answer" qanun in-between phrases; riqq doubles qanun rhythm in second half (0:11–0:20).
- Melody maqam-based (Maqam Hijaz, roughly D E♭ F♯ G A B♭ C [D]).

"ZEINA" MELODY, FIRST STATEMENT

0:21–1:06

- Percussion instruments (tabla, riqq, etc.) enter here, establishing slow-tempoed masmoudi rhythmic groove: ‖ D D - t D - t - ‖.
- Highly ornamented main melody played by nay, with string section (violins, cellos) "answering" in the spaces between nay phrases.
- Strings (violins, cellos, plus qanun) take over lead melody in some parts (0:42–0:46, 0:56–1:06).

"ZEINA" MELODY, SECOND STATEMENT

1:07–1:51

- As before, but with variations and rhythmic reinforcement from the quarter-tone accordion.

FAST ZAAR SECTION

1:52–2:59

- Zaar rhythm ‖ D - - t D - t -‖ in percussion section played at a much faster tempo than the preceding masmoudi rhythm. Sagat (finger cymbals) prominent.
- Quarter-tone accordion takes lead melody for **A** sections (1:55–2:11, 2:28–2:44); melodic call-and-response between nay-plus-strings and accordion in **B** sections (2:12–2:27, 2:44–2:59).

REPRISE OF "ZEINA" MELODY

3:00–end

- Following brief pause and qanun flourish, the masmoudi rhythm is reestablished.
- Melody now played in heterophony (variant versions of a single melody) between the accordion and other instruments as the music fades out at end of excerpt.

The Post-Independence Era

The political climate in Egypt in 1950 that surrounded the release of films like *Zannouba* was a tense one. Many Egyptians had grown increasingly weary of King Faruq (whose favorite dancer, incidentally, was Samia Gamal) and what they regarded as his puppet monarchy. Britain's continuing stronghold over Egypt fostered ever-greater resentment and resistance among the Egyptian population. The declaration of the Jewish state of Israel in 1948 proved especially inflammatory in both regards. The British had supported the founding of Israel, and Faruq's ineffectiveness in blocking this development, combined with Egypt's dismal failure in the 1948 war against Israel, had a devastating impact.

The eventual outcome of all of this was the "bloodless revolution" of 1952, which was led by an Egyptian military commander named Gamal 'Abd al-Nasser. 'Abd al-Nasser and his secretly organized Revolutionary Command Council (RCC) orchestrated a largely peaceful takeover of Egypt. They marched into government offices, national radio stations, and the offices of major utility providers and took control of these institutions with little resistance. They were greeted with broad popular support. Faruq and the constitutional monarchy fell, British troops left the country in large numbers, and the Arab Republic of Egypt was declared an independent nation in that same year (1952). 'Abd al-Nasser ascended to the presidency in 1954 and remained in that position until his death in 1970.

Cultural nationalism and the baladi folk ideal in post-revolutionary Egypt

'Abd al-Nasser's cultural nationalism agenda placed a great emphasis on the support and promotion of Egyptian baladi, or "folk" culture. Ambitious initiatives aimed at preserving and cultivating "authentic folk culture" were undertaken. Baladi became an important symbol of both the new nationalist Egyptian identity and the roots of that identity in the Egyptian past. This applied to music, dance, and folk rituals and ceremonies of all kinds.

Contrastingly, the raqs sharqi world of professional female dance entertainment suffered under 'Abd al-Nasser. Growing anti-Western sentiment and the institutionalization of Arab-Islamic mores into the new Egyptian nationalist ideology contributed to the closing or destruction of many of Cairo's major casinos, nightclubs, cinemas, and places of Western entertainment. Casino Badiaa shut down, and Badiaa Masabni herself left Egypt and returned to her native Lebanon. Summarizing the situation, anthropologist Karin van Nieuwkerk explains that "['Abd al-]Nasser's postrevolutionary Arab nationalism and Islamic socialism prompted a reappraisal of Arabic culture. Folk art, folk music, and folk dance, all of which glorified traditional Arabic culture, were revived. Belly dancers [i.e., Egyptian raqs sharqi dancers] were seen as a bad advertisement for Arabic Muslim womanhood" (van Nieuwkerk 1995:48).

fallahin (fah-la-HEEN)

Musicians, at least the leading media stars of the Egyptian music world, fared much better than raqs sharqi dancers. Both Muhammad 'Abd al-Wahhab and Umm Kulthum benefited from 'Abd al-Nasser's patronage. In 'Abd al-Nasser's Egypt, 'Abd al-Wahhab became an icon of Egyptian musical modernity done right (though not one devoid of controversy) while Umm Kulthum was canonized as the embodiment of traditional Egyptian virtues and contemporary pan-Arab ideals.

The 'Abd al-Nasser–Umm Kulthum connection was especially close. Each cultivated a charismatic public persona emphasizing humble roots in the rural countryside and an abiding commitment to the common Egyptian people. Especially central in both cases was identification with the peasant classes, or **fallahin,** who were romantically idealized as authentic (asil) Egyptians of *un*common virtue and held up as models to be emulated by Egyptians of all classes. Umm Kulthum both promoted herself and was promoted by others as an icon of "peasant" virtues. Regarding her work ethic, for example, a longtime musical collaborator of Umm Kulthum fondly recalled how, during recording sessions, she "was the first to arrive and the last to leave. . . . She had the tirelessness of the peasant . . . and exerted the effort of [one] if the case required it" (c.f. Danielson 1997:131).

Singer Umm Kulthum, "The Voice of Egypt."

Farida Fahmy performing with the Reda Troupe in "peasant" costume.

Farida Fahmy and the Reda Troupe

In the late 1950s and especially through the 1960s, a dancer, Farida Fahmy, transcended the conventional "erotic and disdained image of the female dancer" in Egypt (Franken 1998:265) to become a national symbol and a heroic figure of Egyptian virtue almost on a par with the legendary Umm Kulthum herself. Farida was the lead dancer of the famed Reda Troupe, a pioneering folkloric dance troupe formed by her father, Mahmoud Reda, in 1959. The performance medium of the Reda Troupe built from the roots of peasant (*fallahin*) and other folk dances of the Nile Valley, Upper Egypt (the Saaid), and other parts of Egypt. These were combined in formally staged performances with modern elements, Western influences, and a strong current of Egyptian nationalistic pride. Two films made by the Reda Troupe, *Igazat nuss al-sana* (Mid-Year Holiday) of 1961 and *Gharam fi-l-Karnak* (Love in Karnak) of 1964, were especially influential.

'Abd al-Nasser actively promoted the Reda Troupe and showcased them on major state occasions that aimed

Farida Fahmy (Fah-RI-da Fah-MEE)

Reda (Re-DAH)

***Igazat nuss al-sana** (Ah-gah-zaht nos-ahs-sana)*

***Gharam fi-l-Karnak** (Ghah-ram fil karrnuk [roll the double r])*

to emphasize "the integrity, validity, and artistic worth of indigenous Egyptian culture, free in Egyptian eyes from Western themes and ideals" (Franken 1998:277). There was a certain irony in this, in that Western influences and aesthetics were prevalent in the Reda Troupe's approach, and Farida and other performers of the troupe were in fact people quite far removed from the indigenous, rural baladi world of which they became official representatives. Yet this was also a large part of the appeal for Egyptians from many walks of life:

> Farida Fahmy, daughter of a university professor, graduate of the elite English School and Cairo University, whose mother was English and paternal grandfather an estate manager for King Faruq, married to a film director—Farida Fahmy danced in the dress of a Delta peasant girl, covered her head with traditional veils, wore her hair in long plaits that whirled as she danced like any village girl. This was a spectacle indeed, and Egyptians of all ranks were drawn by curiosity, wonder, admiration, and above all a sense of affinity, to see Farida and the Reda dancers. (Franken 1998:278)

Folk dance rhythms in raqs sharqi and belly dance: Fallahi and Saaidi

The popular entertainment worlds of raqs sharqi and international belly dance came strongly under the influence of the Reda Troupe and other folkloric dance troupes that issued in its wake. Raqs sharqi dancers in Egypt and elsewhere in the Arab world, as well as belly dancers worldwide, now incorporate "folkloric dances" of different kinds into their nightclub acts and stage routines. As Egyptian dance historian Marjorie Franken notes, "What began as an elevation of the folk dance of Egypt by a Westernized elite in the nationalism of the postrevolutionary period has ended in the spread and adoption of this dance into various popular entertainments" (Franken 1998:279).

fallahi (fah-lah-HEE)

This popular interest in folklore has resulted in the adoption and adaptation of certain dance rhythms identified with Egyptian folk culture. These include **fallahi** (from *fallahin,* "peasant"), an upbeat rhythm that is traditionally used in accompaniment of songs and dances of celebration performed during agricultural rituals of Nile Delta farmers. It is lively and played at a quick tempo in a simple two-beat (duple) meter (Figure 12.3). (*Note:* The basic rhythmic pattern of fallahi is identical to that of the standard maqsoum [see the "Insights and Perspectives" box on p. 275]; fallahi is played much faster, however.) **CD ex. #3-14** is an illustration of the fallahi rhythm played by a full Arab percussion section. The recording features Hossam Ramzy.

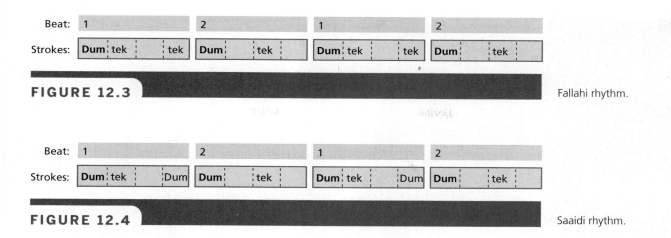

FIGURE 12.3   Fallahi rhythm.

FIGURE 12.4   Saaidi rhythm.

Another very popular folk dance rhythm is **Saaidi** (*Saidi*). Where the fallahi rhythm connotes rural, folk roots of the Nile Delta region, the Saaidi rhythm connotes the traditional baladi culture of Upper Egypt, or the Saaid (Said). This rhythm is closely linked to **tahtib,** a form of martial arts traditionally practiced by men in Upper Egypt that has existed for several thousand years and is represented on tomb paintings from Ancient Egypt. Tahtib opponents wield a long, thick bamboo or wood stave called an *'asaya* (see photo on p. 280). The 'asaya is about 45 inches in length and three to four inches around. It is grasped firmly in one or both fists and is a formidable and dangerous weapon in the hands of a skilled practitioner when used in actual fighting. Most commonly, however, tahtib is practiced as a pastime rather than as a form of true combat. In this recreational format, strict rules are enforced to ensure avoidance of serious injury or death on the part of the tahtib "players." In this respect, tahtib might be compared to fencing in the West, in that both derive from potentially fatal forms of fighting but have been transformed into relatively benign forms of sporting combat.

Beyond the two contexts of actual fighting and sportlike sparring, there is a third type of tahtib called *dance with stick* (*raqs bil-'asaya*). This dance is usually performed prior to or following a tahtib match. It "allows a player to demonstrate skill, inventiveness, and musicality in the manipulation of his weapon, alone or in an ensemble [including other stick players]" (Saleh 2002:631). A large number of different movements and maneuvers are used as the player issues a sequence of blows (stick strikes) and parries (deflections of strikes). These include a variety of leaps, hopping motions, and stances and poses intended to protect different parts of the body from attack (Saleh 2002:631). The sequence of blows, parries, and maneuvers between opponents is delivered in a quasi-choreographed, quasi-improvised manner to the accompaniment of music grounded in the energizing, medium-tempoed groove of the Saaidi rhythm. In traditional contexts, this rhythm is performed on a drum called a *tabl baladi,* which is struck with a stick. (In other contexts, the tabla or other drums are used in substitution.) The two Dum strokes in the middle of the pattern (see Figure 12.4 above) give Saaidi rhythm its distinctive, signature sound. Melodies played on one or more aerophones called *mizmar* are often performed overtop a Saaidi rhythmic accompaniment. The mizmar has a strident, wailing tone that is very characteristic of Upper Egyptian folk music.

The same type of mizmar-plus-percussion texture set to Saaidi rhythm also is used to accompany the "dancing" of Arabian stallions in Upper Egypt. **CD ex. #3-15,** an excerpt of a Hossam Ramzy piece called "Arabian Knights" (a reference to the stallions), offers an illustration of Saaidi rhythm, which is performed here on the standard Arab percussion instruments in the accompaniment of mizmar melody.

Like fallahi, Saaidi has become a staple rhythm of raqs baladi, raqs sharqi, and belly dance. The traditional baladi form of the women's **cane dance** (*raqs 'al-asaya*), which originated in the

Saaidi (Sah-ayi-DEE)

tahtib (tah-TEEB)

raqs bil-'asaya (ra[k]s bil ah-SAH-yah)

mizmar (miz-MAHR)

raqs 'al-asaya (ra[k]s al-ah-SAH-yah)

Tahtib.

The cane dance.

Saaid long ago, derives from tahtib. As dancer and dance scholar Shira explains, the martial art of tahtib "inspired the women of the Said to create their own 'stick' dance. The women's cane dance is a playful parody of the men's martial art. The women's raks al assaya ['asaya] movements are playful, feminine, and flirtatious" (Shira 2000:82). This folk dance, in turn, gave rise to the ubiquitous cane dance, or stick dance, of raqs sharqi and belly dance routines, in which the phallic symbolism of the cane may be played up to humorous effect.

The *Tabla Solo* Dance

An important neo-traditional innovation of the modern era of raqs sharqi and belly dance has been the genre of solo dance known as **Tabla Solo.** The *Tabla Solo* dance was "invented" and first popularized by the Egyptian dancer Nagwa Fu'ad and her long-time tabla accompanist Ahmed Hammouda in the 1970s. (Ahmed's brother, Mahmoud Hammouda, was Hossam Ramzy's Egyptian drumming mentor.) Nagwa Fu'ad was a famous, albeit notorious, dancer. Like Samia Gamal and Tahia Carioca, she was one of the great star dancer/actresses of Egyptian commercial film. The persona she cultivated on screen was an especially licentious one, however. She often was cast as a prostitute who uses the allure of her dancing to seduce another woman's husband. As Franken explains, Nagwa Fu'ad "made explicit the contrast between acceptable female social dance and dangerous, seductive, illicit dance" that has long been articulated in public perceptions of female dancers in Egypt (Franken 1998:268).

Following its introduction by Nagwa Fu'ad and Ahmed Hammouda, the *Tabla Solo,* which essentially comprises an exciting dance suite set to a series of different rhythms played on percussion instruments exclusively (sometimes just on a single tabla), achieved tremendous popularity in the raqs sharqi and belly dance worlds. Today, inclusion of a *Tabla Solo* number is a

Beat:	1		2		1		2	
Strokes:	**Dum**	tek		tek	**Dum**	tek		tek

FIGURE 12.5   Malfuf rhythm.

standard feature of raqs sharqi/belly dance performances. It is, in fact, typically the climactic number of the dance routine.

Tabla Solo in a raqs sharqi dance routine

In a standard, Egyptian-style raqs sharqi performance, the *Tabla Solo* is usually the second-to-last item on the program. The performance normally begins with a quick-tempoed introductory dance set to music featuring a lively, two-beat rhythm called **malfuf** (**CD ex. #3-16** and Figure 12.5, above). As she comes onto the stage, the dancer wears some version of a Hollywood-type raqs sharqi costume—sequined bra, low-slung skirt, bare midriff. She may hold in both hands a diaphonous veil, which trails behind her in the air as she enters. (This feature of the dance is one of many first introduced by Samia Gamal.) Walking and spinning as she swirls the veil around her, she dances for about a minute before discarding it. At this point, malfuf generally segues into a different rhythm, such as maqsoum or masmoudi. The dance becomes highly virtuosic and the music complex, with abundant changes in rhythm, breaks, and stops that show off the dancer's expertise.

malfuf (mahl-FOOF)

Following this opening dance, the dancer leaves the stage and returns in a folkloric costume for a more traditional number. The cane dance is a popular choice, and the music exhibits a strong Saaidi flavor, usually featuring the Saaidi rhythm. The cane dance is followed by two or more additional dance numbers. Each contrasts with the others in terms of style, character, costuming, and music. A variety of tempos and moods, from slow and sultry to fast and feisty, accompanies a diverse array of dance movements: hip circles, shoulder shimmies, figure eights, snake arms (see photo), head slides, stomach rolls. (Visit the Online Learning Center at www.mhhe.com/bakan1 to see illustrative photographs of the dance movements.) Then the dancer leaves the stage and returns once more, this time for the *Tabla Solo* dance, "the final climax in a series of dance climaxes" (Buonaventura 1989:191).

For the *Tabla Solo* dance, the dancer and a solo tabla player (or an ensemble of percussionists led by a tabla player) engage in a playful and mutually reflective duet of rhythmic movement and percussive sound (see the photo on p. 282). The music moves from one rhythm to another to create a kind of rhythmic suite that usually lasts for between two and four minutes. The dancer stands right beside the tabla player throughout the performance, covering little if any floor space while moving all the different parts of her body in a complex polyphony of movement that forms a near-exact visual match to the sonic complexities of the musical rhythm. Every different timbre in the percussive texture is highlighted by a different move, a different part of the body. The virtuosity of expression and integration of dance and rhythmic sound in a first-rate *Tabla Solo* dance are marvels to behold.

There is no true leader or follower in the *Tabla Solo*. At its best, it is an idiom in which movement and sound, dancer and drummer, merge as dual manifestations of a single artistic

A dancer strikes a "snake arms" pose.

A *Tabla Solo* dance performance.

expression. The music is "full of syncopation and offbeat accents, providing an opportunity for playfulness and intense [shoulder] shimmies" on the part of the dancer (Donald 2000:176). Rhythmic accents and flourishes come at a fast and furious pace, and the drummer will often play a single figure several times in a row to give the dancer "a better chance of catching the accents with [her] hips" (Donald 2000:177).

The dancer and tabla player appear almost as two lovers, enticing and wooing each other at one moment, chiding and cajoling one another the next. A humorous, flirtatious atmosphere is generated between the two as they coax and challenge each other through the sequence of rhythmic changes.

The audience is no silent partner in the affair either. As Buonaventura explains,

> This is one of the most popular parts of a dance for the audience, which responds instinctively to the hard-hitting, playful rhythms. The drum solo [*Tabla Solo*] is outgoing and bold, and if a dancer has a good rapport with her *tabla* player it can be the most enjoyable part of the dance for her. When the audience is clapping along and the music is good, she can be inspired by their support and feedback to bring out that aspect of the dance which is uniquely concerned with sharing its humour and playfulness directly with the audience. (Buonaventura 1989:191)

guided listening experience

"Belhadawa Walla Belshaawa?" (*Tabla Solo*), Hossam Ramzy

- CD Track #**3-17**
- Featured performer(s)/group: Hossam Ramzy (all parts)
- Format: Complete track
- Source recording: *Sabla Tolo: Journeys into Pure Egyptian Percussion,* by Hossam Ramzy (ARC Music Productions International Ltd. EUCD 1581)

In the year 2000, Hossam Ramzy produced a wonderful CD on the ARC label featuring 13 original *Tabla Solo* compositions, several of them inspired by and dedicated to great dancers such as Samia Gamal and Tahia Carioca. The title of the album is *Sabla Tolo* (a play on "Tabla Solo"). It is used by belly dancers worldwide to accompany their *Tabla Solo* dance numbers. (Dancers do not always have the luxury of performing with their own percussionists "live.") On this album, Ramzy plays all of the instruments: the various Middle Eastern percussion instruments as well as a host of others. All of the parts were overdubbed in a multitrack recording studio.

One of the pieces featured on *Sabla Tolo* is "Belhadawa Walla Belshaawa?" In the CD booklet, a translation of "Rough or Cool?" is given. "Belhadawa Walla Belshaawa?" features most of the Egyptian dance rhythms introduced in this chapter (Figure 12.6), as well as several others. It offers an excellent opportunity to hear the different rhythms we have been

Masmoudi (0:19–0:38)* — Dum Dum | tek | Dum | tek

Malfuf (0:55–1:02, 1:09–1:16) — Dum | tek | tek | Dum | tek | tek

Fallahi (1:02–1:09, 1:16–1:23) — Dum tek | tek | Dum | tek | Dum tek | tek | Dum | tek

Fast zaar (2:09–2:23) — Dum | tek | Dum | tek | Dum | tek | Dum | tek

Saaidi (2:23–3:18)† — Dum tek | Dum | Dum | tek | Dum tek | Dum | Dum | tek

* The section labeled masmoudi here is identified in the *Sabla Tolo* CD liner notes as maqsoum (as per the varied terminologies for different rhythms discussed earlier in the chapter). The rhythm is notated in "half-time" tempo (compare to Figure 12.2 on p. 274) to better illustrate how it relates to the other dance rhythms in the context of this performance.

† The Saaidi passages feature call-and-response dialogue between the solo tabla and the rest of the ensemble, and also

FIGURE 12.6

Dance rhythms featured in "Belhadawa Walla Belshaawa?"

exploring combined together in an exciting, all-percussion format. As you listen, follow the timeline of the Guided Listening Quick Summary and try to identify these rhythms as they come up. Wherever you can, clap the basic rhythmic patterns of Figure 12.6 together with the recording.

guided listening quick summary

"Belhadawa Walla Belshaawa?" (*Tabla Solo*), Hossam Ramzy (CD ex. #3-17)

0:00–0:19: Introduction

■ Starts with call-and-response between the tabla and the rest of the ensemble (0:00–0:10).

■ Call-and-response opening is followed by a tabla solo (0:11–0:19) that sets up the slow tempo and dance rhythm groove of what immediately follows.

0:19–0:38: Masmoudi (a.k.a. slow maqsoum)

■ Full ensemble re-enters here.

0:39–0:55: Reprise of Introduction

■ Starts with same call-and-response material as at beginning; this time, though, the tabla solo (which starts at 0:49) sets up a fast tempo for the Malfuf section that follows and is quite flashy and virtuosic.

0:55–1:02: Malfuf

1:02–1:09: Fallahi

1:09–1:16: Malfuf

1:16–1:23: Fallahi

1:23–2:09: Several sections featuring other dance rhythms

2:09–2:23: Fast zaar

2:23–3:18: Saaidi

■ Includes some passages with "basic" Saaidi rhythm, as well as others featuring Saaidi rhythmic variants.

■ Some sections with full ensemble; others with call-and-response between tabla and rest of ensemble.

3:18–end: Ending section

■ Like the first part of the Introduction, but at a considerably faster tempo.

From Cairo to Mexico

Listen to the brief excerpt of **CD ex. #3-18.** Can you recognize the rhythm from this short musical snippet? It is malfuf. How about the instruments? They include the standard membranophones and idiophones of the Arab-Egyptian percussion section: tabla, doholla, sagat, and so on. We are clearly in familiar musical terrain for this chapter.

Now listen to CD **ex. #3-19,** which begins exactly like the preceding track but then continues from there. You arrive at 0:09. Surprise! The malfuf groove carries on, but now it is surrounded by the sounds of South American panpipes, a chord progression played on guitar, a melody in a major key. There is not a maqam, an Arab-style melodic ornament, or a nonpercussion Egyptian instrument anywhere to be found. And then you get to 0:25 and, lo and behold, it turns out that everything leading up to this point has just been an elaborate setup for that famous Egyptian—pardon me, *Mexican*—tune "La Cucaracha" (The Cockroach). You would expect this song to be played by a group like the mariachi band featured on **CD ex. #1-21,** but you would not likely think of it as a musical accompaniment to a belly dance routine.

Pablo Cárcamo with his zampoña.

Yet, with its malfuf rhythmic foundation and Egyptian percussion-grounded texture, that is exactly what this arrangement of "La Cucaracha" is intended for. It is one of 20 such numbers featured on one of Hossam Ramzy's most popular recordings, *Latin American Hits for Bellydance* (ARC Music Productions International Ltd. EUCD 1646).

Ramzy's traditional Egyptian malfuf groove (created, once again, with the aid of multitrack overdubbing) gives a fresh face to this old chestnut of a Mexican/international tune. So too does the prominent use of the *zampoña,* or Chilean panpipes, which, along with the guitar and other nonpercussion instruments, are all played (again, overdubbed) by the Chilean multi-instrumentalist, composer, and arranger Pablo Cárcamo. (Ramzy and Cárcamo are the only two musicians who play on the album; Cárcamo is credited with all of the arrangements.)

There is not all that much that needs to be discussed here. The main "point" to get is simply the fusing of the Egyptian rhythms and the song "La Cucaracha" itself. Belly dance music recording artists like Hossam Ramzy are catering to a huge international market of dancers. They and their audiences represent a diverse lot, coming from a wide range of backgrounds and musical tastes. Some want to dance to the most ardently traditional baladi music, others to the more orchestrated sounds of pieces like "Zeina," others to lighthearted transcontinental romps like this version of "La Cucaracha," and a good many more to all of the above. Most people who belly dance or attend belly dance performances—whether in France or Finland, Caracas or Canada—do so for one reason above all others: to have fun. "La Cucaracha," as heard here, is by no means a profound work of musical art. But it *is* fun, and it is very popular within the belly dance world for which it was created. It is, therefore, *an important piece of music,* for the simple reason that it serves its community of listeners in a significant and meaningful way.

Interpretation of the piece's significance may follow a different trajectory as well, one informed by the history of Egyptian dance music we have explored. You will recall that it was the great Muhammad 'Abd al-Wahhab, composer of "Zeina" and cultural hero of the Egyptian people, who first ventured across musical oceans via his dance compositions by infusing Arab-Egyptian music with Latin American rhythms. Ramzy inverts that formula here, infusing a familiar old song *from* Latin America with an Egyptian rhythmic character.

Commenting on the rejuvenating, life-affirming role of belly dance in contemporary Western society, Rosina-Fawzia Al-Rawi states:

> In this historical phase of searching and testing, dancing has regained its role, long lacking, in the official body of socially acknowledged forms of physical expression. It is a sensual instrument that wants to enjoy life in the here and now. By intensifying the moment, dancing facilitates the development and finding of the self beyond any anxieties about the future or burdens from the past. . . . Dancing has thus completed its transformation from the realm of the sacred to the aesthetic and artistic and back to a joyful, sensual, and playful instrument for self-discovery. (Al-Rawi 1999:53)

It is on such a note of joyful playfulness that we end this chapter's journey. So enjoy "La Cucaracha," and get up and dance if you dare!

Summary

In this musicultural journey through the world of Egyptian and Egyptian-derived women's dance and the music that accompanies it, we focused on three domains of dance—raqs baladi, raqs sharqi, and international belly dance—and on common percussion rhythms and instruments used in dance accompaniment. The music we encountered was mainly by a single musical artist, Hossam Ramzy, though it encompassed a wide range of genres and styles. We explored a zaar-inspired percussion piece, an arrangement of a Muhammad 'Abd al-Wahhab dance composition originally created for Samia Gamal in the film *Zannouba,* a *Tabla Solo* composition by Ramzy, and a belly dance arrangement of "La Cucaracha" with Egyptian rhythms and percussion.

Situating the history of Egyptian women's dance in the context of Egyptian cultural and political history, we explored the controversial status of women dancers and their art in Egyptian society and in the Arab-Islamic world more broadly. We also saw how this status has been complicated by Orientalist representations of Middle Eastern dancers in the West, and how agendas of nationalism, internationalism, traditionalism, modernism, folklorization, Arabization, and Westernization have impacted the reputations and the rights and opportunities of dancers during different periods and under different circumstances.

Women's dance and the music that accompanies it are important parts of Egyptian cultural heritage and conceptions of Egyptianness on an international scale, yet their status has traditionally been marginal. This chapter has attempted to both celebrate this great cultural legacy and examine some of the issues and complexities that surround it.

Key Terms

riqq

raqs sharqi

belly dance

tabla (Egyptian)

raqs baladi

zaar

Orientalist (Orientalism)

maqam

Qur'anic recitation

quarter tone

Egyptian nationalism

ghawazi

baladi (folk heritage)

sagat

Dum, tek (drum strokes)

firqa (firqa musiqyya)

takht

masmoudi

maqsoum

fallahin

fallahi

Saaidi

tahtib

cane dance

Tabla Solo (dance/music form)

malfuf

Study Questions

- What are raqs baladi, raqs sharqi, and belly dance? In what ways are these three domains of dance tradition related? In what ways do they differ?

- What are the standard drums and other percussion instruments used in the accompaniment of Egyptian women's dance music? What is the name of the lead drum? What were the main dance rhythms discussed and illustrated in the chapter?

- Who is Hossam Ramzy? What accounts for his significance—and for his controversial status—as a representative of Egyptian musical tradition?

- Why might the choice of Egyptian women's dance and dance music as the basis for an introductory textbook chapter on music of the Middle East be regarded as controversial by some?

- According to Al-Rawi, when and in what form did the ancient forerunners of modern Middle Eastern women's dance likely emerge? How is the legacy of ancient dance rituals carried on in women's gatherings today?

- What is a maqam? Give two examples of maqamat and write out the basic scale of pitches for each.

- What religion and language are dominant throughout the Arab Middle East?

- What foreign powers successively dominated Egypt over the course of many centuries through to the mid-20th century? How did this history of foreign domination ultimately influence the attitudes and cultural values of Egyptian nationalism?

- What is a ghawazi? What are the main theories concerning how the ghawazi first came to Egypt? What is the literal meaning of the word *ghawazi* and how is this significant in terms of understanding the perception of professional female dancers in Egypt?

- What occurs during a zaar ritual? What function does the ritual serve? How does music contribute and what kind of music is played?

- What was the aesthetic ideal for Egyptian music forged by Sayyid Darwish? How did this ideal connect to broader currents of Egyptian nationalism?

- When did the Egyptian film industry emerge and what was its impact?

- What were the significant contributions and innovations of Muhammad 'Abd al-Wahhab, Badiaa Masabni, Samia Gamal, Umm Kulthum, Farida Fahmy, and Nagwa Fu'ad to Egyptian music, dance, culture, and national identity?

- What is a *Tabla Solo* dance and where does it usually occur during a typical raqs sharqi dance routine?

- What is distinctive about the rhythmic approach in the recording of the Mexican song "La Cucaracha" featured in this chapter?

Discussion Questions

- The image of the "belly dancer" has become a significant international emblem of Western popular culture. In what contexts have you encountered belly dance images or references in your own life? What, in your opinion, have such images and references been used to symbolize, and what cultural impressions do they engender?

- Beyond its specific subject matter, a fundamental issue explored in this chapter is the relationship between dance and musical rhythm. How do dancing and the rhythms of music animate one another and define cultural meaning in dance/music contexts with which you are familiar?

Applying What You Have Learned

- Even today, stereotypical "Orientalist" depictions of the Middle East abound in popular culture: on television, in movies, in "Middle Eastern"–influenced pop tunes. Spend some time over the course of a week watching TV and films, listening to the radio, surfing the Internet. Document what kinds of "Middle Eastern" images you encounter (if any). Describe what these reveal about contemporary Western representations of, and attitudes toward, Islamic and Arab cultures. Discuss how what you observe and hear in doing this project relates to, or perhaps contradicts, what you have learned in this chapter.

- Go back and listen to CD musical examples from this chapter in random order. Try to identify the different rhythms you hear by name and try to mark out their basic rhythmic patterns as you listen. Play with creating your own *Tabla Solo*–like composition by stringing together a series of different dance rhythms one after the other without pause.

Resources for Further Study

Visit the Online Learning Center at **www.mhhe.com/bakan1** for learning aids, study help, and additional resources that supplement the content of this chapter.

chapter thirteen

a **musicultural** history of the **Chinese zheng**

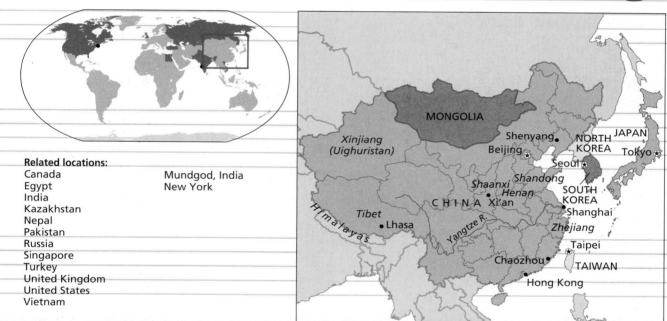

Related locations:

Canada
Egypt
India
Kazakhstan
Nepal
Pakistan
Russia
Singapore
Turkey
United Kingdom
United States
Vietnam

Mundgod, India
New York

**Deng Haiqiong
(Dung High-chee-
ong)**

**zheng (jung [rhymes
with "lung"])**

It has been a long day at the conference. Finally, it is dinnertime, and a lavish banquet has been promised. I, along with several hundred other musicologists gathered in the large dining hall, am famished. All day long we have been listening to each other play music, analyze music, dissect music in every way imaginable. Now it is time to eat. Music can wait until tomorrow.

Yet, this being a musicology conference, there is the obligatory conference banquet musical program, in this case a mini-recital of Chinese music featuring a performer named Deng Haiqiong playing on a zither-type chordophone called the **zheng.** Amidst the clatter of dishes and the chatter of music professors, few of us digging into our just-arrived chicken *cordon bleu* take much notice as an elegant young lady splendidly attired in a full-length

World events	Date	Music events
Earliest Chinese dynasties; emergence of ancient Chinese civilization	**16th century** BCE	
Lifetime of Confucius (551–479 BCE)	**5th century** BCE	Earliest known progenitors of the modern *zheng* (archaeological evidence)
Unification and imperial expansion of China under the Qin dynasty	**3rd century** BCE	Zheng spreads and becomes a popular instrument in many regions of China
	237 BCE	Earliest known written reference to the zheng (Qin era manuscript)
Han dynasty spreads eastward	**202** BCE–**220** CE	Zheng gains in popularity
Confucianism established as foundation of Chinese social order		*Qin* zither becomes instrument of noble and educated classes
Buddhism enters China (1st century CE) and spreads eastward		
Tang dynasty	**618–907**	Huge government music ministry (over 30,000 musicians and dancers from throughout the empire and beyond employed)
Vast imperial expansion; Silk Road		
		Apogee of zheng
		Pipa introduced into Chinese music, becomes closely associated with zheng
Ming dynasty	**1368–1644**	Regional Chinese opera forms flourish
Emergence of large Chinese middle class		Zheng: favored among middle classes (especially young females); important regional opera ensemble instrument
Qing dynasty	**1644–1911**	Beijing Opera (from 18th century)
Last of the Chinese dynasties		Westernization (musically, culturally, politically)
		Regional solo zheng styles (19th century)
Republican era	**1912–1949**	Major cultural reform efforts, including music: Western music as model
Declaration of the Republic of China	**January 1, 1912**	
	1936	"Return of the Fishing Boats", by Lou Shuhua, defines new idiom of solo zheng music
Initial communist period	**1949–1965**	
Chinese communism, under Mao Zedong: People's Republic of China declared	**1949**	
Beginning of Chinese occupation of Tibet	**1950**	First full-fledged zheng curriculum in Chinese music conservatory

World events		Music events
	1952	● Zheng programs at most conservatories, including Beijing, Shanghai
	1955	● "Celebrating the Harvest" (important zheng piece)
Persecution of Tibetans ●	**1956**	
	1958	● New school of piano-inspired zheng compositions and performers (mainly in Shanghai), including Fan Shange ("Spring on Snowy Mountains") and other female virtuosos
Dalai Lama flees to India ●	**1959**	
International council accuses China of ● genocide against Tibetans	**1961**	
	1964	● *The Red Lantern* (Revolutionary Chinese opera)
Cultural Revolution era ●	**1966–1976**	● Censorship of music and freedom of expression in all domains
Period of severe oppression and repression ●		
"Ethnic minorities" (Tibetans, Uighurs) ● especially hard hit		● Period of relative stagnation in zheng's development
Death of Mao Zedong, followed by period ● of political instability	**1976**	
Period of Openness ●	**Late 1970s–present**	● Zheng renaissance (especially "national," conservatory style): new compositional styles, organizations, international attention for zheng artists
Deng Xiaoping comes to power; ● introduces new, "open" policy on the arts	**1979**	
	1980s	● "New Wave" music movement: increasing modernization, Westernization, interest in reviving ancient Chinese musical traditions
	1980	● Beijing Zheng Association founded
	1986	● National Zheng Symposium established
	1988	● "Music from the Muqam" composed
Tiananmen Square uprising and massacre ●	**1989**	
	1995	● Deng Haiqiong wins National Zheng Competition of China
	2002	● Deng Haiqiong releases CD *Ning*

red dress is introduced. She walks purposefully to the center of the hall and sits down behind her instrument. (At this point, listen to **Online Musical Illustration #26** as you continue reading.) She begins to play, filling the room with a richly beautiful, harp-like sonority. In an instant, the audience is captivated, fully attentive, focused in on this wondrous sound and the charismatic performer behind its creation. Tones rise out of the zheng like strings of pearls, then rush back down like waterfalls. Delicate melodies and subtle ornamental touches evoke an air of exquisite refinement as all of us in attendance are transported to a realm of profound beauty and elegance.

■ ■ ■

Introduction

The musicultural focus of this chapter is a particular music instrument, the zheng, which we will discuss through the lens of Chinese history and the political movements and ideologies that have shaped it. Though the history of the zheng since ancient times will be surveyed, primary attention is devoted to the virtuosic tradition of solo zheng playing that has developed in state-sponsored music conservatories of mainland China since the 20th century. This is a tradition of which Deng Haiqiong is representative, and several of the recordings we will listen to and discuss feature her artistry.

The conservatory solo zheng style was predated and influenced by a number of important **regional styles of solo zheng music** in the 19th century, and these are discussed as well. Other traditional Chinese music instruments such as the **pipa** and the **qin** are also introduced in the course of the discussion, as well as related forms of music and drama such as **Beijing Opera** (a.k.a. Peking Opera). Overall, though, we will stay quite narrowly focused on the zheng. The range and diversity of Chinese musical culture is immense, as one would expect of a country that is so vast, has a population of well over a billion people (the world's largest), and is host to a civilization whose documented history dates back several millennia. By focusing on a single, important Chinese music instrument, we will be able to appreciate the richness and

pipa (pee-pah)

qin (chin)

complexity of Chinese music, culture, and history within a manageable scope. Resources for exploring other dimensions of Chinese music and culture are included at the Online Learning Center at www.mhhe.com/bakan1.

China: An Overview

The musicultural world of the zheng in mainland China is framed by the Chinese nation and its long historical and cultural development from antiquity to the present. We therefore begin with the following overview to establish a context for the main body of the chapter that follows it.

The nation-state of modern China

The People's Republic of China (PRC) is the most populous nation on earth, with an estimated population of 1.3 billion. It is also the world's third-largest nation in geographical size. Only the landmasses of Russia and Canada are larger. Along its massive border, China meets up with nations of five major world regions (North Asia, Central Asia, East Asia, South Asia, and mainland Southeast Asia). These nations include Russia, Mongolia, Kazakhstan, Vietnam, India, Nepal, Pakistan, and Korea. The histories of all these countries—as well as others including Japan, the United Kingdom, France, the United States, and Canada—intertwine with China's own at multiple levels, and this is reflected in histories of politics, religion, arts and culture, and trade. Ancient Chinese cultural traditions that disappeared from China long ago live on in Japan and Korea. These include the great court orchestra traditions *gagaku* (Japan) (**CD ex. #1-2** and p. 4) and *aak* (Korea) and the religion of Zen Buddhism. The histories of Taiwan, an island located off the eastern coast of China, and Hong Kong, a tiny island located just to the south of the Chinese mainland, are also complexly entwined with China's own. The modern histories of both Taiwan and Hong Kong are marked by tensions with the People's Republic of China, though much is shared between all three culturally.

The capital of the People's Republic of China (henceforth, also China) is Beijing (formerly Peking). It was here that Communist China's founding father, Mao Zedong, declared the People's Republic in 1949. Since that time, China has been governed, in effect, as a single-party communist republic.

Mao Zedong (Mao Dse[r] Dong ["Mao" rhymes with "how"; "Ze" to rhyme with "sir," but stop before you reach the "r"])

Several hundred miles south of Beijing is the coastal city of Shanghai. Beijing, with an estimated population of 14 million, and Shanghai, with some 17 million people, are China's two largest metropolises. There are many other large cities as well. In fact, 35 Chinese cities have populations of a million people or more.

The east-central and southeastern portions of China are very densely populated and heavily urbanized and industrialized, though agriculture remains the principal source of livelihood for the majority of Chinese people even today. The urbanized eastern coast and the cities along major waterways, especially the great Yangtze River (Chang Jiang), collectively account for a very large portion of China's total population, despite covering a relatively small geographical area within this vast land. The mountainous southwest of the country (including significant portions of the Himalaya Mountains along the western border), by contrast, is sparsely populated, as are the steppe (high plateau) and mountain regions of the northwest, where the majority of China's 55 recognized "ethnic minority" populations reside.

Yangtze/Chang Jiang (Yaang-tzee/Chaang Jee-ang)

Mandarin Chinese is China's official language, though many other languages and regional dialects are spoken as well. This great linguistic diversity is reflected in tremendous cultural diversity, whether expressed through music, belief systems, or culinary practices. Ethnically, China is dominated by its majority **Han Chinese** population, who account for approximately 92 percent of the populace. The remaining 8 percent of the population (about 100 million people) is mainly made up of "ethnic minority" groups, including the Uighur (Uygur, Uyghur) and Tibetan peoples. Though regarded as Chinese minorities by the Han Chinese–dominated political authorities, many of these so-called minority groups regard themselves as occupied peoples and have been engaged in long struggles for independence from China. As

Uighur (Wee-gur)

A giant statue of Mao Zedong dominates the scene at a patriotic rally in China.

ethnomusicologist and Chinese music authority Alan Thrasher notes, "Among the many non-Han peoples, ethnic minorities who have been pushed into the mountains, deserts and other less desirable space, the more usual response to Han unification [than acceptance] has been resistance and often bloody rebellion." Moreover, musical traditions among these minority groups "share few roots with the 'great tradition' of the Han," and China's appropriation of minority traditions for the sake of projecting a desired image of multicultural diversity and national unity is often resented by minority populations (Thrasher 2005). This issue figures significantly in the discussions of some of the music explored in this chapter.

From antiquity to the present

The civilization of China is among the world's oldest, dating back more than 3,500 years. It is to the ancient civilization of China that we owe such inventions as paper, wheel-carts, grid maps, accurate time-measurement devices, guns, gunpowder, and cannons. In the area of medical science, the Chinese had developed a full understanding of the body's blood circulation system, circadian rhythms ("biological clocks"), and the dietary causes of deficiency diseases some two thousand years before such foundational features of human biology were "discovered" by Europeans. Even the equal-tempered, chromatic scale of Western music, with its 12 equally spaced pitch intervals (see Chapter 4, pp. 46–47), has Chinese roots. It was reportedly worked out by a Chinese music scholar using bamboo pitch pipes in the 16th century before being adopted into the mainstream of Western music during the 17th century (Fletcher 2001:325). Institutions such as government music ministries and state music conservatories and research institutes were likely also "inventions" of the ancient Chinese.

For the vast majority of its history, China was ruled by imperial dynasties. A long succession of dynasties—including the Zhou, Qin, Han, Tang, Song, Ming, and Qing—rose and ultimately fell during the course of the dynastic period. Some of these were among the largest, most powerful, and most culturally influential empires ever. Throughout virtually the entire history of imperial China, music was regarded as an important component of political life. Rulers recognized, respected, and exploited what they perceived as music's special capacity to reflect, influ-

Zhou (Joe)

Qin (Chin)

Han (Hahn)

Tang (Tahng)

Qing (Cheeng)

ence, and model an idealized Chinese social order. The history of imperial music ministries and other official music institutions such as conservatories covers a span of more than 3,000 years.

China's long dynastic era came to an end with the collapse of the Qing dynasty (1644–1911). This was followed by the declaration of the Republic of China (established on January 1, 1912), which eventually came under the rule of former general Jiang Jieshi (better known in the West as Chiang Kai-shek) and his Chinese Nationalist Party regime. The Nationalists' agenda centered on modernizing China and developing a new Chinese nationalism rooted in economic, social, and cultural reform. Music was key to the reform effort.

Jiang Jieshi (Jee-ang Jee-yeh-shir)

Jiang Jieshi's rule, however, was chronically unstable. Invaded by Japan, which progressively occupied large parts of China throughout much of the first half of the 20th century, Jiang also was confronted by the challenges of Western imperialism and the emergence and ascent of the **Chinese Communist Party (CCP)** under Mao Zedong.

Mao and the Communists gained political control of China in 1949, founding the People's Republic of China as a socialist (communist) state. From the inception of the PRC to the present, Chinese socialism has placed great emphasis on the importance of state patronage and control of music in efforts to encode and promote official state ideology. National music conservatories and music research institutes have figured prominently.

The history of the People's Republic of China may be divided into three principal periods. In each, the relation of politics and music has been highly significant, though in somewhat different ways. These periods are

- The initial communist period of Mao Zedong's regime, 1949–1965, which saw the profound reformation of Chinese society and culture under Communist rule.
- The **Cultural Revolution** era of 1966–1976, which witnessed unprecedented levels of intolerance for any deviation from the state ideology and a concomitant movement toward extreme restrictions on cultural and artistic expression, both for Han and minority populations.
- The **Period of Openness,** which began to take shape in the turbulent years of the late 1970s following Mao Zedong's death in 1976 and fully crystallized around 1980 under the rule of Deng Xiaoping. Deng brought about major economic reforms with the introduction of free enterprise, increased the involvement of China in global economic and cultural markets, and loosened existing constraints in a variety of civil, cultural, social, artistic, and religious spheres, though not without problems or costs.

Deng Xiaoping (Dung Hsee-ow-ping)

With the above historical overview in mind, we now turn our attention to the musicultural life of the zheng in the context of Chinese history.

An Introduction to the Zheng

The zheng is a Chinese *board zither chordophone*. As with other instruments of this type, its construction features a series of strings laid lengthwise across a wooden frame (the "board") that is attached to its own resonating chamber. The zheng is historically related to several other important Asian board zither chordophones, including the Japanese **koto** (**CD ex. #1-35**), the Korean *kayagum,* the Mongolian *jatag,* and the Vietnamese *dan tranh.* The archaeological record suggests that the ancestral version of the modern zheng was invented more than 2,500 years ago, possibly in southeastern China (Lawergren 2000:80–83). Thus, the historical legacy of the zheng, or *guzheng* ("ancient zheng"), as it is also known, traces back to the age of the great Chinese philosopher Confucius (551–479 BCE). Today, the zheng is a tremendously popular instrument in the PRC, as well as in Taiwan and Hong Kong and among Chinese musicians and music enthusiasts worldwide. (The zheng and its culture beyond mainland China, however, are beyond the scope of this chapter.) Moreover, the tradition and repertoire of the

The Japanese koto.

se (like "sir," but stop before you reach the "r")

solo zheng has contributed as much to our notions in the West of what Chinese instrumental music is and what it sounds like as any other musical idiom (Jones 1995:80).

The oldest forms of the zheng consisted of five silk strings mounted on a bamboo frame. Later developments yielded a wooden-framed zheng with 12 or 13 strings that was similar in construction to another ancient Chinese board zither, the 25-string *se.* Over time, the zheng evolved into its various modern forms, which typically feature a wooden frame and either 16 strings (three-octave range) or 21 strings (four-octave range). The 21-string instrument is the one most commonly used today.

Zheng strings, which are now usually made from a combination of nylon and steel (silk, copper, and steel strings were used in earlier times, and steel strings are still used for more traditional musical styles), are laid horizontally across a slightly rounded wooden soundboard that is mounted directly over the instrument's frame/resonator and attached to pegs at both ends. The strings are supported by *movable bridges,* which may be made of wood, ivory, plastic, or other materials. The positioning of the bridges is adjusted for different tunings. The frame rests on a wooden stand with four legs, behind which the performer plays from a seated position. (See Figure 13.1 and the photo on p. 292.)

The Musical Guided Tour for this chapter provides an introduction to the zheng, illustrating basic scales, techniques, melodic ornaments, and playing styles that we will encounter in Guided Listening Experience selections later on. Deng Haiqiong (or Haiqiong Deng, as she is known in the West) is the performer. She is among the leading zheng players of her generation from mainland China. Haiqiong was born in 1975 and started playing the zheng at age eight. She is a graduate of the Shanghai Conservatory of Music and also studied at the Chinese Conservatory in Beijing. In 1995, she won first prize in the highly prestigious National Zheng Competition of China. Since that time, she has concertized in China, Japan, Singapore, and the United States, including a recital at New York's famed Carnegie Hall. She also has studied ethnomusicology at the graduate level in the United States.

The transcript on page 297 corresponds to the audio Musical Guided Tour. As you listen to this tour at the Online Learning Center (www.mhhe.com/bakan1), follow along with this transcript.

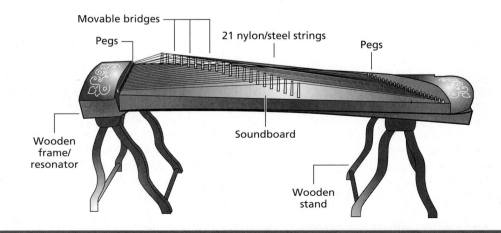

Movable bridges

Pegs

21 nylon/steel strings

Pegs

Wooden frame/resonator

Soundboard

Wooden stand

Zheng.

FIGURE 13.1

(*The tour begins with Deng Haiqiong performing the final portion of a solo zheng piece called "Fighting the Typhoon."*)

The 21-string zheng which you just heard has a range of four octaves [♪]. Altering the positions of the movable bridges on the instrument allows for several different pentatonic [five tone per octave] tunings of the 21 strings. The most commonly used tuning on the zheng produces a scale of D E F♯ A B (D), which sounds like this [♪]. This scale is essentially identical in structure to the Western pentatonic scale to which you were introduced in Chapter 4. Two other zheng tunings are very common as well. These produce the following scales: D E G A B (D), which sounds like this [♪]; and D E G A C (D), which sounds like this [♪].

In traditional zheng playing styles, only the thumb, index finger, and middle finger of the right hand are used to pluck and stroke the strings. The performer usually attaches small, plastic plectra (which are like miniature guitar picks) to the fingertips to produce a clear, bright timbre. Listen now as Haiqiong illustrates a single-line melody using the traditional, one-hand plucking style [♪].

Here is another example of one-hand plucking technique, but this time Haiqiong simultaneously plucks two strings that are an octave apart on most of the melody notes; in other words, she plays the melody in octaves (*da cuo*). This is common in zheng music [♪].

Since the 1950s, techniques involving plucking and stroking the strings of the zheng with both hands, rather than with just the right hand, have become standard. To a significant degree, such techniques reflect Western musical influences, especially influences from Western piano music. Here are a few illustrations of two-hand plucking techniques on the zheng:

■ First, a melody harmonized in two-note chords (*xiao cuo*) [♪].

■ Second, a melody embellished by arpeggiated chords (*payin*) [♪].

■ Third, a melody played in the right-hand part with accompanying chords and arpeggios in the left-hand part [♪].

In the last musical illustration, Haiqiong sustained the notes of the right-hand melody part using a tremolo, or "roll," technique called *yao zhi*. Here's what the tremolo sounds like on its own [♪]. A more rhythmic technique for sustaining notes (*da zhi yao*) is used in many older zheng pieces; it involves a quick back-and-forth thumb motion and sounds like this [♪]. Also popular is the "four-point fingering" technique (*si dian*), which features a quick alternation of middle finger (M), thumb (T), and index finger (I) plucks, in the following pattern: M T I T M T I T, etc. Here is an illustration of what that sounds like [♪].

Melodic **ornamentation** is very highly developed in zheng performance and there are many different kinds of ornaments. Especially striking is the large variety of **gua-zou** (goo-wa zoh), or *glissandos*. These are rapid ascending or descending sweeps across the strings. Here are four of the main types:

■ First, the short gua-zou, consisting of a sweep of a few notes that lands on a main melody note [♪].

■ Second, the long gua-zou, which is often described by Chinese musicians as the "falling water" ornament, for reasons that will likely be apparent to you from the following musical illustration [♪].

■ Third, the strong gua-zou, which is heavily accented and almost attacklike [♪].

■ Fourth, the gua-zou played on the left-hand side of the strings (that is, to the left of the movable bridges), which creates this very distinctive effect [♪].

A host of other zheng ornaments are created by pressing into the string with the fingers of the left hand while the right hand plucks. The main types of left-hand ornaments are

■ First, the up-glide (*shang hua-yin*) [♪].

■ Second, the down-glide (*xia hua-yin*) [♪].

The Zheng in Imperial China

The origin of the name *zheng* is not known. One theory is that it is onomatopoeic, reflecting the timbre of the instrument when its strings are plucked. Another theory has to do with the possible relationship of the instrument's name to a different translation of the word *zheng*, which is "dispute." Legend has it that during the ancient era of the Qin dynasty (3rd century BCE), two sisters in the imperial palace got into a heated argument over a 25-string se zither and broke the instrument in half. This yielded two instruments, one with 12 strings, the other with 13. Amused by the incident, the emperor named these new "half" instruments "zheng" in acknowledgement of the "dispute" that had given rise to them. (According to some versions of the story, the 13-string instrument was eventually given as a gift by the Qin emperor to the imperial house of Japan, giving rise to the 13-string Japanese koto. The 12-string model, meanwhile, ended up in Korea, where it became the prototype of the 12-string Korean kayagum).

The earliest written document containing a reference to the zheng is from a Qin era manuscript of 237 BCE, which describes groups of musicians in rural areas of China who "beat clay drums and earthen jars, play *zheng* and slap their thighs to accompany songs" (Han Mei 2005). This ancient zheng seemingly made a favorable impression on Qin imperialists. It was quite loud and portable and could be adapted to different musical situations. It became a favored Qin instrument, and as the Qin's dynastic realm expanded, so too did the zheng's geographical and musical diffusion. It was incorporated into ensembles, became a popular instrument for accompanying singing of various types, and was employed in a wide range of entertainment and ritual contexts, from imperial banquets to village ceremonies and sacrificial rites.

With Qin imperial expansion came the emergence of what has been described by some scholars as the advent of the first "popular music" culture in China (Lawergren 2000:83). Musical styles whose uses transcended their specific places and cultures of origin, and which blended together elements from different regions and idioms to create new forms of musical expression, began to proliferate as contact between formally separate cultures and traditions increased. The zheng was a key instrument in this emergent, ancient "popular music" culture. As it took root in different areas of Qin China, regional styles of zheng began to emerge. Some zheng regional styles today (for example, in Shaanxi, Henan, and Chaozhou) are believed, by local musicians in those areas and by Chinese music historians alike, to retain musical elements passed down through the millennia from the Qin era. Members of the Shaanxi zheng school in particular refer to their regional tradition as "Qin zheng style" as a way of claiming links to this historical legacy.

Shaanxi
(Shahn-hsee)

Chaozhou
(Chow-joe)

Painting of a court dance performance from the Tang dynasty era. The dancers in the center are accompanied by a women's court orchestra (rear left and rear right) performing on a variety of traditional Chinese instruments.

The Han dynasty era

During the Han dynasty (202 BCE–220 CE), a grand epoch of Chinese civilization during which **Confucianism** was established as the foundation of the Chinese social order (see "Insights and Perspectives" box on p. 300), the zheng continued to develop and gain popularity as an instrument of entertainment and public ritual. It was played at weddings, banquets, and funerals, sometimes even on horseback (Cheng 1991:9). Archaeological evidence indicates that music played on the zheng and other ancient instruments was used to accompany elaborate entertainments and rituals that also involved singing, acrobatics, and dance. Though the painting above dates from the later dynastic period of the Tang (see below), the elaborate entertainments of Han court life were likely similar in spirit.

The zheng during Han times was played by professional court musicians, women, slaves, and common folk and favored by members of diverse social classes—courtesans and poets, soldiers and servants. Though cast as a "vulgar" instrument by some Han poets and literati, it was hailed by others as embodying a high moral character befitting of gentlemen and heroes (Rault-Leyrat 1987:35). Moreover, though it appears that the zheng was mainly an ensemble instrument used in entertainment contexts in Han China, it is possible that a solo tradition of zheng playing also dates back this far. The solo zheng tradition may have developed in association with Confucian practices of using music for purposes of self-cultivation, practices that have been more extensively documented in the history of another Chinese board zither chordophone, the qin (see "Insights and Perspectives" box on p. 300). Disciplined self-cultivation and self-refinement at the individual level were seen as key to the development and maintenance of a morally virtuous social order on the larger scale of society, which was in turn the hallmark ideal of Confucian social and political philosophy.

The Tang dynasty era

The zheng reached its apogee in imperial China during the period of the Tang dynasty (618–907 CE), another golden age in China's cultural history (Rault-Leyrat 1987:80). At its

Confucianism, Buddhism, and the Qin Zither

The teachings of Confucius, only moderately influential during his lifetime (551–479 BCE) and largely ignored for over 200 years of political instability and frequent warring following his death, became the cornerstone of Chinese society and social policy under the rule of the Han dynasty. Another important influence on Chinese social and cultural developments during this period was Buddhism, which originated in India and entered China from the west, gradually spreading eastward throughout much of the country beginning in the 1st century CE.

Confucianism insisted upon the need for social control and direction at every level. Hierarchical social stratification, deference to authority, codification of behavior across the full range of social classes, and the primacy of fulfilling one's duty to society above all other considerations underscored its fundamental goal: the establishment, preservation, and perpetuation of a morally virtuous social order. All facets of society—from family dynamics and political administration to the arts, religious belief and ritual, and cultural and intellectual life—were bound up in the Confucian code of moral virtue as "right" social order.

Painting of two junzi playing music together in an idyllic natural setting. The seated musician on the left is playing a qin. A photograph of Deng Haiqiong playing the qin may be seen at the Online Learning Center at www.mhhe.com/bakan1.

Confucius had claimed that music, properly employed, had great value as a medium for establishing and sustaining a good and moral society. He believed that music had an inherent capacity to cultivate inner character, to mold people's minds and hearts in ways that would make them more committed to—and better capable of—serving the common good. This was true for emperor, sage, and peasant alike. For each social class, certain types of music were regarded as being most appropriate and beneficial. Governmental regulation, control, and institutionalization of music and musical activities were deemed essential for matching the right kinds of music to the right kinds of people. Under the Han, a large governmental music bureau was established to oversee such regulation.

At the top of the Confucian social hierarchy were the *junzi* (jün-dse [to rhyme with "sir," but stop before you reach the "r"]), or "superior individuals." These were men from the ruling and educated classes thought to possess the requisite moral propriety, intellect, and practical wisdom to guide Han society (and music) along the proper path to order and virtue. The junzi instrument *par excellence* was the seven-string *qin,* a board zither chordophone with no bridges that is smaller than the zheng and has a much softer dynamic range. The qin was an instrument of the gentleman scholar. It was usually played solo, often in solitude. Playing the qin was seen as an aid to enlightenment, disciplined thinking, and self-reflection. Many Chinese works of art and poems depict the figure of a junzi with qin engaged in quiet contemplation. Confucius himself is believed to have played the qin.

CD ex. #3-20 features a portion of a solo performance played on the qin. The melody of this instrumental piece is based on an ancient Buddhist chant. With its slow and contemplative style and the use of signature qin musical techniques such as the bell-like harmonics heard from 0:39–0:56, this is a good example of the traditional qin musical art. The performer is Tao Chu Sheng, a qin master from Taiwan.

height, the Tang government music ministry employed 30,000 musicians and dancers from throughout the Chinese empire and beyond (South Asia, Central Asia, Southeast Asia). The popular and adaptable zheng thrived in this era of musical experimentation and cosmopolitanism. It was incorporated into many different kinds of ensembles and used in a wide range of contexts. New features were added (e.g., additional strings) and novel playing techniques were introduced. The zheng's increased stature in this era of opulence was symbolized in features of its decoration and design, from silver-engraved wooden frames to jade bridges. The earliest known examples of notated zheng music also date from this era (Cheng 1991:16).

The zheng was combined with a variety of other instruments in Tang court ensembles. Some of these instruments, including the qin, were of ancient Chinese origin. Others, which also gained popularity in regional folk music traditions outside of the court, had come to China from foreign lands the imperial Chinese had encountered through trade and conquest. Especially important in this regard was the massive **Silk Road,** which connected China to peoples and lands as distant as Central Asia, India, Egypt, and Turkey.

It was via the Silk Road that the *pipa,* a pear-shaped, plucked chordophone with four strings, was introduced into Chinese musical culture, ultimately becoming one of the most important of all Chinese instruments. From Tang times forward, the pipa and the zheng were closely associated with one another, accompanying sung poetry, performing instrumental duets, and playing together in different types of ensembles and various performance contexts.

The pipa, here played by Yiyi Wang.

CD ex. #3-21 is an excerpt of a duet for zheng and pipa. The performers are Deng Haiqiong (zheng) and Hou Yuehua (pipa). The excerpt begins with the pipa, which has an almost banjo-like timbre. Note the dramatic tremolo "rolls" (*yao zhi*). (This technique was originally associated with the pipa, and was later adapted for zheng; the zheng version was demonstrated earlier in the Musical Guided Tour.) The zheng makes its entrance at 0:17 with a short, descending gua-zou (glissando). From 0:45 until the music fades out at the end of the excerpt, the two instruments are featured playing together.

Hou Yuehua (Ho Yoo-e-hwah)

CD ex. #3-22 is a selection for an ensemble that includes zheng and pipa together with other traditional Chinese instruments including the *xiao,* an end-blown bamboo flute; the erhu, a two-string fiddle; and percussion instruments. (Additional photos of Chinese instruments may be viewed at the Online Learning Center at www.mhhe.com/bakan1.) The xiao flute is the first instrument heard; then the pipa joins the xiao at 0:05. After a pause, the full ensemble comes in at 0:27. Though this is a modern arrangement and the music cannot be said to be representative of Tang court or folk music tradition, the combination of instruments is similar to that described in accounts of certain ensembles of the Tang era.

xiao (hsee-ow)
erhu (err-hoo)

Another important Tang period development was that women began playing the zheng in greater numbers, generating an association between this instrument and female performers that is also reflected in the zheng music culture of modern times, as we shall see. Moreover, whereas female zheng players of earlier eras had typically been of low social status (prostitutes, concubines, servants), records from the Tang era indicate that the instrument gained popularity among girls and women of the upper classes, who played it—often solo—for both entertainment and self-cultivation (Rault-Leyrat 1987:83). The growing association of the

Common to the different styles of traditional Chinese opera (see the final paragraph of p. 303) was a format in which a dramatic story was enacted by costumed performers wearing makeup who combined heightened speech, song, dance, mime, acting, and acrobatics in their presentation. The use of stage props was minimal, and the action tended to be highly stylized (as opposed to realistic). Traditional, regional Chinese opera styles featured four standard character types: male (*sheng*), female (*dan*), painted-face male (*jing*), and clown (*chou*). (The parts of the female characters were often played by boys or adult female impersonators.)

The most widely known type of Chinese opera is Beijing Opera (or Peking Opera), which had its origins in the capital in the late 18th century but did not fully crystallize until the 19th century. Like other forms of traditional Chinese opera, Beijing Opera is highly stylized. There are 26 ways to laugh, 20 different types of beard, and 39 ways of manipulating the beard (Han and Mark 1980:21). The accompanying instrumental ensemble in traditional Beijing Opera features a small, two-string fiddle with a piercing timbre called the *jinghu* (meaning "Beijing fiddle"), as well as other chordophones including the pipa. Additional melodic instruments (chordophones and aerophones) are also included, and there is a percussion section (gongs, cymbals, wooden clappers). The leader of the ensemble performs on a drum called a *danpi gu*, which creates a unique clicking sound.

Beijing Opera experienced its golden age in the early decades of the 20th century, spanning the decline of the Qing dynasty and the early years of the Republican era. Indeed, Beijing Opera served as a powerful vehicle of social and political change during that transitional period of Chinese history (see Mackerras 1997).

During the Communist era, especially in the 1960s and early- to mid-1970s, Beijing Opera and other Chinese opera genres were either discredited or else radically transformed in accordance with the stringent political priorities and agendas of Chinese socialism of that period. Contemporary themes, plots, and costumes, as well as realistic staging, were used to modernize the look of the performances and to advance socialist propaganda. The heightened speech of the old dramas was replaced by ordinary Mandarin speech. The traditional division of the characters into four types and most of the conventional stylized and symbolic

zheng with women was tied to an identification of the instrument with romantic subjects: the beauty of nature, the beauty of women, sentimental feelings of love, memories of sadness and longing.

Xuanzong (Hsü-en-dsong)

The Tang emperor Xuanzong played an important role in cultivating the zheng as a "women's instrument," and in promoting women's performance on other instruments, such as the pipa, as well. Under his patronage, hundreds of women in the imperial palace were given expert training on the zheng by leading (male) court musicians. Ensembles of well-trained female musicians entertained guests at royal banquets and in other contexts (see the painting on p. 299).

Altogether, Emperor Xuanzong did much to better the lot of musicians in the imperial court. The social status of zheng masters and other musicians, traditionally low despite the important role accorded to music in imperial China, improved significantly under his rule (Cheng 1991:9).

The Ming and Qing dynasty eras

Following a period after the Tang and subsequent Song dynasty eras when it declined in popularity, the zheng became very popular again in the 14th century during the Ming dynasty gestures were removed. In the new style, traditional Beijing Opera melodies alternated with revolutionary songs espousing the virtues of Chinese communism. The music also was often modified through the addition of Western instruments and musical influences (e.g., Western harmonies).

A classic example of this type of Revolutionary Chinese Opera that derived from the original Beijing Opera form was *The Red Lantern* (1964), the plot of which concerns three generations in a family of Chinese revolutionaries during the China–Japan war of 1937–1945. Productions of *The Red Lantern* were common during the Cultural Revolution era of 1966–1976. After that period, it was not performed for many years. It was revived, however, in 1995. **CD ex. #1-4,** which we listened to earlier in connection with Chapter 2, features an excerpt from a 1997 recording of a song from *The Red Lantern* sung by the well-known vocalist Wei Li. Although this is an example of a Revolutionary Opera song rather than a song from a traditional Beijing Opera, the musical style of the arrangement is essentially traditional. The melodic instruments (there is no percussion in this excerpt) are led by the *jinghu* fiddle and the pipa also is heard. A texture of variant versions of a single melody (heterophony) predominates, with especially close interaction between the jinghu and the vocalist, who weave in and out of each other's melodic lines in interesting ways. The heterophonic texture heard here is characteristic of Beijing Opera musical style, as it is of much Chinese ensemble music.

Scene from a traditional Beijing Opera.

Scene from a Revolutionary Chinese Opera.

(1368–1644). The Ming witnessed the rise of a large Chinese middle class, and a zheng was a standard item to have in the home. There was even a popular saying in Ming times that claimed: "Almost every household has a painted drum and a silver *zheng* can be found everywhere" (Cheng 1991:11). Girls and young women were especially encouraged to study and play the instrument.

The Ming was also an era when various regional styles of *Chinese opera* (*xi, xiqu,* or *xiju*) flourished in different areas of the country. The zheng was an important instrument in the ensembles that accompanied Chinese regional opera performances, from Shandong and Henan in the north to Chaozhou and Hakka in the south. This was true during the consequent Qing dynasty as well, which saw a continued efflorescence of Chinese opera forms (see "Insights and Perspectives" box on preceding page and above). Distinctive zheng playing techniques and styles of melodic ornamentation were developed in each region to capture the nuances of regional languages and dialects, especially in connection with local types of opera and song and their related instrumental music styles. These developments were important to the eventual emergence of identifiable regional styles of *solo* zheng playing, to which we turn our attention in the next section of the chapter.

xi, xiqu, xiju (hsee, hsee-chew, hsee-jü)

TABLE 13.1	Major developments of the zheng and its musical culture during the dynastic era (pre-1912).

Qin Dynasty Era (3rd century BCE)

- 237 BCE: First written documentation of zheng
- Zheng prominent in emergent "popular music" culture of China
- Possible origins of regional styles

Han Dynasty Era (202 BCE–220 CE)

- Zheng played in many different contexts and types of ensembles
- Possible origins of regional solo traditions

Tang Dynasty Era (618–907)

- Zheng reaches its "apogee"
- Played in many new ensemble contexts, introduction of new features of instrument design and construction, elaborate instrument decoration (silver engraving, jade bridges), new playing techniques
- Earliest known examples of music notation for zheng
- Close association with the pipa established
- Women zheng players and women's court ensembles (Emperor Xuanzong)

Ming Dynasty Era (1368–1644)

- Reemergence of zheng in popularity after a period of post-Tang decline; girls and young women especially encouraged to play
- Zheng becomes important instrument in regional Chinese opera ensembles

Qing Dynasty Era (1644–1911)

- Continued importance of zheng in regional Chinese opera ensembles
- Crystallization of regional solo playing styles and traditions in Shandong, Henan, etc. (discussed below)
- Pieces in *baban* form central to solo zheng traditions (discussed below)

Regional Styles: Traditional Solo Zheng Music

During the later Qing dynasty era, a number of distinct regional styles of solo zheng music and performance practice crystallized in different parts of China. These developed out of existing regional traditions of folk opera, sung poetry, musically accompanied storytelling, and instrumental ensemble music involving the zheng; they also reflected a long history of mixing between folk, popular, and court music traditions. By the mid- to late-19th century, distinctive regional solo zheng styles were recognized in areas including Shandong, Henan, Shaanxi, Chaozhou, Hakka, and Zhejiang. These regional styles still exist today though, in many respects, they have been absorbed into or eclipsed by the "national" style of the conservatories, to which we shall return.

Each regional style has its own, distinctive **yun,** or "regional character." The yun of Henan zheng, for example, is known for its liveliness, short descending melodic phrases, and, as was demonstrated earlier in the Musical Guided Tour, a preference for wide rather than narrow vibrato. The dramatic vocal rises and falls of Henan spoken dialect (especially as reflected in Henan folk opera) are mirrored by similarly dramatic up- and down-glide ornaments in Henan zheng playing.

yun (yün)

Common to the various regional zheng styles is a shared basis in pieces that represent a form called **baban.** In the Guided Listening Experience that follows, we explore one such piece.

baban (bah-bahn)

guided listening experience

"Autumn Moon over the Han Palace," Deng Haiqiong

- CD Track #**3-23**
- Featured performer(s)/group: Deng Haiqiong (zheng)
- Format: Excerpt
- Source recording: *Ning,* by Hai-qiong Deng [Deng Haiqiong] (Celebrity Music CMCD 9464)

"Autumn Moon over the Han Palace" is one of the best-known traditional zheng pieces in the baban form. The version heard here, performed by Deng Haiqiong, is representative of the Shandong regional zheng style. Archaeological evidence indicates that the zheng has been a part of musical life in Shandong since at least the 3rd century CE (Cheng 1991:88).

Haiqiong plays the piece on a 16-string zheng with steel strings, rather than on the more common 21-string zheng with metal-wound nylon strings that we heard in the Musical Guided Tour. The smaller zheng with steel strings is generally preferred for traditional pieces like this one because

- Plucked tones on steel strings are able to resonate (sustain) longer than plucked tones on metal-wound nylon strings, allowing for subtle nuances in melodic ornamentation that the traditional pieces demand.
- These compositions do not exceed the three-octave range of the 16-string instrument, unlike many modern compositions that employ the full, four-octave range of the 21-string zheng.

Though not a representative of the Shandong zheng tradition herself, Haiqiong learned "Autumn Moon over the Han Palace" from one of the most revered 20th-century Shandong zheng masters, Gao Zicheng (b. 1918). She first learned to play the piece on her own with the aid of a cassette recording of it by Gao. She would listen to this recording on her portable tape player through headphones over and over again and try to emulate what she heard. Later, while a student at the high school for performing arts in Xi'an, she got an opportunity to work on the piece directly with Gao Zicheng. But in teaching Haiqiong "Autumn Moon," Gao did not so much teach her to play the piece as simply play it *for* her in-between lengthy discourses on various aspects of the life, culture, and musical world of Shandong. And what music "teaching" there was *per se* consisted mainly of Gao playing the piece straight through from start to finish, then listening to Haiqiong play it back for him in the same manner. He had little to say to her at all in the way of specifics concerning her performance or interpretation.

Gao Zicheng (Gow Dser-chung)

Xi'an (Hsee-ahn)

"He would listen to me play through the piece," Haiqiong recalled to me during an interview, "and then say, 'No, something's totally incorrect.' Then he would play the whole piece again, but I really couldn't hear the difference and he wouldn't explain [laughs]. . . . I really didn't understand at that age. My other teachers [at the conservatory] were much more systematic and

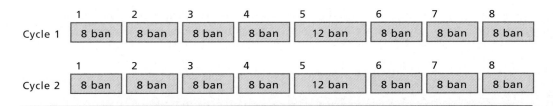

	1	2	3	4	5	6	7	8
Cycle 1	8 ban	8 ban	8 ban	8 ban	12 ban	8 ban	8 ban	8 ban

	1	2	3	4	5	6	7	8
Cycle 2	8 ban	8 ban	8 ban	8 ban	12 ban	8 ban	8 ban	8 ban

Baban form outline.

FIGURE 13.2

analytical. It was so different. But later, when I was older, I realized what he was trying to teach me. That it's not about technique. It's about where the music comes from, its feeling and its cultural background. . . . When I was little [i.e., a teenager], I thought, 'This is such a simple piece. It's boring, not challenging.' But as I grow older I realize you can never get bored playing this piece. There's always something more. It's not always necessary to be complicated and technical for [good] musical expression. Just being simple is sometimes more effective. That's what I learned from playing this piece and, looking back, from studying with Gao Zicheng."

Haiqiong's love of the piece "Autumn Moon over the Han Palace" extends to a deeper appreciation of the baban tradition to which it belongs. "These baban pieces are just so perfect, though they are very simple," she explains. "You cannot imagine a single note being added or taken away."

The standard formal design of a baban piece consists of a melody with eight phrases (Figure 13.2). The basic unit of measurement for each phrase is called a *ban*. The term *ban* has no real English-language equivalent. Each *ban* essentially consists of two beats, a strong beat (*ban*) followed by a weak beat (*yan*). This *ban-yan,* strong-weak, pattern continues throughout the whole form.

In "Autumn Moon over the Han Palace" and most other baban pieces, phrases 1–4 and 6–8 are all the same length: eight *ban*. Phrase 5, however, is longer, consisting of 12 *ban* instead of just eight. Thus, the baban form in its entirety has a length of 68 *ban*: 56 *ban* for phrases 1–4 and 6–8 (i.e., 8 × 7 = 56), plus 12 *ban* for phrase 5 (56 + 12 = 68). In a standard performance, the entire 68-ban form is played twice in succession without pause (Figure 13.2).

The 68-ban form of baban serves as a framework for many different melodies. Each is subject to different styles of ornamentation and embellishment. These define, at one level, the music's regional character (*yun*) and, at another level, the style and interpretation of the individual performer of the piece.

In her own interpretation of "Autumn Moon over the Han Palace," Haiqiong aimed to capture both the *yun* of traditional Shandong zheng playing and the unique stylistic approach of Gao Zicheng within that Shandong tradition. Beyond that, she simply allowed her musical personality to come through. "The more I play the piece, I don't worry about the style anymore," she explains. "It's just there."

yijing (ee-jing)

Haiqiong is, however, guided significantly in her playing by the desire to capture the culturally designated emotional quality, or **yijing,** of the composition. This piece is identified with an yijing of "sadness," but Haiqiong is quick to emphasize that this is a different brand of emotion than is generally implied by the English word *sadness*.

"The yijing is of a sadness that's in your heart, that you keep inside yourself," she explains. "It's very gentle, moderate, and controlled. This sense of moderation is what has to come through when you play the piece. More important than expressing 'sadness' through the music for me is expressing this mood of moderation, of a certain sense of peacefulness and restraint."

Listen now to the excerpt of Deng Haiqiong's rendition of "Autumn Moon over the Han Palace" on **CD ex. #3-23,** which includes one full cycle of the 68-ban baban form melody (on the original recording, the entire form is repeated once). Follow along with the Guided Listening Quick Summary on the next page. Use the summary's timeline to track the eight phrases of the baban form. Also, take note of the many different kinds of melodic ornaments that occur, the first few of which are charted out. Listen carefully, and you will hear that virtually every note of the melody is ornamented in one way or another!

---

guided listening quick summary

"Autumn Moon over the Han Palace," Deng Haiqiong (CD ex. #3-23)

The piece is in the standard 68-*ban* baban form and uses the tuning of one of the three standard zheng modes: D E G A B (D).

0:00–0:20: Phrase 1 (Length of phrase = 8 ban)
Examples of melodic ornaments in Phrase 1:

- 0:00: gua-zou (glissando)
- 0:02: up-glide (*shang hua-yin*)
- 0:03: down-up round-glide (*hui hua-yin*)
- 0:05: down-glide (*xia hua-yin*)
- 0:12: vibrato "shake" (*rou*)

0:21–0:38: Phrase 2 (Length of phrase = 8 ban)
0:39–0:56: Phrase 3 (Length of phrase = 8 ban)
0:56–1:12: Phrase 4 (Length of phrase = 8 ban)
1:13–1:37: Phrase 5 (Length of phrase = 12 ban)
1:37–1:53: Phrase 6 (Length of phrase = 8 ban)
1:54–2:08: Phrase 7 (Length of phrase = 8 ban)
2:09–2:25: Phrase 8 (Length of phrase = 8 ban)

Emergence and Development of the Conservatory Solo Zheng Style in Mainland China

The conservatory tradition (*xueyuan pai*) of solo zheng playing of which Deng Haiqiong is representative has its direct roots in the Republican era of Chinese history, 1912–1949. This era covers the years following the collapse of the Qing dynasty at the end of 1911 through to the establishment of the People's Republic of China as a communist state under the leadership of Mao Zedong in 1949. During this period, China experienced great political instability and massive social and cultural reform. Modernization was seen as key to reform efforts on all levels, and modernizing China equated largely with appropriating Western technological, economic, and cultural systems and resources for purposes of Chinese nationalism and economic growth.

Music, which had had a long history of explicit use for political purposes throughout Chinese dynastic history, became a major focus of reform efforts during the post-dynastic Republican period too. Chinese traditional musics were essentially cast as backward and regressive, while Western music (especially that of European Classical and Romantic era composers of the 18th and 19th centuries) was prized as an adopted icon of Chinese modernity and progressiveness. Some reformers believed that wholesale replacement of Chinese music by Western music was the proper path for modern Chinese musical nationalism. This attitude was fueled by a prevalent notion that Western music was inherently superior to Chinese music, a notion that still persists even today, according to ethnomusicologist Stephen Jones. Conservatory "students of traditional Chinese instruments are plainly considered inferior to students of Western music," Jones writes. "For many urban Chinese, their traditional music is 'backward', less 'scientific' than Western music" (Jones 1995:62).

xueyuan pai (hsoo-e-yoo-en pie)

Liu Tianhua (Lee-oo Tee-en-hwah)

Buoyed by such prejudices, music conservatories, symphony orchestras, and other institutions devoted to the cultivation of Western music were established in Chinese cities such as Shanghai and Beijing during the first half of the 20th century. Expatriate Western musicians, as well as Chinese musicians who had studied at major music schools in Europe, North America, and Japan, taught at the conservatories.

There was another important school of thought in the music reform arena of Republican China, however. Members of this school, led by Liu Tianhua, argued that traditional Chinese musics and instruments should not be discarded, but rather should be reformed in accordance with modern, nationalistic ideals to become the basis of a new, national Chinese music. (See Stock [1996] on musicultural life in China during this period of reform.) Many leading representatives of this camp, like their counterparts on the other side of the music reform debate, had studied Western music abroad. They sought to "improve" the quality of traditional Chinese music by modernizing it, which largely equated with incorporating Western elements: standardized tunings, Western-style harmonies and textures, modifications to traditional Chinese instruments inspired by the modern technologies of Western instruments (e.g., the piano). Collecting, transcribing, and publishing traditional folk music from different regions of China were regarded as key to the reform effort. Folk music was to provide the base upon which a new Chinese national music would be created with the aid of more "advanced" (i.e., mainly Western-derived) musical resources. This was to be a music imbued with Chinese "national characteristics," a music that would ideally evolve to be "the equal of Western music" in the aspirations of its most ambitious advocates (Wong 2002:382). One significant outgrowth of this branch of reform was that regional masters of instruments like the zheng and pipa were hired as part-time music instructors at some urban conservatories, institutions that had initially been devoted almost exclusively to Western music.

Meanwhile, musical life outside the cities continued much as it had before, and regional music traditions such as those associated with the solo zheng continued as part of local musicultural scenes. Some regional zheng players straddled both worlds, continuing to function as local musicians in their home communities while also teaching part-time at the urban conservatories, where their "folk art" was passed on and developed by a new generation of conservatory-trained musicians. These formally trained conservatory musicians, with backgrounds in both Chinese and Western music, developed and ultimately published a body of traditional and neo-traditional solo zheng music. Collections of notated zheng pieces representing different regional repertoires were compiled. Also, new pieces based on traditional tunes and forms but modified in ways that reflected the new musical values and approaches of the reform movement were created. The most important and influential of these neo-traditional compositions was "Return of the Fishing Boats" (1936), by Lou Shuhua.

Lou Shuhua (Lo Shoo-hwah)

guided listening experience

"Return of the Fishing Boats," by Lou Shuhua

- CD Tracks #**3-24** and **3-25**
- Featured performer(s)/group: Xiao Ying (zheng)
- Format: Two excerpts
- Source recording: *Classical Folk Music from China,* by Heart of the Dragon Ensemble (ARC Music Productions International Ltd. EUCD 1908)

The most significant innovation of Lou Shuhua's "Return of the Fishing Boats" relative to the more traditional solo zheng repertoire was that it broke away from the baban form. In its melodic character and ornamentation, tempo, rhythm, and overall style, the first part of the piece (**CD ex. #3-24**) closely resembles a conventional baban work like "Autumn Moon over the Han Palace." Indeed, it sounds at the start as though the entire development of "Return of the Fishing Boats" will occur over an underlying framework of the 68-*ban* baban form.

This is not what happens, however. Rather, the baban-esque quality established at the outset disappears in the final part of the piece (**CD ex. #3-25**), where a recurring, highly embellished melodic figure (ostinato) becomes the sole foundation of the musical development. Moreover, this new melody, instead of moving from note to note in stepwise (conjunct) fashion, as was customary in traditional baban pieces, leaps from note to note across larger intervals as it climbs up and down the scale (D E F♯ A B [D]) in a sequential way. This creates a type of melodic contour that was novel for zheng music of its time, but that would become very common in later zheng pieces, many of which were directly influenced by the style of this one.

Another innovation introduced in the last section of "Return of the Fishing Boats" is the frequent and dramatic use of short, descending sweeps across the strings—that is, of *gua-zou,* or glissandos. Though use of gua-zou ornamentation to decorate and enhance melodies played on the zheng was by no means new, the almost overwhelming profusion of glissandos heard in the concluding part of this piece was unprecedented.

Finally, "Return of the Fishing Boats" charted new territory for solo zheng music in its treatment of tempo. When the recurring melodic figure is first presented (beginning of **CD ex. #3-25**), it is introduced at a very slow tempo. Almost immediately, though, the music begins to speed up, getting faster, and faster, and faster still in a progressive acceleration that continues for almost a full minute until the section comes to a close with a flourish of ascending and descending glissandos. Throughout this passage, the dynamic level and intensity continually increase along with the tempo. The kind of spectacular acceleration and growing musical intensity featured in this section of "Return of the Fishing Boats" marked a new stylistic development for zheng music, again, one that would have widespread influence on later zheng pieces. (We will encounter something similar in the last piece we explore in this chapter, "Music from the Muqam" [**CD ex. #3-30**]).

All of the musical excitement generated by the recurring melodic figure, profuse use of glissandos, and dramatic tempo acceleration in the final section of "Return of the Fishing Boats" was created for programmatic effect. Specifically, it was used to evoke the motion and sound of the fishing boats of the piece's title as they are rowed faster and faster by fishermen returning from their work at the end of the day. Programmaticism is a common feature of much Chinese music, but the brand of highly explicit musical symbolism used in this work represents a significant departure from earlier zheng styles. Indeed, the type of programmaticism evident here is suggestive of European programmatic music of 19th-century Romantic composers, which almost surely influenced Lou Shuhua in his approach to this piece, whether directly or indirectly.

guided listening quick summary

"Return of the Fishing Boats," by Lou Shuhua (CD exs. #3-24 and 3-25)

Zheng tuning: D E F♯ A B (D)

EXCERPT 1. OPENING SECTION OF PIECE (CD EX. #3-24)

- Traditional musical style similar to that of baban-form pieces like "Autumn Moon over the Han Palace": slow tempo, conventional ornaments, single-line melody, relaxed and contemplative mood.

EXCERPT 2. CLOSING SECTION OF PIECE (CD EX. #3-25)

- Departure from traditional zheng musical style on multiple levels evident.

- Baban form no longer present.

- Recurring melodic figure (ostinato) used as basis for musical development; this approach, and the melodic contour itself (not stepwise), represents break from tradition.

- Elaborate use of *gua-zou* (glissando) ornamentation unconventional for this time; likewise true of the dramatic use of acceleration of tempo and the explicit programmaticism of the music.

Music and the conservatory solo zheng tradition in Communist China, 1949–1965

With the rise to power of Mao Zedong and the Chinese Communist Party (CCP) in 1949, efforts to reform Chinese music continued, but now with a thick overlay of explicit political content tied to the doctrines of Chinese socialism. According to Mao Zedong, all music and arts in the "New China" were to expressly serve the goals of the socialist state: to elevate and valorize the peasantry and proletarian (working class) masses, promote revolutionary ideals, and glorify the revolution, communism, and Mao himself. Communist songs for the masses like "On the Golden Hill in Beijing" (sung by Deng Haiqiong's mother, Li Xiuqin, with zheng accompaniment by Haiqiong, on **CD ex. #3-26**) were created in abundance and used to propagate Chinese state ideology and policies. With its melody based, at least ostensibly, on a Tibetan folksong, the text of "On the Golden Hill in Beijing" (see below) invokes several standard themes of Chinese communist rhetoric. These include

- The literal and metaphorical glorification of Mao Zedong and the CCP.

- The rationalization of CCP policies regarding China's "ethnic minorities" (in this case, Tibetans, many of whom regarded this song as "an offensive official reaction to the threatening antagonism" they felt toward the Chinese state [Baranovitch 2003:65]).

- The "emancipation" of the peasant masses.

- The ideal of building socialism for China.

A mass children's choir and orchestra perform a song entitled "We Are Successors to Communism" in Beijing (1965).

"On the Golden Hill in Beijing" (partial text translation, adapted from Baranovitch 2003:62) (CD ex. #3-26)

> *Rays of light from the golden hill in Beijing illuminate the four directions.*
>
> *Nurtured by the thought of Mao Zedong, we grow up.*
>
> *The emancipated peasants have good morale, and new Xijang [Tibet] is building socialism.*
>
> *Songs of praise are offered to Chairman Mao, songs of praise are offered to the Chinese Communist Party.*

Under Mao's rule, the government gradually became the sole official patron and controller of the arts, artistic activities, and arts-related institutions in Communist China. Organizations including the Chinese Musicians' Association (CMA), centered in Beijing, were established "to develop a body of music for the masses (peasants, workers, and soldiers) that . . . would reflect China's national aspirations and its achievements under communism" (Wong 2002:386). Regional and national music conservatories and research institutes played a major role in cultivating and promoting the new, official musical culture of the Chinese communist state. By 1952, conservatories were being established throughout the mainland, with the flagship institutions in Beijing and Shanghai.

As during the preceding Republican era, both Western and Chinese music were taught at the conservatories. Western music and instruments (especially the violin and the piano) continued to have the highest prestige, but Chinese music and instruments, including the zheng, made gradual advances in prominence and stature. The first full-fledged Chinese conservatory curriculum in zheng was established at the Shenyang Conservatory in 1950. A year later, in 1951, the prestigious Shanghai Conservatory instituted a major in zheng performance, and in the years that followed full-time zheng instructors were appointed at conservatories throughout China.

Extensive collection, research, and "development" of folk, minority, and historical traditions constituted a major component of the communist agenda for Chinese music. Government-sponsored music research institutes sent scholars, composers, and "music workers" out to towns, villages, and rural areas throughout China to collect data on traditional music genres so that they could be "preserved, studied, reformed, and modernized to serve the state and the people" (Wong 2002:387–88).

Within the new, socialist musical environment of the urban conservatories and music institutes, the zheng was promoted as a "genuine folk instrument" (Zheng 1983) and many new works for solo zheng were composed. Like "Return of the Fishing Boats," these new pieces were generally based (or at least said to be based) on traditional folk songs or folk music styles or forms. However, the musical departures from traditional folk roots were now more pronounced and more clearly indebted to Western influences. Additionally, these pieces were generally linked to titles and *programs* (i.e., descriptions of what the music was properly supposed to represent and evoke) informed by dominant themes of socialist ideology: celebration of the Chinese peasantry and proletariat, glorification of the revolution and Chinese communism, paying of homage to Mao Zedong and the CCP. Especially important and influential among the new solo zheng compositions of the period was "Celebrating the Harvest" (1955), which made extensive use of a piano-inspired, two-hand plucking technique on the zheng that would become a standard feature of much later zheng music.

In 1958, a government initiative to increase the official stature of Chinese music led several talented pianists at the Shanghai Conservatory to switch to the zheng as their main instrument. Among these was Fan Shang'e, who was also significant as a representative of a new generation of female zheng players who soon came to replace the older, male regional masters as the most renowned players of the instrument. The virtuosic, "pianistic" potential of the zheng was greatly developed by this new generation of performers. Solo zheng pieces became increasingly demanding technically, requiring new, flashier playing techniques. The zheng itself was modified to meet the new musical demands. It was during this period that the 21-string zheng, with its expanded four-octave range, replaced its three-octave, 16-string predecessor as the standard form of the instrument in the conservatories.

Fan Shang'e (Fan Shaang-uh)

The important composer and zheng player Fan Shang'e.

"Spring on Snowy Mountains," by Fan Shang'e

- CD Track #**3-27**
- Featured performer(s)/group: Xiao Ying (zheng)
- Format: Excerpt
- Source recording: *The Art of the Chinese Harp: Guzheng,* by Xiao Ying (ARC Music Productions International Ltd. EUCD 1877)

The virtuosic, piano-inspired approach to solo zheng composition that emerged out of Shanghai and other conservatories in the post-1958 era is well represented by the piece "Spring on Snowy Mountains," by Fan Shang'e (who now resides in Toronto). Here again, a Tibetan folksong is cited as the source of the piece's melody, but aside from the possible connection of the "Spring on Snowy Mountains" main melody to an actual Tibetan tune, the piece has little, if anything, to do with traditional Tibetan folk music. (Visit the Online Learning Center at www.mhhe.com/bakan1 for references to Tibetan music recordings and resources.)

The socialist program linked to "Spring on Snowy Mountains," which describes a scene of Tibetans happily singing and dancing in their beautiful, mountainous land in a spirit of welcome toward Chinese communist rule, has even less bearing on Tibetan realities. Tibetans during this time were severely oppressed under Chinese occupation. Through instrumental music like this and propoganda songs such as "On the Golden Hill in Beijing," the Chinese government, via its music-based initiatives, endeavored to invent and promote an image of national harmony and inclusiveness that was starkly at odds with political realities (see "Insights and Perspectives" box on p. 313).

What is most interesting and novel about this piece in comparison to earlier solo zheng music is the highly developed two-hand playing technique. Instead of a predominantly single-line melodic texture with right-hand plucking and ornamental embellishments produced by left-hand string pressing, "Spring on Snowy Mountains" features a two-part texture in which the right hand plucks out the main melody on the high-pitched strings while the left hand provides accompaniment in the form of arpeggiated chords (*payin*) in the lower register. This more complex, two-level texture is clearly the result of Western piano and harp music influence. It is not at all surprising that music such as this was largely the product of a new breed of zheng virtuosos like Fan Shang'e who had begun their careers as pianists.

Some of the most striking parts of "Spring on Snowy Mountains" feature a texture in which the right hand plays the melody in notes that are sustained by tremolos (*yao zhi*) overtop arpeggiated, left-hand chordal accompaniment embellished by frequent glissandos. The section of the piece included on **CD ex. #3-27** begins with an example of this type of texture (0:00–0:45). This is followed by a short, lovely passage featuring harp-like, descending arpeggios (0:45–1:01). The final portion of the excerpt is in a lively dance rhythm meant to evoke images of "happy Tibetans" performing their traditional folk dances (1:02–end).

The novel zheng style represented by "Spring on Snowy Mountains" and other works of this period, including the very famous solo zheng composition "Fighting the Typhoon" (1965; passages from this piece were featured in both Online Musical Illustration #26 and the chapter's Musical Guided Tour), was considered extremely difficult to master in terms of its technical demands when it was introduced in the late 1950s/1960s. However, in the hyper-virtuosic environment of contemporary zheng playing inhabited by the likes of Deng Haiqiong and Xiao Ying (the performer heard on this recording of "Spring on Snowy Mountains"), mastery of pieces of this level of difficulty has become just a basic requirement of performance competence on the instrument.

The Chinese Occupation of Tibet and the Plight of Tibetan Buddhists

Communist China's gradual takeover and occupation of Tibet, beginning in 1950 and intensifying after 1956, led to brutal persecution of Tibetans, especially monks of Tibetan Buddhist monastic orders. It was this persecution that led the Dalai Lama, the renowned spiritual leader of Tibetan Buddhism (and winner of the 1989 Nobel Peace Prize), to flee Tibet for exile in India in 1959. In the wake of his departure, upwards of a hundred thousand Tibetan Buddhists fled Tibet to escape persecution so brutal that China was accused of committing genocide against the Tibetan people by an international council in 1961.

Still today, the Dalai Lama and multitudes of Tibetan Buddhists remain political refugees from their homeland, now China's so-called Autonomous Region of Tibet. Their chants and music have been the subject of much interest among ethnomusicologists and scholars of religion (see references at the Online Learning Center: www.mhhe.com/bakan1). An example of Tibetan Buddhist chant performed by monks of the Drepung Gomang Monastery is featured on **CD ex. #3-28.** The original Drepung Gomang Monastery was founded near Lhasa, the capital of Tibet, in 1416. In the wake of the destruction of Tibetan Buddhist monasteries during the Chinese communist invasion, some 300 monks of the Gomang order escaped China, fleeing to neighboring India to live in exile. Under the sponsorship of the Dalai Lama, the Drepung Gomang Monastery was rebuilt in Mundgod, India, in 1969.

This recording of the Drepung Gomang monks features an extraordinary type of chant vocalization called *gyü-ke,* in which the monks manipulate their voices to produce an extremely low-pitched and powerful vocal sound rich in overtones. In gyü-ke, each voice produces multiple tones (multiphonics), so that both the super-low notes described and also high-pitched, almost bell-like overtones sound together to produce a sound that is not only unique in the world of music, but also profoundly spiritual from a Tibetan Buddhist perspective. From that perspective, gyü-ke is perceived as a sonic realization of everything that exists in the universe.

Though unique in sound and cultural meaning, Tibetan Buddhist chant such as that heard in **CD ex. #3-28** involves "overtone singing" techniques similar to those to which we were introduced earlier from Mongolia (**CD ex. #1-5**) and Tuva (**CD ex. #1-18**).

Monks of the Drepung Gomang Monastery.

guided listening quick summary

"Spring on Snowy Mountains," by Fan Shang'e (CD ex. #3-27)

Zheng tuning: D E G A B (D)

The Cultural Revolution era

The Cultural Revolution (1966–1976) is generally depicted as a dark period in China's modern history. The purported aim of the Cultural Revolution was to rid Chinese culture of anything "alien to the egalitarian spirit of [Chinese] socialism" (Fletcher 2001:344). In effect, this translated into brutally oppressive policies aimed at many sectors of Chinese society. Freedom of intellectual and artistic expression was severely constrained. Individuals and groups accused of going against the grain of state ideology were sent off to work camps in the country to be "reformed." (Many were tortured or even executed.) Beijing Opera and other Chinese opera and theater forms were placed in a virtual stranglehold. Most Beijing Opera productions were banned outright, and those that were allowed were so profoundly saturated with Cultural Revolution–inspired politicization that they barely resembled the operas of earlier periods. Religion (or "superstition," as it was known), already subject to severe repression prior to the Cultural Revolution, was now squelched to unprecedented degrees. Oppression of ethnic minority groups also escalated, devastating peoples such as Uighurs and Tibetans living in their Chinese-occupied homelands.

For all of its atrocities, however, the Cultural Revolution was not quite the cultural vacuum that popular accounts often make it out to have been. Musical life, though restrained, continued. People sang revolutionary songs. They were allowed to learn and play instruments (though only certain approved pieces). There was considerable activity in the domains of both amateur and children's music making. In rural areas far from the centers of bureaucratic power, cultural life in some cases went on much as it always had, existing largely beyond the scrutiny of the centralized political authorities.

With respect to the zheng in conservatory music culture, Te-yuan Cheng, an authority on the instrument and its history, claims that the Cultural Revolution "choked off new composition" and that activities related to the zheng essentially "came to a halt" (Cheng 1991:192, 249). This is perhaps an overstatement, though it does seem clear that the evolution of the zheng was severely impeded. A relatively small number of new solo zheng compositions were composed, and the titles and programs linked to these pieces, not surprisingly, were characterized by an especially intense political character. These included "Molten Iron Pouring in a Stream" (a disturbing title if ever there was one) and "Little Sister Hero of the Plains." The latter of these programatically depicts a Mongolian child protecting her commune's sheep in the midst of a blizzard while singing songs in praise of the Cultural Revolution (Cheng 1991:191).

The Rise of Deng Xiaoping and the Period of Openness

The death of Mao Zedong in 1976 and the fall of the Gang of Four, a group of ultraradical CCP leaders (including Mao's wife, Jiang Qing, who had been a catalyst in the effort to place extreme constraints on artistic expression during the preceding decade), brought to an end the Cultural Revolution. In its wake came a period of major social upheaval and instability. Rampant persecution, widespread poverty and disease, and large-scale societal frustration with China's increased international isolation and resultant economic failures led the Chinese populace to call for major political, economic, and social reforms. Deng Xiaoping, a CCP senior official who had been demoted during the Cultural Revolution, reemerged to become the new leader of China and ushered the troubled nation into the so-called Period of Openness era that crystallized in the early 1980s.

Deng's regime was in effect a high-wire act of radical political experimentation. His goal was to maintain the communist political order amid an environment of free enterprise and engagement with global markets of which China had not previously been a part. In many respects, his experiment achieved great successes, its continuing legacy still evident in China's remarkable ascent as an international economic power in recent decades. In other respects, it failed miserably, the most notorious example being the Tiananmen Square massacre of 1989, where the old draconian tactics of authoritarian rule that lurked beneath the public facade of a more liberal and tolerant government were brutally exposed (see below). The shockwaves of

Cui Jian and the Tiananmen Square Uprisings

The Chinese rock star Cui Jian (Tsway Jee-en) has been described by author and musician Dennis Rea as "Bob Dylan, John Lennon, and Kurt Cobain all rolled into one, a one-man rock and roll revolution whose poignant songs of alienation spoke volumes to a generation searching for meaning in a rapidly changing and increasingly globalized China." His best-known song, "Nothing to My Name" ("Yi Wu Suo You") was adopted as an unofficial anthem of the Chinese democracy movement that reached its climax in a massive hunger-strike protest at Beijing's Tiananmen Square in 1989. Cui Jian and his band ADO performed this song and others at the protest. The image of him defiantly rallying the protesters with his music, in Rea's words, "symbolized a generation's struggles and aspirations." The Tiananmen Square uprising began as a peaceful protest led by college students and other alienated Chinese youth who were frustrated by the institutionalized corruption, rampant materialism, widening social stratification, and "bankrupt ideology" of late 1980s "open" China under Deng Xiaoping and the CCP. It ended in bloodshed and tragedy when army tanks rolled into the Square and opened fire on the assembled masses, killing many. More than any other single incident, this tragic event came to symbolize the troubling vestiges of old, authoritarian rule in the ostensibly new and open society of post-1970s China (Rea 2006; see also Baranovitch 2003).

Cui Jian.

change initiated by Deng resonate still today, as China's balancing act between capitalist enterprise and communist ideology grows ever more complex.

The arts, the zheng, and musicultural life in post-1970s China

In 1979, Deng Xiaoping introduced his policy for the arts in a new, more "open" China as part of a sweeping agenda for the modernization of the country and Chinese socialism. Framing his words in relation to the preceding era of severe government control and censorship of the arts, he stated that

> our nation has a long history, a vast domain, a huge population, many different peoples, a great range of occupations . . . and a variety of customs, cultural traditions and artistic interests. If only we can educate and enlighten the people and enable them to enjoy beauty and recreation, then they will find their own place in the sphere of the arts. . . . In their leadership of artistic and literary work, the [Communist] party will not simply issue orders and commands, nor will it demand that literature or art submit to political work on a temporary, a concrete or a direct basis. . . . The complex spiritual labor of artistic and literary creation truly requires that writers and artists give free rein to their individual creative endeavors. Whatever they write or create can only be investigated and resolved by artists. There will be no interference in these matters. . . . (Deng Xiaoping, c.f. Cheng 1991:194)

The new policies of openness, combined with the release of the pressure valve of controls on artistic freedom that had held Chinese musicians in its grip during the preceding era, yielded a Chinese musical renaissance. International mass media entertainment—popular music, music videos, commercial films, and television shows—flooded into mainland China from Hong Kong, Taiwan, the West, and elsewhere. A booming local Chinese popular music culture and industry emerged as well, producing superstar figures such as the rock musician Cui Jian (see "Insights and Perspectives" box on p. 315). Traditional, pre-revolutionary Beijing Opera and other styles of regional drama were revived and flourished. Formerly suppressed folk, ritual, religious, and minority music traditions, as well as court music traditions of the dynastic period that had been roundly condemned under earlier communist regimes, were allowed to reemerge and were officially embraced as integral dimensions of China's multicultural society. Extensive research on living rural traditions and musics and dances of China's ethnic minorities was conducted at state music institutions (Witzleben 2002:90). Conservatory-trained virtuoso performers on both Western instruments (piano, violin) and Chinese instruments (zheng, pipa, erhu) appeared on concert stages worldwide and were featured on internationally distributed recordings.

Tan Dun (Tahn Doo-en)

Composer Tan Dun receiving his Academy Award for the score of *Crouching Tiger, Hidden Dragon.*

Attitudes toward Western art music (the "classical" music traditions of the West) relative to Chinese music also underwent a transformation. The works of contemporary, experimental Western composers of the 20th century, formerly censored or at least frowned upon in official Chinese cultural circles, now came to be appreciated and to exert a significant influence on contemporary developments in Chinese conservatory music culture and its offshoots. Numerous gifted, young Chinese composers were sent abroad to study at major university music schools and conservatories, where they learned the techniques and methods of Western new music composition. The integration of diverse Chinese, Western, and other musical elements in the works of these composers yielded the "New Wave" movement in modern Chinese music. Tan Dun, the Academy Award–winning composer of the musical score for the internationally acclaimed Chinese film *Crouching Tiger, Hidden Dragon,* is the best-known of the New Wave Chinese composers. His composition "Desert Capriccio" (**CD ex. #3-29**) is a quite lovely work from that film. The soloist is the American cellist (of Chinese descent) Yo-Yo Ma. He is accompanied by an ensemble of Chinese instruments including the erhu, the pipa, and a fascinating ancient instrument called the *sheng,* which is a "mouth organ" with 17 bamboo pipes arranged in an incomplete circle formation.

The zheng and its conservatory-based musical tradition blossomed in post-1970s China. The founding of the Beijing Zheng Association in 1980 and the establishment of the National Zheng Symposium in 1986 (at which Deng Haiqiong performed "Autumn Moon over the Han Palace" in a tribute performance for Gao Zicheng) were important institutional benchmarks of the instrument's ascent. The emergence of novel compositional styles representing entirely new levels of virtuosity, experimentalism, and cosmopolitanism (especially in the incorporation of adapted, modern Western compositional techniques) was a major development. So too was a revival of interest in researching, preserving, and cultivating older regional styles of zheng music. Gifted female zheng artists, the majority of them associated with the Shanghai Conservatory, increasingly came to dominate the zheng performance world. New, experimental types of zheng, such as the 49-string "butterfly zheng"—named for its distinctive shape— were invented (though they generally did not achieve wide popularity). Collectively, these many and varied developments marked the arrival and evolution of a post-traditional age for the zheng in mainland China.

Sheng being played.

sheng (shung [rhymes with "lung"])

Yet while the musical renaissance of the Period of Openness, in the zheng world and beyond, brought many positive and exciting developments in the wake of the Cultural Revolution, it was by no means devoid of problems. As in virtually every other era of Chinese history, close links between musical and political life underscored both the good and the bad. On the one hand, China's increasing integration into the global economy afforded new opportunities for musicians from the PRC to study and perform abroad, widening their musical horizons and providing abundant new professional opportunities. On the other hand, as China moved aggressively toward its own version of a free market economy, government support of state institutions such as music conservatories generally decreased. This compelled many talented, conservatory-trained musicians to pursue international careers not only out of a desire to seek new opportunities but also out of economic necessity.

Another problem has had to do with a new variation on the old theme of cultural appropriation of folk and minority musics by the state conservatory music culture. "The People's Republic of China, a multi-ethnic state that takes pride in its wealth of diverse traditions," writes Sabine Trebinjac, an ethnomusicologist who specializes in music of the Uighur people of northwestern China, "is also anxious to affirm the existence of a national musical tradition, which involves manufacturing heavily sinicized [i.e., Chinese-ified] versions of the products of other cultures," in particular, cultures such as the Uighurs and Tibetans, who are much less likely to view themselves as Chinese people than as people living against their will under Chinese rule (Trebinjac 2005). Ethnic groups such as the Tibetans and Uighurs have suffered greatly at the hands of Chinese authorities. While their contemporary situations are perhaps better than they were, say, during the Cultural Revolution, acute tensions, troubling civil rights issues, and struggles for national sovereignty and independence continue.

A significant portion of the repertoire of solo instrumental music of the modern conservatory tradition, including solo zheng music, consists of heavily sinicized/Westernized compositions "based on" minority music traditions of peoples such as the Uighurs and Tibetans. Many of these pieces are extremely well crafted and very effective on a purely musical level. They

TABLE 13.2 Major developments of the zheng and its musical culture during the modern era (post-1912).

Republican Era (1912–1948)

- Zheng taught at urban conservatories

- Neo-traditional musical style for solo zheng pieces ("Return of the Fishing Boats," Lou Shuhua, 1936): departure from baban form, new techniques, explicit programmaticism, music of a more dramatic character

Initial Period of Communist Era (1949–1965)

- Establishment of zheng programs in most major conservatories, including Beijing and Shanghai (early 1950s)

- Significant Western influences (especially piano-derived) on zheng music and playing styles; pianistic two-hand playing techniques; titles and programs of pieces linked to communist ideology ("Celebrating the Harvest," 1955)

- Increasingly pianistic, virtuosic style of solo zheng playing post-1958 (Fan Shang'e, "Spring on Snowy Mountains"); 21-string zheng replaces 16-string zheng as standard instrument around the same time; Shanghai Conservatory leads the way

Cultural Revolution Era (1966–1976)

- Development of zheng stifled during this oppressive period; new pieces that emerge exceedingly ideological ("Molten Iron Pouring in a Stream," "Little Sister Hero of the Plains")

Period of Openness (Late 1970s–Present)

- Modern zheng renaissance: new techniques, playing styles, and compositional styles ("Music from the Muqam," discussed in next section of chapter); openness to contemporary Western music influences and experimentation among "New Wave" and other composers (e.g., Tan Dun)

- Major professional organizations founded and conferences established (Beijing Zheng Association, 1980; National Zheng Symposium, 1986)

- Women zheng artists dominant (especially out of Shanghai Conservatory)

- Major new instrument innovations and experiments (e.g., 49-string "butterfly zheng"), though standard 21-string zheng remains predominant

- Numerous leading conservatory-trained zheng players establish international careers (e.g., Deng Haiqiong)

project a positive image of a unified, inclusive, multicultural Chinese nation that is very much in keeping with the public image the Chinese government endeavors to promote to both its own citizenry and the broader world. Alas, the positive image projected still contradicts much harsher sociopolitical realities. The peoples ostensibly represented through music of this kind—Uighurs, Tibetans, members of other minority groups in China—typically resent having their musical traditions, and by extension themselves, cast in this light. This is important to keep in mind as we turn now to a final Guided Listening Experience focusing on a Uighur music-inspired Chinese zheng piece entitled "Music from the Muqam."

"Music from the Muqam," by Zhou Ji, Shao Guangchen, and Li Mei

- CD Track #**3-30**
- Featured performer(s)/group: Deng Haiqiong (zheng), Quek Ling Kiong (*dap* [drum])
- Format: Excerpt
- Source recording: *Ning,* by Hai-qiong Deng [Deng Haiqiong] (Celebrity Music CMCD 9464)

"Music from the Muqam" is a composition for solo zheng with drum accompaniment. It was created in 1988 by three Han Chinese composers from the far northwestern region of China called Xinjiang (East Turkistan or Uighuristan by Uighur nationalists), where the majority of Uighur people live. One of the composers, Li Mei, was a teacher of Haiqiong.

The piece takes its inspiration and key elements of its style and design from a Uighur tradition known as the Dolan Muqam. This is one of several Uighur regional traditions of **muqam** music that collectively constitute the core foundation of Uighur musical art. Some of these, like the venerable Twelve Muqam (*On Iqqi Muqam*) are believed to descend from the Uighur royal courts of olden times and are repositories of rich cultural lore and symbolism. For example, *Muqam Raq,* one of the Twelve Muqam, is symbolically tied to a Uighur legend in which the protagonist wanders through the labyrinth of a network of a thousand caves, each of which presents him with some treasure and mystery. The "wanderer" is considered to be on the way to discovering new treasures of traditional Uighur wisdom (Czekanowska 1983:104).

In contrast, the Dolan Muqam is pure village style, representing the rough, raw end of Uighur music. The Dolan were traditionally the poorest, most despised class of Uighurs. Under Chinese imperial rule, they served the Chinese administration as indentured serfs, and they were well-known for their enthusiasm for rebellion.

Muqam is a local pronunciation of the Arabic *maqam.* In Arab music, *maqam* essentially means "mode" and the term is integrally linked to a wide range of music traditions (see Chapter 12, p. 259). In the Uighur music context, however (and in Central Asia generally), *muqam*

Li Mei (Lee May)

muqam (moo-KAHM)

insights and perspectives

Uighur History and Culture

More than six million Uighurs live in the so-called Xinjiang-Uighur Autonomous Region of northwestern China, accounting for some 45 percent of the region's total population. The Uighur are Muslims who long ago converted from Buddhism and before that practiced shamanistic religions. They speak a Turkic language and their cultural and musical traditions draw more from Persian (Iranian), Arabic, and Turkic (including Uzbek and Tajik) sources than from Chinese ones. In ancient times, the Uighur occupied a strategic position along the Silk Road and prospered greatly through favored trade relations with imperial China during some dynastic eras. It was in the ancestral homelands of the Uighur that Chinese traders crossed paths with the likes of European imperialists and explorers such as Alexander the Great and Marco Polo. It was also along the Silk Road through Uighur lands that Central Asian prototypes of instruments such as the pipa and erhu first came to China. Uighur music ensembles are documented as having resided and performed at the Chinese imperial courts during dynastic times.

has a different meaning, referring to a particular type of *large-scale precomposed suite of songs and instrumental music.*

A muqam performance begins with a free rhythm introduction (with or without singing) followed by a series of pieces performed in different meters at progressively faster tempos. The instrumentation is not standardized, but generally features either a solo vocalist accompanying himself on a plucked chordophone (e.g., a *rawap;* see the photo above) or a lead vocalist accompanied by a small chorus of singers and a small ensemble of instrumentalists. The percussive rhythmic accompaniment is provided by a frame drum called a **dap** (see photo). The head of the dap is made of donkey hide or snake skin.

Though they are not Uighurs themselves, Li Mei and the other two composers of "Music from the Muqam" have all studied and researched the muqam traditions extensively. Li Mei grew up in Xinjiang and was trained as a zheng player in the Chinese conservatory system. She eventually went on to advanced musicological studies of Uighur music at the graduate level. Haiqiong believes that Li Mei's life experiences in Xinjiang and her extensive record of musical and scholarly study of Uighur music set her apart from many other Chinese composers—especially composers of earlier eras—who have composed modern-style pieces based on "minority" source music materials.

"The earlier pieces based on minority music," states Haiqiong, "always have a similar kind of 'happy' feeling. They all describe the beauty of nature and scenery and people living a happy life with much singing and dancing. When I was little, that was what I believed [the lives of members of China's ethnic minority groups were like]. But 'Music from the Muqam' is different. It's a really great piece. Li Mei and her collaborators brought some deeper feeling and expression to it, and new ways of performing on the zheng. It completely changed my perceptions of the possibilities of zheng performance."

"Music from the Muqam" employs an unusual zheng tuning: D F♯ G A C (two "extra" pitches, B and E, appear occasionally as well). According to Haiqiong, this tuning reproduces the melodic character of a traditional Uighur mode. She also explains that certain rhythmic patterns, melodic ornaments, and elements of formal design in "Music from the Muqam" likewise represent direct Uighur music influences. Of particular interest on the rhythmic level is the prominent use of meters with five beats per measure. Meters of five and seven are common in Uighur music, where they generate what the Uighur refer to as *aksak,* literally "limping," rhythms (Rachel Harris, personal correspondence with the author, 2006).

Despite these clearly identifiable Uighur influences, "Music from the Muqam" is firmly centered in the virtuosic style of contemporary, conservatory zheng music, and therefore reflects a high level of Western musical influence as well. Even the Uighur-inspired tuning of the zheng is evidence of this, since the "Uighur mode" employed is recast in equal-tempered (evenly spaced) intervals unrelated to traditional Uighur musical practice.

"Music from the Muqam" consists of three main formal sections: A, B, and A. The excerpt found on **CD ex.#3-30** features the B section of the piece only. It begins with a hauntingly beautiful zheng melody that builds through several phrases (0:00–1:54). Many of the melodic ornaments, such as the various forms of *gua-zou* (glissandos), are standard to Chinese zheng style and familiar to us from earlier examples; others are not. Especially distinctive is an ornament in which strings tuned to the pitch A are bent slightly upward (almost to the pitch B) on certain notes (e.g., at 0:06). This, according to Haiqiong, is an inflection inspired by traditional melodic ornamentation in Uighur music. Haiqiong also explains that the ostinato, duple-meter rhythmic pattern of the dap frame drum in this section is characteristically Uighur. Noteworthy, too, but for a different reason, are the chords played on the zheng. Many of these consist of four pitches, rather than the customary three- or two-pitch chords of earlier zheng music styles. This exemplifies the presence of more modern streams of Western musical influence than we have encountered previously in the chapter's musical examples. Moreover, in Haiqiong's assessment, these more complex chords represent a distinctively innovative feature of the composition.

The second part of the excerpt begins at 1:55. Following a transitional, free rhythm moment where time seems to hang suspended in mid-air (1:55–2:04), aksak rhythms come to the fore, replacing the steady duple-meter rhythms of the preceding section. From 2:05, the music moves along mainly in a five-beat, aksak meter with unpredictable accents. It builds progressively—in volume, tempo, and overall intensity—to a dazzling, glissando-laden climax at the end. This kind of dramatic buildup has no parallel in traditional Uighur music, though it has many in both standard zheng pieces (e.g., "Return of the Fishing Boats") and Western music. Throughout this second part of the example, the zheng and the dap proceed in lock-step rhythmic unison, and the precise synchronization of their rhythms is impressive. So too is the flair of Haiqiong's performance here, which puts the expressive range of the zheng on brilliant display.

guided listening quick summary

"Music from the Muqam," Deng Haiqiong (CD ex. #3-30)

Zheng tuning: D F♯ G A C (D) (nontraditional). Two additional pitches, B and E, also occur intermittently (produced by pressing into the A and D strings, respectively, so that their pitches "bend" upward).

PART I OF EXCERPT

0:00–1:54

■ Steady, duple-meter rhythm; rhythm of *dap* (frame drum) characteristically "Uighur."

■ Many standard zheng melodic ornaments used (e.g., *gua-zou*), but so too are a variety of other ornaments that are not conventional for the zheng and reflect traditional Uighur musical practices (e.g., the upward bend of the pitch A heard at 0:06 and elsewhere in the piece).

- Chords often include four pitches, suggesting more modern Western influences than are evident in most earlier zheng pieces.

PART II OF EXCERPT

1:55–end

- Begins with transitional moment of free rhythm; creates impression of suspension of time.
- Aksak ("limping") rhythms replace the steady, duple-meter rhythms of the earlier portion of the piece.
- From 2:05, five-beat meter is established and maintained (except for two measures of six-beat meter at 2:21), though the rhythmic accents are varied and unpredictable.
- Progressive, gradual acceleration and intensification leading to an exciting climax at the end.
- Impressive rhythmic synchrony between zheng and dap, and dazzling displays of zheng virtuosity by Deng Haiqiong.

Summary

In the course of this chapter, we tracked the history of the zheng and its music from the Qin dynasty of the 3rd century BCE to contemporary times. Primary attention was devoted to the history of the zheng during the modern era, especially to the tradition of solo zheng playing associated with the government-sponsored, conservatory music culture of mainland China in the 20th century and since. Deng Haiqiong, the featured performer in several of the chapter's musical examples, was cast as a representative of that tradition. The integral historical link between regional solo zheng traditions and the conservatory style these traditions fed into was examined. So too was the important relationship between Chinese traditional and Western musics, a relationship that has influenced the development of zheng music on many levels.

The approach of the chapter was essentially historical, linking well-known zheng compositions of different eras to significant musical, political, and cultural events and movements. In tracking the evolution of zheng music from one period to the next—from traditional styles ("Autumn Moon over the Han Palace"), to neo-traditional styles ("Return of the Fishing Boats," "Spring on Snowy Mountains"), to post-traditional styles ("Music from the Muqam")—we saw how stylistic continuity and change in music may be seen to reflect continuity and change much more broadly at societal and cultural levels. Issues of "ethnic minority" representation, gender roles, political control and ideological use of music, traditionalism and modernity (including Westernization), and creative freedoms and constraints during different historical periods were all shown to be implicated in the particular course of development that the zheng has followed over the more than two thousand years of its existence.

Key Terms

zheng
regional styles of solo zheng music
pipa
qin
Beijing Opera
Mandarin Chinese (language)

Han Chinese (majority ethnic group)
Chinese Communist Party (CCP)
Cultural Revolution
Period of Openness
koto
ornamentation (different types)
gua-zou (glissando ornaments)

Confucianism
Silk Road
yun
baban (form)
yijing
muqam
dap

Study Questions

- Who is Deng Haiqiong? What instrument does she play? What have been some of her significant professional accomplishments?

- What are China's two most populous cities (also the locations of the country's leading music conservatories)?

- Which of the many imperial dynasties of China were discussed in this chapter? What developments in zheng music and culture were associated with each?

- How is the zheng constructed? What were some of the main zheng playing and ornamentation techniques discussed?

- What other zither-type chordophones besides the zheng are found in China and other nations of East and Southeast Asia (Japan, Korea, Mongolia, Vietnam)?

- What were the principal regional styles of solo zheng playing discussed in the chapter? Of what regional style is "Autumn Moon over the Han Palace" representative? What is the name of the *musical form* of this piece (and most other traditional zheng compositions)?

- What was the Silk Road? What was its significance to the development of Chinese music and culture during the dynastic era?

- What musical innovations were introduced and/or developed in the following compositions: "Return of the Fishing Boats," "Spring on Snowy Mountains," "Music from the Muqam"? Who were the composers of these important works?

- What have been the three main historical periods of the People's Republic of China (est. 1949)? What major political developments were associated with each period and what developments in Chinese musical culture (and the conservatory-based culture of the zheng especially) occurred during each?

- How does the history of Beijing Opera since the 19th century reflect larger social and political movements in Chinese history?

- Who is Tan Dun and what is his significance as a composer?

- How has the appropriation of Uighur, Tibetan, and other "minority" musics into the musical culture of the Chinese conservatories been approached during different periods? What sorts of issues and controversies surround such appropriations, both musically and sociopolitically?

Discussion Questions

- A major issue explored in this chapter is the relationship between musical developments and political movements in Chinese history. Relationships between music and politics run deep in societies throughout the world. Where do you see instances of music being used in political contexts in your own society? Are the political uses of music of which you are aware explicit or implicit, obvious or subtle? Why do you think music has been closely aligned with so many political regimes and institutions in so many societies throughout history?

- In this chapter, a single instrument, the zheng, was taken as a lens through which to view large currents in the history of Chinese society, culture, and politics. A similar approach might be productive in studies of American or other Western societies. What might a historical, ethnomusicological approach to the study of the electric guitar reveal about larger issues in American social history? What could we learn about the cultures and histories of Europe or the Americas through a sociopolitically informed history of the piano?

Applying What You Have Learned

- The People's Republic of China today is a nation in the midst of tremendous economic, political, social, and cultural transformation. Contemporary Chinese musicultural life reflects this climate of change profoundly, with burgeoning movements in rock, punk, hip-hop, avant-garde, and other musical styles that were formerly not allowed. Use Internet keyword searches (e.g., "Chinese rock music," "Chinese punk music," etc.) to research the contemporary music scene in mainland China. Write an annotated Webography chronicling your findings. Conclude with some general comments in which you apply what you have learned about historical processes of tradition and transformation in Chinese music to your assessment of current musical trends and directions in China.

Resources for Further Study

Visit the Online Learning Center at **www.mhhe.com/bakan1** for learning aids, study help, and additional resources that supplement the content of this chapter.

climbing **Jacob's Ladder:**
modern musical reflections
of an ancient **Jewish mystical text**

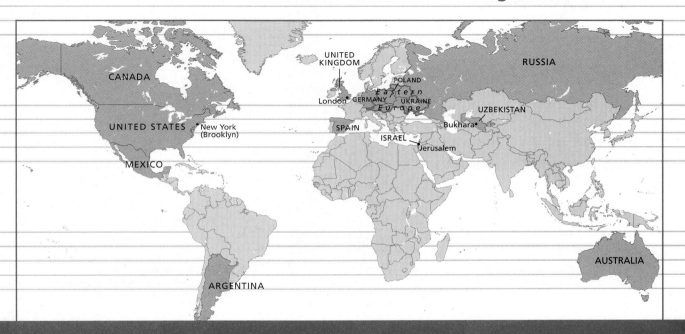

The holy master, the Baal Shem Tov, while lying on his deathbed, gathered together his disciples, and requested that they sing a song together. As they sang the song, the Baal Shem Tov's soul was slowly drifting from this world. As they neared the end of the tune, the Baal Shem Tov whispered a prayer, and his soul departed his body, entering eternity through a song. He lived music; his life reads like a harmonious melody; he ascended through music, and finally, became music.

DovBer Pinson, *Inner Rhythms: The Kabbalah of Music*

A passage of ancient, sacred verse chanted by an elderly musician in Uzbekistan. A mystical prayer that is traditionally intoned only by men being sung by a female Israeli vocalist. A contemporary techno recording by a British band featuring heavily processed digital samples of the voice of a cantor from the 1920s.

World events		Music events
Abraham, first patriarch of the Jewish people (in the Torah), migrates to Canaan (modern-day Israel/Palestine)	2nd millennium BCE	
Hyksos Dynasty, Ancient Egypt (third Jewish patriarch, Jacob)	c. 1650–1550 BCE	
Israelite kingdom founded (Jerusalem)	c. 1000 BCE	King David, legendary musician and poet of the Hebrew Bible, was second king of the Israelite kingdom
Israelite kingdom conquered by the Babylonians; First Temple destroyed; Jews exiled to Babylonian territories	587 BCE	
Jews allowed to return to their homeland (renamed Judea—province of Persian empire)	539 BCE	
Second Temple rebuilt in Jerusalem during Persian rule period		
Judea comes under control of Greek empire	332 BCE	
Judea (Palestine) comes under Roman control	37 BCE	
Second Temple destroyed by Romans	70 CE	
Jews expelled from Judea, sent into exile	132 CE	Contemporary diversity of Jewish musics reflective of long diasporic history dating back to this era
Jewish diaspora; beginnings of Rabbinic Judaism, synagogues		
Writing of the Zohar, according to Kabbalistic traditionalists	2nd century CE	
Writing of the Zohar (attributed to Moses de León), according to academic historians	13th century CE	Music an important part of Kabbalistic practice traditionally, including musical renderings of passages from the Zohar

Zohar (ZOE-har)

Kabbalah (Kah-bah-LAH)

deveikut (d'vay-KOOT)

ratso v'shov (ROT-zaw v'SHAWV [Hebrew, but with Yiddish pronunciation])

On the surface, it is difficult to imagine a more eclectic mix of musical productions. Yet the **Zohar,** a central literary work of the Jewish mystical tradition of **Kabbalah** that serves as the common point of reference for all of these performances, is not about surfaces; it is, rather, about the hidden spiritual dimensions *beneath* the surface of perceivable reality.

Music based on or inspired by the Zohar is the focus of this chapter. We will explore several works that are very different from one another, but that all share at least one foundational feature: they are rooted, musically and symbolically, in this central text of Kabbalah. The principal cultural element explored, then, is the Zohar itself. The chapter's musicultural focus is musical symbolism, which is approached in relation to the following guiding question: How are symbolic musical devices—of melodic contour, contrasting textures and dynamics, musical settings of chanted or sung texts—employed, in essence, to invoke the Zohar and bring it to musical life?

A prevalent theme of certain Kabbalistic practices stemming from the Zohar is a transcendent, spiritual ideal of **deveikut,** meaning "to be one with the Divine" (Pinson 2000:33). For Jews who seek this ideal, the path to deveikut is not a straight one, but rather involves a lifelong process of *ratso v'shov,* "going out from and coming back to" this earthly world in aspiring to an ultimate state of direct communion with God.

World events		Music events
New age of Zoharic thought and Kabbalah under Isaac Luria	**16th century**	
Chassidic Judaism in Central and Eastern Europe (Baal Shem Tov)	**18th century**	Music important in Chassidic worship and spirituality; secular, instrumental styles such as klezmer eventually associated with Chassidic culture as well
Reform Judaism (begins in Germany)	**19th century**	Reform principles inspired more liberal attitudes toward use of music in connection with Jewish practice and expressions of faith
Mass migrations of Jews from Europe and Russia to U.S. (especially New York City), Canada, Britain, Palestine (under British control), Australia, other countries Major global shift of world Jewish demographics, culture	**1881–1948**	Shifting demographics and cultural developments reflected in the international landscape of Jewish music
	1928	Pinchas Pinchik, a Jewish cantor and immigrant to the U.S. from the Ukraine, records "Roso De Shabbos" (on text from the Zohar)
World War II; Holocaust	**1939–1945**	
Modern nation of Israel declared	**1948**	
	1997	British techno group Zöhar formed
	1999	Ruth Wieder Magan releases CD *Songs to the Invisible God,* featuring "Roza DeShabbos"
	2001	Zöhar releases CD *onethreeseven,* featuring "Ehad"

Music, song, and sung prayer may be performed both to facilitate the pursuit of deveikut and to symbolize it. *Melodic direction* is often key to this symbolism. The spiritual aspirant is "seen," through alternately ascending and descending melodies, going out from and coming back to the world on a "ladder of perfection" leading from the earth to the heavens and back again. And travel occurs in the opposite direction as well, as the God of the Zohar, "in His . . . knowable aspects" (Blumenthal 1978:130), is portrayed as descending *from* the heavens to seek communion with the human world, then returning to the heavenly realms in His own process of ratso v'shov, or going out and coming back.

All this traveling between different cosmic realms is highly significant, for in Zoharic thought, "God and man stand in a reciprocal relationship, each benefiting the other, each doing something that allows the other to achieve full existence. . . . The Zohar teaches that God, having committed himself to creation, now needs it" (Blumenthal 1978:154, 156). Exploring how this relationship plays out in music stemming from the Zohar is our interest here.

Jewish Music and Jewish Musics

In approaching this chapter, it is important to note at the outset that some of the music we will examine, though created and performed principally by people who are Jewish, is not necessarily "Jewish music" in the sense of being tied to some universal standard of Jewish religious practices and conventions, Kabbalistic or otherwise. For example, the selection we will focus on in the chapter's final Guided Listening Experience, Zöhar's "Ehad" (**CD ex. #3-33**), could be interpreted as a strictly secular piece of popular music; its status as a composition emerging from the Zoharic tradition of Kabbalah, which is advanced here, is certainly open to question. One of the other pieces, Ruth Weider Magan's "Roza DeShabbos" (**CD ex. #3-32**), *is* a performance that clearly contains Jewish religious content, intent, and affect. Moreover, its connection to the tradition of the Zohar is undeniable. However, its status in some sectors of Jewish society is very controversial for reasons having to do with conflicting ideas about what kinds of spiritual/musical practices are or are not appropriate for Jewish women.

We will explore these two pieces in detail later in the chapter. For now, though, just listen to them and allow yourself to form your own impressions of what they are and what you think they may "represent," musically and culturally. In particular, consider the following question as you listen: How do these two pieces (either one of them or both together) conform to or contradict any preconceptions you may have had about "Jewish music" prior to hearing them?

Zöhar's "Ehad" and Ruth Wieder Magan's "Roza DeShabbos" are, each in its own way, controversial and provocative choices for an introductory textbook chapter on "Jewish music" such as this one, but as with certain other chapters in this book (e.g., Chapter 12), the decision here to focus on music that challenges tidy notions of what constitutes "the tradition" at issue is intentional. There is no single Jewish culture, history, or identity; and though Judaism is a religion, the ways in which this religion is interpreted and practiced are as diverse as Jewish people themselves. Indeed, as historian Raymond Scheindlin and others have commented, "the Jewish people and the Jewish religion are not at all the same thing, certainly not in modern times" (Scheindlin

Jewish men reading from the Torah during a religious service.

1998:xii). The diversity of music covered in this chapter, though all stemming from a single source, the Zohar, reflects these realities, and opens the door to exploring important themes and challenges of tradition and transformation in Jewish experience, past and present.

Further to the matter of Jewish diversity, another important point that warrants mention here is the complex relationship of peoplehood and nationhood in Jewish history. The connection between the Jewish people and a Jewish national homeland is fundamentally different than what we have encountered elsewhere in this book. Whereas all of the other chapters (i.e., of Part II) began their musicultural explorations from a more-or-less specified geographical location—China, India, western Africa, Cuba, Bali, Egypt, Ireland—before venturing off on musical journeys to various other lands and nations, this chapter works differently.

A Jewish music ensemble from Bukhara, Uzbekistan.

For almost two thousand years prior to the founding of the modern Jewish nation-state of Israel in 1948, the Jews were predominantly a diasporic people, living away from their ancestral homeland (i.e., the land of present-day Israel). They shared a pre-diasporic history, a unique monotheistic religious belief system, and certain fundamental tenets of law and culture, ethics and morality, and intellectual life. All of these were closely tied to the foundational sacred scripture of the Jewish religion, the **Torah,** the heart of the **Hebrew Bible** (see "Insights and Perspectives" box on p. 330). The Torah, together with a perpetual hope for the arrival of a universal age of redemption under the divine order of God, an age when all Jews would be able to return to their sacred, ancestral homeland of Israel, were key factors that defined the Jews as a people—the Jewish people—for millennia.

**Torah
(Toe-RAH [English pronunciation: TOE-rah])**

But Jews throughout the **Jewish diaspora** were perhaps as importantly defined, as a people, by their relationships with the *other* peoples among whom they lived. For many diasporic Jewish communities in different places and during different times, involuntary separation and exclusion from the "mainstream" of their surrounding societies was as much a part of their Jewishness as being Jewish itself. Moreover, Jews throughout the diaspora were strongly influenced by, and in turn influenced, the societies and cultures surrounding them on many levels, including musical ones. The history of "Jewish music" cannot be directly traced back to the age of the kingdoms of the Israelites thousands of years ago (though there is ample historical evidence to suggest that music played an important role in the Jewish culture of that ancient time). Indeed, most scholars agree that no form of Jewish music that survives today has been in existence for more than a couple of centuries. Jewish music, or, more accurately, Jewish *musics* have developed, evolved, and diversified across the vast range of the Jewish diaspora, and collectively reflect the immense diversity of all with which they have come in contact.

The Chassidic Jewish reggae musician Matisyahu.

The multiple, eclectic traditions that today fall under the large umbrella of "Jewish music"—from devotional songs of prayer performed by colorfully attired Jewish ensembles from Central Asia (see photo at top of page); to the lively, instrumental dance tunes of *klezmer* bands (Chapter 6, p. 82; **CD ex. #1-46**); to the Radical Jewish Culture movement music of John Zorn and the Chassidic reggae of Matisyahu—speak to this diversity. It is far more than we can cover here, but a list of resources is included at the Online Learning Center at www.mhhe.com/bakan1 for those interested in further exploration.

The Hebrew Bible consists of three main parts: the Torah, the books of the Prophets, and the Hagiographa (or Sacred Writings). The seminal core of this immense work is the Torah itself, which is comprised of the Five Books of Moses (*Pentateuch*) (PEN-ta-tookh [from Greek]). The Torah provides what modern historians have described as an allegorical history (though many Jews take it to be more a *literal* history) of the ancient Jews (Israelites) and their God, from the time of God's creation of the universe through to the death of the prophet and Biblical hero Moses. (A prophet is a person who is believed to speak directly with God.) It also furnishes the fundamental basis of all Jewish religious law and custom, which are described as having issued directly from God.

Prophets, the second part of the Hebrew Bible, continues the historical narrative of the Torah through to the destruction of the First Temple of the Israelites in the holy city of Jerusalem (in 587 BCE). This event marked the end of Israelite sovereignty in the Biblical era. Prophets also includes the speeches of the prophets of Israel—Isaiah, Jeremiah, Ezekiel, Zechariah (Ze-KHAR-ya)—important religious leaders and social commentators (and often champions of social justice) who operated outside the confines of the Israelite Temple hierarchy. Hagiographa, the third part of the Hebrew Bible, includes miscellaneous books such as the Book of Psalms, Lamentations (lamenting the destruction of Jerusalem at the end of the Israelite kingdom era), and Ecclesiastes (a meditation that explores the essential meaning of life).

All of the great sacred texts of Judaism of later periods, including the Talmud (TAL-mud), the Mishnah, the Midrashim (Meed-ra-SHEEM), and, most important for us, the Zohar and other works in the Kabbalistic tradition, represent different instances of, and approaches to, interpretation of the Hebrew Bible. It is also noteworthy that the Hebrew Bible is identified as the Old Testament of the Christian Bible, and is regarded as a sacred text in Islam as well.

Jewish History and the Zohar

Though none of the music of this chapter can be directly traced back to Biblical times or even to later periods of Jewish antiquity, the long and multifaceted history of the Jewish people from Biblical times to the present prefigures and underscores all of this music in significant ways. The selective overview of Jewish history that follows highlights certain important developments that provide an essential cultural-historical background for understanding and appreciating the far-flung Zoharic musical odyssey that follows it.

Early Jewish history

The two principal repositories of information on the ancient history of the Jewish people are (1) archaeological evidence and other non-Biblical sources and (2) the Hebrew Bible. The two corroborate one another in many key respects.

The history of the Jews begins with the first patriarch, Abraham the Hebrew, who the Torah tells us began his life in Ur (in Mesopotamia, probably in present-day Iraq) and, at the command of the God of the Hebrews (Yahweh), migrated to the land of Canaan—modern-day Israel/Palestine—to become the father of the Hebrew people. The Torah indicates that Abraham's migration to Canaan would have taken place sometime during the second millennium BCE, which is consistent with non-Biblical sources that indicate large-scale migrations of seminomadic peoples from regions in Mesopotamia to Canaan around that time.

According to the Torah, the descendants of Abraham, most notably his grandson Jacob, the third patriarch of the Jews, and Jacob's own 12 sons (the fathers of the 12 tribes of Israel in the

Habiru and Hebrew

The name "Hebrew" itself is interesting, since archaeological sources from Egypt in the second millennium BCE make reference to a social class of seminomadic peoples (as opposed to a specific ethnic group or clan) called Habiru during that era. This may explain the historical origin of the word Hebrew that we now associate specifically with the Jewish people and their ancient, scriptural language, Biblical **Hebrew** (Scheindlin 1998:4).

Torah) eventually migrated to Egypt. One of Jacob's sons, Joseph, rose to a position of power in Egyptian politics, and with Joseph's aid, his father and brothers also prospered. This is again interesting relative to the non-Biblical record. There are archaeological sources that indicate that the Hyksos dynasty in ancient Egypt that began circa 1650 BCE and lasted for approximately a hundred years was ruled by foreigners who had come to Egypt from Canaan. Perhaps Joseph's rise to power in Egypt corresponded with this development.

Hyksos (HICK-sos)

Descendants of Joseph and his kin fared less well than their predecessors, becoming slaves of the Egyptians. Eventually they were able to leave Egypt, and they returned to Canaan (led by Moses, according to the Biblical version of history) by about 1220 BCE. There they established the Israelite kingdom, circa 1000 BCE. The Israelite kings David (also a legendary musician and poet) and Solomon, heroic figures of the Hebrew Bible, reigned over this kingdom during its golden age. After a long string of conquests by larger, neighboring powers (Egyptian, Assyrian, Babylonian) and a period of gradual decline and division after Solomon's reign, the Israelites were finally conquered and their kingdom liquidated by the Babylonians in 587 BCE.

The Israelites were subsequently exiled to Babylonian territories, where they "created religious institutions that would enable them to keep the memory of their kingdom and the dream of its restoration alive for centuries" (Scheindlin 1998:22–23). This dream, these religious institutions, the Hebrew Bible, and the monotheistic religion of Judaism itself would become unifying foundations of diasporic Judaism in this and later ages.

Under the Persians (who conquered the Babylonians shortly after the Babylonians conquered the Israelites), Jews were allowed to return to their homeland, now redesignated as the Persian province of Judea, beginning in 539 BCE. Many did not return, however, continuing to live in diaspora in Babylonia, Egypt, and other places. According to Scheindlin, it is from this period onward that "it becomes appropriate to begin speaking of the Jewish people, meaning all those who, throughout history and around the globe, have regarded themselves as linked to one another and to the people of the ancient Israelite kingdom, either by ethnicity, culture, intellectual heritage, or religion" (Scheindlin 1998:28).

Judea became a quasi-autonomous province where Jews were free to practice their religion and culture under the Persians. Then, in the 4th century BCE, Judea (and ultimately the entire Persian empire, including virtually all other lands to which diasporic Jews had relocated up to that time) came under Greek rule (332 BCE). Henceforth, "the interplay between Jewish and Hellenic [Greek] ideals was to become one of the characteristic themes of all Western civilization" (Scheindlin 1998:33). Next (in 37 BCE) came the era of Roman control of Judea (which came also to be known as Palestine). Over time, Jewish-Roman relations deteriorated, leading to the destruction of the Second Temple in Jerusalem in 70 CE and the expulsion of the entire Jewish population of Judea following an unsuccessful revolt against Roman rule (132 CE).

With this exiling of the Jews began almost two thousand years of continuous diasporic existence for the vast majority of Jewish people. Though Jews were eventually allowed to return to the

A woman prays at the Wailing Wall in Jerusalem, Israel; this holy wall is all that remains of the Second Temple destroyed by the Romans in 70 CE.

Shimon Bar Yochai (SHEE-moan Bar Yo-KHAI [rhymes with "high"])

Chassidism (KHA-sid-is-um [NB: Anglicized word based on Hebrew])

land that the Torah claimed had been promised to them by God, that land was ruled by a succession of foreign powers from Roman times until the declaration of the modern state of Israel in 1948. Throughout that long period and even since 1948, the majority of the world's Jewish population has lived outside of the country now called Israel.

Rabbinic Judaism, the Zohar, Kabbalah, and Reform Judaism

From Roman times forward to the present, Jewish religious practice mainly took the form of **Rabbinic Judaism,** which centered on study of the Torah. The **synagogue** (from a Greek word meaning "assembly") was established as the communal center of Jewish religious life and ritual observance. **Rabbis,** specialists in Jewish religious traditions and law, served as the leaders of synagogue congregations. They also created the canonical texts of Biblical interpretation, such as the Mishnah and the Talmud. These explained and reframed the eternal teachings and laws of the Torah, placing them in the context of the new times, places, and conditions of Jewish life.

The stream of Judaism that would ultimately come to be known as Kabbalah also experienced important developments during the Roman period. Kabbalists claim that the Zohar was actually written during the 2nd century CE as a chronicle of divine revelations and teachings attributed to a legendary mystic of that period named Shimon Bar Yochai. This massive work is not so much a book as a sprawling compendium of mystical commentaries on the Hebrew Bible and other sacred texts. The original language in which the Zohar was written is **Aramaic,** which was the main language spoken by Jews of this period.

Most modern scholarly sources on the Zohar refute the Kabbalists' claim of its origin in this early period, suggesting rather that it was written during the late 13th century, more than a thousand years later than was formerly believed. Principal authorship of the Zohar, according to this theory, is attributed to a 13th-century Spanish Kabbalist named Moses de León. Scholars suggest that he wrote the Zohar in Aramaic and concealed his identity as its author so that people would think it was an ancient work that he had discovered (Scheindlin 1998:116).

The next great age of Zoharic thought came in the 16th century, when a group of Kabbalists led by Isaac Luria created a new approach to interpreting the Zohar that explained the historical suffering of the Jews in relation to cataclysmic cosmic events that would ultimately find resolution in a future age of universal redemption under the rule of God (Scheindlin 1998:132). All of the musical works in this chapter are linked closely to this Lurianic conception of the Zohar, as we shall see.

The Lurianic approach to the Zohar had a profound influence on the final major stage of historical development in Kabbalistic Judaism, **Chassidism,** which arose in Central and Eastern Europe during the 18th century. Chassidism was a populist movement that privileged a joyful, ecstatic brand of Jewish religious experience over the learned, scholarly, and rationalist approaches of Rabbinic Judaism that had mainly prevailed in Europe up to that time. The Chassidic movement took its inspiration from the Baal Shem Tov, a sage who stressed that joy, not asceticism, was the key to pursuing a righteous path to God. The complex, scholarly, esoteric texts of the Kabbalah, including the Zohar itself and works inspired by it that came out of the Lurianic school and others, were transformed into simple teachings designed to be accessible and engaging for

At the risk of oversimplification, it may be said that mystic forms of spirituality, such as Kabbalah in Judaism and Sufism in Islam (see Chapter 12), focus more on direct, personal experience of the divine than on understandings rooted in reason and intellect. Where Rabbinic Judaism, as represented especially in works like the Talmud, approaches the interpretation of the Torah mainly from rational, philosophical perspectives on Jewish law and custom, Kabbalistic Judaism is more often characterized by a contrasting emphasis on a mystical, experiential pursuit of hidden truths that Kabbalists believe are there to be revealed beneath the "surface" of the Torah itself (a subject to which we will return).

the commoner classes of Jews to whom Chassidism was largely directed. (These teachings were disseminated mainly in the vernacular Central/ Eastern European language of **Yiddish,** which combined German with elements of Hebrew, Russian, Polish, and other languages.) Music, dance, and all manner of joyful celebration were central to Chassidic practice and philosophy. This, together with its populist orientation and simplified messages of Zoharic/Lurianic-inspired hope for a glorious Jewish future, proved highly appealing to many European Jews, especially in the wake of growing anti-Semitism—hatred and persecution of Jews—in Europe during this period.

Another important development of Judaism in Europe was the emergence of **Reform Judaism,** which began in Germany in the 19th century. Reform Judaism, like Chassidism, challenged the established conventions of European Rabbinic Judaism, but did so in very different ways. The Reform movement maintained that the conventional rituals and laws of Judaism needed to be adjusted and transformed to keep pace with changing times and social conditions; in other words, they needed to be modernized. New forms of worship and customs were introduced.

The progressive, modernist spirit of Reform Judaism persists to the present and is embedded, explicitly or implicitly, in music we will explore in this chapter. Interestingly, many important contemporary ideas and practices linked to Reform Judaism, including musical ones, draw heavily from Chassidic traditions and new approaches to the tradition of Kabbalah.

רבינו ישראל ב"ר אליעזר (בעש"ט)

לשנה טובה תכתבו

Painting of the Baal Shem Tov.

Modern Jewish history

The late 19th and early 20th centuries witnessed a major shift in the demographics of Jewish diaspora culture. In the face of escalating anti-Semitism, growing poverty, political strife, and diminished opportunities, large numbers of Jews migrated from Central and Eastern Europe and Russia to the United States, Canada, and other lands (the United Kingdom, Argentina, Mexico, Australia, and also Palestine, which was under British control from 1917–1948). Mass migration from Eastern Europe to the United States from 1881 through to the outbreak of World War II in 1939 brought millions of Jewish immigrants. New York City emerged as the new center of Jewish culture on an international scale. One outcome of this was that the world headquarters of Chassidism was moved from Eastern Europe to Brooklyn, New York, and with it the Chassidic legacy of the Kabbalah and the Zohar.

The history of the Jewish people in the middle of the 20th century was dominated by the unspeakable atrocities of the **Holocaust** during World War II (in which six million Jews perished at the hands of the Nazis) and by the establishment of the modern nation of Israel in 1948. Today, Israel is both a rich and vibrant country and one plagued by immense challenges. The ongoing struggles between Israel and its Arab neighbors, the incessant climate of terrorist danger, and the extraordinary problems that define Palestinian-Israeli relations contribute to Israel's status as a volatile and troubled nation. On the other hand, Israel is a land of great cultural, intellectual, and spiritual richness and diversity and a beacon of hope and opportunity for many Jews worldwide. It is also a major hub of a thriving pan-Jewish, international musical culture with comparable centers in New York, London, and other locations. Israel is today home to many great musicians, one of whom, Ruth Wieder Magan, is a focus of this chapter.

Climbing Jacob's Ladder: Musical Symbolism and the Melodious Voice in Kabbalistic Prayer

In Genesis (or in Hebrew, *Bereshith*), the first book of the Torah, is contained the story of Jacob's Ladder, one of the best-known portions of the Hebrew Bible. In the story, Jacob, patriarch and prophet of the Jewish people, has a dream of divine revelation. He sees a ladder that reaches from the earth to the heavens, and God's messengers (angels) are climbing up and down upon it. Then he hears the voice of God. It is a pivotal moment in the narrative of the Torah and in the Torah's historical chronicling of the Jewish people.

Jacob's Ladder (the ladder of holiness, the ladder of perfection) has important metaphorical significance in the prayer tradition of Kabbalah. "Prayer is likened, say the kabbalists, to the ladder in the dream of Jacob, which stands on the ground, and reaches into the sky," explains DovBer Pinson, a Chassidic Jew and the author of the book *Inner Rhythms: The Kabbalah of Music* (2000). "Thus," Pinson continues, "the course of prayer is to connect ourselves to God one step at a time, climbing the ladder of perfection. At the outset of prayer one starts off on the lowest rung, and eventually one climbs until he is joined and becomes 'one with One,'" that is, united in heart and soul with God, or deveikut (Pinson 2000:79).

This metaphor of climbing Jacob's Ladder is importantly symbolized through the melodious use of the voice in prayer. The different notes of the musical scale to which a prayer melody is set become, metaphorically, rungs on the ladder of holiness. As Pinson writes, "Kabbalah teaches that the various notes in the octave represent the various levels in a person's love for God. The higher the note, the loftier and deeper is the love being expressed" (Pinson 2000:34). Moreover, the melodies of prayer, potentially even more than the words of prayer themselves, may provide pathways to the deepest and most profound levels of spiritual expression, communication, and transcendence. "[W]hen the thought that one wishes to share is something beyond the rational, a profound expression of love, for example, the most direct communication is through song. Understanding this in the human realm brings us to an understanding of the Divine realm. When the Torah is read, the expression of Divinity coming through the *melody* of the reading is in fact higher than that of the actual *letters* of the holy Torah" (Pinson 2000:4).

Passages from other sacred Jewish texts besides the Torah, including the Zohar, also are set to melodies, and in these contexts, too, the use of melody figures importantly in the expression of spirituality. In the following Guided Listening Experience, we explore a chanted (melodically recited) setting of a passage from the Zohar in which melodic shape and direction serve to create a Jacob's Ladder-like musical portrait in prayer.

Painting of the Biblical scene of Jacob's Ladder.

guided listening experience

"V'amazirim" (Zoharic chant), Isaac Kataev

- ■ CD Track #**3-31**
- ■ Featured performer(s)/group: Isaac Kataev (voice)
- ■ Format: Complete track
- ■ Source recording: "Zohar" (title of selection on the original recording), from *Bukhara: Musical Crossroads of Asia* (Smithsonian Folkways CD SF 40050)

The Central Asian city of Bukhara (in Uzbekistan) is home to Jewish communities and traditions dating back centuries. These communities thrived under benevolent Islamic rulers, especially during the 14th and 15th centuries, when great epic works were written in a distinctive Judeo-Persian language. The Jews of Bukhara mainly spoke the language of their surrounding culture, Tajik, a dialect of Persian (Persia was the former name of modern-day Iran).

In modern times, the Jewish culture of Bukhara has been greatly diminished, but its traditions, including Kabbalistic ones linked to the Zohar specifically, have passed down through the generations to individuals like the late Isaac Kataev, who have preserved them. **CD ex. #3-31** **Kataev (Ka-TAH-yev)**

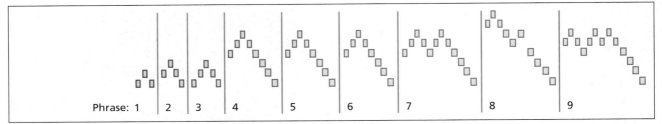

Phrase: 1 | 2 | 3 | 4 | 5 | 6 | 7 | 8 | 9

Ladder-like melodic contour in Isaac Kataev's "V'amazirim."

FIGURE 14.1

features Kataev performing a passage from the Zohar, V'amazirim Yazhaeru Kezohar Harakiah (These People Will Be Radiant Like the Light of Heaven). Though it cannot be known for sure, the style of prayerful, melodious recitation of the Zohar represented here may provide a glimpse of how the Zohar was "performed" by Jews in Bukhara centuries ago (and also reflects melodic and rhythmic influences of non-Jewish, Central Asian court music traditions—see Levin 2005).

Isaac Kataev.

On a purely musical level, one of the most interesting features of Kataev's rendition of "V'amazirim" is its *melodic contour,* both that of its individual melodic phrases *and* of the performance overall (Figure 14.1). In true Jacob's Ladder fashion, each phrase of the melody climbs up the scale of pitches and then climbs back down again, always ending on the starting pitch (i.e., the tonic) of B. In addition, the melodic range *overall* climbs progressively higher over the course of the performance. Phrase 1 (0:00–0:09), for example, begins and ends on the tonic, B, traveling upward and downward a few melodic steps in-between. Phrase 2 (0:10–0:19) then begins on the *second* scale degree, C♯, and from there ascends a step higher in pitch than Phrase 1 did before climbing back down to end on the tonic, B. A progressive, phrase-by-phrase, overall melodic ascent unfolds from that point forward. The climax occurs in Phrase 8 (1:52–2:09), which starts on a *high* B (an octave above the starting note of the piece), then pushes upward higher still to a D before gradually winding its way back down the ladder to the low B again. The concluding passage, Phrase 9 (2:10–2:39), rounds out the performance.

On both micro and macro levels of melodic design, then, Kataev's performance illustrates the principle of Jacob's Ladder-like ascents and descents. On the micro level, this occurs in the melodic rises and falls of each individual phrase; on the macro level, it is evident in the progressive, gradual rise in pitch and expansion of pitch range that occurs over the course of the piece, phrase after phrase. As the voice of prayer travels, we witness its journey as a continual series of "going out and coming back" excursions, with each excursion reaching higher rungs on the ladder of holiness than the ones preceding (Figure 14.1).

guided listening quick summary

"V'amazirim," Isaac Kataev (CD ex. #3-31)

PHRASE 1

0:00–0:09

■ Starts on tonic note, B, ascends (to D), then returns to B.

PHRASE 2

0:10–0:19

- Starts on second degree of scale, C♯ (after a lead-in "pick-up" note of B), rises a step higher than Phrase 1 did, then returns to and ends on B.

PHRASE 3

0:20–0:34

- No significant change from Phrase 2.

PHRASE 4

0:35–0:56

- Melody jumps to higher range territory; F♯ and G♯ (the fifth and sixth scale degrees, or "steps" of the ladder) become the main pitches.

PHRASES 5–7

0:57–1:51

- No significant change from Phrase 4.

PHRASE 8

1:52–2:09

- Climax of performance arrives at 1:52, where the melody begins on a *high* B (one octave above the starting note), ascends higher yet (to a high D), then gradually descends more than an octave to end on the piece's opening pitch, the low B.

PHRASE 9

2:10–2:39

- Conclusion of performance.

Melodic symbolism in "We Are Climbing Jacob's Ladder"

The Jacob's Ladder-like use of melodic symbolism in performances such as Isaac Kataev's "V'ama-zirim" is not uniquely Jewish. Indeed, similar symbolic devices are used in many other traditions of music as well, including some Christian spiritual songs. Appropriately enough, the Christian spiritual "We Are Climbing Jacob's Ladder" offers a clear and accessible illustration of this type of musical symbolism.

The Musical Guided Tour for this chapter breaks down the opening verse of "We Are Climbing Jacob's Ladder" phrase by phrase, showing how the contour of the melody rises progressively before ultimately descending back to the opening tonic pitch (B). The overall profile of the melodic contour is similar to that of "V'amazirim" in **CD ex. #3-31** (see Figure 14.2 on p. 338) (though this is not to imply that there is any direct relationship between the two works; there is none). The transcript in the box on page 338 corresponds to the audio Musical Guided Tour. As you listen to this tour at the Online Learning Center (www.mhhe.com/bakan1), follow along with this transcript.

The upward and downward melodic motion that accompanies the climbing imagery of the "We Are Climbing Jacob's Ladder" text illustrates a musical symbolism technique that is found in many world music traditions. A common English-language term for this technique is **word painting.** In word painting, the words of the text are evoked in the sound and design of the music itself (i.e., the words are "painted" in musical tones), in this case with the climbing up and down

This is the first verse of "We Are Climbing Jacob's Ladder." The song is sung here in the key of B major.

Here is Phrase 1. Note how the melody begins on the tonic note, B, rises up to an F♯, then descends back to B [♪].

Now here's Phrase 2, which begins on the *second* degree of the scale, C♯, then rises up to a G♯ before ending up one scale step below on an F♯ [♪].

The verse ends with Phrase 3, which starts a full octave above the starting note on a *high* B, then winds its way back down the scale a full octave to the low B starting pitch to conclude [♪].

Now, here is a performance of the complete first verse, start to finish [♪]:

(Phrase 1): *We are climbing Jacob's ladder.*

(Phrase 2): *We are climbing Jacob's ladder.*

(Phrase 3): *We are climbing Jacob's ladder. We're soldiers of the cross.*

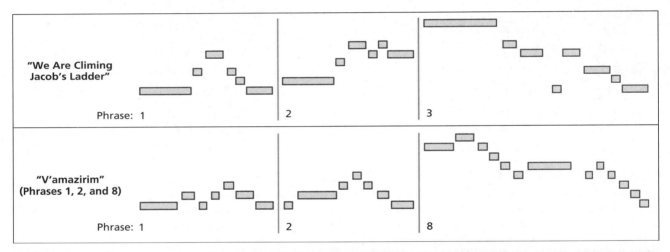

Similarities in melodic contour of "V'amazirim" and "We Are Climbing Jacob's Ladder."

FIGURE 14.2

of the "soldiers of the cross" made manifest in the ascending and descending lines of the melody. We will encounter more complex instances of word painting in music explored later in the chapter.

Music, the Zohar, and the Secrets of the Torah

According to the traditions of Kabbalah, the Torah consists of two dimensions: a "body," which is the Torah proper, and an invisible "inner dimension" or "soul," which is the domain of Kabbalah. For those who follow its teachings, Kabbalah thus represents the hidden dimension of the Torah. Kabbalistic texts like the Zohar, say the Kabbalists, contain the "secrets, mysteries, mysteries of mysteries, and many dimensions of soul within soul" that reside beneath the surface level of the Torah's actual written text (Ginsburgh 2002). These are not readily revealed, for the Zohar is an exceedingly complex literary work. Unlike the Torah itself, whose secrets it aims to reveal, the Zohar does not proceed in anything like a linear fashion. Instead, it jumps about in a seemingly haphazard manner among different themes, ideas, scriptural references, and moralizing anecdotes, which often appear to have little, if anything, to do with each other. Beyond careful reading and analysis of the Zohar, Kabbalists employ a variety of related techniques—meditation, mystical numerology (i.e., **gematria,** in which hidden meanings are believed to emerge when numerical values are assigned to Hebrew letters in complex, arithmetic procedures), and fasting and other forms of bodily deprivation—to open themselves to the complexly construed divine revelations of the Zohar and, in turn, of the Torah.

gematria (ge-MA-tree-yah)

Music is recognized as a particularly important medium used by Kabbalists in their pursuit of divine revelations. "Knowledge of the secret of music leads one to knowledge of the secret of the Torah," as one 13th-century Kabbalist wrote (see Shiloah 1992:132). It therefore follows that musical performances *of* passages from the Zohar, delivered mainly in the context of prayer, occupy a prominent place in Kabbalistic methods.

We have already been introduced to one passage of the Zohar for which there exists a tradition of setting the text to music in prayer (V'amazirim). Another Zoharic passage that has served as the basis of many different musical settings is **Roza D'Shabbos** (The Secret of the Sabbath).

Roza D'Shabbos (RAW-za d'SHAH-bus [Hebrew, but with Yiddish pronunciation])

Roza D'Shabbos: The Secret of the Sabbath

The passage of the Zohar known as Roza D'Shabbos is one that forecasts a coming age of universal redemption under the divine rule of God, and that provides a prescription, as it were, for bringing about this glorious future age. In order to help you understand the text of Roza D'Shabbos and appreciate the musical works originating from it that we will examine, the following primer on Zoharic basics is offered.

Background information on the Zohar and Roza D'Shabbos

A major, perhaps *the* major, concern of the Zohar is unraveling the mysteries of the creation of the universe described in the Torah. One of the great challenges of this unraveling is to account for the seeming paradox of God's infinite, unfathomable nothingness, on the one hand, and His more manifest presence as the God of the Creation and the finite world, on the other (Koskoff 2001:34).

The Zohar explains that **Hashem,** the one true God in Judaism, is everywhere and in everything that is, has been, and ever will be, and yet he is also "nothing." At the most exalted level, He is **Ain Sof,** "the God of Nothingness," "the Invisible God," "God Without End." Ain Sof is completely unknowable, unimaginable. Only by descending through a series of 10 lower spheres of His own divine being—the **Ten Sefirot,** or rays of divine radiance—does this unknowable God become knowable as God of the Creation, the Torah, and the earthly and heavenly realms (see Figure 14.3, p. 340).

Hashem (Hah-SHEM)
Ain Sof (Ayn-SOAF)
Sefirot (S'fee-ROTE)

In the Zohar, the lowest of the Sefirot, the one closest to earth, is called **Malchut,** meaning "Kingdom." Herein dwells the **Shechinah,** who is characterized as a female, receiving aspect of God's omnidimensional Oneness. She is the divine embodiment of neutrality, an empty vessel capable of absorbing all of Hashem's higher aspects and attributes and thus of implanting the "divine spark" of His essence in all of God's creations. The Creation is portrayed in the Zohar as resulting from an act of divine intercourse between Hashem (in his male aspect) and the Shechinah. Through this union, we learn, the Shechinah became "one with One," one with Hashem, in the moment of the Creation, which accounts for her status as the queen, daughter, and bride of God, the mother of all Jews (Scholem 1995[1941]:230).

Malchut (Mall-KHOOT)
Shechinah (Sh'khee-NAH)

But the Shechinah is a queen and mother in exile. Long ago, says the Zohar, the combined effects of human failings (beginning with Adam and Eve in the Garden of Eden) and impurities in

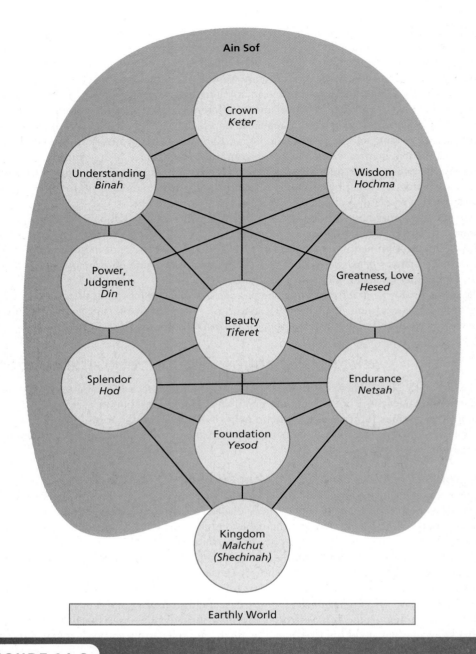

Ain Sof

Crown
Keter

Understanding
Binah

Wisdom
Hochma

Power,
Judgment
Din

Greatness, Love
Hesed

Beauty
Tiferet

Splendor
Hod

Endurance
Netsah

Foundation
Yesod

Kingdom
Malchut
(Shechinah)

Earthly World

The Ten Sefirot.

Source: Adapted from
Koskoff 2001:35. Used by
permission of Ellen Koskoff.

FIGURE 14.3

the divine rays of the higher Sefirot combined to obscure God's radiant light, which disrupted the divine order of the universe. As a result, Malchut and the earthly world below it were severed from the higher Sefirot above, and the Shechinah was separated from the higher aspects of Hashem. With that calamitous moment of cosmic fracture, claims the Zohar, came the tragic consequences of divine fragmentation that continue to affect us today.

But there is hope for a better future, we learn from the Zohar. The potential for a reunification of Malchut and the earthly world with the higher Sefirot exists, and Hashem and the Shechinah can be reunited. If this occurs, an age of universal healing and redemption will occur. The responsibility for all this, however, lies not with God, but with humankind. Only when all people everywhere (or, at least, all Jewish people), through their prayers, good deeds, and total devotion to God, have purified the world to the point that God's rays of divine light are reflected back up to Him in full radiance will Hashem and the Shechinah once again be united. Only then will the cosmic balance of the universe be restored, paving the way for the coming age of redemption, when Hashem will reveal Himself in the world and rule from this heaven-on-earth as King of Kings.

Divine reunification and universal redemption in Roza D'Shabbos

The Zoharic passage Roza D'Shabbos depicts, in highly metaphorical terms, the reunification of Hashem and the Shechinah that initiates the long-yearned-for coming age of universal redemption. It unfolds as a narrative of ascending and descending flights between divine and earthly realms that are traveled by entities both divine and human. Hashem is "seen" descending to unite with the Shechinah. The Shechinah ascends in holiness as she is restored to grace by again becoming "one with God." And prompting all of this divine motion to occur in the first place, the Jewish people themselves are portrayed metaphorically as climbing the rungs of the ladder of holiness toward communion with God through their prayers.

Here is an English translation of the Roza D'Shabbos text, followed by an interpretation that explains the meanings of the text's metaphorical language. In the translation (from Aramaic), the Shechinah is referred to as She or Her. Hashem is referred to in several different ways: as The Holy One, the Holy King, the Holy Transcendent King, and sometimes simply as One, or Him. One of the important names for God used by Jews in prayer, the Hebrew *Adonai,* appears only once, in the last line of the first stanza: "God is One and His Name is One."—"Adonai Echad oo-Sh'mo Echad." This line of text, taken from the Torah, is paramount to Jewish law and belief.

Echad, Ehad (e-KHAD)

The Holy One, Blessed Be He, who is One

does not sit on His Throne of Glory above

until She enters into the mystery of One with Him

as being one within One

As it is written, the secret of

"God is One and His Name is One."

In the secret of Shabbat, She, on Shabbat

Shabbat (Sha-BAHT)

enters into the mystery of One, the mystery of

One resting in Her

through the evening prayer rising into Shabbat.

Then it is that the Throne of Glory

merges into the mystery of One

and is made ready for the Holy

Transcendent King to sit upon.

As Shabbat enters She merges into One

and is separated from evil.

All judgments against Her are canceled

and She abides in union with the holy light

and is crowned with many crowns

before the Holy King.

> *Then all the powers of wrath and the accusers vanish*
> *and in all the worlds no other power reigns.*

(Adapted from a translation by Ruth Wieder Magan [personal correspondence with the author, 2002]; used by permission of Ruth Wieder Magan.)

To summarize, then, we learn in Roza D'Shabbos that God's universe exists in a perpetual state of disharmony ("The Holy One . . . does not sit on His Throne of Glory above") and will remain that way until such time as Hashem and the Shechinah can once again be united as they were at the time of the Creation ("until She enters into the mystery of One with Him, as being one within One"). The holy union that will lead to this unification ("the mystery of One resting in Her") will be initiated neither by Hashem nor the Shechinah, however, but rather by the Jewish people, whose long-awaited, uniform, and total submission to God will be signaled by their Sabbath (Shabbat) prayers rising up in purity for God to hear ("through the evening prayer rising into Shabbat"). Only then will Hashem come down into the world to rule as the King of Kings, and will all evil disappear and all of God's creations again become "one within One" in God.

Pinchas Pinchik (PIN-khass PIN-chick)

Pinchas Pinchik's "Roso De Shabbos" (Roza D'Shabbos): A tone-poem about holiness

In the past, and still today, the Roza D'Shabbos passage of the Zohar was recited as a prayer by Chassidic Jews as a prelude to their Friday evening Shabbat (Shabbos) religious services. (Shabbat is the Jewish Sabbath, the day of rest and holiest day of the week; it begins every Friday evening at sundown and ends an hour after sunset on Saturday.) In this context, Roza D'Shabbos is performed as a kind of "Kabbalistic meditation" murmured under the breath in barely audible tones.

In the early 1900s, a renowned **cantor** (the solo singer and leader of congregational chanting in Jewish religious services), Pinchas (Pierre) Pinchik, became deeply interested in Chassidic music from his native Ukraine and other areas of Eastern Europe. Though not a Chassid himself, he drew upon this music as source and inspiration for his own compositions and singing style. For the first half of the text of Roza D'Shabbos (ending with the line meaning "and is made ready for the Holy Transcendent King to sit upon"), Pinchik created a powerful and beautiful melody, transforming this former "silent prayer" into what the American cantor Sam Weiss has aptly described as "a tone-poem about holiness" (Weiss 1994:15).

A historic recording of this composition, featuring Pinchik singing and accompanying himself on the organ, was produced in 1928, three years after Pinchik emigrated from the Ukraine to the United States during the mass migrations of that period. That recording has since been re-released on an excellent CD entitled *Mysteries of the Sabbath: Classic Cantorial Recordings: 1907–47* (Yazoo Records 7002). In his notes accompanying the recording, Weiss writes evocatively of Pinchik's "soaring flights heavenward" that are "tempered by chastened returns earthward," of moments where the melody seems to "outline the rungs on the ladder of holiness" as it climbs upward and back down again (Weiss 1994:15).

guided listening experience

"Roza DeShabbos," Ruth Wieder Magan (after Pinchas Pinchik)

- CD Track #**3-32**
- Featured performer(s)/group: Ruth Wieder Magan (voice)
- Format: Complete track
- Source recording: *Songs to the Invisible God,* by Ruth Wieder Magan (Sounds True STA M111D)

Much of the spirit of Pinchas Pinchik's original recording of "Roso De Shabbos" lives on in a relatively recent recording of the same piece (here titled "Roza DeShabbos") by the outstanding Israeli vocalist Ruth Wieder Magan. Wieder Magan's "Roza," to which we listened earlier, appears as the opening track on her 1999 CD *Songs to the Invisible God*. The Hebrew title of *Songs to the Invisible God* is *Ayin Zoher*. *Ayin* (*Ain*) means "nothingness," a reference to the nothingness of *Ain Sof*, the "Invisible God" of the English title. *Zoher* means "brightly glowing," referring to the Zohar itself (a common English translation of the full title of the Zohar, *Sefer ha-Zohar*, is "The Book of Radiance").

Ruth Wieder Magan lives in Israel but was born and raised in Australia by parents who were survivors of the Holocaust. She is a classically trained singer and voice teacher, a co-founding member of an innovative Israeli theater company (Theatre Company Jerusalem), a wife and mother, and a self-described feminist. Most importantly for our purposes, perhaps, Wieder Magan is a serious student of the Zohar and the tradition and practice of Kabbalah more broadly, despite the fact that the study of Kabbalah has historically been "a masculine doctrine, made for men and by men" (Scholem 1995[1941]:37).

Ruth Wieder Magan.

For Wieder Magan, the release of *Songs to the Invisible God* followed nearly a quarter-century of intensive study of the Zohar, other sacred texts, and the Jewish prayer tradition. She counts many learned and respected rabbis among her teachers. The recording itself is a testament to her seriousness of purpose; her committed spirituality seems to shine through on every note. In the accompanying CD booklet of *Songs,* the music is described as an "original blend of ancient prayers and folksongs with poetry and theatre—delicately and intensely woven into burning, bruising, beautiful sounds."

Wieder Magan sings "Roza DeShabbos" in the original Aramaic language of the Zohar (i.e., with quoted passages from the Torah in Hebrew). Other than the use of female voice and the absence of the organ, her version adheres quite closely to Pinchik's original. But although she consciously models her own performance after Pinchik's, Wieder Magan is by no means afraid to move away from his model to follow her own interpretive and spiritual vision.

Wieder Magan's "Roza" features several passages in which the melody seems to climb heavenward and descend earthward. Other elements—changes in dynamics, rhythm, voice timbre, and emotional intensity—serve to enhance these musical episodes of "going out and coming back" from different points of earthly and heavenly departure. The piece and performance as a whole paint a vivid picture of the Zoharic text they evoke, while adding deeper dimensions to its meaning and interpretation. The approaches to musical symbolism evident in this compelling performance are especially clear in certain passages, which are identified and described below and summarized in the Guided Listening Quick Summary on pages 344–45.

One interesting instance of musical symbolism occurs beginning at 0:40, on the line (in translation) "as being one within One," a reference to the Shechinah becoming encompassed in the supreme Oneness of God through their divine union. The first part of the line, "as being one," is uttered at a moderate dynamic level in speechlike fashion, but at "within One," the melody swoops upward, the voice diminishing in volume as it ascends (0:43–0:45). By the top of her ascent, Wieder Magan's voice is almost inaudible as she holds a pristine, unornamented note of very high pitch for three full seconds (0:45–0:48). Then, quite suddenly, the dynamic level returns to moderate and the melody tumbles downward to conclude the phrase (0:48–0:53). Heavenward flight and earthward return are vividly portrayed not just in the melody but also in the dynamics: as the voice climbs upward it almost disappears, approaching inaudibility as it travels away from the world and toward the invisible "nothingness" of *Ain Sof*. Then it comes back to normal volume for the climb back down to the lower realms.

Another heavenward musical flight occurs in the passage from 1:00–1:25. In contrast to the previous one, however, it unfolds with great intensity. From 1:03–1:14, the volume *increases* dramatically with the melody rising a full octave on the word "Echad"—meaning "One," that is, the One true God—then continues to increase as Wieder Magan holds the top note for a very long time (seven seconds). The volume and intensity then diminish for the last part of the phrase (1:15–1:25), where the Hebrew words for "and His Name is One" ("oo-Sh'mo Echad") are intoned. The climactic moment on the highest-pitched note seems to symbolize the "arrival" of God on the scene at this point. The great intensity here is also a testament to the paramount commandment of "Adonai Echad"—"God is One"—that is emphatically proclaimed.

A third interesting passage is the one heard at 2:21–2:31. Here, the symbolism of melodic descent seems to evoke the descent of Hashem into the Shechinah's sphere and their subsequent divine union. On the line meaning "the mystery of One resting in Her" (2:21–2:31), which metaphorically represents Hashem and the Shechinah uniting in love, there is a decrease in intensity as the melody descends to a very low-pitched note at the end of the phrase. The mood created here by the music is very gentle, a lover's caress, as it were.

Finally, and perhaps most intriguing of all, we come to the section of the piece featuring the line meaning "through the evening prayer rising into Shabbat" (2:32–2:45). It is here that the text invokes the Zoharic ideal of the prayers of the Jewish people ascending to the heavens in full and unified purity and devotion. Through this prayer, the divine act of love between Hashem and the Shechinah leading to universal redemption is finally made possible. Why, though, is this line about prayer *rising* set to a *descending* rather than an ascending melodic line (2:32–2:41)? The "answer" arrives immediately following the singing of the line of text itself in the form of an ascending, *wordless* melody that climbs an octave up the scale, step by step, as if rising up the ladder of holiness for God to hear (2:42–2:45).

The poignancy of the symbolism in this passage is suggested by the following comments of Pinson. "In the Kabbalah," he writes, "it is explained that words, though they are designed to reveal, are actually a concealment. . . . When we find ourselves with a pure thought, a deeply felt emotion, and no words which will communicate it without dilution of the original feeling, we sing. A wordless melody from the soul, with the notes becoming a channel from the essence of my soul, to the essence of yours. . . . Music has the unique ability to be apprehended by one's rational mind yet at the same time, communicate something which is above logic and human understanding" (Pinson 2000:11–12).

---

guided listening quick summary

"Roza DeShabbos," Ruth Wieder Magan (CD ex. #3-32)

As you listen, focus especially on those portions of the selection featuring the key examples of musical word painting outlined below.

KEY EXAMPLE 1

0:40–0:53

- Literal meaning of text line: ". . . as being one within One."
- Meaning in context: Shechinah is encompassed in supreme Oneness of God through their divine union.
- Musical word painting: Dramatic decrease in volume (decrescendo) as voice swoops upward in pitch on "within One" (0:43–0:45). On the long-held high note at the top of the ascent, sound

essentially disappears into silence (0:45–0:48), then returns to moderate dynamic level as melody descends (0:48–0:53). Elegant heavenward flight–earthward return symbolism in both the melodic contour and the use of dynamics.

KEY EXAMPLE 2

1:00–1:25

- Literal meaning of text line: "God is One and His Name is One." ("Adonai Echad oo-sh'mo Echad.")

- Meaning in context: This pronouncement represents the foundational premise of Jewish faith.

- Musical word painting: From 1:03–1:14, Wieder Magan crescendos dramatically on the word "Echad" ("One," as in the One true God) then holds the note out very loud and long (seven seconds). This seemingly symbolizes "arrival" of God as a manifest presence in the scenario. This dramatic "heavenward flight" is followed by "earthward return" in second half of phrase (1:15–1:25), with its descending melody and lower dynamic level.

KEY EXAMPLE 3

2:21–2:31

- Literal meaning of text line: ". . . the mystery of One resting in her."

- Meaning in context: Evocation of divine union of Hashem and the Shechinah.

- Musical word painting: Calming descent into the low register of Wieder Magan's voice at this decisive moment of universal redemption; a lover's caress in sound, so to speak.

KEY EXAMPLE 4

2:32–2:45

- Literal meaning of text line: ". . . through the evening prayer rising into Shabbat."

- Meaning in context: It is the heavenward ascent of the prayers of Jewish people on Shabbat that inspires the redemptive, divine union of Hashem and the Shechinah.

- Musical word painting: Linking of the *descending* melody to which this text is set (2:32–2:41) with a message concerning the profound importance of prayer *ascending* may seem paradoxical at first. The rising, wordless melody that immediately follows, however (2:42–2:45), reflects this message with more direct symbolism, while also showing how melody itself is more spiritually powerful even than the words of prayer.

Ruth Wieder Magan: Dusting off the surfaces of tradition

There can be little doubt that Ruth Wieder Magan's performance of "Roza DeShabbos" is not just a powerful musical statement, but also a powerful expression of the artist's Jewish faith. The question of whether or not such a performance is *appropriate* as an expression of Jewish faith, however, is a subject of debate and controversy in some sectors of Jewish society.

The source of controversy stems from differing attitudes regarding gender. In some Chassidic and ultra-Orthodox forms of Judaism, the principle of **kol isha** ("the voice of a woman") dictates that women should not sing prayers in the presence of men. The rationale for this is that a woman's voice has the potential to distract men from their all-important prayers. Since religious practice prescribes that prayer is principally the duty of men (although women most certainly pray as well), this is a genuinely serious concern.

kol isha (kohl ee-SHAH)

Furthermore, for a woman to sing publicly in the presence of men is to defy fundamental notions of "women's modesty" that are highly prized in orthodox forms of Judaism. The model Jewish woman, in this orthodox vision, is one who strives to approach in her own life the divine

Exuberance and Ecstasy in Chassidic Men's Devotional Singing

In contrast to Chassidic women, Chassidic men may appear as anything but modest in their ritual expressions of faith through singing. As Koskoff explains, in men's singing the musical pursuit of deveikut—that is, of a Kabbalah-inspired ideal of communion with the divine—may involve "loud clapping, shouting, thumping, . . . speeding up, swaying, and, at times, dancing. Arms begin to flail, drinking becomes more obvious. . . . After many repetitions, many sips of vodka, and wilder and wilder bodily gestures, swooning or unconsciousness may take place. . . . These behaviors are inevitably interpreted as overstimulation in the face of the divine, and those who achieve unconsciousness are treated with special deference" (Koskoff 2001:110–11).

ideal of the Shechinah—the epitome of female modesty, whose pure form of neutrality is essential to all God's creations. The woman's role in the redemption of the world is to embody this modesty, humility, and neutrality in devotion to God.

The *kol isha* concept transfers to the *sight* of a woman as well. Therefore, in Chassidic and other Orthodox synagogues, the women are separated from the men, congregating in the "women's gallery," which is set off by a screen, a sheet, or often nowadays, heavily tinted but transparent black plastic panels (Koskoff 2001:7). From the perspective of a person with modern, Western sensibilities, *kol isha* may seem backward and repressive, but most Chassidic women regard it as neither. As ethnomusicologist Ellen Koskoff explains, they regard symbols of *kol isha* such as the plastic panels as necessary for the protection of their modesty. If Jewish women are to pursue the ideal of the Shechinah, then their own modesty must be secured at all costs. And from such a vantage point, lacking access to certain highly prized values of the modern West, such as "freedom of self-expression" or "equal opportunity," is seen as a small price to pay for ensuring the realization of one's divine purpose on earth.

Chassidic women, then, "must be self-conscious and conscious of others, always aware of their social and religious context," according to Koskoff (2001:139). Although men can "express their spiritual feelings without . . . limitation, even within a mixed-gender, public context" (see "Insights and Perspectives" box above), women "can sing only for and among each other" (Koskoff 2001:139). Given these constraints, the following response to Ruth Wieder Magan's recording of "Roza DeShabbos" by a Chassidic rabbi (Rabbi Schneur Oirechman of Tallahassee, Florida) is not surprising: "I don't like this, women coming and trying to sing the prayers, trying to change the role of women prescribed in the Torah. The role of the Jewish woman is to be modest, and her role in the world is very important" (Oirechman, personal correspondence with the author, 2002).

Jewish women like Wieder Magan have their own views on their "role in the world," however. A serious student of Kabbalah and other Jewish sacred traditions, she does not consider her musical work to be in any way defiant or blasphemous. On the contrary, she describes it as a *return* to tradition.

"What my work has been about," she explains, "is going to my tradition and freeing its captive female voice, to draw that voice out through careful study of the texts and songs and reclaim it, drawing it into myself. . . . In both the Talmud and the *Zohar*, I believe there is a definite feminine voice. Both are non-linear texts: their movement circles and spirals in and out of many worlds and many, many layers of interpretation. . . . I believe that this spiraling movement is definitely feminine in nature. It is the center of the creative power behind the great Jewish texts and liturgy" (Wieder Magan 2000:272).

Schneur Oirechman (Sh'noor OY-rekh-min [Yiddish pronunciation])

Kabbalah *à la* Madonna

If Ruth Wieder Magan is a controversial figure in the world of Kabbalah, then what is one to make of pop superstar Madonna?

The wisdom and teachings of Kabbalah have influenced many of the great figures in Western intellectual and cultural history, Jewish and non-Jewish alike. Isaac Newton, William Shakespeare, and Sigmund Freud, for example, were all familiar with Kabbalah to some degree, and it is reasonable to suggest (as some have) that Kabbalistic influences are present in their work.

In more recent years, the teachings of Kabbalah have been embraced by "New Age" spiritual seekers. People and groups from many walks of life now claim to be devotees of Kabbalah. The most famous of these neo-Kabbalists is probably Madonna, who became involved with the study of Jewish mysticism in the mid-1990s. In a 2003 *USA Today* online article, she describes the impact of Kabbalah on her life:

Madonna speaking at a Kabbalah Centre event in Israel.

"Kabbalah helped me understand that there is a bigger picture and that being well-intentioned is great, but if you don't live your life according to the laws of the universe, you bring chaos into your life. . . . I was raised to believe that the privilege of being American means you can be whatever you want. But the question is, to what end? What's the point of reaching the top? I started that search when I was pregnant with my daughter, because I suddenly realized I was going to be responsible for shaping another person's life. Studying [Kabbalah] has given me clarity and affected my life in every way" (Madonna, quoted in Gundersen 2003).

The organization with which Madonna's Kabbalistic journey has been associated is the Kabbalah Centre, which states outright that it is *not* a Jewish organization (much like many modern yoga training centers in the West have no direct connection to the traditions of Hinduism from which yoga derives). Madonna, like anyone, is and should be free to pursue the spiritual path of her choice. It is important to realize, however, that the school of Kabbalistic thought with which she is identified is essentially separate from Jewish traditions of Kabbalah *per se* (Judah Cohen, personal correspondence with the author, 2005).

"As a woman," Wieder Magan continues, "I must revolutionize this masculine form in order to sing it. Being a woman gives me a big advantage. It makes it easier for me to dust off the surfaces of the tradition, peel back its layers. I can go in and sense the core of the music, its primary source" (Magan 2000:272–73).

Zohar Remix

Ruth Wieder Magan's "Roza DeShabbos" is not the only relatively recent musical production to take Pinchas Pinchik's historic 1928 "Roso De Shabbos" recording as source and inspiration. The imprint of Pinchik's "Roso" is present in an entirely different way in "Ehad" (an alternate spelling of *Echad*), by the innovative group Zöhar (**CD ex. #3-33**).

Our exploration of Zöhar's "Ehad" takes us to London, England. Zöhar is the brainchild of two self-described "young London Jewish lads," Erran Baron Cohen and Andrew Kremer, who,

Erran Baron Cohen of Zöhar. He also composed the musical score for the film *Borat,* starring his brother Sacha Baron Cohen.

after meeting in 1997, collaborated in developing a rather unique style of techno-Judaic fusion music. Upon first getting to know each other, Baron Cohen and Kremer discovered that they shared a dual passion for underground urban club music (techno, electronica, rap, hip-hop, acid jazz), on the one hand, and traditional Jewish and Arab music, on the other (see "Insights and Perspectives" box on p. 349 regarding techno and electronica). It was their common desire to unite these seemingly disparate musical worlds in the creation of a new medium of musical expression that led to the formation of Zöhar.

While Kremer's interest in traditional Jewish music did not really come to fruition until he was already a young man and a working musician on the London dance club scene, Baron Cohen's love of the music developed much earlier. He grew up in a Jewish household. From childhood, he took great joy in listening to classic recordings from his parents' record collection that featured the great Jewish cantors. Pinchik's "Roso De Shabbos" was likely one of the records that he grew up listening to. But Baron Cohen's musical tastes were eclectic. Jewish music was by no means his only passion. He found himself equally enamored of the contemporary sounds of techno and other electronic and electro-acoustic dance music styles of the London underground scene. He became a part of that scene during the late 1980s and 1990s, but this new musical life did not temper his enthusiasm for the Jewish music of his youth.

One night at a London area club, Baron Cohen heard something that struck him as quite remarkable: a techno dance mix in which the electronically transformed and manipulated, digitally sampled voice of a famous Israeli singer, Ofra Haza, was featured prominently. Baron Cohen recognized Haza's voice immediately, and in that same instant emerged his concept for the techno-Judaic fusion approach that would crystallize with Zöhar. With the aid of sophisticated digital sampling technology and contributions of like-minded musical colleagues such as Kremer, Zöhar drummer Neil Conti, and percussionist Simone Haggiag, Baron Cohen was able to fashion all kinds of intriguing "collaborations" with great singers, living and otherwise.

Zöhar's music draws upon many different sources, from techno, electronica, jazz, and funk to Middle Eastern dance music (see Chapter 12) and klezmer. But the key element of the group's unique fusion approach is their merging of techno grooves and textures with digitally sampled and manipulated vocal tracks culled from historic recordings. Often these "source recordings" are of renowned Jewish cantors like Pinchas Pinchik, who is "featured"—in digitally sampled form—on "Ehad," the opening track of the group's 2001 album, *onethreeseven.* All of the digital samples of Pinchik's voice heard in "Ehad" are derived from his 1928 recording of "Roso De Shabbos."

The Zohar in Zöhar's "Ehad"

While the range of musical influences and sources that come to bear in "Ehad" may be readily discerned from the biographies of the music's creators and the sound of the music itself, the extent to which an *actual* Zoharic underpinning may (or may not) inform the music's plan and design is rather more difficult to determine. Nothing in the CD booklet accompanying *onethreeseven* or other available literature on Zöhar indicates that Baron Cohen or Kremer are serious students of the Zohar or other aspects of Kabbalah; on the other hand, nothing indicates specifically that they are not. In either case, a Kabbalistic orientation of some kind is evident in the band's

Techno and Electronica

Techno has become a widely used and difficult-to-pinpoint term applied to a great range of contemporary electronic dance music. The term originated with a style that came out of the inner city of Detroit in the 1980s, in which DJs (disc jockeys) would mix together sparse, funky electronic grooves with futuristic, "sci-fi" sounds. The first big techno hit was "Big Fun," by Inner City (a.k.a. DJ Kevin Saunderson), released in 1989. The infatuation of DJs and club musicians of the London underground scene with Detroit techno led to the establishment of a large British techno scene beginning around 1989. From Britain, the movement spread throughout Europe, Asia, and, ultimately, back to North America, where techno entered the "mainstream" of popular music culture in the 1990s (as opposed to its limited Detroit/inner-city circulation in the '80s) (see Strauss 2001).

Nowadays, the term *techno* is used almost interchangeably with *electronica* as a kind of generic tag for a wide range of electronic dance music genres and subgenres: technofunk, ambient, house, acid house, jungle, trip-hop, techno itself (the "original" Detroit and London sounds), and so on. The dividing line between techno, rap, and hip-hop also has become extremely blurry. Today, DJs, musicians, club-going dancers, and others mix and match musics of all imaginable kinds together, taking advantage of the powerful boundary-blurring potential of modern electronic technologies to exploit both modern sounds *and* musical sounds that have been drawn into the mix from the past.

name and in the *onethreeseven* CD cover art (see below). The cover includes an illustration of the "cosmic tree" of the Sefirot; a collage featuring passages of Jewish sacred scripture; and the title "onethreeseven" itself, a reference to the numerical equivalent (137) of the word "Kabbalah" in the gematria system of Kabbalistic numerology.

These clues, together with what I, at least, hear in the music of "Ehad," have led to the essentially Zoharic interpretation of the piece that follows in our final Guided Listening Experience. The basic premise of the interpretation is that "Ehad," like the Pinchik recording that is embedded within its eclectic mixture of electro-acoustic timbres and textures, is a Zoharic tone-poem in its own right. Here, however, the musical symbolism mainly emerges through sections with contrasting textures rather than through melodic symbolism, word painting, or other devices we have encountered thus far. It is principally the different combinations of instruments, "voices," sounds, timbres, and rhythms of "Ehad" that tell its Zohar-derived story.

As for the story itself, the interpretation advanced here is that "Ehad" picks up where Roza D'Shabbos left off in the Zohar's tale of universal redemption. It begins in the divine afterglow

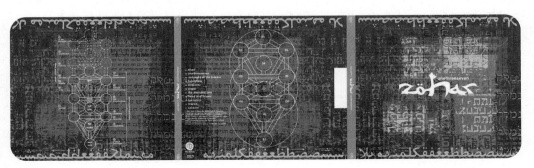

Cover of Zöhar's CD *onethreeseven*.

of the reunification of Hashem and the Shechinah, then continues with the long-awaited and triumphant arrival of Hashem in His new paradise on earth, where He may finally rule as King of Kings in a redeemed and reunited universe. The rest of the story told in the music chronicles a series of heavenward flights and earthward returns, with the heavily processed, digitally sampled voice of Pinchik in the role of the now-manifest Hashem, and the "voice" of a solo synthesizer (played by Baron Cohen) taking the part of a soul striving for, and ultimately achieving, deveikut, or communion with the Divine.

guided listening experience ┠─────────────────────────

"Ehad," Zöhar

- CD Track #**3-33**
- Featured performer(s)/group: Zöhar, with Erran Baron Cohen (piano, synthesizers), Andrew Kremer (bass), Neil Conti (drums), Simone Haggiag (percussion)
- Format: Complete track
- Source recording: *onethreeseven,* by Zöhar (Mondorhythmica/Ark 21 Records 186 850 032 2)

The first and key vocal utterance of "Ehad" occurs at 0:09, where Pinchas Pinchik's digitally sampled voice is heard rising up in pitch and diminishing in volume to near-nothingness against a serene background of acoustic piano and bass. The voice glides upward into the heavens on the word "Echad" ("Ehad"), or "One," on this "Echad glide." A heavenly, ethereal musical atmosphere befitting the afterglow of Hashem's divine reunification with the Shechinah is created in this gentle opening.

Then, with dramatic suddenness, the jarring boom of an electronic drum "bomb" disturbs the celestial serenity at about 0:14. This bomb, together with a second appearance of the sampled Echad glide that occurs simultaneously with it, serves to announce Hashem's manifest arrival in His redeemed, earthly world. A funky rhythmic groove featuring drumset, a *darabukkah* (goblet-shaped, Middle Eastern drum—see also Chapter 12), and an increasingly active bass part contribute to the new musical texture, all reinforcing the sense that we have been musically transported to a new, earthbound setting.

Meanwhile, the piano part continues as before, its calm, elevated demeanor suggesting the merging of heavenly and earthly worlds in the newly reunited cosmic order. By the time the "voice of Hashem" reenters at 0:31, now singing a series of melodic phrases built from skillfully merged, digitally sampled snippets from Pinchik's original "Roso," divine voice and earthly groove are totally in sync. Hashem has taken charge and the music is flowing.

The level of integration grows even deeper beginning at 0:47, where the Echad glide returns and is repeated several times in succession. It becomes the "hook" for the piece overall from here on out, the musical and textual centerpoint around which the composition as a whole builds. Literally and figuratively, the spirit of interaction becomes decidedly celebratory as Hashem jams with the band and they with Him. From this point onward, the piece, much like the Pinchik version of "Roso" that inspired it, unfolds as a series of "soaring flights heavenward" and "chastened returns earthward," with the Echad glide as the central pivot.

At 1:19, both the voice and the percussive groove suddenly cut out, leaving in their wake just the serene, piano-bass musical environment of the opening. This time, though, when the Echad glide returns over the piano and bass at 1:31, Hashem, rather than being brought down to earth as before, instead ascends heavenward on the wings of a surprising, celestial-sounding, modulating synthesizer chord at 1:33. Hashem then disappears into the infinite nothingness of the heavens.

Following this moment of heavenward flight, the scene shifts abruptly back to the earthly realm, where the jam session continues with renewed vigor at 1:37. Eight measures of straight-up, hard-driving rhythmic groove set the stage for a synthesizer solo beginning at 1:53. The timbre of the synthesizer and the plaintive, yearning quality of its melody suggest a voice of prayer. And it is more specifically a *Jewish* voice of prayer, as is symbolized in the music's distinctively Jewish/Middle Eastern modal character here.

Presumably pleased by what He hears rising up from below, Hashem returns earthward with His signature Echad glide to engage in a call-and-response dialogue with this synthesized voice of prayer (2:25–2:40). But at 2:41, the divine voice begins to become unhinged from the rhythmic underpinning. With each successive Echad glide, voice and rhythmic groove become progressively more disengaged. Then, at 2:47, the prayerful voice of the synthesizer likewise takes leave of the music's rhythmic foundation. A suspension of the groove, the disappearance of all but the reverberating echo of the voice of Hashem, and the transformation of the synthesizer's timbre into that of a chorus of angels from 2:57–3:12 collectively serve to transport us heavenward once again, where the righteous soul embodied in the synthesizer's "voice" has apparently joined together with Hashem in the heavenly realm; in other words, it has achieved deveikut, oneness with the Divine.

At 3:13, we are again plummeted back to earth, where music of pure groove becomes the signature of an unprecedented spirit of celebration. The intensity builds, summoning Hashem's earthward return. He arrives at 4:49 for a final, triumphant reprise of the Echad glide hook, following which the piece concludes with the Holy One disappearing into the stratosphere one last time, again accompanied by the "heavenly angel" tones of the synthesizer.

guided listening quick summary

"Ehad," by Zöhar (CD ex. #3-33)

INTRODUCTION

0:00–0:13

- Serene atmosphere created by acoustic piano and bass at beginning.
- First Echad glide (digitally sampled voice of Pinchik) heard at 0:09, ascending in pitch as it diminishes in volume to near-silence.
- Musical atmosphere evokes Hashem-Shechinah union afterglow.

EARTHWARD DESCENT I

0:14–1:18

- Electronic drum bomb at 0:14 and simultaneous Echad glide, followed immediately by drumset/darabbukah/bass funk groove, announce Hashem's manifest arrival in the earthly world.
- Serene piano part continues.
- Hashem (Pinchik's digitally sampled voice) gets fully in sync with the band from 0:31 on.
- Multiple repetitions of Echad glide, which becomes the "hook" of the song (0:47).

HEAVENWARD ASCENT I

1:19–1:36

- Voice and rhythmic groove cut out, leaving just the "ethereal" texture of acoustic piano and bass heard at the start.
- Return of Hashem in the form of the Echad glide at 1:31, but this time He soars heavenward on wings of a celestial synthesizer chord (1:33) rather than remaining earthbound.

Summary

Musically, historically, culturally, and geographically, our journey through musical worlds emanating from the Zohar has taken us a great distance: from the Jacob's Ladder-like melodic symbolism of Isaac Kataev's "V'amazirim" (Bukhara), to the elaborate word painting of Ruth Wieder Magan's "Roza DeShabbos" (Israel), to the varied and evocative electro-acoustic tapestries of Zöhar's "Ehad" (England).

Despite their wide and eclectic musicultural range, all of these different examples of "Jewish music" were shown to have a common point of departure in their shared reliance on the Zohar and its fundamental message of hope for a future age of universal redemption. We saw this message of hope enduring and transforming not just in the music explored, but also through many episodes and eras of Jewish history. It projects forward and backward in time and space from the Zohar itself: backward to the divine revelations believed by Kabbalists to have been experienced by Shimon Bar Yochai, to the golden age of the Israelite kingdoms of Biblical times, and to the very creation of the universe as described in the Torah; forward from Shimon Bar Yochai to Moses de León, Isaac Luria, the Chassidic traditions of Kabbalah in Eastern Europe and then New York, and the modernist (and post-modernist) movements of Jewish reform that underscore the musical, cultural, and religious foundations of musical artists like Ruth Wieder Magan and Zöhar.

Ascent and descent, going out and coming back, travel between worldly and heavenly realms, and, most important of all, the prospect of hope—these are the pervasive themes that unify the diverse Zoharic musical journeys we explored in this chapter. Jewish music, Jewish *musics,* are alive and well in our contemporary world. Like music traditions the world over, from Mali to Mumbai and Bali to Boston, they endure and find vitality and sustenance in the very processes of their own transformation.

Key Terms

Zohar
Kabbalah
deveikut
Torah
Hebrew Bible
Jewish diaspora
Hebrew (language)
Rabbinic Judaism
synagogue

rabbis
Aramaic
Chassidism
Yiddish
Reform Judaism
Holocaust
word painting
gematria

Roza D'Shabbos (passage
  of Zohar)
Hashem
Ain Sof
Ten Sefirot
Malchut
Shechinah
cantor
kol isha

Study Questions

- What is the meaning of deveikut?

- What is Kabbalah?

- How did Jews retain their identity as a people through many centuries of diasporic existence?

- Why is it more appropriate to speak of Jewish *musics* than of Jewish music?

- Can any existing traditions of Jewish music be traced back to the musical culture of the ancient Israelites in Biblical times?

- What kind of a text is the Zohar and what are the theories regarding its origin? In what ways were Shimon Bar Yochai, Moses de León, Isaac Luria, and the Chassidic movement significant to the Zohar's history?

- Who are Ain Sof, Hashem, Adonai, the Shechinah? What are the Ten Sefirot?

- How does Isaac Kataev's performance of "V'amazirim" evoke heavenward ascent and earthward return through its melodic contour?

- What is word painting, and how does Ruth Wieder Magan use this important technique of musical symbolism to evoke the Zoharic text of "Roza DeShabbos"?

- Why is a wordless melody considered more spiritually powerful than a melody with words in Kabbalistic prayer?

- Who was Pinchas Pinchik and what is his significance relative to this chapter?

- Why is Ruth Wieder Magan's recording of "Roza DeShabbos" deemed controversial in some sectors of Jewish society?

- What is kol isha?

- What types of musical symbolism does the group Zöhar use in "Ehad"? What is especially interesting and innovative about their use of digital sampling technology in that piece?

Discussion Questions

- Early in this chapter, historian Raymond Scheindlin was quoted as saying that "the Jewish people and the Jewish religion are not at all the same thing, certainly not in modern times" (Scheindlin 1998:xii). What implications does this statement have for understanding Jewish culture and Judaism, and Jewish musics? By extension, what questions and issues does it raise in relation to the identities, cultures, and musics of peoples who practice other religious faiths: Christianity, Islam, Hinduism, Buddhism?

- For different reasons, Ruth Wieder Magan's "Roza DeShabbos" and Zöhar's "Ehad" are unconventional, even radical, examples of "Jewish music." What are the advantages and disadvantages of exploring these examples in an introductory chapter such as this one?

Applying What You Have Learned

- Word painting is one of the most common symbolic devices used in music throughout the world. Listen to a variety of songs in different styles from your personal music collection. Focus on the words and how they are set to the music. Identify one or more examples of word painting in each song you listen to. Describe how the words are brought to life and "painted" through symbolic uses of melodic direction, rhythmic presentation, dynamics, or other musical elements.

Resources for Further Study

Visit the Online Learning Center at **www.mhhe.com/bakan1** for learning aids, study help, and additional resources that supplement the content of this chapter.

glossary

accents: (Ch. 3) Notes in music that are given special emphasis, usually by being played louder than other notes surrounding them.

acoustic: (Ch. 5) Not amplified, as in acoustic guitar (versus electric guitar).

aerophones: (Ch. 5) Instruments in which the sounds are generated from vibrations created by the action of air passing through a tube or some other kind of resonator (e.g., flute, trumpet, *didjeridu*, human voice).

African diaspora: (Ch. 10) The dispersion of millions of people from Africa—especially western Africa—to other parts of the world, especially the Americas (the United States, Brazil, the Caribbean, etc.); largely a result of the Euro-American slave trade, at least initially. Today, the African diaspora is global in scope and its worldwide musical impact cannot be overestimated.

Africanisms (musical): (Ch. 10) Readily identifiable musicultural characteristics that are widely shared across sub-Saharan Africa and are prominent in musics of the *African diaspora* as well.

Agama Tirta [Ah-gah-muh TEER-tuh]: (Ch. 7) Balinese Hindu religion, representing a syncretism of Hindu, Buddhist, and indigenous Balinese religious elements; literally means "Religion of Holy Water."

Ain Sof [Ayn-SOAF]: (Ch. 14) The "God of Nothingness," or "Invisible God," in Kabbalah. Unknowable, unfathomable aspect of the supreme deity. See also *Ten Sefirot, Hashem*.

Akan [AH-kahn]: (Ch. 10) A large ethnic group of West Africa concentrated principally in the modern nation of Ghana.

alap [ah-LAHP]: (Ch. 8) The nonmetric, improvisatory exploration of a *raga* that constitutes the opening portion of a typical *Hindustani raga* performance; an exploratory journey through the raga's melodic essence and range of possibility.

amplitude: (Ch. 3) The loudness of a tone; basis of dynamics in music.

Aramaic: (Ch. 14) Original language in which the *Zohar* was written.

arpeggio [ahr-PEH-jee-oh]: (Ch. 4) A chord in which the pitches are performed in sequence (one after the other) rather than all at once. An arpeggio (arpeggiated chord) also may be referred to as a "broken chord."

arranging: (Ch. 2) The craft of taking an existing musical work and transforming it into something new, while still retaining its core musical identity.

articulation: (Ch. 4) Refers to the way in which a given tone or series of tones is actually played or sung, for example, with short notes (*staccato*) versus with smooth and sustained notes (*legato*).

atma: (Ch. 7) Human soul (Balinese).

atumpan [AH-toom-pahn]: (Ch. 10) A set of two large drums used by the *Akan* for drum speech and also in other contexts (such as in the *Fontomfrom* royal music ensemble).

baban [bah-bahn]: (Ch. 13) Traditional Chinese melodic form with eight main melodic phrases; most traditional solo *zheng* pieces are in this form (e.g., "Autumn Moon over the Han Palace").

Bahasa Indonesia [Bah-HAH-suh In-doh-NEE-see-uh]: (Ch. 7) The national Indonesian language.

bala [BAH-lah]: (Ch. 10) Xylophone-like idiophone of the *Mande* people of West Africa; one of several instruments historically identified with the musical traditions of *jeliya*.

baladi [bah-lah-dee]: (Ch. 12) Folk heritage (Egypt).

Bali Aga: (Ch. 7) The indigenous people of Bali, whose culture and religion predate the arrival of Hinduism and Buddhism. Bali Aga mainly live in remote Balinese villages (e.g., Tenganan) and have distinctive, ancient forms of *gamelan* (e.g., gamelan selonding).

banjar [BAHN-jahr]: (Ch. 7) Balinese village ward, hamlet, neighborhood organization; responsible for core communal, religious, and social activities of its membership, including cremations and other mortuary rituals; most *gamelan* clubs (sekehe gong) are organized at the banjar level.

barhat [bar-hut]: (Ch. 8) Growth, specifically referring to the musical growth that occurs during a *Hindustani raga* performance.

batá [bah-TAH]: (Ch. 11) Sacred drums used in rituals of the *Santería* (Orisha) religion.

beat: (Ch. 3) Underlying pulse; fundamental unit of rhythmic organization.

Beijing Opera: (Ch. 13) Best-known type of Chinese opera. Like other types, it features heightened speech, song, dance, mime, acting, and acrobatics. The heavily socialism-laden "revolutionary operas" of the 1960s and 1970s (e.g., *The Red Lantern*) represented a radical transformation of the genre during that period.

belly dance: (Ch. 12) Generic term in English for virtually all forms of Middle Eastern and Middle Eastern–derived women's dance; in this text, refers more specifically to Western/international derivates and offshoots of *raqs sharqi* and *raqs baladi*.

bhajan [BUH-jin]: (Ch. 8) A particular class of Hindu devotional songs and hymns with close ties to the historical development of Indian classical music.

bhangra [BHAHNG-rah]: (Ch. 8) Originally a folk music tradition of the Punjab region; now more widely known in its contemporary popular music style; often featured in Indian "Bollywoood" films.

big band mambo: (Ch. 11) The highly syncretic *mambo* style of the 1950s indentified with New York–based bandleaders such as Tito Puente, Machito, and Tito Rodríguez (see also *mambo kings*). Incorporated more Afro-Cuban and American jazz and popular music elements than did the earlier Cuban mambo style.

birimintingo [beer-uh-men-TEEN-go]:   (Ch. 10) The soloistic style of instrumental performance used on instruments like the *kora, bala,* and *koni* in Mande *jeliya* music.

blues scale: (Ch. 4) A distinctive type of *scale* associated with blues and blues-derived musics that combines elements of major, minor, pentatonic, and traditional African scales.

bodhrán [BOH-rawn]:   (Ch. 9) Irish handheld frame drum with a goat skin head. (Synthetic heads are sometimes used in place of goat skin today.)

bongó [bon-GO]:   (Ch. 11) Pair of small, single-headed drums used in percussion sections of many types of Latin dance bands. Held between the knees and played with the fingers.

call-and-response: (Ch. 6) Back-and-forth alternation between different instrument or voice parts.

cane dance: (Ch. 12) Popular women's dance form in which the dancer perfoms with a cane. Different variants found in *raqs baladi, raqs sharqi, belly dance.* Derives originally from the *tahtib* martial art of Saaid (Upper Egypt).

cantor: (Ch. 14) The solo singer and leader of congregational chanting in Jewish religious services.

ceílí [KAY-lee]:   (Ch. 9) Informal social gathering involving dancing, usually held at an Irish pub or dance hall.

Celtic [KEL-tick]:   (Ch. 9) Refers to a complex of historically related cultures that today mainly survive in Ireland, Scotland, Wales, Brittany, and certain regions of eastern Canada. This cultural complex is principally defined by the Celtic family of languages, though other shared aspects of Celtic culture broadly defined, including music, are significant as well.

Central Javanese court gamelan: (Ch. 7) The great *gamelan* traditions associated with the royal courts of the cities of Yogyakarta and Surakarta; along with Balinese *gamelan gong kebyar,* the best-known type of gamelan internationally.

cha cha chá: (Ch. 11) A Cuban dance-music genre characterized by relatively simple dance rhythms and singing; originated with Enrique Jorrin around 1950 and eventually gained international popularity. In the hands of Tito Puente and other New York bandleaders, the cha cha chá took on a new musical identity, leading to the style of arrangements like Puente's original recorded version of "Oye Como Va" (1963).

charanga [cha-RAHN-gah]:   (Ch. 11) "Sweet-sounding" Cuban ensemble associated with the *danzón, danzón-mambo,* early Cuban *cha cha chá,* and other dance music styles. Usually included flute, violins, piano, bass, and percussion (plus singers).

Chassidism [KHA-sid-is-um]:   (Ch. 14) Form of *Kabbalah*-inspired Judaism that arose in Central and Eastern Europe during the 18th century. Stressed populist appeal, joy in worship, and ecstatic experience over more learned, rationalist religious approaches. Took inspiration from the Baal Shem Tov. Remains a vital movement in Judaism today.

Chinese Communist Party: (Ch. 13) The ruling party of the People's Republic of China from 1949–present. Originally led by Mao Zedong until his death in 1976, the party and its policies experienced profound transformations under the leadership of Deng Xiaoping beginning in the late 1970s.

chord: (Ch. 4) A group of two or more notes of different pitch that are sounded simultaneously (or that are perceived as belonging to a single unit even when not sounded simultaneously—see *arpeggio*).

chord progression: (Ch. 4) The sequence of movement from one chord to another in a musical work or performance.

chordophones: (Ch. 5) Instruments in which the sound is activated by the vibration of a string or strings over a resonating chamber (e.g., guitar, violin, piano, *zheng*).

classicization: (Ch. 7) In *kreasi beleganjur* music, the adoption and adaptation of three-part forms (fast-slow-fast) derived from older, classical Balinese *gamelan* traditions.

clave [KLAH-vay]:   (Ch. 11) Fundamental rhythm of *Latin dance music;* comes in four different varieties; often played on *claves,* but even if not actually played its presence is always implied.

claves: (Ch. 11) Instrument consisting of a pair of thick, round sticks that are struck together. Identified with the *clave* rhythm.

composition: (Ch. 2) A musical work; the process of creating a musical work; the process of planning out the design of a musical work prior to its performance.

Confucianism: (Ch. 13) The sociopolitical doctrine and philosophy originating with the writings of Confucius, which stressed rigid social hierarchy, civic responsibility, and a particular conception of morally virtuous social order. Basis of Chinese society for many centuries from the Han dynasty era forward.

conga [KOAN-gah] **drums (congas):**   (Ch. 11) Large, barrel-shaped drums of Afro-Cuban origin and West African (Congolese) derivation. Usually played in sets of three drums, either by three separate players or by just one performer. Used in *rumba* and in most styles of *Latin dance music.*

crescendo: (Ch. 5) Getting louder.

Cultural Revolution: (Ch. 13) Final period of Mao Zedong's leadership of China, 1966–1976. Unprecedented levels of intolerance for any deviation from communist state ideology; extreme restrictions on cultural and artistic expression.

culture: (Ch. 2) As defined in 1871 by anthropologist Edward Tylor, "that complex whole which includes knowledge, belief, art, law, morals, custom, and any other capabilities and habits acquired by man [humankind] as a member of society."

cultures: (Ch. 2) Social entities that are defined by particular complexes of ideas, beliefs, and practices: religions, ideologies, philosophies, sciences, moral and ethical principles, artistic creations, ritual performances.

cycle: (Ch. 6) A recurring musical unit (pattern, sequence), but typically longer than an *ostinato;* basis of cyclic musical forms like the *gong cycles* of Indonesian *gamelan* music and *talas* of *Hindustani raga.*

danzón [dan-SOHN]: (Ch. 11) Creolized Cuban dance-music genre that essentially became the national dance of Cuba in the 1920s; important forerunner of the *danzón-mambo* and the *cha cha chá.* Closely identified with the *charanga* ensemble.

danzón-mambo: (Ch. 11) More Afro-Cubanized version of the earlier *danzón;* created and popularized by Arcaño y sus Maravillas. Maravillas band members the López brothers ("Cachao" and Orestes) were the true innovators of the style, which ultimately influenced both *cha cha chá* and later forms of *mambo.*

dap: (Ch. 13) Traditional Uighur frame drum. Drum head is usually made of donkey hide or snake skin.

decrescendo: (Ch. 5) Getting softer.

deveikut [d'vay-KOOT]: (Ch. 14) "To be one with the Divine"; a key concept of *Kabbalah.*

diaspora: (Ch. 2) An international network of communities linked together by identification with a common ancestral homeland and culture. People in diaspora exist in a condition of living away from their "homeland," often with no guarantee, or even likelihood, of return.

didjeridu [DIJ-er-ee-DOO]: (Ch. 5) Aboriginal Australian aerophone instrument; traditionally constructed from a termite-hollowed eucalyptus branch.

digital sampling: (Ch. 5) Technology that allows for any existing sound to be recorded, stored as digital data, and then reproduced either "verbatim" or in electronically manipulated form.

drone: (Ch. 6) A continuous, sustained tone.

drum speech: (Ch. 10) Linguistic use of certain types of West African drums (e.g., *atumpan*) in certain contexts (e.g., reciting proverbs), which is made possible by the use of *tonal languages.*

drumset: (Ch. 5) "Compound" instrument consisting of a combination of *membranophones* (drums) and *idiophones* (cymbals).

Dum, tek: (Ch. 12) The syllables for the two principal drum strokes used on *tabla* and other Egyptian/Arab percussion instruments. The *Dum* is low-pitched and deep; the *tek,* high-pitched and piercing.

duration: (Ch. 3) The length of a tone; basis of *rhythm* in music.

dynamic range: (Ch. 5) Range of dynamic levels (levels of relative loudness) in a musical work or performance.

Egyptian nationalism: (Ch. 12) Nationalist movement that crystallized beginning in the 19th century and gained momentum through the 20th century. Inspired by Egyptian opposition to foreign domination and defined by currents of Egyptian localism, pan-Arabism, and Islamism. Musicians such as Sayyid Darwish, Muhammad 'Abd al-Wahhab, and Umm Kulthum, as well as the dancer Farida Fahmy, were prominent nationalist icons.

eighth notes: (Ch. 3) Level of rhythmic *subdivision* where there are two evenly spaced notes per *quarter note.*

electronophones: (Ch. 5) Instruments that rely on electronic sound generation/modification to produce their timbres.

ensembles: (Ch. 5) Music groups (instruments, voices, or combined).

ethnocentrism: (Ch. 1) Imposition of one set of culturally grounded perspectives, biases, and assumptions (e.g., Western) on peoples and practices of other cultures.

ethnomusicology: (Ch. 2) An interdisciplinary academic field that draws on musicology, anthropology, and other disciplines in order to study the world's musics; ethnomusicologists are interested in understanding music as a *musicultural* phenomenon.

fallahi [fah-lah-HEE]: (Ch. 12) Upbeat dance rhythm traditionally used in accompaniment of Egyptian rural folk dances; also used to evoke "peasant" image in *raqs sharqi, belly dance,* and Egyptian folkloric dance.

fallahin [fah-la-HEEN]: (Ch. 12) Literally, "peasant"; refers also to a metaphorical, romanticized cultural ideal of authentic (asil) Egyptianness.

fieldwork: (Ch. 2) In *ethnomusicology,* a hallmark of research involving living for an extended period of time among the people whose lives and music one studies; often encompasses learning and performing their music as well.

firqa musiqyya [fir-[k]AH moo-si-ki-YAH]: (Ch. 12) Large ensemble, involving both traditional Middle Eastern instruments of the *takht* ensemble and Western instruments.

five propositions (about music): (Ch. 1) In this text, the propositions that music is based in sound, that the sounds of music are organized in some way, that music is a form of humanly organized sound, that it is a product of human intention and perception, and that the term *music* itself is inescapably Western.

Fon: (Ch. 10) One of the major ethnic groups in the West African nation of Benin; Angélique Kidjo is of Fon heritage and many of her songs are in the Fon language (e.g., "Okan Bale").

Fontomfrom [Fon-tom-frahm]: (Ch. 10) *Akan* royal drum ensemble, featuring several drums (*from, atumpan,* eguankoba) and the gongon iron bell.

form: (Ch. 6) The sequential ordering of a piece of music as it unfolds; the resultant shape and design of the music;

a specific, conventional type of musical design (e.g., *12-bar blues, verse-chorus form*).

free rhythm: (Ch. 3) Refers to music in which there is no discernible *beat* or *meter.*

frequency: (Ch. 3) The highness or lowness of a note; basis of pitch in music.

Gaelic [GAH-lick]: (Ch. 9) See *Irish Gaelic.*

gamelan [gah-muh-lahn]: (Ch. 7) Generic Indonesian term for "ensemble," "orchestra"; used in reference to a diverse class of mainly percussion-dominated music ensembles found on Bali, Java, and several other Indonesian islands.

gamelan beleganjur [buh-luh-gahn-YOOR]: (Ch. 7) "Gamelan of walking warriors"; Balinese processional ensemble consisting of multiple gongs, drums, and cymbals, played in ritualistic contexts (e.g., cremation processions) and in modern music contests.

gamelan gong kebyar [kuh-BYAHR]: (Ch. 7) Best-known type of Balinese *gamelan.* Instrumentation features *gangsa* metallophones; gongs of many types, sizes, and functions; drums, cymbals, and other instruments. Associated with virtuosic kebyar musical style.

gangsa [GAHNG-suh]: (Ch. 7) Keyed metallophone instrument in a Balinese *gamelan.*

gat [like English "gut"]: (Ch. 8) The main part of a *Hindustani raga* performance following the *alap;* a *tala* (metric cycle) serves as its metric/rhythmic foundation; the entry of a rhythmic accompaniment part (usually played on *tabla*) marks the commencement of the gat.

gematria [ge-MA-tree-yah]: (Ch. 14) Mystical numerology tradition in *Kabbalah.*

gerak [GUH-rahk]: (Ch. 7) Literally means "movement"; specifically in this text, refers to the choreographed movements performed by the musicians in beleganjur contests; associated with *kreasi beleganjur.*

gharana [gha-RAH-nah]: (Ch. 8) A "musical family" that preserves, cultivates, and develops a particular "school" of *raga* performance, often over the course of many generations.

ghawazi [gha-WAH-zee]: (Ch. 12) Specifically, a hereditary class of professional female dancers in Egypt; more broadly, a designation for all professional female dancers in Egypt and throughout the Middle East; term literally means "outsider" or "invader."

gilak [GEE-lahk]: (Ch. 7) Common, eight-beat *gong cycle* used in beleganjur and other Balinese music traditions.

gong ageng [gohng ah-GUHNG]: (Ch. 7) "Great gong"; the largest gong (or gongs, if two) in a *gamelan.*

gong cycle: (Ch. 7) A recurring sequence of gong strokes (usually employing two or more gongs) that provides the musical foundation of a *gamelan* piece.

griot [GREE-oh]: (Ch. 10) Generic term (from French) covering a diverse range of African hereditary praise song/music traditions, including that of the Mande *jeli.*

gua-zou [goo-wa zoh]: (Ch. 13) General term for a wide variety of glissando-type ornaments used in *zheng* and other Chinese instrumental traditions.

guru: (Ch. 8) Teacher, mentor (in this text, specifically of Indian classical music).

Han Chinese: (Ch. 13) Chinese ethnic majority, accounting for approximately 92 percent of the population of the People's Republic of China.

harmonics: (Ch. 5) The overtones, or partials, of a tone (as distinct from the fundamental of that tone).

harmonization: (Ch. 4) Procedure (and result) of building *chords* from the individual notes of a melody.

harmonized texture: (Ch. 6) Texture resulting when notes of different pitch occur together to form *chords,* or "harmonies."

harmony: (Ch. 4) A *chord* that "makes sense" within the context of its musical style.

Hashem [Hah-SHEM]: (Ch. 14) Literally means "The Name"; refers to God, as conceived of in Judaism.

Hebrew: (Ch. 14) The ancient Jewish language of the *Torah* and other scriptural writings; modern Hebrew is the national language of Israel.

Hebrew Bible: (Ch. 14) The foundational scriptures of Judaism, consisting of the *Torah,* the books of the Prophets, and the Hagiographa (or Sacred Writings). (Identified in Christianity as the Old Testament of the Christian Bible.)

heterophony: (Ch. 6) Variant versions of a single melodic line performed simultaneously.

Hindustani raga [Hin-dus-TAH-nee RAH-gah (or RAHG)]: (Ch. 8) The *raga* tradition of North India.

HIP (human intention and perception) approach: (Ch. 1) An approach to the study and exploration of world music (advocated in this text) that privileges inclusiveness over exclusiveness and emphasizes the idea that music is inseparable from the people who make and experience it.

Holocaust: (Ch. 14) The genocidal slaughter of six million Jews at the hands of the Nazis in Europe during World War II.

Hornbostel-Sachs classification system: (Ch. 5) Music instrument classification system (originally published in 1914) that classifies the world's instruments into four main categories: *chordophones, aerophones, membranophones,* and *idiophones.* A fifth category, *electronophones,* has since been added.

hornpipe: (Ch. 9) Commonly used dance rhythm in Irish music.

horn section: (Ch. 11) The trumpet, trombone, and saxophone players in a Latin dance band.

identity: (Ch. 2) Defined by people's ideas about who they are and what unites them with, or distinguishes them from, other people and entities: individuals, families, communities, institutions, *cultures, societies, nations,* supernatural powers.

idiophones: (Ch. 5) Instruments in which the vibration of the body of the instrument itself produces the sound (e.g., shaker, cymbal, xylophone).

improvisation: (Ch. 2) The process of composing in the moment of performance; takes different forms in different music traditions (e.g., jazz, *Hindustani raga*).

instrumentation: (Ch. 5) The types of instruments and the number of each employed in a given musical work or performance. Potentially includes voices.

interlocking: (Ch. 6) Division of a single melodic or rhythmic line between two or more instruments/voices.

interpretation: (Ch. 2) The process through which music performers—or music listeners—take an existing composition and in a sense make it their own through the experience of performing or listening to it.

interval: (Ch. 4) The distance in pitch between one note and another.

Irish diaspora: (Ch. 9) The dispersion of millions of people from Ireland to other countries, especially the United States and Canada, where large diasporic communities ultimately formed. The Irish diaspora commenced in response to the *Irish potato famine.*

Irish Gaelic [GAH-lick]: (Ch. 9) The traditional *Celtic* language of Ireland; mainly spoken in the Gaeltacht areas of the country. The Gaelic language subfamily also includes Scottish Gaelic and Manx Gaelic. *Sean nós* songs are sung in Irish Gaelic.

Irish music revival: (Ch. 9) Major musicultural phenomenon of the 1960s and henceforth that both preserved and transformed *Irish traditional music* on many levels, in Ireland itself and internationally.

Irish potato famine: (Ch. 9) Devastating famine that began in the 1840s. Led to decimation of the Irish population, the *Irish diaspora,* violent resistance to British control of Ireland, and the beginnings of Irish nationalism.

Irish traditional music: (Ch. 9) Umbrella term for a wide range of musics—traditional, neo-traditional, post-traditional—that share a common basis in rural, Irish folk music.

Irish wooden flute: (Ch. 9) A relatively large and low-pitched *aerophone* with a distinctive *timbre* that is a standard instrument in *Irish traditional music.*

jeli [JAY-lee] (pl. jelilu): (Ch. 10) A Mande *griot.* Most of the leading jelilu are descended from a hereditary jeli family (Kouyate, Diabate, Sissoko). Those who are instrumentalists play specific jeli instruments such as *kora, bala,* and *koni.*

jeliya [jay-lee-yuh]: (Ch. 10) The artistic culture of the *jeli,* including its *praise songs* and instrumental music traditions.

Jewish diaspora: (Ch. 14) The global dispersion of the Jewish people from their ancestral homeland (in modern-day Israel), with a history dating back millennia.

jig: (Ch. 9) Commonly used dance rhythm in Irish music.

Kabbalah [Kah-bah-LAH]: (Ch. 14) The Jewish mystical tradition, including its canonical works like the *Zohar.*

Karnatak [Kar-NAH-tuck]: (Ch. 8) The culture of South India; in this text, specifically refers to the great South Indian classical music tradition.

kebyarization: (Ch. 7) In *kreasi beleganjur* music, the incorporation of musical elements and stylistic influences derived from *gamelan gong kebyar* music.

Kecak [ke-CHAHK]: (Ch. 7) Balinese dance-drama that employs a gamelan suara (*gamelan* of voices) as its sole musical accompaniment; music features complex interlocking rhythms derived from the *kilitan telu.*

keeping tal: (Ch. 8) Practice of outlining the metric cycle of a *tala* using a combination of claps, waves, and finger touches to mark the various beats.

key: (Ch. 4) Term that indicates the fundamental *scale* from which a piece of music is built (e.g., a piece in the key of C major is based on a C-major scale).

kilitan telu [kee-lee-TAHN tuh-LOO]: (Ch. 7) Set of three interlocking rhythmic patterns that are an integral component of much Balinese music; basis of the interlocking cymbal patterns in *gamelan beleganjur* music and of the interlocking vocal patterns in *Kecak.*

kol isha [kohl ee-SHAH]: (Ch. 14) Literally means "the voice of a woman." Refers to the belief in some domains of Jewish society that women should not sing prayers in the presence of men.

koni [koh-nee]: (Ch. 10) Banjo-like plucked chordophone of the *Mande; jeli* instrument. Bassekou Kouyate is one of its best-known exponents.

kora: (Ch. 10) 21-string *Mande* spike harp chordophone; *jeli* instrument. Sidiki, Toumani, and Mamadou Diabate represent one of the great lineages of kora players.

koto: (Ch. 13) Japanese board zither chordophone with 13 strings. Historically related to the Chinese *zheng.*

kreasi beleganjur [kray-YAH-see buh-luh-gahn-YOOR]: (Ch. 7) Modern, contest style of beleganjur music; first developed in 1986 in Denpasar, Bali.

kumbengo [koom-BAYN-go]: (Ch. 10) The accompaniment style of instrumental performance used on instruments like the *kora, bala,* and *koni* in Mande *jeliya* music.

Latin Dance: (Ch. 11) Dance-music genre that is a hybrid of diverse contemporary music styles—pop, rock, hip-hop, techno, Latino pop—and *mambo, cha cha chá,* and Dominican merengue. Identified specifically with Tito Puente Jr. in this text.

Latin dance music: (Ch. 11) Generically, all dance music traditions of Latin America; more specifically in this text, refers to a particular lineage of dance-music traditions rooted in Cuban forms.

Latin rock: (Ch. 11) Hybrid of *Latin dance music* styles (*rumba, cha cha chá, mambo,* etc.) and rock music. Term is most closely identified with the music of Santana.

Latino/American: (Ch. 11) The slash between the words implies "and/or" in the widest sense; that is, it points to the fluidity and multiplicity of Latino and American identities, musiculturally and otherwise.

layered ostinatos: (Ch. 6) "Stacking" of two or more *ostinatos* one atop the other.

legato [le-GAH-toe]: (Ch. 4) Italian term for a type of articulation in which the notes are sustained; opposite of *staccato.*

major scale: (Ch. 4) A common type of *scale* in Western music with seven pitches per octave. The ascending and descending forms of the scale employ the same set of pitches.

Malchut [Mall-KHOOT]: (Ch. 14) The lowest of the *Ten Sefirot* in the *Zohar,* wherein the *Shechinah* is thought to reside.

malfuf [mahl-FOOF]: (Ch. 12) Lively, quick-tempoed Egyptian dance rhythm often heard in the opening numbers of *raqs sharqi* and *belly dance* routines.

malpal: (Ch. 7) Hard-driving, highly energetic style of beleganjur playing used at crossroads along the procession route during Balinese cremation processions.

mambo: (Ch. 11) Highly Afro-Cubanized form of *Latin dance music* that was crystallized by Pérez Prado but is today principally identified with 1950s New York Latin big bands like Machito and the Afro-Cubans and the bands of Tito Puente and Tito Rodríguez.

mambo kings: (Ch. 11) The leaders of the top Latin dance bands of New York in the 1950s, who were responsible for the "mambo craze" of that era: Machito, Tito Puente, Tito Rodríguez.

Mandarin Chinese: (Ch. 13) China's official national language.

Mande [MAHN-day]: (Ch. 10) Major ethnic group of western Africa, concentrated in areas of Mali, Senegal, Guinea, Guinea-Bissau, and Gambia. Principal subgroups are the Maninka (Mali, Guinea) and Mandinka (Senegal, Gambia).

maqam [mah-KAHM]: (Ch. 12) Term for "mode" in Arab music; part of a large modal system comprising many maqamat (plural of maqam).

maqsoum [mak-SOOM]: (Ch. 12) Popular dance rhythm in Egyptian women's dance.

masmoudi [mas-MOO-dee]: (Ch. 12) Very commonly used Egyptian dance rhythm; comes in several different varieties and may be played at different tempos.

measure: (Ch. 3) One unit, or group, of beats in music that has *meter* (i.e., in metric music).

medley: (Ch. 9) A musical form in which two or more pieces (e.g., Irish dance tunes) are performed one after the other without pause.

melody: (Ch. 4) A sequence of pitches that defines the identity of a song or other piece of music as it unfolds; a "tune." Every melody has distinctive features including range, direction, character, and contour.

membranophones: (Ch. 5) Instruments in which the vibration of a membrane (natural or synthetic) stretched tightly across a frame resonator produces the sound (e.g., drums).

meter: (Ch. 3) The systematic grouping of individual *beats* into larger groupings; a specific pattern of grouped beats (e.g., duple meter, triple meter).

metric cycle: (Ch. 3) Like a *meter,* but longer (e.g., *gong cycle* in Indonesian *gamelan* music, *tala* cycle in *Hindustani raga*).

microtones: (Ch. 4) Tiny pitch *intervals,* as found in the pitch systems of Middle Eastern, Indian, and other music traditions that recognize more than the 12 divisions of the *octave* identified in the Western chromatic *scale.*

minor scales: (Ch. 4) Like the *major scale,* minor scales have seven pitches per octave, but they differ in that the *interval* between the second and third scale degrees is always smaller than in the major scale. Additionally, the ascending and descending forms of a minor scale may use different sets of pitches.

mode: (Ch. 4) A comprehensive, multidimensional musical system—based on but not limited to a specific *scale* of pitches—that guides composers/performers on how to generate musical works and performances *in* that mode. May encompass both musical dimensions (pitches, ornaments, melodic procedures) and extramusical dimensions (associations with particular times of day, seasons, emotions).

modulation: (Ch. 4) Changing *key* (or changing *mode*) in the course of a composition.

mrdangam [mir-DUNG-ahm]: (Ch. 8) Double-headed South Indian drum used in *Karnatak* music performance.

multiple-melody texture: (Ch. 6) Texture in which two or more essentially separate melodic lines are performed simultaneously.

multitrack recording: (Ch. 5) Involves technologies that make it possible to layer dozens upon dozens of separate musical tracks one atop the other using computers or other equipment.

muqam [moo-KAHM]: (Ch. 13) In Uighur music (and Central Asian traditions more broadly), refers to a large-scale, precomposed suite of songs and instrumental music.

music instrument: (Ch. 5) Any sound-generating medium used to produce tones in the making of music.

musical syncretism: (Ch. 2) The merging of formerly distinct musical styles and idioms into new forms of musical expression.

musicultural: (Ch. 2) Conception of music in which *music as sound* and *music as culture* are regarded as mutually reinforcing and essentially inseparable from one another.

Nada Brahma: (Ch. 8) "The Sound of God" (Brahma); the divine source of all sound and thus of all ragas. *Raga* performance, at its highest level, is ultimately a pursuit of the ideal of Nada Brahma.

nation-state/nation: (Ch. 2) A nation-state is defined by a national society and culture *and* a national homeland (e.g., Canada); a nation *may* be defined in an identical manner, but some nations do not have political autonomy over the geographical area they claim as their homeland (e.g., as of this writing, Palestine).

nationalist music: (Ch. 2) Music tied to movements of nationalism and concepts of and ideas about national identities.

Newyorican: (Ch. 11) New York resident of Puerto Rican descent; includes both New York natives (e.g., Tito Puente) and Puerto Rican immigrants to New York (e.g., Tito Rodríguez).

octave [OCK-tiv]: (Ch. 4) The phenomenon accounting for why the "same" pitch may occur in multiple—that is, higher and lower—versions (e.g., why a note on the pitch C sung by a woman sounds higher than a note on the pitch C sung by a man).

ombak [OAM-bahk]: (Ch. 7) Means "wave"; refers to the acoustical beating effect generated by instruments with *paired tuning* in a Balinese *gamelan*.

Orientalist (Orientalism): (Ch. 12) Exoticized (and often marginalizing) representations of "Eastern" (i.e., "Oriental") people and cultures. Orientalist characterizations of Egypt spanned from 19th-century French paintings to 20th-century Hollywood movies, and the image of the Middle Eastern female dancer (belly dancer) was a consistently prominent image.

ornamentation: (Ch. 4, 13) Decoration, or adornment, of the main notes in a *melody* by additional notes and ornamental figures (e.g., pitch bends, glissandos).

ornaments: (Ch. 9) A general term relating to the decoration of melodies in music traditions worldwide (see *ornamentation*); in the chapter, relates specifically to ornaments used in Irish music such as the roll, cran, treble, cut, and triplet.

ostinato [ah-sti-NAH-toe]: (Ch. 6) A short, recurring musical figure; may be repeated exactly or with variations as the music unfolds. Generally, the smallest unit of musical organization upon which formal musical designs are built (as in ostinato-based forms).

overdubbing: (Ch. 5) The process of separately recording and then combining multiple recorded tracks using *multitrack recording*.

paired tuning: (Ch. 7) The tuning of the pitches of the "male" and "female" instruments of a Balinese *gamelan* to slightly different *frequencies;* striking the "same" pitch simultaneously on a male-female pair creates *ombak;* female instruments of each pair are tuned lower than their male counterparts.

pan-Irish: (Ch. 9) Pertaining to Irish identity and culture (including music) in Ireland itself, transnationally throughout the *Irish diaspora,* and worldwide across the expansive range of Irish and Irish diasporic influence.

pentatonic scale: (Ch. 4) Five-tone *scale* (five tones per octave). The version discussed in the chapter is closely related to the *major scale,* though there are many different forms of pentatonic scales in other world music traditions as well.

Period of Openness: (Ch. 13) Modern period of Chinese socialism, initiated by Deng Xiaoping in late 1970s/early 1980s. Yielded profound transformations of Chinese society, including introduction of free enterprise economy, China's immersion in global markets, and liberalization of policies on the arts.

pipa [pee-pah]: (Ch. 13) Pear-shaped, plucked chordophone with four strings. Chinese instrument of Central Asian heritage; close historical association with the *zheng*.

polyphonic: (Ch. 6) Music with two or more distinct parts.

polyrhythm: (Ch. 6) Music in which there are several different parts or layers, with each defined by its distinctive rhythmic character rather than by melodies or chords.

polyvocality: (Ch. 10) Comprising "many voices"; in the chapter, relates to the conversational dimension of much West African music, wherein many voices—vocal and/or instrumental—may speak and be heard all at once, expressing a unified diversity of views and perspectives.

praise songs: (Ch. 10) In the *jeliya* tradition of the *Mande* and in other African *griot* traditions, a class of songs that were traditionally sung to honor royalty exclusively, but that are now often performed in honor of modern politicians or other wealthy patrons who are not of royal lineage as well.

qin [chin]: (Ch. 13) Ancient Chinese zither-type chordophone with seven strings, no bridges; quintessential instrument of the Chinese gentleman/scholar (junzi) during the dynastic era. Confucius is said to have played this instrument.

quarter notes: (Ch. 3) Notes whose duration often defines the *beat* in music; see also *eighth notes* and *sixteenth notes*.

Qur'an [Koar-AHN]: (Ch. 1, 12) The holy book of Islam; principal sacred text of that religion.

Qur'anic [Koar-AH-nik] **recitation:** (Ch. 12) The melodious art of reciting the Qur'an. Though it sounds musical to Western listeners and uses *maqam*-like melodies similar to those found in Middle Eastern music, it is categorically *not* music according to most Muslims.

quarter tone: (Ch. 12) Microtonal interval that falls halfway between the smallest intervals (semitones) in the conventional Western pitch system (i.e., halfway between consecutive keys on a piano). Quarter-tone intervals are used in *maqam*-based music of the Middle East.

Rabbinic Judaism: (Ch. 14) The principal tradition(s) of Jewish religious practice from Roman times to the present, focusing on study of the *Torah* and related texts and on congregational worship in *synagogues* led by *rabbis*.

rabbis: (Ch. 14) Specialists in Jewish religious traditions and law who serve as the leaders of *synagogue* congregations; historically, it was rabbis who also created the canonical texts of Biblical interpretation, such as the Mishnah and the Talmud.

Radio Éireann [AIR-ahn]: (Ch. 9) Ireland's national radio station.

raga: (Ch. 8) In Indian classical music, a complete and self-contained melodic system that serves as the basis for all the melodic materials in any composition or performance created *in* that raga.

Raga Nat Bhairav [RAH-gah nut BHAY-ruv]: (Ch. 8) A well-known raga in the Bhairav family of morning ragas; combines elements of two ragas—Raga Bhairav and Raga Nat. First popularized by Ravi Shankar in the 1940s.

ranges: (Ch. 4) Refers to the different octave registers (pitch ranges) in which different instruments and voice types perform (e.g., the range of a tuba is much lower than the range of a flute).

raqs baladi [ra[k]s bah-lah-dee]: (Ch. 12) Egyptian (and other Middle Eastern) "folk dance"; the term implies rural culture or origins; encompasses traditional dance of women's gatherings and certain other types of folk rituals and ceremonial performances.

raqs sharqi [ra[k]s shar[k]ee]: (Ch. 12) The professional entertainment medium of women's dance, associated with Egyptian weddings, nightclub and cabaret performance, and commercial film and other mass media.

reel: (Ch. 9) The most commonly used dance rhythm in Irish music.

Reform Judaism: (Ch. 14) An important movement in Judaism that first developed in Germany in the 19th century; premised on the notion that the conventional rituals and laws of Judaism need to be adjusted and transformed in accordance with changing (modern) times and social conditions.

regional styles of solo zheng music: (Ch. 13) A complex of distinctive playing styles, repertoires, and performance traditions on the *zheng* that crystallized in the late 19th century in regions of China including Shandong, Henan, Shaanxi, Chaozhou, Hakka, and Zhejiang.

reyong: (Ch. 7) In the *gamelan beleganjur*, a set of four small, hand-held gongs (each played by a separate performer) played in interlocking style; main function is to elaborate the music's core melody.

rhythm: (Ch. 3) In music, the organization of sounds and silences in time.

rhythm section: (Ch. 11) The pianist, bassist, and percussionists in a Latin dance band.

riffs: (Ch. 11) Short, recurring patterns (ostinatos) that are repeated over and over, often with variations, and layered one atop the other. Important feature of arrangements in *mambo, salsa,* and other *Latin dance music* styles.

riqq [ri[k]]: (Ch. 12) Arab tambourine.

rituals: (Ch. 2) Special events during which individuals or communities enact, through performance, their core beliefs, values, and ideals.

Roza D'Shabbos [RAW-za d'SHAH-bus]: (Ch. 14) Passage from the *Zohar* that forecasts a coming age of universal redemption under the divine rule of *Hashem*. Basis of several musical works explored in this text.

rumba [ROOM-bah]: (Ch. 11) Traditional Afro-Cuban secular dance music featuring singing and music played on *conga* drums and other instruments.

Saaidi [sah-ayi-DEE]: (Ch. 12) Dance rhythm associated with the traditional *baladi* culture of the Saaid (Upper Egypt); the rhythm is derived from those used in accompaniment of the martial art/men's dance forms of *tahtib*.

sagat [sah-gaht]: (Ch. 12) Finger cymbals, often played by female dancers as they perform.

salsa: (Ch. 11) Major form of *Latin dance music* that emerged in New York in the 1970s. Strongly rooted in Cuban *son*.

sam [like English "some"]: (Ch. 8) The first beat of a *tala* cycle (and, simultaneously, the last beat of the preceding cycle).

Santería [San-te-REE-yah]: (Ch. 11) Afro-Cuban religion based on traditional West African religious practices of the Yoruba people syncretized with Catholicism. Sacred ritual music employing the *batá* drums is central. (Also known as Orisha [Oricha] religion).

sataro: (Ch. 10) Improvisatory, partially speechlike style of singing in *jeliya* vocal art. Kassemady Diabate is a master of sataro.

sauta [sow-tah]: (Ch. 10) An important musical mode in *Mande* music, using a *scale* that is roughly equivalent to F G A B C D E (F) in Western music.

scale: (Ch. 4) An ascending and/or descending series of notes of different pitch. Songs and other pieces of music are typically "built" from the notes of particular scales. The chromatic, major, pentatonic, minor, and blues scales are important types in Western and related music traditions.

sean nós [SHAWN nohs]: (Ch. 9) The "old way" songs , sung in *Irish Gaelic;* revered as the cornerstone of *Irish traditional music.*

session (Irish music session): (Ch. 9) Informal gathering where musicians playing different instruments come together to perform traditional Irish tunes and newer tunes modeled after them, but not generally to accompany dancing.

Shechinah [Sh'khee-NAH]: (Ch. 14) In the *Zohar* and other Kabbalistic works, the "female," receiving aspect of *Hashem*, whose domain is *Malchut*, the lowest of the *Ten Sefirot*. The Shechinah's reunification with Hashem is central to the Zoharic passage *Roza D'Shabbos*.

Silk Road: (Ch. 13) Expansive trade route of antiquity that connected China to lands as distant as Central Asia, India, Egypt, and Turkey.

single-line texture: (Ch. 6) Music with only a single part, for example, a single melody. Note that this one part may be performed by multiple performers, and may employ a wide array of different voices, instruments, and octave ranges. (See also *unison*.)

sitar [si-TAHR]: (Ch. 8) North Indian plucked chordophone instrument; one of the main melodic instruments in Hindustani music; principal instrument of Ravi Shankar; iconic symbol of "Indian music" internationally.

sixteenth notes: (Ch. 3) Level of rhythmic *subdivision* where there are four evenly spaced notes per *quarter note.*

social institutions: (Ch. 2) Institutions (governmental, economic, legal, religious, family-centered, activity- or interest-based, service-oriented, etc.) whose functions and interactions largely define the structure of a *society.*

society: (Ch. 2) A group of persons regarded as forming a single community; the society-based concept of a "community" is defined largely by the *social institutions* of which it is comprised.

son [sohn]: (Ch. 11) Afro-Cuban dance-music style that gained popularity from the 1920s onward, influencing related styles such as *danzón, danzón-mambo,* and *mambo* and prefiguring later developments like *salsa* and Latin jazz. Also historically important as a symbol of Cuban nationalism. Central historical figure was Arsenio Rodríguez.

staccato [stah-KAH-toe]: (Ch. 4) Italian term for a type of articulation in which the notes are performed in a short, clipped manner; opposite of *legato.*

subdivision: (Ch. 3) The dividing of beats into smaller rhythmic units.

synagogue: (Ch. 14) Jewish house of worship.

syncopation: (Ch. 3) An *accent* or other note that falls in-between main *beats.*

tabla [TUB-lah]: (Ch. 12) Lead drum in Egyptian dance music. This single-headed, goblet-shaped drum should not be confused with the Indian instrument of the same name. The Egyptian tabla is also known by several other names (darabukkah, dumbek, doumbec).

tabla [TUB-lah]: (Ch. 8) The principal percussion instrument in North Indian music (not to be confused with the Egyptian tabla, an entirely different instrument). Consists of two drums—the higher-pitched tabla and lower-pitched dahina. Master performers include the late Alla Rakha and his son Zakir Hussain.

Tabla Solo: (Ch. 12) Neo-traditional dance genre "invented" in the 1970s by Nagwa Fu'ad and her tabla accompanist Ahmed Hammouda; involves close coordination and interaction between dancer and drummer(s); often the highlight of a *raqs sharqi* or *belly dance* routine.

tahtib [tah-TEEB]: (Ch. 12) Traditional male martial arts form/dance of the Saaid region of Egypt (i.e., Upper Egypt).

The *Saaidi* rhythm and the various forms of the women's *cane dance* all have their origins in tahtib.

takht [tah-kht]: (Ch. 12) Main instrumental ensemble for Arab "classical" music (tarab). Includes the 'ud, nay, qanun, violin, and *riqq,* sometimes supplemented by *tabla* (i.e., Egyptian).

tala [TAH-lah (or TAHL)]: (Ch. 8) Metric cycle in Indian music.

tambura [tum-BOO-rah]: (Ch. 8) Chorodophone instrument used to provide drone in Indian music; Hindustani and Karnatak versions are distinct.

tek: (Ch. 12) See *Dum/tek.*

tempo: (Ch. 3) The rate at which the beats pass in music.

Ten Sefirot: (Ch. 14) In the *Zohar,* the 10 rays of divine radiance through which *Ain Sof* becomes knowable as the God of the Creation, the *Torah,* and the earthly and heavenly realms.

texture: (Ch. 6) Refers to the relationships and interactions between the different parts and elements in a musical work or performance.

theka [TAY-kah]: (Ch. 8) The basic pattern of drum strokes (e.g., on the Indian *tabla*) that outlines a *tala* in its most skeletal form.

tihai [ti-HA-EE]: (Ch. 8) Rhythmic cadence (ending), in which the same rhythmic pattern is played three times in succession, generating complex rhythmic relationships with the underlying *tala* cycle in the process.

timbales [teem-BAH-lays]: (Ch. 11) Latin "drum set" featuring two or more relatively high-pitched metal-sided drums (the timbales), plus cowbells, woodblock, cymbal(s), and sometimes additional drums and other percussion instruments.

timbre [TAM-ber]: (Ch. 3) Sound quality, or "tone color"; what particular notes, instruments, or voices "sound like."

tintal [TEEN-tahl]: (Ch. 8) A 16-beat metric cycle (i.e., *tala*) used in *Hindustani raga* and other types of North Indian music.

tinwhistle: (Ch. 9) Small, end-blown flute with six finger-holes used in Irish music. Usually made of metal (tin or other), but may alternately be made of wood or plastic. Also known as the pennywhistle.

tonal languages: (Ch. 10) Languages in which the meaning of words is determined not just by the actual sounds of their syllables, but also by the specific patterns of pitch, rhythm, and timbral inflection with which they are articulated. Many West African languages (such as the Akan language Twi) are tonal; so too are other world languages, including *Mandarin Chinese.*

tone: (Ch. 1) A sound whose principal identity is a musical identity, as defined by people (though not necessarily all people) who make or experience that sound.

tonic: (Ch. 4) The first, fundamental pitch of a *scale* (e.g., the pitch C relative to a C-major scale or a piece in the *key* of C major).

Torah [Toe-RAH (Hebrew), TOE-rah (English)]: (Ch. 14) The foundational sacred scripture of the Jewish religion; heart of the *Hebrew Bible.*

tradition: (Ch. 2) In this text, a process of creative transformation whose most remarkable feature is the continuity it nurtures and sustains.

12-bar blues: (Ch. 6) Cyclic form defined by a standard-length *cycle* (12 measures) and *chord progression*. Employed in most blues tunes and in many other blues-derived musical contexts as well.

uilleann [YOO-lee-yin] **pipes:** (Ch. 9) The Irish version of the bagpipe, regarded as the most distinctively Irish music instrument.

unison: (Ch. 6) The same part performed by two or more instruments/voices.

Unity in Diversity: (Ch. 7) The national slogan of the Republic of Indonesia; important relative to Indonesian policies of cultural diversity, preservation and development of indigenous cultural traditions, and nationalism.

vadi [VAH-dee]: (Ch. 8) The tonic, or fundamental, pitch of a *raga*.

Vedas [VAY-dahs]: (Ch. 8) The four ancient Sanskrit scriptures of Hinduism, believed by Hindus to be of divine origin; some (including Ravi Shankar) claim that Vedic chant was the original basis of Indian classical music (though this claim is widely disputed).

verse-chorus form: (Ch. 6) Very common formal design in Western popular music and many other world music traditions. Features two main types of formal sections—verse and chorus—often with additional sections as well (introductions, interludes, bridges, transitions, ending sections).

vina [VEE-nah]: (Ch. 8) South Indian plucked chordophone instrument; one of the main melodic instruments in *Karnatak* music.

virtual communities: (Ch. 2) Transnational communities forged in the electronic sphere of cyberspace (e.g., on the Internet) rather than in more conventional ways.

word painting: (Ch. 14) A type of musical symbolism in which the text set to music is evoked in the sound and design of the music itself (e.g., through melodic direction, dynamics, textural contrasts).

Yiddish: (Ch. 14) A language historically spoken by Jews of Central/Eastern Europe (and still spoken today) that combines German with elements of Hebrew, Russian, Polish, and other languages.

yijing [ee-jing]: (Ch. 13) Designated emotional quality of a musical work (e.g., yijing of "sadness" for "Autumn Moon over the Han Palace"). Usually complex and multifaceted rather than simple and straightforward.

yun [yün]: (Ch. 13) Distinctive regional character of a piece of music or particular musical style (e.g., Shandong yun versus Henan yun in *zheng* music).

zaar [zahr]: (Ch. 12) Ancient healing ritual (performed mainly for and by women) rooted in shamanistic practices and involving spirit possession and trance. In modern times, the ritual has been folklorized, and zaar-derived rhythms and dance elements are commonly used in *raqs baladi, raqs sharqi* and *belly dance.*

zheng [jung]: (Ch. 13) Chinese board zither chordophone of ancient heritage. Most common form of instrument today has 21 strings and movable bridges; historically related to several other Asian zither-type chordophones (Japanese *koto,* Korean kayagum, Mongolian jatag, Vietnamese dan tranh); Deng Haiqiong is a leading zheng performer.

Zohar [ZOE-har]: (Ch. 14) Canonical text of *Kabbalah;* takes the form of a sprawling compendium of mystical commentaries on the *Hebrew Bible* and other sacred texts.

references cited in the text

Al-Rawi, Rosina-Fawzia. 1999. *Grandmother's Secrets: The Ancient Rituals and Healing Power of Belly Dancing.* Translated by Monique Arav. Brooklyn, NY: Interlink.

Amira, John, and Steven Cornelius. 1992. *The Music of Santería: Traditional Rhythms of the Batá Drums.* Crown Point, IN: White Cliffs Media Company.

Anderson, Benedict. 1991. *Imagined Communities: Reflections on the Origin and Spread of Nationalism.* 2nd ed., revised and extended. London and New York: Verso. First edition published 1983.

Arnold, Alison (ed.). 2000. *South Asia: The Indian Subcontinent.* Vol. 5 of *The Garland Encyclopedia of World Music.* New York and London: Garland Publishing, Inc.

Bakan, Michael B. 1999. *Music of Death and New Creation: Experiences in the World of Balinese Gamelan Beleganjur.* Chicago and London: University of Chicago Press.

Baranovitch, Nimrod. 2003. *China's New Voices: Popular Music, Ethnicity, Gender, and Politics, 1978–1997.* Berkeley and Los Angeles: University of California Press.

Barnard, Alan. 2000. *History and Theory in Anthropology.* Cambridge and New York: Cambridge University Press.

Bensignor, François, and Eric Audra. 1999. "Benin and Togo." In *World Music: The Rough Guide.* Vol. 1. New edition, ed. Simon Broughton, Mark Ellingham, and Richard Trillo. London: The Rough Guides, pp. 432–36.

Blacking, John. 1973. *How Musical Is Man?* Seattle: University of Washington Press.

———. 1995. *Music, Culture, & Experience: Selected Papers of John Blacking.* Chicago and London: University of Chicago Press.

Blumenthal, David R. 1978. *Understanding Jewish Mysticism (A Source Reader): The Merkabah Tradition and the Zoharic Tradition.* New York: KTAV Publishing House, Inc.

Buonaventura, Wendy. 1989. *Serpent of the Nile: Women and Dance in the Arab World.* London: Saqi Books.

Charry, Eric. 2000. *Mande Music.* Chicago and London: University of Chicago Press.

Cheng, Te-yuan. 1991. *Zheng, Tradition and Change.* Ph.D. dissertation, University of Maryland, Baltimore County.

Czekanowska, Anna. 1983. "Apects of the Classical Music of Uighur People: Legend versus Reality." *Asian Music* 14(1):94–110.

Danielson, Virginia. 1997. *The Voice of Egypt: Umm Kulthūm, Arabic Song, and Egyptian Society in the Twentieth Century.* Chicago and London: University of Chicago Press.

———. 2002. "Stardom in Egyptian Music: Four Case Studies." In *The Middle East,* ed. Virginia Danielson, Scott Marcus, and Dwight Reynolds. Vol. 6 of *The Garland Encyclopedia of World Music.* New York and London: Routledge, pp. 597–601.

Dibia, I Wayan. 1996. *Kecak: The Vocal Chant of Bali.* Denpasar (Bali): Hartanto Art Books Studio.

Donald, Mary Ellen. 2000. "Basic Rhythms for a Cabaret Belly Dance Routine." In *The Belly Dance Book: Rediscovering the Oldest Dance,* ed. Tazz Richards. Concord, CA: Backbeat Press, pp. 176–77.

Duran, Lucy. 2000. *The Rough Guide to the Music of Mali & Guinea.* CD booklet. World Music Network/ Rough Guides RGNET 1048 CD.

Eiseman, Fred B. 1990. *Sekala and Niskala,* vol. II, *Essays on Society, Tradition, and Craft.* Berkeley, CA, and Singapore: Periplus Editions.

Ephland, John. 1991 [1976]. *Shakti, with John McLaughlin.* CD booklet. New York: Columbia/Legacy CK 46868.

Fairley, Jan. 2000. "Cuba: Son and Afro-Cuban Music." In *World Music: The Rough Guide.* Vol. 2. New edition, ed. Simon Broughton and Mark Ellingham. London: The Rough Guides, pp. 386–407.

Farrell, Gerry. 1997. *Indian Music and the West.* New York: Oxford University Press.

———. 2000. "Music and Internationalization." In *South Asia: The Indian Subcontinent,* ed. Alison Arnold. Vol. 5 of *The Garland Encyclopedia of World Music.* New York and London: Garland Publishing, Inc., pp. 560–69.

Fletcher, Peter. 2001. *World Musics in Context.* New York: Oxford University Press.

Fong-Torres, Ben. 1998. *Abraxas.* CD booklet. New York: Sony Music Entertainment, Inc.

Franken, Marjorie. 1998. "Farida Fahmy and the Dancer's Image in Egyptian Film." In *Images of Enchantment: Visual and Performing Arts of the Middle East,* ed. Sherifa Zuhur. Cairo: American University in Cairo Press, pp. 265–81.

Frishkopf, Michael. 2002. "Islamic Hymnody in Egypt: *Al-Inshād al-Dīnī.*" In *The Middle East,* ed. Virginia Danielson, Scott Marcus, and Dwight Reynolds. Vol. 6 of *The Garland Encyclopedia of World Music.* New York and London: Routledge, pp. 165–75.

Gerard, Charley. 2001. *Music from Cuba: Mongo Santamaría, Chocolate Armenteros and Other State-side Cuban Musicians.* Westport, CT and London: Praeger.

Gerard, Charley, and Marty Sheller. 1989. *Salsa! The Rhythm of Latin Music.* Crown Point, IN: White Cliffs Media Company.

Ginsburgh, Yitzchak. 2002. "The Inner Dimension: A Gateway to the Wisdom of Kabbalah and Chassidut." www.inner.org (accessed 2002).

Gundersen, Edna. 2003. "Madonna's Epiphany." *USA Today* (online version), www.usatoday.com/life/2003-04-17-madonna-main_x.htm (accessed 2003).

Han, Kuo-huang, and Lindy Li Mark. 1980. "Evolution and Revolution in Chinese Music." In *Musics of Many Cultures: An Introduction,* ed. Elizabeth May. Berkeley and Los Angeles: University of California Press, pp. 10–31.

Han Mei. 2005. "Zheng." *Grove Music Online,* ed. L. Macy, www.grovemusic.com (accessed April 1, 2005).

Hast, Dorothea E., James Cowdery, and Stan Scott. 1999. *Exploring the World of Music.* Dubuque, IA: Kendall/Hunt.

Hornbostel, Erich M. von, and Curt Sachs. 1992[1914]. "Classification of Musical Instruments." English trans. version. In *Ethnomusicology: An Introduction,* ed. Helen Myers. New York: W.W. Norton & Co., pp. 444–61.

Jones, Stephen. 1995. *Folk Music of China: Living Instrumental Traditions.* Oxford: Clarendon Press.

Keita, Seckou. 2002. *Mali.* CD booklet, with liner notes by Jalikunda/Diz Heller. ARC Music Productions International Ltd. EUCD 1779.

Khan, Ali Akbar, and George Ruckert (editors). 1998. *The Classical Music of North India.* Vol. 1. New Delhi: Munshiram Manoharlal Publishers Pvt. Ltd.

Khan, Hafez Inayat. 1991. *The Mysticism of Sound, and Music.* Boston: Shambhala.

Kidjo, Angélique. 2004. Angélique Kidjo official Web site, www.angeliquekidjo.com.

King, Anthony. 1972. "The Construction and Tuning of the Kora." *African Language Studies* 13:113–36.

Knight, Roderic. 2001. "Kora." ed. Stanley Sadie and John Tyrrell. In *The New Grove Dictionary of Music and Musicians.* Vol 13. London: Macmillan, pp. 796–99. (Also in *Grove Music Online,* ed. L. Macy, www.grovemusic.com.)

Koskoff, Ellen. 2001. *Music in Lubavitcher Life.* Urbana and Chicago: University of Illinois Press.

Kuter, Lois. 2000. "Celtic Music." In *Europe,* ed. Timothy Rice, James Porter, and Chris Goertzen. Vol. 8 of *The Garland Encyclopedia of World Music.* New York and London: Garland Publishing, Inc., pp. 319–23.

Lane, Edward William. 1978 [1895]. *An Account of the Manners and Customs of the Modern Egyptians (Written in Egypt During the Years 1833–1835).* The Hague and London: East-West Publications. (Orig. pub: Cairo: Livres de France, 1836.)

Lawergren, Bo. 2000. "Strings." In *Music in the Age of Confucius,* ed. Jenny F. So. Washington, DC: Freer Gallery of Art and Arthur M. Sackler Gallery, Smithsonian Institution, pp. 65–85.

Levin, Theodore. 2005. "Jewish Music: Tajikistan and Uzbekistan (Bukhara)," *Grove Music Online,* ed. L. Macy, www.grovemusic.com (accessed June 7, 2005).

Leymarie, Isabelle. 2002. "Latin Jazz." *Latin Jazz: La Combinación Perfecta.* CD booklet. Washington, DC: Smithsonian Folkways Recordings SFW 40802.

Loza, Steven. 1993. *Barrio Rhythm: Mexican American Music in Los Angeles.* Urbana and Chicago: University of Illinois Press.

———. 1999. *Tito Puente and the Making of Latin Music.* Urbana and Chicago: University of Illinois Press.

Lüscher, Barbara (Aischa). 2000. "The Golden Age of Egyptian Oriental Dance." In *The Belly Dance Book: Rediscovering the Oldest Dance,* ed. Tazz Richards. Concord, CA: Backbeat Press, pp. 18–23.

Mackerras, Colin. 1997. *Peking Opera.* Hong Kong: Oxford University Press.

Mahal, Taj. 2004. Taj Mahal official Web site, www.taj-mo-roots.com/kulanjan.html.

Manuel, Peter (with Kenneth Bilby and Michael Largey). 1995. *Caribbean Currents: Caribbean Music from Rumba to Reggae.* Philadelphia: Temple University Press.

McCourt, Frank. 1996. *Angela's Ashes: A Memoir.* New York: Scribner.

———. 1999. "Crossing the Bridge." CD booklet essay. In *Crossing the Bridge,* Eileen Ivers. Sony Classical SK 60746.

Metting, Fred. 2001. *The Unbroken Circle: Tradition and Innovation in the Music of Ry Cooder and Taj Mahal.* Lanham, MD, and London: Scarecrow Press.

Molloy, Michael. 2002. *Experiencing the World's Religions: Tradition, Challenge, and Change.* 2nd ed. New York: McGraw-Hill.

Moloney, Michael. 1992. *Irish Music in America: Continuity and Change.* Ph.D. dissertation, University of Pennsylvania.

Moore, Robin. 1997. *Nationalizing Blackness:* Afrocubanismo *and Aristic Revolution in Havana, 1920–1940.* Pittsburgh: University of Pittsburgh Press.

Moyo, Dumisani "Ramadu," and Diz Heller. 2002. *Izambulelo: Traditional and Contemporary Music from Zimbabwe.* CD booklet. ARC Music Productions International Ltd. EUCD 1704.

Nelson Davies, Kristina. 2002. "The Qur'ān Recited." In *The Middle East,* ed. Virginia Danielson, Scott Marcus, and Dwight Reynolds. Vol. 6 of *The Garland Encyclopedia of World Music.* New York and London: Routledge, pp. 157–63.

Nettl, Bruno. 2006. *The Study of Ethnomusicology: Thirty-one Issues and Concepts.* Urbana and Chicago: University of Illinois Press.

Nolan, Ronan. 2003. "Seamus Ennis 1919–1982." Rambling House (Irish music Web site), www.iol.ie/~ronolan/ennis.html (accessed 2005).

O'Connor, Nuala. 1999. "Ireland." In *World Music: The Rough Guide.* Vol. 1. New edition, ed. Simon Broughton, Mark Ellingham, and Richard Trillo. London: The Rough Guides, pp. 170–88.

Olsen, Dale. 1996. *Music of the Warao of Venezuela: Song People of the Rain Forest.* Gainesville: University Press of Florida.

Pinson, DovBer. 2000. *Inner Rhythms: The Kabbalah of Music.* Northvale, NJ, and Jerusalem: Jason Aronson, Inc.

Porter, Lewis. 1998. *John Coltrane: His Life and Music.* Ann Arbor: University of Michigan Press.

Puente, Tito Jr. 2004. Tito Puente Jr. official Web site, www.titopuentejr.net/biography.html.

Racy, A. J. 2003. *Making Music in the Arab World: The Culture and Artistry of Ṭarab.* Cambridge and New York: Cambridge University Press.

Racy, Ali Jihad. 1981. "Music in Contemporary Cairo: A Comparative Overview." *Asian Music* 13(1):4–26.

Radano, Ronald, and Philip V. Bohlman (editors). 2000. *Music and the Racial Imagination.* Chicago and London: University of Chicago Press.

Ramzy, Hossam. 1995. *Zeina: Best of Mohammed Abdul Wahab.* CD booklet. ARC Music Productions International Ltd. EUCD 1231.

Rault-Leyrat, Lucie. 1987. *La Cithare Chinoise* Zheng, *Un Vol D'oies Sauvages Sur Les Cordes de Soie . . . .* Paris: Le Léopard D'Or.

Rea, Dennis. 2006. "Live at the Forbidden City." www.dennisrea.com/cuijian.html (accessed 2006).

Rice, Timothy. 1994. *May It Fill Your Soul: Experiencing Bulgarian Music.* Chicago and London: University of Chicago Press.

Roberts, John Storm. 1979. *The Latin Tinge: The Impact of Latin American Music on the United States.* New York: Oxford University Press.

Ruckert, George, and Richard Widdess. 2000. "Hindustani Raga." In *South Asia: The Indian Subcontinent,* ed. Alison Arnold. Vol. 5 of *The Garland Encyclopedia of World Music.* New York and London: Garland Publishing, Inc., pp. 64–88.

Saleh, Magda. 2002. "Dance in Egypt." In *The Middle East,* ed. Virginia Danielson, Scott Marcus, and Dwight Reynolds. Vol. 6 of *The Garland Encyclopedia of World Music.* New York and London: Routledge, pp. 623–33.

Sanabria, Bobby, and Ben Socolov. 1990. "Tito Puente: Long Live the King." *Hip: Highlights in Percussion for the Percussion Enthusiast* 5, pp. 1–7, 22–23.

Scheindlin, Raymond P. 1998. *A Short History of the Jewish People: From Legendary Times to Modern Statehood.* New York: Macmillan.

Scholem, Gershom. 1995[1941]. *Major Trends in Jewish Mysticism.* New York: Schocken Books.

Shankar, Ravi. 1968. *My Music, My Life.* New York: Simon and Schuster.

———. 1999. *Raga Mala: The Autobiography of Ravi Shankar,* ed. George Harrison. New York: Welcome Rain Publishers.

Shields, Hugh, and Paulette Gershen. 2000. "Ireland." In *Europe,* ed. Timothy Rice, James Porter, and Chris Goertzen. Vol. 8 of *The Garland Encyclopedia of World Music.* New York and London: Garland Publishing, Inc., pp. 378–97.

Shiloah, Amnon. 1992. *Jewish Musical Traditions.* Detroit: Wayne State University Press.

Shira. 2000. "Props for Oriental Dance." In *The Belly Dance Book: Rediscovering the Oldest Dance,* ed. Tazz Richards. Concord, CA: Backbeat Press, pp. 80–92.

Slawek, Stephen. 1991. "Ravi Shankar as Mediator between a Traditional Music and Modernity." In *Ethnomusicology and Modern Music History,* ed. Stephen Blum, Philip V. Bohlman, and Daniel M. Neuman. Urbana: University of Illionis Press, pp. 161–80.

Spiller, Henry. 2004. *Gamelan: The Traditional Sounds of Indonesia.* Santa Barbara, CA, Denver, and Oxford: ABC-CLIO.

Starr, Larry, and Christopher Alan Waterman. 2003. *American Popular Music: From Minstrelsy to MTV.* New York: Oxford University Press.

Stock, Jonathon P. J. 1996. *Musical Creativity in Twentieth-Century China: Abing, His Music, and Its Changing Meanings.* Rochester, NY: University of Rochester Press.

Strauss, Neil. 2001. "A Brief History of Electronica." In *Rolling Stone: The Decades of Rock & Roll.* San Francisco: Rolling Stone Press/Chronicle Books, pp. 275–79.

Tenzer, Michael. 1998 [1991]. *Balinese Music.* Berkeley, CA, and Singapore: Periplus Editions.

———. 2000. *Gamelan Gong Kebyar: The Art of Twentieth-Century Balinese Music.* Chicago and London: University of Chicago Press.

Thrasher, Alan. 2005. "China." *Grove Music Online,* ed. L. Macy, www.grovemusic.com (accessed April 1, 2005).

Touma, Habib Hassan. 1996. *The Music of the Arabs.* New expanded ed. Translated by Laurie Schwartz. Portland: Amadeus Press.

Trebinjac, Sabine. 2005. "China (Minority Traditions: North and West China)." *Grove Music Online,* ed. L. Macy, www.grovemusic.com (accessed April 1, 2005).

van Nieuwkerk, Karin. 1995. *"A Trade Like Any Other": Female Singers and Dancers in Egypt.* Austin: University of Texas Press.

Vetter, Roger. 1996. *Rhythms of Life, Songs of Wisdom.* CD booklet. Smithsonian Folkways SF CD 40463.

Weiss, Sam. 1994. *Mysteries of the Sabbath: Classic Cantorial Recordings: 1907–47.* CD booklet. Yazoo Records Yazoo 7002.

Wieder Magan, Ruth. 2000. "Ruth Wieder-Magan, Composer and Performer of *Songs to the Invisible God* (interview)." Interview by Andrew Young. *Nashim* 3: 271–76.

Witzleben, J. Lawrence. 2002. "China: A Musical Profile." In *East Asia: China, Japan, and Korea,* ed. Robert C. Provine, Yosihiko Tokumaru, and J. Lawrence Witzleben. Vol. 7 of *The Garland Encyclopedia of World Music.* New York and London: Routledge, pp. 87–93.

Wong, Isabel K. F. 2002. "Nationalism, Westernization, and Modernization." In *East Asia: China, Japan, and Korea,* ed. Robert C. Provine, Yosihiko Tokumaru, and J. Lawrence Witzleben. Vol. 7 of *The Garland Encyclopedia of World Music.* New York and London: Routledge, pp. 379–90.

Zemp, Hugo. 1978. "'Are'are Classification of Musical Types and Instruments." *Ethnomusicology* 22(1):37–67.

———. 1979. "Aspects of 'Are'are Musical Theory." *Ethnomusicology* 23(1):5–48.

Zheng, Cao. 1983. "A Discussion of the History of the Guzheng." Translated by Yohana Knobloch. *Asian Music* 14(2):1–16.

Credits

Chapter 1

p. 1, Michael B. Bakan; p. 3, George Newson/Lebrecht/The Image Works; p. 4, Imperial Household Agency; p. 5, Paul Doyle/Alamy.

Chapter 2

p. 9, © Dinodia Images/Alamy; p. 11 (top), Dale A. Olsen; (bottom), ARC Music Productions International Ltd.; p. 12 (top), ARC Music Productions International Ltd.; (bottom), Sean Williams; p. 13, Owen Franken/Corbis; pp. 14, 15, 16, Michael B. Bakan; p. 17, Guy Le Querrec/Magnum Photos; pp. 18, 19, AFP/Getty Images; p. 20, AP Images/ Jose Goitia; p. 21 (top), Jack Fields/ Corbis; (bottom), Bildarchiv Preussischer Kulturbesitz/Art Resource, NY; p. 22, AP Images/STR; p. 23 (top), photo by Allan Marett, courtesy of Smithsonian Folkways Recordings, used by permission. From rear cover of CD booklet accompanying Bunggridj-bunggridj: Wangga Songs by Alan Maralung-Northern Australia SF CD 40430; (bottom), Michael Redig; p. 24, Simon Isabelle/SIPA; p. 26 (top to bottom), Bettmann/Corbis, Frank Gunderson, Arvind Garg/Corbis; p. 28, Jennifer Cheek-Pantaleon.

Chapter 3

p. 31, Jacob Silberberg/Getty Images; p. 37, Rich Miller; p. 38, ARC Music Productions International Ltd.; p. 39 (top), Getty Images; (bottom), ARC Music Productions International Ltd.; p. 40, Courtesy of Geetha Bennett.

Chapter 4

p. 43, © Wolfgang Kaehler/Corbis; p. 45, © Chris Roberts; p. 47, Wolfgang Kaehler/Corbis; p. 51, Michael Redig.

Chapter 5

p. 57, © Shepard Sherbell/Corbis SABA; p. 59, Michael B. Bakan; p. 64, Michael Redig; p. 67 (top), Michael Redig; (left), CMCD/Getty Images; (right), ARC Music Productions International Ltd; p. 68 (top), Michael Redig; (bottom), Michael B. Bakan; pp. 69, 70, 72, Michael Redig.

Chapter 6

p. 75, Michael B. Bakan; p. 76, ARC Music Productions International Ltd.; p. 78, Avery Research Center at the College of Charleston; p. 79, Diego Goldberg/Sygma/Corbis; p. 80, Images of Africa Photobank/Alamy; p. 82, ARC Music Productions International Ltd.; p. 83, ARC Music Productions International Ltd.

Chapter 7

p. 89, Marilyn Campbell-Bakan; p. 91, Barbara Anello; p. 92, Harry Gruyaert/ Magnum Photos; pp. 93, 95, Michael B. Bakan; p. 96, Michael Redig; p. 98, Ian Berry/Magnum Photos; p. 99, Michael B. Bakan; p. 100, Michael B. Bakan; p. 104, Bruno Barbey/Magnum Photos; p. 105 (top), courtesy Marilyn Campbell-Bakan; (bottom), Michael B. Bakan; pp. 107, 108, Michael B. Bakan; p. 111, photo by George Riordan. Used courtesy of Florida State University College of Music; p. 112 (left), S.I.N./Corbis; (right), The McGraw-Hill Companies, Inc./Christopher Kerrigan, photographer.

Chapter 8

p. 120, John Reader/Time Life Pictures/ Getty Images; p. 122 (top), Dinodia/ Alamy; (bottom), ARC Music Productions International Ltd.; p. 123 (top), Michael Harder/Alamy; (bottom), Mono pole-Pathé/Photofest; p. 124, Dinodia Photo Library; p. 125, Wesleyan University Library, Special Collections & Archives; p. 127, AP Images/Rajesh Nirgude; p. 129, Michael Redig; p. 130 (top, left to right), Indiapicture/Alamy, Diondia/ Alamy; (bottom, left to right), Michael Redig, AFP/Getty Images, India Images/ Alamy; p. 138, Mary Katherine Aldin; p. 142, Guy Le Querrec/Magnum Photos; p. 143, Ravi Shankar Center/Corbis; p. 145, Andrew Putler/Redferns; p. 147, Andrew Lepley/Redferns.

Chapter 9

p. 156, Sean Williams; p. 157, Corbis; p. 158, Michael Redig; p. 161 (top), Bettmann/Corbis; (bottom), Michael Redig; p. 162, reproduced courtesy of the James Hardiman Library, NUI, Galway, Ireland; p. 163, Michael Redig; p. 165 (left), Michael Redig; (right), C Squared Studios/Getty Images; p. 171 (top), courtesy Gael Linn; (bottom), Michael Redig; p. 172, AP Images/Kim Garnick; p. 174, Val Wilmer/Redferns; p. 176, ArenaPal/Topham/The Image Works; p. 177, Leon Morris/Redferns; p. 179, Andrew Lepley/Redferns.

Chapter 10

p. 187, ArenaPal/Topham/The Image Works; p. 188, Roderic Knight; p. 189, David Redfern/Redferns; p. 191, Black Star/Alamy; p. 192, Roger Vetter; p. 196, Visual & Written SL/Alamy; p. 197 (left), Roger Vetter; (right), Michael Redig; p. 198, Roderic Knight; p. 199, Philip Ryalls/Redferns; p. 200, Roderic Knight; p. 201 (left), Philip Ryalls/Redferns; (right), ARC Music Productions International Ltd; p. 205, Paul Bergen/Redferns; p. 210, AP Images/Jason DeCrow; p. 211, Philip Scalia/Alamy.

Chapter 11

p. 218, Leon Morris/Redferns; p. 223 (top), AP Images/Jose Goitia; (bottom), Michael Redig; p. 224, Peter Turnley/ Corbis; p. 225, Michael Redig; p. 226, Hulton Deutsch Collection/Corbis; p. 227, Michael Redig; p. 229, Frank Driggs Collection/Getty Images; p. 230, Courtesy Everett Collection; p. 231, C Squared Studios/Getty Images; p. 232, courtesy of Margaret Puente; p. 235, The McGraw-Hill Companies, Inc./John Flournoy, photographer; p. 236, Getty Images; p. 243, AFP/Getty Images; p. 244, AP Images/Dean Cox.

Chapter 12

p. 252, photo by Ali Al Gabry, courtesy, Aisha Ali; p. 253, ARC Music Productions International Ltd.; p. 256 (top, left to right), Bettmann/Corbis, Michael Redig; (bottom), Alfred/SIPA; p. 257, Gavin Graham Gallery, London, UK/The Bridgeman Art Library; p. 258, Michael Redig; p. 259, Shepard Sherbell/Corbis; p. 262, The Art Archive/Dagli Orti; p. 264 (top), AP Images/STR; (bottom), Michael Redig; pp. 266, 269, Michael Redig; p. 270 (top), AFP/Getty Images; (bottom), courtesy Everett Collection; p. 273 (left), Michael Redig; (right), J. C. Sugarman; p. 277, Bettmann/Corbis; p. 278, Mahmoud Reda, courtesy Aisha Ali; p. 280 (left), Time Life Pictures/Getty Images; (right), Michael Redig; pp. 281, 282, Michael Redig; p. 284, ARC Music Productions International Ltd.

Index

banjo, 63, 176
bansuri, 130
"B.A.Ph.PET" (Michael Bakan), 111–113
baqawathar, 121
barhat, 120, 133–134
Baron Cohen, Erran, 347–352
Barretto, Ray, 241
bass drum, 70
bassoon, 66
batá, 223, 231
Bauzá, Mario, 221, 229, 230
bayan, 131–132
beat (pulse), 34
Beatles, 27, 120, 121, 127, 143–144, 210, 242
bebop jazz, 230
Beethoven, Ludwig van, 217
    Symphony No. 9, 4, 27, 39, 53, 54
Beijing Opera, 11, 292, 302–303, 314, 316
Beijing Zheng Association, 317
beleganjur. See gamelan beleganjur
Belfast, Northern Ireland, 156
"Belhadawa Walla Belshaawa?" (Hossam Ramzy), 282–284
belly dance, 21, 252, 253, 256, 260, 262, 264, 269, 270, 278–280, 284–285
Benary, Barbara, 110
Benin, 209–211
berani, 16
Beratha, I Wayan, 16
Berry, Chuck, 226
Bhairav family of ragas, 146
bhajan, 121
bhangra, 39, 123, 147
Bhatt, Vishwa Mohan, 120, 145
    "Raga Nat Bhairav," 133–134, 138–141, 149
bhuta, 102–103
Big 3 Palladium Orchestra, 246–247
big band jazz, 230
big band mambo (New York mambo style), 227, 228–229
bird sounds, 4
birimintingo, 203
Black Ivory Soul (Angélique Kidjo), 210–211

"Black Magic Woman" (Santana), 234, 237
Blades, Rubén, 221, 243
blue notes, 50, 62
blues, 189, 196, 204, 205, 235, 242
    four-beat meters, 37
    as music of tradition, 28
    shuffle rhythm, 35
    slide guitar technique in, 139
    12-bar, 80–81
blues scale, 50, 54, 62
Bobo, Willie, 236
bodhrán (Irish frame drum), 171, 173, 175
Bollywood, 123
bongó, 227, 228, 231
Bose, Kumar, 140
bossa nova, 53, 54, 77
Bothy Band, The, 170, 172, 174, 176
bouzouki, Irish, 175, 176–179
Brahma, the Creator, 20–21, 92
Brahmin caste, 126
Brando, Marlon, 232
Brazil
    bossa nova, 53, 54, 77
    diasporic communities of, 17
    samba, 17, 18, 189
"Brek Dan/Break Dance" (I Ketut Sukarata), 107
bridge
    African kora, 197, 198
    guitar, 65
    song, 83
    violin, 66
British Broadcasting Corporation (BBC), 69
Britten, Benjamin, 110
Brown, James, 17, 39, 147, 210
Buddhism, 293, 300
    in India, 122
    in Tibet, 313
Bulgaria
    gaida (Bulgarian bagpipe), 19
bullroarer, as aerophone, 66
Buonaventura, Wendy, 254
button box accordion, 171
buzzer, 69
Byrd, Donald, 212

C

Cabaret dance, 253
cadences, 167

Cage, John, 110
    4'33", 1–5
call-and-response, 78–79
    Egyptian women's dance music, 283
    rumba, 224
    West African music, 196
calypso, 210–211
Camillo, Michel, 243
Canada
    diasporic communities of, 18
    as nation-state, 16
cane dance, 279–280, 281
cantor, 342–348
Cárcamo, Pablo, 284–285
Carioca, Tahia, 269, 280, 282
Casino Badiaa productions, 268–269, 277
castanets, 68
caste system
    in Bali, 100
    in India, 100, 126
Castro, Fidel, 240
ceílí (Irish social gathering), 159
Celtic, 162, 164
Celtic hornpipe rhythm, 35
Central Javanese court gamelan, 12, 14, 77, 91, 92–95
Ceoltóirí Cualann (group), 159, 170, 171, 174
cha cha chá, 218, 219, 222, 224, 225–227, 230–234, 236, 237, 240, 245, 246
chanting. See human voice
charanga, 225–226
Charry, Eric, 204, 205
Chassidic reggae, 329
Chassidism, 332–333, 342–346
Cheng, Te-yuan, 314
Cherish the Ladies (group), 180
Cherry, Don, 147
Chiang Kai-shek, 295
Chicano musicians, 235
Chieftains, The (group), 159, 170–173, 174, 177, 180
    "Dingle Set, The" (medley), 172–173
Chimnoy, Sri, 144
China, 289–322. See also zheng
    Beijing Opera, 11, 292, 302–303, 314, 316

Chinese Communist Party (CCP), 293, 295, 307, 310–314, 318
Cultural Revolution, 295, 303, 314–315, 317, 318
dynasties, 294–295, 298–304, 307
instruments, 63, 292, 301, 316–317, 319–320. See also zheng (Chinese chordophone)
metric cycles, 39
Muslims in, 314, 317–318, 319
nation-state, 293–294, 318
nationalism in, 295, 307–308
overview, 293–295
Period of Openness, 295, 315–318
post-1970s, 316–318
rhythms, 321
Silk Road, 301, 319
Tibet and, 313, 314, 317–318
Tiananmen Square uprisings, 315
timeline of world and music events, 290–291
Uighurs and, 314, 317–318, 319
Chinese Communist Party (CCP), 293, 295, 307, 310–314, 318
choir (ensemble of singers), 60
chord (notes of different pitch played together)
    arpeggio, 53–54
    defined, 53
    harmonization of melody, 53–54
    Irish traditional music, 165–167, 171, 175
    non-Western music, 54
    progressions, 53
    single chord, 53
    West African music, 203
chord progression (movement of chords), 53
chordal accompaniment, 53, 77
chordophones, 63–66, 73
    Indian raga, 124–125, 129–131, 134